CW00923550

CATHOLIC RECORD SOCIETY
PUBLICATIONS

RECORDS SERIES
VOLUME 84

Casus aliqui ad Angliam pertinentes.

The first page of Ampleforth MS 131, reproduced by kind permission of the
Rt Rev. Dom Cuthbert Madden OSB, Abbot of Ampleforth

Caroline Casuistry

The Cases of Conscience of Fr Thomas Southwell SJ

Edited by
PETER HOLMES

PUBLISHED FOR
THE CATHOLIC RECORD SOCIETY
BY
THE BOYDELL PRESS
2012

First published 2012

ISBN 978–0–902832–27–5

A Catholic Record Society publication
published by The Boydell Press
an imprint of Boydell & Brewer Ltd
PO Box 9, Woodbridge, Suffolk IP12 3DF, UK
and of Boydell & Brewer Inc.
668 Mt Hope Avenue, Rochester, NY 14620–2731, USA
website: www.boydellandbrewer.com

A CIP catalogue record for this book is available
from the British Library

The publisher has no responsibility for the continued existence or
accuracy of URLs for external or third-party internet websites referred to
in this book, and does not guarantee that any content
on such websites is, or will remain, accurate or appropriate

Papers used by Boydell & Brewer Ltd are natural, recyclable products
made from wood grown in sustainable forests

MIX
Paper from
responsible sources
FSC® C013604

Printed and bound in Great Britain by
CPI Group (UK) Ltd, Croydon, CR0 4YY

CONTENTS

ACKNOWLEDGEMENTS

I should begin by recording here my debt to the late Abbot Placid Spearritt OSB, when he was Librarian and Archivist of Ampleforth Abbey, for his assistance and hospitality when I visited Ampleforth in about 1977 to look at the manuscript used in this edition for the first time, and for providing me subsequently with a microfilm, at the expense of the Abbey, which he had made at the University of York. In addition, the present archivist, Fr Anselm OSB, has been most helpful in furnishing information and photographs of the document. The Rt Rev. Dom Cuthbert Madden OSB, Fr Abbot of Ampleforth, kindly gave permission for the manuscript to be used in this edition, as did the Bodleian Library, University of Oxford, for the other source principally used here. The staff of the University Library at Cambridge have also been most helpful, as also the staff at the Suffolk Record Office, Bury St Edmunds. I owe a great debt also to Dr Peter Doyle, volumes editor of the Catholic Record Society, for carefully checking my translation and saving me from some important errors. Responsibility for the final product, of course, remains with me.

INTRODUCTION

The manuscript sources and their presentation in this edition

The cases of conscience edited below are taken from two sources. The first, MS 131 (described in this edition as A) at Ampleforth Abbey, Yorkshire, is a seventeenth-century manuscript book in Latin composed of the following six main elements:[1]

1. 'Casus aliqui ad Angliam pertinentes' (Some cases which concern England), fos. 1–13. A collection of 30 cases, edited here.
2. 'Casus de Matrimonio R. P. Tho: Southw:' (Cases concerning marriage by the Reverend Father Thomas Southwell), fos. 13ᵛff. A collection of 63 cases, included here.
3. 'De sponsalibus' (Concerning betrothals), fos. 57ff. A collection of 6 cases, also included here.
4. 'Casus spectantes ad ipsos sacerdotes in Anglia' (Cases regarding the priests themselves in England), fos. 63ff. A collection of 22 cases, edited here.
5. 'Casus spectantes ad ipsos poenitentes' (Cases regarding the penitents themselves), fos. 71ff. A collection of 58 cases, edited here.
6. A list of faculties; a list of feasts and fasts; a brief note from Cardinal Cajetan's *Summa* published in Venice in 1601, and various miscellaneous theological items, fos. 103ᵛff; the first two elements of which are included here, the others not.

The second source is MS Sancroft 37 of the Bodleian Library, Oxford (described in this edition as S). This is a similar sort of booklet, written in the seventeenth century in Latin, containing seven elements, some the same as those listed above, some different:

1. 'Casus aliqui ad Angliam pertinentes' (as above), fos. 1–15.
2. 'Casus aliqui de Ieiunio Ecclesiastico' (Some cases concerning the fasts of the Church), fos. 16ff. A collection of 12 cases, edited here.
3. 'De horis canonicis' (Concerning canonical hours), fos. 21ᵛff. A collection of 42 cases, not included here.
4. 'De matrimonio' (as above), fos. 37ᵛff.
5. 'De sponsalibus' (as above), fos. 74ᵛff.

---

[1] There is a brief note, on the leaf before the one which has been numbered fo.1 here, headed 'Delectatio Morosa'. This note does not seem to be part of what follows, but has been transcribed and translated as a footnote to Case M60 below, where it seems relevant; see note 659 (pp. 261–2).

6. 'De Voto' (Concerning vows), fos. 79ff. A collection of 60 cases, not edited here.

7. A short digest of points on marriage, largely drawn from 'De matri-monio', fos. 104ff, which culminates in 'De Osculis' (Concerning kisses), the latter edited here.

Below, the cases which are presented to the reader are done so in three sections. First, the English Cases: sections 1, 4, and 5 in A; and section 1 in S. Second, the Cases concerning Marriage: sections 2 and 3 in A; and sections 4, 5, and part of 7 in S. Third, the Cases concerning Ecclesiastical Fasts, which are in S, section 2. As can be seen, almost all of the Ampleforth manuscript has been edited here, and this has been treated as the master text. It is, on the whole, a fuller text for these cases than the Bodleian manuscript, especially on the English cases, since it includes 80 additional cases, and also from Case 7 (fo. 4), the Bodleian manuscript does not contain the question or brief heading of the case, only the resolution. On the marriage cases, for the first 28 cases, the Bodleian manuscript contains a fuller text, mainly because it gives copious reference material, which Ampleforth leaves out, but then after that the two manuscripts are very close for the remainder of the marriage cases. The differences between the manuscripts most of the time are largely a matter of Latin sentence structure and vocabulary. In editing the Latin text, the editor has simply tried to give as full a text as possible, with footnotes recording the additional elements to be found in S that seem useful, or recording the sections where S differs markedly from A, and that help our understanding or the translation. However, minor differences of vocabulary (for example, *tantum* for *solum*) are not recorded in the footnotes. No attempt is made to show where S omits sections of A. The contractions in the Latin have largely been expanded, except that the references are left in their original, highly abbreviated form; the principal abbreviations used are explained in Abbreviations, below. Punctuation has not been modified and capitalisation has been left as far as possible as in the original. 'J' has been changed into 'i' in all cases. The spelling of the original has been retained, which leads to some inconsistencies (over *immo/imo*, for example), and over spelling proper names (*Rebellus/Rebellius*, for example). Some parts of the Latin text are underlined in the original, and this underlining is preserved here. The translation does not give a translation of the references, but a key to them is given in Southwell's Authorities, below.

In referring to the cases, the English cases are numbered as they are found in the two manuscripts: 1–30 and then 70–151. The marriage cases carry the prefix M and are designated M1–69, with an appendix consisting of 'De Osculis', which has the code MA. The cases concerning ecclesiastical fasts have the prefix F. The translation of each case follows immediately after its Latin presentation.

Authorship

The cases concerning marriage are referred to in the Ampleforth manuscript as the work of 'R. P. Tho: Southw:', who has been identified by Hugh Aveling as Thomas Southwell, SJ.[2] This attribution seems reasonably certain, as will be shown below, and can be used to assign the other cases edited here also to Southwell. It is probable, in other words, that all the cases in both manuscripts are the work of the same man: at certain points there are cross-references from one section to another which confirm this.[3] There is also, it is worth noting, a reference in these cases to a further work, 'De Lege' (Concerning Law), which is also to be found in the Sancroft collection in the Bodleian, but in a different manuscript; and hence this should also be added to the list of Southwell's works.[4] There are also references at Cases 78 and M4 to a work by our author on the sacraments, which I take to be MS 305 in the Library of the University of Liège. This document is described in their catalogue as 'Commentarius in quaestiones sexagesimam usque ad octogesimam tertiam D. Thomae, de Sacramentis in genere, de baptismo, de confirmatione et Eucharistia autore R. P. Thoma Southvello 'Couvent des Jésuites anglais', a work of 423 pages, which Southwell was apparently preparing for publication at the time of his death.[5]

The approximate date of composition of the cases, which can be worked out from internal evidence, also ties in with what we know of

[2] H. Aveling, 'The Marriages of Catholic Recusants 1559–1642', *Journal of Ecclesiastical History* 14 (1963), 70; *idem*, 'The Catholic Recusants of the West Riding of Yorkshire 1558–1790', *Proceedings of the Leeds Philosophical and Literary Society* 10 (1962–3), 250–1.

[3] See Case 101 (a reference back to Cases 13 and 14); and Case 29 (a reference to 'De Voto', Case 32, not edited here). Perhaps most helpful in terms of establishing authorship of the English cases are the cross-references in the 'Casus de Matrimonio', attributed in its title, as has been said, to Southwell (Ampleforth MS, fo. 39ᵛ), back to the English cases; see M25, M28, M37, M42, M57. There are also references to 'De Voto' in the marriage cases: M33, M53, and possibly M32.

[4] The reference is in Case 28 which reads: 'As I have said concerning law, Cases 19 and 50' ('Ut dixi de leg: cas: 19 et 50'). This I interpret as a reference to Bodleian Library MS Sancroft 96, a short casuistical discussion of various problems 'De Lege', which is written in what may be the same hand as some of Sancroft MS 37 edited here. There are also two references to 'De Lege' in the marriage cases M20 and M57.

[5] Bibliothèque de l'Université de Liège, *Catalogue des Manuscrits* (Liège, 1875), p. 204, MS no. 305; C. Sommervogel, *Bibliothèque de la Compagnie de Jésus* (Brussels, 1890), I, 755. Charles Dodd, writing a century after, says that Southwell, 'had laid the design of a curious performance, when he was taken off in his prime', and this is taken to refer to the 'de Sacramentis': C. Dodd, *The Church History* (Brussels, 1739), III, 110.

the life of Thomas Southwell, and therefore helps confirm his authorship. The dates 1626, 1628 and 1631 are mentioned in the text.[6] Case 21 provides the best indication as to date, where it says that in 1641 and 1644 the fast of St Mark will fall on one of the five days of Easter. This provides a *terminus ad quem* independent of the date of Southwell's death (December 1637). The fast of St Mark last fell before 1641 at Easter in 1633 (when Easter day was April 21 as in 1644). Hence, the text itself tells us, the cases of conscience were composed after St Mark's 1633 and before 1641; and we may add, before December 1637 if they are the work of Southwell. In the marriage cases, there are a number of very specific references made to a work printed in 1633: *Nouae declarationes Congregationis S. R. E. Cardinalium ad decreta Sacros. Concilii Tridentini ex bibliotheca Card. R. Bellarmini*, edited by Laurent Durand.[7] It is, of course, likely that the separate elements which make up the two manuscripts, and which make up the present edition itself, were composed at different times, although perhaps unlikely that they would cover a span of more than a few years. There are no cross-references in the marriage cases to the two sections of English cases (Cases 70–150) that stand in the Ampleforth MS after the marriage cases, but there are a number of references to the earlier English cases; this suggests that these later English cases were composed after the marriage cases. The cross-references in 'De matrimonio' to 'De Lege', 'De Voto' and 'De Sacramentis' probably also place the composition of these marriage cases before these three (unless later editing went on).

Thomas Bacon, who adopted the pseudonym Southwell (1592–1637), was born in Sculthorpe, near Fakenham, in Norfolk, and was educated at King's Lynn. Thomas's father John is described as a 'schismatic', who was reconciled at some point to the Catholic Church. John certainly brought up his family as Catholics, since Thomas and three of his brothers (John, Nathanial and George, who all also took the alias Southwell) and a sister, Frances, were smuggled out of Norfolk and sent to Catholic Europe to study, as a result of which all four of them, like Thomas, entered religion. John and Nathanial also became Jesuits like Thomas, Frances became a Franciscan nun at Brussels,[8] George became a Benedictine, which may explain the presence of one of the manuscript collections of these cases in the library at Ampleforth. Thomas studied at St Omers and the English College, Rome, entered the Society of Jesus, and became a highly respected Professor of Theology at the English College of the Society of Jesus at Liège. Here he was teaching

6   Case 9 (1626), Case 101 (1628), Case 129 (1631), Case M20 (1631).
7   Cases M20, M21, M22, M23, M24, M26, M38, M44.
8   R. Trappes-Lomax, *The English Franciscan Nuns* (Catholic Record Society, 24, 1922), 8.

at the theologate, or house of higher studies, of the English province, which was in effect a training college for English Jesuits, some of whom would return to England as missionary priests. Southwell is known to have written and published a small number of theological works and was probably the person described by Sir Tobie Matthew (in conversation with Sir Francis Bacon, possibly a distant kinsman) as 'the most prodigious wit that ever I knew of any nation and of this side of the sea'.[9] He died at 45, and had he lived longer would certainly have published a great deal more. His brothers, John, Nathanial and George, all worked on the mission in England, which may perhaps have given Thomas, whose adult life was tranquil, scholarly and passed in exile, a personal reason to ponder the casuistical problems which faced the Catholic priest and his flock in England. The obvious explanation for the composition of the cases, though, is that they were teaching notes, used by Southwell when he taught courses in pastoral theology at Liège.[10] They are therefore very similar to the two Elizabethan collections of cases of conscience dating from the late 1570s and early 1580s, the first composed at the English College at Douai-Rheims, and the second edited by Robert Persons and William Allen.[11] The existence of Southwell's cases in two separate collections of manuscripts suggests also that they circulated more widely among the community of English Catholics. Indeed, Hugh Aveling suggests that copies of these cases were taken to England by missionary

[9]   J. P. Fiel, 'Bacon-Shakespeare: the Tobie Matthew Postscript', *Shakespeare Quarterly* 18 (1967), 73–6. Strange to say, this precise quotation has been used by those who think Francis Bacon wrote Shakespeare. Cf. L. P. Smith (ed.), *The Life and Letters of Sir Henry Wotton* (Oxford, 1907), II, 393–6.
[10]   Thomas McCoog's article in *New Oxford Dictionary of National Biography*; idem (ed.), *English and Welsh Jesuits 1555–1650* (Part II, Catholic Record Society, 1995), 298–300; idem (ed.), *Monumenta Anglia* (Monumenta Historica Societatis Iesu 143, Rome, 1992), 482–4; A. Kenny (ed.), *The Responsa Scholarum of the English College, Rome*, I (Catholic Record Society, 1962), 239–40; G. Oliver, *Collections towards Illustrating the Biography of the Scotch, English and Irish Members of the Society of Jesus* (London, 1845); H. Foley, *Records of the English Province of the Society of Jesus*, V (London, 1879), 520–1. Cf. E. Henson (ed.), *The English College at Madrid 1611–1767* (Catholic Record Society, 1929), 85; idem, *Registers of the English College at Valladolid 1589–1862* (Catholic Record Society, 1930), 117, 123 and note; N. Southwell, P. Ribadeneira and P. Alegambe (successive eds.), *Bibliotheca scriptorum Societatis Iesu* (Rome, 1676 and ed. A. F. Allison, London, 1969); T. A. Birrell (ed.), *Florus Anglo-Bavaricus* (London, 1970), Introduction, and 33, 50. The manuscripts themselves add a little more biographical detail where they state that the author was in Spain at some point after 1628 (Case 101), and also that he studied at Seville (Case 124). The references to the author being 'here in Belgium' (Case M22) and 'here in Liège' (Case M55) helps confirm Southwell's authorship. The author also confirms he is a Jesuit in Case M32.
[11]   See below under 'The cases and their Elizabethan counterparts', p. xxiv.

priests as works of reference, less bulky than the weighty printed casuistical tomes on which Southwell's notes are based.[12]

The English cases

The English cases of conscience edited below are chiefly of interest
because of the light they cast on the difficulties facing Catholic priests
and layfolk in England in the reign of Charles I. These difficulties of
course arose from the fact that Catholicism was forbidden by the law of
the land, and severe penalties were threatened against those who were
discovered to be Catholics. The cases are divided, as has been said,
into three principal groups: the first 30 cases have the general heading
'Cases which concern England', and hence concern both the laity and
clergy. The first two cases deal with how a Catholic might avoid detection in Protestant England: Case 1 asks whether, when interrogated, it
is lawful to use dissimulation or equivocation in such circumstances;
Case 2 whether, when eating in the company of 'heretics', or English
Protestants, it is lawful for a Catholic to break the fast or say grace with
them in order to avoid discovery. Cases 3 to 8 continue in the same
vein, but concern the involvement of Catholics directly, by their own
actions, in the religious ceremonies of Protestants. Attendance at Protestant churches is discussed in Cases 3 and 4; presence at Protestant
marriages, funerals and baptisms in Cases 5, 6 (especially as godparents)
and 7 (involving the baptism of their own children). Case 8 returns to the
problems thrown up in Case 2, dealing with presence at informal, spon-
taneous religious singing or praying while travelling with Protestants,
and the dangers of discovery in such circumstances. Cases 9, 10 and 11
deal with the famous Oath of Allegiance, devised by James I after the
Gunpowder Plot of 1605 ostensibly to test the loyalty of Catholics, but
actually to force them to deny papal power. Case 12 moves on to look at
the question of whether Catholics may exercise their rights of patronage
as landowners and appoint Protestant parish clergy, a case which again
concerns how Catholics relate to the Church of England. Cases 13, 14
and 15 are cases which look at whether Catholics may allow Protestant
guests or members of their household to break the Catholic fasts. Case
16 asks whether Catholics might allow their children to live in Protestant
households. Like the previous three cases, this case deals with a problem
posed by early-modern social conventions, which involved regular
hospitality, and also sending children away to live in other 'families'
or households. Case 17 deals again with a question of detection, asking
about Catholic attendance at specific Catholic services. Cases 18 and 19

---

[12] Aveling, 'Marriages of Catholic Recusants', 69–70.

deal specifically with the problems faced by Catholic priests at work in secret in England: the first concerns their penitential role, the second the Catholic ornaments and vestments that are required, when they may be difficult to come by. Cases 20 and 21 deal with fast-keeping. Cases 22, 23 and 24 are marriage cases. Case 25 is a technical question about what Roman decrees are to be observed in England; this links to a theme to some extent at play in the previous five cases, which has to do with how far the Council of Trent's decrees, never formally adopted in England as a result of Elizabeth I's accession, overrule the ancient traditions of the medieval English Church. Cases 26 and 27 return to the sort of problems faced by priests at work in England that had been discussed at 18 and 19: 26 deals with vestments, and 27 with the difficulties of saying Mass in small chapels. Cases 28 and 29 return to marriage; the latter case seems not to be a particularly English one. The final case in this group (30) looks again at questions of separation and communion, asking whether heretics and schismatics may attend Catholic services. All in all, although there is a certain flow to the order in which these cases are taken, and they can be grouped together in some sub-sets, nevertheless they do seem to be a rather miscellaneous collection, perhaps for pedagogical reasons. They may be cases suggested to the master by his students, or part of a type of revision guide or test.

The second group of English cases edited here answers 22 questions which are said to relate to 'priests themselves' in England. These are Cases 70 to 92, so numbered because they follow the sixty-nine marriage cases in the Ampleforth manuscript, which are edited later in this present volume. Cases 70–72 look at the subterfuges that priests may be forced to adopt to avoid capture; denying their names, going in disguise, and avoiding performing ceremonies. These cases therefore deal with the same sort of problems as Cases 1 and 2 in the first group. Case 74 overlaps with Case 18, and discusses probabilism and the priest's role as a confessor, which will be discussed briefly later in this Introduction. Cases 75 and 76 deal with the priest's role in baptism, and suggest perhaps the sort of emergencies which might arise under persecution, although the questions seem rather general. Case 77 certainly deals with the problems faced by priests operating in England, in secret and without easy access to the support of bishops, in this instance in relation to the sacraments of confirmation and ordination. Case 78 deals with a similar dilemma, and the possibility that a priest might need to celebrate Mass without having fasted, and without access to a chalice. Related cases, suggesting the need for priests to respond to emergencies, follow: May a priest celebrate Mass more than once in a day (79)? How far may a priest improvise in administering the last rites and the Eucharist (80)? May a priest avoid performing his sacramental duties when in danger (81)? How extensive are the powers of a 'simple' priest in the confessional (82)? Question

83 asks how far a priest may bend the rules in administering the last rites during a time of plague. There were serious plagues in England in 1625 and 1636, the latter being the plague which Fr Henry Morse SJ describes from first-hand experience as a Catholic priest in London, in his autobiography.[13] Case 84 is a little difficult to link to England and concerns ordination, but Cases 85 and 86 are certainly of English relevance, dealing with the priest's role in mixed marriages, which links to Case 28. Cases 87, 88 and 89 discuss what priests may do to escape imprisonment, and Case 90 discusses how priests should deal in the confessional with people trying to avoid persecution at the hands of the legal authorities. These last four cases are therefore a little reminiscent of the cases in the first group which dealt with what a Catholic might do to avoid persecution at the hands of the Protestant authorities; and Case 91 is rather close to Cases 2 and 8, and asks what a priest should do when he finds himself in the company of heretics and they blaspheme or attack Catholicism. The final case here (92) looks at the reconciliation of relapsed priests to the Church.

The third, and longest group of 'English' cases is headed 'Cases regarding the penitents themselves' and consists of 58 cases: although not actually designated as such, they deal to a large extent, but not exclusively, with cases which might be encountered in England. The heading of these cases, taken in relation to the two headings of the previous groups of cases, seems to suggest that they will concern the laity. But, of course, clergymen can be penitents, and Case 93, discussing the lawfulness of engaging in disputations with Protestants (a fairly common event at the time), was, as the case itself says, of as much interest to the clergy as to the laity. Cases 94 and 95 return to the Oath of Allegiance, and put a different slant on the questions posed on this topic in the first group of cases (especially 9, 10, 11). Cases 96 and 97 look at baptism and godparents, in the context of religious division and the persecution of Catholics (rather like Cases 5, 6, 7, 16 in the first group; and 75, 76 in the second). Confirmation and whether it is essential is discussed in 98 (confirmation had also been looked at in 77). Marriage is returned to in 99 (already raised in 22, 23, 24, 85, 86). In the first group of cases, discussion of marriage had been followed by a case (25) on the Council of Trent, whose decrees on marriage overruled medieval practice in this matter, and the same is true here, when Case 100 again looks at Trent. This then leads to three cases on fasting (101–3), since the old English fasts

---

[13] Philip Caraman, *Henry Morse: Priest of the Plague* (London, 1957). Thomas Southwell's brother John collaborated with Morse in the production of a broadsheet seeking charitable relief from fellow Catholics for those suffering in the plague of 1636: *To the Catholics of England* (Menston, 1973). It is possible that this case suggests a date of 1636 for its composition.

had set the country, in the days before the 'Counter-Reformation', somewhat apart from some other parts of Christendom. Three highly diverting cases on fighting and duelling follow (104–6), an issue much discussed by contemporary casuists on the Continent. The next two cases deal with wills (107, 108), using examples of legacies to pious uses. Cases 109–15 deal with the ownership by the laity of ecclesiastical property, and thus overlap with Case 12. The important question of the ownership of the property of dissolved monasteries is discussed in 109 and 115; there is a case on tithes (110) and the others concern advowsons and the patronage of benefices. One more marriage case follows (116). There is then a group of cases (117–25) which get at the canonical heart of the question of relations between Catholics and Protestants, the subject which at a practical level had lain behind most of the cases here. These cases look at definitions of heresy, schism, excommunication and prohibited books, especially in the light of the Bull *In Coena Domini*.[14] Four cases follow on witchcraft, astrology and superstition (126–9), topical moral matters, but not specifically English. What is not surprising is Southwell's absolute belief in witchcraft, which is confirmed in the marriage cases, where it is mentioned as a cause of impotence.[15] He seems to see astrology as a fraud, however. Three cases on blasphemy (130–2) are also rather generalised. The next case and one of the longest in the collection (133) discusses the vexed question of the vow made by English seminarists that they would return to England after their training, and how far it would prevent them from entering a religious order, like the Jesuits. This was a subject for contemporary debate within the English Catholic community. There are then five further cases on vows: 134 on perjury; 135 on vows within marriage; 136 on vows and fasting (harking back to 20–1 and 101–3); 137 on vows not to gamble, and 138 on the vows of children. Cases 139–40 deal with gambling again. The final cases (141–51) are economic cases and deal with the doctrine of the just price in relation to market value (141–4, 149), questions broadly speaking of usury (145–8, 150), and finally monopolies (151). Again, these cases, like those on witchcraft, are not central to English Catholic concerns but are interesting in so far as they relate to aspects of European social and intellectual history which have been much discussed in recent years by historians.

---

14 See note 137 to the translation of Case 118, pp. 96–7.
15 Cases M49, M50.

The cases concerning marriage

With the cases concering marriage we move into different territory, which takes Southwell away from his exclusively English focus in the cases just discussed.[16] There are, however, frequent references throughout these cases to England, and referral back to the English cases. The really tricky problem for Southwell and his students on matrimonial matters lay in the Council of Trent, which had thoroughly reformed Church law on the subject; so much so that Southwell refers to the 'new law' of Trent contrasting it with the 'old law' which had previously obtained. As Southwell frequently explains, when it came to marriage much of pre-existing Canon Law was swept away by the great reforming Council and its twenty-fourth session.[17] However, Southwell is very clear, as were other English Catholics, that since the Council of Trent had closed after the death of Queen Mary I, its decrees had never been accepted in this country. Every schoolboy knows that one of the great agents of Counter-Reformation was this Council, yet here paradoxically is a Jesuit casuist announcing that the English Church was not bound by its rules. However, given the difficulties of the Catholic Church in England in the early seventeenth century – the absence of church courts, indeed the absence of parish priests and the need to marry, by and large, in Protestant churches – how far the Council of Trent applied was probably the least of their problems. These sixty-nine marriage cases contain before Case 64 the sub-heading Concerning Betrothals, and the final five cases deal with this; however, it is important to bear in mind that in the previous discussions betrothal was sometimes in Southwell's mind as much as marriage. For betrothal and what we understand as marriage were both in a sense 'contracts of marriage', the first concerning the future, the second concerning the present.[18] This was not unconnected with the discussion of Trent because, for example, before Trent (and hence still in England), copulation turned betrothal into marriage with no need for any further ceremony.

The first three cases on marriage (M1, M2, M3) define the 'form' and 'matter' of the sacrament of matrimony. Southwell, in the spirit of a good medievalist, comes close to defining marriage as a civil contract. The flavour of these discussions is highly academic and theoretical, and it is important to remember that Southwell was essentially teaching academic theology in these cases as well as addressing practical problems. Case M4 looks at the 'deliberation', or conscientious thought and consultation

---

16 The essential guide to Catholic marriage in England at this time is Aveling, 'Marriages of Catholic Recusants'.
17 A. L. Richter (ed.), *Canones et Decreta Concilii Tridentini* (Leipzig, 1853), 214–326.
18 R. A. Houlbrooke, *The English Family 1450–1700* (London, 1984), chap. 4, esp. 78ff.

required before marriage is contracted, and this is followed by a resolution of a case concerning those who may enter the marriage contract deceitfully, and whether internal consent is sufficient to validate marriage (M5 and M6). If marriage is essentially a contract does it matter if one (or both) of the parties agrees through fear, or erroneously? (Cases M7, M8, M9, M10, M11, M12) Conditional marriage is discussed in the next five cases (M13–M18). Such marriages were apparently quite common at the time, the contract or agreement to marriage being limited by a condition without the fulfilment of which the marriage would not take place.[19] It is worth bearing in mind here again that a marriage contract could either be what we would call a marriage, or alternatively it could be a betrothal, a marriage 'for the future', and this makes conditional marriage more easy to understand. Case 19 looks at marriage without parental knowledge or permission, already the subject of discussion in the English cases. Cases M20–M26 look at the Tridentine requirement to be married before a parish priest and after the reading on three occasions of the banns. This, of course, was irrelevant in England, where Trent did not apply, and in any case was very difficult there; all this had been discussed in the English cases. A further impediment to marriage is discussed in Case M27: one which arises through fear, when a spouse is intimidated into marriage. Case M28 looks at the way in which a marriage can be validated when some secret impediment has been removed. A more general discussion of the impediments to marriage follows in M29, where it is decided that the Pope and the Church (through its Council) alone can prescribe impediments to Christian marriages. The 'diriment' impediments are listed in Case 30; these are the impediments which should prevent marriage, and have the power to render a marriage null and void if it has been contracted. Marriage to a slave is discussed in Case M31, and the power of religious vows to invalidate marriage in Cases M32 and M33. The impediment of consanguinity is discussed in the next three cases (M34–M36), with a discussion of the exceptions raised by examples from the Old Testament. Spiritual kinship, the relationship between godparents and godchildren, is discussed in Cases M37–M39; this is of English importance because of the changes brought about by the Council of Trent. Legal kinship, which arises through adoption, is discussed in M40. Impediments arising from the crimes of adultery and the murder of a spouse are debated in M41; and in M42 marriage to a heretic is condemned, as it had been in the English cases, to which Southwell makes a cross-reference. Case M43 discusses re-marriage, and Cases M44–M45 deal with the impediment of public honesty, which prevented

[19] *Ibid.*, 79.

marriage after a betrothal or an unconsummated marriage between one of the spouses and close relatives of the other. This then leads to a discussion of affinity in Cases M46–M48, the relationship created between people by their relatives' marriages, which also acted as an impediment to marriages, and had been changed at Trent. The need for a priest to treat marriage guidance in a sensitive way is highlighted by the discussion of impotence and how far it can render marriage null and void in Cases M49–M51. Impotence brings in again the question of witchcraft, which was often blamed for it. Abduction of brides and its power to create an impediment to lawful marriage is discussed in M52. A discussion of the 'impeding' or prohibitory impediments (those which make a marriage unlawful but not invalid) begins in M53. The canonical times of year when marriage is allowed are described in M54, followed by a discussion in M55 of who has the power to dispense with impediments. Sexual matters emerge again in a discussion of conjugal rights, and what may interfere with them (Cases M57–M60), with Southwell encouraging his trainee priests to take a commonsensibly robust view of such matters. Divorce concludes the discussion in Cases M61–M63.

The manuscripts at this point have a large heading, 'De Sponsalibus' (Concerning Betrothals), and the final six cases (M64–M69) discuss this matter. Southwell admits from the very beginning that the discussion of marriage in the earlier cases covered a number of topics relevant to betrothal – deliberation, deception, consent, fear and error, for example. We might add that consanguinity and affinity, and other impediments, also apply. The process of 'getting married' in the early-modern period was a lengthy and complicated one, and it is difficult to separate marriage from betrothal.

The marriage cases, as edited here, conclude with a brief discussion (designated MA here) entitled 'De Osculis' (Concerning Kisses), which is drawn from the Bodleian manuscript, in a brief section which recapitulates some points from the earlier marriage cases, and which is not edited here. The discussion of kisses takes a decidedly un-puritanical approach, and concludes with some rambling and not entirely coherent notes on sexual morality. The reference at the beginning of the discussion to the custom of the 'fatherland' ('patriae consuetudinem') may take us back to English matters, bearing in mind Erasmus's well-known comments on the kissing habits of the English.

The cases concerning ecclesiastical fasts

In the Sancroft manuscript there are twelve cases about fasting, edited here. These are more general in their scope than the cases on fasts in the earlier, English collections, although the first case (F1), on the age at which people should fast, explicitly mentions England. The next five cases (F2–F6) look at the types of people who may be excused from fasting. Case 7 looks at the consumption of eggs and dairy products in Lent, and discusses the role of local custom in fasting regulations. There is no explicit reference to England here, indeed Southwell mentions Belgium instead, but it was generally the custom, especially in the North of England, to avoid such foods in Lent,[20] and Southwell's resolution probably reflects this. The remaining cases discuss the types of food and drink which were acceptable while fasting (F8), and how fasting and abstinence affected the meals which were eaten at different times of day (F9–F12). Case F11 mentions the tendency of the British to have larger collations than the French. These cases are a reminder of the continuing strength in the English Catholic tradition of the minute regulation of dietary customs. As an appendix to them, a brief calendar of feast days and statement of rules with regards to fasting and feasting is included, drawn from the Ampleforth manuscript.

Faculties

As an appendix, a list of faculties which is found at the end of the Ampleforth manuscript is included here. They are undated, but mention the 'king of England', so must be post-1603, and perhaps are more or less contemporaneous with these cases of conscience. They are granted by an unnamed Cardinal Protector of the English. It is also unclear for whom precisely they were intended, whether for all the clergy or just some of them. Once a priest had been trained, perhaps using the cases of conscience edited here, his freedom to apply the casuistical judgements and principles he had learned from his professors was guided by the 'faculties' he was granted. For example, it will be seen from the faculties that they allow a departure from the normal canonical requirements on the part of missionary priests of a sort which is discussed at greater length in the cases of conscience. Celebrating Mass and administering the other sacraments will need to be performed in difficult circumstances, and the faculties allow modifications. Fasting and marriage matters also involve faculties to grant dispensations. There is also a faculty to read prohibited books, excepting works of astrology and the writings of Machiavelli and also, a little surprisingly, of Charles Dumoulin (1500–1566),[21] the maverick French jurist and critic of the Council of Trent. There is no extended discussion of faculties in the historical literature, of which I am aware, but other examples from roughly this era are to be found printed

---

[20] P. J. Holmes, *Elizabethan Casuistry* (Catholic Record Society, 1981), 40–1.
[21] R. Filhol, 'Charles Dumoulin', in *Dictionnaire de droit canonique*, ed. R. Naz (Paris, 1953), V, 41–67.

in a number of sources and invite comparison with those included here.[22] The question of the faculties granted to priests, both secular and religious, became an important issue in the great controversies surrounding the appointment from 1625 of, first, William Bishop, then Richard Smith as successive bishops of Chalcedon, to act as Catholic bishops in England. Thomas Southwell played a significant role in these controversies, publishing a work opposing Smith in 1629, on which he collaborated with a Belgian, Antonio Goffar, who was himself a publisher of works of casuistry.[23] A number of the cases in this collection should be read in the light of these controversies, especially the cases on confirmation and jurisdiction.[24]

The cases and their Elizabethan counterparts

These Caroline cases of conscience invite comparison with the Elizabethan cases of conscience edited in the early 1580s by William Allen and Robert Persons and also those used at roughly the same time in the seminary at Douai-Rheims to train English priests.[25] In fact, it seems at times that Southwell was deliberately bringing these earlier casuist discussions up to date. Southwell refers on several occasions in the cases given below to the manual edited by Allen and Persons in the early 1580s, which, of course, shows the enduring influence of their work, although Southwell is keen on occasion to point out how he differs from these writers. It is worth going through the five references that Southwell makes to the work of Allen and Persons to demonstrate this.[26] In Case 26, Southwell, with some slight hesitation, concludes that priests may perform the sacraments without the correct canonical vestments, a sign that life for a priest in England under persecution might be difficult; he does so by saying that 'Cardinal Allen and Father Persons once responded in this way', and he gives a reference to 'Casus 8 De Poenitentia', which

---

[22] On faculties, see Philip Hughes, *Rome and the Counter-Reformation in England* (London, 1942), esp. 296–7, 344ff, 418–19; T. F. Knox, *The First and Second Douai Diaries* (London, 1878), 354–5, 364–7; idem, *Letters of William Cardinal Allen* (London, 1882), 359–62; A. O. Meyer, *England and the Catholic Church under Queen Elizabeth*, trans. J. R. McKee (London, 1916), 486–9.

[23] A. Goffar, *Vindiciae pro Nicolao Smitheo* (Louvain, 1631). On Southwell's part in this book, see A. F. Allison and D. M. Rogers, *The Contemporary Printed Literature of the English Counter-Reformation 1558–1640* (London, 1989), I, 7–8; A. F. Allison, 'Richard Smith's Gallican Backers and Jesuit Opponents I', *Recusant History* 18 (1987), 373.

[24] Cases 77 and 82, for example. Southwell's attitude towards the bishops of Chalcedon is also probably connected to his views on the Council of Trent's reception in England, since the bishops took their stand on Tridentine rules with regard to faculties.

[25] See Holmes, *Elizabethan Casuistry*.

[26] The reference to 'Alanus' as an authority in Case 78 does not seem to be a reference to the work of Allen and Persons, but may refer to Alain de Lille.

can be identified through this reference in the Allen-Persons manual.[27] In Case 109, on the question of whether Catholics may buy and sell former monastic property and benefices in England, Southwell immediately reports that Allen and Persons say that both are lawful as things at present are in England, but adds that they give no reason, and then proceeds to supply his own. This suggests a degree of academic rivalry across the generations, but also a real substantive disagreement over this very serious matter. Allen and Persons in the early 1580s had envisaged the retention in lay hands of monastic land as a temporary arrangement; half a century later, Southwell disagrees. It is not so much that Allen and Persons give no reason, nor indeed that they agree in substance with Southwell. The fact is that he sees this ownership as permanent, if regrettable; they see it as temporary.[28] In the crisp resolution which Southwell gives to Case 111, which deals with the question of whether Catholics may buy and rent the products of ecclesiastical benefices held by heretics, and also whether they may maintain the fabric of the churches currently occupied by heretics, there is another reference to Allen and Persons, and Southwell says they support his view entirely.[29] Southwell's answer here is brief, and Allen and Persons are more prolix, so perhaps Southwell intended his readers (or listeners) to refer to the earlier work, but on the other hand, he gives no specific reference to it. Southwell flatly contradicts his two forerunners in Case 112, which is a discussion of whether the Catholic patron of a living may present a heretic to the Protestant bishop for appointment, in order that a crypto-Catholic or a luke-warm Protestant is appointed rather than a thorough-going puritan. He says that Allen and Persons had replied that neither was lawful, but that he, Southwell, considers both are lawful. It is worth adding that the Elizabethan casuists were particularly vehement in this conclusion, saying it would be to 'present a wolf, rapacious and thirsting for the blood of the flock'.[30] In the same way, finally, Southwell refers to Allen and Persons in order to disagree with them in his discussion of Case 114. They had, Southwell claimed, denied that it was lawful for the Catholic patron of a church living to receive payment from a heretic he appointed to it, and also for a heretic minister who is converted to sell the benefice; Southwell, in contrast, thought that both could be justified. In fact, Southwell does not entirely do justice to the subtlety of the argument used by Allen and Persons, who were willing in certain circumstances to allow this simony, especially in the second case if the money was put to pious uses, which

---

[27] Holmes, *Elizabethan Casuistry*, 87 (A-P II, I, 8).
[28] *Ibid.*, 96–8, 100–1 (A-P II, I, 21 and II, II, 3).
[29] *Ibid.*, 109–10 (A-P II, II, 10–11).
[30] *Ibid.*, 114 (A-P II, II, 14).

is not very different from what Southwell says. However, he is right to emphasise that there is a broad disagreement here.[31]

In addition to these specific references, of the cases edited here roughly a third discuss questions very close to some of the cases which had been considered by the Elizabethan casuists. As might be expected, many of the decisions made by Southwell are broadly similar, but there are two significant shifts in emphasis.[32] First, the casuists of the Elizabethan era were more willing than Southwell to allow latitude on matters of separation from heretics, especially on recusancy, in order to enable Catholics to survive persecution in England. Southwell condemns attendance at church, except for noblemen who accompany the Queen, and is reluctant to allow servants and children to go with their masters and parents to Anglican divine service. In the Allen-Persons cases of about 1581, on the other hand, the authors (particularly the anonymous author of the 'Solutions') had been prepared to countenance a certain degree of occasional conformity.[33] This question was the subject of a great deal of debate among Elizabethan Catholics, and the 'official' line on the subject of occasional conformity had hardened quite quickly after the Allen-Persons cases were written.[34] Southwell wrote – as he says himself – after a specific papal condemnation of conformity by Paul V in a brief of 1606, and also at a time when the profession of Catholicism was less likely to have fatal consequences. Persons himself took an extremely firm line on 'church-papistry' in a book published in Latin in 1607, to which Southwell himself refers three times in these cases.[35] Southwell is able to describe his own strict line on recusancy as 'the salutary practice used on this matter in England'; salutary because it is 'of great importance to preserve the purity of faith of Catholics', necessary to avoid perversion, and because attendance at church is a 'distinguishing mark' of heresy.

---

[31] *Ibid.*, 116–17 (A-P II, II, 17–19).

[32] *Ibid.*, Introduction, pp. 1–5; P. Holmes, *Resistance and Compromise* (Cambridge, 2009), 99–125.

[33] Below, Cases 2–8, 14–16, 22, 30, 85–6, 91, 97; cf. Holmes, *Elizabethan Casuistry*, A-P I, 6 (pp. 74–7); II, I, 4 (pp. 84–6); I, I, 14 (pp. 91–2); II, I, 18–19 (pp. 94–5); II, II, 1 (p. 99); II, II, 20 (pp. 117–18); II, II, 25–6 (pp. 120–1); D-R. B8 (pp. 20–1); F3 (p. 38); F5 (pp. 39–40); I1 (p. 48); I2 (p. 49); I6 (p. 50); I8 (p. 51); K5 (p. 57).

[34] The story of how Catholic doctrine on recusancy and conformity developed under Elizabeth and James can be traced in G. Crosignani, T. M. McCoog, M. Questier (and P. Holmes) (eds.), *Recusancy and Conformity in Early Modern England* (Toronto, 2010); Holmes, *Resistance and Compromise*, 79–125, 198–9; Elliot Rose, *Cases of Conscience* (Cambridge, 1975), esp. Part 1, chaps. 6 and 7.

[35] R. Persons, *Quaestiones duae de sacris alienis non adeundis* (St Omers, 1607), referred to in Case 3 and twice in Case 4. Cf. Ginevra Crosignani, *'De Adeundis Ecclesiis Protestantium'. Thomas Wright, Robert Persons, S. J. e il Dibattito sul Conformismo Occasionale nell'Inghilterra dell'Eta Moderna* (Institutum Historicum Societatis Iesu, Rome, 2004).

Such occasional attendance by Catholics might be acceptable in some
countries, but not generally in England, Southwell suggests, and there
only very rarely, for very good reasons, and privately, in order to avoid
causing scandal.[36] Similarly, Southwell is less inclined to allow Catholics
to conceal their religious identity by the use of equivocation than Persons
and Allen had been, although he does not condemn such subterfuges
entirely.[37] To be discovered as a Catholic was simply less dangerous in
the 1630s than it had been half a century before. 'Often there is really no
particular danger in hearing Mass', Southwell is able to say.[38] However,
he emphasises that there are still iniquitous laws which forbid Catholicism in England, in contrast with Germany, France and Poland, where
there is 'a mixture of religions', and 'liberty of conscience'; and he uses
this as a reason for opposing mixed marriages in England, contrary to the
practice (at least according to some) in Germany.[39] One important sign of
how the persecution of Catholics in England had changed by Southwell's
time is the fact that his doctrine tends to be laxer in relation to priests
than the laity; this is not a tendency evident in the Elizabethan casuists.
Under Elizabeth, the clergy had made up the bulk of the martyrs, but the
laity had also suffered very severely. By the Stuart period, the number
of executions for Catholicism had decreased considerably, but the clergy
were by then somewhat more likely to suffer death, and in other ways,
than the laity. As Southwell says, 'ordinarily secular people are not in
such danger' as priests, 'but priests are ordinarily in grave and probable
danger of imprisonment, exile etc.'[40] Hence, when Southwell discusses
the use of equivocation to avoid detection, his doctrine is laxer when it
comes to priests than in a different case when he deals only with the laity.
This is not hypocrisy or inconsistency, but is based on the good casuist
doctrine that we have a right to protect our lives, even if we break some
less important aspects of our moral code in the process: priests are more
likely to be able to use this as a reason than the laity.[41] The priests in
addition have a greater call on our moral sympathy because their work
is for the common good, and not just for their own individual concerns;
the shortage of priests in England, 'where priests are rare and in hiding
... itself is a sort of necessity', sufficient to allow the rules governing
ritual to be relaxed.[42] Thus, Southwell considers (after some debate) that

[36] Case 4.
[37] Cases 1, 2, 70; cf. Holmes, *Elizabethan Casuistry*, A-P I, I (pp. 63–6); I, 4 (pp. 69–71);
I, 7 (p. 77); D-R. F3 (p. 48); F5 (pp. 39–40); I1 (p. 48); J5 (pp. 54–5); K5 (p. 57).
[38] Case 17.
[39] Cases 22 and 85.
[40] Case 81.
[41] Compare Case 1 with Case 70.
[42] Case 27.

it might be possible for a priest to escape from prison after having sworn that he will not do so, even if the result is that the Catholic laity in the prison may suffer as a result.[43] Southwell does not oppose all equivocation and dissimulation in all circumstances, however, and is willing to allow a bride to conceal the fact that she has lost her virginity by giving evasive answers when questioned, and by employing subterfuges on her wedding night to avoid her husband discovering it –it will be better for him not to know, Southwell feels.[44]

The second major difference between the doctrine of the Elizabethan casuists and that of Southwell follows from the last, but leads to advice which seems in a way to run rather counter to the somewhat stricter line adopted by Southwell which has just been discussed in the last paragraph. This approach develops when he discusses matters which are concerned rather more broadly with the position of the Catholic community as a minority in English society. By Southwell's day the position of the Catholic Church in England was more clearly defined than it had been half a century earlier. On both sides – both Catholic and Protestant – the fact that Catholicism might remain the religion of a small minority of Englishmen was gradually being accepted. Southwell's resolutions reflect this change. Allen and Persons had been reluctant to admit that Catholic lay patrons should present heretic ministers to their benefices, while Southwell encourages patrons to appoint what we might call conservative Anglicans since they will do less harm than those of puritan views.[45] Southwell was better able to face the realities of the Catholic situation in England than the Elizabethan casuists had been. Allen and Persons considered the possession by laymen of former monastic property a temporary situation which would be ended at the restoration of Catholicism. Fifty years on, Southwell decided that the Pope could dispense with heretic nobles who held abbey lands, and mentioned the famous dispensation brought to England in the reign of Mary I by Cardinal Pole, which the Elizabethan writers had chosen to ignore.[46]

A faintly eirenic tone can be detected in Southwell's cases. He admits clearly the right of Charles I to the throne of England, while Persons and Allen had (without denying her title directly) cast doubt upon the legality of Elizabeth's government.[47] Southwell is even prepared to renounce the inquisitorial rights of the Catholic Church over Protestants; he admits

---

[43] Case 89.
[44] Case M67.
[45] Cases 12, 112, 113, 114; cf. Holmes, *Elizabethan Casuistry*, A-P II, II, 7 (pp. 106–7); II, II, 14 (p. 114); II, II, 16 (pp. 115–16); II, II, 19 (p. 117); D-R. H2 (p. 46); H3 (p. 47).
[46] Cases 109, 115; cf. Holmes, *Elizabethan Casuistry*, A-P II, I, 21 (pp. 96–8); II, II, 3 (pp. 100–1); II, II, 13 (pp. 111–14); D-R. B21 (pp. 26–7); G2 (pp. 43–4).
[47] Case 94; cf. Holmes, *Elizabethan Casuistry*, A-P I, 1 (pp. 63–6); II, II, 27 (p. 121).

that some heretics labour in 'invincible ignorance' after nearly a century
of the English schism, and hence do not suffer the censures usually
allotted to the heretic, and are not excommunicated by the Bull *In Coena
Domini*.[48] In another case, Southwell accepts as a probable opinion that
heretics are 'truly and properly Christians', and hence should be treated
with humanity in the event of a shipwreck.[49] Even contact with 'notorious persecutors of the clergy' in England might be considered only
a venial sin, Southwell decides, citing Thomas Sanchez, and departing
from the standard view followed generally by Elizabethans, and based
on a canonical source, the Extravagant *Ad Evitanda* of Pope Martin V,
which had condemned as a mortal sin associating with such people.[50]
As Southwell says, life would be difficult if we had to avoid all contact
with justices of the peace, mayors, and judges on the ground that they
were associated with persecution in some way. Southwell seems almost
to accept that the position of Catholicism as a minority sect in England
is, if not permanent, at least likely to last a long time. Hence he allows
priests to perform confirmation services, while under Elizabeth the casuists did not consider this case, and merely decided that confirmation
was not an essential ceremony since there were no bishops in England
to administer it.[51] Southwell's judgement here follows the decision at
the end of Elizabeth's reign (after Allen and Persons wrote) to send an
archpriest to England with faculties allowing him to perform this sacrament. It may also be connected to Southwell's opposition at roughly the
time these cases were being composed to the appointment of an English
Catholic bishop with the title Bishop of Chalcedon. Southwell discusses
at some length under what circumstances the books of heretics can be
read by a priest, and again his doctrine here seems a good deal softer
(within the limits imposed by the laws of the Church) than that of the
earlier casuists.[52] In the marriage cases, there is an interesting discussion
of the difficulties people, both heretics and Catholics, face in some parts
of Europe – Southwell mentions Holland – if they wish to abide by the
canon of the Council of Trent requiring the presence of a Catholic parish
priest to validate a marriage. Southwell suggests tentatively that the Pope
might 'with tacit indulgence' allow such marriages to be valid, saying
that 'some agreement often develops between heretics and Catholics that
they should live according to their religion, which the Pope is judged to
approve in order to secure the well-being of Catholics'.[53]

---

[48]   Cases 117, 118, 119.
[49]   Case 125.
[50]   Case 120; cf. Rose, *Cases of Conscience*, esp. 86–8.
[51]   Case 77; cf. Holmes, *Elizabethan Casuistry*, D-R. B11 (p. 22).
[52]   Case 123; cf. Holmes, *Elizabethan Casuistry*, A-P II, I, 16 (pp. 92–3).
[53]   Case M20.

Of the cases dealt with by Southwell that had not been discussed by the Elizabethan casuists, some consider problems which were new to Catholics in the seventeenth century. The Oath of Allegiance, which was imposed on the Catholics by James I after the Gunpowder Plot and which aroused a great controversy, is discussed at some length in four cases.[54] The line taken is, as might be expected from a Jesuit, wholly hostile to the Oath, and this was indeed very much the doctrine of the mainstream English Catholic movement, Jesuit or not. It is interesting to note, however, that even here Southwell was able to use the powerful tool of casuistry to attempt to make life a little easier for Catholics in England. The central doctrine was that a Catholic should die rather than take the Oath, as some indeed did, since it denied the papal power in temporals, which was a matter of faith.[55] Nor could the Catholic practise equivocation with respect to the Oath, using the sort of subterfuges that were permissible to avoid capture when interrogated; not because the Oath itself required the swearer to say he was not using equivocation for that was redundant in an oath,[56] but simply because the papal power in temporals was so significant a part of Catholic doctrine. However, Southwell would allow a Catholic to ask for a delay before he refused the Oath, in order to have time to arrange his affairs in such a way as to protect his dependants.[57] Southwell also argues that a Catholic might send a friend or servant to an official to get him a passport or licence of some sort, knowing that this friend would need to swear the Oath in order to obtain the document.[58] In addition, Southwell is prepared, with some reluctance, to say that it might be lawful to bribe an official so that he falsely says you have taken the Oath of Allegiance; but only in circumstances where scandal can be avoided. His reasoning is that you are then asking the official to commit the lesser evil (of lying) in preference to the greater evil (of persecuting you). Southwell in the same case is much clearer, however, in concluding that it is lawful for a Catholic to bribe an official into not offering him the Oath in the first place: this is to buy off ill-treatment, which is always lawful.[59] Southwell is clearly pulled in two directions by the Oath of Allegiance, as Allen and Persons had been by the question of recusancy in the 1580s. On the one hand, it was important to demonstrate complete hostility to the Oath; on the other hand, it was necessary to exploit any possible loop-hole which might preserve lives. Another subject for further domestic controversy among

[54] Cases 9, 10, 11, 95.
[55] Case 9.
[56] Case 70.
[57] Case 95.
[58] Case 11.
[59] Case 10.

Catholics at the time – the question of the vocations of seminarists – is also resolved, in one of the longest of these cases.[60] Southwell decides in the end, after a very careful refutation of a contrary judgement by the great casuist 'Navarre' (or Martin ab Azpilcueta), that the seminarists' oath – that they will return to England after their education – does not prevent them entering the Society of Jesus or other religious orders, as Southwell himself had.

Probabilism

There is also a difference in academic approach between Southwell and his Elizabethan counterparts. Allen and Persons' resolutions are prefaced by a brief methodological introduction, which mainly emphasises the differences between, on the one hand, divine law, which included the law of nature, and, on the other hand, human law, which included the Canon Law, the law of the Church. The essential message here was that Canon Law was overruled by the law of nature, which allowed Catholic priests and the laity to do what they had to in order to survive; and that papal dispensations of some sort were needed in the future to bridge the gap between the law of the Church and the law of nature. The Allen and Persons text then relies on clear argument with occasional references to the Bible, the Canon Law and a few respected canonists. It is true that the roughly contemporary Douai-Rheims cases rely much more heavily on the authority of other casuists, especially Martin ab Azpilcueta, who is referred to 143 times, but also the old English canonist William Lyndwood (1375?–1446), who is referenced 19 times. But in the 1580s the great academic discipline of casuistry was only just getting into its stride.[61] Thomas Southwell writes, in contrast, as a skilled and learned casuist, in a great Catholic, and especially Jesuit, tradition which had by his time about two generations of publications under its belt. This tradition had also developed a methodology, which has been labelled probabilism.[62]

Southwell is writing self-consciously in this probabilist context.[63] What he wishes to arrive at is a judgement ('sententia') on moral prob-

---

[60] Case 133.

[61] P. Holmes, 'Casuistry', *The Philosophers' Magazine* 2 (1998), 16–17.

[62] It is interesting that one of Southwell's successors as Professor of Theology at Liège, Anthony Bonville *alias* Tyrrell, was a major authority on probabilism in the 1660s; see Birrell, *Florus Anglo-Bavaricus*, 50.

[63] On probabilism, see M. W. F. Stone, 'Scrupulosity and Conscience: Probabilism in Early Modern Scholastic Ethics', in *Contexts of Conscience in Early Modern Europe 1500–1700*, ed. Harald E. Braun and Edward Vallance (London, 2004), 1–16; Albert R. Jonsen and Stephen Toulmin, *The Abuse of Casuistry: a History of Moral Reasoning* (London, 1983), 164–75; James Franklin, *The Science of Conjecture: Evidence and*

lems which is safe, one on which a confessor or priest giving pastoral guidance can rely, and one which will not lead Catholics into sin. He explains the problems involved in this quest for casuist certainty in three cases here, which all show a desire to discuss the nature of the probabilist approach. In Case 18 he asks what a priest in England should do if he is asked about a moral problem and, because the persecution of Catholics in England disrupts the normal life of a priest, the priest does not have books or advisors at hand to guide him. Would the priest sin if he gave advice based on an 'improbable' opinion? It is worth emphasising that 'probability' did not quite have its modern meaning for Southwell. 'Probability' for a seventeenth-century casuist meant primarily what could be supported by proof. When a case is discussed by Southwell, he generally gives an answer and then 'proves' (Latin: *probare*) the answer, usually in a clause or sentence beginning 'because' (Latin: *quia*). This proof will generally consist either of a piece of logical argument (proof *a priori*, based perhaps on the meaning of the words used in the question, *ex ipsis terminis*[64]), then appeal to divine/natural law, or to the law of the Church. Above all this proof needed the support of some authorities: the Bible in the case of divine law; the Canon Law, papal Bulls or conciliar decrees in the case of ecclesiastical law. But it also needed the corroboration of learned theological support, from other casuists, either consulted directly or through their printed books and manuscripts. Hence the dilemma in Case 18, when a priest in hiding in some far-flung part of England had access to neither. Southwell concludes that then it might be necessary in such circumstances for a priest to follow an improbable path (that is, give an opinion or judgement which lacks proof, or is based on his own unsupported judgement), but that the priest should certainly avoid doing so in cases which might cause irreparable harm (matrimonial cases and those involving exorcism are mentioned), and that the priest should not be rushed into giving a decision in order to show off.

In Case 74, a longer resolution is given of a similar question: whether a confessor is bound to follow the probable judgement of a penitent. The case begins with a definition of probable opinion, and one which shows Southwell at his cautious, commonsensical best. There is nothing provocative about Southwell's probabalism. For him, a probable judgement is one which rests on a solid and grave foundation, and one on the opposite side of which there is nothing convincing to be said. Southwell backs his definition up with reference to two authorities: Thomas Sanchez, his great favourite from among the casuists, and Vincenzo

Probability before Pascal (Baltimore, 2001), esp. chap. 4; John Harty, 'Probabilism', in *The Catholic Encyclopedia*, XII (New York, 1911).
[64] Case 74, for example.

Filliucci, both Jesuits. It is enough for a judgement to be probable for it to have the support of one upright and learned doctor; however, the doctor concerned should not be an 'ancient' one, but instead one from among the more recent authors. Since he is a modern author, such a person will have had a chance to study a larger body of casuistical literature and also to have considered more cases. Southwell then proceeds to the substantial question and concludes that a confessor should not feel compelled to absolve a penitent who has relied on a probable opinion, if it might be a lax one. In Case 73, Southwell treads a similar path. He says at first that it would be a grave sin to use doubtful matter or form in the administration of the sacraments, even if it were probable, except as we have just seen in the sacrament of penance. The reason given is that such an action might invalidate the sacrament. He then adds that it is lawful to follow a probable opinion in providing the matter of the other sacraments, and this, he says explicitly, might be a doubtful opinion. The reason is that urgent necessity or a serious reason justifies this risk. Although he does not say so explicitly in this particular case, it is worth emphasising that the danger under which priests worked in England at the time he was writing provided such an urgent necessity.

Probabilism was soon to be attacked because it allowed, as Southwell clearly states here, a moral decision to be made on the basis of one judgement by a respected theologian, which might be lax and might even be doubtful. A probable opinion might be, simply, probable, in the modern meaning of the word; in one of the cases on fasting, Southwell uses the Latin *verisimilis* (literally 'like the truth') as a synonym for *probabilis*, which perhaps shows this.[65] Some probable opinions were stronger than others; some could be described as 'less probable'.[66] There was nothing very odd about this if we consider casuistical judgements as the fallible work of mere human beings; but it did lead to misunderstandings, best shown in the satire of Pascal.[67] Pascal would probably have found much ammunition in the work of Southwell, and indeed many of the casuists Pascal attacks are favourites with our author. Pascal makes great fun of a long list of (largely) Jesuit authors with unpronounceable names that the casuists he lampoons refer to; and his list contains many of the writers who are referenced by Southwell and who are to be found in our list of authorities printed after the end of this Introduction.[68] Pascal attacks the method of probabilism,[69] the use of equivocation,[70] the 'contrat Mohatra'

---

[65] See Case F3.
[66] See, for example, Case 84, where the phrase 'minimal probability' is used.
[67] B. Pascal, *Les Provinciales*, ed. Louis Cognet (Paris, 1965).
[68] *Ibid.*, 91–3: 'tous ces gens-là étaient-ils chretiens?' ('were all these people Christians?').
[69] *Ibid.*, esp. 85ff.
[70] *Ibid.*, 164ff.

(the Mohatra contract) and other concealed usury,[71] the laxity in sexual matters,[72] the defence of simony,[73] and the abuse of self-defence ('celui qui a reçu un soufflet peut poursuivre à l'heure son ennemi, et même à coups d'épée', according to Lessius, quoted by Pascal).[74] All of this is in Southwell, if he is read with Pascal's jaundiced eye and controversial bitterness against the Jesuits.

In fact, Southwell's approach throughout the cases resolved in this collection is arguably closer to the probabiliorism which within half a century of Southwell's death had to some extent replaced probabilism in Catholic theology. It is interesting to read Southwell's brief aside on the subject of duelling. After a technical discussion of the possible lawfulness of the duel, Southwell confides in his readers that he had found from experience that when giving advice to noblemen on subjects like the duel it was best to keep the message simple, and not allow them any opening to justify duelling by giving an over-sophisticated message. He attacks his fellow-Jesuit, Paul Laymann, an authority he otherwise treats with respect, for giving a rather subtle judgement on duelling which could be misinterpreted in this way.[75] Similarly, in the marriage cases there is an interesting discussion of the limits of probabilism in a case on a variant of the Martin Guerre problem: 'what certainty is sufficient concerning the death of the first spouse in order for a second marriage to be lawfully undertaken?' Mere probability or conjecture is not enough in a question so serious, because it affects the rights of a third party, and might involve inflicting grave harm on those involved. What is required in such a case is 'moral certainty'. But then the casuist approach reasserts itself, and Southwell admits that this may be true of the law courts, but that in the forum of conscience 'some notable probability or presumption is enough'. This is especially true if it is a woman contemplating a second marriage and she is driven to it by hardship, because as the legal adage has it 'what necessity forces must be judged free from blame'.[76]

Southwell is always keen to demonstrate that his arguments have the support of a good number of writers – hence his use of frequent citation and a slightly irksome tendency to over-use references. In Case 25, for example, he supports a comment by listing fifteen writers who also hold his opinion; in Case 124, there is a similar list of eleven authorities,

---

[71]   *Ibid.*, 139–41; compare Case 150.
[72]   *Ibid.*, letter 10.
[73]   *Ibid.*, letter 12.
[74]   'He who has received a slap in the face may immediately pursue his enemy, and even strike him with a sword', Pascal, *Les Provinciales*, 237–8; compare Case 106, although Southwell's doctrine is a good deal more sensible.
[75]   Case 105.
[76]   Case M43.

named one after the other. In the course of resolving the twelve cases here on fasting Southwell makes 200 separate references to 36 authorities. One of his most common expressions when giving a reference to an authority is to add that this authority writes 'from the common view' (*ex communi*), or some other similar phrase. Southwell is always keen to show that his judgements are not only probable but that they are 'more probable' than the alternative, in part because they have so much learned support.

It is worth concluding that the development of casuistry in the Catholic Church in the sixteenth and seventeenth centuries took place against a background of religious turmoil which would tend to encourage the development of a probabilist approach. The really interesting point about all the English Catholic casuist literature from Elizabeth I to Charles I is that English Catholic moral theologians were trying to find a way in which Catholics could survive in England. This might involve breaking canons with regard to Catholic ritual; it would necessitate subterfuges to avoid arrest, and it could justify actions which might be of questionable morality in normal circumstances. Hence, a laxer casuistical framework might be useful, one based on probabilism. It might be argued, more broadly, that the development of a rather relativistic moral theology in probabilism in sixteenth- and seventeenth-century Catholic Europe owed something to considerations of the moral dilemmas faced by Catholic missionaries and communities in divided Europe, not to mention the wider global context of Catholic expansion. By the 1630s, when laxism was, according to the enemies of the Jesuits, on the increase, and its great agent was their probabilist casuistry, in fact Southwell's doctrine was in some ways more rigorous than that of his predecessors of the 1580s; the tide had turned by then in England. He was less willing, as has been shown above, than they were to allow 'Church papistry', equivocation and other subterfuges. The great watchword for Southwell was often 'scandal'; the law of charity (hence the law of God, which trumped every merely human canon) demanded that Catholics, especially priests, should avoid giving scandal to their fellow-Catholics. The over-subtle interpretation of probable opinions in order to avoid arrest or detection, or to bend the rules of ceremonial or Catholic practice, could offend, even unsettle, the faith of other Catholics. On the other hand, Southwell's doctrine on the separation of Catholics from heretics does, as has also been argued above, seem less rigorous than that of his predecessors; the tide was not all flowing in one direction.

SOUTHWELL'S AUTHORITIES

There are just over 2600 separate references to about 115[77] authorities made in the course of the 193 cases edited below. As was customary in such works, these annotations were contained in the body of the text in often highly abbreviated form. A good number of the references are, as it were, second-hand; that is, Southwell merely mentions the name of an authority, and then says what other author cites this writer. The great majority of the references are to other moral theologians of the period, especially Jesuits. The top ten favourite authors are: Thomas Sanchez (420 references); Paul Laymann (240); Martin Bonacina (192); Giles de Coninck (186); Adam Tanner (127); Basilius Pontius (92); Francis Suarez (84); Leonard Lessius (84); Martin Azpilcueta, known as Navarre (69); Vincenzo Filliucci (54); Antonino Diana (45). All except three of these writers Southwell relied upon principally were Jesuits: the exceptions are Diana, of the Theatine Order and famous for his laxism; Pontius, an Augustinian and used especially by Southwell for his marriage cases; and Azpilcueta (Navarre), who was the great founding father of early-modern casuistry, an Augustinian canon (although he was related to Francis Xavier). All except one (also Navarre, who died in 1586) died in or after 1610, fulfilling Southwell's requirement that a probable opinion should be based on the work of a later writer. It is highly likely that a majority of these, his favourite, authors were known to Southwell personally. In addition to the works of fellow-casuists, Southwell also cited what might be called official sources: the Bible (40 times); papal Bulls, briefs and enactments of various sorts (54); Canon Law and the Gloss[78] (177) and the decrees of various councils of the Church (98). Among the 'official' sources we should also, of course, mention the great medieval theologians, Peter Lombard and St Thomas Aquinas. Although Aquinas is only directly referred to 39 times, and Lombard not once, their work stands behind much of the casuistry of the other writers listed here, whose works are often explicitly couched as commentaries on the *Summa Theologica* of Aquinas or the *Sententiae* of Lombard. The only English authors cited by Southwell are William Allen and Robert Persons (6 times for the cases discussed above); Persons alone (3 times); Gregory Sayer (8 times); and, for different reasons, Alexander of Hales,

---

[77] Not counting each individual Pope and each individual Council that Southwell cites.
[78] The codified canon law text-book, or *Corpus Iuris Canonici*, used by Southwell was probably the three-volume work published at Rome in 1582 by order of Pope Gregory XIII. The 'Gloss' refers to the medieval commentaries, the work of a number of highly respected canonists, which were published alongside the canons themselves, and which had themselves acquired a sort of 'canonical' status.

Roger Widdrington and Matthew Kellison (once each). As an English casuist, Southwell was, at least as far as he was concerned, ploughing a lonely furrow.

A full list of Southwell's references to authorities follows, with as many of the authors identified as possible; a few of the identifications are provisional, especially where there are only one or two references, and these are general ones not assigned by Southwell to a particular work. As has been said, Southwell quite often refers to an author simply by name, generally because he has (as he acknowledges) taken the reference from another of his authorities; in the list that follows, if this applies to an author who is referred to only once, or a few times, in the text, this is indicated. No attempt has been made to check all of Southwell's references, although those which have been checked have been found to be accurate. The dates and places of publication of the works cited below are just a guide and are not meant to imply that this was the edition used by Southwell; they generally relate to a work the editor has consulted to check the reference. If an author is a member of the Society of Jesus, it is mentioned, but not in the case of other religious orders, largely to emphasise the use Southwell made of his colleagues' work. The numbers listed after each entry refer to the cases edited here; if there is a further number in brackets, it shows the number of times that author is referenced in that individual case. The English cases are referred to by the number they are given in the text (and by Southwell). I have added the prefix M to the marriage cases, and MA to the Appendix to these cases; and the prefix F is attached to the cases concerning fasts.

Abbas, *see* Panormitanus.
Adrian VI, Pope (1459–1523), *Quaestiones in quartam sententiarum* (Paris, 1528). 2 refs: 98, 113.
Agrippa, Heinrich Cornelius (1486?–1535), *De occulta philosophia* (Cologne, 1533). 1 ref.: 128. *De sacramento matrimonii*: 1 ref.: M42.
Alanus. Alain de Lille (1128–1202). 1 ref. (no work specified): 78.
Allen and Persons. Cardinal William Allen (1532–1594) and Robert Persons, SJ (1546–1610), MS Cases of Conscience, 1581 (see P. J. Holmes, *Elizabethan Casuistry* (Catholic Record Society, 1981)). 6 refs: 26, 78, 109, 111, 112, 114.
Angelus. Carletus Angelus de Clavasio (1411?–1495), *Summa Angelica*. 12 refs: 78, 84, 126, 146, 149, M9, M28, M35, M40, M48, F1, F12.
Antoninus, St, Archbishop of Florence (1389–1459). 1 ref. (no work specified): M43.
Aquinas (1225–1274), St Thomas, *Summa Theologica*. 16 refs: 6, 29, 98 (2), 101, 103, 131, 141, 144, 149, F1 (2), F2, F7, F8 (2). *Supplementum tertiae partis*: 23 refs: M4 (2), M9, M14, M18 (2), M31 (2),

M34, M35 (2), M37 (2), M41, M42 (2), M44, M49, M50, M53, M60, M64 (2).

Aragon. Peter of Aragon (fl. 1600). 1 ref. (no work specified): 124.

Argent, *see* Silber.

Armilla, *see* Fumo.

Augustine (386–429), St, *De bono viduitatis*. 1 ref: M18. *Letter 180.* 2 refs: 17, 19. *De Virgine Maria.* 1 ref: M32.

Azor, John, SJ (1535–1603), *Institutionum moralium* (Louvain, 1610–1616). 42 refs: 1 (2), 2 (2), 3, 4 (2), 13, 14, 25, 27 (2), 70, 71, 101, 102, 115, 123, 128, 132, 133 (4), 136, M32, F1 (2), F2, F3, F5, F6, F7 (3), F9, F10, F11 (3), F12 (2).

Azpilcueta, *see* Navarre.

Baldus de Ubaldis (1327–1400). 1 ref. (no work specified): 107.

Bannes, Dominic (1527?–1604). 5 refs. (no work specified): 93, 124, 142, 146, 149.

Barclay, William (1546–1608). 1 ref. (no work specified, but in favour of the Oath of Allegiance): 9.

Baronius, Cesare (1538–1607), *Annales* (1588–1607). 1 ref: 9.

Becanus, Martin, SJ (1563–1624), *Manuale controversiorum* (Mainz, 1625). 10 refs: 7, 9, 23, 25, 100 (3), 125 (3).

Bellarmine, Robert, SJ (1542–1641) St. *Apologia pro iuramento fidelitatis.* 1 ref: 9; *De Controversiis matrionialibus.* 7 refs: M1 (2), M19 (3), M29, M35. *De Monachis.* 1 ref: M32. Lectures at Louvain. 1 ref: 147. For *Declarationes ex Bibliotheca Bellarmini, see* Durand.

Bible. 40 refs: 4 (4 Kings 5), 4 (1 Corin. 8), 9 (1 Corin. 5; 2 Thess. 3; 2 John; Tit. 3; Matt. 18), 16 (1 Tim. 5), 22 (Exod. 34; Deut. 7; 3 Kings 11; Ezra. 9), 95 (Luke 20, 25), 144 (41 Gen.), M1 (Ephes. 5), M2 (Ephes. 5), M25 (John 22), M29 (1 Corin. 7), M35 (Levit. 18, 20; Deut. 25; Gen. 20, 29, 38; Exod. 6), M42 (Exod. 34; Deut. 7; 1 Kings 11; 1 Corin. 7; 2 Corin. 6), M43 (Matt. 19), M46 (1 Corin. 6), M48 (2 Kings 20), M56 (Levit. 20; Ezek. 18), M59 (Gen. 38), M61 (Matt. 19), M63 (Matt. 5), M68 (1 Corin. 7).

Binsfield, Peter (c. 1540–1603). 1 ref. (no work specified): M26.

Boethius (480–524). 1 ref. (no work specified): 107.

Bonacina, Martin, SJ (1585–1631), *Opera omnia sive tractatio absolutissima omnium conscientiae casuum* (Paris, 1633). 192 refs: 1, 3, 4 (2), 10, 11, 13, 18, 23, 25 (2), 27, 28, 70, 73, 77 (2), 78, 98, 101, 107 (2), M1 (2), M2 (4), M3, M4 (2), M5 (3), M6, M7 (3), M8 (4), M9 (3), M10, M11 (3), M12 (2), M13, M14 (2), M15, M16, M17, M18 (2), M19 (3), M20, M21 (2), M22 (2), M23 (2), M24 (4), M26 (2), M27 (3), M28 (2), M29, M30, M31, M32 (2), M33 (2), M34, M35, M36 (2), M37 (2), M38 (5), M39, M40 (2), M41 (4), M42, M43 (3), M44 (3), M45 (2), M46, M47 (2), M48 (4), M49 (3), M50 (2), M52 (4), M53 (3), M54 (2), M55 (3), M56 (2), M57 (2), M58 (2), M59 (4),

M60 (3), M61 (3), M62 (2), M63, M64 (4), M65 (2), M66, M67, M68 (5), M69 (3), F1 (2), F3 (2), F4 (2), F6 (3), F7 (2), F8 (2), F9 (2), F10, F11, F12 (2).

Bonaventure, St (1221–1274). 2 refs. (no work specified): M35.

Cagnazzo, Giovanni (d. 1521), *Summa Tabiena* (Bologna, 1517). 2 refs: 136, M49.

Caietan, Thomas de Vio (1469–1534), *Opuscula omnia* (Louvain, 1587). 2 refs: 28, M28. *Summae theologicae D. Thomae Aquinatis* (Louvain, 1581). 21 refs: 24, 89, 93, 98, 125, 128, 144, 146, 147, M2, M28, M35 (3), M41, M51, MA, F1 (2), F6, F9.

Cano, Melchior (1509?–1560), *De locis theologicis* (Cologne, 1585). 3 refs: M1, M2, M3.

Canon Law. 177 refs: 9, 10, 16, 18 (Gloss), 19, 20, 21 (2), 22, 25, 27, 28 (3), 29, 30, 75, 77 (3), 92 (2), 93, 94, 96, 99 (Gloss), 100, 101, 132, 133 (4, plus Gloss), M1, M2, M4 (2), M5 (3), M6 (7), M8 (5), M9 (3), M10, M16, M17, M19 (8), M24 (2), M26 (2), M28 (4), M31 (3), M32 (12), M33 (2), M37 (5), M38 (3), M40 (3), M41 (13), M43 (6), M44 (7), M45 (2), M48 (6), M49 (4), M50 (3), M51 (2), M52 (7), M53 (2), M54, M55 (2), M58 (4), M63 (2), M64 (4), M65, M68 (3), M69 (3), F7 (1, plus Gloss).

Cardinals, Declarations of, *see* Durand and Gallemart.

Castanega, Martin de (fl. 1511–1551). 1 ref. (no work specified): 128.

Castro-Palao, Ferdinand, SJ (1581–1633), *Operis moralis* (Louvain, 1631–41). 6 refs: 1, 13, 14, 17, 101, M55.

Catechism, Roman. 1 ref: M53.

Cicero (106–43 BC), *De Officiis*. 1 ref: 144.

Civil Law. 19 refs: 107 (2), M1, M4, M7 (2), M10 (3), M22, M23, M34 (2), M36, M38, M40 (3), M52.

Comitolus, Paulus, SJ (1547–1626), *Responsa moralia* (Lyons, 1609). 3 refs: 82, M26, M60.

Coninck, Giles de, SJ (1571–1633), *De sacramentis ac Commentariorum, ac disputationum in universam doctrinam D. Thomae de sacramentis* (Antwerp, 1619). 186 refs: 1 (3), 2, 3, 4 (2), 5, 8 (2), 10, 19 (2), 23, 70, 71, 77, 81 (2), 84, 85, 96, 104, 105, M1 (2), M2 (3), M3 (3), M4 (2), M5, M6 (3), M7 (5), M8 (4), M9 (3), M10 (3), M11, M12 (2), M13 (2), M14 (3), M15, M16 (2), M17 (2), M18 (2), M19 (3), M20 (3), M21, M22 (2), M23 (2), M24 (5), M25 (4), M26 (3), M27 (3), M28, M29 (2), M30, M31 (2), M32 (2), M33 (2), M34 (2), M35 (2), M36 (2), M37, M38 (3), M39, M40 (3), M41 (4), M42, M43 (3), M44 (2), M45 (2), M46, M47 (2), M49, M50 (4), M51, M52 (2), M53 (3), M54 (2), M55 (2), M56 (3), M57 (3), M58 (3), M59 (2), M60 (2), M61 (2), M62 (2), M63 (3), M64 (4), M65 (2), M66 (2), M67 (3), M68 (4), M69 (4).

Conradus. Conrad Summenhart (1458–1502), *De contractibus* (1500). 2 refs: 74, 144.

Cornel, *see* Agrippa.

Councils etc., decrees etc. 98 refs: Agatha, 22, M35 (2); Aurillac, M35 (2); Carthage, 6, 22, M32; Chalcedon, 22, M32; Eliberitanum, 22; Florence, 77 (2), 84, M1 (2), M3, M5, M6; Laodicea, 6, 22; Lateran, 9, 24, 132 (2), M25, M36, M46; Diocesan Synod of Liège (1618), 21; Lyons, 9; Nicaea, M42; Pamiers, M35 (2); Rome, M32; Sens, 70; Sixth General Synod (Third Council of Constantinople), F7; Toledo (various), 94, M32 (3); Tours, M32; Trebur, M32; Trent (*and see* Cardinals, Declarations of), 23, 24, 77, 82, 105, 124 (2), 139, M1 (2), M2 (2), M6, M9, M19, M20 (2), M21, M22, M23, M24, M25 (3), M26, M28, M29, M32, M35 (2), M36, M37 (3), M38 (5), M43, M44 (4), M45, M46, M48, M52 (3), M53, M54 (2), M55, M61, M63, M65.

Covarrubias y Leyva, Diego (1512–1577). *Opera omnia* (Antwerp, 1627). 4 refs: 89, 98, 107, 140.

de Loaisa, Garcias (1479–1546). 2 refs. (no work specified): 139, 146.

Decius, Philippus (1454–1536/7). 1 ref. (no work specified): 140.

Delrius. Del Rio, Martin Antoine (1551–1608). 1 ref. (no work specified): 128.

Diana, Antonino (1585–1663), *Resolutiones morales* (1629). 45 refs: 19 (6), 25, M2, M5, M8 (2), M21, M22, M26, M27, M33, M41 (2), M44, M50, M52 (2), M53, M55, M57, M59 (2), M60 (3), M67, F1, F3, F4, F5, F7, F8 (2), F9, F10, F11 (3), F12 (2).

Dionysius the Areopagite (5th century). 1 ref. (no work specified): M37.

Durand, Laurent (fl. 1610–1640), *Nouae declarationes Congregationis S. R. E. Cardinalium ad decreta Sacros. Concilii Tridentini ex bibliotheca Card. R. Bellarmini* (Lyons, 1633). 10 refs: M20, M21, M22 (2), M23, M24, M26 (2), M38, M44.

Durandus. Durand, Guillaume (1230–1296). 3 refs. (no work specified): M31, M35 (2).

Estius. William Hessels van Est (1542–1613), *In quatuor libros sententiarum commentaria* (Douai, 1616). 4 refs: 84, M1, M3, M35.

Faber, Philip (1564–1630), *Philosophia naturalis Ioan. Duns Scoti: ex quatuor libris sententiarum* (Venice, 1616). 1 ref: 74.

Fagundez, Stephen, SJ (1577–1645), *Tractatus in quinque Ecclesiae praecepta* (Louvain, 1626). 15 refs: 4, 15, 101, 102 (2), F1, F3 (2), F7 (2), F8 (2), F10, F11, F12.

Farinacci, Prospero (1554–1618). 2 refs. (no work specified): M26, M33.

Filliucci, Vincenzo, SJ (1566–1622), *Quaestionum moralium de Christianis officiis in casibus conscientiae* (Louvain, 1622). 54 refs: 1 (2), 4, 19 (2), 70, 71, 73, 74 (3), 77 (2), 78 (2), 79, 84, 89, 90, 91, 92, 101, 104 (5), 124, M47 (2), M49, M60, MA (2), F1 (2), F2, F4 (2), F5, F6 (2), F7 (3), F8, F9 (2), F10, F11 (3), F12 (2).

Fumo, Bartolomeo (d. 1545), *Summa Aurea Armilla* (Antwerp, 1541). 7 refs: 107, 132, 147, 149, M41, M43, MA.

Gallemart, Ioannes (d. 1625), *Sacros Concilii Tridentini canones et decreta, item declarationes cardinalium* (Cologne, 1621). 1 ref: M44.

Gamachaeus, Philippus (1528–1625), *Summa theologica* (Paris, 1634). 4 refs: 8, 25, 77 (2).

Garcias, *see* de Loaisa.

Graffeus. Graffi, Giacomo (1548–1620), *Decisionum aureum casuum conscientiae* (1600). 4 refs: 26, 120, 123, F7.

Gretser, Jacob, SJ (1562–1625). 1 ref. (no work specified): 9.

Guttier. Gutierrez Placentinus, Johannes (fl. 1587). 2 refs. (no work specified): 124, M47.

Hadrian, *see* Adrian.

Halensis. Alexander of Hales (c. 1186–1245) 1 ref. (no work specified): F8.

Henriquez, Enrique, SJ (1536–1608), *Theologiae moralis summa* (Salamanca, 1591–3). 19 refs: 70, 77, 79, 80, 84, 98, 99 (2), 121 (2), 124 (2), M2, M18, M28, M41, M47, M52 (2).

Homobonus (?). 1 ref. (no work specified): M55.

Hostiensis, *see* Segusio.

Hugolino. Hugguccio of Pisa (b. 1210). 6 refs. (no work specified): 120, 123 (5).

Iavellus, Chrysostomus (d. 1540). 1 ref. (no work specified): 120.

Justinian, *see* Civil Law

K/Kon/Koninck, *see* Coninck.

Kellison, Matthew (1561–1642), *Commentarii ac disputationes in tertiam partem summae theologicae St Thomae Aquinatis* (Douai, 1632). 1 ref: M20.

Laymann, Paul, SJ (1574–1635), *Theologia moralis in quinque libros* (Munich, 1634). 240 refs: 1, 2, 3, 4 (2), 5, 6, 11 (2), 12, 13, 14, 19 (11), 22 (3), 25, 26, 27, 70, 71, 72, 77, 78, 80, 84, 85, 88, 96 (3), 98, 100 (3), 101, 102, 105 (2), 106, 107, 109, 117, 119, 120 (2), 121 (2), 122, 123, 133 (5), 136, M1 (2), M2 (3), M3, M5 (5), M6, M7 (4), M8 (3), M9 (2), M10, M11 (3), M12, M13, M14, M16, M17 (2), M18 (2), M19 (3), M20 (3), M21, M22, M23, M24 (2), M25 (6), M26 (2), M27 (3), M28 (2), M29, M30, M31 (2), M32 (3), M34 (2), M35 (2), M36, M37, M38 (5), M39, M40 (3), M41 (4), M42, M43 (3), M44 (3), M45 (2), M46, M47, M48, M49 (4), M50 (2), M51, M52 (3), M53 (3), M54 (2), M55 (2), M56, M57 (2), M58 (2), M59 (4), M60 (6), M61 (3), M62 (3), M63 (2), M64 (5), M65, M66 (2), M68 (5), M69 (3), F1 (2), F2, F3, F4 (2), F5, F6, F7 (5), F8, F9 (3), F10, F11 (4), F12 (2).

Ledesma, Petrus de (1544–1616). 7 refs. (no work specified): 124, 132, 142, M9, M41, F3, F5.

Lessius, Leonard, SJ (1554–1623), *De iustitia et iure* (Louvain, 1605).
  84 refs: 13, 14 (2), 25, 70, 87 (2), 88, 89 (3), 90, 104 (2), 105 (2), 107
  (2), 109, 113 (2), 115, 125, 126, 127 (2), 128 (4), 134, 135, 138 (4),
  139 (5), 140, 141, 142 (2), 144 (2), 145, 146, 147 (2), 148, 149, 150,
  151, M5 (4), M7 (4), M8 (3), M11, M16, M17 (2), M32, M59, M67,
  MA, F1 (2), F2, F3 (3), F7 (2), F8, F12.
Lopez, Ludovicus (d. 1595?). 4 refs. (no work specified): 132, M43,
  M45, F12.
Lorca, Petrus de (1554–1606), *De legibus* (Madrid, 1614). 3 refs: 1, 23,
  25.
Major, John (Scotus) (1467–1550), *Quartus sententiarum* (Paris, 1509).
  5 refs: 74, 78 (2), M35, F11.
Malderus, Joannes (1563–1633), *De virtutibus … ad secundam secundae
  D. Thomae* (Antwerp, 1613). 4 refs: 23, 25, 106, 133.
Malta, Knights of, statutes. 1 ref: 21.
Manuel. Emmanuel, commentator on Aquinas. 2 refs. (no work speci-
  fied): 124, 142.
Medina, Juan de (1490–1547), *De poenitentia, restitutione, et contrac-
  tibus* (Ingolstadt, 1581). 8 refs: 133, 139, 142, 146, F5, F10, F11, F12.
Mendoza. Antonio Escobar y Mendoza, SJ (1589–1669). 1 ref. (no work
  specified): 146.
Molfesius, Andreas (fl. 1619). 1 ref. (no work specified): M55.
Molina, Luis, SJ (1533–1600), *De iustitia et iure* (Louvain, 1605). 22
  refs: 10, 87, 100, 102, 104, 105 (2), 107 (2), 108, 136, 144, 147 (2),
  149 (2) M5, M17, M52 (3), M62.
Navarre. Martin ab Azpilcueta (1492–1586), *Enchiridion sive manuale
  confessariorum* (Lyons, 1575). 69 refs: 14, 25, 70, 74, 79, 82, 85, 90,
  96, 98, 99, 106, 115, 120, 123, 124 (2), 125, 128, 132 (2), 133 (7), 139,
  142, 146, 147, M1, M5 (2), M8 (2), M9 (2), M10, M11, M14, M21,
  M22, M26 (2), M27 (2), M28, M33, M41, M46, M48 (2), M49, M52,
  M53 (2), M60, MA, F1 (2), F2, F6, F8 (2), F10, F11, F12 (2).
Palude, Petrus de (1277–1342). 3 refs. (no work specified): M2, M9, F1.
Panormitanus, Nicolaus de Tedeschis (1386–1445), *Lectura super
  quarto et quinto Decretalium* (Venice, 1475). 3 refs: 20, F7, F8.
Parra, Petrus de, SJ (fl. 1580). 1 ref. (no work specified): 147.
Pedraza, Juan de (fl. 1567). 1 ref. (no work specified): 146.
Peres, P. Perez, Antonio, SJ (d. 1649). 1 ref. (no work specified): 101.
Persons, Robert, SJ (1546–1610), *Quaestiones duae de sacris alienis*
  (1607). 3 refs: 3, 4 (2); *and see under* Allen and Persons.
Pliny the Elder (23–79), *Naturalis Historia.* 1 ref: 128.
Polanchus, Iohannes, SJ (1517–1576), *Breve directorium ad confessarii
  munus* (Rome, 1554). 1 ref: 74.
Pontius, Basilius (d. 1629), *De sacramento matrimonii* (Louvain, 1640).
  92 refs: 29, M1 (2), M2 (3), M4 (3), M5 (3), M6 (3), M7 (3), M9, M10

(2), M11, M13, M14, M16, M17, M18, M19 (2), M21 (2), M22 (5), M23, M24 (2), M25, M26, M27, M29, M31, M32 (2), M33 (4), M35 (2), M38 (2), M40, M41 (4), M42, M44, M46, M47, M48 (3), M49 (4), M51 (3), M53 (2), M54, M55 (2), M57, M59, M61, M62, M63, M64, M66, M67, M68 (4), M69 (2).

Popes: Briefs, Bulls, papal injunctions/laws etc. 54 refs: Bulls of 1560, 1582, 1592: 105. Alexander II: M33. Alexander III: 75, M56. Boniface VIII: 9 (*Unam Sanctam*), M53. Calixtus II: M32. Clement [I]: 6. Clement VIII: M20, M26 (3), M27. Eugenius IV: 77 (2), 84, F3. Fabianus: 6. St Gregory: 9, 77, M32. Gregory II: 9. Gregory III: 9. Gregory VII: 9. Gregory IX: M16, M17, M34 (2). Gregory XIII: M32. Innocent I: M32. Innocent II: M32. Innocent III: M35, M43. John XXII: M25. [Martin V], Extravagant *Ad Evitanda*: 120. Nicholas I: M64. Paul V in 1606 and 1607: 3 (2), 5, 9. Paul V (*Ritual*): M21 (2). Pius V: M26, M34, M45 (3). Siricius: M32. Sixtus V: M49. Urban VIII in 1626: 9, 129. Urban VIII in 1631: M20. Zacharias: M33.

Praepositus, *see* San Giorgio.

Rebellus, Ferdinand (d. 1608), *Opus de obligationibus* (Louvain, 1608). 11 refs: 107, 144, 147, M2, M17 (2), M22, M27, M44, M48, M52.

Reginaldus, Valerius, SJ (1543/5–1623), *Praxis fori poenitentialis* (Lyons, 1616). 14 refs: 8, 14 (2), 28, 77, 98, 101, 125 (2), M55, F3, F6, F8, F11.

Rodriguez, Manuel (1545–1619), *Summa casuum conscientiae* (Douai, 1614). 11 refs: 25, 28, 74, 144, M8, M26, M28, M33, M49, M52, M60.

Rosella, *see* Trovamala.

Sa, Manuel de, SJ (1528/30–1596), *Aphorismi confessariorum* (Venice, 1595). 31 refs: 6, 27, 74, 80, 82, 84 (2), 85, 89 (2), 90, 91, 92, 121 (2), 124, 132, 142, 144, 146, 147, M22, M41, M44, M47, M48, M52, M60, MA, F1, F6.

Salas, Juan de, SJ (1553–1612), *Tractatus de legibus in primam secundae* (Louvain, 1611). 8 refs: 20, 25 (2), 29, 72, 73, 74, M55. *Commentarii in secundam secundae D. Thomae* (Louvain, 1617). 24 refs: 139 (2), 140 (3), 141, 142 (2), 144, 145, 146 (2), 147 (3), 148, 149 (6), 150, 151.

Salon, Miguel (fl. 1590). 1 ref. (no work specified): 146.

San Giorgio, Joannes de, *alias* Praepositus (d. c. 1378), *Quaestiones*. 26 refs: 19 (4), 79, 83, 84 (4), 85, 96, M14, M16 (2), M17, M20 (2), M22, M26, M49, M52 (3), M61 (2).

Sanchez, Thomas, SJ (1550–1610), 'Manuscript seen at Seville'. 1 ref: 124. *Opus morale in praecepta Decalogi* [running title: *Summa*] (Antwerp, 1631–2). 419 refs: 1 (3), 2, 3, 4 (2), 6, 7, 10, 11, 13, 17 (2), 18, 22, 28 (2), 29 (2), 70 (2), 71, 74 (4), 78, 85 (2), 89, 93 (2), 96, 99, 102, 103, 104 (4), 107 (2), 116 (2), 117, 118 (4), 119, 120 (3), 121,

122, 123 (11), 124 (4), 126 (4), 127 (2), 128 (4), 129 (2), 130, 131, 132 (3), 133 (4), 134, 135, 136, 137 (2), M1 (3), M2 (3), M3 (2), M4 (5), M5 (6), M6 (8), M7 (8), M8 (8), M9 (4), M10 (4), M11 (2), M12, M13 (8), M14 (2), M15 (3), M16 (2), M17 (3), M18 (2), M19 (5), M20 (2), M21 (4), M22 (6), M23 (2), M24 (9), M25 (2), M26 (5), M27, M28 (2), M29 (3), M30, M31 (6), M32 (5), M33 (3), M34 (4), M35 (5), M36 (2), M37 (3), M38 (13), M39, M40 (5), M41(6), M42 (3), M43 (5), M44 (4), M45 (4), M46 (3), M47 (3), M48 (5), M49 (11), M50 (6), M51 (5), M52 (4), M53 (4), M54 (3), M55 (5), M56 (5), M57 (4), M58 (2), M59 (6), M60 (7), M61 (5), M62 (2), M63 (4), M64 (7), M65, M66 (4), M67 (2), M68 (5), M69 (7), F1 (2), F2 (2), F3 (2), F4 (6), F5 (5), F6 (2), F7 (2), F8, F9 (3), F10, F12 (2).

Sanchius, Joannes (d. 1620). 1 ref. (no work specified): F9.

Sayer, Gregory (1560–1602), C*lavis regia sacerdotum casuum conscientiae* [running title: *Thes. Casuum Consc.*] (Münster, 1628). 8 refs: 74, 105, 120, 121, 123 (2), 125 (2), F11.

Scotus, *see* Major.

Segusio, Henricus de (c. 1200–1271), 'Hostiensis'. 1 ref. (no work specified): F7.

Serrarius, Nicholas, SJ (1545–1609), *Opusculum de matrimonio Catholicorum cum haereticis* (Cologne, 1609). 3 refs: 22 (2), 85.

Silber, Eucharius (fl. 1480–1510). 1 ref. (no work specified): M2.

Soto, Dominic (1494–1566), *Commentariorum in quartam sententiarum* (Salamanca, 1569). 23 refs: 28, 84, 89, 98, 100, 142, 144, 146, M1, M5 (3), M9, M14, M18, M28, M32, M35 (2), M48 (2), M53, MA.

Soto, Petrus de (d. 1563), *Lectiones de Matrimonio*. 3 refs: M29, M35, M36, MA.

Southwell, Thomas, cross-references to his own MS works. 29 refs: 28, 29, 101, 125, 133, M4, M18, M20, M22, M25, M26, M27, M28, M31, M32, M33 (3), M37, M32, M42, M47, M49, M53 (2), M55 (2), M57 (2).

Suarez, Francisco, SJ (1548–1617), *Defensio fidei catholicae et apostolicae adversus Anglicanae sectae errores* (Coimbra, 1613). 5 refs: 3, 7, 8, 9, 94. *Tractatus de legibus, ac deo legislatore* (Mainz, 1619). 9 refs: 20, 23, 25, 26, 29 (2), 72, 100 (2). *Opus de triplici virtute* (Aschaffenburg, 1622). 7 refs: 1 (2), 10, 11, 71, 81 (2). *Commentariorum et disputationum in tertiam partem* (5 vols., Munich, 1616–17). 52 refs: 6, 11, 18, 19 (3), 73, 74, 75, 77 (2), 78 (5), 79, 80, 82, 83, 87, 92, 98, 118 (3), 119, 120 (3), 122, 123, 124, 125 (3), 126, M1 (2), M3 (2), M4, M22 (2), M24, M32, M33 (2), M37 (2), M38 (2). *Opus de virtute* (3 vols., Munich, 1623–5). 11 refs: 70 102, 109, 113 (2), 117, 131, 132 (2), 138, F7.

Sylvester. Silvestro Mazzolani da Priero (1460–1523), *Summa summarum*. 10 refs: 20, 74, 79, 84, 99, 107, 144, M43, M48, M60.

Tabiena, *see* Cagnazzo.

Tanner, Adam, SJ (1572–1632), *Theologia scholastica* (4 vols., Ingolstadt, 1626–7). 127 refs: 1 (2), 2 (2), 5, 6, 9, 10, 14, 17, 19, 22, 23, 24, 25, 70, 71, 77 (3), 78, 80, 81 (2), 84, 85 (2), 90, 93, 96 (3), 98, 101, 117 (2), 121 (4), 122, 123, 124 (2),125 (3), 128, 130, 132 (2), 138 (2), 139 (3), 140, M1 (2), M2 (2), M3 (2), M4 (3), M5, M6 (2), M8 (3), M9, M11, M14 (2), M18, M19 (6), M20, M21, M22 (3), M26, M28 (2), M29 (2), M32, M33 (2), M35 (2), M36, M38 (3), M40 (2), M43, M44, M45, M49 (4), M50, M51, M52, M53, M55, M56 (3), M62, M68 (5), M69, F3 (2), F6.

Tertullian (c. 160 – c. 225). 1 ref. (no work specified): M37.

Toletus, Franciscus, Cardinal, SJ (1532–1596), *Summa casuum conscientiae* (Douai, 1633). 11 refs: 25, 70, 77, 120, 123, 142, 146, M45, F3, F7, F10.

Trovamala, Giovanni Baptista (15th century), *Summa Rosella*. 2 refs: 147, F8.

Turrianus, Franciscus, SJ (1509–1584), *De fide; de scandalo*. 2 refs: 9, 13.

Valentia, Gregorius de, SJ (1550–1603), *Commentarium theologicorum* (1591–7). 18 refs: 18, 25, 70, 74, 75, 77 (2), 85, 89, 91, 101, 104, 138, 142, 144, 146, M22 (2), F6.

Vazquez, Gabriel, SJ (1549–1604), *Commentariorum, ac disputationum in primam [- tertiam] partem Sancti Thomae* (9 vols., Louvain, 1631). 36 refs: 9, 11 (2), 23, 28, 78, 84 (3), 89, 102, 107, M1 (2), M2 (2), M4 (4), M5 (2), M10 (2), M11, M18, M28 (2), M32, M33, M46, M55, M58, M60 (2), M64.

Vega, Christopher, SJ (d. 1672). 3 refs. (no work specified): 117, 124, M49.

Veracruz, Alonso de la (c. 1507–1584). 3 refs. (no work specified): 128, M33, M48.

Victoria, Franciscus de (1492–1546), *Relectiones de iure belli* (1539). 4 refs: 106, 117, M2, M41. [*De arte magica*]. 1 ref. (no work specified): 128.

Vincent of Spain (13th-century glossator). 1 ref: 84.

Vivaldi, Martinus Alphonsus (1545–1605). 1 ref. (no work specified): 124.

Widdrington, Roger (1563–1640). 1 ref. (no work specified, but in favour of Oath of Allegiance): 9.

Zambrano, Melchior (fl. 1604), *Decissio casuum ocurrentium in articulo mortis* (1604). 5 refs: 76 (2), 78, 80, 82.

ABBREVIATIONS

The following list is of abbreviations Southwell used in his references. Abbreviations that he used for the names of authors and for their works should be clear from the list of Southell's Authorities above.

a. *articulus*, article, chapter, section.
arg. *argumentum*, argument (used to introduce certain references to the Canon and Civil Law).
bapt. *baptismus*, baptism (*de baptismo*, concerning baptism).
c. *see* cap.
C. *concilium*, Council.
cap. *capitulum*, chapter (sometimes indicating a reference to the Canon Law).
cas. *casus*, case (of conscience).
CC. *concilia*, Councils.
cens. *censura*, censure, punishment (*de censuris*, concerning censures).
char. *charitas*, charity (*de charitate*, concerning charity; a subdivision of a work of moral theology, divided according to the Virtues).
cit. *citatus*, as already cited.
can. *canon*, canon, a law of the Church, especially a decree of a Council.
d. *divisio*, division; *and see* db.
db. *dubium, dubitatio*, doubt.
Decalog. *decalogus*, Decalogue, Ten Commandments.
disp., *see* dp.
dist. *distinctio*, distinction, division.
dp. *disputatio*, debate.
dub. *dubium, dubitatio*, doubt.
ep. *epistola*, letter.
Euchar. *Eucharistia*, Eucharist (*de Eucharistia*, concerning the Eucharist).
ff. *fecerunt*, they decreed (used to introduce a piece of Civil Law).
fid. *fides*, faith (*de fide*, concerning faith; a subdivision of a work of moral theology, divided according to the Virtues).
ib., ibi: *ibid.*, in the same place.
imped. *impedimentum*, legal impediment to marriage (*de impedimentis*, concerning the impediments to marriage).
iust. *iustitia*, justice (*de iustitia*, concerning justice).
l. *liber*, book.
l. *lex*, law (often indicating a reference to the Civil Law).
leg. *lege*, in *de lege*, concerning law.

li. *liber*, book.

matrim. *matrimonium*, marriage (*de matrimonio*, concerning marriage).

mor. *moralis*, moral.

n. *numerus*, number.

p. *see* par.

par. *pars*, part.

peccat. *peccatum*, sin (*de peccato*, concerning sin).

praecep. *praeceptum*, precept, commandment (works of moral theology were often commentaries on the Ten Commandments).

pun. *punctum*, point.

q. *quaestio*, question.

reg. *regula*, rule or legal maxim (used with certain references to the Canon Law).

resol. *resolutio*, resolution of a case of conscience.

S. *Sanctus*, Saint (S. T: St Thomas Aquinas).

s. *sectio*, section.

Sa. *see* sum.

Sacram. *Sacramentum*, Sacrament.

sent. *sententia*, judgement (sometimes an indication that a commentary on Peter Lombard's *Libri quattuor Sententiarum* is being referred to).

sum. *summa*, summary (sometimes an indication that a commentary on St Thomas Aquinas's *Summa* is being referred to, or the work itself).

sup. *supra*, above.

tit. *titulus*, title, section.

tom. *tomus*, volume, or section.

tract./trac. *tractatus*, tract, discussion.

ult./vlt. *vltimus*, last.

v. *see* verb.

verb. *verbum*, word (*sub verbo* ..., under the word ...).

WORKS CITED
in the Introduction

Allison, A. F., 'Richard Smith's Gallican Backers and Jesuit Opponents I', *Recusant History* 18 (1987).
———— and Rogers, D. M., *The Contemporary Printed Literature of the English Counter-Reformation 1558–1640*, I (London, 1989).
Aveling, H., 'The Catholic Recusants of the West Riding of Yorkshire 1558–1790', *Proceedings of the Leeds Philosophical and Literary Society* 10 (1962–3).
————, 'The Marriages of Catholic Recusants 1559–1642', *Journal of Ecclesiastical History* 14 (1963).
Bibliothèque de l'Université de Liège, *Catalogue des Manuscrits* (Liège, 1875).
Birrell, T. A. (ed.), *Florus Anglo-Bavaricus* (London, 1970).
Caraman, Philip, *Henry Morse: Priest of the Plague* (London, 1957).
Crosignani, Ginevra, *'De Adeundis Ecclesiis Protestantium'. Thomas Wright, Robert Persons, S. J. e il Dibattito sul Conformismo Occasionale nell'Inghilterra dell'Eta Moderna* (Institutum Historicum Societatis Iesu, Rome, 2004).
Crosignani, G., McCoog, T. M., Questier, M. (and Holmes, P.) (eds.), *Recusancy and Conformity in Early Modern England* (Toronto, 2010).
Dodd, C., *The Church History* (Brussels, 1739).
Fiel, J. P., 'Bacon-Shakespeare: the Tobie Matthew Postscript', *Shakespeare Quarterly* 18 (1967).
Filhol, R., 'Charles Dumoulin', in *Dictionnaire de droit canonique*, ed. R. Naz, V (Paris, 1953).
Foley, H., *Records of the English Province of the Society of Jesus*, V (London, 1879).
Franklin, James, *The Science of Conjecture: Evidence and Probability before Pascal* (Baltimore, 2001).
Goffar, A., [and Southwell, T.], *Vindiciae pro Nicolao Smitheo* (Louvain, 1631).
Harty, John, 'Probabilism', in *The Catholic Encyclopedia*, XII (New York, 1911).
Henson, E. (ed.), *The English College at Madrid 1611–1767* (Catholic Record Society, 29, 1929).
————, *Registers of the English College at Valladolid 1589–1862* (Catholic Record Society, 30, 1930).
Holmes, P. J., 'Casuistry', *The Philosophers' Magazine* 2 (1998).
————, *Elizabethan Casuistry* (Catholic Record Society, 1981).
————, *Resistance and Compromise* (Cambridge, 2009).

Houlbrooke, R. A., *The English Family 1450–1700* (London, 1984).
Hughes, Philip, *Rome and the Counter-Reformation in England* (London, 1942).
Jonsen, Albert R. and Toulmin, Stephen, *The Abuse of Casuistry: a History of Moral Reasoning* (London, 1983).
Kenny, A. (ed.), *The Responsa Scholarum of the English College, Rome*, I (Catholic Record Society, 54, 1962).
Knox, T. F., *The First and Second Douai Diaries* (London, 1878).
——, *Letters of William Cardinal Allen* (London, 1882).
McCoog, Thomas, *English and Welsh Jesuits 1555–1650* (Catholic Record Society, 75, 1995).
—— (ed.), *Monumenta Anglia* (Monumenta Historica Societatis Iesu 143, Rome, 1992).
——, 'Thomas Southwell', in *New Oxford Dictionary of National Biography* (Oxford, 2004).
Meyer, A. O., *England and the Catholic Church under Queen Elizabeth*, trans. J. R. McKee (London, 1916).
Oliver, G., *Collections towards Illustrating the Biography of the Scotch, English and Irish Members of the Society of Jesus* (London, 1845).
Pascal, B., *Les Provinciales*, ed. Louis Cognet (Paris, 1965).
Persons, Robert, *Quaestiones duae de sacris alienis non adeundis* (St Omers, 1607).[79]
Richter, A. L. (ed.), *Canones et Decreta Concilii Tridentini* (Leipzig, 1853).
Rose, Elliott, *Cases of Conscience* (Cambridge, 1975).
Smith, L. P. (ed.), *The Life and Letters of Sir Henry Wotton* (Oxford, 1907).
Sommervogel, C., *Bibliothèque de la Compagnie de Jésus* (Brussels, 1890).
Southwell, John and Morse, Henry, *To the Catholics of England* (London reprint, 1973).
Southwell, N., Ribadeneira P. and Alegambe, P. (successive eds.), *Bibliotheca scriptorum Societatis Iesu* (Rome, 1676 and ed. A. F. Allison, London, 1969).
Southwell, T., *see* Goffar, A.
Stone, M. W. F., 'Scrupulosity and Conscience: Probabilism in Early Modern Scholastic Ethics', in *Contexts of Conscience in Early Modern Europe 1500–1700*, ed. Harald E. Braun and Edward Vallance (London, 2004).
Trappes-Lomax, R., *The English Franciscan Nuns* (Catholic Record Society, 24, 1922).

---

[79] This includes *De non audiendis haereticorum concionibus* (Case 3); the *De Poenitentia* (Case 126) is in the Allen-Persons manual of 1581 (p. xxxviii above).

THE CASES

The English Cases

Casus aliqui ad Angliam pertinentes
(Some cases which concern England)

[1] Casus 1us. <u>Vtrum sit licitum ad vitanda pericula negare se aut Papistam:</u> aut saltem interrogatum id dissimulare. <u>Respondeo</u> nunquam esse
licitum fidem negare v.g. dicendo se catholicum aut Papistam non esse.
hoc enim malum est intrinsece. ita Laym. l. 2. tr. 1. c. 11. Conink. de fid.
dp. 5. db. 5. Bonac. de Praecep. dp. 3. q. 2. p. 3. Sanch. in Decalog. l. 2.
c. 4. Azor. Filucius. <u>Immo nec licet ita aequiuocando</u> eam dissimulare,
vt quoad externam verborum speciem vere eam negare videaris. hoc
enim in hac materia est illicitum, quia etiam impium est sola apparentia
externa velle eam negare. ita Conink. Tan. de fide. q. 7. n. 115. Suar. de
fid. dp. 14. s. 3. n.7. Cast. Palao de fid. dp. 1. punct. 16. <u>neque de hoc
simulationis genere loquuntur</u> Sanch. et Laym. dum dicunt eam licere,
sed de mera occultatione aut detrectatione responsionis et similibus.

    <u>Fidem occultare licitum est iuxta omnes,</u> immo consultum saepe et
necessarium. <u>quod si interrogeris: distinguendum</u> vel priuata autoritate
interrogeris vel publica. <u>si primum, licitum erit</u> declinare responsum,
dicendo v.g. quid ad te, etc. <u>Sin publica,</u> sunt qui dicunt quod si haereticus in odium fidei interroget, quod non tenearis respondere per se
loquendo, quia cum talis potestatem interrogandi non habeat contemni
potest, ac si priuatus esset ita Coninck. Palao citati, et Lorca apud ipsos.
<u>Alii dicunt tunc fidem</u> ei confitendam alias derogari eius dignitati et
existimationi ita Sanch. Azor. Filiuc. Bon: sed in re non discrepant. Quia
moraliter loquendo semper erit talis obligatio, vt bene Suar cit. n. 6.
et Tan. n. 120. et sic in Anglia credo practice sentiendum, quia saltem
foret grauis offensio et vilipensio fidei si Catholicus maxime grauis
non auderet fidem suam profiteri. at si cessarent haec extrinseca iudicio
prudentis viri, tunc credo veram priorem sententiam.

Case 1. *Is it lawful to deny that one is a Papist in order to avoid danger,
or at least, when interrogated, is it lawful to dissimulate?*
    I reply that it is never lawful to deny the faith, for example by saying
that one is not a Catholic (or a Papist), for this is intrinsically evil;
thus, Laymann, Coninck, Bonacina, Sanchez, Azor and Filliucci [refs].
Indeed, it is not lawful in such a case to dissimulate, using equivocation,
so that you really seem to deny it according to the external appearance
of the words you use. For in this matter to do so is unlawful, because it
is also impious to wish to deny the faith by external appearance alone;
thus, Coninck, Tanner, Suarez and Castro-Palao [refs]. When Sanchez

3

and Laymann say it is lawful, they are not writing about this type of
dissimulation, but only about the simple concealment or refusal of an
answer, and things of that sort.

According to everyone it is lawful to conceal one's faith; indeed
it is often prudent and necessary to do so. If you are interrogated, it
is important to distinguish between whether you are interrogated by
someone with private or public authority. If it is done by a person in a
private capacity, it is lawful to decline making a response, saying, 'What
is it to you?' etc. But if you are interrogated by some person with public
authority (1) there are those who say that if a heretic interrogates you
out of hatred of the faith, considering the matter narrowly in itself, you
are not bound to respond because since this person does not have the
right to interrogate you, he may be treated with contempt as if he were a
private person; thus, Coninck, Castro-Palao, as cited above, and Lorca,
who is cited by them. Others say (2) that in this case the faith must be
confessed to him, otherwise his dignity and reputation would be diminished; thus, Sanchez, Azor, Filliucci, Bonacina. But these writers do not
disagree with the previous ones in essentials, because considering the
matter in a broader context, as one of morality, there will always be this
obligation to confess the faith, as Suarez and Tanner show well [refs].
And so in England I believe the case must in practice be judged in this
second way (2), because at the least, grave offence may be given and
the faith will be despised, if a Catholic, especially an important one,
does not dare to profess his faith. But if these extrinsic considerations
(of scandal) are not present, according to the judgement of a prudent
man, then I believe the prior judgement (1) is the true one.

[2] Casus 2. <u>An liceat in Anglia comedere carnes diebus prohibitis in
hospitiis et mensis</u> haereticorum, ad vitandum detectionis periculum:
et capite aperto interesse benedictioni mensae ritu haereticorum.
<u>Respondeo id esse licitum. Nam praeceptum</u> Ecclesiae non obligat ad
abstinendum cum tanto periculo, [fo. 1ᵛ] sed neque est signum distinctiuum Religionis, aut Professio haeresis: cum Catholici diebus prohibitis vesci carnibus et possint et soleant ob varias causas. Solum ergo
occultatur fides quod licitum est. ita Laym. Bonac. Conink. Sanch. Azor.
citati. Excipe cum Tan. n. 118. nisi in odium fidei id alicui praeciperetur,
tunc enim mors potius esset sustinenda. <u>Interesse Benedictioni mensae
etiam aperto capite non est illicitum,</u> tum quia vrbanitas et publica tran-
quillitas id exigit, vt in simili docet Tan. n. 125. tum quia vnusquisque
tunc solet more suo mensae benedicere, vnde stare aperto capite praecise non est argumentum quod cum iis in precibus communices. et hoc
ad minimum docet Azor par. 1. l. 8. c. 11. q. 2.

Case 2. *Is it lawful in England, in order to avoid the danger of detection,*

to eat meat on prohibited days in the inns and at the tables of heretics,
and to be present bareheaded when grace is said at table according to
the heretics' rite?

I reply that it is lawful, for the teaching of the Church does not oblige
us to abstain from this when in such danger. Neither is it a distinctive
sign of our religion nor a profession of heresy, since Catholics may,
and are accustomed to, eat meat on prohibited days for various reasons.
Therefore, to do this only involves concealing one's faith, which is
lawful; thus, Laymann, Bonacina, Coninck, Sanchez and Azor in the
places cited. The exception is, as Tanner says [ref.], if anyone should be
ordered to do this out of hatred of the faith, for then he must suffer death
rather than do so. To be present, even bareheaded, when grace is said
at table is not unlawful, first because urbanity and public tranquillity
demand it, as Tanner teaches in a similar case [ref.]; and second because
everyone is accustomed then to bless the table in his own manner, and
so to stand with a bare head is not positively an argument that you are
communicating with heretics in their prayers. And Azor's doctrine is the
same, down to the smallest point [ref.].

[3] 3ᵘˢ. An liceat Catholico adire templa haereticorum precibus et
concionibus interesse; saltem si praemittatur protestatio quod id facias
mere ciuilis obedientiae causa vt statutis regiis obediatur. Respondeo id
nullo modo licitum esse. ita declarauit Paulus V. 10. calend Oct. 1606.
et sequuntur omnes theologi. Sanch. n. 27. Conin. Bonac. Lay. Suar.
l. 6. contra Sect. Angl. c. 9. Azor. p. 3. explicans quae locis prioribus
obscurius dixerat. Ratio est quia ire in vigore statuti facti ad promou-
endam haeresim et supprimendam fidem (vt fit in Anglia) ibique interesse more caeterorum quoad externam saltem compositionem, est vere
communicare in ritibus et haeresim profiteri. Quid enim ad externam
communicationem amplius requiri potest? ad haec, cohonestantur
coetus haereticorum: et aperitur via plurimorum peruersioni et scandalo. Quae rationes non militant iis in locis vbi Catholici eunt mere
sponte, spectandi causa, et ita vt exterius se gerere possint, vt meros
spectatores, proque libito discedere et vbi prohiberi facile possunt ii,
qui periculum essent subituri. Est ergo hoc in Anglia intrinsece malum
et signum distinctiuum.

Eadem est ratio de audienda concione, vt [fo. 2] etiam declarauit
Paulus V. quia haec in Anglia est pars potissima cultus haereticalis et
eam audire est vere haeresim profiteri, vt optime P. Personius in libello
de non audiend. haereticorum concionibus. n. 23.

Case 3. *Is it lawful for a Catholic to go to the churches of heretics and*
to be present at their prayers and sermons, at least if a prior protesta-

tion is made, that you do it purely out of civil obedience in order to obey the royal statutes?

I reply that this is in no way lawful, as Paul V declared on 22 September 1606. All theologians follow this; Sanchez, Coninck, Bonacina, Laymann, Suarez, and Azor [refs], who explains what he had said more obscurely in earlier writings. The reason is that to go on the strength of a statute which was passed in order to promote heresy and suppress the faith (as is the case in England) and there to be present in the manner of the rest of the congregation as far at least as external deportment is concerned, is truly to communicate with heretics in their rites and to profess heresy. For, what more could be required to constitute 'external communication'? By doing this the meetings of heretics are honoured, and a way is opened to the perversion and scandal of many. These reasons have no force in those places where Catholics only go to church once for the sake of being spectators, and thus are able to conduct themselves as outsiders and mere spectators, and may freely leave; and also in places where those Catholics who might be in danger as a result of going to church can easily be prevented from doing so. However, in England this is intrinsically bad and a distinguishing sign of heresy.

The same reason applies to listening to a sermon, as Paul V also declared, because in England that is the most powerful part of the heretic cult, and to hear a sermon is truly to profess heresy, as Father Persons shows very well in his little book, *Concerning not hearing the sermons of heretics* [ref.].

[4] 4us. An liceat temporalis negotii aut officii peragendi causa adire in Anglia haereticorum Ecclesias, v.g. vt vir nobilis ensem ferat ante Regem ad Sacellum: vt filius parentem famulus herum obsequii causa comitetur. Respondeo licitum esse per se loquendo adire templa mere ciuilis officii causa. tunc enim ipsum seruitium praestandum satis declarat non animo illam sectam profitendi accedere, sed alio, idque probat vulgare exemplum Naaman Syri 4 Reg. c. 5. ita Sanch. Laym. Azor. Conin. Bon. Filuc et P. Personius libel. de non adeund. haer: Eccles. n. 14.

Limitatur tamen 1°. modo non communices in ritibus, psallendo v.g. cum illis, etc. 2°. modo non adsit, graue peruersionis periculum, quod non semper aderit. 3°. et principaliter modo plus non fiat quam exigat ratio illius officii aut negoti. Hinc existimo nullo pacto concedendum vt famuli et pueri heris et parentibus toto concionis tempore assistant, sed satis esse si eos eo deducant. plus enim non exigit officii illius ratio: et ex alia parte aperiretur ianua magnis periculis et incommodis si plus concederetur. Atque ita se habet praxis, vt contrarium foret scandalosum.

Similiter nec videtur licitum Comitibus Prouinciarum comitari Iudices regios ad templa, assistendo cum iis toto tempore, quia seruitium id non exigit, satis est si ad fores vsque templi deducant, vt fecerunt aliqui. Ensifero regis videtur concedi posse vt expectet paratus omni momento ad reuersionem casu quo Regi liberet discedere, id enim et ratio officii, et Maiestas regia videntur exposcere.[1] et ita expresse docet P. Personius Sanch. et alii, et satis probatur exemplo Naaman Domino inter adorandum deseruientis Vide Laym. l. 2. tr. 1. c. 11. n. 5. Sanch. l. 2. mor. c. 4. n. 27. Azor. p. 1. l. 8. c. 27. q. 7. Conink. dp. 15. n. 62. Bonac. de praecep. dp. 3. q. 2. n. 27. Filuc. tr. 22. n. 91.

[fo. 2ᵛ] Petes, quid si herus[2] aliquis vere indigeat comitatu sui famuli toto tempore precum et concionis ob peculiarem necessitatem ciuilem? Respondeo nisi esset casus valde extraordinarius et euidens, saltem ob scandalum pusillorum, non deberet fieri, sed omnino relinquendum potius famulatum, multi enim inde ex ignorantia vel infirmitate occasionem sumerent parui pendendi salutarem hanc Angliae praxim, quae tamen maximi est momenti ad fidei puritatem in catholicis conseruandam. quare etiam cum incommodo est abstinendum iuxta illud Apostoli. 1. Cor. 8. si esca scandalizat fratrem meum, non manducabo carnem in aeternum. maxime cum de bono communi hic agatur. deinde vt res sunt in Anglia moraliter fieri non potest sine peruersionis periculo et communicatione in ritibus. denique cum in Anglia itio ad haereticorum preces publicas recepta sit vt signum distinctiuum et haeresis professio, debet esse causa grauissima, et valde euidens, quaeque rarissime in priuatis maxime eueniet, vt haec turpitudo ab ea diuellatur.

Case 4. *Is it lawful in England in order to perform some temporal business or office, to go to the churches of heretics; for example, as a noble man to bear a sword before the king on the way to his chapel, or as a child to accompany a parent, or as a servant to accompany a master for the sake of obedience?*

I reply that speaking of the action in itself, it is lawful to go to a church merely for the sake of a civil duty. For then the need to perform that service is sufficient to declare that you do not go in order to benefit that sect but for another reason, and the example commonly given of Naaman the Syrian in 4 Kings, chapter 5 proves this; thus Sanchez, Laymann, Azor, Coninck, Bonacina, Filliucci, and Father Persons' little book, *Concerning not going to the churches of heretics* [refs].

There are, however, three restrictions: first, that you do not communicate with them in their rites, for example by singing with them, etc.; second, that there is no serious danger of perversion, which there will

---

1 S reads: *reposcere*
2 S reads: *haeres*

not always be; thirdly, and principally, that more is not done than is required by reason of that business or office. Hence I judge that it could on no account be conceded that servants and children might assist their masters or parents for the whole period of the sermon, but it is enough that they accompany them there. For the nature of their office does not demand that they do more, and if more were conceded by them, it would open a door to great danger and trouble. And this is the practice, so the contrary would be scandalous.

Similarly, it does not seem lawful for the local gentry to accompany royal justices to church, staying with them for the whole time they are there, because the role of the gentry does not require it, and it is enough that they accompany the justices to the doors of the church as some do. It seems that it may be conceded to the king's sword bearer that he should wait ready at any moment to go, if the king should wish to leave, for both the nature of his office and the royal majesty seem to demand that. And thus Fathers Persons, Sanchez and others expressly teach, and it is sufficiently proved by the example of Naaman, who served his master while he worshipped; see Laymann, Sanchez, Azor, Coninck, Bonacina, and Filliucci [refs].

You will ask, what if a master truly needs the company of his servant for the duration of the prayers and sermon, for some particular non-religious reason? I reply: unless it is a most extraordinary and evident case, at least because of the scandal it would give to the weaker minded, it should not be done, but instead the servant should completely give up his employment. For many, out of ignorance or infirmity might as a result use the example to under-value the salutary practice used in this matter in England, which is however of great importance in order to preserve the purity of the faith of Catholics. For which reason such behaviour must be given up even if it results in trouble, according to I Corinthians 8 ('if meat scandalizes my brother I will not eat meat for eternity'), especially since it is a matter of the common good. In addition, as things are in England it cannot morally be done without the danger of perversion, and without communicating in their rites. Finally, since to go to the public prayers of heretics is understood in England to be a distinguishing mark and profession of heresy, it should only be done for a most serious and most clear reason, and one which occurs most rarely, and above all in private, so that this dishonour should be removed from such an action.

[5] 5[us]. An liceat Catholico in anglia interesse nuptiis, sepulturis et baptismis dum ritu haereticorum celebrantur. Respondeo illa nullo modo licere in Anglia, et colligitur ex Breui Pauli V. vbi 3ª. distincte prohibet. 1. ad haereticorum templa accedere. 2. eorum conciones audire. 3. cum

ipsis in ritibus communicare. Hoc 3. fieret in praesenti,[3] quare qui praesens est assistere debet toti illi actioni indiuiduae prout fit, atque adeo
actioni haereticali cooperari, quod sane est in ea communicare: quod
vel inde patet, quia si quis ita assisteret actui personae excommunicatae
non toleratae, censeretur iuxta omnes proprie cum eodem communicare, et excommunicationem minorem contrahere. Neque obstat quod
in Germania dicantur ab aliquibus Catholici licite interesse his officiis
humanitatis causa, vt docet Tan. de fid. q. 7. [fo. 3] n. 125. Laym.[4] et
Coninck cit. nimirum quatenus sunt actus ciuiles. 1º. quia statuta parla-
mentiaria effecerunt vt in Anglia adire istas preces sit signum distinctiuum, atque ita consuetudo iam merito obtinuit, secus in Germania. 2º.
quia in Germania ita accedunt, vt possint profiteri, et exterius in ipso
assistendi modo ostendere se mere ciuilitatis causa interesse, vt coho-
nestent amicorum nuptias et sepulturas, et haereticorum[5] mere spectare,
vt nihil ad se pertinentes atque ita omnes intelligunt secus in Anglia.

Case 5. *Is it lawful for a Catholic in England to be present at weddings,
funerals or baptisms when they are celebrated according to the rites of
heretics?*

I reply that this is in no way lawful in England. This judgement is
based on the brief of Paul V where he distinctly prohibits three things:
first, going to the churches of heretics; second, hearing their sermons;
third, communicating with them in their rites. This third point applies
in the present case because these acts are performed using the prayers
and rites of heretics; hence, whoever is present must take part in the
whole of that individual act as it is performed, and so cooperate in a
heretical act, which truly is to communicate in it. Following from this,
it is clear that if anyone assists in that way in the action of a person
who is excommunicated and not to be tolerated, he is judged properly
according to everyone to communicate with that person, and himself
to incur the minor excommunication. Neither is it an objection that in
Germany Catholics are said by some to be present lawfully in these
ceremonies for reasons of politeness, in so far as they are civil acts, as
Tanner, Laymann and Coninck teach [refs]. This is because, first, the
parliamentary statutes mean that to go to those prayers in England is
a distinguishing sign of religion, and thus this worthy custom (of not
going to these services) prevails there, which is different from that used
in Germany. The second reason is that in Germany people go to these
ceremonies in such a way that they can make it clear publicly, and show

---

3   S adds: *quia actus hi fiunt cum precibus et ritibus haereticis*
4   S adds: *l. 5. tr. 2. c. 9. n. 6.*
5   S adds: *ritus*

in the way they conduct themselves that they are there merely for the
sake of civility, so that they may do honour to the weddings and funerals
of friends, and merely watch the rites of heretics, as rites which do not
concern them at all, and everyone understands that this is the case; but
it is different in England.

[6] 6ᵘˢ. Vtrum Catholicus in Anglia possit licite esse patrinus, per se vel
alium in Baptismo ab haereticis collato et e contra. Respondeo Catholicum non posse per se interesse eorum Baptismis, vt iam dictum est.
2°. nec posse alium suo nomine eo mittere, saltem nisi vrgente aliqua
necessitate, quia cum ille peccaturus sit id faciendo, induceret eum ad
peccatum. Caeterum cum suscipere puerum in se bonum sit, possetque
bene fieri ab illis si vellent, ideo graui ex causa potest aliquem mittere,
maxime alias paratum, quod si ille male faciat, sibi imputet, quia non
tenebatur ipse tanto cum incommodo id curare, vt in materia de scandalo docent communiter theologi. Quod si non esset opus aliquem
mittere, sed tantum quasi permittere, vt aliquis ex iis qui alioqui sunt
interfuturi, ipsius nomine id agant, refundendo in ipsum obligationem
patrini, sic non videtur vllo modo illicitum, sed potius bonum vt ipse
obligationem subeat. Consultius tamen quam minimum cum haereticis
in huiusmodi habere commercium, vt docent SS. PP. Clem. l. 2. const.
c. 62. Fabianus Papa. ep. 1. col. 2. CC. Laodicenum can. 37. Carthag.
4. c. 70. Denique haereticum patrinum facere semper illicitum⁶ censent
Tan. cit. et Sanch.⁷ c. 9. n. 12. sed verius ait Lay. l. 5. tr. 2. c. 9. n. 6. id
posse ex causa fieri. quia inter christianos nullum [fo. 3ᵛ] est periculum
pro infante, cum non soleant a patrinis institui, vt docet S. Tho. 3. p. q.
67. a. 8. et Suar. ibid. imo obligationem illam ex desuetudine extinctam
putat Sa. verb. Baptis. n. 17. cauenda tamen offensio.

Case 6. *May a Catholic in England lawfully be a godfather, personally
or by proxy through another, in a baptism arranged by heretics; and
may heretics act as godparents to Catholics?*
    I reply that a Catholic cannot himself attend their baptisms, as has
already been said. Secondly, neither can he send someone else in his
place, at least not unless there is an urgent necessity, because since he
himself would sin by going, to send another would be to lead the other
person into sin. On the other hand, since it is good in itself to stand
godparent to a child, and may be well done by those who wish to do
it, for a serious reason, one may send someone else to do it, especially
if they are otherwise prepared to go. Because if the proxy should act

---

⁶ S adds: *in Baptismo Catholicorum*
⁷ S adds: *l. 2. mor:*

badly by doing this, it is to be imputed to him, and the Catholic is not bound with such trouble to concern himself about it, as the theologians commonly teach when they discuss scandal. Hence, if it were not a case of sending someone, but only of the Catholic permitting, as it were, someone from among those who were going anyway to be there, to do it in the name of the Catholic, charging him with the obligation of acting as godfather, this does not seem in any way unlawful, but rather it is good that the latter undertake that obligation. However, it is more prudent in such matters to have the minimum of contact with heretics, as is taught by the Holy Fathers Clement and Fabian, and the Councils of Laodicea and Carthage [refs]. Finally, to make a heretic a godfather in the baptism of Catholics is never lawful according to the judgement of Tanner and Sanchez [refs]. But more truly Laymann [refs] says that it can be done for a reason, because among Christians there is no danger to the child, since children are not accustomed to be educated by their godparents, as St Thomas Aquinas and Suarez teach [refs]. Indeed, Sa [ref.] thinks the obligation (not to make a heretic a godparent) is extinct through disuse, although it is necessary to avoid giving offence.

[7] 7us. An possint Catholici in Anglia mittere proles suas baptizandas, et initiandas ab haereticis eorum ritu, aut rogare Ministrum, vt nominem eorum in librum referat, ac testetur eas esse baptizatas? Respondeo id minime licere foret enim cooperari actioni malae haereticali, eamque procurare, quod sane malum est, idque non solum quia alieni peccati causa es, sed quia aduersatur professioni fidei. ita Suar: contra Sect. Ang. l. 6. c 9. n. 29. Sanch. l. 2. mor. c. 9. n. 10. Becan. 2. 2. q. 5. n. 19. at mera permissio ex graui causa excusari potest, vt si vxor permittat marito, Pater auo, vt faciat more suo eam baptizari ad vitanda alia incommoda. Petere a Ministro[8] vt nomen[9] in libro scribat, licitum est. iuuat etiam ad varios fines bonos. similiter vt testetur infantem esse baptizatum, quia id verum est. quod si mentiendo plus diceret v.g. se baptizasse eum, non videtur multum curandum, modo non incitetur ad hoc, et prudenter occurratur scandalis, si quae inde essent nata sequi[10].

Case 7. *May Catholics in England send their children to be baptised and initiated by the heretics according to their rites; or may they ask the heretic minister to put the children's names in the parish register and attest that they have been baptised?*

I reply that this is by no means lawful, for it would be to co-operate

---

8   S adds: *haeretico*
9   S adds: *prolis baptizatae*
10 S reads from the comma: *quae possent inde sequi*

in an evil heretical action, and to procure one, which clearly is evil, and not only because you are the cause of another's sin, but also because it is contrary to the profession of faith; thus, Suarez, Sanchez and Becanus [refs]. But the mere permission of such an action may be excused for a serious reason; for example, if, in order to avoid other troubles, a wife should permit her husband, or a father permit a grandfather to use his customs in baptising a child. To ask a heretic minister to write the name of the baptised child in the register is lawful, and also contributes to various good ends; and similarly to ask him to testify that the child has been baptised is lawful, because it is true. Indeed if the minister should lie and say more, for example that he himself baptised the child, it does not seem to matter much, as long as he is not incited to do this, and the scandals which might follow from this are prudently avoided.

[8] 8ᵘˢ. Quid faciendum Sacerdoti alteriue Catholico, qui in itinere aut alibi cum haereticis versaretur, illi autem inciperent psalmos et preces suas decantare, etiam flexis genibus, et nisi ipse etiam flectat se periculo detectionis exponeret? Respondeo nullo modo licere precari aut psallere cum Haereticis, eorum scilicet preces et psalmos, hoc enim foret haeresim profiteri.¹¹ vt optime Suar. l. 6. cit. c. 9. n. 27. et 29. Conink de fid. dp. 15. n. 30. 56. 61. Reginald. l. 17. n. 31. et 33. Gamach: de fide q. 3. prope fin: Immo nec licet ita se gerere vt videatur exterius ista facere, vt recte Coninck. et Gamach. cit. Caeterum si graue imminet periculum, nec possis eos deserere, vt si essent in nauicula, non videtur illicitum [fo. 4¹²] si te ad orandum componas secreto et catholice, loci enim circumstantia facit, vt non sit haeresis professio ita orare: quandoquidem omnes omnium Religionum cultores ius ibi orandi habeant aequaliter.

Case 8. *What must a priest or other Catholic do, if he is in the company of heretics on a journey or elsewhere, and they begin to sing their psalms and prayers, even on bended knee, and unless he also kneels he would expose himself to the danger of detection?*

I reply that even if there is a danger that he would reveal himself by not doing so, it is in no way lawful for such a person to kneel, pray or to sing psalms with heretics, that is, by using their prayers and psalms, for this would be to profess heresy, as Suarez, Coninck, Reginaldus and Gamachaeus show well [refs]. Neither should he behave in such a way that it seems externally that he is doing these things, as Coninck and Gamachaeus in the places cited rightly say. However, if grave danger

---

¹¹ S reads instead of the last sentence: *non posse inquam talem cum illis flectere, psallere, et preces eorum recitare, etiamsi periculum sit ne inde detegatur.*
¹² A has the following heading above this page: *De Iuramento fidelitatis*, which refers to the next case.

threatens, and you cannot leave these people, for example if you are in a boat, it does not seem unlawful if you contrive to say Catholic prayers secretly, for the circumstances of place mean that it is not a profession of heresy to pray then, since the worshippers of all religions have equally a right to pray in such a place.

[9] 9us.¹³ An liceat iuramentum Anglicanum fidelitatis dictum praestare, protestando saltem quod meram ciuilem intendas obedientiam? Respondeo nullo modo licitum esse iuramentum illud praestare,¹⁴ sed potius moriendum. ita definiuit Paulus V. in duobus Breuibus ad Catholicos Anglos anno 1606. et 1607. Eiusque sententiam grauissimis verbis confirmat Vrbanus 8. in 3. Breuibus datis anno 1626. ad Regem Galliae, Episcopum Calcedonensem et Catholicos Anglos. Et contra tam expressum indubiumque Pontificis Decretum nulla potest esse ab autoritate vnius fortasse aut alterius priuati hominis in contrarium probabilitas, vt in materia de conscientia docent theologi omnes, specialiter Vasq. ibi. dp. 62. c. 4. Tan. q. 4. db. 3. Turrian: de fide dp. 55. db. 3. Pontificem sequuntur Suar. Bell. Grets. Becan: caeterique huius aetatis Doctores. Et qui contrarium asserere ausi sunt, pauci sunt, obscuri et Apostolica Sede proscripti, vt Barclayus, Wideringtonus et quidam alii. Fundamentum est quia de fide est posse Ecclesiam poenis etiam temporalibus coercere improbos ob bonum spirituale, priuando eos omni ciuili commercio cum caeteris, vt nocere desinant et corrigantur, et praecipiendo bonis nec cibum cum iis sumere. 1. Cor: 5. iis non commisceri 2. ad Thess. 3. nec Aue iis dicere 2. Ioan: haereticos deuitare ad Tit. 3. vnde hanc vim habere excommunicationem maiorem docent omnes theologi reclamante nemine, et iidem omnes, vt fidei certum docent potestatem excommunicandi ab ipso Christo et iure diuino Ecclesiae competere ex illo Mat. 18. sit tibi tanquam Ethnicus etc. In iuramento autem aperte negatur posse Pontificem hac segregationis poena punire Reges impios, aperte ergo negatur fides Catholica.

Et quoad depositionem Regum in particulari posse Ecclesiam ea vti, definitum est in Con: Later. cap. 3. in Con. Lugd. 1. cap. ad Apostolicae de sent. et re iudi. in 6. et c. 1. de hom. item in 6. a Greg. 7º. apud Baron. ann: 1076. a Bonifac. 8. Extrau: Vnam Sanctam de maiorit. et obed. et a Sacris canonibus cap. Nos Sanctorum et cap. iuratos 15. q. 6. [fo. 4ᵛ] Eam de facto exercuerunt S. Greg. 1. 12. ep. 82.¹⁵ Greg. 2. et 3. deponentes Leonem Isauricum, Zacharias, Childericum. Leo 3us. creans Imperatorem Carolum Mag. Greg. 7. deponens Henricum, Alex:

---

¹³ S has a large heading to this case (and no others in the MS): *De Iuramento Fidelitatis*
¹⁴ S adds: *etiamsi protesteris non nisi meram ciuilem obedientiam a te intendi*
¹⁵ S reads: *ep. 62.*

3. Fredericum 1ᵐ. Innoc: 3. Ottonem. Innoc. 4. Freder: 2ᵐ. Paulus 2. Georgium Pogebratium. Paulus 3. Henricum 8. Pius 5. Elizabetham Sixtus 5. Henricum Nauaristum. Porro protestatio illa in contrarium nihil iuuaret, quia facta sunt contraria. abiuratur enim clarissime potestas Ecclesiae, idque in plano verborum sensu idque sine vlla aequiuocatione, vt in forma dicitur.

Case 9. *Is it lawful to swear the English oath called the Oath of Allegiance, at least if you protest that you are doing so merely to demonstrate your civil obedience?*

I reply that it is in no way lawful and you should suffer death rather than take that oath. This was settled by Paul V in two briefs directed to English Catholics in 1606 and 1607. Urban VIII confirmed his judgement with the weightiest words in three briefs of 1626 to the King of France, the Bishop of Chalcedon and the English Catholics. Against such a clear and indubitable decree of the Pope there can be no probable judgement to the contrary on the authority of perhaps one or another private man, as, on the subject of conscience, all theologians teach, especially Vazquez, Tanner and Turrianus [refs]. Suarez, Bellarmine, Gretser, Becanus and many other doctors of this age also follow the Pope. Those who have dared to assert the contrary are few, obscure and proscribed by the Apostolic See, such as Barclay, Widdrington and some others. The fundamental point is that it is a matter of faith to hold that the Church may, even with temporal penalties, discipline the wicked for the sake of spiritual welfare, depriving them of all civil contact with others, so that they cease to do harm and are corrected, and commanding the good: 'Do not eat food with them' (1 Corinthians, 5); 'do not mix with them' (2 Thessalonians, 3); 'do not say "good day" to them' (2 John 10); 'Avoid heretics' (Titus, 3). All theologians with no exceptions teach that the major excommunication draws its power from these texts, and they all teach that it is certain and a matter of faith that the power of excommunication derives from Christ himself and belongs by divine right to the Church, according to Matthew, 18: 'may he be like a heathen to you etc.' However, in the Oath it is openly denied that the Pope may punish impious kings with that penalty of segregation, and therefore the Catholic faith is openly denied.

And as far as the deposition of kings in particular is concerned, that the Church may use this power was made clear in the Lateran Council, the Council of Lyons, in the 'Sext' of the Canon Law, by Gregory VII (in Baronius under the year 1076), by Boniface VIII in the Extravagant *Vnam Sanctam*, and in holy canons [refs].

This power has been exercised as a matter of fact by Gregory I [ref.]; Gregory II and III deposing Leo the Isaurian; Zacharias against Childeric; Leo III creating Charlemagne Emperor; Gregory VII deposing Henry;

Alexander III against Frederick I; Innocent III against Otto; Innocent
IV against Frederick II; Paul II against George of Podebrady; Paul III
against Henry VIII; Pius V against Elizabeth; and Sixtus V against
Henry of Navarre. Moreover, the proposed protestation contradicting
the Oath's content cannot help, because the facts are contrary. For the
Oath most clearly denies in plain words the power of the Church, and
the words of the Oath also say that it is sworn with no equivocation.

[10] 10ᵘˢ. An officiato regio iuramentum exigenti dare possis pecuniam
vt supersedeat. et rogare vt dicat te illud praestitisse? Respondeo licitum
esse sine dubio dare pecuniam vt supersedeat, hoc enim est tantum
redimere vexationem iniustam quod iuxta omnes licitum est etiam in
rebus sacris, vt docent omnes arg. cap. Dilectus 28. de Simon: Vlterius
etiam licitum est petere vt dicat te officio functum, iurasse fidelitatem
vel quid simile. hoc enim bonum est. Quod si aliqui male id interpre-
tantur, id leuiter faciunt, nec teneris cum graui incommodo id curare.
Ratio est quia non tenemur abstinere ab actione¹⁶ licita et nobis vtili
cum graui nostra iactura, quod alii scandalizentur, sed quantum sine
magno possumus incommodo, nec enim charitas ad plus obligat. vt bene
Tan. to: 3. dp. 2. q. 6. n. 108. et Suar. de char: dp. 10. s. 3. n. 10. cum
ista proximi necessitas¹⁷ nec sit extrema, nec adeo etiam grauis.¹⁸ vnde
addo vlterius posse hoc fieri etiamsi praeuideat officialem mentiendo
plus dicturum v. g. quod iuramentum ipsum fidelitatis acceperis. requiritur tamen causa valde grauis, vtque grauioribus scandalis modo aliquo
prudenti occurratur.

Posset adhuc forte alicui non illicitum videri directe petere ab offi-
ciali, vt dicat te, ipsum fidelitatis iuramentum praestitisse saudes enim ei
minus peccatum, ne faciat maius. minus enim est ita mentiri etiam cum
aliquo religionis damno, quam exigere iuramentum, quo peccatur et
contra ipsam fidem immediate, et contra iustitiam, cooperando iniquis-
simae Catholici spoliationi, et incarcerationi. Porro licere suadere [fo.
5¹⁹] minus malum tenent probabiliter Mol. Sanch. Bonac. citan. conclus.
12. aliique complures. Respondeo tamen hoc non videri licitum practice et moraliter, quia moraliter loquendo hoc non fiet quin ipse petens
cooperetur ad hoc ipsum aliis persuadendum ita se gerendo ac si vere
iurasset, et mendacium illud tacite approbando ac confirmando: hoc
autem est aperte impium et contra fidei professionem, ipsumque libella-

---

¹⁶ A has in slightly larger, bold letters in the margin here: *Scandalum*
¹⁷ S reads instead of the last four words: *illa proximeitas*
¹⁸ S adds: *vt colligitur ex Sua: ibid. dp. 9. l. 2. n. 4.*
¹⁹ A has the heading at the top of this page: *De Patrono bonorum Ecclesiasticorum*, a
reference to case 12.

ticorum crimen vt ostendit Coninck cit:[20] n. 117. si tamen ponatur casus Metaphysicus quod solum repraesentes ei minus malum, illudque qua tale suadeas, paratus ipse veritatem confiteri caueaturque scandalum, non videtur improbabile id excusari posse.

Case 10. *When a royal official demands that you take the Oath, may you give him money, so that he omits doing so, and may you ask him to say that you have taken it?*

I reply that without doubt it is lawful to give him money so that he omits administering the oath to you, for this is only to buy off ill-treatment, which according to everyone is lawful, even in sacred matters, as everyone teaches following canon law [ref.]. Furthermore, it is even lawful to ask him to say that you have done your duty, or that you have sworn your allegiance or something similar, for this is good. If some people should interpret what you do badly, they do so lightly, and you are not bound to be concerned if it helps you avoid serious trouble. The reason is that we are not bound with serious damage to ourselves to abstain from a lawful action and one which is useful to us, on the grounds that others are scandalised by it, but only to do as much as we can without causing great harm to ourselves. For charity does not oblige us to do more, as Tanner and Suarez show well [refs], since in this case the necessity of our neighbour is not extreme nor even very grave, as is gathered from Suarez [ref.]. Whence I add further that this may be done, even if you foresee that the official will say more and lie, for example saying that you have taken the Oath of Allegiance. A very serious reason for doing so, however, is required and one that avoids in some prudent way causing more serious scandal.

It may perhaps in addition seem to some that it is not unlawful to ask the official to say plainly that you have taken the Oath of Allegiance, for you are persuading him to commit a smaller sin to avoid committing a greater one: for it is a smaller sin for him to lie in this way, even if it does some harm to religion, than to demand that you take the Oath, as a result of which sin is committed immediately and against the faith itself, and against justice, by co-operating in the spoliation and incarceration of a Catholic. Furthermore, that it is lawful to persuade someone to commit a lesser evil is held as probable by Molina, Sanchez, Bonacina, citing many others. I reply, however, that this does not seem lawful in practical and moral terms, because speaking morally this cannot be done unless the Catholic co-operates in persuading others, and hence behaves as if he truly swore the Oath, and tacitly approves and confirms this lie. But this is openly impious and against the profession of faith, and

<hr/>

[20] S reads instead of the last word: *de fide dp: 15.*

is the crime of the *libellatici*,[21] as Coninck shows [ref.]. If however the metaphysical case is posed that you only represent to him a lesser evil, and you persuade him to do it as such, while you are prepared to confess the faith, and scandal is avoided, it does not seem improbable that it may be excused.

[11] 11[us]. An liceat mittere amicum vel famulum haereticum ad officiales pro obtinendis licentiis seu passaportis, quae certum est non concedenda, nisi ipsi prius iuramentum praestent?

Respondeo posse id fieri graui ex causa, quamuis enim nunquam liceat ab aliquo petere id quod sine peccato praestare nequit quantumcunque sit paratus, vt docet Laym.[22] cum Sanch. Vasq. Suar. et aliis seu[23] communiter; at licet graui ex causa petere ab aliquo quod ex se fieri potest recte, sed de facto ab ipso non nisi male fiet. sic licet petere iuramentum ab eo, qui per falsos Deos est iuraturus, petere mutuum ab vsurario: petere a malefico vt soluat maleficium, plus autem hic non fit, ita Laym. l. 2. trac: 3. c. 13. n. 3. et 4: Suar. de Sacra: dp.18. s. 1. Bonac. de peccatis dp. 2. q. 4. p. 2.[24] Vasq. de scandalo et alii passim.

Case 11. *Is it lawful to send a heretic friend or servant to officials to obtain licences or passports which it is certain will not be issued to them, unless they first take the Oath?*

I reply that for a grave cause, it can be done. For although it is never lawful to ask someone to do something which he cannot do without sin, however much he may be prepared to do it (as Laymann [ref.] teaches, with Sanchez, Vazquez, Suarez and others, and as is commonly held), it is nevertheless lawful for a serious reason to ask someone to do something which he could rightly do, although in fact the person making the request could only perform it by acting wrongly. Thus it is lawful to ask someone who will swear by false gods to take an oath; to seek a loan from a usurer; and to ask a witch to remove witchcraft. This case however involves nothing more, as Laymann, Suarez, Bonacina, Kon, Vazquez and others teach [refs].

[12] 12[us]. An Catholici habentes ius patronatus in beneficiis possint praesentare Episcopis Ministros aliquos haereticos ex moderatioribus, eo animo vt minus noceant, quam alii qui alioquin essent instituendi. et

---

[21] *Libellatici*: Christians in third-century Rome who, under persecution, purchased certificates from a magistrate in which they were said, falsely, to have sacrificed after the pagan fashion. See www.newadvent.org/cathen (*Catholic Encyclopaedia*).

[22] S adds: *l. 2. tr. 3. c. 13. n. 3.et 4.*

[23] S reads: *fere*

[24] S adds: *Kon.*

an possint absque Simoniae vitio pacisci cum iis de certa aliqua pecuniae Summa? Respondeo licitum esse talem ministrum praesentare Episcopo haeretico 1º. quia suadetur tantum minus malum ei, qui actu paratus est maius facere et quidem in eodem genere, quod plerique censent licitum. 2º. quia praesentare Laicum et indignum non est malum intrinsece, viz: si praesentes mere, vt ius tuum conserues eo quod alium praesentare nequeas. tunc enim solum defendis ius tuum relinquens Episcopo vt ipse eum reiiciat, et meliorem [fo. 5ᵛ] substituat puta Catholicum Sacerdotem: quod quia non faciet vnquam, ipsi imputabitur non patrono.

Dices hoc esse agnoscere potestatem Episcopi. Respondeo minime. solum enim agnoscis in ipso potestatem facti, sicut et ille qui iustitiam petit a Tyranno.

Licitum est etiam pacisci de pecuniae summa,[25] idque secluso Apostolico omni priuilegio ex ipsa rei natura. nam quoad ius Ecclesiae positiuum prohibens[26] pactionem in spiritualibus certum videtur quod cesset, cum finis eius adaequatus totaliter cesset in Anglia,[27] idque non negatiue, sed contrarie hoc est ita vt religioni et cultui diuino magis noceret illud seruari dum haeretici beneficia sine diminutione occupant, quam si in Catholicorum subsidium diminuerentur. cessat ergo lex vt cum communi docet Laym. de leg. c. 21. n. 2. quoad vero ius naturale diuinum hoc solum obligat ne pecunias accipias vt pretium beneficii qua spirituale est. hoc autem facile hic vitatur, patronus pecuniam accipit alio titulo, viz: vt furi et inuasori iniusto eripiat, quantum potest, vt eo minus Ecclesia perdat, similesque alii tituli facile inueniri possunt. potest autem impendi in quosuis vsus pios arbitrio patroni, vt sunt Sacerdotes alere proprios liberos in Catholicis regionibus educare: compensare damna propria et mulctas, quae tulit ob fidem Catholicam et similia arbitrio prudentis. Denique in Catholicos egentes, vnde si vere egeat sibi poterit cum Confessarii consilio partem vel etiam totum applicare.

Case 12. *May Catholics who own the advowson of benefices present heretic ministers of the more moderate sort to the bishops, in the hope that they may be less harmful than others who would otherwise be instituted? And may they without committing the crime of simony make a financial agreement with the person they present?*

I reply that it is lawful to present such a minister to the heretic bishop. First, because this is only to persuade the bishop to do something less harmful when he was prepared to commit a worse act, and indeed one of

---

25   S adds: *sine metu Simoniae*
26   S adds: *omnem*
27   S reads from the comma: *cum finis eius totalis in Anglia cesset adaequate*

the same sort, which most think is lawful. Second, because to present a layman and one who is unworthy is not intrinsically bad, if you present him merely in order to preserve your right, when you cannot present anyone else. For then you only defend your right, leaving the bishop free to reject him and substitute someone better, for example a Catholic priest, which if he does not ever do, it will be imputed to him rather than to you as the patron.

You will say that this is to acknowledge the power of the bishop. I reply, no, for you only acknowledge in him a power which is a fact, as a person does who asks for justice from a tyrant.

It is also lawful by the very nature of the subject for a Catholic to make an arrangement to receive a sum of money without fear of simony, and to do so without any papal privilege. For as concerns the positive law of the Church which prohibits all bargains in spiritual matters, it certainly seems that it does not apply in this case, since the whole purpose of the law is not adequately achieved in England. Furthermore, not only is its purpose not achieved, but the reverse results, so that religion and divine worship are harmed more by obeying the law when the heretics enjoy the benefices with undiminished income, than if their income were to be diminished to relieve Catholics. Therefore the law ceases to apply, as is the common view taught by Laymann [ref.]. In truth, as far as the divine law of nature is concerned, it only obliges you not to accept money as payment for the benefice, because it is spiritual. However, this is easily avoided in this case, if we consider that the patron accepts money by another title, namely so that he takes as much as he can from a furious and unjust invader, so that the Church will lose so much the less; other similar explanations can easily be found. Moreover, the money may be spent on whatever pious uses the patron wishes; for example to maintain priests, to educate his own children in Catholic countries, to compensate himself for the damages and the taxes which he endures for the Catholic faith, and on other matters according to the judgement of a prudent person. Finally he may spend the money on needy Catholics, and so if he is truly needy himself he can, on the advice of a confessor, use it in part or in whole for his own needs.

[13] 13us. An liceat famulis catholicis carnes in die ieiunii parare ac ministrare heris ieiunium violaturis? Negant licere Vasq. Opusc. de scandalo a.1 db. 3 . Turrian: vlt. de scandalo, quia cum esus carnium indifferens non sit sed plane hic et nunc illicitus; nullo modo inquiunt, fas est eas apponere. Respondeo tamen id licitum esse, si id officii non nisi cum suo incommodo detractare queant, vt plerumque fit. ita caeteri passim. Less. de iust. l. 4. c. 2. db. 4. Bonac. de peccatis dp. 2. q. 4. p. 2. Laym. l. 2. tr. 3. c. 13. n. 4. Azor. p. 1. l. 7. c. 20. q. 11. Sanch. [fo. 6] l. 1. mor. c. 7. n. 35. Ferdin. a Castro-Palao. de char: q. 6. p. 11. ratio

est quia appositio carnium est indifferens, potest enim Dominus, si velit ea bene vti, eas vel reiiciendo, vel pauperibus aut aegrotis donando quod satis est vt famuli excusentur.

Case 13. *Is it lawful for Catholic servants to prepare meat on fast days and serve it to their masters who are about to violate the fast? (Vazquez and Turrianus [refs] deny that it is lawful, saying that since eating meat is not an indifferent matter, but is plainly at certain times and under certain circumstances unlawful; so, they say, it is in no way right to serve it.)*

I reply that nevertheless it is lawful if they cannot avoid this duty except with great trouble to themselves, as many may not. This is the view generally of others: Lessius, Bonacina, Laymann, Azor, Sanchez and Ferdinand Castro-Palao [refs]. The reason is that serving meat is an indifferent matter, for the master may if he wants, use it well, either by rejecting the meat or by giving it to the poor or the sick, and so the servants are satisfactorily excused.

[14] 14us. An liceat Catholico in Anglia haereticis siue amicis siue aliis magnae authoritatis viris hospitio exceptis praebere carnes in mensa,[28] eosque ad comedendum inuitare posito quod aliter iis non satisfieret? Respondeo 1°. non posse carnes apponi, si commode negari queant; et peccant grauiter qui tam facile id faciunt, quia cooperantur peccato alieno sine causa, et quidem valde propinque. ac haec res est mali exempli vnde et restringenda ita communiter Autores Aliqui tamen vt Less. et Laym cum Nauar. dicunt quod si[29] esset alibi[30] comesturus licitum sit eas apponere, quod tamen ita intelligo vt leuior causa tunc sufficiat. alias ipsum alibi coenaturum esse, non est satis vt ego cooperer, vt bene Palao cit.[31] p. 9. 2°. certum est si carnes negare non possis sine magno incommodo, quia nimirum te propterea vexaturus aut elaturus,[32] etc. licitum fore eas apponere quia Ecclesiae praeceptum non obligat cum tanto incommodo: modo non petantur in contemptum fidei ita Autores passim. 3°. Dico solam amicitiam non sufficere vt carnes vel coenam suppedites ei, quem constat obligatum, nisi timeatur offensio alicuius momenti. Regin. l. 4. n. 195. et 198. 4°. si sit vir potens ad quem excipiendum ius habes, vel etiam debitum aliquod ob tuum notabile commodum: nec credatur ipse contentus futurus nisi carnibus appositis; credo posse eas apponi, quia non teneris eas negare cum tanto incommodo. Non enim

---

28   S adds: *in die ieiunii*
29   S adds: *hospes*
30   S adds: *carnes*
31   S substitutes for the last word: *de char: dp. 6.*
32   S reads: *eiecturus sit*

inducis ad comedendum, sed materiam praebes, qua posset ipse bene
vti. et sane quoad hoc eadem videtur ratio ac de famulis, quos tamen
illarum ministrantes omnes fere excusant, vt super vidimus. Duo tamen
addenda 1º. si possit in alium diem non prohibitum differri inuitatio, id
faciendum esse. 2º. Dandam esse operam vt simul apponantur pisces,
alioquin nimis directe prouocantur ad peccandum.

Inuitare ad edendas carnes non[33] licet, quia nunquam licet etiam a
paratissimo petere quod nequeat fieri sine peccato [fo. 6ᵛ] vt cum aliis
supra citatis docet Tan. de charit. q. 6. n. 100. at inuitare solum ceremoniae causa, vt animum ostendas hospitalem, non videtur malum, quia
plus non est quam cibum offerre, relinquendo ei liberum esum maxime,
si adsint cibi non vetiti, vnde Less. cit. db. 3. Reginal. 1. 4. n. 195. et
Azor. tom. 2. 1. 12. c. 18. dum inuitationem condemnant, significanter
et caute dicunt se loqui de inuitatione simpliciter et absolute, quaeque[34]
futura causa comestionis.

Case 14. *Is it lawful for a Catholic in England, having received as
guests heretics who are friends, or other men of great authority, to
provide them at table with meat and to invite them to eat, if it is understood that nothing else would satisfy them?*

I reply firstly that he may not serve meat if he can conveniently refuse,
and those who so freely do this, sin gravely, since they co-operate, and
indeed very directly and without cause, in the sin of another. It also
sets a bad example, and should therefore be stopped according to the
common view of our authors. However, some like Lessius and Laymann,
who follows Navarre, say that if the guest were prepared to eat meat
somewhere else, it would be lawful to serve it; which, however, I understand as saying that a rather weak reason (the fact that he is prepared
to eat elsewhere) should be sufficient for doing this; but I believe this
is not sufficient reason for me to co-operate, as Castro-Palao shows
well [refs]. Secondly, it is certain that if you cannot refuse giving them
food without great trouble, because you will certainly be persecuted, or
evicted, or revealed as a Catholic, it is lawful to serve them with it, since
the law of the Church does not oblige if it will cause such trouble. This
is as long as the request for food is not made in contempt of the faith, as
our authors teach throughout. Thirdly, I say that friendship alone is not
enough to justify providing meat or dinner to a person, even if it may
be acknowledged you are obliged to him, unless it is a case where you
are afraid of causing offence of some moment; see Reginaldus [ref.].
Fourthly, if he is a powerful man, whom you have a duty to entertain or

[33] S reads: *nunquam*
[34] S inserts: *credatur*

to whom you are also very much indebted, and it is believed that he will
not be happy unless served meat, then I think you may do so, because
you are not bound to deny it if it will cause such trouble. For you do
not induce him to eat, but merely provide the material which he himself
could use well. The same indeed seems also to be the reason in the case
of the servants who serve the food, for almost everyone excuses them,
as we saw above. Two points, however, need to be added: first, if the
invitation can be put off to a day when meat is not prohibited, it must
be done; second, care should be taken to serve fish at the same time,
otherwise the guests are too directly provoked to sin.

   To invite people to eat meat is not lawful, for it is never lawful to
invite someone to do something which they cannot do without sin, even
if they are prepared to do so, as Tanner along with others cited above
teaches [ref.]. But to invite someone only for the sake of ceremony, so
that you show a hospitable spirit, does not seem evil because you are
doing no more than offering food, leaving him free to eat, especially if
there are foods which are not prohibited available. Hence, while Lessius,
Reginaldus and Azor [refs] condemn an invitation, it is significant that
they say cautiously that they are talking simply and absolutely of an
invitation which it is believed will be the cause of eating.

[15] 15us. <u>An liceat Paterfamilias filiis et famulis permittere vt ieiunium violent</u>: aut praebere mercenariis cibos vetitos quos domi suae
essent comesturi; si id ipsi petant, vel sit ei commodius? <u>Respondeo
teneri</u> Patremfamilias curare vt domestici[35] seruent ieiunium, et videtur
peccatum mortale permittere[36] omnibus praebere copiam coenae et
ciborum prohibitorum, vt docet Reginal. n. 196. caeterique cit. Non
tamen ad hoc tenetur cum magno suo incommodo, vnde si famuli essent
haeretici damnumque timeret eos cohibendo, posset permittere vt iis
satisfiat. ita Autores cit.[37] Addunt aliqui satis esse si credas si negentur,
grauius peccaturos murmurando, clam comestando, etc. ita Les. nec
videtur improbabile. contrarium tamen credo probabilius cum Faiundez
in 4 praecept c. 10. n. 11. quia licet passim iis suadere minus malum ad
impediendum maius, non tamen cooperari ad illud ordinarie loquendo
(nisi in casu aliquo, quo censeri posset voluntas partis laesae, vt id in
gratiam ipsius faciam, vt in furtis contingit.) quia suasio est tantum
conditionalis: at executio est absoluta, videtur licita mere ad impediendum operantis peccatum. <u>Tandem dico nec mercenariis posse dari
cibos vetitos</u>, quos domi essent comesturi eo mere titulo quod pretii

---

35 S adds: *viz: liberi et famuli*
36 S adds: *promiscue*
37 S adds: *et Fagundez in 4° praec: c. 10. n. 11.*

sint vilioris, sed concurrere debet aliud incommodum et ita vniuersim ex causae et necessitatis magnitudine aestimandum est totum hoc negotium, vt recte etiam monet Suar. de charit. dp. 10. s. 3. n. 9. et s. 4. n. 5.

Case 15. *Is it lawful for the head of the household to allow his children and servants to violate the fast, or to provide forbidden food for workers to eat in their own homes, if they ask for it, or if it is more convenient for him?*

I reply that the head of the family is bound to take care that his household (his children and servants) observe the fasts, and it seems to be a mortal sin to allow all of them indiscriminately to be supplied with large meals and forbidden food, as Reginald and others teach [refs]. He is not however bound to this if it will result in great trouble for himself; hence if the servants are heretics and he fears harm will come from prohibiting them, he may permit that they should be satisfied; thus the authors cited and Fagundez [ref.]. Some, for example Lessius, add that it is enough if he believes that, if they are forbidden, they will sin more gravely by grumbling and eating in secret etc., nor does it seem improbable. The contrary however I believe, with Fagundez [ref.], is more probable, because it is always lawful to persuade people to commit a lesser evil in order to prevent a greater, however I may not, ordinarily speaking, co-operate in their sin (except in some particular case, in which the will of the injured party could be assessed, so that I do it for his own good, as happens in the case of thefts[38]), because the persuading is only conditional while the execution is absolute, and so it (the persuading) seems lawful only to prevent the agent's sinning. Finally I say that forbidden foods cannot be given to workers, who will eat them at home, merely because they are cheaper, but this factor should coincide with the avoidance of some other harm to justify the action; and thus the whole matter is entirely to be judged according to the magnitude of the reason and of the necessity, as Suarez also rightly warns [ref.].

[16] 16. An liceat Catholico in Anglia egestatis causa filios suos apud haereticos amicos aut consanguineos collocare cum peruersionis periculo? Respondeo [fo. 7] videri penitus illicitum ita liberos peruersionis periculo exponere. Quis enim non dicet esse contra charitatem liberis debitam iis eos obiicere periculis et malis ob temporale aliquod commodum, quae certo vel saltem probabiliter sint eos redditura in aeternum miseros, peiori loco quam bestias, quam si nati non fuissent, aut in curis interfecti? Nec sufficit dicere eos culpa sua id incursuros,

---

38 The meaning here is not very clear.

quia charitas hoc etiam impedire debet maxime in filiis, quorum qui curam non habet est infideli deterior iuxta Apostolum. 1. Tim . 5. Nec sufficit iterum dicere teneri quidem, sed non cum graui incommodo extraordinaria. at praestare alimentum more aliorum[39] parentum, et prouidere prout fert status, non debet censeri tale incommodum, vt ob illud vitandum possint filios hac ratione idolo[40] sacrificare. Multo minus lautioris fortunae captandae gratia possunt ita collocari. confirmatur iubent canones parente apostatante filios ei abstrahi ne peruertantur. cap. Iudaeorum filios 28. q. 1. ergo multo magis volunt ne parentes catholici proles suas haereticis corrumpendas permittant.

Case 16. *Is it lawful for a Catholic in England on account of his extreme poverty to lodge his children with heretic friends or relations if there is danger of their perversion there?*

I reply that it seems completely unlawful to expose children to the danger of perversion in this way. For who will not say that it is contrary to the charity owed to children to throw them, for the sake of some temporal benefits, into dangers and evils, which certainly or at least probably would hand them over to miseries for eternity, in a worse place than beasts, worse than if they had not been born, or worse than if they were to be killed in a painful way? Nor is it enough to say that it would be their fault if they were perverted, because we should also prevent this out of charity, especially in the case of children; for the person who does not take care of children, is worse than an infidel, as the Apostle says in 1 Timothy 5. Nor is it enough to say again that a man is obliged to avoid this, but not if it causes serious, extraordinary trouble. For to be able to afford to provide food like other parents, and to look after them according to their status in society, should not be thought so much trouble that in order to avoid it, the children should be sacrificed to the idol Moloch. Much less may the children be lodged in this way with heretics, in the hope of acquiring better prospects for them. This is confirmed because the canons order that children should be taken from an apostate parent lest they are perverted [ref.]; therefore it is much more clearly the intention of the canons that Catholic parents should not allow their children to be corrupted by heretics.

[17] 17[us]. An teneantur Catholici audire Sacrum diebus festis in Anglia, confiteri et communicare in Paschate, non obstante metu poenalium statutorum, quando nullum speciale adest periculum? Respondeo in particulari casu si vrgeat speciale periculum graue, non est dubium

---

[39] S reads: *iure caeterorum*
[40] S reads: *Moloch*, where there is a gap of about an inch in A.

quin cesset obligatio iuxta omnes Doctores in materia de legibus. At vbi illud non vrget dico ob generale periculum ortum ex regni legibus non excusari Catholicos ab his praeceptis, et contrarium dicere foret meo iudicio valde absurdum et improbabile, 1º. quia saepe in particulari nullum vere subest periculum si sacrum audias, quare metus tunc leuis erit et inanis, non iustus qui excuset, nam vt recte Sanch. de Matr: l. 4. dp. 1. n. 15. metus iustus debet esse opinio mali [fo. 7ᵛ] futuri fortis et probabilis, et infra n. 6. cum Couar. ait, quod valde remota non timentur. Certum autem est saepe periculum vel nullum esse, vel non nisi valde remotum vt quando filius vel famulus audiret sacrum in domo paterna aut herili. et 2º. quia etiam aliquod periculum subeundum est quando cum praecepto humano concurrit necessitas aliqua boni communis, vt tenent omnes. Sanch. l. 1. mor. c.18. Tan. de leg. q. 6. n. 88. Palao de leg. dp. 1. p. 21. viz: quando legis neglectus vergeret in Religionis detrimentum, vt optime Laym. de leg. c. 14. n. 6. si autem Catholici non frequentarent Missam, confessionem, etc. certum est maximum inde secuturum religionis detrimentum. ergo periculum illud generale et remotum non potest facere quin ad rem adeo necessariam obligentur. Sane S. Aug. ep. 180. docet experientia compertum[41] iis in locis periisse fidem, quibus quotidianum dominici corporis ministerium, id est Missae Sacrificium defuit.

Case 17. *Are Catholics in England bound to hear Mass on feast days, to confess and to take communion at Easter, despite the fear of the penal statutes, when there is no special danger?*

I reply that in the particular case that a special grave danger threatens us, there is no doubt that a legal obligation ceases, according to all Doctors when they discuss the subject of laws. But when a particular danger does not threaten us, I say that Catholics are not excused from these religious commandments on account of the general danger arising from the laws of the kingdom, and to say the contrary seems in my judgement most absurd and improbable. The first reason is that often there is really no particular danger in hearing Mass, and so your excuse then would be a light and stupid fear and not a just fear; not, as Sanchez [ref.] rightly says it should be, a just fear based on a strong and probable opinion of the evil to come. He agrees with Covarrubias [ref.] when he says we should not be afraid of things which are truly remote. Moreover it is certain that in this case fear often is either non-existent or nothing but truly remote, for example when a child or a servant hears Mass in the home of a parent or master. The second reason is that even some danger must be undergone when the requirements of the common good

---

[41] S inserts: *esse*

coincide with a human law, as all hold, including Sanchez, Tannner and Castro-Palao [refs]; that is, when neglect of the law tends towards the harming of religion, as Laymann shows well [ref.]. If however Catholics do not frequent Mass, confession etc., it is certain that trouble will as a result follow to the detriment of religion. Therefore such a general and remote danger cannot mean that a man is not obliged to do such a necessary thing. St Augustine in his 180th letter teaches this well, having learnt from experience that where there was no daily administration of the body of our Lord, that is the sacrifice of the Mass, the faith perished.

[18] 18. Quid faciet Sacerdos in casu subitaneo, vbi nec libri nec viri docti consuli possunt: an peccabit si opinionem improbabilem sequatur et iuxta eam det consilium? Respondeo non semper teneri hominem ad vtendum tota ea diligentia, quae in se sufficiens sit ad vincendum dubium quia locus et tempus saepe id non patientur. sufficiet ergo in eo casu facere quod potest, et sic immunis erit a peccato, etiamsi improbabilem capiat viam, quia ignorantia erit inuoluntaria. ita Sanch. l. 1. Mor. c. 9. n. 25. et c. 10. n. 5. et 8. Suar. de censur. dp. 40. s. 5. n.14. Valen. l. 2. dp. 2. q. 14. p. 4. q1a. 4. Bonac. de peccat. dp. 2. q. 4. p. 7. n. 12. At non excusabitur, immo grauissime peccare poterit, qui leuiter, et sine necessitate se praecipitat ad huiusmodi dubia dissoluenda praesertim si res magni momenti sit, si tangat iura aliena si damnum afferat irreparabile, vt in Matrimoniis [fo. 8] et possessorio dimittendo facile contingit. vnde in huiusmodi vix admitti debet quod sit Sacerdoti necessarium ita subito se resoluere, multo minus erit causa iusta ita subito respondi ne alioqui videatur minus doctus, etc. cum e consilio signum potius sit doctrinae et prudentiae mature et lente quantum res ipsa permittit procedere.

Case 18. *What should a priest in England do if he is faced with a case unexpectedly proposed to him, when neither books nor learned men can be consulted: will he sin if he follows an improbable opinion and gives advice according to that?*

I reply that a man is not always bound to use all the diligence which would be sufficient by itself to overcome doubt, because the place and time often do not allow it. Therefore it will be enough in this case for him to do what he can, and thus he will be immune from sin, even if he takes the improbable path, because his ignorance is involuntary; thus Sanchez, Suarez, Valentia, and Bonacina [refs]. But he will not be excused, and he could even sin most gravely if he should throw himself lightly and without necessity into solving doubts in this way, especially if the matter is of great moment, or if it touches the rights of third parties, or if it might cause irreparable harm, as easily may happen in matrimonial cases and in cases involving the casting out of devils from those possessed. Hence in cases of this sort it should hardly be accepted as necessary for the priest to have to resolve them very quickly. Much less will there be a just reason to reply very quickly in order not to appear less learned etc., since in giving advice it is a better proof of doctrine and prudence to proceed maturely and slowly as much as the matter itself permits.

[19] 19. An liceat in Anglia ex necessitate celebrare Sacrum sine ara, calice consecratis: sine vestibus benedictis sine mappis, lumine, crucifixo, missali, mirilio, ante luce aut post meridiem? Respondeo celebrare sine vasis et ornamentis nullo modo est licitum, ne quidem ad dandum moribundo viaticum, quia ius diuinum celebrare non obligat, nisi vbi decentia pro tanti sacrificii dignitate seruari possit, vt cum communi docet Laym. l. 5. tr. 5. c. 6. n. 17. Suar. dp. 82. s. 3. Conink. 3. p. 9. 83. n. 250. caeterum pro praxi haec ritu⁴² digna sunt.

Primo Probabile satis est posse aram consecrari sine reliquiis, nec iis ablatis consecrationem amittere. ita Suar.⁴³ dp. 8l. s. 5. Conin. n. 4. 240. 2º. Calicis cuppam esse debere ex argento aut saltem stanno; non ex plumbo, quia⁴⁴ bibulum, et sordes contrahit. ita Tan. et Praepost. nedum ex aere iuxta omnes. 3º. licitum esse ex causa iusta celebrare sine vna aut altera ex vestibus minoribus, stola, manipulo aut cingulo aut sine benedictis non tamen sine necessitate. Lay. n. 17. Filuc. tr. 5. n. 149. Suar. s. 3. cit. Diana. de celeb. Miss. resol. 57. 4º. Mappae altaris requiruntur duae vel vna duplicata, sed in necessitate sufficeret vna, nec opus est vt sit benedicta. Lay. n. 11. Praepos. q. 83. a. 3. db. 4. possetque tunc ad vsus profanos redire. Lay. n. 11. et 17. 5º. Lumen debet esse ex cera, in necessitate tamen sufficeret vnum ex oleo, vel seuo.⁴⁵ Lay. Diana resol. 67. Filuc. Reginald. Bonac. 6º. Crucifixus ex causa non magna potest omitti, solum enim obligat ex vi rubricarum Lay. n. 17. 7º. Curandum vt adsit minister, qui mas esse debet iuxta canones. posset tamen Sacerdos ex necessitate, si valde expediret non omittere Missam, sine Ministro celebrare Praepos. dub. 7. Lay. c. 6. n. 13. Diana resolutione 43. alios citans. denique consuetudo in Anglia adhibendi ex necessitate foeminam ad ministrandum non est [fo. 8ᵛ⁴⁶] illicita censenda aut irrationabilis quia saepe alii non adsunt nec adesse possunt: ex alia parte res est magni momenti vt in familiis, vbi degunt Sacerdotes, conseruetur celebratio quotidiana, vt ex S. Aug. ep. 180.

---

⁴² S reads: *scitu*
⁴³ S adds: *3. p. t. 3.*
⁴⁴ S adds: *est*
⁴⁵ S reads: *sebo*
⁴⁶ A has the heading above this page: *De ieiunio feriae sextae in Anglia*, referring to the next case.

supra cit:[47] Denique quia canon ille viz: cap. 1. de cohabitat. cler. et mul. videtur loqui de ecclesiis publicis vbi sunt cancelli, intra quos consistere foeminas ibidem prohibetur, quod in Anglia vbique cessat. 8°. Missale etiam est necessarium, sed qui constantis esset memoriae, et bene sciret Missam memoriter, posset ex causa cessante scandalo sine eo celebrare. Lay. n. 17. Praepos. db 4. posset etiam se iuuare scribendo praecipua. 9°. Quoad[48] probabile est in Anglia etiam seclusis priuilegiis posse celebrari duabus horis ante ortum solis, vel citius ob grauem causam. Praepos. q. 83. a. 2. db. 4. Dian. cit. resol 33. Lay. c. 4. n. 2. Immo media nocte vt detur infirmo viaticum Diana. Lay. n. 3. similiter et post meridiem vna hora inchoare licet etiam seclusis priuilegiis ex causa, quia non est notabilis erratio Lay. n. 4. Diana. resol. 34. vide Tanner.

Case 19. *Is it lawful in England out of necessity to celebrate Mass without a consecrated altar or chalice, without vestments that have been blessed, without altar cloths, an altar light, a crucifix, a missal or an assistant, before daylight or after mid-day?*

I reply that it is not lawful in any way to celebrate without vessels and ornaments, not even to give the viaticum to a dying man, because the divine law to celebrate does not oblige except in places where the decencies required to respect the dignity of such a sacrifice may be observed, as is the common view taught by Laymann, Suarez and Coninck. In practice the following are suitable for the rite.

Firstly, it is, according to probable judgement, satisfactory for an altar to be consecrated without relics, and it is not necessary to avoid performing the consecration because the relics are lacking; thus, Suarez and Coninck [refs]. Secondly, the cup of the chalice should be made of silver, or at least of tin, but not of lead, because it is absorbent and when wet it becomes dirty (thus, Tanner and Praepositus), much less of bronze, according to all. Thirdly, it is lawful for a just cause to celebrate Mass without one or other of the minor vestments (stole, maniple or girdle) or without consecrated vestments, but only in cases of necessity; thus, Laymann, Filliucci, Suarez and Diana [refs]. Fourthly, two altar cloths are required, or one folded double, but in necessity one is sufficient; nor is it necessary that it should be blessed, according to Laymann and Praepositus [refs]; and it may afterwards be returned to profane uses, according to Laymann [ref.]. Fifthly, a light should be of wax, but in cases of necessity of oil or tallow; thus, Laymann, Diana, Filliucci, Reginald, Bonacina [refs]. Sixthly, a crucifix may, for a reason which is not serious, be omitted, for the obligation to use one is only derived

---

[47] S adds: *diximus*
[48] S inserts: *horam*

from the rubrics, as Laymann says [ref.]. Seventhly, care must be taken that there is a server, who must be male according to the canons. It is possible however, when it is most important not to omit the Mass, for a priest to celebrate without a server, as Praepositus, Laymann and Diana say, citing others [refs]. Lastly, the custom in England of using a woman in cases of necessity to serve is not to be judged unreasonable or unlawful, because often there are no males there, and they cannot be present. On the other side of the question it is of great importance that in households where priests are living the daily celebration of Mass should be preserved, as we have said above from St Augustine's 180th letter. Finally, because that canon [ref.] about the cohabitation of women and the clergy seems to speak about public churches where there are chancels, in which it is forbidden for women to be present at the same time as priests, which in England is not at present the case anywhere. Eighthly, a missal is also necessary, but whoever is of sound memory and knows the Mass well from memory may if there is no scandal perform the Mass without a missal, as Laymann and Praepositus say [refs]. He may also help himself by writing down the principal points. Ninthly, as far as time goes, it is probable in England even without privileges that Mass may be celebrated two hours before sunrise, or earlier for a grave cause, as Praepositus, Diana and Laymann say [refs]; indeed, in the middle of the night, in order to give viaticum to someone who is ill, according to Diana and Laymann [refs]. Similarly it is lawful for a good reason to start the Mass an hour after midday even without privileges, because this is not a notable aberration from the prescribed times, as Laymann, Diana and Tanner say [refs].

[20] 20. An teneantur Catholici in Anglia ieiunare feriis sextis per totum annum: caeteraque festa ac ieiunia antiqua Ecclesiae Anglicanae adhuc retinere. Respondeo Legem semel legitime latam (eadem est ratio de consuetudine vim legis habente) durare donec abrogetur etiam extincta potestate, quae eam tulit, vt docet Panor. cap. a nobis l. de sent. excom. Syl. v. statut. n. 12. Suar. l. 1. de leg. c. 10. Salas disp. 1. de leg. n. 60. cap. fin. de offic. Legat. Cum ergo haec ieiunia[49] semel fuerint legitima autoritate introducta; vt supponitur, sequitur quod adhuc obligent, nisi aliunde constet de abrogatione. Itaque tenentur ieiunare feriis sextis, et ad similia, in quibus constat nullum specialem factam mutationem. Alia est ratio de multis festis antiquis, quia iam consuetudo contaria inualuit.

Case 20. *Are Catholics in England bound to fast on Fridays throughout the year? And should the other ancient feasts and fasts of the English Church be still kept?*

---

[49] S adds: *et festa*

I reply that once a law has been legitimately made (and the same is the case with a custom which has the force of law), it endures until it is abolished, even when the power which made it is extinguished, as Panormitanus, Sylvester, Suarez and Salas teach [refs]. Since therefore these fast and feasts were introduced in the past by legitimate authority, as is supposed, it follows that they still oblige, unless it is otherwise agreed that they have been abolished. Therefore Catholics in England are bound to fast on Fridays, and to do other things to which it is agreed there has been no change specially made. The judgement is different concerning many of the ancient holidays, because now a contrary custom prevails.

[21] 21. <u>Quid faciendum de ieiunio S. Marci quando incidit in vnum ex primis 5. diebus Paschae. Respondeo Casus iste</u> eueniet anno 1641. et iterum anno 1644. dico igitur videtur mihi vel omittendum, vel potius cum officio transferendum. Ratio est, quia ita fit in aliis ecclesiis vicinis, [fo. 9⁵⁰] Belgicis v.g. et sic statuitur in Synod. Dioeces. Leod: ann: 1618. tit. 11. c. 7. et in statutis⁵¹ Melitensium, viz: vt transferatur post octauam Paschae. Credibile autem est Angliam quoad hoc alios imitatam, et in dubio hoc praesumendum iuxta reg. inspicimus de reg. iuris in 6°.⁵² et hoc eo magis quod ieiunium in tempore Paschali exorbitet a iure communi cap. Scire dist. 76. vnde in dubio restringi debet saltem vt non censeatur obligare pro una septima quae solemnior est et reputatur pro vno die cum ipso festo, vt patet ex Praefatione Missae. Certum autem est si incideret in ipsam Domenicam Paschatis, non deberi tunc seruari. Dixi in dubio, quia si certo constaret aliter⁵³ fuisse institutum nunc illud foret sequendum.

Case 21. *What is to be done about the Fast of St Mark when it falls on one of the first five days of Easter?*⁵⁴
I reply that this case will happen in 1641 and again in 1644. I say therefore that it seems to me that it should either be omitted or preferably it should be transferred, along with the associated office. The reason is that this is how it is done in other neighbouring churches, for example Belgium; and it was decreed in the diocesan synod of Liège in 1618, [ref.] and by the decrees of the knights of Malta, that it should be

---

⁵⁰ A has the following heading at the top of this page: *De ieiunio S. Marci in Pasch.*
⁵¹ S inserts: *militum*
⁵² S reads: *iuxta reg: 45. in 6°. Inspicimus in obscuris.*
⁵³ S reads: *in Anglia*
⁵⁴ St Mark's (25 April) was a day of abstinence, but Easter involved a week of celebration, which, being a moveable feast, might conflict with St Mark's. This discussion is important for providing a date for the composition of the cases: see the Introduction, p. xiii.

transferred until after the octave of Easter. Moreover it is credible that England in this matter imitated the practice of other countries, and in cases of doubt this is to be presumed, according to what is laid down in the Decretals of Boniface VIII [ref.]. This is more likely because to fast at Easter is to depart from the common law [ref.]. Hence, if there is any doubt, it should at least be postponed, so that it is not judged that it should oblige during Easter week, which is more solemn and has a greater reputation than the single day associated with this holy day, as is clear from the Preface to the Mass. It is however certain that if it falls on Easter Sunday itself it should not then be kept. I have said 'if there is any doubt', because if it is agreed that certainly it was established otherwise in England, that rule should now be followed.

[22] 22. An liceat Catholico in Anglia contrahere matrimonium cum haeretica, aut Catholicae cum haeretico. An possint parentes tales nuptias filiis procurare, et sacerdotes eis assistere et benedicere? Respondeo Matrimonia Catholici cum haeretica[55] esse per se loquendo illicita: tum ex ipsa rei natura ob magna pericula et incommoda, vt satis indicat scriptura tam seuere ea olim Iudaeis interdicens hoc nomine Exod. 34. Deut. 7. 3. Reg. 11.[56] tum etiam iure Ecclesiastico ex C. Calced. act. 15. can: 14. Eliberino. can. 16. Laod: can. 31. Carth. 3. can. 12. Agathensi cap. 26. ita passim Theologi apud Sanchem l. 7[57] dp. 72. Non tamen ita illicita quin ex graui causa permitti possint dispensante saltem Pontifice, vnde et constat eum aliquando dispensare. Addunt aliqui in Germania, Gallia, Polonia, similibusque locis, vbi est mixtura religionum,[58] vsu receptum[59] vt haec matrimonia facile ineantur. Caeterum Scriptores Germani Laym. de imped: c. 19. n. 2. Tan: de matr. q. 4. n. 89. Serrar: opusc. de hac re tom. 2. c. 2. §. 6. 7. et 13. negant hoc facile licere, aiuntque experientia compertum magna illis subesse animarum pericula, ob quae vitari debeant.

[fo. 9v60] A fortiori igitur in Anglia censeri debent illicita nec nisi difficillime permitti, vbi personae malitiam armat et sustentat animorum[61] iniquitas. Vel enim vir est catholicus, vxor haeretica: et sic in familiam haereticam propagatur haeresis; vel haec catholica, ille haereticus; et sic timendum ne compellatur ad leges regni seruandas in profi-

---

55 S adds: *aut Catholicae cum haeretico*
56 S adds: *1 Esd: 9.*
57 S adds: *de Matrim.*
58 S adds: *(praesertim permissa a Principe)*
59 S adds: *esse*
60 A has this heading at the top of the page, which carries on over to the top of fo. 10: *An Catholicus cum haeretica possit contrahere Matrimonium. An impedimenta antiqua sint sublata in Anglia, at an ibi valeat matrimonium clandestinum.*
61 S reads: *legum*

tenda haeresim. denique vtrolibet modo sit, periculum est peruersionis prolium, quod ingentis sane est momenti:[62] hinc per se loquendo peccant parentes haec matrimonia procurantes: item sacerdotes his assistentes, nisi hi inuite, et ob graue incommodum vitandum assistendo excusentur. Causa excusans est 1º. promissio vel spes certa conuersionis, si nequeat differri contractus Lay. cit. Tan. n. 88. Serr. canones enim hunc casum excipiunt.[63] 2º. causa valde eximia. talis porro non est vt lautius et opulentius nubas. Potius tale censeri quod[64] res non sit integra: vt si foemina esset grauida, etc.[65] cum enim hoc malum morte ipsa non multo leuius sentiatur, multum videtur excusare posse,[66] modo[67] caueatur caueatur[68] periculum peruersionis, nec pacto se obliget catholica pars ad consentiendum vt liberorum pars vlla haretice educetur, quin integrum sibi seruet ad eas rite instituendas incumbere quantum potest.[69] Caeterum hae nuptiae non videntur debere benedici a Sacerdote ritu illo solemni Ecclesiae, etiam quando licite contrahentur vt docet Laym. in append. c. de matrim. catholici cum haeretica c. 9. n. 8. etsi alii aliter sentiant.

Case 22. *Is it lawful for a Catholic in England to contract marriage with a heretic woman, or for a Catholic woman to marry a heretic man? May parents arrange such marriages for their children, and may priests perform and bless them?*

I reply that the marriages of a Catholic man with a heretic woman, or of a Catholic woman with a heretic man, are in themselves unlawful. First they are unlawful by their very nature, because of the great danger and trouble they bring, as Scripture sufficiently makes clear by in the past forbidding the Jews so severely to do this; namely in Exodus, 34; Deuteronomy, 7; 3 Kings, 11; 1 Ezra, 9. Second, it is also unlawful by the law of the Church, as decreed by the councils of Chalcedon, Eliberitanum, Laodicea, Carthage, and Agatha [refs], as all theologians show, as cited in Sanchez [ref.]. It is not however so unlawful that it may not be permitted for a serious reason, at least with a dispensation from the Pope, which he sometimes agrees to grant. Some authors add that in

---

[62] S reads instead of the sentence from 'Vel': *Quid quod praeter periculum peruersionis partis Catholicae, maius forte sit periculum peruersionis liberorum.*
[63] S inserts here: *Excusat*
[64] S reads: *quando*
[65] S adds: *vel quid simile*
[66] S reads instead of the last fourteen words: *ad quod sequi posset malum non multo leuius morti, nisi contraheres.*
[67] S adds: *semper*
[68] Thus in A.
[69] S reads instead of the last clause, from 'nec pacto': *te obliges, vt pars vlla liberorum subducatur iuri tuo eos Catholice educandi.*

Germany, France, Poland and such-like places where there is a mixture of religions, especially if it is permitted by the ruler, it is the accepted usage that such marriages are contracted without difficulty. However, German writers like Laymann, Tanner and Serrarius [refs] deny that mixed marriages are easily lawful, and they say that experience has taught that those who marry in this way risk great danger to their souls, for which reason such marriages should be avoided.

Therefore especially in England, where the iniquity of the laws arms and sustains the malice of the individual, such marriages should be judged to be unlawful and only permitted with great difficulty. For whether the man is Catholic and the woman heretic and thus heresy is continued in a heretic family, or if she is Catholic and he is heretic and thus it must be feared that she will be compelled to obey the laws of the kingdom in professing heresy; in short, whichever way it may be, there is danger of the perversion of the children, which is indeed of immense importance. Hence, speaking of such marriages in themselves, the parents sin mortally by arranging them. Priests also sin by performing these marriages, unless they do it against their will and to avoid a serious difficulty, in which case they would be excused.

The reasons which excuse are: first, where there is a promise or certain hope of conversion, and if the marriage cannot be deferred, according to Laymann, Tanner and Serrarius [refs], for the canons make an exception in this case. Second, for exceptional reasons, which do not include marrying someone higher in the social scale or someone richer. Rather, it is judged to be an exceptional reason if the matter is one over which the law has not yet made a decision; for example, if the woman is pregnant, or something similar. For since an evil not much better than death would follow if they did not marry, then it seems very clear that the marriage may be excused. However, the danger of perversion is always to be avoided. Nor should the Catholic party on any account agree to any of the children being educated in a heretic fashion, but the Catholic should honestly ensure, that they are educated as far as possible correctly. Moreover, it does not seem that these marriages should be blessed by a priest using the solemn rite of the Church even when they have been lawfully contracted, as Laymann teaches [refs], even if others judge differently.

[23] 23. Vtrum impedimenta iuris antiqui per Tridentinum sublata vim adhuc habeant in Anglia, v.g. Titius vxore mortua ducere vellet eam quam vxor post consummatum cum[70] matrimonium de sacro fonte suscepit. Respondeo [fo. 10] sublata censet Malderus expresse l. 2 q.

---

[70] S adds: eo

90. a. 4. db. 2. cuius autoritas rem facit non improbabilem. verius tamen est ea sublata non esse.[71] quia reuocatorio legis, quae fieri debet non per modum merae gratiae (talis enim a quouis priuato statim acceptari poterit pro libito.) sed per modum legis omnes vniformiter obligantis debet esse promulgata et acceptata plane eo modo, quo aliae leges, alias regula communis actionum pro omnibus esse nequit ita Vasq. l. 2. tom. 2. dp. 158. n. 24. Bonac. de leg. dp. 1. q. 1. p. 4. n. 13.[72] Becanus de leg. c. 6. q. 6. Tan. de leg. q. 5. n. 106.[73] et alii. cum ergo Tridentinum in Anglia nondum sit receptum, nec obliget quoad alia[74] sane nec censeri potest acceptatum quoad hoc.[75]

Case 23. *Do the impediments of the ancient law, removed by the Council of Trent, still have force in England? For example, may Titius, after the death of his wife, marry the woman for whom his former wife acted as godmother after the consummation of their marriage?*

I reply that the explicit judgement of Malderus is that these impediments have been removed [ref.], and his authority makes the matter not improbable. However, it is more true that they are not removed. Thus the impediments of the ancient law, removed by Trent, still have force in England, and for example Titius may not in that country, after the death of his wife, marry the woman for whom his late wife after the consummation of the marriage acted as godmother. This is because the revocation of a law should not be done on the basis of mere whim (for if this were the case a law could be accepted immediately by a private person at his pleasure) but by the law obliging everyone uniformly, and this law should be promulgated and accepted openly in such a way as to disqualify other laws, and other rules of common action for everyone; thus, Vazquez, Bonacina, Lorca, Becanus, Tanner, Suarez and others [refs]. Since therefore the decrees of the Council Trent have not yet been accepted in England, and do not oblige in many other cases, it is clearly not to be taken that they can be accepted in this case either.

[24] 24. <u>Sintne valida ac licita in Anglia matrimonia clandestina?</u> <u>Respondeo Nota</u> dupliciter dici matrimonium clandestinum, aut quia contractum sine Parocho et testibus aut contractum sine denuntiatio-

---

[71] S reads from the beginning: *Impedimenta iuris Antiqui per Trident. sublata vim adhuc habere in Anglia, v.g. Titius ibi nequit, mortua vxore, eam ducere, quam vxor post consummatum cum eo matrimonium de sacro fonte suscepit. Ratio est*

[72] S adds: *Lorca.*

[73] S adds: *Suar. l. 6 de legibus c. 27.*

[74] There is a gap of about an inch in A, and S adds: *multa*

[75] S adds: *Contrarium tenet non improbabiliter Malderus l. 2. q. 90. a. 4.*

nibus. De hoc posteriori modo parum videtur esse difficultatis[76] in Anglia, nam certum est valere vbique gentium. In Anglia insuper videtur licitum quia non sunt Parochiae Catholicae, in quibus fieri possint proclamationes. Igitur ex necessitate excusantur seruando tamen Catholicorum consuetudines, si quae existant. De priori[77] certum est matrimonium esse validum, quia Decretum irritans Tridentinum nunquam fuit in Parochiis Anglicanis promulgatum, quod tamen speciatim et expresse requiritur in ipso Concilio loco citato.

At contractum clam sine testibus est ibi illicitum tum iure ipso naturae ob pericula, tum iure antiquo Ecclesiae, quae hasce nuptias semper est detestata, vt testatur Trid: s. 24. c. 1. et patet ex multis iuribus 3°. q. 5. et ex C. Londin:[78] sub Innoc. 3. vbi iubetur vt in facie Ecclesiae et coram Sacerdote copulentur. Excusaret tamen vrgens aliqua necessitas vt cum Caiet. docet Tann: q. 3. n. 111. et facilius adhuc excusari possunt ab adhibendo sacerdote ob pericula speciatim, modo adsint alii testes.

Case 24. *Are clandestine marriages valid and lawful in England?*

I reply that it should be noted that there are two ways in which a marriage can be said to be clandestine: either because it was contracted without a parish priest and witnesses, or because it was contracted without banns. Concerning this second type, there seems to be little difficulty in England, for it is certain that it is valid among all nations. In England moreover it seems lawful because there are no Catholic parishes in which it is possible to read the banns. Therefore, people marrying in this way out of necessity are excused, as long as they observe the customs of Catholics, if there are any such. Concerning the first type, it is certain that it is valid, because the Tridentine decree invalidating them was never proclaimed in the parishes of England, which was specially and expressly required by the Council itself, in the place cited.

But to marry secretly without witnesses is unlawful there, both by the law of nature itself due to the danger involved, and by the ancient law of the Church, which has always detested such marriages, as the Council of Trent [ref.] bears witness, and as is clear from many laws [ref.] and from the Lateran Council under Innocent III where it was decreed that marriage should take place in the face of the Church and in the presence of a priest. Some urgent necessity however would excuse, as Tanner teaches with Caietan [ref.], and moreover those marrying can more easily be excused for not having a priest because of the special danger of doing so, as long as there are other witnesses present.

---

[76] S reads instead of the last four words: *non videtur dubium quin matrimonia clandestina sint valida*

[77] S adds: *modo*

[78] Thus in both MSS, but would seem to be a miscopy of *Lateran:*

[25] [fo. 10ᵛ] 25. Quousque teneantur Catholici in Anglia, Sacerdotes maxime ad obseruantiam Decretorum et Constitutionum Apostolicarum, quae de nouo emanant Romae in dies. Respondeo si sint Decreta peculiariter ad Anglos destinata obtemperandum esse⁷⁹ cum fuerint idonee intimata vt colligitur ex Suar. de leg. lib.8. c. 24. an. 7. et Lorca de leg. dp. 18. si tamen difficultas occurrat in acceptatione poterit supplicari, et executio tantisper suspendi, vt habet communis argum. cap. si quando. de rescript. ita Salas de leg. dp. 13. s. 4. Bonac. de leg. dp. 1.q. l. p. 4. n. 27. et alii passim quod si Pontifex informatus adhuc persistat, seruari debet Decretum.

Quoad Decreta toti Ecclesiae communia, credo quod si sit specialis difficultas in iis acceptandis, non teneantur in Anglia ea statim acceptare. quod si non acceptentur, nec ad ea seruanda tenebuntur, donec ii, ad quos spectat, executionem vrgeant. quia leges etiam Pontificiae cum hac tacita conditione feruntur si acceptentur. 1º. quia hoc⁸⁰ consentaneum moderationi Ecclesiae. 2º. quia regionum consuetudo potest legem abrogare iure communi: ergo a fortiori obligationem ab initio impedire: et ita tenent Less. de iust. l. 2. c. 22. db.13. Azor. l. 5. p.1ᵃᵉ. c. 4. Valent. de leg. q. 5. p. 5. q. 4. Bonac. cit. Tan. q. 5. db. 4. Rodrig. tom. 1. q. 6. et 10. Nau. Ench. c. 23. n. 40. Salas.

Case 25. *How far are Catholics, especially priests in England, bound to observe the Decrees and Apostolic Constitutions, which newly emanate from Rome every day?*

I reply that if they are decrees specifically for the English they should be obeyed when they have been suitably published, as is gathered from Suarez and Lorca [refs]. If however a difficulty occurs in accepting the decree, it may be appealed, and the execution suspended in the mean time, as is the common view based on the canon law; thus, Salas, Bonacina and many others [refs]. If the Pontiff, having been informed, still persists, the decree should be obeyed.

As regards decrees which are common to the whole Church, if there is a special difficulty in accepting them, people in England are not bound to do so immediately, and if they are not accepted, people are not bound to obey them, until those that they concern insist on the execution of them. This is because laws, even Pontifical ones, are made with this tacit condition, that they should be accepted. First, because that is in agreement with the usual way of doing things in the Church. Second, because according to the common law, the custom of a region may abrogate such laws, therefore it is even clearer that it may remove the

---

⁷⁹ S reads instead of the last two words: *debere sacerdotes inibi existentes iisdem obtemperare*
⁸⁰ S adds: *est*

obligation from the beginning; thus, Lessius, Azor, Valentia, Bonacina, Tanner, Rodriguez, Navarre, Becanus, Toletus, Reginald, Diana; and Laymann, Malderus, Gamachaeus and Salas do not disagree [refs].

[26] 26. An possit Sacerdos Baptismum, Extremam Vnctionem, Sacrae Eucharistiae ministrationem, purificationem mulierum, aquae Benedictionem, similiaque exercere sine [fo. 11] vestibus sacris, quando commode haberi non possunt. Respondeo consuetudinem Ecclesiae vim legis habentem esse vt in Sacramentorum administratione[81] adhibeatur stola et superpiliceum, vt patet ex instructionibus generalibus Ritualis Romani initio. Graffeus tamen l. 2. c. 41. n. 3. videtur solam stolam sub mortali exigere in administratione Eucharistiae vnde a fortiori idem de reliquis dici potest, saltem in Anglia. Et sane cum stola possit facile fere parari, non videtur facile committendum, vt sine ea vnquam ista fiant. Dato tamen casu quo nullo modo haberi possent, vt in domibus pauperculorum; existimo posse ita fieri sine vestibus sacris. ita responderunt olim Card. Alanus et P. Personius casu 8. De Poenitentia est indubitatum item et de Baptismo non solemni, cum et a laico possit ministrari: et ex his deducitur argumentum satis probabile ad reliqua, quia necessitas spiritualis praeponderare debet praecepto positiuo rituum, praesertim in regno haeresi infecto, vbi non semel sed frequenter occurrit necessitas, sicut olim in Ecclesia primitiua. Ad hoc facit quod probabiliter doceant aliqui etiam laicum posse moribundo ministrare Sacram communionem, cessante scandalo. ita Lay. de Euch. c.7. in fine cum Suar. et aliis. ergo a fortiori Sacerdos hoc et similia poterit sine vestitu Sacro.

Case 26. *May a priest perform baptism, extreme unction, the administration of the holy Eucharist, the purification of women, the blessing of water and similar ceremonies, without consecrated vestments when they cannot conveniently be had?*

I reply that the custom of the Church which has the force of law is that in the administration of baptism, extreme unction, the Eucharist, the purification of women, the blessing of water and similar things, the stole and the surplice should be used, as is clear from the general instructions at the beginning of the Roman Ritual. Graffeus [ref.], however, seems only to demand the stole under pain of mortal sin in the administration of the Eucharist, and this may be said even more strongly about the rest, at least in England. And truly since a stole can quite easily be obtained, it does not seem easy to agree that these ceremonies should ever be performed without one. Given however a case in which these

---

[81] S reads instead of the last three words: *in administratione Baptismi, Extremae Vnctionis, Eucharistiae, Purificationis mulierum, aquae Benedictionis, et similium*

things cannot in any way be had, as in the houses of paupers, I think that these ceremonies may be performed without consecrated vestments. This was the reply once of Cardinal Allen and Father Persons in *Concerning Penance,* case 8. It is not to be doubted that this is also true in the case of a baptism which is not a solemn one, since such a baptism may also be administered by a layman. And from these points is deduced an argument which is probable enough for the rest, since spiritual necessity should be considered more important than the rules governing ritual, especially in a kingdom infected with heresy, where necessity occurs not once but frequently, as once it did in the primitive Church. This is supported when we consider that some teach as a probable judgement that even a layperson may minister holy communion to a dying person, if there is no scandal; thus, Laymann, Suarez and others [refs]. Therefore there is an even stronger case for saying a priest may do this and similar things without consecrated vestments.

[27] 27. <u>Si post offertorium Missae peractum superueniant aliqui</u> <u>cupientes communicare,</u> quomodo illis subueniendum, vbi non asseruatur Venerabile Sacramentum. <u>Respondeo</u> si veniant ante consecrationem poterit[82] nouas hostias adiicere, easque mentaliter oblatas (hoc enim in eo casu sufficit) consecrare. si post consecrationem;[83] poterit partem suae hostiae dare iis. vt docet Lay. l. 5. tr. 5. c. 4. n. 6. Bonac. de Euch. [fo. 11ᵛ] q. 5. n. 14. Sa. et alii. Denique si neque hoc fieri possit magnaque sit concurrentium necessitas iudicio prudentis, poterit alterum sacrum dicere. ita Lay. cit. vbi speciatim de Anglia loquitur cum Azor. p. 1. l. 10. c. 24. q. 6, et ait etiam diebus non festis hoc fieri posse. Nam cap. consulius ti. de celeb. Miss. excipitur casus necessitatis; in Anglia autem vbi Sacerdotes rari sunt, et in latebris, ipsa paucitas est quaedam necessitas, vt bene Azor, quare possunt rationabili de causa, habita ratione consuetudinis et aedificationis saepius ibi in die celebrare.

Case 27. *If after the offertory has been performed during the Mass, people arrive who want to take communion, in what way may they be helped where the Blessed Sacrament is not reserved?*

I reply that if they come before the consecration the priest could add new hosts and having offered them mentally (for in this case, that would suffice) consecrate them. If they come after the consecration, he could give part of his own host to them, as Laymann, Bonacina, Sa and others teach [refs]. Indeed, if this could not be done, and according to the judgement of a prudent man the necessity of the people coming along late was great, he could say another Mass. Thus, Laymann, where he

---

82 S substitutes for the last word: *posse Sacerdotem*
83 S adds: *veniant*

specially discusses England, with Azor [ref.], and says that even on days
which are not feast days this may be done. For the canon [ref.] allows
exceptions in cases of necessity. Moreover in England where priests are
rare and in hiding, this shortage of priests is itself a sort of necessity, as
Azor shows well. Hence priests may for a reasonable cause, for example
for reasons of custom and edification, celebrate Mass more frequently
in the day there.

[28] 28. Quid faciendum iis, qui more haereticorum matrimonium
contrahunt in gradibus ab Ecclesia prohibitis, si alter postea ad fidem
conuertatur, nec sine magnis incommodis possint seperari? An possit
pars Catholica defectus conscientia reddere debitum antequam obtineatur dispensatio? an ea obtenta necessarium sit vt pars altera moneatur
de nullitate atque ita iterum contrahant? an vero sufficiat copula coniugalis ad matrimonium conualidandum, parte non monita?

Respondeo matrimonium illud haud dubie esse nullum, cum teneantur Haeretici in Anglia[84] legibus Ecclesiae olim ibi receptis nec
illorum consuetudo potest contrarium praescribere, cum sit irrationabilis
et iniquissima. Vnde consequenter dico non posse coniugem illum[85]
reddere debitum,[86] ne quidem ad vitandam mortem, quia esset fornicatio; quamuis enim metus mortis cessare faciat legem humanam quoad
actiones praeceptas aut prohibitas, at non quoad vim irritantem, quia
non expedit bono communi.[87] Debet ergo donec obtineatur dispensatio
vel peregrinari, vel aegrotam se fingere, vel alio modo copulam subter-
fugere, vt docet Sanch. l. 2. de matr. d. 29.[88] n. 13. aiens[89] certissimum
esse, quod etsi iuris tantum humani sit impedimentum, nihilominus non
liceat copulari. argm. c. litteras 13. de restit. spoliat. et c. inquisioni de
sent. Excom:

[fo. 12] Dico tamen[90] obtenta iam occulte dispensatione, si absque
periculo moneri possit coniux;[91] et renouari,[92] id omnino faciendum,
quia est modus tutissimus, et stylus Curiae Romanae fauet. Caeterum
posito quod id fieri nequeat absque periculo, velitque Catholicus[93]
(quod fere suadendum erit) in matrimonio persistere, dico satis esse
copulam coniugalem ad matrimonium conualidandum, aut alium actum

---

84 S adds: *obtemperare*
85 S substitutes for last two words: *alteram partem, etiamsi conuertatur*
86 S adds: *antequam obtineatur dispensatio*
87 S adds: *vt dixi de leg: cas: 19. et 50.*
88 S reads: *disp. 39.*
89 S adds: *n. 8.*
90 S reads: *2º.*
91 S adds: *de nullitate prioris matrimonii*
92 S adds: *contractus*
93 S reads: *Catholica pars*

ei aequipollentem. <u>Probatur 1º. ex cap.</u> proposuit et c. fin: de coniugio seruorum vbi plane deciditur, si ingenuus cognita coniugis conditione seruili, nihilominus maritale affectu ad eam accedat, conualidari matrimonium eo ipso, absque eo quod serua moneatur de nullitate aut de nouo contrahat. <u>probatur 2º.</u> a priori quia quia⁹⁴ copula maritalis est verus consensus de praesente non verbo, sed facto, vt loquuntur iura, est enim realis corporum traditio mutua, idque non animo fornicario, seu quamdiu libeat, sed cum affectu coniunctionis perpetuae vt passim docent iura. c. is qui de Sponsalibus c. 3. de condit. apposit: c. ad id de Sponsalib:⁹⁵ ergo cum copula ista cum affectu maritali exerceatur, sitque iam inter personas habiles, nec opus sit in Anglia Parocho et testibus, sane nulla videtur ratio cur vim non habeat ad constituendum ex nunc verum matrimonium.

    <u>Dices 1º. esse consensum ex errore,</u> quia alter coniux accedit eo ductus errore, quod iam ante ex contractu praeterito sit obligatus, alias forte id non facturus. <u>Respondeo esto accedat ex</u> hoc errore, at hic non est error substantiae (qui solus matrimonium vitiat, iuxta communem) immo nec alicuius qualitatis magni momenti. Consentis enim nunc in eandem, in quam olim consenseras, et quam sponte elegeras: hoc per se loquendo apud prudentes, non potest esse tanti momenti ac consentire in corruptam, leprosam aut ignobilem, quam credebas virginem, sanam,⁹⁶ et generosam, et tamen hoc in casu valet matrimonium iuxta vniuersos fere Doctores.

    <u>Dices 2º. Coniugem ignarum tantum</u> intendere ratificare primum <u>matrimonium,</u>⁹⁷ non vero contrahere de nouo. <u>Respondeo eum intendere</u> tradere suum corpus nunc, atque adeo non mere ratificare actum priorem, sed illum potius repetere ac renouare, [fo. 12ᵛ⁹⁸] quod sufficit ad nouum contractum, si prior non valuerit, modo personae nunc sint habiles, cessetque vis ac metus, atque error in substantia. <u>Dices⁹⁹ qui soluit alteri</u> pecuniam putans eam debitam, cum non sit, errat in substantia, et non obligare¹⁰⁰ stare pacto suo. ergo et reddere debitum coniugale putando deberi, est error in substantia. <u>Respondeo nego</u> sequentiam¹⁰¹, quia quod in vno¹⁰² contractu est substantiale, est¹⁰³ accidentale in altero, vt bene

---

⁹⁴   Thus in A.
⁹⁵   S adds: *et alibi*
⁹⁶   S adds: *opulentam*
⁹⁷   Interlineated here in A: *contractum*
⁹⁸   In A there is a heading at the top of the page which continues across fo. 13 and reads: *Vtrum copulam carnalem exercentes censendi matrimonium contraxisse.*
⁹⁹   S adds: *3º.*
¹⁰⁰ S reads: *obligatur*
¹⁰¹ S reads: *consequentiam*
¹⁰² S reads: *tuo*
¹⁰³ S adds: *tantum*

Vasq. l. 2. d. 30. n. 27. <u>Porro in matrimonio</u> nihil est substantiale, nisi ipsae personae seu corpora contrahentium, in his autem hic non erratur. Et hanc sententiam probabilem docent Sanch. cit d. 36. n. 9. Reginald.[104] Caiet. Rodrig. Sotus et Bonacin: de matr. q. 2 p. 9. n. 7.

Case 28. *What should be done with those who contract marriage in the manner of heretics in the degrees prohibited by the Church, if one of them afterwards is converted to the faith, and they cannot separate without great trouble? May the Catholic spouse, if he is weak in conscience, perform his marital duties before a dispensation has been obtained? Once it has been obtained, is it necessary that the other party should be warned about the nullity of the marriage and should they contract marriage again? Is marital copulation sufficient to validate the marriage, with one spouse not being warned about the nullity?*

I reply that without doubt that marriage is null, since heretics in England are bound to obey the law of the Church which was once received there, and the custom of heretics cannot prescribe the contrary, since it is unreasonable and most iniquitous. Consequently, I say that the spouse cannot, even if converted, perform his marital duties, before a dispensation has been obtained, not even to avoid death, because it would be fornication. For although the fear of death overrides human law, as far as actions laid down or forbidden are concerned, it does not do so in the case of a law with the power to invalidate a marriage, because in this case, such an action does not contribute to the common good, as I have said in *Concerning Laws*, cases 19 and 50. This person should therefore either go on a pilgrimage or pretend to be ill, or in some other way avoid copulation until a dispensation has been obtained, as Sanchez teaches [ref.], saying it is most certain that even if the impediment to the marriage were only a matter of human law, it would nevertheless not be lawful, according to canon law, to copulate [ref.].

I say, however, that if, having secretly obtained the dispensation, the spouse can be without danger warned about the nullity of the prior marriage, and the contract renewed, it certainly should be done, because it is the safest method, and the custom and practice of the Roman Curia favour it. For the rest, if it is understood that this cannot be done without danger, and the Catholic spouse wants to persist in the marriage (which usually s/he should be advised to do) I say that marital copulation, or some equivalent act, is enough to validate the marriage. This is proved first by the canon law [ref.] where it is clearly laid down that if a

---

104 S reads from here: *et Bona: citat. et tenent Sotus in 4. dist. 29. q. 2. a. 1. db. vlt. et dist. 28. q. 1. a. 2. conc. 3. Caiet. t. 1. opusc. tract. 12. q. 2. et in Summa verb. matrim: Rodrig: t. 1. Sum: cap: 219. n. 2.*

freeman, having learned of the servile condition of his spouse nevertheless approaches her with true marital affection, the marriage is validated
by that action, without the slave-girl being warned of the nullity or a
new contract being made. It is proved secondly from the definitions
of our terminology, because marital copulation is true consent 'for the
present' not by word but by deed, to use the language of the laws, for it
is the real mutual surrender of bodies, and is done without the intention
to commit fornication, or to have temporary pleasure, but with the affection of a lasting union, as the laws teach throughout [refs]. Therefore
since this copulation is performed with marital passion, and between
people who are now suitable, and since it is not necessary in England for
a parish priest or witnesses to validate a marriage, there does not seem
to be any reason in truth why it should not have the power to constitute
this from now on as a true marriage.

You will say, firstly, that in this case it is consent given in error,
because the other spouse agreed to have marital relations through error,
as a result of the obligation created by the marriage contract made in the
past, and that otherwise perhaps the spouse would not have consented.
I reply: let us agree that s/he agreed through this error, but this error is
not an error of substance (which alone can vitiate marriage according to
all) and indeed not an error of any great moment at all. For you consent
now to the same thing that you consented to in the past, and one which
you freely choose. This, speaking of the matter in itself, according to
prudent men, cannot be of such moment as when a person consents to
marry a corrupt, leprous, or ignoble person whom they believe to be a
healthy, rich virgin of gentle birth; but, according to almost all doctors,
in that case the marriage is still valid.

You will say secondly that the ignorant spouse only intended to ratify
the first marriage, not truly to make a new contract. I reply that s/he
intended to deliver up her/his body now, and in such a way as not only
to ratify a prior act, but rather to repeat and renew it, which is sufficient
for a new contract, if the prior one is not valid, as long as the people
are now suitable, and no force or fear is involved, and there is no error
in substance. You will say thirdly, that when a man gives money to
another, thinking he owes him the money, when he does not, he errs
in substance and is not bound to honour his agreement. Therefore to
perform these marital duties, thinking that you should, is an error in
substance. I reply that I deny the logic of the argument, because what
is substantial in one contract, is only accidental in the other, as Vazquez
shows well [ref.]. But in matrimony, nothing is substantial except the
very persons or the bodies of the contracting parties; in these however
there is in this case no error. And this judgement is taught as probable
by Sanchez, Reginaldus, Caietan, Rodriguez, Soto and Bonacina [refs].

[29] 29. Vtrum sponsi in Anglia copulam carnalem exercentes censendi sint matrimonium contraxisse, de qua re S. T. 3. p. q. 40. in suppl: a. 2. Sanch. l. 3. d. 40. Respondeo Ecclesiam praesumere in foro externo quod animo maritali accedant, cum non sit credendum eos voluisse fornicari, quare nullam probationem in contrarium admittet,[105] vt habetur c. Is. qui 30. de spons: et c. vnic. de despons. impub. in 6°. In foro autem conscientiae, si vere adfuerit animus maritalis, erit matrimonium, nec opus erit aliis signis aut nutibus tunc (modo praecesserit fides data) vt recte Sotus[106] vt manifestum est ex iuribus. Vnde et in foro conscientiae erit matrimonium, si copulentur[107] citra seminationem, si animo maritali id fecerint; licet non quoad externam praesumptionem. At si alteruter certo sciat se non animo maritali accessisse, non erit in conscientia matrimonium iuxta omnes; esto peccarit grauiter tam fornicando, quam alterum decipiendo. Vnde si secundam ducat legitime, standum erit huic secundo matrimonio. Quod si dubitet an animus fuerit maritalis, prae-sumendum est pro valore matrimonii in foro conscientiae. Siquidem ordinarie non solent homines exterius facere totum id, quod requiritur ad valorem actus, sine animo faciendi, vt Suar. et alii docent in materia de voto,[108] et quia matrimonium est res fauorabilis, maxime si [fo. 13] accedant aliae coniecturae, in quo etiam censeo rationem esse habendam partis damnum passae. estque ex mente Sanch. l. 1. de matr. d. 9. n. 13.[109] nihilominus si adsint speciales coniecturae in hoc dubio, vt si in calore libidinis promiserit ad extorquendam copulam, vel quid simile, tunc si vere dubitet an consenserit de praesente, an tantum de futuro, idque etiam in ipsa copula, probabile est, et forte probabilius[110] quod non sit matrimonium maxime si sit ipsi incommodum, aut mali euentus timeantur, vt vniuersim de omni dubio docet Salas l. 2. tr. 8. d. vn. s. 25. quia quoties agitur de incurrendo nouo onere, quocunque ex capite redditur dubium, probabile videtur[111] possessionem stare pro libertate, et huic fauendum, quicquid sit de praesumptione fori externi. Caeterum illud cauendum ne dubium sit leue, et de industria affectatum ad obli-gationem matrimonii subterfugiendam.[112]

---

[105] S reads instead of the last five words: *nullam probationem admittet quin censendi sint matrimonium contraxisse*
[106] S adds: *cit. versic: dubia. Quicquid in Contrarium indicet Pontius l. 2. de matr: c. 12. n. 3.*
[107] S adds: *etiam*
[108] S reads: *vt cum Suar: et aliis dixi casu 32 de Voto:*
[109] S adds: *et alibi*
[110] S adds: *vt existimo*
[111] S reads: *valde est*
[112] S adds: *quod prudentis iudicio relinquendum.*

Case 29. *Are betrothed couples in England who commit carnal copulation to be judged to have contracted matrimony? (On which, see St Thomas Aquinas and Sanchez [refs].)*

I reply that in the Church courts the presumption is that they did copulate with marital intent, since it is not to be believed that they wanted to fornicate; and in this matter no proof to the contrary is admissible, and they must be judged to have contracted matrimony, as the canon law shows [refs]. In the court of conscience, also, if there truly was marital intent, it will result in marriage, nor will there be need then of other signs or words of agreement, only that betrothal preceded it, as Soto rightly says [refs], and is clear from the laws, although Pontius says something to the contrary. Therefore, in conscience (although not as far as the law courts are concerned) it will also be marriage if they copulate without semination, if they do it with marital intent. But if one or the other knows certainly that he did it without marital intent it will not in conscience be matrimony, according to everyone, although that person sinned gravely as much by fornicating as by deceiving the other party. Therefore, if he then legitimately married another person, that second marriage would stand. If he doubts whether his intent was marital or not, the presumption must be in favour of the validity of the marriage in conscience, since ordinarily men who externally perform everything which is required for the validity of an act, do so intentionally; as, with Suarez and others, I have said in Case 32 in *Concerning Vows,* and also because marriage is a pleasing thing, especially if there are other reasons supporting this presumption. I also believe that the decision must go in favour of the party who may suffer harm, and that is the view of Sanchez [ref.]. Nevertheless if there are special reasons supporting this doubt, as for example if in the heat of lust he made a promise in order to extort copulation, or something similar, then if he truly doubts whether he gave consent to marriage 'for the present', or only 'for the future', through the act of copulation, it is probable and perhaps 'more probable', as I believe, that it should not be considered marriage, especially if it is troublesome to him, or an evil outcome is feared, a principle which Salas teaches universally on the subject of doubt [ref.]. Another reason is that when it is a matter of incurring a new burden, and for whatever reason a doubt has arisen, it seems probable that it is right to make a decision in favour of liberty, whatever is the presumption in legal terms. However, it is necessary to beware that the doubt is not slight or one which is craftily feigned to avoid the obligations of marriage; a decision on this should be left to the judgement of a prudent man.

[30] <u>An possint admitti ad Sacrum vel concionem haeretici, aut schismatici nondum</u> Ecclesiae reconciliati, de qua re Laym. de encom: c.

5. Conink. de sacr. d. 14. db. 2. 3. et n. 58. Bonac. de censuris d. 2. q. 2. p. 1. §. 1. et p. 3. Respondeo quoad concionem nulla est difficultas siue ex parte accedentium, siue admittentium, cum id iura permittant etiam vitandis c. responso de sen. excom: et cum aliis Conink cit. quoad Missam et diuina officia si sit vere haereticus non deberet admitti, quia est illi illicitum, cum sit vere excommunicatus, vnde qui sine necessitate eum admitteret, cooperaretur eius peccato. si tamen se ingerat, non peccant Catholici cum eo communicando, toleratus quippe est, vtpote nondum denuntiatus; at vero schismatici, id est animo catholici, vel alii qui creduntur non ita contumaces, vt excommunicationem incurrant, quales credo esse in Anglia plurimos, possunt admitti prout dictauerit prudentia ad communem aedificationem magis expedire.

Finis.

Case 30. *May heretics or schismatics who are not yet reconciled to the Church be admitted to Mass or to a sermon? (On which matter, see Laymann, Coninck and Bonacina [refs].)*

I reply that there is no difficulty as far as a sermon is concerned, whether in the case of the persons coming to the sermon, or of the persons admitting them to it, since the laws permit this even for those who should be avoided, as Coninck and others say [ref.]. As far as Mass and divine offices are concerned, if the person is truly a heretic, he should not be admitted, for it is unlawful for him since he is truly excommunicated; therefore whoever without necessity admits him has co-operated in his sin. If however, the heretic does gain admittance, Catholics do not sin by communicating with him, and he should certainly be tolerated since he is not yet denounced. But in truth, schismatics, that is those who are in their hearts Catholics or others who are believed not to be so contumacious that they have incurred excommunication (and I believe there are many such people in England), may be admitted, as far as prudence dictates should more significantly contribute to the common edification.

The End

[fo. 63] **CASUS spectantes ad ipsos Sacerdotes in Anglia (Cases regarding the priests themselves in England)**

[70] 70. An Sacerdotes in Anglia possint licite negare se esse sacerdotes, nomina vera, patriam, etc. sive in iudicio, sive extra? et quid si petatur vt praedicta omnia iuramento confirment.

Respondeo sacerdotes posse licite praedicta omnia negare, eaque iuramento confirmare, modo licita aliqua amphibologia, vel aequivocatione aut restrictione mentali vtantur. Quia non tenentur veritatem dicere cum tanto damno suo, sed possunt illam celare vel dissimulare; cum hoc ex iusta causa non sit malum; immo possunt vti sola aequivocatione, vel restrictione mentali: Ita docent Valent. tom. 3. D. 5. q. 13. pun. 2º. ex Navar aliisque antiquioribus. Lessius l. 2. c. 42. dub. 6. Suar. tom. 2º. de relig. l. 3 de iuramento c. 9. et 10. Sanchez in Summa l. 3. c. 6. Filu. tom. 2º. trac. 25. c. 11. Tan. tom. 3. D. 6. q. 2. dub. 1º. Tol. l. 5. c. 58. Bonac. Dub. 4. de iuramento. q. 1ª. pun. 12. quia vti pura mentali reservatione in iusta causa non est mentiri, quia proferens non it contra mentem: et si Azor. Henriq. et Coninck l. 1. de nubibus supernaturalibus D. 10. dub. 3º. Laym. l. 4. tr. 3. de iuramento c. 13 et alii id affirment. quos non sequimur, sed priores Theologos. Quare vt optime docet Sanchez. cit. licitum est iurare ex iusta causa (quae vt supponitur semper debet esse gravis[113], et si cogens excludat omnem aequiuocationem per quemcumque reduplicationem (etiam in infinitum complicatam.) quia adhuc ius habet iurans vti licita restrictione: viz. vt tibi dicam, quatenus tenear, aut alia simili, quae cum externis verbis verum sensum faciat.

Case 70. *May priests in England lawfully deny that they are priests, deny their true names and their country etc., either in court or otherwise? And what if they are asked to confirm these things under oath?*
I reply that priests may lawfully deny all these things, and confirm them with an oath, provided they use some lawful amphibology; that is, equivocation, or mental reservation. This is because they are not bound to tell the truth if it involves such danger to themselves, but may conceal or dissimulate it, since it is not evil to do this for a just cause. Indeed they may use either equivocation alone, or mental reservation. This is taught by Valentia (using Navarre and other more ancient writers); Lessius; Suarez; Sanchez; Filliucci; Tanner; Toletus; and Bonacina [refs]. The reason is that to use mental reservation pure and simple in a just cause is not to lie, because the speaker says nothing contrary to what is in his mind; although Azor, Henriquez, Coninck, Laymann and others say that it is lying. [refs]. But we do not follow them, and we prefer the former theologians, because, as Sanchez in the place cited teaches well, it is lawful to swear in this way for a just reason (which it is accepted must always be a serious reason), even if the oath forces the swearer to exclude all equivocation by whatever repetition of words (and round and round in circles forever),[114] and, in swearing the oath,

---

[113] The sense requires a second bracket here.
[114] The best example of such a clause was that used in the Oath of Allegiance of 1606,

the swearer has a right to use the lawful mental reservation of phrases like, 'as I will tell you', 'as far as I am bound', or other similar things, which when combined with the spoken words, make the meaning true.

[71] 71. An liceat Sacerdoti vestes clericales et saeculares assumere; et an ad evitandum periculum mortis aut carceris possit licite induere vestes, quas gerunt Ministri haeretici, etiam in concionibus suis, et templis? Respondeo haec omnia licite fieri posse, quia non tenetur sacerdos cum tanto suo damno vestes clericales gestare; neque intrinsece malum est vestes Ministrorum iusta de causa induere, cum sint indifferentes, licet ex contrario fine instituantur ad [fo. 63ᵛ] distinctionem cultarum: vt in simili casu de vestibus Iudaeorum et aliorum infidelium docent ex communi sententia Sanchez, Azor, Tanner, Filiuc, et Laym: citati. Suarez li. 14. de fide, Coninck D. 15. Dub. 3. Si tamen certis quibusdam vestibus in concionibus et templis vterentur ministri haeretici, directe institutis ad cultum suum falsum profitendum (quales sunt illae vestes, quibus vtuntur Iudaei, et Mahometani dum sacrificant) non possunt sacerdotes talibus vti licite, nec sine gravi peccato, vt Authores citati: quia talis vsus iudicatur, et est, vera professio falsi cultus, sicut est oblatio thuris, vel genuflexio coram idolo.

Case 71. *May a priest wear both clerical and secular clothes, and in order to avoid the danger of death and imprisonment may he lawfully even wear the clothes that heretic ministers wear when preaching their sermons, and when in their churches?*

I reply that all these things may lawfully be done, because a priest is not bound to wear his clerical clothes with such danger to himself. Nor is it intrinsically evil to put on the clothes of ministers for a just cause, since they are things indifferent, although they were instituted for a contrary end, as a distinguishing mark of their cult, as is taught in a similar case concerning the clothes of Jews and of other infidels by Sanchez, Azor, Tanner, Filliucci, Laymann, Suarez and Coninck, following the common judgement [refs]. If however heretic ministers, while preaching their sermons, and in their temples, use certain vestments of whatever sort which are directly instituted to profess their false cult (of which sort are those clothes the Jews and Moslems use while they sacrifice), priests cannot lawfully use them without grave sin, as the authors cited say, because such use is judged to be, and is, a true

which required those who swore it to swear that they were doing so without equivocation: an illogicality, according to Southwell. The same clause was also used in other oaths devised when Catholics were questioned.

profession of a false cult, just as the offering of incense, or genuflection to an idol is.

[72] 72. <u>An possint Sacerdotes in Anglia non recitare officium</u>, non celebrare missam, diebus festis, non audire missam etc. <u>Respondeo praedicta omnia licite omitti posse, quando</u> adest periculum probabile vitae, vel incarcerationis, vel alterius gravis mali; quia praecepta Ecclesiae communiter non obligant in probabili periculo gravis mali temporalis, vt ex communi sententia fuse docent et probant Suarez. 1. 3. de legibus. c. 3. conclusione 3. Salas D. 11. de leg. c. 1. con. 2. Laym. 1. 1°. tract. 4. c. 14. assert. 2ª. Quando autem tale periculum probabile gravis mali censeri debet, prudenti viri boni iudicio relinquitur, vt in similibus.

Case 72. *May priests in England omit to recite the Office, to celebrate Mass; and on feast days, omit to hear Mass, etc.?*

I reply that all the aforesaid things may lawfully be omitted, when there is probable danger to life, or of incarceration, or of other serious harm, because the precepts of the Church do not commonly oblige when there is probable danger of serious temporal harm, as from the common judgement Suarez, Salas and Laymann teach and prove at length [refs]. When, however, such probable danger of serious harm is thought to be present, should be left, as in similar matters, to the good judgement of a prudent man.

[73] 73. <u>An liceat sequi opinionem</u> probabilem in materia Sacramentorum relicto probabiliori et tutiori? <u>Respondeo 1º. esse grave peccatum</u> vti materia dubia, vel forma dubia, etsi probabili in Sacramentis nisi sit causa sufficiens, quia sic exponitur Sacramentum periculo irritationis et proximum prodendi fructum expetitum, vtrumque autem grave est, hoc contra charitatem, illud religionem, ita ex communi sententia Salas 1ª. 2ae. tract. 8. D. vnica. 1. 5. n. 6. Suarez tom. 3. in 3am. partem D. 16. par. 2 ª. et tom. 4. D. 26. 5. 6. Filiuc. tom 1º. tract. 1º. c. 4. n. 69. Bonac. D. 2ª. de peccatis q. 4. pun. 9. n. 19. <u>Excipiunt tamen dicti Autores dubiam iurisdictionem</u> in Sacramento poenitentiae. Dicunt enim sacerdotem posse licite conferre absolutionem poenitenti, quando est probabilis opinio [fo. 64] de eius iurisdictione, etsi contraria sit probabilior, et tutior, quia in hoc casu nullum est periculum irritandi Sacramentum, tum quia censetur Ecclesiam dare iurisdictionem iuxta legem barbarorum tum quia poenitens semper confitetur aliquid, in quod directam iurisdictionem habet quilibet sacerdos, vt fusius ostendunt Autores citati. <u>Respondeo 2º. licere sequi practice</u> opinionem probabilem in conficiendis Sacramentis quando datur gravis causa, vel urgens necessitas. ita Doctores cit. quia tunc necessitas illa gravis excusat omne periculum irritationis. sic communiter dicunt posse iusta de causa Episcopum

vto[115] solo oleo in Sacramento Confirmationis (quod est tantum materia probabilis, et dubia) si fieri nequit balsamum, quod, oleo permixtum, est materia certa.

Case 73. *Is it lawful to follow a probable opinion concerning the matter*[116] *of the sacraments, having ignored a more probable and safer opinion?*
I reply firstly that it is a grave sin to use doubtful (even if it is probable) matter or form, in administering the sacraments, unless there is a sufficient cause, because by doing so the sacrament is exposed to the danger of invalidity, and a neighbour is exposed to the danger of losing the benefits which he expects from the sacrament; both of which are serious, the latter being contrary to charity, the former to religion. Thus, from the common judgement, Salas, Suarez, Filliucci and Bonacina [refs]. The said authors make an exception however in the case of doubtful jurisdiction in the sacrament of penance. For they say that a priest may lawfully confer absolution on a penitent when his jurisdiction is based on a probable opinion, even if the contrary opinion is more probable and safer. This is because in this case there is no danger of invalidating the sacrament; both because the Church is judged to give jurisdiction according to the law of barbarians,[117] and because the penitent always confesses something, over which every priest has direct jurisdiction, as the authors cited show more fully. I reply secondly that it is lawful in practice to follow the probable opinion in providing the matter of the sacraments when there is a serious reason or urgent necessity to do so, as the doctors cited say, because then that serious necessity excuses all danger of invalidating the sacrament. Thus it is commonly said that a bishop may for a just cause use oil alone in the sacrament of confirmation (which is only probable, and doubtful, matter) if it cannot be done with balsam, which when mixed with oil, is the certain matter.

[74] 74. Quaenam opinio censenda probabilis; et an confessarius teneatur sequi opinionem probabilem poenitentis. Respondeo 1º. opinionem illam esse probabilem, quae innitetur ratione alicuius momenti, aut gravi et solido fundamento, ita vt pro opposita parte nil sit convincens. ita Sanchez. l. 1º. c. 9. n. 6. in Summa Filiuc. to. 2º. tract. 21. c. 4. n. 133.

115 Thus for *vti*
116 The 'matter' of the sacraments refers (to simplify) to the materials used in administering them; the 'form' to the words used.
117 *Lex barbarorum*: the ancient Germanic customary law. The meaning here is obscure, but possibly Southwell wishes to say that a sort of feudalism applies to the devolution of jurisdiction to the level of the priest, the priest being entrusted by his superior with a degree of autonomy, like a lord of the manor under a feudal king.

et patet ex ipsis terminis. Porro vnius Doctoris probi ac docti autoritas
reddit opinionem probabilem, quia tanti viri autoritas, non est leve, sed
grave fundamentum. ita Sanchez cit. n. 7. et Filiuc n. 134. Valen: 1ᵃ. 2ᵃᵉ.
q. 14. punc. 4. Sa in verbo Dubium ex Navarr. Debet tamen talis Doctor
non esse ex antiquis, sed recentioribus, vt notant Doctores citati de quo
verosimile sit quod viderit, et examinaverit omnia quae apponi possent,
et quod posset illa solvere. Respondeo 2ᵒ. Confessarius post auditam
confessionem non posse sine causa sufficiente denegare absolutionem
poenitenti, qui sequitur opinionem probabilem; posse tamen ex causa
sufficienti, et iusta illum non absoluere. Primam partem tenent Suar. 3.
p. to. 4. D. 32. s. 5. Vq. 1. 2ᵃᵉ. D. 62. c. 7. Sanch. in Summa l. 1ᵒ. c. 9.
Salas 1. 2ᵃᵉ. tr. 8. D. vnica s. 9. Filiuc. to. 1ᵒ. tr. 7. c. 12. Suirus in clave
regia l. 1ᵒ. c. 9. Rodrig. in sum.[fo. 64ᵛ] c. 62. to. 1ᵒ. quia poenitens
sequendo opinionem probabilem est probabiliter dispositus sufficienter,
ergo tenetur confessarius eum absolvere, quia alioquin faceret contra
charitatem, imponendo ei sine causa sufficienti, grave onus, confessionem repetendi, et defraudando eum fructu Sacramenti.

Posteriorem partem, tenent etiam dicti Doctores fere omnes sed prae-
cipue Faber l. 4ᵒ. sent. a. 19. q. vnica. D. 33. c. 2 n. 15. dicens poenitentem teneri sequi opinionem sacerdotis tutiorem. Scotus ibi. Polanchus
in decretorio[118] c. 1. §. de prudentia confessoris, docet confessarium ex
commissione posse non absoluere poenitentem, etsi habeat opinionem
probabilem. idemque docent conradus, Sylvester et alii apud Sanchez.
Probatur tum quia durum et absurdum est, quod confessor doctus, qui
locum et vicem Dei gerit cogatur semper ab indocto poenitente, qui velit
ipse [poenitentiam][119] sententiam sequi in illo sacro tribunali, in quo
confessor ipse est Iudex, et poenitens, reus; tum quia confessarius potest
habere gravem et iustam causam, vel ob bonum nomen suum tuendum,
vel bonum ipsius poenitentis procurandum cur nolit sequi opinionem
probabilem poenitentis, sed propriam. tum demum, quia alioquin multa
et gravia incommoda sequeruntur in praxi; quia poenitentes sequi
volunt laxissimam, etsi vtcumque probabilem, quae tandem ruinam et
scandalum pariunt, ex quibus patet poenitentem, qui non vult parere
confessario ex iusta et gravi causa, conformitatem ad suam sententiam
exigentis, non esse debite dispositum; vel dici potest in hoc casu dari
iustum bellum vtricunque, vt in aliis per accidens dici solet.

Case 74. *Which opinion is to be judged probable; and is a confessor
bound to follow the probable opinion of a penitent?*

---

[118] Thus for *directorio?*
[119] Bracketed thus in MS, indicating probably that the copyist has written the wrong
word and is correcting it, or is correcting the text he is copying.

I reply firstly that an opinion is probable which relies upon a reason of some moment, or on a grave and solid foundation, so that on the opposite side there is nothing convincing. Thus, Sanchez and Filliucci [refs] and it is clear from the words 'probable opinion' themselves. Further, the authority of one upright and learned doctor renders an opinion probable, because the authority of such a man is not a light but a grave foundation; thus, Sanchez, Filliucci, Valentia and Sa, using Navarre [refs]. This doctor however should not be from the ancient authors, but from the more recent authors, as the doctors cited note. This seems likely because such a doctor will have seen and examined all the questions which can be asked and everything which can solve them. I reply secondly that a confessor after hearing a confession first (1) cannot without sufficient cause deny absolution to a penitent who is following a probable opinion; but second (2), he can, if there is a just and sufficient cause, refuse to absolve him. The first part (1) is held by Suarez, Vazquez, Sanchez, Salas, Filliucci, Sayer, and Rodriguez [refs], because the penitent following the probable opinion is probably sufficiently well disposed, and therefore the confessor is bound to absolve him; because otherwise the confessor would act against charity, by imposing on the penitent without sufficient cause the grave burden of having to repeat the confession, and by defrauding the penitent of the benefit of the sacrament.

The second part (2) almost all the said doctors also hold, but especially Faber [ref.], who says the penitent is bound to follow the safer opinion of the priest; and Major agrees [ref.]. Polanchus [ref.] teaches that a confessor by virtue of his commission may refuse to absolve a penitent, even if the latter has a probable opinion, and the same is taught by Conradus, Sylvester, and others cited by Sanchez. This is also proved because it is hard and absurd to say that a learned confessor, who bears the place and office of God, should be always bound by an unlearned penitent who wants to follow his own opinion in that sacred tribunal in which the confessor himself is the judge and the penitent the defendant. It is also proved, because the confessor may have a grave and just reason (either to preserve his good name, or to procure the good of the penitent himself), why he does not wish to follow the probable opinion of the penitent but his own. Finally, because otherwise many grave troubles might follow in practice, if penitents wish to follow an opinion which is most lax, even if in whatsoever manner it is probable; troubles which at length bring forth ruin and scandal. From which it is clear that a penitent is not suitably disposed if he does not wish to obey a confessor who, for a just and grave reason, wishes the penitent to conform to the demands of his judgement. Alternatively, it may be said in this case that a 'just war' can be declared against those on both sides of the argument, as it happens is often said in other cases![120]

[75] 75. <u>An teneatur Sacerdos in Anglia</u> re-baptizare sub conditione illum, de quo est verum et grave dubium an sit baptizatus? <u>Respondeo teneri sub mortali</u>, vt aperte definitur ab Alexand. III. c. de quibus de baptismo, et eius effectu, et tenent omnes, quos sequuntur Suar. 3. p. to. 3. D. 22. s. 2. Valen. D. 4. punc. 4. Vq. D. 147. c. 4. quia [fo. 65] alioquin exponitur proximus periculo salutis, quod esset grave peccatum. quare quocunque ex capite baptismus reddatur vere dubius in prudenti iudicio, licet alter[121] pars videatur probabilior, repetendus est sub conditione, vt siquis baptizetur in pede, vel una tantum gutta aquae, vel et in pectore, quia hae partes sunt dubiae iuxta Theologos. sed si in capite solo, quia haec pars est certa secundum omnes et ritum Ecclesiae.

Case 75. *Is a priest in England bound to rebaptise conditionally someone about whom there is a true and grave doubt whether he has already been baptised or not?*
I reply that he is bound under pain of mortal sin, as is clearly defined by Alexander III [ref.], and everyone holds; see Suarez, Valentia, and Vazquez [refs]. This is because otherwise a neighbour is exposed to a danger concerning his salvation, which would be a grave sin. Therefore, wherever baptism is given except on the head, it is rendered truly doubtful according to prudent judgement, although some other part of the body may seem more probable; it is to be repeated conditionally, for example, if a person had been baptised on the foot, or with only one drop of water, or on the breast, because these parts of the body are doubtful, according to theologians. But it should not be repeated if the person had been baptised on the head only, because this part is certain, according to all, and according to the rite of the Church.

[76] 76. <u>An in extrema necessitate teneatur sacerdos</u> in Anglia ministrare baptismum causativum mortis, et an tunc sit irregularis, praesertim si mala fide ministret? <u>Respondeo 1º. licite posse administrari</u>, et deberi in casu quo certum sit puerum, vel amentem moriturum vi baptismi, si tamen certum sit eum alias moriturum, licet acceleratio mortis sit magna. ita cum aliis, Zambranus dub. 12. de baptismo con. 4. quia hic non est volita mors baptizandi per se, sed tantum permissa, adeoque praeponderat aeterna salus baptizandi. <u>Per magnam accelerationem</u> intelligo, vnam, vel forte duas horas: <u>non puto tamen licitum</u> proiicere

---

120   This translation, suggesting professorial humour, is speculative.
121   For *altera*?

puerum ex alto in puteum quia talis proiectio est actio per se directe tendens ad occidendum puerum, adeoque in tali casu incurreretur irre-gularitas, vt ex communi doctrina videtur certum. Respondeo 2°. sacer-dotem baptizantem in dicto casu licito, non fore irregularem, licet mala fide id putaret; quia irregularitas imponitur delicto in re, quod hic non est, licet sit in conscientia erronea, vt ex aliis optime docet Zambran. cit.

Case 76. *Is a priest in England bound to perform a baptism, in extreme necessity, when it will cause death, and is he then irregular, especially if he performed it in bad faith?*

I reply firstly that he may lawfully administer it and he must do so in a case where it is certain that the child or senseless person will die as a result of the baptism, provided it is certain that he was about to die in any case, even though the acceleration of death caused by the baptism is great: thus, with others, Zambrano [ref.]. The reason is that in this case the death of the person baptised is not deliberately caused by the person performing the baptism, but only permitted, and so the eternal benefit of baptism is a more serious consideration. By 'great acceleration' I understand one or perhaps two hours. I do not think however that in such a case it is lawful to project the child from a height into a font, for such projection is an action in itself directly tending to the killing of the child, and so in such a case the priest would incur irregularity, as from common doctrine seems certain. I reply secondly that a priest baptising in the said lawful case will not be irregular, even if he acted mentally in bad faith, because irregularity is imposed for an actual crime, which this is not, although it is erroneous in conscience, as is best taught by Zambrano, following others, in the place cited.

[77] 77. <u>An possit simplex sacerdos in Anglia ex dispensatione</u> Papae consecrare Chrysma, et conferre sacramentum confirmationis et sacros ordines? <u>Respondeo 1º. simplicem sacerdotem ex dispensatione</u> Papae posse valide et licite conferre sacramentum confirmationis. ita omnes fere Theologi, quos sequuntur omnes nostri Suar. to. 3. 3ᵃᵉ. partis. D. 36. s. 2. Henriq. Valent. Tollet. [fo. 65ᵛ] Reginaldus, Coninck. Tan. to. 3. D. 4. q. 4. dub. 3°. Laym. Filiuc. etc. Bonac. D. 3. de confirma-tione q. vnica pun. 2. Gamach. 3. p. to. 3°. c. 8. de ministro confir-mationis, et canonistae cum glossa. d. 95 c. pervenit. et extrav. de consuetudine c. 4°. <u>Probatur quia Christus potuit instituere vt minister ordinarius ex</u> sua consecratione esset Episcopus, et extraordinarius ex Papae dispensatione, sacerdos simplex. in hoc enim nulla repugnat, sed ita de facto instituit. ergo. probatur minor 1°. quia S. Gregor. mag. ep. 26. l. 3°. (et heturd: 95. c. pervenit) talem facultatem concessit sacer-dotibus Sardiniae. 2º. concil. Florent. in decreto Eugenii 4. narrat per Apostolicae sedis dispensationem simplicem sacerdotem, chrysmate

per Episcopo confecto administrasse confirmationis sacramentum. 3º. Trident. s. 7. et can. 3º. de confirm: definit, ordinarium ministrum esse solum Episcopum, atque significat extraordinarium posse esse solum simplicem sacerdotem. 4º. idem docet concilium senonense nationale totius Galliae, in decretis morum c. 28. 5º. denique Gregor. XIII. idem concessit quibusdam presbyteris in India, vt referunt Gamach. et Filiuc. cit. imo Gamach affirmat Adrianus VI. eandem potestatem dedisse Franciscanis, ergo.

Respondeo 2º. quoad confectionem chrysmatis idem esse probabile, sic docent Valen. 3. p. D. 5. q. 1. de confirmatione. pun. 2º. Suar. Tan. Bonac. citati; oppositum tamen est probabilius, vt iidem docent. tum quia Florent. in decreto Eugenii 4. assignat pro materia, oleum, et balsamum ab Episcopo benedictum: tum quia Ecclesiae praxis ita docet, quae nunquam concedit facultatem presbyteris consecrandi chrysma. Respondeo 3º. probabilius esse non posse simplicem sacerdotem ex concessione Papae conferre ordines maiores, sed tantum minores. 1ª. pars est communis theologorum, quos sequitur Tan. to. 4º. D. 7 de ordine q. 3. dub 2. quia Ecclesiae praxis non agnoscit talem potestatem esse in Papa. 2ª. etiam pars [fo. 66] est communis et certa, quia talis potestas concessa est abbatibus pro suis monachis, vt constat ex c. quoniam. d. 69. et ex c. cum contingat de aetate, et qualitate ordinandorum. probabile tamen est, quod simplex sacerdos ex concessione papae possit esse minister ordinum maiorum subdiaconatus, Diaconatus, et presbyteratus, nam ita docent graves canonistae et theologi, quos refert Vq. 3. p. to. 3º. D. 243. c. 4. qui rem relinquit indecisam. sine dubio est probabile, tum ex privilegiis Cistersiensis, tum quia Florent. videtur admittere ministrum extraordinarium in hoc Sacramento; tum quia eadem videtur ratio ac de confirmatione, tum quia Tan. cit. dicit, auditum esse a viris fide dignis, id esse concessum Franciscanis; quare ipse Tan. putat hanc sententiam esse satis probabilem.

Case 77. *May a simple priest in England by virtue of a papal dispensation consecrate chrism, and confer the sacraments of confirmation and holy orders?*

I reply that a simple priest by virtue of a papal dispensation may validly and lawfully confer the sacrament of confirmation; thus, almost all theologians, including all our authors (Suarez, Henriquez, Valentia, Toletus, Reginaldus, Coninck, Tanner, Laymann, Filliucci, Bonacina and Gamachaeus) [refs], as well as canonists, and the Gloss [ref.]. This is proved because Christ could institute that the ordinary minister by his consecration would be a bishop, and the extraordinary minister might by papal dispensation be a simple priest. For there is nothing in this repugnant to Christ, and in fact Christ instituted it, which proves this point. The minor is proved: first because St Gregory the Great [ref.] conceded such a faculty to priests in Sardinia. Secondly, the Council of Florence by the decree of Eugene IV [ref.] declares that with the dispensation of the Apostolic See a simple priest may administer the sacrament of confirmation with chrism provided by a bishop. Thirdly, the Council of Trent [ref.] lays it down that only the bishop is the ordinary minister, and so indicates that the extraordinary minister can be a mere simple priest. Fourthly, the same doctrine was taught by the national council of the whole of France held at Sens [ref.]. Fifthly and finally, Gregory XIII conceded the same to certain priests in India, to which Gamachaeus and Filliucci, in the places cited, refer, and furthermore Gamachaeus affirms that Adrian VI gave the same power to the Franciscans. Therefore this judgement is proved.

I reply secondly that as far as the preparation of chrism is concerned the same is probable, which is what Valentia, Suarez, Tanner and Bonacina teach [refs]. But the opposite is more probable as the same writers teach; because the Council of Florence by the decree of Eugene IV assigns as matter, oil and balsam blessed by a bishop; and also because the practice of the Church teaches this, for the Church never conceded to priests the faculty of consecrating chrism. I reply thirdly that it is more probable that a simple priest with a papal concession (1) may not confer the major orders, but (2) only the minor orders. The first part (1) of this reply is the common view of theologians, whom Tanner follows [ref.], because the practice of the Church does not recognize that the Pope has such a power. The second part (2) is also common and certain doctrine, because such a power is conceded to abbots for their monks, as is clear from the canon law [refs]. However, it is probable that a simple priest with papal permission may administer the major orders, the subdiaconate, diaconate, and priesthood, for this is the doctrine of grave canonists and theologians, to whom Vazquez refers [ref.], although he leaves the matter undecided. Without doubt it is probable for the following reasons: first, from the privileges of the Cistercians; second, because the Council of Florence seems to admit that an extraordinary minister may administer this sacrament; third, because the same seems also to be the reason with respect to confirmation; fourth, because Tanner says in the place cited that he heard from men worthy of trust that the same had been conceded to the Franciscans, for which reason, Tanner himself thinks that this judgement is probable enough.

[78] 78. In quibus casibus possit sacerdos in Anglia non ieiunus celebrare? et an licite possit hostiam consecrare sine calice ex dispensatione Papae? Respondeo non ieiunum in aliquibus casibus posse licite celebrare. 1°. ratione integritatis sacrificii, vt si celebrans moriatur vel destituatur sensibus debet alius substitui vt perficiat sacrificium, quod si non inveniatur qui sit ieiunus, potest substitui non ieiunus. Item si quis

post consecrationem recordetur se non esse ieiunum debet pergere. Item si aquam pro vino consecravit, et id advertat tantum post sumptionem aquae, vt saepe fit, debet vinum consecrare, et sumere. hos 3. casus ex communi sententia admittit Suar. 3. p. to. 3. D. 68. q. 6. Vq. ibi, d. 211. c. 5. et omnes communiter. 2°. ex parte scandali nam siquis sacerdos non esset ieiunus posset tamen licite celebrare ad evitandum scandalum, quia tunc servat praeceptum humanum, vel ieiunium, vt optime Suar. cit. s. 15. Tan. et Laym: citandi. putat tamen Suar. casum vix posse contingere; Ego tamen non video cur non possit in praxi. V.g. in celebraturo primitias [fo. 66ᵛ] in oppido non magno, et invitasset fere omnes, at ex obliuione comedisset aliquid. 3ᵒ. ratione necessitatis, potest enim quis celebrare non ieiunus, vt seipsum communicet in articulo mortis. Zambran. c. 3. de Eucharistia dub. 6. n. 1°. at Bonac. d. 4. de Euchar. q. 6. pun. 2°. n. 24. id negat, sed non recte quia cum illa persona teneatur etiam non ieiuna communicare, poterit etiam celebrare. Denique probabile est practice posse sacerdotem non ieiunum celebrare, vt det viaticum moribundo; ita docent Maior, et alii et probabile putat Suar. cit. Filiuc. to. 1°. tr. 4°. de eucharistia c. 6. n. 21. tum quia sacerdos potest consecrare sine confessione praemissa; tum quia communio est de iure Diuino ex communi, et ieiunium de Ecclesiastico, ergo illud praevalebit. oppositum tamen est communius et probabilius, docent Vq. Suar. et Filiuc. cit. quia sic habet praxis Ecclesiae, quod maximum est in his rebus.

Porro nunquam licet per se consecrare vnam speciem sine alia sine dispensatione Papae, cum illa, licet. 1ᵐ. tenent omnes contra Maior, vt certum, quia est saltem contra gravissimum Ecclesiae praeceptum. 2ᵐ. vero tenent multi graves Theologi Gabriel, Alanus, et Sanchez. et Angelus contra Suar. 3. p. to. 3. D. 43. s. 4. qui id putat probabile. idque ego docui in materia Euchar: quia integritas sacrificii in vtraque specie, est tantum de iure Ecclesiastico.

Case 78. *In what cases may a priest who has not fasted celebrate Mass? And may he, by virtue of a papal dispensation, lawfully consecrate the host, without consecrating the chalice?*
I reply that in some cases a priest who has not fasted may lawfully celebrate. First, by reason of the integrity of the sacrifice; if, for example, the celebrant should die or take leave of his senses, another priest ought to be substituted in order to complete the sacrifice, and if someone cannot be found who has fasted, someone who has not fasted may be substituted. In addition, if someone after the consecration of the host remembers that he has not fasted, he should continue. Further, if he has consecrated water instead of wine, and if he notices this only after drinking it, as often is the case, he should consecrate some wine and drink that. These three cases by common judgement, Suarez, Vazquez,

and all writers commonly admit [refs] Secondly for reasons of scandal; thus, if a priest has not fasted, he may nevertheless lawfully celebrate Mass in order to avoid scandal, for then he upholds a human law, that is, fasting, as Suarez shows best; Tanner and Laymann must also be cited here [ref.]. Suarez thinks however that this case is hardly likely to happen. I however do not see why it could not in practice happen, for example, the priest, being about to celebrate the first fruits in a small town, had invited almost everyone, and he absent-mindedly had eaten something. Thirdly, out of necessity, for anyone may celebrate without having fasted in order to give himself communion at the moment of death. Zambrano and Bonacina [refs] deny this, but not rightly because since that person is bound to take communion even if he has not fasted, he may also celebrate Mass. Finally it is probable in practice that a priest may celebrate without having fasted in order to give a viaticum to a dying man; thus Major and others teach, and Suarez and Filliucci in the place cited think it is probable [ref.]. The reasons for this are: first, because the priest can consecrate without a previous confession; and second, because communion is a matter of divine law according to the common view, and fasting is a matter of ecclesiastical law, therefore the former will prevail. The opposite judgement, however, is more common and more probable, as Vazquez, Suarez and Filliucci teach in the places cited, because this is the practice of the Church, which is the most important consideration in these matters.

On the next question (1) it never is lawful in itself to consecrate one species without the other, without having a papal dispensation, but (2) with it, it is lawful. All writers apart from Major hold the first point (1) to be certain, because it is at the least against the most grave precept of the Church. The second point (2) many grave theologians (Gabriel Vasquez, Alanus, Sanchez and Angelus) hold to be true, although Suarez disagrees [ref.] and thinks it to be merely probable. And I have taught the same (2) in *The matter of the Eucharist*, because the integrity of the sacrifice in both species is only a matter of ecclesiastical law.

[79] 79. <u>An licite possit sacerdos in Anglia</u> saepius eodem die, ieiunus tamen, celebrare, et quoties? <u>Respondeo posse, si sit gravis necessitas</u> vt ex C. consuluistis, de celebratione missarum docent Henrique. l. 9. de missa. c. 3°. Nau. c. 25 summa, n. 87. Sylvester, verbo missa. 1°. gravi causa <u>v.g. alioquin infirmus</u> moreretur sine viatico. 2°. si sit penuria sacerdotum, vt in Anglia: vt docet Filiuc. c. 4°. de Euchar. q. 6. et si persona nobilis, vel multi peregrini, vel copiosus populus careret alioquin sacro, die festo: denique quotiescunque occurrunt causae graves, et iustae iudicio boni viri. <u>Eadem autem causa quae sufficit</u> ad celebrandum bis eodem die, sufficit vt ter, vel quater, vt cum Suar. docent Tanner, Coninck et Praepos.

Case 79. *May a priest in England, who has however fasted, lawfully celebrate Mass a number of times in the same day, and how often?*
I reply that he may if there is grave necessity, as Henriquez, Navarre and Sylvester teach [refs], from canon law [ref.]. Firstly, he may do so for a serious reason; for example, if otherwise a sick person might die without the viaticum. Secondly, he may do so, if there is a shortage of priests, as there is in England, as Filliucci teaches [ref.], and a noble person, or many pilgrims, or a large number of people otherwise would not hear Mass on a feast day if he did not do so. Finally, whenever according to the judgement of a good man, grave and just causes occur. The same reason, moreover, which allows a priest to celebrate twice in one day, is also sufficient to allow him to do so three or four times, as Tanner, Coninck and Praepositus teach, with Suarez.

[80] [fo. 67] 80. An possit Sacerdos vel Laicus seipsum communicare in articulo mortis, quando non possit celebrare? et an possit particulam suae hostiae consecratae dare laico extra gravem necessitatem et an possit mittere Laico Eucharistiam [incho][122] per Laicum; et an liceat missam inchoatam relinquere? Respondeo haec omnia licite fieri posse. ita Suar. Sa. verbo Euchar. Tan. d 5. q. 8. dub. 8. Laym. tr. 5. de Euchar. c. 6 et 7°. quia non sunt intrinsece mala, nec prohibita, sed bona, ergo licita. Quoad interruptionem missae, recte docet Laym. cit. cum Zambran. causas debere esse graves, etiam ante consecrationem, et graviores post consecrationem; puta si alicui morti proximo sacramentum sit ministrandum, vt confessio, Extrema vnctio, vel baptismus parvulo moribundo (non autem Eucharistia) quia in his casibus salus proximi excusat illum ab interruptione: debet autem quam citissime redire, et perficere sacrificium: immo Henriq. docet ex communi, licere ex gravi aliqua necessitate propria corporali, vel ad occidendum illum, qui iniuste vult te occidere, modo non habeas alium modum defendendi te, vt in praxi contingere potest tunc autem redire potes et perficere sacrificium, si non excessisti limites iustae defensionis.

Case 80. *May a priest or a layman give himself communion at the time of death, when he cannot celebrate Mass? And may he give a small piece of his own consecrated host to a lay person without grave necessity; and may he send the Eucharist to a layperson by means of a lay person; and is it lawful to leave the Mass unfinished?*
I reply that all these things may lawfully be done; thus, Suarez, Sa, Tanner and Laymann [refs]. This is because they are not intrinsically bad, nor prohibited, but good and therefore lawful. As far as the interruption

---

[122]   Bracketed thus in MS, indicating a correction.

of the Mass is concerned, Laymann in the place cited, with Zambrano, rightly teaches that the reasons for doing so even before the consecration should be serious ones, and more serious after the consecration. For example, if a sacrament must be ministered to someone close to death; such as confession, extreme unction, or baptism for a dying baby (but not the Eucharist), because in these cases the salvation of a neighbour excuses him for the interruption. He should however return as quickly as possible, and complete the sacrifice. Indeed, Henriquez teaches according to the common doctrine, that it is even lawful, when your physical safety is seriously threatened, to kill someone who is coming unjustly to kill you, as long as you have no other way of defending yourself, as in practice might happen, and then for you to return and complete the sacrifice, as long as you do not exceed the limits of just self-defence.

[81]¹²³ An et qui sub peccato mortali teneatur Sacerdos in Anglia ministrare Sacramenta? et quae? Respondeo 1º. Sacerdotes omnes in Anglia teneri sub mortali audire confessiones eorum, qui sunt in extrema necessitate; et baptizare parvulos si sit certa spes eos iuvandi etiam cum manifesto vitae periculo (extrema necessitas spiritualis proxima dicitur, quando est in certo periculo damnationis aeternae constitutus, a quo nequit se moraliter eripere) quia mors corporalis sacerdotis leve bonum est respectu salutis aeternae alterius, adeoque postponenda: Debet autem esse spes certa subveniendi proximo in tali necessitate; quia si sit spes dubia, et incerta, non obligabitur quis ad tantum periculum, cum tanto damno certo et evidenti suo. [fo. 67ᵛ] vnde facile excusantur sacerdotes in Anglia, quia communiter nulla fere est spes convertendi haereticos, at periculum proprium est maximum et certum. ergo. ita docet ex communi, et certa sententia. Suar. 2. 2ᵃᵉ. D. 9. de charitate. sec. 2. Tan. to. 3. D. 2. q. 3 dub. 4º. Coninck D. 25 de charit: Dub. 7º. Puto tamen sacerdotem non teneri ad dandum illis alia sacramenta cum tali periculo, nisi forte extremam vnctionem, cum nullum aliud applicari possit, quia non sunt necessaria ad salutem, adeoque sine illis salvari possunt illis carentes. Respondeo 2º. in gravi solum et privata necessitate proximi (in qua nempe quis nequit absque magna difficultate saluti suae consulere) nullum sacerdotem teneri ministrare haec Sacramenta cum probabili vitae periculo. tenetur tamen cum magno aliquo damno coporali iuxta prudentis iudicium aestimando. ita ex communi Suar. Tan. Coninck citati. 1ᵃ. pars probatur quia contrarium nequit efficaciter probari; adeoque cum sit graue onus, sacerdotibus non est imponendum sine evidenti ratione contra suave iugum charitatis. 2ᵃ. etiam

pars probatur quia damnum aliquod grave temporale est postponendum gravi damno spirituali proximi. Dixi in privata necessitate; quia gravis necessitas spiritualis communis praeferenda est bono privato proprio et magno quale est vita vt docent ex communi Autores citati. vnde communiter, et ordinarie Sacerdotes in Anglia non tenentur administrare Sacramenta sub mortali, quia ordinarie saeculares non sunt in [tam][124] gravi necessitate, at sacerdotes ordinarie sunt in gravi et probabili periculo incarcerationis exilii etc.

Case 81. *Is a priest in England bound under mortal sin to administer the sacraments; to whom; and which sacraments?*

I reply first that all priests in England are bound under mortal sin to hear the confessions of those who are in *extreme necessity*, and to baptize babies if there is certain hope of helping them, even with manifest danger to their lives. This *extreme*, close, spiritual *necessity* is said to exist when a person is found to be in certain danger of eternal damnation from which s/he cannot morally escape. The reason for this is that the bodily death of a priest is of less importance than the eternal salvation of another person, and hence the latter takes precedence. There should however be certain hope of helping your neighbour who is in such necessity, because if there is doubtful and uncertain hope, no one will be obliged to undergo such danger, with such certain and evident harm to himself. As a result, priests in England are easily excused, because commonly there is hardly any hope of converting heretics, but their own danger is very great and certain, which proves the point. Thus, Suarez, Tanner and Coninck [refs] teach, from the common and certain judgement. I think however that a priest is not bound to give the other sacraments if it involves such danger (except perhaps extreme unction, when nothing else may be employed), because the other sacraments are not necessary to salvation, and so those who lack them may be saved without them. I reply secondly that in a case which only involves the grave and *private necessity* of a neighbour (in which case certainly no one may very easily give priority to his own safety) (1) no priest is bound to administer these sacraments if it will probably endanger his life, but (2) he is bound to do so, when there is what a prudent man would judge to be the risk of some great physical harm (short of death). Thus, following the common opinion, Suarez, Tanner and Coninck in the places cited. The first part (1) is proved because the contrary cannot effectively be proved; and so, since it is a heavy burden, it is not to be imposed on priests without a clear reason contrary to the sweet yoke of charity. The second part (2) is also proved because some grave temporal

---

[124] Bracketed thus in MS, indicating a correction.

harm to oneself is to be considered less important than the grave spiritual harm of a neighbour. I have said above *'private necessity'*, because a grave spiritual necessity involving the common good is to be preferred to your own great, private good, such as your own life, as the authors cited teach following the common doctrine. So, commonly and ordinarily, priests in England are not bound to administer sacraments under mortal sin because ordinarily secular people are not in such grave necessity, but priests are ordinarily in grave and probable danger of imprisonment, exile etc.

[82] 82. An simplex sacerdos in Anglia absolvere possit a casibus reservatis, illum, qui possit adire superiorem sed non vult. Respondeo posse sacerdotes tales absolvere iuxta probabilem sententiam. nam ita docet [an][125] Navar. l. 5. consiliorum consilio [fo. 68] 23. Sa, verbo absolutio n. 4. Comitolus in suis responsis moralibus q. 22. Tan. d. 6. de poent. q. 9. d. 3. citans multos qui nullam limitationem ponunt. Probatur quia Trid. s. 14. c. 7. affirmat simpliciter et sine limitatione nullam esse casuum reservationem in articulo mortis, et quoslibet poenitentes a quibuslibet sacerdotibus absolui posse, idque semper custoditum fuisse ab Ecclesia igitur sic simpliciter, et sine limitatione id intelligendum est. Oppositum tamen est probabilius communiter et per se, quod ex communi sententia tenet Suar. to. 4. D. 26. s. 4. et acriter Zambran c. 4. de poent. dub. 4. vbi dicit contrariam esse omnino falsam; sed excessit ex nimio zelo propriae opinionis, vt ex dictis constet.

Case 82. *May a simple priest in England absolve in reserved cases someone who could go to a superior but does not want to do so?*

I reply that such priests may absolve someone in this position, according to a probable judgement, for Navarre, Sa, Comitolus, and Tanner teach this, citing many who impose no limitation [refs]. This is proved because the Council of Trent [ref.] affirms simply and without limitation that there is no reservation of cases at the point death, when a penitent may be absolved by any priest, and this was always the custom followed by the Church, and therefore, is to be understood simply and without limitation. The opposite however is more probable, commonly and in itself; Suarez holds this, from the common doctrine [ref.], and Zambrano does so vehemently, [ref.] when he says the contrary is completely false; but he goes too far out of too much zeal for his own opinion, as is clear from what he says.

[83] 83. An possit licite sacerdos in Anglia tempore pestis administrare sacramentum Extremae Vnctionis in vnica tantum vnctione? Respondeo

---

125 Bracketed thus in MS, indicating a correction.

quod non. quia iuxta communem, et practice certam, requiruntur essentialiter quinque vnctiones 5. sensum, vt fuse probat Suar. to. 4. 3ᵃᵉ. p.
D. 41. s. 3. Praepos. q. vnica de extrema vnct. dub. 9. contraria iam
publice defendere.

Case 83. *May a priest in England in the time of plague lawfully administer the sacrament of extreme unction in only one anointing?*

I reply that he may not, because according to the common, and
in practice certain, judgement, five anointings of the five senses are
essentially required, as Suarez proves at length [ref.]. Praepositus [ref.],
however, has publicly defended the contrary.

[84] 84.¹²⁶ An Reordinandus sit sacerdos qui non tetigit physice calicem,
aut patenam, vel qui calicem tetigit, in quo non erat vinum, vel qui sine
diaconatu vel subdiaconatu aut per saltum ordinatus fuit? Respondeo
reordinandus Sacerdos ille qui nullam partem tetigit physice (id est) nec
calicem, nec patenam, quia cum hoc Sacramentum sit maximae necessitatis, debet esse moralis certitudo de eius validitate, quae esse nequit nisi
aliquod instrumentum physice tangatur, quia communis satis sententia
requirit, contactum physicum, quam sequitur Coninck d. 20. de sacramento ordinis Dub. 7. citans D. Tho. et alios theologos. Respondeo
2º. si tamen quis tetigisset calicem physice, et non patenam non esset
reordinandus; tum quia verior sententia tenet non esse vllum contactum
physicum necessarium, quam sequuntur Vq: 3. p. to. 3. d. 24. c. 21.
Sa verbo ordo. n. 3. Praepos. quaestione vnica de Sacramento [fo. 68ᵛ]
ordinis dub. 1º. Estius in 4º. d. 24. §. 2. Laym. tr. 9. c. 4. qui alios citant;
tum etiam, quia ita in terminis docent Praepos. et Sa. cit. et Sotus in
4º. d. 24. q. 1. a 2º. et Angelus verbo Ordo. 1º. n. 10. Sylvester v. ordo
2º. q. 5. et Vq. putat contrarium esse improbabile, et Praepositus dicit
Praelatos non reordinare tales, et hanc sententiam esse sibi moraliter
certam. atque Coninck cit. id etiam putat sat probabile vnde videtur
moraliter certum. quare a fortiori non erit necesse tangere hostiam, nec
ambabus manibus vt iidem etiam docent. Respondeo 3º. si quis solum
patenam tangeret, res esset magis dubia, quia de hoc casu in terminis
non loquuntur Doctores tam clare. idem tamen esse dicendum colligitur
ex Sa citato. et Filiuc tr. 9. c. 21. n. 35 et 38. Vq. etc. vnde attenta
minima probabilitate contrariae sententiae de contactu physico puto
practice certum, satis esse tangere solum patenam coniunctam calici,
et forte solam hostiam ob eandem rationem. Respondeo 4º. Sacerdotem

---

¹²⁶ In the MS the initial question is actually copied by mistake after the first sentence
of the response (from *Respondeo* to *theologos*). I have restored the order here, to be
consistent with the other cases.

illum esse reordinandum, cui pro materia traditus fuit solus calix cum patena sine vino, ita fuse probat Tan. to. 4. d. 7. de ordine. q. 2. dub 4. et breviter Praepos. supra n. 91. quia licet contraria sententia Henriq. l. 1. c. 6. n. 1°. sit speculative probabilis, est tamen contra communem, et fere certam sententiam, quae colligitur ex Florent. in decreto Eugenii 4. vbi definitur, quod presbyteratus traditur per calicis cum vino, et patenae cum pane, porrectionem: vnde nec valeret ordinatio, si traderetur patena sine pane, quia vtrumque coniunctum requiritur vt materia. Respondeo 5º. non esse reordinandum qui fit sacerdos sine subdiaconatu, vel diaconatu, vel per saltum colligitur vt certum ex Innoc. III. C. vn: de clerico per saltum ordinato; vbi glossa cum vincentio, clare docet valide recipi sacrum ordinem sacerdotii etsi [fo. 69] nullum habeat de minoribus, excepto Episcopali, quem nemo recipere potest, nisi saltem sacerdos. similiter Episcopus valide sine diaconatu, vel subdiaconatu sed non sine sacerdotio, quia Episcopalis character dependet a sacerdotali, at alii characteres non dependent a se mutuo. ita tenere videntur omnes Theologi.

Case 84. *Should a priest be reordained if, when he was ordained, he did not physically touch the chalice or the paten; or if he touched a chalice in which there was no wine; or if he was ordained priest without being a deacon or subdeacon, or by skipping another order?*

I reply that a priest should be reordained if he touched neither part physically; that is neither the chalice nor the paten. This is because, since this sacrament is of the greatest necessity, there should be moral certainty of its validity, which there cannot be unless one of the vessels is physically touched, and because according to a judgement which is common enough, physical contact is required; this judgement is followed by Coninck [ref.], citing St Thomas Aquinas and other theologians. I reply secondly that if, however, he touched the chalice physically and not the paten, he is not to be reordained, because the truer judgement holds that no physical contact is necessary, which Vazquez, Sa, Praepositus, Estius and Laymann [ref.] follow, citing others; Praepositus and Sa [refs] also teach this, in terms, in the places cited; and so do Soto, Angelus and Sylvester [refs]. Vazquez thinks the contrary is improbable and Praepositus says prelates are not to reordain such people, and that this judgement is for him morally certain, and Coninck in the place cited also thinks it is probable enough; and so it seems morally certain. So it is even clearer that it will not be necessary to touch the host, nor to touch it with both hands, as the same authors also teach. I reply thirdly that if someone only touched the paten, the matter is more doubtful, because the doctors do not speak in terms so clearly about this case. The same however is to be said here as on the previous points, as is gathered from Sa as cited, Filliucci [ref.] and Vazquez etc. Hence, having considered the minimal probability of the contrary judgement about physical contact, I think it is practically certain that it is enough to touch the paten alone if it is joined to chalice, and perhaps the host alone for the same reason. I reply fourthly that the priest must be reordained, if as far as the matter of the sacrament is concerned, he was given the chalice with the paten, but without wine; Tanner proves this at length [ref.] and also Praepositus briefly [ref.]. This is because, although the contrary judgement of Henriquez is speculatively probable, it is, however, contrary to the common and almost certain judgement which is collected from the decree of Eugene IV, at the Council of Florence, where it is defined that when someone is made a priest he should be given a chalice with wine, and a paten with bread. Hence, the ordination is not valid if he is given a paten without bread, because both together are required as matter. I reply fifthly that he is not to be reordained if he was made a priest without the subdiaconate or the diaconate, or by omitting another order, which is gathered as certain from the canon of Innocent III [ref.], where the Gloss with Vincent clearly teaches that the sacred order of priest may be received even by someone who is not in minor orders, although no one is to receive the episcopal order unless he has been at least a priest. Similarly a bishop is validly ordained without having received the diaconate or subdiaconate, but not without the priesthood, because the episcopal character depends on the priestly character, but the other characters have no dependence on one another. All theologians seem to hold this.

[85] 85. An potest licite sacerdos in Anglia assistere matrimonio haeretici et Catholicae, vel econtra: vel Catholicorum, qui invitis vel insciis parentibus contrahunt. Respondeo 1º. talia matrimonia in Anglia esse mortaliter illicita, tum quia sunt contra praxim Ecclesiae, tum quia pars Catholica exponitur periculo perversionis: tum quia non potest proles educari more catholico iuxta gravem obligationem vtriusque parentis: ita dicerent a fortiori de Anglia, qui id dicunt etiam in Germania, vbi est libertas conscientiae. nempe Serra. opusc. de matrimonio. catholicorum cum haereticis c. 2. q. 2. Tan. to. 4º. d. 8. q. 4. dub. 5. Laym. tr. 10. parte 4. Valent. to. 4. d. 10. q. 5. pun. 3. Conin. d. 31. de matrimonio. dub. 3. ex Navar. in Summa c. 22. n. 48. vnde in Anglia nunquam videtur occurrere posse casum in quo sint licita, quia nunquam potest deesse moraliter periculum perversionis adeoque neque Sanchius neque vllus alius id dixit de Anglia. Ex quo patet Sacerdotem assistentem matrimonio tali sine dispensatione Papae contracto, peccare mortaliter; sicut etiam peccant parentes si id possint impedire, quia cooperantur peccato gravi contrahentium. Respondeo 2º. tunc sacerdotem peccare mortaliter assistendo matrimonio quod contrahitur invitis parentibus, quando ipsi filii peccant mortaliter sic contrahendo, quia tunc sacerdos cooperatur

gravi peccato filiorum. <u>Porro licet filii per se iure naturae non teneantur</u> obedire parentibus in hoc statu capescendo, quia iure naturae debent esse liberi in re tam difficili; tenentur tamen per accidens aliquando, quando parentes habent graves [fo. 69ᵛ] causas iudicio prudenti discernendas, ipsis non invitis contrahere, vt fuse Sanch. et aliis probat Praepos. q. 3. de S. matr. At si desit gravis causa, solum erit peccatum veniale, et saepe nullum vt docent citati Doctores et Sa. Verbo filius n. 24. eandemque doctrinam tradit Tan. d. 8. de matrimonio. q. 3. dub. 6. addens etiam ex communi non posse filios exhaereditari, licet invitis parentibus et insciis matrimonia etiam indigna ineant: puto tamen patriae cuiusque regni standum esse consuetudini.

Case 85. *May a priest in England lawfully officiate at the marriage of a heretic man with a Catholic woman, or of a Catholic man with a heretic woman; or at the marriage of Catholics who marry without the approval or knowledge of their parents?*

I reply firstly that such marriages in England are mortally unlawful, first because they are against the practice of the Church; second, because the Catholic party is exposed to the danger of perversion; third, because the offspring cannot be educated in a Catholic fashion according to the grave obligation which is on both parents. Those who take this view even in Germany where there is liberty of conscience would also do so even more strongly with reference to England; that is, Serrarius, Tanner, Laymann, Valentia and Coninck, using Navarre [refs]. So in England it never seems possible for a case to occur in which these things are lawful, because the danger of perversion can never morally be absent, and so neither Sanchez nor any other says it of England. From which it is clear that a priest officiating at such a marriage contracted without a papal dispensation, sins mortally; just as the parents also sin if they could impede the marriage and do not do so, because they are co-operating in the grave sin of the people contracting the marriage. I reply secondly that the priest also sins mortally by officiating at a marriage which is contracted against the wishes of the parents, when the children themselves sin mortally by marrying in that way, because then the priest co-operates in the grave sin of the children. Further, although the children according to the law of nature are not bound in normal circumstances to obey their parents in the matter of taking a marriage partner, because by the law of nature they should be free in such a difficult matter; they are however sometimes bound in certain circumstances to obey their parents, when in the judgement of a prudent man, their parents have grave cause to decide that the children should not marry against their wishes, as more fully Praepositus proves, with Sanchez and others [ref.]. But if there is no grave cause it will only be a venial sin and often no sin at all, as the doctors we have cited, and also Sa, teach [ref.]. The same doctrine Tanner [ref.] teaches, adding also, following the common view, that the children cannot be disinherited even if they also make an unworthy marriage against the will and knowledge of their parents. I think however that it is important to stand by the custom of each country and kingdom.

[86] 86. An possit sacerdos in Anglia benedicere matrimoniis clandestinis, et Catholicorum cum haereticis illicite initis. Respondeo per se loquendo vtrumque fieri posse; primum, quia sic solum optat sacerdos vt bonos habeant eventus. 2^m. quia sic solum fit favor parti Catholicae. De neutro casu agunt Doctores; sed vt credo resolutionem nostram non negarent.

Case 86. *May a priest in England bless clandestine marriages, and those between Catholics and heretics, which have been entered into unlawfully?*

I reply that, speaking of the matter in itself, both can be done; first, because in doing this the priest is only expressing the wish that these marriages should have good outcomes. Second, because he only does this to favour the Catholic party. The doctors discuss neither case, but I believe they would not disagree with our resolution.

[87] 87. An possit licite sacerdos in Anglia verberare, vulnerare, vel occidere satellites, vulgo Pursuivantes, si nequeat alia via evadere, et an esset in dictis casibus irregularis? Respondeo dicta omnia licere, si absit scandalum (quod aliquando adesse, vel abesse potest iuxta prudentium iudicium,[127] quia ius naturale dictat posse homines vim vi repellere, ita ex communi probant Mol. to. 4. de iure tr. 3. d. 11. 16. et 17. Less. l. 2 de iustitia c. 9. Dub. 8. 11. et 12. Respondeo 2°. sacerdotem non esse irregularem in praedictis casibus, quia haec non contrahitur nisi ex peccato mortali cum sit ex delicto: atqui, vt supponitur hic non est peccatum mortale. ergo. ita Less. cit. Suar. to. 5. de cens. d. 46. s. 1. et 2^a.

Case 87. *May a priest in England lawfully beat, wound, or kill guards, vulgarly called 'pursuivants', if he cannot in any other way escape? And is he irregular in the said cases?*

I reply that all the said things are lawful if there is no scandal (which sometimes there is and sometimes there may not be, according to the judgement of prudent men), because the law of nature lays down that it is possible for men to repel force with force; Molina and Lessius prove this, from the common view [refs]. I reply secondly that a priest is not

---

127   The sense requires a second, closing bracket here.

irregular in the aforesaid cases, because irregularity is not contracted except on account of mortal sin, which is the result of a crime; and as is supposed this is not a mortal sin, which proves the point. Thus, Lessius in the place cited and Suarez [ref.].

[88] 88. An possit licite Sacerdos in Anglia inebriare satellites qui eum iniuste caperent, si nequeat alia via evadere? Respondeo licere, vt bene docet Less. l. 4. de iust. c. 3. dub. 4. et ex parte Laym l. 3. s. 4. de temperantia n. 4. quia licet non possit intendere ebrietatem, hoc enim per se est intrinsece malum, possit tamen intendere hilaritatem alterius ex qua sequi possit ipsius liberatio, haec enim non est intrinsece [fo. 70] mala, licet fiat permittendo alterius ebrietatem.

Case 88. *May a priest in England lawfully inebriate pursuivants who have unjustly captured him, if there is no other way of escaping from them?*
I reply that it is lawful as Lessius [ref.] teaches well, and in part Laymann [ref.]. This is because although he should not intend to cause drunkenness, for this is intrinsically evil, he might, however, intend to make another person merry and this is not intrinsically evil, even if his own liberty might follow as a result of permitting the drunkenness of another person.

[89] 89. An sacerdos in Anglia iniuste incarceratus possit fugere, quando talis fuga esset graviter nociva Laicis Catholicis ibidem incarceratis? et quid si promisisset se non fugiturum, et quid si iurasset? Respondeo 1º. Sacerdotem posse fugere quando maius ei damnum imminet si maneret, quam Catholicis si [maneret][128] fugeret. quia tunc habet ius fugiendi et Catholici tenentur suum damnum minus postponere ipsius maiori damno iuxta regulam charitatis. Imo forte potest fugere, etsi maius damnum illis immineret, quia habet ius ad fugam, adeoque illa damna sequuntur per accidens ex eius fuga, vt in simili. Respondeo 2º. posse etiam fugere licet promisisset se non fugiturum, si absit scandalum, quia promissio non obligat cum tanto detrimento vitae propriae: at si sit scandalum, vt semper est in Anglia, non potest fugere, etsi morte multandus sit, quia grave peccatum est scandalum sacerdotem fidem fallere in re tam gravi: quod a fortiore verum est si id iuraverit, quia tunc iuramentum est de re licita, adeoque de re obligatoria. haec omnia colliguntur ex Lessio. l. 2. de iustitia c. 31. dub. 5. Filiuc. to. 2. tr. 4. c. 9. et 17. Valen. 2. 2ae. D. 5. q. 13. de re. §. 4. Sa. verbo reus, et ex communi, si tamen cessaret scandalum, vt cessare potest extra Angliam, multi Doctores apud Sanchem

---

[128] Bracketed thus in MS, indicating a correction.

l. 3. sum. c. 11. n. 26. et 27. et apud Lessium l. 2. de iustitia c. 42. dub.
6. ut Caiet. Sotus Covar. et Vq 12. d. 124. c. 5. et Sa verbo iuramentum.
n. 11. tenent non teneri talem redire ad carcerem iniustum, licet iuraverit
se rediturum, quorum sententiam probabilem, et securam in praxi dicit
Lessius propter Doctores. at contraria est omnino vera, quam tenet Less.
et Sanchez cit. cum communi.

Case 89. *May a priest in England who has been unjustly imprisoned
escape when such an escape would be gravely harmful to Catholic lay
people imprisoned in the same place; and what if he had promised not
to escape; and what if he had sworn not to do so?*

I reply firstly that a priest may flee when greater danger threatens
him if he should remain, than threatens Catholics if he should flee. For
then he would have a right to escape and Catholics should count as less
important their own harm compared with the greater harm of another,
according to the law of charity. Further, perhaps he can flee even if
greater harm threatens them than threatens him, because he has a right
to escape, and their harm would follow by accident from his flight,
as in similar cases. Secondly I reply that he may also flee even if he
had promised that he would not flee, if there is no scandal, because a
promise does not oblige with such harm to one's own life. But if there
should be scandal, as there always is in England, he cannot flee, even
if he should be punished with death, because the scandal caused if a
priest breaks his word in such a grave thing is a serious sin. This is all
the more clearly true if he had sworn not to escape, because then the
oath is about a lawful matter, and so it obliges us concerning that matter.
All these things are gathered from Lessius, Filliucci, Valentia and Sa
[refs], and from the common doctrine. If however there is no scandal,
as can be the case outside England, many doctors cited by Sanchez and
Lessius, such as Caietan, Soto, Covarrubias, Vazquez and Sa [refs] hold
that such a person is not bound to return to a prison where he is unjustly
imprisoned, even if he had sworn an oath that he would return; and this
judgement is probable and secure in practice, Lessius says, because the
doctors support it. But the contrary is entirely true, which Lessius and
Sanchez in the places cited hold with the common view.

[90] 90. An possit confessarius in Anglia absoluere reum, qui Iudici
interroganti iuridice (id est post semiplenam probationem) non vult
fateri veritatem in causis gravioribus v. g. confiscationis bonorum,
perpetui carceris, gravis mutilationis, exilii, vel mortis, quando spem
habet probabilem evadendi? [fo. 70^v] Respondeo probabile esse posse
absoluere. ita docent Sa verbo Reus. et cum Navar. Lessius l. 2. de
iustitia. c. 31. dub. 3. Tan. to. 3. d. 4. q. 4. dub. 5. Filiuc. to. 2. tr.
4. c. 9. q. 4. quia praeceptum confitendi veritatem in his casibus est

nimis durum, et grave, adeoque cum tanto periculo non obligat vt fusius probant citati.

Case 90. *May a confessor in England absolve a person who is in court accused of a serious offence, the punishment for which is, for example, the confiscation of goods, perpetual imprisonment, serious mutilation, exile or death, and the accused does not wish to tell the truth to a judge who is interrogating him during the course of a judicial process (after, that is, 'half proof'[129]) when he has a probable hope of escaping if he does not tell the truth?*

I reply that it is probable that he may absolve him; as Sa, Lessius, Tanner, and Filliucci teach, with Navarre [refs]. This is because the precept that we should confess the truth in these cases is excessively hard and onerous, and so it does not oblige if it involves such danger, as those cited above prove more fully.

[91] 91. An possit sacerdos in Anglia tacere quando in itinere vel mensa audit haereticos blasphemantes, contra Deum, vel religionem, et enormia mendacia proferentes contra Papam, Ecclesiasticos, vel religiosos. Respondeo per se loquendo posse tacere, quia per se loquendo nullus fructus sequeretur ex correctione. Dein quia certum est moraliter, sacerdotem tali correptione magnum prericulum propriae vitae, incarcerationis etc. subiturum, adeoque licet illi essent emendandi nisi tamen essent in extrema necessitate, et non essent alias postea emendandi, non teneretur cum tanto damno suo illos corriperre. Denique omittere correptionem etiam debitam ex neglegentia, metu, vel tepiditate, tantum est peccatum veniale. Dixi per se quia per accidens ratione scandali, potest teneri sacerdos illos corripere, vt si adessent aliqui, qui scirent talem esse sacerdotem, et scandalizarentur, quia non defendit causam Dei. hic tamen casus est valde rarus, quia facile tolli potest scandalum explicando Catholicis in illis casibus non teneri sacerdotem corripere haereticos, de quibus non est spes fructus, sed periculum maioris mali. satis esset id paulo post mensam explicare, vt credo, quia parum pro nihilo reputatur. haec resolutio colligitur ex communi doctrina Theologorum de correptione fraterna, quam sequuntur Valens. 2. 2ᵃᵉ. D. 13. q. 11. pun. 2. Filiuc to. 2°. tr. 28. c. 5. et 6. q. 8. et Sa verbo Correptio.

Case 91. *May a priest in England be silent when he is on a journey or at table and he hears heretics blaspheming against God, or religion, and telling enormous lies about the Pope, the clergy or the religious?*

---

[129] 'Half proof' was a Civil Law term, meaning sufficient proof to allow the continuation of a trial or enquiry; it was also used by the Spanish Inquisition to justify the future use of torture. Southwell is perhaps suggesting the threat of torture here too.

I reply that considering the matter *in itself*, he may be silent because no good would come from correcting the blasphemers, and also because it is morally certain that the priest, if he did chastise the blasphemers, would place himself in great danger of suffering death or imprisonment etc. In addition, although the blasphemers ought to be corrected, unless they are in great need of this, and if they could not be otherwise corrected afterwards, he is not bound with such danger to himself to chastise them. Finally to avoid giving them the chastisement, even if they deserve it, out of negligence, fear or indifference, is only a venial sin. I have said '*in itself*', because in some cases, by reason of scandal, the priest may be bound to chastise them; for example, if someone had been present there who knew the person was a priest and would have been scandalised because he did not defend the cause of God. However, this case is most rare, because he can easily remove scandal by explaining to the Catholics that in these cases, a priest is not bound to chastise heretics from whom there is no hope of a good outcome, but danger of greater evil. It would be enough to explain this immediately after the meal, as I believe, because the short delay would be of no importance.[130] This resolution is collected from the common doctrine of theologians on the subject of fraternal chastisement, which Valentia, Filliuci and Sa [refs], follow.

[92] 92. An sacerdos relapsus sit statim post reconciliationem admittendus ad altare? et an schismatici et haeretici reconciliandi sint absque iuramento de non relabendo? et an [fo. 71] expediat in praxi exigere tale iuramentum? Respondeo 1º. non debere sacerdotem relapsum statim admitti ad celebrandum, tum quia prius agere debet poenitentiam, tum quia alioquin iuste scandalizarentur alii, et proniores redderentur ad lapsum imitandum. Respondeo 2º. si haeretici et schismatici sint publice absolvendi, debent iurare se velle parere Ecclesiae vt constat ex C. ex tenore; et ex C. de caetero de sententia excommunicationis. et ex communi docent Suar. to. 5. de censuris d. 9. s. 2. Filiuc to. 1º. tr. 12. c. 10. q. 10. qui idem etiam docent de absolutione in foro conscientiae. Addunt tamen esse peccatum veniale solum non exigere tale iuramentum, quia res est levis, cum solum fit ad formam accidentalem absolvendi. Respondeo tamen 3º. cum Sa verbo absolutio ab excommunicatione n. 18. nullum esse peccatum tale iuramentum omittere in foro Sacramentali: tum quia ita servatur in praxi; tum quia non est cur novum onus valde grave sine evidenti necessitate imponatur poenitentibus.

---

[130] *Parum pro nihilo reputatur*: a legal aphorism, 'little counts as nothing'.

Case 92. *Should a relapsed priest immediately after his reconciliation be admitted to the altar; and should schismatics and heretics be reconciled without an oath that they will not relapse; and is it expedient in practice to demand such an oath?*

I reply firstly that a relapsed priest should not be allowed immediately to celebrate Mass, because he should first perform some penance, and also because otherwise other people would justly be scandalized, and made more prone to imitate his lapse. I reply secondly that if schismatics and heretics are to be publicly absolved they should swear that they intend to obey the Church, as is clear from the canons [refs], and as Suarez and Filliucci teach from the common doctrine [refs]. These authors also teach the same about absolution in the court of conscience. However, they add that it is only a venial sin not to ask for such an oath, because the matter is not grave, since it is only done to observe the formalities of absolution. I reply however thirdly with Sa [ref.] that omitting to demand in the confessional that the penitent take such an oath is not a sin, because that is what is done in practice, and also because there is no reason why such a heavy, new burden should be imposed on penitents without evident necessity.

Casus Spectantes ad ipsos Poenitentes
(Cases regarding the penitents themselves)

[93] 93. <u>An liceat Catholicis laicis, vel sacerdotibus in</u> Anglia disputare de rebus fidei cum haereticis, et quid de laicis indoctis, qui vt liberentur e carcere, promittant se velle conferre cum ministris haereticis de rebus fidei? <u>Respondeo per se loquendo non licere etiam doctis</u> publice vel privatim vt constat ex C. 2°. § inhibemus de haereticis in 6°. <u>Probabile tamen est, Laicos doctos</u> non comprendi vt docet Caiet. Ban. Pet. Ledesm. apud Sanchem citandum. quia in illis legis ratio nempe periculum perversionis non militat, at oppositum est commune, et probabilius quia lex est vniuersalis, et de omnibus personis laicis loquitur vniversaliter ergo. <u>debet tamen esse disputatio fraternalis</u> (id est) quae ad veritatem persuadendam, vel confirmandam suscipitur nec sufficit materialis, quae exercitii gratia, vel ingenii fit. [fo. 71ᵛ] Porro laicus stricte sumitur, cum lex sit poenalis, et restringenda. vnde qui habent 1ᵃᵐ. tonsuram, non comprenduntur quia sunt clerici. Similiter nec religiosi, quamvis non habent ordinem vllum, quia non sunt laici. Si tamen hi vel illi sint indocti peccabunt graviter contra legem naturae, cum se exponunt periculo errandi. <u>Rursus lex illa non obligat</u> laicos in casu necessitatis, vel vtilitatis si sint docti, imo potest teneri aliquando laicus doctus disputare lege charitatis, si esset spes magna fructus notabilis.

Denique in locis, quibus haeretici grassantur vt in Germania et Anglia lex praedicta est abrogata pro laicis doctis per contrariam consuetudinem. haec omnia cum aliis docet Sanch. l. 2. sum. c. 6. Tan. to. 3. d. 1 de fide q. 9. dub. 5. Ex quibus inferatur, graviter peccare laicos indoctos in Anglia qui promittunt se velle conferre cum ministris haereticis in rebus fidei, tum quia ostendunt se dubios in fide, tum quia scandalizant alios; tum quia exponunt se periculo perversionis. At si sint docti non peccabunt, quia praedictae rationes in iis deficiunt, potest tamen esse scandalum nisi sint notorie docti; quod si adsit et non tollatur, nunquam poterunt promittere se velle conferre. haec ex communi Theologorum.

Case 93. *Is it lawful for Catholics in England, whether laymen or priests, to participate in disputations with heretics about matters of faith, and what about unlearned laymen who in order to be released from prison promise that they will confer with heretic ministers about matters of faith?*

I reply that in itself it is not lawful even for learned men publicly or privately to do so, as is clear from the canon law [ref.]. It is however probable that learned laymen are not included in this prohibition, as Caietan, Bannes, and Petrus de Ledesma teach, according to Sanchez, who must be cited. This is because in the case of learned men, the reason for this law, which is the danger of their perversion, does not apply. But the opposite opinion is common and more probable, because the law is universal, and therefore speaks of all laymen universally. It should however be a fraternal disputation; that is, one which is undertaken in order to persuade people of, or confirm them in, the truth, and it is not a sufficient reason to hold such a debate that it is done as an intellectual exercise. Moreover, 'layman' is taken strictly, since the law is penal and must be applied strictly. Hence, those who have had the first tonsure are not included because they are clerics. Similarly, the religious are not included, even if they have not been ordained at all, because they are not laymen. If however the former or the latter are unlearned they will sin gravely against the law of nature by doing so, since they expose themselves to the danger of making an error. Again, the law does not bind the laity in a case of necessity, or of utility, if they are learned; indeed, sometimes a learned layman may be bound to dispute by the law of charity if there were great hope of notable benefits resulting from it. Finally, in places where the heretics flourish, as in Germany and England, the aforesaid law is abrogated for learned laymen by contrary custom. All this with other matters is taught by Sanchez and Tanner [refs]. From which it is inferred that unlearned laymen sin gravely in England if they promise that they will confer with heretic ministers about matters of faith. This is first because they show they might have doubts about the faith; second because they scandalise others; and third because they expose themselves to the danger of perversion. But if they are learned, they do not sin, because the aforesaid reasons are lacking in their case. There may however be scandal unless they are known to be learned; and if there is scandal and it cannot be removed, they should never promise that they will confer. This is the common view of theologians.

[94] 94. An liceat iuramentum mere ciuile, in quo solum agnoscatur rex Angliae, vt verus rex, ac Dominus totius Angliae in temporalibus? Respondeo iuramentum fidelitatis mere civile licere, et praestandum esse a Catholicis, si offeratur: ita Suar. l. de iuramento fidelitatis ex certa doctrina et praxi Hispaniae in conciliis Toletanis; quia quae Caesaris, reddenda sunt Caesari, iuxta praeceptum Domini, et legem naturae, atqui rex Angliae, est verus rex et Dominus in temporalibus, vt certum. ergo id licite iurari potest. consequentia patet, nam quod verum est, iuramento confirmari potest, vt ex terminis patet, et docent omnes in materia de Iuramento.

Case 94. *Is it lawful to take a merely civil oath, in which the King of England is only recognised as true king and lord of the whole of England in temporal matters?*

I reply that a merely civil oath of loyalty is lawful and should be taken by Catholics if offered; thus, Suarez, [ref.] based on true doctrine, and the practice in Spain as defined in the councils of Toledo. This is because the things that are Caesar's should be rendered unto Caesar,[131] according to the commandment of the Lord and the law of nature, but the king of England is true king and lord in temporals, as is certain, therefore such an oath may lawfully be sworn. This conclusion is clear, for what is true can be confirmed by an oath, as is clear from the meaning of the words themselves, and as all teach on the subject of oaths.

[95] [fo. 72] 95. An Catholicus vocatus ad praestandum iuramentum fidelitatis possit a iudice licite petere dilationem, et interstitium respondendi? Respondeo licere, quia talis petitio est indifferens in se, quia in illo interstitio potest disponere de rebus suis domi, vel alia via, se praedicta difficultate liberare. nec tenetur cum tanto damno suo sinistram aliorum opinionem impedire, sed ius habet illam permittendi.

Case 95. *May a Catholic who is called upon to take the Oath of Allegiance ask the judge for a delay and postponement in replying?*

I reply that it is lawful because such a request is indifferent in itself,

[131] Luke 20. 25.

and in that interval the Catholic may dispose of his affairs at home, or
in another way free himself from the difficulties associated with the
Oath.[132] Nor is he bound, if it will result in such harm to himself, to
impede the unfavourable opinion of others, but he has a right to permit
it.

[96] 96. An in Anglia liceat non adhibere Patrinum in baptismo privato
in necessitate conferendo, et an vir et vxor possint simul esse patrini
in eodem baptismo et an possint esse patrini filii sui tempore necessitatis et, an tunc cognationem spiritualem contrahant, amittantque ius
exigendi debitum? Respondeo non esse vllum peccatum non adhibere
patrinum tempore necessitatis in baptismo privato. ita Tan. to. 4. d. 5.
dub. 1º. n. 23. et Laym. l. 5. tr. 2. c. 9. n. 5. ex communi quia patrinus
solum requiritur in baptismo solenni. Respondeo 2º. virum et vxorem
posse licite simul esse patrinos in eodem baptismo, quia id nullibi prohibetur vnde nec cognationem spiritualem contrahent. ita Tan. supra. n.
29. ex Navar. et Sanch. l. 7. de matr. d. 49. n. 5. citans multos: at Suar.
apud eundem putat esse peccatum veniale, quod non placet. Respondeo
3º. maritum et vxorem posse licite esse patrinos suae prolis tempore
necessitatis sed non extra illud. 1ᵐ. patet ex C. ad limina 30. q. 1ᵃ. 2ᵐ.
patet ex c. peruenit. et c. dictum est, ibidem. docentque ex communi
Tan. et Layman citati. Respondeo 4º. coniuges illos, posse et reddere,
et petere debitum, colligitur ex C.cit. ad limina. docetque ex communi
Layman. l. 5. tr. 10. c. 8. q. 3. Imo licet sua culpa gravi, et extra necessitate parentes essent patrini, et contraherent cognationem spiritualem
possent tamen licite petere debitum, et e contra, vt contra communem
sententiam aperte probat K. d. 34. de matrimonio. dub 8. Praepos. q.
6. de matrimonio. dub. 14. [fo. 72ᵛ] quia contrarium nequit efficaciter
probari ex iure; est vero durissimum pro praxi ergo.

Case 96. *Is it lawful in England not to have a godparent in a private
baptism performed in a case of necessity? May a husband and wife
be godparents at the same time in the same baptism and may they be
godparents to their own child in a time of necessity; and do they then
contract spiritual kinship and lose their right to demand the performance by their spouse of the marital duties?*

I reply there is no sin in not having a godparent in a time of necessity in a private baptism; thus, Tanner and Laymann, [refs] from the
common doctrine. This is because a godparent is only required in a
solemn baptism. I reply secondly that a husband and wife may at the

---

[132] The Latin reads 'aforesaid difficulties', presumably referring to a previous case on
the Oath of Allegiance.

same time lawfully be godparents in the same baptism because it is nowhere prohibited, and so they do not contract spiritual kinship as a result; thus, Tanner, from Navarre, and Sanchez, citing many [refs]. But Suarez, referred to by the same author, thinks it is a venial sin, which is an unconvincing opinion. I reply thirdly that (1) a husband and wife may lawfully be godparents of their own child in a time of necessity, but (2) not otherwise. The first (1) is clear from canon law [ref.] and the second (2) from other canons [ref.]; and Tanner and Laymann teach this from the common doctrine in the places cited. I reply fourthly that those spouses may perform and ask for their marital duties, as is gathered from a canon [ref.], and as Laymann [ref.] teaches from the common view. Further, even if it is their own serious fault and without necessity that the parents become godparents, and contract spiritual kinship, they can lawfully ask for their marital rights and enjoy them, as Rebellus and Praepositus [refs] prove openly, against the common opinion, on the grounds that the opposite cannot effectively be proved from the law, and it is truly most hard in practice, which proves our point.

[97] 97. An Catholici coniuges qui sub parentum protestantium tutela degunt, et ab iis maxime dependent in temporalibus, possint, ad evitandam gravem parentum offensionem, et propria damna temporalia etiam gravia permittere filios suos a ministris haereticis, et ritu haeretico baptizari? Et an possint tacere licet rebaptizentur? et an liceat vocare ministrum qui baptizati nomen ponat in libro, et pretio conductus, dicat se, illum baptizasse more haeretico? Respondeo 1º. si non sint baptizati filii, posse parentes id permittere quia non tenentur cum tam gravi damno id impedire cum validus sit baptismus, et filiis gratiam conferat. Respondeo 2º. si filii prius sint baptizati more catholico, non possunt id vllo modo permittere, quia illa reiteratio baptismi est maxima Sacramenti iniuria, quam tenentur evitare, quantum poterunt, cum damno suo quocumque vt ego credo, hoc enim videtur pium, contrarium impium. possunt enim parentes explicare veritatem, dicentes prolem fuisse baptizatam in necessitate qua vllam personam nominent, quod si vi agere vellent protestantes, tum Catholici parentes id permittere possunt; fecerunt enim, quod potuerunt, nec videntur obligati vim vi repellere cum tanto damno suo. Respondeo 3º. licere vocare ministrum, eique pretium dare vt baptizati nomen scribat in libro, quia hoc non est malum, sed necessarium ob multos fines. illicitum tamen est eidem pretium dare vt divulget se puerum baptizasse more haeretico, quia hoc est malum et scandalosum, et signum protestativum communicationis in ritibus haereticis. Possunt tamen licite ei dari pretium pro scripto nominis, quod si ille posse dicere velit se puerum baptizasse more haeretico non tenebuntur parentes Catholici [fo. 73] contrarium dicere, cum tanto damno suo: si tamen aliquod scandalum inde oriatur, tenebuntur illud tollere,

vt constat; quae hic diximus colliguntur ex receptis theologorum princi-
piis, licet nullum de his in particulari disputantem invenirem.

Case 97. *May Catholic spouses who live under the tutelage of Protestant parents, and greatly depend on them in temporal matters, permit
their own children to be baptised according to the heretic rite by heretic
ministers, in order to avoid giving grave offence to these parents, and
also to avoid their own grave temporal harm? And may they be silent
although the children are being rebaptised? And is it lawful to ask the
minister to put the baptised child's name in the register, and bribe him
to say that he baptised the child in the heretic fashion?*

I reply firstly that if the children have not already been baptised, the
parents may permit this, because they are not bound to impede it if it
would cause such grave harm, since the baptism is valid and confers
grace on the children. I reply secondly that if the children have previously been baptised in the Catholic fashion it can in no way be permitted,
because that repetition of the baptism is the greatest injury to the sacrament, which they are bound to avoid, as much as they can, whatever
harm it may cause to themselves, as I believe, for this seems pious and
the contrary impious. For parents may explain the truth, saying that the
child was baptised in the sort of necessity which requires everyone to be
given a name. If the Protestants wish to act with force, then the Catholic
parents may permit it; for they have done what they can, and they do not
seem to be bound to repel force with force if it would cause such harm
to themselves. I reply thirdly it is lawful to ask the minister and give him
money so that he writes the name of the baptised child in the register,
because that is not evil, but necessary for many ends. It is unlawful
however to give him money so that he declares publicly that he had
baptised the child in the heretic fashion, because that is evil and scandalous, and is a sign bearing witness to communication in heretic rites.
They may however give him money to write the name in the register,
and if he wishes to say that he baptised the child in the heretic fashion,
the Catholic parents are not bound to say the contrary, with such harm
to themselves. If however some scandal should arise from it, they will
be bound to remove the scandal, as is clear. What we have said here is
drawn from the received principles of theologians, although I have not
found any one of them that debates these matters in particular.

[98] 98. An et quale peccatum in Anglia voluntarie omittere Sacramentum
confirmationis? Respondeo per se loquendo solum esse veniale quia
nullum est praeceptum Diuinum vel Ecclesiasticum obligans, adeoque
si absit contemptus, et scandalum, solum erit veniale illud omittere, licet
commode fieri posset, quia est quaedam spiritualis prodigalitas: haec est
communis et vera sententia. D. Tho. in 4. D. 7. a. 1º. q. 2: et 3. p. q. 65.

a. 4. et q. 72. a. 1º. ad 3ᵐ. et a. 8. q. 48. quam sequuntur Sot. in 4. d. 7. 9. vnica a. 4. Adrianus ibi. q. 1ª. a. 1º. Caiet. Sum. V. confirmatio. Bonac. d. 3. q. vnica, pun. 2º. Navar. in Manuali c. 22. n. 8. Covar. l. 1º variarum. c. 1. n. 5. vel to. 4. d. 5. q. 2. punc. 3. Suar. 3. p. to. 3. d. 38. S. 1ª. Tan. to. 4. d. 4. q. 4. dub. 2. Henrique. Reginald, et Layman: et hoc est verum etiam tempore persecutionis, quando fides confitenda est coram tyranno, vt docent citati. quia licet confirmatio tribuat vires et robur ad profitendum et confirmandam fidem; possunt tamen huiusmodi vires obtineri per alia media, orationem, confessionem, Eucharistiam, et alia opera pia. Scio graves Theologos contrarium docere, sed eorum argumenta solvuntur a citatis ad autoritates Patrum et Canonum. Dicendum est, quod loquuntur de necessitate congruentia, sive ad melius esse, sicut equus necessarius est ad iter, non autem de necessitate simpliciter, sicut cibum est ad vitam, vti loquitur D. Tho. citatus.

Case 98. *Is it a sin, and of what sort, to omit voluntarily the sacrament of confirmation in England?*

I reply that speaking of the subject in itself, it is only a venial sin, because there is no divine or ecclesiastical commandment which obliges us in this matter, and so if contempt and scandal are not present, it will only be a venial sin to omit it, provided this can be done in a proper fashion, because confirmation is a sort of spiritual prodigality; this is the common and true judgement, according to St Thomas Aquinas [ref.], who is followed by Soto, Adrian, Caietan, Bonacina, Navarre, Covarrubias, Suarez, Tanner, Henriquez, Reginaldus and Laymann [refs]. And this is also true in a time of persecution when faith must be confessed before a tyrant, as those cited teach. This is because, although confirmation provides strength and power for professing and confirming the faith, this sort of strength may be obtained by other means; by prayer, confession, the Eucharist and other pious works. I know that grave theologians teach the contrary, but their arguments are shown to be wrong by those who have been cited, as the authoritative opinion of the fathers, and of canon law; it must be said that what they speak of concerns 'congruent necessity', or what is best for a specific purpose, as a horse is necessary for a journey, but not of 'simple necessity', as food is necessary to life, as St Thomas Aquinas says in the place cited.

[99] 99. An matrimonium vere dubium, iudicandum sit validum?
Respondeo ex quacunque causa matrimonium sit vere dubium, iudicandum esse invalidum in foro conscientiae, quia standum est pro libertate dubitantis, sicut in votis dubiis iuxta communem. ita Henrique. l. 11. de matr. c. 11. n. 5. Sylvest. v. matr. 2. n. 15. Navar apud Henriquem: in foro tamen extrinseco praesumitur [fo. 73ᵛ] validum, vt omnes communiter docent, et probant ex gloss: c. ex literis, de probationibus. Scio

tamen multos tenere esse validum in foro conscientiae, quos sequitur
Sanch. l. 1°. de sponsalibus d. 18. n. 6. quod etiam puto probabile.

Case 99. *Is a marriage which is truly doubtful to be judged valid?*
I reply that a marriage which is truly doubtful for whatever reason
is to be judged invalid in conscience, because it is necessary to support
the liberty of the doubting party, as is the case with all doubtful vows,
according to the common view; thus, Henriquez, Sylvester, and Navarre
cited by Henriquez [refs]. In the law courts, however, it is presumed to
be valid, as all commonly teach and prove from the Gloss [ref.]. I know
however that many, whom Sanchez follows [ref.], think it is valid in
conscience, which I think is also probable.

[100] An, et in quibus Tridentinum obliget in Anglia? Respondeo obligare in Anglia quoad omnia decreta per se loquendo etiam irritantia;
quia communis et vera sententia, quam confirmat stilus curiae Romanae,
docet leges Pontificias Romae solenniter promulgatas obligare etiam
alias provincias per se loquendo, nec necessarium esse promulgationem
in singulis provinciis. ita Suar. l. 4. de leg. c. 14. de lege positiva cano-
nica. et l. 5. c. 33 de lege irritante. Becan. tr. 3. de lege humana c. 6.
Layman tr. 4. de lege c. 2. apud quos citantur alii. Lex tamen Pontificia
irritans contractus, alioquin iure naturali validos, vel inferiorem iurisdictionem, v. g. in ordine ad sacramentum poenitentiae, benigna interpretatione, censeri debet non sortiri effectum suum antequam in dioecesi
promulgata sit. ita Layman cit. et Becan. c. 5. vbi docet etiam cum
Soto, et aliis, legem revocatoriam privilegiorum non habere effectum,
licet promulgetur in curia, donec promulgetur in patria Dioecesi: nec
videtur consuetudo, nec mens Pontificum, tum quia multa alioqin seque-
rentur incommoda in praxi. imo probabile est leges Pontificias non obligare vbique, nisi in provinciis et dioecesi promulgentur, nec sufficere
promulgationem Romae factam ad Germanos, vel Polonos obligandos.
ita docent Becan. cit. c. 3. Molina tr. 2. de iustitia d. 13 q. 5. qui citant
alios. vnde potest quis esse tutus in conscientia, si hanc opinionem
probabilem sequatur in praxi, vt recte Becan. cit. n. 6. Denique lex cano-
nica si per consuetudinem toleratam, non acceptetur tandem non obligat,
licet fore in initio culpabiliter fuerit non observata, vt ex communi docet
Suar. 4°. de lege. c. 16. n. 9. ex quibus colliges, quando excusari potest
non-observatio Tridentini in Anglia.

Case 100. *Does the Council of Trent oblige in England, and in what
matters?*
I reply that it obliges in England as much as all decrees do, speaking
of them *perse*, even those which invalidate, because the commonly
held, and true, judgement, which the practice of the Roman curia

confirms, teaches that pontifical laws solemnly promulgated in Rome also oblige other provinces, speaking of the matter in itself, and promulgation in every single province is not necessary. Thus, Suarez, Becanus, Laymann, who cite others [refs]. However, a pontifical law invalidating contracts which are otherwise valid by the law of nature, or invalidating an inferior jurisdiction, for example with reference to the sacrament of penance, should be thought by benign interpretation not to produce its effect before it has been promulgated in the diocese. Thus, Laymann in the place cited and Becanus [ref.], where he teaches, as do Soto and others, that a law revoking privileges, even though it is promulgated in the curia, does not have effect, until it is promulgated in the home diocese; and it does not seem the custom, nor the pontifical intention to disagree with this, because many difficulties would otherwise in practice follow. Indeed, it is probable that pontifical laws do not oblige everywhere, unless they have been promulgated in the provinces and dioceses, and promulgation in Rome is not enough to oblige the Germans or Poles. Thus, Becanus and Molina teach, [refs] citing others. As result, anyone may be safe in conscience if he follows this probable opinion in practice, as Becanus [ref.] rightly says. Finally, a canon law even if it is tolerated by custom, but is not after a time accepted, does not oblige, although at the beginning it would have been blameworthy not to have observed it, as Suarez teaches from the common view [ref.]. From which you may gather when the non-observance of Trent may be excused in England.

[101] [fo. 74] An Catholici qui ob infirmitatem, carnes edunt diebus ieiunii, possint licite aliis qui mensae assident vel etiam famulis haereticis, earundem esum permittere: vel an potius debeant a communi mensa abstinere, et relictas carnes sibi soli reservare: et an sit mortale comedere ova, et lacticinia in quadragesima, vbi non est consuetudo contraria. Respondeo haec omnia licere ex causa gravi excusante, sed non sine illa. patet ex resolutione casus 13. et 14. vnde puto in hospitiis posse aliquem comedere carnes relictas, quia nequit illas commode servare iuxta mores Angliae. Respondeo 2º. iure communi esse praeceptum abstinendi ab ovis et lacticiniis in quadragesima vbi non est licite introducta consuetudo contraria. patet ex C. Denique d. 4. quod est D. Gregorii ad S. Aug. ex quo videas antiquam consuetudinem abstinendi ab ovis, et lacticiniis in Anglia, introductam esse cum ista fide catholica. tum quia est communis omnium. At Fagund. 4. praecept. Eccl. c. 2. n. 12 et 13. citans Palaum: et P. Peres putat ex vi iuris communis non esse mortale, absque vlla causa vesci ovis et lacticiniis tempore quadragesimario etiam vbi viget consuetudo, illis non vescendi, quia putat illa esse prohibita sub veniali adeoque quamcumque causam sufficere ad excusandam etiam a veniali. sed haec sententia videtur

improbabilis et non tuta in praxi, vnde merito expuncta est ab inquisitione Hispanica anno 1628., vt intellexi dum ibi tunc eram, tum quia est contra communem, et receptam sententiam omnium aliorum Theologorum qui intelligunt praedictum c. Denique, hoc modo; tum quia res ipsa est gravissima, adeoque sub gravissima obligatione ligat, sicut ligat obligatio non comedendi carnes. videantur Tan. 3. d. q. 3. dub. 5. n. 88. Valen. to. 3. d. 9. q. 2. de ieiunio pun. 3. Azor to. 1°. l. 10. q. 1. Reginal. l. 4. c. 13. s. 1. n. 144. Filiuc tr. 27. p. 2. c. 3. q. 1. Layman. l. 4. tr. 8. c. 18. n. 3. Bonac. d. vltima de 1°. praecepto. q. 1. pun. 2. n. 2. et D. Tho. 2. 2ᵃᵉ. q. 147. a. 8. ad 2ᵐ. docens in ieiunio quadragesimario [fo. 74ᵛ] interdici venialiter, etiam ova, et lacticinia. Addunt tamen huic consuetudini abrogatum esse in aliquibus locis, cui standum est, vt omnes docent in Germania et Belgio.

Case 101. *May Catholics, who on account of infirmity eat meat on fast days, lawfully allow others who are sitting at the table, or even heretic servants, to eat the same; or should they rather abstain from the common table and reserve the meat provided for themselves alone; and is it a mortal sin to eat eggs and dairy foods in Lent in places where there is no contrary custom?*

I reply that all these things are lawful and may be excused for a serious reason, but not without one. This is clear from the resolution of Cases 13 and 14. Hence I think that in inns anyone may eat the meat which is provided, because it cannot conveniently be put aside, according to the customs of England. I reply secondly that the precept which prohibits the eating of eggs and dairy foods in Lent is a matter of common law, which applies where the contrary custom has not lawfully been introduced. This is clear from the canon, *c. Denique*, which is based on a letter from Pope Gregory to St Augustine, from which you see that the ancient custom of abstaining from eggs and dairy foods in England was introduced there with the Catholic faith; and also because this is the judgement which is common to all. But Fagundez [ref.], citing Castro-Palao and P. Peres, thinks that it is not a mortal sin on the strength of the common law to eat eggs and dairy foods in Lent without any reason, even where the custom of not eating them is in force, because he thinks that it is prohibited under pain of venial sin, and further, that many reasons may be sufficient to excuse even from this venial sin. But this judgement seems improbable and not safe in practice. Hence it was rightly suppressed by the Spanish Inquisition in 1628, as I learned when I was there at that time: first because it is against the common and received judgement of all other theologians who understand the aforesaid canon, *c. Denique*, in the former way; and second because the matter itself is most grave, and hence it binds under most grave obligation, just as the obligation not to eat meat binds. Tanner,

Valentia, Azor, Reginaldus, Filliucci, Laymann, Bonacina should be consulted, and St Thomas Aquinas [refs] teaches that in the Lenten fast, dairy foods including eggs, are prohibited as a venial sin, but in addition that in some places this custom is abrogated, and this should be observed, as all teach in Germany and Belgium.

[102] <u>An uxor Catholica possit licite violare ieiunium</u> vt obediat marito, id praecipienti? et an vovens ieiunare omnibus feriis 6. per totam vitam, nil cogitans de die natiuitatis Domini, teneatur eo die ieiunare quando cadit in feriam 6. <u>Respondeo. 1ᵐ.</u> esse licitum, si timeatur vel sequatur notabile gravamen uxoris, vel offensio mariti, non vero si levis tantum. ita Layman. ex communi. l. 4. tr. 8. c. 8. n. 4. quia ieiunium Ecclesiae non obligat cum tanto detrimento maiori boni. <u>At si</u> maritus prohiberet ieiunare in contemptum religionis id esset intrinsece malum, vt constat, ideoque nec posset vxor parere, vt omnes docent. <u>Respondeo 2º.</u> in casu voti praedicti, ieiunandum esse probabiliter. ita Sanch. l. 4. Sum. c. 11. n. 61. Suar. l. 4. de voto. c. 20. Vasq. l. 2ᵃᵉ. q. d. 3 c. 4. n. 16. quia talis circumstantia videtur implicite voluntaria. <u>Negant tamen probabilius</u> Molin. to. 2. de iustitia d. 272. Azor. to. 1º. l. 11. c. 40. q. 3. Fagund. in 4. praecept. l. 6. n. 6. quia vovens taliter ieiunare, non censetur vovere ieiunium, nisi iuxta vsum Ecclesiae, qui non ieiunat in die nativitatis vnde fit, eum, qui vovet ieiunare diebus dominicis, irrito vovere, vt ex Suar; docet Sanch. sum. l. 2. c. 39. n. 16. et sic votum ieiunandi per totum annum, non intelligitur de Dominicis vt docet Fagund. cit: <u>c. a finale de observatione non est contra</u> nos, quia intelligitur de astrictis voto specialiter et certo ieiunandi in die nativitatis non vero de voto generali, vt in casu nostro.

Case 102. *May a Catholic wife lawfully break the fast in order to obey her husband when he commands her to do so? And is someone who has vowed to fast on every Friday throughout his whole life, not thinking about Christmas Day, bound to fast on that day when it falls on a Friday?*

I reply that the first is lawful if there is fear of, or there occurs, serious trouble for the wife, or offence to the husband, but not truly if it is only slight trouble or offence. Thus, Laymann, following the common doctrine, [ref.] because the fasts of the Church do not oblige, if they cause such damage to a greater good. But if the husband should prohibit the wife's fasting out of contempt for religion, it would be intrinsically bad, as is clear, and so the wife could not obey her husband in such a case, as all teach. I reply secondly in the case of the aforesaid vow, it is probable that this person must fast. Thus, Sanchez, Suarez and Vazquez [refs] because such a state of affairs seems implicitly one which should be left to the freedom of the individual. However, Molina, Azor and

Fagundez [refs] deny this, and their teaching is more probable, because if a person makes a vow to fast in such a way, that person is judged to be vowing to fast only according to the use of the Church, which is not to fast on Christmas Day. Hence it follows that someone who vows to fast on Sundays, vows invalidly, as Sanchez teaches from Suarez [ref.], and thus a vow to fast throughout the whole year is not understood to mean Sundays, as Fagundez teaches in the place cited. The canon law [ref.] is not against us, because it is understood to concern those who have bound themselves strictly by a vow to fast especially and certainly on Christmas Day, and in truth, it does not concern a general vow, as in our case.

[103] <u>An vovens ieiunare feria 5 in Anglia, vbi sunt</u> prohibita lacticinia satisfaciat etiam in quadragesima? et quid de ieiuniis indictis per iubilaeum, vel confessarium. <u>Respondeo, his omnibus ieiuniis satisfieri</u> [per][133] comedendo lacticinia [fo. 75] et in quadragesima, vt docet Sanch. sum. l. 4. c. 11. n. 53. cum aliis. quia praeceptum ieiunii vt sic, impletur per lacticinia. ergo.

Case 103. *Should someone who vows to fast on Thursdays in England where dairy products are prohibited, also do so in Lent?[134] And what about fasts ordained by the Jubilee or by a confessor?*
 I reply that all these fasts may be fulfilled while eating milk stuffs, even in Lent, as Sanchez teaches [ref.] with others, because the precept ordering us to fast, as such, is fulfilled while eating dairy foods, which proves our point.

[104] Quid Duellum tum publicum, tum privatum? et an sit in Anglia licitum ad defensionem vitae, vel bonorum temporalium? Respondeo 1°. Duellum est pugna 2, vel plurium ex condicto ita Filiuc to. 1°. tr. 15. c. 5. n. 107. ex communi Theologorum dicitur pugna cum periculo occisionis, vel mutilationis, vel vulnerum; vnde concertatio, quae vel inter mulieres fieret, convulsione capillorum, vel inter pueros, aut viros pugnis solum, aut alio instrumento non periculoso, vt recte docet Filiuc. cit. non esset proprie, Duellum. Condictio autem includit et tempus, et locum determinatum communiter (aliquando tamen sufficeret indeterminatum, vt si duo conueniant, vt vbicumque sibi occurrent pugnabunt, erit proprium duellum, vt recte Filiuc. to. 2. tr. 29. c. 8. n. 135.) ita vt requiratur vtrumque copulative, nec alterutrum solum sufficiet, vt colligitur ex Filiuc. cit. et Sanch. l. 2. sum. c. 39. n. 28. ad condicionem etiam requiritur vt intercedat tempus inter conuentionem et pugnam.

---

133 Bracketed thus in MS, indicating a correction.
134 During Lent the fast was relaxed on Thursdays.

vnde non sufficit vt invitatio fiat in rixam ad pugnam, sed fieri debet praemeditate; vnde si occurrenti sibi et provocanti ad pugnam educto ense, et mortem minanti alter acceptet et pugnet incontinenter non est duellum, quia non est ex condicto vt docent Sanch. et Filiuc. cit. potest quidem provocatus ad duellum dicere se paratum ad defendendum se quandocumque provocans invaserit: vel se paratum fore si per Ecclesiae decreta liceret; vel provocantem experturum quicum negotium habeat si palam, et non proditorie aggrediatur vt docent Sanch. cit. et Less. l. 2. de iustitia. c. 9. Dub. 12. Sed non potest dicere, nocti me tali via domum reversurum, si habes aliquid contra me, ego non declinabo viam, nec illam deseram. quia hoc esset designare [fo. 75^v] locum et tempus, saltem in generali; adeoque esset pugna ex condicto, vnde censetur implicite acceptare duellum, etsi explicite recuset, vt colligitur ex communi.

Respondeo 2$^{\underline{o}}$. duellum publicum esse quod fit cum patrinis, et armis designatis: privatum est, quod fit sine his solennitatibus, indeterminato tamen loco, et tempore vt dictum.

Respondeo 3$^{\underline{o}}$. Catholicum in Anglia posse licite acceptare duellum, et ad illud provocare, si alioquin vitam perderet, aut bona temporalia alicuius momenti vt ex communi docent Sanch. Less. Filiuc. cit. Molin. tr. 3. de iustitia d. 17. K. 2. 2^{ae}. d. 32. D. 2. et Valent. to. 3. d. 3. q. 17. pun. 1°. quia vtrumque est tantum defendere vitam et bona, ab iniusto invasore, quod non est proprie duellum, sed iusta defensio; vnde in his casibus non loquuntur leges prohibentes duellum.

Case 104. *What is a duel, whether public or private? And is it lawful in England in order to defend life or temporal goods?*

I reply firstly that a duel is a fight between two or more people, by agreement; thus, Filliucci [ref.], according to the common view of theologians. It is said to be a fight with danger of death, of mutilation or of wounding. Hence, a conflict between women, with hair pulling, or between boys, or men, only using their fists, or some other weapon which is not dangerous, is not properly a duel, as Filliucci rightly teaches in the place cited. Moreover, the agreement will include a common decision on both the time and the place for the fight (sometimes however a decision about time and place is not necessary, so that if two men agree that they will fight wherever they may meet, this will be a genuine duel, as Filliucci rightly says [ref.]), so that the two parties are required to agree together, and one deciding unilaterally to fight the other would not suffice, as is gathered from Filliucci in the place cited, and Sanchez [ref.]. It is also a requirement that some time should intervene between the agreement and the fight. Hence it is not sufficient that the invitation to fight is made in a quarrel, but it must be done premeditatively. Hence if someone meets a man who provokes him into fighting with a drawn sword and threatens to kill him, and the first person accepts and immediately fights, it is not a duel, because it is not done as the result of an agreement, as Sanchez and Filliucci teach in the places cited. The party who is challenged to a duel may say that he is prepared to defend himself whenever the challenger will attack; or that he will be prepared if by the decrees of the Church it should be lawful; or that he will fight the challenger, whatever business he has with him, if it is done publicly, and he does not attack traitorously, as Sanchez teaches in the place cited, and Lessius [ref.]. But he may not say: 'tonight I will return home on such and such a road, if you have anything against me, I will not turn aside from the road or run away,' because that would be to designate place and time, at least in general; and so it would in that case be a fight by agreement, and he would be judged to have implicitly accepted a duel, even if he explicitly refused, as may be gathered from the common view.

I reply secondly that a public duel is one that is done with seconds and designated weapons; a private duel is one that is done without these solemnities, but with an agreement as to place and time, as has been said.

I reply thirdly that a Catholic in England may lawfully accept a duel, and challenge someone into fighting one, if otherwise he would lose his life, or temporal goods of some importance; as, from the common view, Sanchez, Lessius, Filliucci, Molina, Coninck and Valentia teach [refs]. This is because in both cases this is only a matter of defending life and goods, from an unjust attacker, which is not properly a duel, but just defence; hence in these cases the laws prohibiting a duel do not speak.

[105] An liceat provocare ad duellum, aut illud admittere ad honorem tuendum? et an occidens alium in duello, vel hastiludio teneatur restituere damna illata vxori vel filio occisi? Respondeo 1º. neutrum licere in vllo casu imaginabili extra bellum, vt tenet communis et certa sententia. probatur quia Ecclesia gravissime sub poenis excommunicationis, infamiae etc. prohibuit, tam publica duella, vt Trident. sess. 25. c. 29. de reform. et Pius IV. bulla edita anno 1560; quam etiam privata, vtrumque enim complectuntur duellum. Greg. XIII. anno 1582. et Clem. VIII. anno 1592. quae extant apud Surium in thesauro l. 3. c. 31. iussisse vero potuit ob innumera incommoda animarum, et corporum, vt sunt odium et vindictae, mutilationes neces etc. prohibere duella omnia, ita vt obliget tale praeceptum cum dispendio famae, honoris et officii temporalis, vt recte docet Less. et K. cit. haec ratio [fo. 76] semper vrgenda est, et reddenda viris nobilibus quia facilius ab iis capitur, quam vlla alia subtilior, vt ego experimento didici. vnde in nullo casu neque rarissimo admitti debet duellum licere, quia si in vno admittatur semel, non est cur negetur in alio. quare perniciose pro praxi, locutus mihi videtur Layman

l. 3. s. 5. tr. 3. p. 3. c. 3. n. 3. et 4. rarissimos aliquos casus excipiens, quos nullus alius ausus est excipere. Respondeo 2º. provocatus ab alio, si provocantem occidat in duello, vel hastiludio, iuxta leges receptas ad nullam restitutionem teneri; quia occisus non invitus descendit ad pugnam atque consentienti non fit iniuria. ergo. ita Molin. supra d. 38. et 7. Less. dub. 21. idem est, quando duo provocant se invicem, et pari consensu pugnam ineunt, vt docet Less. cit. Laym. supra c. 6. n. 5. Quando vero vnus eorum, alterum provocat, et alter descendit solum ad defendendum suum honorem mundanum, tum provocans tenetur ad restitutionem omnium damnorum, vt extra dubium esse docet Molin. d. 82. n. 2. quia provocatus invitus descendit in arenam.

Case 105. *Is it lawful to challenge someone to fight a duel, or to accept such a challenge in order to protect one's honour; and should someone who kills another in a duel or joust be bound to compensate the wife or son of the dead person for their loss?*

I reply firstly that neither is lawful in any case imaginable outside war, as the common and certain judgement holds. This is proved because the Church most gravely under the penalties of excommunication and infamy has prohibited both types of duel: public duels by the Council of Trent [ref.], and by Pius IV in the bull published in 1560; and private duels by Gregory XIII in 1582, and Clement VIII in 1592, which are to be found in Sayer [ref.]. On account of the innumerable troubles for both the soul and the body, such as hatred, revenge, mutilation, death etc., that duels cause, the Church certainly is entitled to make an order that all duels be prohibited; and as a result such a command obliges on pain of the loss of fame, honour and temporal office, as Lessius and Coninck rightly teach in the places cited. This doctrine must always be urged and repeated to noblemen because it is more easily understood by them than anything more subtle, as I have learnt by experience. Hence in no case, not even the most rare, should it be admitted that duelling is lawful, because if it is once admitted in one case, there is no reason why it should be denied in another. For which reason it seems to me that Laymann [ref.] spoke perniciously in practice by excepting some very rare cases, which no one else has dared to except. I reply secondly that if someone is challenged by another and kills him in a duel or joust, according to the accepted legal view, he is not bound to make any restitution, because the dead person did not take part in the fight unwillingly; and no injury is done to someone who consents to being harmed, which proves our point. Thus, Molina and Lessius [refs] The same is true when two people challenge one another and enter the fight with equal consent, as Lessius teaches in the place cited, and Laymann [ref.]. When indeed one person challenges another and the latter fights him only to defend his worldly honour, then the one who challenges is bound to make restitution for all the damage which results, as Molina [ref.] teaches as a matter beyond doubt, because the person who accepted the challenge entered the arena to fight unwillingly.

[106] An liceat post acceptam alapam statim repercutere. Respondeo licitum esse incontinenter repercutere, quia iniuria nondum est plane recepta, adeoque repercussio est repulsio propriae iniuriae. ita Navar. c. 15. manual n. 3. Victoria. relec. de iure belli n. 5. Mald. 2. 2ae. tr. 3. dub. 14. c. 1. §. 2. miles. Layman cit. qui citat Navar. qui etiam ait licere currere post percussorem et repercutere, quantum est ad honorem recuperandum quod mihi non displicet.

Case 106. *Is it lawful to hit back immediately after having received a blow?*

I reply that it is lawful to hit back intemperately, because the injury is not yet truly received, and so the hitting back is a repulsion of your own injury. Thus Navarre, Victoria, Malderus [refs], and Laymann, who cites Navarre, who also says that it is lawful to run after the person who has hit you and hit him back, doing as much as is necessary to recover your honour, which does not displease me.

[107] An testamentum ad causam piam vel non piam sit validum in foro conscientiae si desint solennitates a iure positivo requisitae? Respondeo in vtroque casu esse validum quia iure naturali standum est voluntati testatoris, [fo. 76ᵛ] nec vlla solennitas externa requiritur sed sufficit potestas in disponente, et capacitas in acceptante. solennitates autem externae sunt solum pro foro externo ad litem tollendam. ita Mol. tr. 2. de iustitia d. 81. Less. l. 2. c. 19. dub. 2. et 3. alios citantes, et addentes in conscientia posse aliquem vti secreta compensatione si alio modo nequit obtinere legatum. Probabilis tamen est contraria sententia, prae-cipue quoad causas non pias, vt videre est in citatis, quia iura videntur irritare huiusmodi decreta in foro conscientiae pro bono communi; vnde hac via poterit se defendere haeres a solutione praedictorum legatorum, tam quoad causas pias, quam non pias.

1º. Petrus relinquit filiae suae 1000 si nupserit, et 500, si ingrediatur religionem, quaeritur an si monialis fiat debeantur ei mille, vel solum 500?

2º. Paulus absolute legavit filiae suae 1000 in die quo nuberet solv-enda; quaeritur an ei debeantur si profiteatur religionem, quae dicitur matrimonium spirituale?

3º. Petro relinquitur haereditas, relinquendam tamen Paulo si Petrus sine liberis discesserit: quaeritur si Petrus fiat religiosus, an ei, sive monasterio debeatur haereditas, an vero Paulo? Responde.

4o. An legatum relictum pro virginibus in matrimoniis collocandis possit distribui Virginibus religionem ingredientibus? Respondeo in his omnibus casibus conditiones esse implendas vt sonant. vnde in 1º. casu solum debentur 500. in 2º. nil debetur, nisi dos sufficiens pro monasterio. (si eam aliunde non habeat ex praesumpta voluntate parentis, qui sine dubio noluisset filiam suam sufficientum dote carere pro vita religiosa.) in 3º. casu haereditas Paulo debetur, et non Petro, nec monasterio. in 4º. legatum nequit distribui Virginibus ingredientibus religionem. haec resolutio traditur a Rebel. l. 18. de iustitia [fo. 77] q. 16. Sanch. l. 7. de sponsal. d. 33. n. 30. et d. 34. n. 11. et 13. Layman. tr. 5. de vltis volunt. q. 4. n. 12. Filiuc. tr. 33. c. 10. q. 7 et Vque tr. de testam. c. 8. p. 2. dub. 6. Mol: tr. 2. de iustitia d. 207. Covar. l. 1. var. resolutiones, qui citat multos iuristas et canonistas. Ratio omnium est, quia in conditionibus honestis (quales praedictae omnes) ius naturale dictat, quod voluntati et menti testatoris standum sit, quia haec est causa dans vim et valorem testamentis, et legatis. Authentica illa de Sanctissimis Episcopis, et nisi rogati, solum habent vim in foro externo civili et iudiciali, et ex praesumptione, non autem in iure canonico, nec in foro conscientiae (nedum in Anglia, quae ius civile non sequitur.[135] Contraria tamen sententia in his 4. casibus est probabilis in praxi; nam ita docet Sylvest. v. haered. 4. n. vlto et v. legatum l. n. 9. Armil. v. haered. n. 22. Sa v. legatum n. 34. Bonac. d. 3. de contractibus in genere q. 1. p. 4. n. 10. Less. l. 2. de iust. c. 18. dub. 15. Bonac. vero cit. expresse docet 1ᵐ. 2ᵐ. et 3ᵐ. casum. nota autem Baldus, et Boetius apud Sanch. cit. tenent expresse 3ᵐ. casum, estque sat favorabilis religiosis favetque pietati, eamque sequeretur, si haberet tam bonas rationes quam prima sententia.

Case 107. *Is a will leaving property for pious, or non-pious, uses valid in conscience if it lacks the formalities required by positive law?*

I reply that in both cases it is valid because by the law of nature it is necessary to stand by the will of the testator, and no external formalities are required: power in the person who disposes, and capacity in the person who accepts are sufficient. External formalities moreover are only necessary for public purposes, to avoid litigation. Thus, Molina and Lessius [refs], citing others and adding that in conscience a person may compensate himself secretly if he cannot obtain his legacy by any other means. The contrary judgement however is probable, especially in relation to non-pious uses, as may be seen in the authors cited, because the laws seem to invalidate wills of this sort in conscience, for the sake of the common good; hence in this way an heir could defend himself from

---

135   The sense requires a second, closing bracket here.

the payment of the aforesaid legacies both for pious and for non-pious uses.

1. Peter leaves his daughter 1,000 if she should marry, and 500 if she should enter religion; the question is, if she becomes a nun is she owed 1,000 or only 500?

2. Paul leaves his daughter 1,000 to be paid unconditionally on the day she marries; the question is, is the money due to her if she should become a professed religious, in what is called a spiritual marriage?

3. An inheritance is left to Peter which must however be left to Paul if Peter should die without children. What if Peter becomes a monk; should the inheritance be left to him, or to the monastery, or indeed to Paul? Reply!

4. May a legacy left to girls for their marriage settlement be given to them if they enter religion?

I reply in all these cases that the terms of the will should be implemented according to the meaning of the words used. Hence, in case 1, only 500 is owed. In case 2, nothing is owed, unless it is a dowry sufficient for the monastery (if she should not have it from another source; this is as a result of what may be presumed to be the will of her parent, who without doubt would not have wanted his daughter to lack a dowry sufficient for the religious life). In case 3, the inheritance is owed to Paul and not to Peter, nor to the monastery. In case 4, the legacy cannot be given to the girls entering religion. This resolution is handed down by Rebellus, Sanchez, Laymann, Filliucci, Vazquez, Molina, and Covarrubias [refs], who cite many jurists and canonists. The main reason in all these cases is that if the wills are honestly made (as are all the aforesaid ones) the law of nature dictates that it is necessary to stand by the will and intention of the testator, because this is what gives strength and validity to wills and legacies. The *Novellae* of Justinian which run counter to this judgement [ref.] only have power legally in the Roman-law courts, and by usurpation, but not in canon law or in conscience (not to say in England which does not follow the civil law). The contrary judgement in these four cases is however probable in practice, for thus Sylvester, Armilla, Sa, Bonacina and Lessius teach [refs]. Bonacina indeed in the place cited expressly teaches this in cases 1, 2, and 3. Note, moreover, that Baldus and Boethius, in Sanchez as cited, hold this contrary view expressly in case 3, and such a judgement is favourable enough to the religious and favours piety, and it would be followed if it had such good reasons to support it as the first judgement.

[108] Petrus moribundus legavit 100. monasterio in quo eius filia vixit, v. g. Leodii, accidit autem, quod illo tempore quo relinquitur legatum filia parente inscio, migrat Traiectum, quaeritur an illa 100. debeantur monasterio Leodensi in quo tunc credebatur vivere, vel Traiectensi, in

quo revera est deinceps victura? Respondeo solvenda esse monasterio Traiectensi quia legatum est dividendum in dubio at dandum est omnino ei, pro quo stant coniecturae, quod ei relinquere voluerit testator, cum mens testatoris in legatis sit sequenda, vt ex terminis constat, et optime [fo. 77ᵛ] docet Mol. tr. 2. de iustitia d. 107. at dubium non est quin Petrus solum reliquerit illa 100 monasterio Leodensi intuitu filiae, quam in eo credebat esse. ergo.

Case 108. *Peter, on the point of death, left 100 to the monastery in which his daughter was living, for example Liège. However, it happened that at the time the legacy was left to the daughter, she migrated to Maastricht, without the parent knowing. The question is whether the 100 is owed to the monastery of Liège in which at that time she had been believed to be living, or to that of Maastricht, in which in truth she was thenceforth going to live?*

I reply that it is to be paid to the monastery of Maastricht, because although the legacy ought to be divided if there is any doubt, in this case it is to be given entirely to the monastery which it can be inferred from the will was the intended recipient, because the testator wished to leave it the money. This is because the intention of the testator in legacies is to be followed, as is clear from the words ('testator' and 'legacy') themselves, and is best taught by Molina [ref.]. But there is no doubt that Peter only left the 100 to the monastery at Liège in consideration of his daughter, because she had been believed to be a member of it. This proves our judgement.

[109] An liceat Catholicis in Anglia possessiones monasteriorum, vel alia Ecclesiastica beneficia emere vel vendere. Respondeo vtrumque licere, vt res nunc se habent in Anglia, vt bene docent Allanus, et Personius in suis responsis, rationem tamen non dant; ego sequentem do, quia, vt docet communis sententia, quam sequuntur Suar. to. 1º. de relig. l. 4. de simon. c. 24. Lessius l. 2. de iust. c. 25. dub. 2 et 3. Layman tr. 10. c. vltimo de simonia, §. 5. q. 1ª. ius percipiendi in beneficiis Ecclesiasticis non est invendibile iure divino, sed tantum Ecclesiastico atque iam in Anglia hoc ius servari nequit, adeoque ex benigna interpretatione Ecclesiae videtur abrogatum. confirmatur quia talis emptio videtur ex mente Ecclesiae, quia Catholici facilius suo tempore restituent; et talis venditio videtur iusta ad vitanda alia damna gravia.

Case 109. *Is it lawful for Catholics in England to buy and sell the possessions of monasteries or other ecclesiastical benefices?*

I reply that both are lawful as things now are in England, as Allen and Persons teach well in their responses. They however give no reason, but I give one as follows. This is that, as the common judgement teaches

and Suarez, Lessius and Laymann follow [refs], the sale of the right
to ecclesiastical benefices is not prohibited by divine law, but only by
ecclesiastical law, and now in England that law cannot be obeyed, and
so by the benign interpretation of the Church it seems to be repealed.
This is confirmed because the purchase of such property seems to be in
the interest of the Church, because Catholics may more easily restore it
when the time comes; and the selling of it seems just, in order to avoid
other grave harm.

[110] An Catholici in Anglia peccent solvendo decimas et alios huiusmodi reditus Ecclesiasticos haereticis ministris? et an possint eorum
aliquid licite defraudare ad distribuendum in pios usus Catholicorum?
Respondeo 1º. non peccare solvendo quia sic solum propriam vexationem gravem redimunt, quia vel inviti cogentur solvere. Respondeo
2º. licere defraudationem si sine scandalo fiat, quia haeretici iniuste
possident dicta beneficia, et contra intentionem fundatorum.

Case 110. *Do Catholics in England sin by paying tithes and other
ecclesiastical payments of this sort to heretic ministers? And may they
defraud them lawfully of anything to distribute it for the pious uses of
Catholics?*
    I reply firstly that they do not sin by making these payments, because
by doing this they are only buying off their own grave vexation, and
because they will certainly be forced against their will to pay them.
I reply secondly that defrauding is lawful if it may be done without
scandal, because the heretics unjustly possess these benefices, and
against the intention of their founders.

[111] An liceat Catholicis in Anglia emere beneficiorum fructus, frumenta
etc. ab haereticis ministris, cum illa reuera non sint eorum? et an liceat
conducere eorum beneficia? et an possint et teneantur Catholici templa,
quae sunt in manibus haereticorum sarta tecta tenere? Respondeo 1º.
licere 1ᵐ. et 2ᵐ. vt constat ex casu. Respondeo 2º. posse, et teneri Catholicos quae ad ipsos spectant sarta tecta tueri, quia hoc est opus bonum, et
per se proficuum Religioni Catholicae licet illis abutantur [fo. 78] haeretici, quod ab illis non est intentum, sed sequitur per accidens ex malitia
haereticorum. haec etiam est resolutio Allani et Personii, quoad omnia.

Case 111. *Is it lawful for Catholics in England to buy from heretic ministers the product of their benefices, for example, corn etc., since it does
not truly belong to the ministers? And is it lawful to rent their benefices?
And may Catholics maintain the fabric of the churches, which are in the
hands of heretics; and are they bound to do so?*
    I reply firstly that the first and second actions are lawful as is clear

from the question itself. I reply secondly that Catholics may, and are bound, to maintain the fabric of their local churches, because it is a good work, and advantageous to the Catholic religion. This is true even though the heretics abuse the churches, because this is not intended by the Catholics, but follows by accident from the malice of the heretics. This is also the resolution on all these points of Allen and Persons.

[112] An liceat Catholicis in Anglia, ministrum haereticum promovere ad beneficia, quorum ipsi habent vocationem seu patronatum, seu praesentare pseudoepiscopo? et an absolute liceat precibus aut literis promovere ad excludendum nequiorem? Respondent Allanus et Personius neutras licere: putarem tamen vtrumque licere: 1^m. quidem, quia sic tantum defenditur ius patronatus, quod non tenetur Catholicus amittere: nec hoc est agnoscere pseudoepiscopum vt superiorem, et legitimum, sed solum vi cogi, ipsi ac si esset superior, ministros praesentare. Dein alius praesentabitur adeoque malum aequale sequetur. 2^m. vero est licitum tum quia sic redimitur propria vexatio gravis, tum quia maius malum impeditur et minus permittitur.

Case 112. *Is it lawful for Catholics in England to promote a heretic minister to a benefice of which they have the advowson or patronage, or to present him to the pseudo-bishop? And is it absolutely lawful to support his appointment with entreaties and letters in order to exclude a worse candidate?*

Allen and Persons reply that neither is lawful. I however should have thought that both are lawful. In the first case, certainly, because this is only to defend one's right as a patron, which a Catholic is not bound to give up. Neither is it to acknowledge the pseudo-bishop as superior and legitimate, but only to be constrained by force to present ministers to him as if he were superior. Further, if you do not do so another person will be presented, and so an equal evil will follow. In the second case, it is certainly lawful because by doing this, first your own grave ill-treatment is averted, and second, a greater evil is impeded and a lesser evil is permitted.

[113] An Catholicis in Anglia liceat ius patronatus ad Ecclesiastica beneficia vendere? et an ipsa beneficia Ecclesiastica possint licite pro aliis beneficiis Ecclesiasticis commutari, vel pro aliis bonis saecularibus? Respondeo 1°. cum communi quam sequitur Suar. to. 1°. de relig. l. 4. de summa c. 28. ius patronatus (id est) ius ad praesentandum aliquem ad beneficia Ecclesiastica posse vendi, vendito fundo, vel re, cui annectitur, quia licet ex se sit aliquid spiritale vendique directe non possit, vendito tamen fundo, vel re cui inest, venditur consequenter, et indirecte: nequit tamen res aliqua carius ob hoc ius vendi, quia esset simonia, sicut est

<u>vendere</u> carius calicem aureum, quia est consecratus. <u>Respondeo 2º.</u> <u>non</u>
<u>esse</u> illicitum in Anglia commutationem beneficiorum pro beneficiis,
quia talis commutatio non est prohibita iure divino, sed solum Ecclesiastico. vt ex communi probat Suar. cit. c. 31. et non est illicita vllo
modo [fo. 78ᵛ] si fiat cum facultate superioris, vt docet, et probat etiam
ex communi in c. 32. Less. l. 2. c. 35. dub. 2. et 4. atque haec lex Ecclesiastica iam non habet vim, sed est abrogata in Anglia, ergo. <u>Respondeo</u>
<u>3º.</u> <u>licite etiam posse mutari beneficia</u> pro rebus temporalibus in Anglia,
modo non intendatur vendere, vel communitare[136] spirituale pro temporale sed tantum ius percipiendi fructus. probatur quia vt optime Less.
cit. dub. 2. venditio aut commutatio beneficiorum etiam pro temporalibus non est simonia iuris Divini nisi quis intendat ius fructus vendere
mediante officio, vt optime Hadrian. sed tantum est simonia iuris Eccle-
stiastici sed vt saepe dictum, ius Ecclesiasticum in Anglia iam non habet
vim quoad beneficia, sed abrogatum videtur, ergo.

Case 113. *Is it lawful for Catholics in England to sell the right of*
patronage to ecclesiastical benefices? And may these ecclesiastical
benefices lawfully be exchanged for other ecclesiastical benefices, or
for other secular goods?

I reply first with the common view, which Suarez follows [ref.], that
the right of patronage, that is, the right of presenting someone to an
ecclesiastical benefice, may be sold, along with the sale of the land, or
of the property to which it is annexed. This is because, although in itself
it is something spiritual and it may not be directly sold, by the sale of
the land or property of which it forms a part, it is sold indirectly, as a
consequence of something else being sold. However, no property can be
sold more dearly on account of its connection to this right of patronage,
because that would be simony, just as it is simony to sell a golden
chalice more dearly because it is consecrated. I reply secondly that the
exchange of benefices for benefices in England is not unlawful, because
such exchange is not prohibited by divine law but only by ecclesiastical law, as from the common view Suarez proves [ref.]. And it is not
unlawful in any way if it is done with the permission of a superior, as
Suarez and Lessius [ref.] teach and prove also from the common view.
And this ecclesiastical law now has no force but is abrogated in England,
which proves the point. I reply thirdly that it is also possible lawfully
to exchange benefices for temporal property in England, provided that
the intention is not to sell or exchange spiritual for temporal goods, but
only to sell or exchange the right of receiving an income. This is proved
because, as Lessius shows well [ref.], the sale or exchange of benefices

---

136   A slip of the pen for *commutare*?

even for temporal property is not simony according to divine law, unless a man intends to sell the right to an income derived from a religious office (as Adrian argues well); but otherwise it is only simony according to ecclesiastical law. However, as has often been said, the ecclesiastical law now has no force in England as far as benefices are concerned, but seems to be abrogated, which proves the point.

[114] An Catholicus in Anglia habens ius patronatus possit componere cum ministro, vt sibi aliquam partem beneficii, vel pensionem relinquat? et an tales pensiones possint retineri a Catholicis? et an minister haereticus beneficium habens possit illud resignare haeretico, quando convertitur et cum eo componere pro praesenti aliqua pecunia. Respondeo 1º. haec omnia videri in Anglia illicita, quia videntur simoniaca, vti sunt extra Angliam iuxta omnes Theologos. ita Allanus, et Personius. Ego tamen probabilem putarem, haec tria licere, iuxta doctrinam a me traditam supra; 1ᵐ. est, patronum Catholicum posse sic pacisci, et componere pro pensione sibi danda, quia iuxta omnes hoc fieri potest a Papa adeoque non est intrinsece malum aut contra ius Divinum sed tantum contra ius Ecclesiasticum quod in hac re locum non habet, vt saepe dictum. 2ᵐ. est, tales pensiones esse restituendas pauperibus Catholicis, quia haec est praesumpta voluntas Ecclesiae, et fundatorum. 3ᵐ. est, posse licite ministrum iam conversum eadem ratione pacisci, et pecuniam praesentem pro se, si sit pauper extorquere, vel pro aliis pauperibus Catholicis [fo. 79] quia haec videtur mens praesumpta Ecclesiae.

Case 114. *May a Catholic in England who has the right of patronage, make an agreement with the minister, so that the minister leaves him some part of the benefice or a pension? And may such pensions be kept by Catholics? And if a heretic minister having a benefice is converted may he resign it to a heretic, and make an agreement with him for the immediate payment of some money?*

I reply that all these things seem to be unlawful in England, because they seem to be simoniacal, as they are outside England, according to all theologians; thus, Allen and Persons. However, I should think it probable that these three things are lawful, according to the doctrine handed down by me above. In the first case, the Catholic patron may bargain in this way and make an agreement for a pension to be given to him, because according to everyone this may be done by the Pope, and so it is not intrinsically evil and against divine law, but only against ecclesiastical law, which in this matter has no place, as has often been said. In the second case, such pensions are to be restored to poor Catholics, because this is presumed to be the will of the Church and of the founders. In the third case, the minister who is now converted may lawfully by the same reasoning bargain, and extort an immediate payment for himself, if he is poor, or for other poor Catholics, for that seems to be the presumed intention of the Church.

[115] An Papa possit dispensare, vel permittere, si Anglia convertatur vt possessiones omnes, et reditus Ecclesiastici qui iam sunt in manibus nobilium haereticorum, ab iisdem, et eorum haeredibus detineantur. Respondeo affirmative quoad vtrumque: quia possunt occurrere causae gravissimae ob quas talis dispensatio sit expediens, imo et necessaria ad quietem, et pacem totius regni, et ad introductionem fidei Catholicae ergo cum Papa in spiritualibus supremam habeat potestatem, vt ex fide certum est, potest valide et licite ea vti in tali dispensatione. confirmatur quia voluntas praesumpta fundatorum est, vt pro tali necessitate fiat talis dispensatio, et ii qui ius habent ad talia bona essent irrationaliter inviti, si resisterent, ergo. sic docet Azor to. 1°. moralis l. 5. c. 15. q. 5. in simili casu. ait enim ex iusta causa posse Papam dispensare vt alienentur domus, praedia, et res Ecclesiasticae. hanc resolutionem tenet breviter Less. l. 2. c. 4. dub. 7. et favet Navar. in c. non liceat de spoliis clericorum. q. 15. fine. 2ᵐ. etiam probatur quia vniuscuiusque conscientiae, liberam relinquere dictorum bonorum restitutionem, est solum permittere minus malum, quod licitum est, ad evitandum maius, vt ex communi Theologorum. ergo. vnde legimus id factum esse a Cardinale Polo tempore Reginae Mariae.

Case 115. *May the Pope grant a dispensation, or give permission that, if England should be converted, all ecclesiastical possessions and revenues which are now in the hands of heretic nobles, should be retained by them and their heirs?*

I reply affirmatively in both cases, because there might occur most grave reasons which would make such a dispensation expedient, and indeed necessary, for the peace and quiet of the whole kingdom, and for the introduction of the Catholic faith. Therefore since the Pope has supreme power in spiritual matters, which is certain and an article of faith, he may validly and lawfully use his power in granting such a dispensation. This is confirmed because the presumed will of the founders is that such a dispensation should be made for such a necessity, and those who have the right to such goods would be acting unreasonably in their opposition if they resisted. This proves the point. Thus Azor teaches [ref.] in the same case, for he says that for a just cause the Pope may grant a dispensation that houses, estates and property of the Church might be alienated. This resolution is held briefly by Lessius [ref.], and Navarre [ref.] favours it. The answer to the second part of the question is also proved, because to leave the restitution of the said goods to the free decision of each person's conscience, is only to permit a lesser evil in order to avoid a greater, which is lawful according to the common judgment of theologians. This proves that point. Hence we read that this was done by Cardinal Pole in the time of Queen Mary.

[116] An Catholici in Anglia contrahentes in 3. vel 4. gradu per dispensationem absque iusta causa concessam valide contraxerunt. Respondeo tales, certum est, invalide contraxisse. patet, quia vt ex communi et certa docet Sanch l. 8. de matr. d. 17. n. 4. quoties inferiori permittitur potestas dispensandi in lege seperioris, intelligitur, si existat iusta causa. adeoque si haec desit dispensatio est irrita, nec vllus Theologus dissentit vt testatur Sanch. ergo.

Case 116. *Have Catholics in England who have contracted marriage in the third or fourth degree by virtue of a dispensation which has been granted without just cause, contracted validly?*

I reply that it is certain that such people have contracted marriage invalidly. This is clear because, as Sanchez teaches [ref.], following the common and certain view, it is understood that the power granted to an inferior authority to dispense with the law of a superior authority is only to be exercised if there is just cause to do so, and hence if this just cause is not present the dispensation is invalid; and no theologian dissents, as Sanchez testifies. This proves the judgement.

[117] An de facto reperiantur in Anglia haeretici tantum materiales qui invincibili laborant ignorantia circa veram religionem, adeoque fidem infusam habeant, nec sint excommunicati, et quomodo dignoscantur? Respondeo multos huiusmodi in Anglia reperiri, qui fidem infusam in baptismo [fo. 79ᵛ] receptam retinent, nec sunt excommunicati, esto sint exterius haeretici quoad ritus et ceremonias. ita clare Sanch. sum: l. 9. c. 1. n. 8. et Tan. to. 3. d. 1. de fide. q. 8. dub. 1. n. 10. citans Victoriam et Vegam, et Layman. c. 13. de haeresi n. 4 et 5. Probatur quia ad haeresim formalem requiritur pertinacia, vt omnes docent. Suar. d. 19. s. 3. et Tan. cit. dub. 5. atqui multi in Anglia possunt habere invincibilem ignorantiam circa veram religionem ergo non habent pertinaciam ergo non amittunt fidem, Nec sunt excommunicati. Regula autem dignoscendi tales ignorantes est ista iuxta citatos. si veritas Catholicae religionis, et falsitas sectae suae non sit sufficienter illis proposita, habent invincibilem ignorantiam; quando autem haec propositio sit sufficiens, discernet doctus Theologus ex circumstantiis iuxta capacitatem maiorem vel minorem personarum.

Case 117. *Are there in fact to be found in England heretics who are only material heretics and who labour in invincible ignorance about the true religion, but have had the faith infused into them at baptism, and are not excommunicated? And how are they to be recognised?*

I reply that many people of this sort are to be found in England; they retain the faith received and infused in baptism and are not excommunicated, although they are externally heretics as far as rites and ceremonies are concerned. Thus Sanchez teaches clearly, and Tanner, who cites Victoria, Vega and Laymann [refs]. This is proved, because for formal heresy, pertinacity is required, as Sanchez, Tanner and all theologians teach [refs], but many in England may be invincibly ignorant about the true religion; therefore they are not pertinacious, and therefore they have not lost their faith, and they are not excommunicated. Moreover, the rule used to distinguish such ignorant people is this, according to the writers cited: if the truth of the Catholic religion and the falsity of their own sect has not been sufficiently proposed to them, they have invincible ignorance. To which individual cases, however, this description applies, a learned theologian will decide, according to the circumstances and the greater or lesser capacity of the persons concerned.

[118] An omnes haeretici et Apostatae in Anglia sint excommunicati per bullam coenae. Respondeo 1º. Apostatas et haereticos mentales et internos non esse excommunicatos licet sint formales. ita Sanch. l. 2. sum. c. 8. Suar. to. 5. de censuris d. 21. s. 2. ex communi. quia Ecclesia non iudicat de internis, sed solum de externis licet occultissimis. modo tamen ex internis oriantur externa, vt fusius probant Doctores citati. Respondeo 2º. omnes haereticos et Apostatas formales esse excommunicatos per bullam coenae, si tales sint interius in corde et exterius in actu. patet ex bulla coenae, et docent omnes Theologi. Respondeo 3º. excusari multos haereticos in foro conscientiae ab omni excommunicatione (sic autem non sunt excusabiles Apostatae, quia scientes legem Ecclesiae peccant malitiose, et crasse) vel quia habent 1º. invincibilem ignorantiam incurrendae excommunicationis, quae iuxta communem excusat, quam sequuntur Suar. de cens. d. 4. S. 9. et Sanch. l. 1. sum. c. 16. n. 26. et l. 9. de matr. d. 32. n. 9. et 10; vel 2º. quia licet habeant ignorantiam vincibilem, et culpabilem ipsius excommunicationis non est tamen crassa, nec supina, iuxta probabilem sententiam, quam cum aliis sequitur Sanch. cit. d. 32. n. 31. et sqq. esto contraria sententia sit etiam probabilis, quam sequitur Suar. cit d. 4. s. 10. dicens se non audere dicere contrariam Sanch: et [fo. 80] practice, et moraliter probabilem. idem tamen iterum post suam censuram docuit l. 1º. sum. c. 16. n. 7. citans alios.

Case 118. *Are all heretics and apostates in England excommunicated by the bull In Coena Domini?*[137]

---

[137] This Bull was proclaimed annually from the eleventh century in Rome and contained

I reply that that those whose heresy and apostasy is mental and internal are not excommunicated although they are formally heretics; thus, Sanchez and Suarez from the common doctrine [refs]. This is because the Church does not judge internal thoughts, but only external acts, although these may be most secret; provided, however, that external acts do not arise from internal thoughts, as the doctors cited prove at more length. I reply secondly that all formal heretics and apostates are excommunicated by the Bull *In Coena* if they are such both internally in heart and externally in act. This is clear from the Bull *In Coena*, and all theologians teach this. I reply thirdly that many heretics are excused in conscience from all excommunication (those however who are apostates and, knowing the law of the Church, sin maliciously and crassly, cannot be excused). This is either because they are, firstly, invincibly ignorant that they are incurring excommunication, which according to the common judgement excuses, and is the view followed by Suarez and Sanchez [refs]; or, secondly, because although their ignorance is not invincible and they are culpable of this excommunication, their ignorance is nevertheless not crass, nor supine, according to the probable judgement, which with others is followed by Sanchez [ref.]. However, the contrary judgement may also be probable, which Suarez follows [ref.], saying that he does not dare say the contrary, as Sanchez does, and it is both practically and morally probable. However, Sanchez continued to teach the same after his censure [ref.], citing others.

[119] An omnes illi qui in Anglia vocantur Schismatici (id est) qui omnia credunt, quae credit Ecclesia Romana exterius tamen profitentur publicam Angliae religionem sint excommunicati per bullam coenae? Respondeo affirmative, quia in bulla expresse excommunicantur schismatici aeque ac haeretici. ita Suar. de cens. d. 21. s. 2. n. 13. et Sanch. l. 2. sum. c. 36. n. 14. Layman tr. 3. de. charitate. c. 11. n. 5. ratio est, quia Schisma est peccatum, quod exterius proficitur, et completur. ideoque in sola actione externa consistit: secus est de haeresi, quae interius proficitur, adeoque pro sola externa actione schismatis incurritur excommunicatio, sed non pro haeresi sola interna, vt dictum est.

Case 119. *Are all those who in England are called schismatics (that is, those who believe everything which the Roman Church teaches but externally profess the public religion of England) excommunicated by the Bull In Coena Domini?*

a list of anathemas and excommunications against heretics, schismatics, and wrong-doers of all sorts. It was last issued in 1773. See www.newadvent.org/cathen (*Catholic Encyclopaedia*).

I reply affirmatively because in the Bull schismatics are expressly excommunicated in the same way as heretics; thus, Suarez, Sanchez and Laymann [refs]. The reason is because schism is a sin which is committed entirely externally, and so consists only in external action. It is otherwise with heresy which is committed internally. And so excommunication is incurred only for external action in the case of schism, but not in the case of heresy, as has been said.

[120] An Angli Catholici teneantur in Anglia non communicare cum haereticis Anglis et schismaticis, tum in sacris tum in politicis? Respondeo negative ita Sanch. l. 2. sum. c 9. n. 5. eoque communis. probatur quia solum obligantur evitare communicationem cum haereticis denunciatis, et notoriis clericorum percussoribus, vt ex Lateranensi Extrauagante ad evitanda scandala tenet communis, quam sequitur Suar. d. 9. de excom: l. 2. Sanch. l. 2. sum. c. 9. n. 3. et Layman c. 5. de excom: n. 2. atqui Angli haeretici non sunt denunciati; nec notorii etc. ergo. probatur minor quia vt Sanch. cit. docet ex Tolet. Hugolino. Sayro, et Iavello,[138] non censentur vitandi Lutherani, vel alii specialium sectarum expresse in prima excommunicatione bullae coenae, donec nominatim denuncientur: quia denunciatio, seu declaratio publica a Iudice, vel superiore necessario requiritur iuxta citatam extrauagantem vt et ex communi docet Layman. vnde Sanch. cit. n. 4. bene docet cum Navarr. et Graff. iuxta communem sententiam nominatim excommunicatum non esse vitandum, donec expresse denuncietur, vt excommunicatus. imo addit idem esse dandum etsi aliquis declararetur incurrisse omnes censuras, vel esse haereticum, quia debet specialiter, vel expresse denunciari vel declarari excommunicatio ipsa (id est) eum incurrisse excommunicationem [fo. 80ᵛ] At cum haereticis denunciatis, vel notoriis clericorum percussoribus communicare est mortale, et incurritur excommunicationem vt omnes docent et constat ex citata extrauagante. Demum communicare cum dictis, in politicis tantum, et civilibus actionibus ad humanam convictum spectantibus, peccatum est solum veniale, vt ex communi docet Sua. d. 25. de excommunicatione s. 2. quare in Anglia nullum erit peccatum cum notoriis clericorum percussoribus communicare, quales sunt multi Iustitiarii, Iudices Praetores etc, quia excusantur Catholici titulo necessitatis in regno haeretico, vt colligitur ex communi Suar. supra s. 3. et sqq.

Case 120. *Are English Catholics bound in England not to communicate with English heretics and schismatics, both in religious and in political matters?*

---

[138] The MS seems to read 'Lavello', which I take to be a miscopy.

I reply negatively; thus, Sanchez [ref.], and with him the common view. This is proved because they are only obliged to avoid communication with heretics who have been denounced, and with notorious persecutors of the clergy, as the common view based on the Lateran Extravagant *Ad Evitanda*[139] [ref.] holds, which Suarez, Sanchez and Laymann follow [refs]. But English heretics are neither denounced nor notorious etc., which proves the point. This is further proved, because as Sanchez in the place cited teaches, from Toletus, Hugguccio, Sayer and Iavellus, it is not judged that Lutherans should be avoided, or other of the particular sects expressly included in the first excommunication of the Bull *In Coena Domini*, until they are denounced by name; because a denunciation or public declaration by a judge or superior is necessarily required according to the Extravagant cited, as from the common view Laymann teaches. Hence Sanchez [ref.] teaches well with Navarre and Graffeus according to the common judgement, that a person excommunicated by name is not to be avoided until they are expressly denounced as excommunicate. Indeed he adds that the same is to be said even if someone is declared to have incurred every censure, or to be a heretic, because the excommunication itself should be expressly or specially denounced or declared; that is, it should be declared that a particular individual has incurred excommunication. But to communicate with denounced heretics or notorious persecutors of the clergy is a mortal sin and incurs excommunication as all teach and is clear from the Extravagant cited. However, to communicate with the said people in politics alone and civil actions regarding everyday human contact is only a venial sin, as from the common view Suarez teaches [ref.]. So, in England, it will be neither a venial nor a mortal sin to communicate with notorious persecutors of the clergy, as are many justices, judges, mayors etc., because Catholics are excused on the grounds of necessity in a heretic kingdom, as Suarez [ref.] gathers from the common opinion.

[121] An Angli haeretici, et schismatici sint infames et irregulares? et quid de eorum filiis. Respondeo 1º. haereticos et schismaticos toleratos non esse infames in Germania. ita Tan. d. 1. de fid. q. 8. n.126. neque irregulares, ibid n. 12. et to. 4. d. 6. q. 10. n. 201 vtrumque repetit, quia non ob haeresim, vel apostasiam secundum se, sed quatenus iuris infamiam habet annexam, contrahi videtur infamia et irregularitas: atqui in Germania haeresis non infert infamiam ergo. Porro eadem est ratio de Anglia. ergo. Dein valde probabile est occultos haereticos vel

---

[139]   An 'extravagant' constitution, or decree, of Pope Martin V, issued in 1418, which was interpreted as allowing contact between Catholics and heretics. It was much discussed in the Elizabethan Catholic literature, since it made life under persecution in England more bearable; see P. Holmes, *Resistance and Compromise* (Cambridge, 2009), 110–13.

apostatas non incurrere irregularitatem vt tenet Sa, Henriques et Sayr. quos sequitur Layman. c. 4. de irregul. n. 12. vnde multi possunt se hac via defendere ab irregularitate si, vbi petunt dispensationem, delictum negant probari iuxta probabilem sententiam. Sanch. l. 2. sum. c. 11. n. 20. dicentis tale delictum esse occultum. Respondeo 2°. filios haereticorum Anglorum nec irregulares, nec infames, nec incapaces beneficiorum Ecclesiasticorum etc. ita Tan. et Layman. citati Henrique l. 74. c. 5. n. 4. et Sa v. haeret. n. 4. probatur quia tales non sunt [infantes][140] infames. confirmatur, quia ex praxi seminariorum tales ordinari solent, cum tamen nullum extet dispensandi privilegium.

Case 121. *Are English heretics and schismatic to be considered infamous and irregular? And what about their children?*
I reply firstly that the heretics and schismatics who are tolerated in Germany, are not infamous, and neither are they irregular; as Tanner says [refs]. He explains both judgements by arguing that it is not on account of heresy (or apostasy according to him), but in so far as by the laws heresy has infamy annexed to it, that infamy and irregularity seem to be contracted; but in Germany, heresy does not bring infamy with it, which proves the argument. Furthermore, the same reason applies in England, which proves the point. Finally, it is very probable that neither occult heretics nor apostates incur irregularity; as Sa, Henriquez and Sayer hold, whom Laymann follows [ref.]. Hence many may use this argument to defend themselves from accusations of irregularity, if when they seek a dispensation they deny there is any crime to be proved, according to a probable judgement of Sanchez [ref.], who says such a crime is occult. I reply secondly that the children of English heretics are not irregular, nor infamous, nor incapable of holding ecclesiastical benefices etc.; thus Tanner and Laymann as cited, Henriquez [ref.] and Sa [ref.]. This is proved because their parents are not infamous. It is confirmed because the practice of the seminaries is that such children are customariy ordained, when there is, however, no privilege of dispensing with irregularity or infamy.

[122] Qui sint excommunicati Credentes, Fautores, et Defensores Haereticorum. Respondeo praedictos omnes esse excommunicatos si haereticos recipiant, defendant, iisque faueant, [fo. 81] et credant formaliter (id est) quatenus haeretici sunt siue causa haereseos, siue[141] vero, si defendant etc. solum materialiter (id est) quatenus amici, consanguinei etc. ita Sanch. l. 2. sum. c. 10. n. 5. et Suar. cum aliis. Tan. et Laym.

---

[140] Bracketed thus in MS, indicating a correction.
[141] Thus; a better reading might be: *secus*

cit. probatur quia si 1°. modo faveant etc. id faciunt ex motivo haereseos; secus vero si 2°. modo, ergo sunt excommunicati, secus vero si
2°. modo. ergo. Sufficit tamen vnicus actus externus scienter factus ad
incurrendam dictam censuram, quia res est gravissima, vel semel tantum
recipere favere, defendere etc. vt Doctores citati recte docent.

Case 122. *Who are excommunicated: the believers in, the favourers of,
or the defenders of heretics?*

I reply that all the aforesaid are excommunicated if they receive,
defend and favour heretics, and if they believe heresy formally, that
is, in so far as they are themselves heretics or the cause of heresy. It
is different if in truth they only defend etc. heretics materially, that is,
as their friends and relations etc. Thus, Sanchez, Suarez, with Tanner,
Laymann and others [refs]. This is proved because if they favour etc.
heresy in the first way, they do it from heretical motives, but it is
certainly otherwise if they do it in the second way. Therefore, if they do
it in the first way, they are excommunicated, but it is certainly otherwise
if they do it in the second way. This proves the argument. It is sufficient
however to commit intentionally one single external act to incur the said
censure, because the matter is most grave; or to receive, favour, defend
etc. only once, as the doctors cited rightly teach.

[123] Quinam libri haereticorum sunt prohibiti per bullam coenae,
vel per aliam excommunicationem? Respondeo 1°. per bullam coenae
excommunicatos legentes scienter haereticorum libros, haeresim continentes, vel de religione tractantes. Illi autem libri, qui eorum errores
continent dicuntur continere haeresim; vnde etiamsi vnus tantum error
(inquit Suar. to. 5. de cens. d. 21. n. 10.) in toto libro contineatur totus est
prohibitus. consentit Sanch. citandus: addit etiam nec illo errore deleto,
licitum esse librum retinere, quia absolute ex vi huius clausulae, prohibitus est; sed hoc videtur nimis rigidum. De religione tractantes dicuntur
omnes, qui ad fidei expositionem pertinent, sed non qui de Philosophia,
aut aliis artibus inferioribus, vel de historia tractant, ita Suar. cit. et
Sanch. l. 2. sum. c. 10. n. 21. similiter non incurrit hanc excommunicationem legens libros infidelium, vel catholicorum, in quibus inserti
sunt errores haereticorum ad verbum, etsi legat intentione discendi
haeresim. quia tales non sunt libri haereticorum ita Sanch. cit. citans
alios. idemque est, si liber sit Catholici, qui ex ignorantia haereses vel
errores[142] vnde constare debent quod Author sit haereticus, et hac ratione
Erasmi libros legens, ab hac excommunicatione excusatur. non tamen

---

142 Gap of a good inch in MS, where a word meaning something like 'included' presumably should have been written.

requiritur vt Author sit haereticus damnatus, sed satis est, si sit vere
haereticus, idque legenti constet, vt bene Sanch. cit. cum aliis. Item non
excommunicatur legens libros catholici, in quibus sunt annotationes [fo.
81ᵛ] et scholia haereticorum, etsi ea quoque scholia legat, quia tales libri
sunt Catholicorum, non haereticorum. ita Sanch. cit. et Navar. in Man. c.
27. n. 56. Item audientes praedictos libros, etsi sint causa lectionis non
excommunicantur, vt bene docet Sanch. Sᵃ. n. 48. ex Hugolino iuxta¹⁴³
Azor. Sayr. et Graff. (quos sequitur et defendit Laym quia talis mandans
legit moraliter) quia tales non legunt proprie. ergo. Item sciens legere
Graece vel hebraice sed non intelligit quae legit, non incurrit excommunicationem si tales libros legeret, vt bene Sanch. n. 51. quia more
humano ad intelligendum non legit, sed instar psittaci nil intelligens.
ergo. Parvitas materiae in hac re, sicut in aliis excusat, vt bene Sanch.
ex communi iuxta Hugol. et Tol. vnde vna pagina in parvis, et folium in
maioribus non videtur materia sufficiens pro tam gravi censura, vt bene
Sanch. Sᵃ. n. 31. Denique liber manuscriptus haeretici liber est, adeoque
hac censura prohibitus, vt ex Hugol. docet Sanch. n. 28. imo incurret
etiam legens indicem, proemium, praefationem exempla ad lectorem.
ita Sanch. Sᵃ. n. 30. ex Hugol. sed non incurret legens, retinensve epis-
tolam, conciones, aut aliam chartam haeretici solutam, nec in tractatus
formam redactam quia nil horum est proprie, et vsitate loquendo liber.
ita Sanch. Sᵃ. n. 29. iuxta Hugol. Adverte tamen quod Sayr. et Graff
apud Sanch. Sᵃ. n. 34. dicant ad hanc censuram incurrendam requiri
vt liber haeretici tractet ex professo de haeresi aut religione (id est) vt
argumentum libri sit de hoc; secus si ex professo de aliis rebus tractet,
quamvis obiter interserat aliquam haeresim ad aliquid ad religionem
pertinens, quod non videtur improbabile. quae de legente dicta sunt,
locum etiam habent in retinente, imprimente defendente, vt ex bulla
constat, et docent omnes. Respondeo 2º. omnes libros haereticorum esse
prohibitos in indice librorum prohibitorum. duo tamen notat¹⁴⁴ Tan. to.
4. d. 6. q. 11. dub. 5. pro Germania, quae pro Anglia et Belgio [fo.
82] vsui esse possunt. 1ᵐ. est n. 96. vsum se obtinuisse necessitate ita
compellente, vt eiusmodi libris emendandis (loquitur de illis, in quibus
principale argumentum bonum est, in quibus tamen obiter inserta sunt
aliqua, quae ad haeresim, vel impietatem divinationem seu supersti-
tionem spectant. vt de prologis, summariis vel annotationibus, quae a
damnatis autoribus, libris non damnatis apposita sunt) et post emen-
dationem vsurpandis sufficiat privata alicuius viri docti cura et industria. Imo addit viros Laicos doctos, et probe Catholicos talium librorum

---

¹⁴³ There is a bold *X* in the margin of the MS at this point, perhaps indicating that *contra*
would have been a better reading than *iuxta*.
¹⁴⁴ There is a bold *N* in the margin of the MS at this point.

possessores, illos sua autoritate emendare posse vt et docet Layman. Sᵃ.
n. 4. 2ᵐ. est n. 105. vbi libros illos haereticorum, dicit, qui de religione
ex instituto non tractant, cum limitatione, vsu interprete permitti videri.

Case 123. *Which books of heretics are prohibited by the Bull In Coena
Domini, or by another excommunication?*
I reply firstly that by the Bull *In Coena Domini* those knowingly
reading the books of heretics containing heresy or treating of religion
are excommunicated. Further, those books which contain their errors
are said to contain heresy; whence even if there is only one error (says
Suarez [ref.]) contained in the whole book, the whole is prohibited.
Sanchez, who must be cited here, agrees, and he also adds that even if
that error is deleted it is not lawful to keep the book because absolutely
on the strength of that little clause it is prohibited; but that seems too
rigid. Books 'treating of religion' are said to be all those which are
concerned with the exposition of the faith, but not those which treat
of philosophy or the other inferior arts, or history; thus, Suarez in the
place cited and Sanchez [ref.]. Similarly a man does not incur that
excommunication by reading the books of infidels or of Catholics in
which the errors of heretics are inserted, word for word, even if he reads
the book with the intention of learning heresy, because such are not the
books of heretics; thus Sanchez in the place cited, citing others. And the
same is true if the book is written by a Catholic who out of ignorance
included errors or heresies. Hence there should be agreement that the
author is a heretic, and for this reason reading the books of Erasmus is
excused from this excommunication. It is not however required that the
author should be a condemned heretic, but it is enough that he should
truly be a heretic and that this is clear to a reader, as Sanchez shows
well in the place cited, with others. Also a person is not excommunicated through reading Catholic books in which there are annotations and
glosses written by heretics, even if he also reads the glosses, because
such books are those of Catholics and not of heretics; thus, Sanchez as
cited and Navarre [ref.]. Also those listening to the said books, even if
they are the cause of them being read out, are not excommunicated, as
Sanchez [ref.] teaches well, from Hugguccio, against the judgement of
Azor, Sayer and Graffeus (whom Laymann follows and defends on the
grounds that the person who commands that the book should be read,
reads himself, morally), because such people do not, properly speaking,
read. Also someone who knows how to read Greek or Hebrew but who
does not understand what he reads, does not incur excommunication if
he should read such books, as Sanchez shows well [ref.], because he
does not read in the human fashion in order to understand, but in the
manner of a parrot that understands nothing, which proves the argument.
The smallness of the material, in this subject, as in others, excuses,

as Sanchez shows well from the common view, with Hugguccio and
Toletus; so, one page in small books, or a leaf in large books does not
seem sufficient material for such a grave censure, as Sanchez shows
well [ref.]. Next, the manuscript book of a heretic is a book, and so is
prohibited by this censure, as from Hugguccio, Sanchez teaches [ref.].
Indeed a person also incurs excommunication by reading the index, the
preamble, the preface, the contents, and the introduction to the reader;
thus, Sanchez [ref.] following Hugguccio. But he will not incur excommunication by reading or keeping a letter, the sermons, or other loose
page written by a heretic, even if drawn up in the form of a pamphlet,
because none of them is properly speaking a book; thus, Sanchez,
following Hugguccio. Notice, however, that Sayer and Graffeus, cited
in Sanchez [ref.], say that it is required in order to incur this censure
that the book by the heretic treats professedly of heresy or religion, that
is, that the argument of the book should be about this. It is different if
it professedly treats of other matters, even if in passing there has been
inserted some heresy pertaining to something to do with religion; and
this judgement does not seem improbable. What has been said about
reading relates also to keeping, printing and storing books, as is clear
from the Bull, and all teach. I reply secondly that all books of heretics
are prohibited in the Index of Prohibited Books. Tanner [ref.] however
notes two things with regards to Germany, which may be applied to
Belgium and England. The first is [ref.] that the practice has developed,
when necessity compels, of emending such books (he speaks of those
books in which the main argument is good, but in which in passing
some things have been inserted which relate to heresy and impiety, or
to divination and superstition, like the prologues, summaries and annotations which are added by condemned authors to books which are not
themselves condemned) and after this emendation it is satisfactory for
them to be kept privately for some learned man's attention and work. He
adds that learned laymen and the truly Catholic owners of such books,
may amend them on their own authority, as Laymann also teaches [ref.].
His second point [ref.] is that it seems that an expert may be permitted to
use, with certain limitations, those books of heretics which do not deal
essentially with religion.

[124] An Episcopi et Regulares praelati, habentes iurisdictionem quasi
episcopalem, vt Generales Ordinum, Provinciales, et Abbates possint
virtute Trident. S. 24 de reform. c. 6. absoluere ab haeresi occulta et aliis
criminibus occultis Sedi Apostolicae reservatis etiam post annuam publi-
cationem Bullae coenae? Respondeo 1°. probabiliorem esse practice,
sententiam asserentem Episcopos posse absoluere ab haeresi occulta,
et caeteris casibus ac delictis occultis sedi Apostolicae reservatis. ita
enim docet in terminis Navarr. Guttier. Henrique Bannez, Aragon. Sa.

Vivald. Manuel. Ledesma, et Vega apud Sanch. l. 2. sum. c. 11. n. 27.
vbi contrariam sententiam sequitur, at in manuscriptis eius Hispali, ego
legi praedictam sententiam. Navar. Suar. etiam D. 21. de censuris s. 3.
n. 5, ait esse probabiliorem et absolute tenet Tann. to. 4. d. 6. q. 10. dub.
6. n. 121. citans Henrique et Filiucanum: quia ita expresse deciditur
in Trident. s. 24. de reform. c. 6. At probabilius est per derogationem
generalem bullae coenae non derogari privilegiis in iure continentis, vt
generatim de [fo. 82ᵛ] legibus probatur Tann. to. 2. d. 5. q. 7. dub. 3.
Adde per bullam coenae solum revocari illa privilegia, quibus dabatur
facultas absolvendi ab haeresi, vel aliis delictis publicis, et sic stare
posse privilegium a Trident. concessum, quoad occulta, et sic vitatur
iuris correctio, quae semper est odiosa et vitanda. Respondeo 2ᵘ. Tridentini virtute non posse praelatos regulares, nec quidem Generales aut
Provinciales absolvere ab haeresi occulta, vel aliis criminibus occultis
sedi Apostolicae reservatis. ita Sanch. l. 2. sum. c. 11. n. 7. ex communi,
et certa sententia quia nomine Episcopus in Trident. vt ex tenore illius
decreti constat, non intelliguntur omnes qualitercunque habentes iurisdictionem quasi episcopalem: sic enim regulares praelati includerentur
in eo decreto, respectu suorum subditorum; sed solum intelliguntur
habentes talem iurisdictionem in aliqua dioecesi sibi subdita, vnde
quidam Abbates in eo comprehenderentur, vt cum aliis docet Sanch. Sᵃ.
n. 5. etiam respectu saecularium.

Case 124. *May bishops, and regular prelates who have a quasi-episcopal
jurisdiction, such as the generals of orders, provincials and abbots, by
virtue of the Council of Trent [ref.], absolve from occult heresy and
other occult crimes reserved to the Apostolic See, even after the annual
publication of the Bull In Coena Domini?*

I reply firstly that the judgement is more probable in practice which
asserts that bishops may absolve from occult heresy and other occult
cases and crimes reserved to the Apostolic See. For Navarre, Guttier,
Henriquez, Bannez, Aragon, Sa, Vivaldi, Manuel, Ledesma, and Vega,
teach this explicitly, as cited in Sanchez [ref.] (where he follows the
contrary judgement, although in his manuscripts at Seville I read the first
judgement). Navarre and Suarez also say this judgement is more probable; and Tanner absolutely holds it [ref.], citing Henriquez and Filliucci,
because it was decided in this way expressly at Trent [ref.]. But the more
probable judgement is that the general act of repeal contained in the
Bull *In Coena Domini* does not remove privileges with a legal basis, as
is generally the case in matters of law, as Tanner [ref.] shows. In addition, by the Bull *In Coena Domini*, only those privileges are revoked in
which the faculty of absolving from heresy, or other public crimes has
been given; and thus the privilege conceded by Trent may stand, as far
as occult crimes are concerned, and in this way the amendment of laws

is avoided, which is always odious and to be avoided. I reply secondly that by virtue of Trent, regular prelates, and indeed even generals and provincials, may not absolve from occult heresy, or other occult crimes reserved to the Apostolic See; thus Sanchez [ref.] from the common and certain judgement. This is because under the heading 'bishop' at Trent, as is clear from the tenor of that decree, is not included everyone of whatever sort who has quasi-episcopal jurisdiction. For under this heading regular prelates were included in the decree, in respect of their subjects, but they are only understood to have jurisdiction of this sort in a diocese which is subject to them. Hence, many abbots are included in it, as Sanchez [ref.] teaches with others also in respect of seculars.

[125] An bulla coenae obliget in Anglia, et quid de consuetudine qua Dominus fundi vindicat naufragantium. Respondeo 1º. probabilius esse quod obliget, quia lex Ecclesiastica Romae promulgata vbique obligat iuxta commumem sententiam Theologorum quam probat Becan. c. 6. de lege humana. concl. 4. et Tan. q. 5. de lege dub. 3. ass. 3. oppositam tamen probabiliorem putat Becan. cit. c. 3. vide dicta de concil. Trident. in casu. de hac re tractans Tann. d. 6. de pec. q. 10. n. 99. dicit rem est facti non iuris; quam proinde pro locorum varietate expertus rerum melius noret, quam peritus iuris et Becan c. 15. de poen. haeret. q. 8. n. 5. agens de eadem re, dat istam regulam: vbicumque lex vel constitutio Pontificalis vsu recepta est, ibi obligat, vbi recepta non est, non obligat, vt supponitur ex communi Theologorum [fo. 83] (dicitur a vsu recepta quando a maiore parte communitatis recipitur et servatur.) vnde si in Anglia non sit vsu et praxi Catholicorum recepta, non obligabit bulla coenae Tann. et Becan. Respondetur 2º. consuetudinem illam iniquissimam esse. 1º. quia prohibetur in 4ª. excommunicatione bullae coenae, vbi revocatur omnis consuetudo contraria, licet sit immemorialis, et antiquissima praescriptio, et in cap. excom. de [Reginald. to. 1º. l. 9. an. 268]145 rapt. vid. Suar. de cens. d. 21. l. 2. a. n. 26. Reginald. to. 1º. l. 9. an. 268. et Sayr. l. 3. Thesaur. c. 8: 2º. quia tales consuetudines fuerunt iniustae, et contra omnem aequitatem. quia afflicto non est addenda afflictio. vt ex aliis optime Sayr. cit. Less. l. 2. de iust. c. 14. dub. 7. n. 50. et Suar. et Caiet. et Navar. Duo tamen notanda: 1m. ex Reginaldo c. n. 270. nomine Christianorum quibus intendit bulla favere non intelligi haereticos, quia Ecclesia non censetur velle illis, vtpote hostibus, favere. oppositum tamen est probabile, quia haeretici sunt vere et proprie Christiani. 2m. ex Suar. cit. n. 35. licitam fore legem et consuetudinem praescribendi talia bona pro certis vsibus post sufficientem inquisitionem pro veris Dominis inveniendis, quia talis lex esset rationabilis, vt patet.

---

145 Bracketed thus in MS, indicating a correction.

Case 125. *Does the Bull In Coena Domini oblige in England? And what about the custom by which the lord of the manor claims the property of those who have been shipwrecked?*[146]

I reply firstly it is more probable that it obliges, because when the law of the Church has been promulgated in Rome it obliges everywhere, according to the common judgement of theologians, which is proved by Becanus [ref.] and Tanner [ref.]. However, Becanus thinks the opposite is more probable [ref.]; see what he says about the Council of Trent in the case which deals with this matter. Tanner [ref.] says the question is one of fact and not of law, and therefore because of the variety of places, an expert in such facts knows the solution better than someone skilled in the law. And Becanus [ref.], when discussing the same matter, gives this rule: wherever a law or constitution of the Pontiff is received by use it obliges there; where it is not received by use, it does not bind, as is accepted commonly by theologians. It is said to be 'received by use' when it is received and obeyed by the majority of the community. Hence, if is not received in England by the use and practice of Catholics, the Bull *In Coena Domini* does not oblige, according to Tanner and Becanus. It is to be replied to the second part of this question that this custom is most iniquitous. First because it is prohibited in the fourth excommunication of the Bull *In Coena Domini*, where all contrary custom is revoked, even if it dates from time immemorial and is supported by the most ancient prescription; and it is also prohibited by the canon law [ref.], according to Suarez, Reginaldus and Sayer [refs]. Secondly because such customs were unjust and against all equity, because affliction should not be added to the afflicted, as among others is well shown by Sayer in the place cited, Lessius [ref.], Suarez, Caietan, and Navarre. Two things however are to be noted; the first, from Reginaldus [ref.], that the Bull intends to favour Christians and this does not include heretics, because the Church is not judged to wish to favour them, since they are its enemies. The opposite, however, is probable because heretics are truly and properly Christians. The second thing to note, following Suarez [ref.], is that the law and custom of prescribing certain uses for goods from a shipwreck, after a sufficient inquisition to find the true owners has been made, will be lawful, because such a law is reasonable, as is clear.

---

[146] As Southwell says, the fourth excommunication of the Bull *In Coena Domini* anathematized those plundering shipwrecks. English law seemed to allow this practice: 'Where a Ship is perished on the Sea, and no Man escapes alive out of it, this is called *Wreck*: And the Goods in the Ship being brought to Land by the Waves, belong to the King by his Prerogative, or to the Lord of the Manor': Giles Jacob, *A New Law-Dictionary* (6th ed., London, 1750), *s.v.* Wreck.

[126] An liceat maleficium tollere Maleficio, et maleficii signum destruere? <u>Respondeo 1º.</u> <u>esse intrinsece malum, et</u> illicitum exigere ab altero vt maleficium tollat maleficio, si nequeat alio modo licito tolli. vt ex communi[147] certa docet Sanch. l. 2. Sum. c. 41. n. 5. dicens contrariam Aureali, et Angeli esse falsam et erroneam, quia id potest licite, et sine peccato ab altero exigi vel peti, quod potest sine peccato praestari. hoc enim est rem licitam petere, et oppositum petere, est petere peccatum, eique cooperari, vt patet, ergo. Respondeo tamen 2º. licere petere a mago, vt solvat maleficium, si id potest modo licito tollere, licet scias eum nolle tollere nisi modo illicito, seu alio maleficio, vt cum Suar. et Less. docet Sanch. l. 2. cit. n. 13. 14. quia hoc, est petere quod licitum est, et solum [fo. 83ᵛ] permittere alterius malitiam: vt de petente mutuum ab vsuario, et iuramentum ab infideli, per Deos falsos iuraturo, dici solet. <u>Respondeo 3º.</u> <u>licere</u> malefico, vel cuivis signum maleficii amovere, destruere etc. ex animo dissolvendi pactum cum Daemone, et obtinendae sanitatis, vt ex communi recte Sanch. Sª. n. 19. quia hoc modo tollitur pactum cum Daemone et ab eius amicitia receditur ipseque in signo destructo, vel combusto, contemnitur. haec omnia bona sunt, ergo. Imo vt docet Sanch. n. 25. licet signum positivum contrarium apponere modo sit ex se licitum, vel indifferens ad pactum cum Daemone, rescindendum, v.g. si Daemon esset pactus cum malefico, se nociturum, nisi maleficiatus postea se signet signo crucis, aut corpus lavet, licebit se signare, et lavare, non quidem animo se sanandi per illud medium [sed solo animo][148] vel operam Daemonis sed solo animo tollendi signum et dissolvendi pactum, quia res ex se est bona, et licitum medium. ergo.

Case 126. *Is it lawful to remove witchcraft*[149] *by using witchcraft, and lawful to destroy the sign*[150] *of witchcraft?*

    I reply firstly that it is intrinsically evil and unlawful to ask another

---

147   At this point in the MS the word *vera* is crossed out.

148   Bracketed thus in MS, indicating a correction.

149   *Maleficium* causes difficulty for translators, and is often rendered more literally as 'harmful magic'; it would not quite work here, since the discussion turns on removing harm through the use of witchcraft.

150   *Maleficii Signum*. The translation of *signum* is difficult: the word could mean 'seal', 'proof', 'token' or 'symptom'. What Southwell intends is made clearer by consulting Sanchez (*Opus morale*, Antwerp 1631, II, 41, 18–25, 318–19), his main source here. Sanchez uses the example of something buried in a certain place ('dum res aliqua in tali loco defossa permanserit'), or an amulet ('ligatura aliqua'), tokens of the pact between witch and devil, and the agency by which the *maleficium*, or harm caused by witchcraft, is somehow transmitted to the victim. As is clear from later in the case and also from Sanchez, a *signum* might also be some action: using the *sign* of the cross, or washing. Cf. K. Thomas, *Religion and the Rise of Magic* (London, 1978), 519, where he mentions briefly what he calls 'technical aids' used in witchcraft.

to remove witchcraft by using witchcraft, if it cannot be done in any other way, as from the common and certain judgment, Sanchez [ref.] teaches, saying that the contrary judgement of Fumo's *Summa Aurea Armilla* and of Angelus is false and erroneous. This is because it is lawful and without sin to demand or ask someone else to do something which you could yourself do lawfully and without sin, for this is to ask for a lawful thing; and to ask for the opposite is to ask for sin, and to co-operate in it, as is clear. This proves the judgement. I reply secondly that it is, however, lawful to ask a magician[151] to remove witchcraft, if he can remove it using some lawful method, even if you know that he does not intend to remove it except by using an unlawful method or by using some other witchcraft, as with Suarez and Lessius, Sanchez [ref.] teaches. This is because to do so is to ask what is lawful and only permit the wickedness of another, as is generally said about asking for a loan from a usurer, and an oath from an infidel who will swear by false gods. I reply thirdly that it is lawful for a witch or anyone to remove and destroy the sign of witchcraft, with the intention of dissolving the pact with the devil and obtaining health, as from the common judgement Sanchez [ref.] rightly says. This is because in that way the pact with the devil is removed, the devil's friendship is renounced, and the devil is condemned as a result of the sign being destroyed or burnt. All these things are good, which proves the judgement. Indeed, as Sanchez [ref.] teaches, it is lawful to use a positive contrary sign, in order to break the pact with the devil, as long as it is in itself lawful or indifferent. For example, if the devil had made a pact with a witch that the bewitched person would be harmed unless he should afterwards sign himself with the cross or wash his body, then it would be lawful for him to sign himself and wash, not indeed with the intention of curing himself in that way through the work of the devil, but only with the intention of removing the sign and dissolving the pact, because these actions are in themselves good, and a lawful method. This proves the judgement.

[127] An liceat consulere Aegyptios, vt vocant pro fortuna et quid de aliis vanis observantiis? Respondeo 1º. esse mortale illos consulere, credendo ipsis. esse tamen solum veniale ipsis non credendo, ita Sanch. l. 2. sum. c. 38. citans alios. patet, quia 1ᵐ. esset quaedam superstitio gravis: at 2ᵐ. videtur quaedam levis curiositas, ergo. Respondeo 2º. omnes vanas observationes esse ex genere suo peccatum mortale maxime quando opus externum est superstitiosum, vt ex communi Less. l. 2. c. 43. dub. 10. n. 64. ratione tamen ignorantiae vel bonae fidei saepe excusatur a

---

151 *Magus*: the 'cunning man' beloved of Thomas and the other historians of witchcraft; wizard.

mortali, vt idem recte docet. qui etiam recte addit n. 66. obseruantiam
etiam eventus esse ex se mortale; esse tamen saepe veniale ob ignorantiam vel bonam fidem et sic excusantur, qui leviter credunt somniis
[fo. 84] vel timent ne sibi accedant mala, si mane labantur vel calceum
sinistrum induant prius quam dextrum. si calceos induentes sternitent
etc. hanc et doctrinam tradit Sanch. cit. n. 21.

Case 127. *Is it lawful to consult Gypsies, so that they tell your fortune;
and what about other vain observances?*

I reply first that it is a mortal sin to consult them if you believe in
them, but only a venial sin if you do not believe in them; thus, Sanchez
[ref.], citing others. This is clear because in the first case it is a sort of
grave superstition; but the second seems to be a sort of frivolous curi-
osity, which proves the judgement. I reply secondly that all vain observances are by their nature a mortal sin, especially when the external
action is superstitious, as Lessius [ref.] says, from the common judgement. However, if a person acts out of ignorance or in good faith, he is
often excused from mortal sin, as the same writer rightly teaches. He
also rightly adds [ref.] that a reverence for fate is in itself a mortal sin;
however, it is often a venial sin if people act out of ignorance or in good
faith. Hence, people are excused who believe frivolously in dreams; or
if they are afraid that some evil may happen to them if they trip up in the
morning, or put on the left shoe before the right, or sneeze while putting
on their shoes etc. Sanchez also delivers this doctrine in the place cited
[ref.].

[128] An licita sint brevia, seu scripta Antidaemoniaca, et amuleta ex
corolla, gemmis etc. herbis confecta etc. et quid de Salvatoribus Hispa-
nicis? Respondeo 1º. illicita esse, et superstitiosa, si aliqua parerga vana,
inutilia, falsa aut apocrypha contineant, tanquam necessaria, vt docet
ex communi Less. l. 2. c. 43. n. 22. quia tales circumstantiae naturaliter non sunt operativae talis effectus, nec ex virtute Dei vel Ecclesiae
institutione, ergo ex pacto, saltem implicito cum Daemone, ergo sunt
superstitiosae. vnde patet characteres vel imagines astronomicas sub
certa constellatione fabricatas esse superstitiosas. v.g. si quis sub signo
leonis sculpat in auro signi huius figuram, quam dicunt valere contra
phantasmata melancholica, hydropsica, febrem, pestem etc. de quibus
fuse Cornel Agrip. l. de occulta philosophia. et Less. cit. ex communi
et certa sententia, et Sanch Sª. n. 50. citans multos contra vnum Caiet.
vide Tann. to. 3. disp. 5. de relig. q. 9. dub. 2ª. n. 54. vbi defendit
quaedam amuleta, quae ego iuxta Less et Sanch. Sª. condemnanda
puto. Non hinc sequitur missas novenarias in honorem 9. mensis quibus
Christus fuit in vtero Beatissimae Virginis nec missas 30. Gregorianas
ex facto S. Gregorii incoeptas, et vsitatas condemnandas esse, quia non

sunt superstitiosae, nisi in tale numero credatur vim inesse. tunc enim essent superstitiosae vt patet. in honorem igitur talis mysterii vel facti S. Gregorii possint licite celebrari, sicut in honorem [fo. 84ᵛ] Sanctissimae Trinitatis 3ᵃ. Sacra etc. sic de similibus ita optime Sanch. Sᵃ. n. 41. sic etiam defendens missam S Amatoris vt vocant, modo tollatur omnis alia vana observantia. Respondeo 2º. Salvatores Hispanicos qui curant vulneratos et aegros per quasdam preces bonas, et per habitum, non esse damnandos vt superstitiosos quia omnes fere graves Doctores defendunt illos. aliqui enim, vt Veracrux, Castanega,¹⁵² et Victoria, dicunt talem virtutem esse naturalem ipsis, sicut et similem virtutem habuisse Psillos, et Marsos refert Plinius l. 28. c. 3. hist. naturalis et partim consentit Less. cit. aliqui vero, vt Azor, Navar et Delrius, quos sequuntur Sanch. Sᵃ. n. 49, et Less. cit. dicunt illam virtutem esse gratiam gratis datam; alii, esse iis datam ob eximiam eorum fidem.

Case 128. *Are anti-demoniacal amulets or writings lawful; and amulets made of coral or jewels etc., or with herbs etc.; and what about 'Spanish protectors'?*

I reply firstly that they are unlawful and superstitious, if they contain some vain, useless, false or apocryphal additional ornaments, as if they were necessary, as Lessius [ref.] teaches from the common judgement. This is because such things do not produce the effects attributed to them, either naturally, or by the grace of God, or by the institution of the Church; and therefore they must do so through a pact, at least implicit, with the devil; therefore, they are superstitious. Hence it is clear that the astrological engravings or statues made under certain constellations are superstitious; for example, if someone casts in gold, under the sign of Leo, a statue of this sign, which they then say is of value against melancholic phantasms, hydropsy, fever, plague etc. Cornelius Agrippa [ref.] writes about this at more length, and Lessius in the place cited, following the common and certain judgement, and also Sanchez [ref.], who cites many. Against these writers, there is one, Caietan (see Tanner [ref.]), who defends certain amulets, which I think, like Lessius and Sanchez, ought to be condemned. It does not follow from this that the novena of Masses in honour of the nine months in which Christ was in the womb of the Blessed Virgin, or the thirty Gregorian Masses which began as a result of the action of St Gregory, and have become customary now, are to be condemned, because they are not superstitious, unless it is believed that there is a power in these numbers, for then they would be superstitious. Therefore, it is clear that Mass can lawfully be celebrated in honour of the mystery of the Immaculate Conception, or of

---

152 The MS reads 'Castaneda', which seems to be a mistake in copying.

the action of St Gregory, just as three Masses etc. may be celebrated in
honour of the Holy Trinity. Sanchez teaches this well with reference to
similar cases [ref.], and also defends the Mass of St Amator as they call
it, as long as all other vain observances are removed. I reply secondly
that the 'Spanish protectors', which cure the wounded and sick through
some good prayers and by being worn are not to be condemned as
superstitious, because nearly all grave Doctors defend them. For, some,
like Veracruz, Castanega and Victoria say that such power is natural to
them, just as the Psilli and Marsi have a similar power, as Pliny relates
in his *Natural History* [ref.];[153] and Lessius partly agrees in the place
cited. Others in truth, like Azor, Navarre and Delrius, whom Sanchez
follows [ref.], and Lessius in the place cited, say that this power is a
grace freely given; others say it is given to men of pre-eminent faith.

[129] Quid dicendum sit de Astrologia Iudiciaria? disces ex bulla Vrbani
VIII. calend. April. 1631. edita, quae incipit inscrutabilis Iudiciorum
dei altitudo contra Astrologos Iudiciarios: qui nempe praedicunt certo,
vel probabiliter tantum effectus fortuiti ac liberi. vide et Sanch. l. 2. Sᵃ.
c. 38. n. 34. Nota Iudiciarium teneri restituere pretium, si nullum, vel
diligentiam posuerit. ita. Sanch. l. 2. Sᵃ. c. 38. n. 96.

Case 129. *What is to be said about Judicial Astrology?*

You learn the answer to this from the Bull of Urban VIII published
on the 1ˢᵗ April, 1631, which begins *Inscrutabilis iudiciorum Dei altitudo*, which condemns judicial astrologers, or those who claim to
predict as certain, or at least probable, events which are fortuitous and
free; see also Sanchez [ref.]. Note that the judicial astrologer is bound
to make recompense for the cost, if any, or the trouble he has caused;
thus Sanchez [ref.].

[130] Quid blasphemia in Deum, vel Sacramenta? Respondeo 1º.
blasphemiam esse quandam contumeliam adversus Deum, qua sive per
verba, sive facta impie ei tribuitur, quod non convenit, aut detrahetur
quod convenit. ita ex communi Tann. d. 1. de fide q. 8. n. 131.
Respondeo 2º. haec esse blasphemia: malum Deo contingat, iuro per
Iovem (si serio iuret) nego Deum, sive Deus velit sive nolit. non est
in Dei potentia, iustitia etc. taedeat Deum, vel Deo displiceat, Deus
est iniustus etc. in nomine Sacramentorum; per vitam [fo. 85] Dei, per
pudenda Christi, imo et per caput, vngues, corpus, sanguinem, crines

---

153 St Amator (d. 418) was Bishop of Auxerre, famous for miraculous cures. His feast
day is 1 May. Pliny (*Natural History* 28.6) says the Psilli and Marsi proples could cure
snake bites.

Dei, si intelligantur esse membra Dei, vt Deus est: in quo haeretici Angli
praesertim rudiores, et male instructi de mysterio Incarnationis facile
errant; secus vero si intelligantur esse membra Dei, vt incarnatus est, et
factus homo. quia hoc est iurare per membra honesta Christi, quod non
est blasphemium, et sic excusantur Catholici communiter sic iurantes .
vide Sanch. l. 2. Sᵃ. c. 32.

Case 130. *What about blasphemy against God or the sacraments?*

I reply firstly that blasphemy is a sort of insolence towards God,
which either by word or deed impiously attributes something to Him
which is not fitting, or removes something from Him which is fitting;
thus, following the common judgement, Tanner [ref.]. I reply secondly
that these are blasphemies: may evil befall God; I swear by Jove (if
he swears seriously); I deny God; whether God wishes it or not; it is
not in God's power, justice etc.; may it disgust God, or displease God;
God is unjust etc.; in the name of the sacraments; by the life of God;
by the pudenda of Christ; and also by the head, nails, body, blood,
hair of God, if they are understood to be parts of the body of God, as
God. In such matters, the English heretics, especially the more ignorant
ones, and those who are badly instructed concerning the mysteries of
the Incarnation, easily err. It is, however, different if these references
are understood to mean the parts of God's body, as he is when incarnate
and made a man; for that is to swear by the honest members of Christ,
which is not blasphemy. Thus, Catholics are excused commonly when
they swear in that way; see Sanchez [ref.].

[131] An omnes blasphemiae in Deum, vel Sanctos sint eiusdem speciei
et in confessione necessario explicanda? Respondeo 1º. omnes Theologos convenire, blasphemias haereticales (id est) haeresim continentes,
et quae procedunt ex formali odio Dei, vel Sanctorum distingui specie, a
non haereticalibus, et aliis, ideoque haec duo genera esse distincte explicanda. Respondeo 2º. probabilem esse sententiam negantem in vtroque
casu pro aliis blasphemiis, iuxta probabilem sententiam negantem circumstantiam aggravantem esse distincte explicandam ita Sanch. Sᵃ. n. 38.
39. et alii. Respondeo 3º. probabiliorem esse sententiam affirmantem in
vtroque casu, quia blasphemia in Deum est contra latriam; in Sanctos
solum contra Douliam ergo distinguuntur specie cum haec excellentiam
creatam essentialiter respiciat, illa increatam. ita Suar. to. 1º. de relig. 1.
1º. de irrel: c. 6. prope finem et alii. Imo credo blasphemiam in Beatam
Virginem distingui specie incompleta a blasphemia in reliquos Sanctos
vel Angelos, quatenus est mater Dei eximiamque habet excellentiam.
inter Sanctos vero reliquos et Angelos solum est maior dignitas in eadem
specie Douliae, ergo. sunt tamen circumstantiae aggravantes non tamen
explicandae iuxta S. T. et veriorem.

Case 131. *Are all blasphemies against God or the Saints of the same sort, and must they necessarily be explained in confession?*

I reply firstly that all theologians agree that heretical blasphemies, that is those containing heresy, and which proceed from a formal hatred of God or the Saints are to be distinguished in species from non-heretical ones and from other types of blasphemy; and so these two types are to be distinctly explained. I reply secondly that the judgement which says that it is not necessary to explain distinctly the aggravating circumstances is probable in both cases of blasphemy, and others too; thus Sanchez [ref.] and others. I reply thirdly that the judgement which affirms that it is necessary in both cases is more probable, because blasphemy against God is contrary to the worship owed to the divine; blasphemy against the Saints is only contrary to the respect owed to men and created beings. Therefore they are distinguished in species, since the latter essentially respects the excellence of what has been created, the former the uncreated. Thus, Suarez [ref.] and others. Indeed, I believe that blasphemy against the Blessed Virgin is to be distinguished as an incomplete species of sin from blasphemy against the other Saints or Angels, in so far as she is the Mother of God and has outstanding excellence. Between the Saints and Angels, however, there is only greater dignity within the same kind of veneration due to them, which proves the judgement. There are however aggravating circumstances which it is not essential to explain, according to St Thomas Aquinas and the truer judgement.

[132] Quaenam poenae blasphemantibus imponuntur iure canonico? et an sit vllum praeceptum reprehendendi [fo. 85ᵛ] blasphemantem, quando nulla spes emendationis? Respondeo 1º quod c. statuimus de maledicis et concil. Lateran. sub Leone X. s. 9. de reformatione curiae §. ad absoluendum Respondeo inquam, quod nec poenae in illo c. nec decretum concilii vsu recepta esse, vt docet Tan: d. 1ᵃ. de fide q. 8. n. 144. Sanch. l. 2. Sᵃ. c. 32. n. 44. cum Armilla, Sa, Azor et Suario. ideoque hodie non obligare. Navar. tamen in Sum. c. 12. n. 83. Lopes, et Ledesma apud Sanch. cit. docent decretum illud vere obligare, et esse in vsu servandum. rursus c. siquis. 22. q. 1ᵃ. Clericus blasphemus deponendus est. sed lex haec loquitur ad Iudices, adeoque ipso facto non incurritur, nec nunc est in vsu, vt ex communi docet Suar. cit. Respondeo 2º. Navar. et alios tenere quod sub mortali teneatur audiens graviter increpare blasphemantem, si id facere possit sine suo periculo, licet nulla sit spes emendationis, quia ita statuit C. Lateran. concedens ius novum. sed Sanch. Tan. et Suar. cum aliis docent decretum illud iam non esse vsu receptum, nec obligare.

Case 132. *What punishments are imposed by canon law on blasphemers? And is there any precept commanding us to censure a blasphemer when there is no hope of improving him?*
I reply firstly that the Canon Law [ref.] and the decree of the Lateran Council under Leo X [ref.] punishing this have not been received by usage (as Tanner [ref.] and Sanchez [ref.] teach, with Armilla, Sa, Azor, and Sayer), and so today they do not oblige. However, Navarre [ref.], Lopes, Ledesma, as reported by Sanchez in the place cited, teach that that decree truly obliges and is in use and is to be obeyed. Again, another canon [ref.] lays down that a blaspheming clergyman is to be deposed, but this law speaks to judges and so the penalty is not incurred without a trial, and is not now in use, as Suarez teaches in the place cited. I reply secondly that Navarre and others hold that a person is bound under pain of mortal sin to upbraid someone s/he hears uttering grave blasphemies, if it can be done without danger to her/himself, even if there is no hope of the improvement of the blasphemer, because the Lateran Council laid this down, making a new law. But Sanchez, Tanner and Suarez, with others, teach that this decree is not yet received through usage, and does not oblige.

[133] An iuramentum Alumnorum Seminariorum Anglicanorum quod praestant, se absolutis studiis in Angliam ituros etc. impediat ingressum religionis. Navar l. 3. concil. de regularibus affirmat. probat, quia omne iuramentum quod est in bonum tertii est praeferendum vitae religiosae vt constat ex communi apud Sanch. l. 3. S^a. c. 9. n. 19. quam sequitur Laym: c. 6. de iuramento n. 6. et ex communi etiam sententia quam sequitur Sanch. cit. c. 31. n. 3. et Laym cit. asserente iuramentum homini praestitum non posse propria autoritate commutari in aliquid melius, nec in ingressum religionis et ex communi etc. recepta illa regula iuris canonici ex c. quamvis pactum de pact. in 6. et ex c. cum contingat: de iureiurando et ex glossa descripta [fo. 86] nempe iusiurandum homini praestitum servandum est quoties sine peccato sive salutis dispendio fieri posset: alioquin enim fieret iniuria et damnum tertio quod est contra iustitiam. sed iuramentum dictum est in bonum Ecclesiae Anglicanae, ergo praeferendum est voto, vel ingressui religionis.

2$^\text{o}$. probat in Enchiridion ad 3. negando votum religiosum excedere omne aliud bonum, quia martyrium est eo maius, vt ait D. Th. 2. 2$^\text{ae}$. q. 124. n. 3. atqui iuramentum dictum videtur satis obligare martyrio, ergo. Layman. in sum: c. 6. de iur. n. 6. versus exinde patet, citat et sequitur Navar, cum hac limitatione, quod dicti Alumni nequeant sine dispensatione religionem ingredi in qua voto satisfacere nequeunt (qualis est Carthusianorum etc. quae propriae saluti solum ex vi institutionis incumbunt.) quia eorum iuramentum factum est in vtilitatem Anglicanae Ecclesiae. Censet ergo Laym: partim cum Nav. partim contra quatenus

putat dictos Alumnos posse ingredi religionem in qua voto suo satisfacere possunt qualis est Societas, et aliae mendicantes, imo et mona-
chales, vt S. Benedicti. quia omnes hae possunt ire in Angliam. ergo.
Azor. to. 1º l. 11. c. 5. versus absolute reiicet sententiam Navar. quia qui
iusiurandum in melius commutat non est periurus ex c. pervenit 2º. de
iureiurando scilicet promisso non infringit: qui illud in melius mutat. et
c. scripturae de voto.
Ad rationes Nav. Respondetur servum et alios esse aliquo [modo][154]
iustitiae vinculo hominibus abstrictos, ideoque cum alterius damno
non posse eos religionem ingredi. praedictos vero Iuvenes solum esse
iureiurandi nexu Deo obligatos, quod ingressum in religionem impedire non potest. Sanch. l. 4. Sum. c. 19. q. posteriore n. 30. reiicit [fo.
86ᵛ] rationem Azor et aliorum probantium votum vel iuramentum non
infringi, si in melius mutetur; quia hoc verum est si in voto vel iuramento Deo soli facto, non vero in illis homini factis. quia fieret iniuria.
Legitima ergo ratio, inquit est, quia obligationibus his tacite conditio est
nisi transitus ad religionem placeat quod vel inde constat, quia maior
est obligatio homini debita promissionem ineundi matrimonii et tamen
vt l. 1º· de matr. d. 43. n. 3. etc. probavimus ei promissioni, quantu-
mvis iuretur inest haec conditio. haec Sanch. citans multos Casuistas et
Theologos. tenet igitur absolute sententiam Azor. contra Navar. Idem et
verbis generalibus tenet Med. cod. de restitut. q. 3. c. 8. ad 4.
Existimo sententiam Nav. absolute vt sonat esse improbabilem,
quia per se non habet probabile argumentum vt patet sententiam vero
Laymanni esse certissimam in praxi, et verissimam in speculatione:
patet quia Alumni ingredientes religionem eorum qui possunt ire in
Anglia perfectiore modo et statu implent iuramentum suum vel per se
immediate concionando etc. vel mediate per alios, quatenus iuvant alios,
vel concurrunt vt alii eiusdem institui concionentur in Anglia ergo.
Existimo tamen sententiam Azor esse longe veriorem et solidiorem,
tum quia per illud iuramentum Ecclesia Anglicana nullum acquirit ius
in iurantes, qui ei non obligantur sed Deo soli ex vi iuramenti, ergo
potest commutari in religionem tanquam in quid melius. tum quia illa
conditio tacite supponitur annexa tali iuramento vt bene Sanch. cit. tum
quia non iurant se martyrium passuros, vt male supponit Navar. sed satis
adimplent iuramentum si bona fide, finitis studiis, redeant in Anglia et
serio se applicent conversioni animarum, nec tenentur in [fo. 87] ibi tota
vita manere, ex vi iuramenti, at ex vi susceptae religionis tenentur in ea
perfectissima, et difficilissima vita ad mortem vsque durare, adeoque
haec secunda obligatio est gravior, et perfectior priore, ergo prima potest
commutari in secundam autoritate propria, vt optime Sanch. et Azor. cit.

---

[154] Bracketed thus in MS, indicating a correction.

Denique nostram tenet Reverendissimus Malderus, refutans Navar. 2. 2^{ae}. tr. 10. c. 6. de iuramento d. 3. dicens huiusmodi iuramentum tacite habere exceptum, casum ingressus religionis eo quod solum aut principaliter Deo obliget cui, ob perpetuitatem religio gratior est.

Case 133. *Does the oath which the students of the English seminaries take, swearing to go to England etc., when they have finished their studies, prevent them from entering religion?*

Navarre [ref.] says that it does. He proves this by saying that every oath which is for the good of a third party is to be preferred to the religious life, as is clear by the common judgement in Sanchez, whom Laymann [refs] follows. This judgement of Sanchez and Laymann [refs] holds that once an oath has been made to a man it cannot be commuted into something better on one's own authority, and not into the entry into religion; and this is supported by the common judgement, according to the accepted rule of the canon law [ref.] and the explanation of the Gloss [ref.], which is that without a doubt when an oath to a man has been made it is to be kept when this can be done without sin or loss of salvation. For otherwise, injury and harm would be done to the third party, which is contrary to justice. But the said oath is for the good of the English Church and therefore it is to be preferred to a religious vow, or the entry into religion.

Secondly, Navarre proves [ref.] his point by denying that the religious vow exceeds all other goods, because martyrdom is greater than it, as St Thomas Aquinas [ref.] says; but the said oath seems sufficient to oblige to martyrdom, which proves the argument. Laymann [ref.], in contrast, while clarifying, citing and following Navarre, does so with this limitation, that the said alumni cannot without dispensation enter a religious order in which they cannot keep their oath (such as the Carthusians etc. who are only concerned with their own salvation by virtue of their Rule), because their oath is made for the utility of the English Church. Therefore Laymann's judgement is partly with Navarre and partly against, since he thinks that the said alumni may enter a religious order in which they may fulfil their oath, like the Society and the other mendicant orders, and also the monastic orders, like St Benedict's, because all of these may go to England. This establishes the point. Azor [ref.] on the other hand absolutely rejects the judgement of Navarre, arguing that if someone commutes his oath into something better he is not a perjurer according to the canon [ref.]; and secondly, someone who changes an oath into something better does not break the oath or promise, according to a further canon [ref.]

To the reasons given by Navarre it may be replied that a slave and others who are bound to men by some bond of justice, may not enter religion without harming another person. But the aforesaid seminarists are simply obliged to God by swearing an oath, which cannot prevent them entering religion. Sanchez [ref.] rejects the reason of Azor and others who approve of the view that a vow or oath is not broken if it is changed into something better; Sanchez's reason is that this is true of a vow or oath made to God alone, but not of those which are made to man, because injury might be done in that case. Therefore there is a legitimate reason to break the seminarists' vow, he says, because in these obligations there is the tacit condition which says, 'unless I have entered religion'. This judgement is pleasing because it is agreed that the promise of entering matrimony is greater than an obligation owed to a man, but we have proved in our book on marriage, Case 43, n. 3, that when this promise is made it is has within it this same condition. Sanchez, therefore, holds absolutely the judgement of Azor, citing many casuists and theologians, against Navarre. The same judgement, in words which can be applied more generally, Medina [ref.] holds.

I think the judgement of Navarre taken literally and in isolation is improbable, because in itself it does not have a probable argument, as is clear. I think the judgement of Laymann to be in truth most certain in practice and most true in theory. This is shown because students who enter religion, and those of them who can go to England, fulfil their oath in a more perfect way, and in a more perfect condition of life; either immediately by themselves preaching etc., or indirectly, through helping and training others who then go to England to preach. This proves the argument.

I think the judgement of Azor however to be by a long way the truer and more solid one. This is first because by that oath the English Church acquires no right in the oath-takers, who are not obliged to it, but to God alone by virtue of the oath; therefore it may be commuted into religion as into something better. Second, because the condition mentioned above is tacitly supposed to be annexed to such an oath, as Sanchez shows well in the place cited. Third, because they do not swear that they will suffer martyrdom, as Navarre wrongly assumes, but they sufficiently fulfil the oath if with good faith, having finished their studies they return to England and seriously apply themselves to the conversion of souls. Nor are they bound to stay there for their whole life, by virtue of the oath; but by virtue of having taken up religion they are bound to stay as religious until death in that most perfect and difficult life. And so that second obligation is more grave and more perfect than the first one, therefore the first may be commuted into the second on the individual's own authority, as Sanchez and Azor show well in the place cited.

Finally our judgement is held by the Most Reverend Malderus, who refutes Navarre [ref.], and says that an oath of this sort tacitly has as an exception the case of entering religion, because it simply or principally is an obligation owed to God, to whom the religious life is more pleasing, on account of its perpetuity.

[134] An liceat offerre iuramentum ei, qui creditur falso iuraturus? Respondeo non sine grave et iusta causa; quia ex charitate obligatur quisquam evitare peccatum alterius nec illi occasionem peccati prae-bere. licere tamen ex gravi causa. ob magnum commodum tuum asse-quendum, aut magnum malum tuum, aut alienum evitandum. quia tunc solum permittitur peccatum alterius, eo quod habeas ius ad offerendum alteri iuramentum. Sic licet Ethnico securitatis causa deferre iura-mentum licet sit iuraturus per Iovem; quia tum solum petis, vt alter iuret, ad quod ius habes, si adsit causa iusta, quod potest bene praestari et licitum est. alterius igitur malitiae (quam tu iuste permittere potes) est adscribendum, quod periuret, vel per falsum Deum iuret, ita ex communi Less. d. 10. et Sanch. l. 3. Sᵃ. c. 8. citati.

Case 134. *Is it lawful to offer an oath to someone when you believe he will swear falsely?*

I reply: not without grave and just cause, because out of charity everyone is obliged to prevent the sin of another and not to give him an occasion for committing sin. It is however lawful for a grave cause, in order to achieve your own great benefit, or to avoid your own great harm, or that of another, because then it is only to permit the sin of another, since you have the right to offer someone an oath. Thus it is lawful to ask a heathen to swear an oath, to confirm an agreement, although he will swear by Jove, because then you only ask another to swear, which you have a right to do if there is a just cause, which he may perform lawfully and well. Therefore, it is to be ascribed to the malice of another (which you may justly permit) if he perjures himself, or if he swears by false gods. Thus, from the common judgement, Lessius [ref.] and Sanchez [ref.].

[135] An alter coniunx possit omnia vota alterius irritare? Respondeo 1ᵒ. valde probabilem esse sententiam asserentem maritum posse solum ea vota vxoris irritare, quae vel iuri eius in vxorem incommodant, vel ad familiae administrationem pertinent: vxorem non posse mariti vota irritare, nisi eius iuri officiant. ita Less. l. 2. c. 40. d. 15. citans alios. Respondeo 2ᵒ. valde etiam probabile esse maritum posse omnia vxoris vota post [fo. 87ᵛ] initum matrimonium facta irritare. vxorem vero posse irritare omnia et sola illa mariti, quae sibi praeiudicant quoad mode-ratam debiti redditionem vel mutuam cohabitationem, vt sunt vota casti-tatis et longae peregrinationis etc. ita Sanch. l. 4. S. c. 34. prior pars probatur quia vir est absolute caput vxoris etc. ergo. 2ᵃ. probatur quia

vxor habet ius ad debitum coniugale, vt vir eius cum ea cohibitet, ergo potest omnia impedimenta reddere irrita.

Case 135. *May one spouse invalidate all the vows of the other?*

I reply firstly that the judgement is most probable which maintains that the husband may only invalidate those vows of his wife which either infringe his rights over his wife, or pertain to the administration of the family; the wife may not invalidate the vows of her husband unless they obstruct her right. Thus, Lessius [ref.], citing others. I reply secondly that it is also most probable that the husband may invalidate all the vows made by his wife since the beginning of the marriage. The wife in truth may invalidate all, and only, those vows of her husband which prejudice her as far as concern the moderate discharge of his marital duty, or mutual cohabitation; for example, vows of chastity, and of long pilgrimage, etc. Thus, Sanchez [ref.]. The first part is proved because the man is absolutely the head of the wife etc., which proves the point. The second is proved because the wife has a right to her conjugal dues; for example, that her husband live with her. Therefore she may render all impediments to this invalid.

[136] An vovens ieiunare toto anno teneatur ieiunare in Dominicis, et die nativitatis, si cadit in diem Sabbati. <u>Respondetur negative quoad vtrumque</u>, quia intentio implicita voventis est ieiunare iuxta morem Ecclesiae, quae diebus illis non ieiunat. ergo. 1^m. tenet Sanch. l. 2. S. c. 39. n. 20. citans Tabienam. 2^m. tenet Laym. c. 8. de voto. n. 3. citans Molinam et Azor. qui rem tenent sed ob aliam rationem, quam non probo.

Case 136. *Is someone who vows to fast for the whole year bound to fast on Sundays and on Christmas Day if it falls on the Sabbath day?*

A negative reply should be given as far as both are concerned, because the implicit intention of the person making the vow is to fast according to the custom of the Church, which on those days mentioned is not to fast. This proves the point. The first judgement (concerning Sundays) is held by Sanchez [ref.] citing Tabiena; the second (concerning Christmas Day) by Laymann [ref.], citing Molina and Azor, who hold this opinion but for other reasons, with which I do not agree.

[137] An obligent vota non ludendi? <u>Respondeo 1º. certum esse</u> quod vota non ludendi chartis, aleis etc. si fiant ob bonam finem esse valida, et servanda, ita Sanch. 3. S. c. 18. n. 10. quia talis abstinentia est Deo grata evitatque gravia mala, iuramenta, rixas etc. <u>Respondeo 2º</u>. vota, vel iuramenta (eadem enim est ratio) non ludendi cum persona detracta, vel in domo detracta, vel detracto ludo, quando per illa non aufertur

libertas ludendi cum aliis in aliis locis, aliisque ludis, non obligant communiter, quia sunt de rebus indifferentibus nil enim refert si poteris absolute ludere cum aliis et in aliis locis, aliisque ludis, quod cum hoc vel illo ludas. talia tamen vota obligant quando res illae detractae, seu circumstantiae, personae, ludi, aut loci sunt occasiones alicuius mali, rixarum etc. [fo. 88] quia his casibus res illae iam sunt bonae et Deo gratae ita Sanch. cit n. 9.

Case 137. *Do vows not to gamble oblige?*

I reply firstly that it is certain that vows not to play cards or dice etc., if they are made for a good end, are valid and to be observed; thus, Sanchez [ref.]. This is because such abstinence is pleasing to God and avoids grave ills, swearing, and quarrels etc. I reply secondly that vows or oaths (for the reason is the same in both cases) not to play with a disreputable person, or in a disreputable house, or at a disreputable game (when the liberty of playing with others, in other places, and in other games, is not given up by such vows) do not bind according to the common judgment, because they are about things indifferent. For it is of no importance whether you do or do not play with this person or that, if you can perfectly well play with others, and in other places, and with other games. However, such vows oblige when those disreputable aspects, or circumstances, of the people you play with, the games, or the places, are the occasions of some evil, of quarrels etc., because then in these cases the vows themselves are good and pleasing to God; thus, Sanchez [ref.].

[138] An parentes possint irritare vota filiorum. Respondeo 1°. patrem posse irritare omnia vota impuberum (marium vsque ad 14. expletum, faeminarum vsque ad 12. expletam) ita ex communi Less. l. 2. c. 40. de voto. dub. 14. Tan. q. 4. de voto. d. 2. Valen. q. 6. p. 6. et Suar. l. 6. de voto. c.6. colligitur ex c. mulier 32. q. 2. et c. 1°. de regular. in 6. idem dicendum de tutore respectu pupilli. Mater vero non potest nisi mortuo tutore, esse loco tutoris quia non ipsa, sed tutor habet patriam potestatem. ratio, quia ante annum pubertatis filii non videntur apti ad se obligandum Deo, nisi dependenter a voluntate patris, vel tutoris quibus subduntur eorum voluntates. Possunt etiam irritari impuberum vota a praedictis postquam ad aetatem puberum venerint vt bene citati. quia pertractum temporis non amiserunt potestatem quam habuerunt; et vota illa erunt tacite conditionata, nisi parens vel tutor contradixerit, etc. ergo. Quod etiam intelligendum, si se aliquid facturos voverint cum ad pubertatem venerint, vt optime Less. Respondeo 2°. Pater tutor vel tutrix nequeunt vota puberum irritare, nisi vel disciplinae familiae, vel potestati patriae obsint. ita Less. et Tan. ex communi. patet quia horum vota solum subsunt parentibus etc. ratione materiae, et non dominii in

voluntatem vnde vota religionis castitatis, sacrorum Ordinum etc. irritari non possunt: possunt tamen vota ieiunii longae peregrinationis etc. quae ad gubernationem domesticum spectant. Realia et vota iritari possunt (nisi habeant bona Castrensia vel quasi castrensia) [fo. 88ᵛ] a praedictis, vsque ad annum 25. quia ante, non habent administrationem bonorum; secus tamen est de votis realibus quae referuntur in tempus quo erunt sui iuris, quia haec non officiunt administrationi parentum, vel curatorum. vt bene Less. cit. ex communi.

Case 138. *May parents invalidate the vows of their children?*

I reply firstly that a father may invalidate all the vows of those below the age of puberty (of males before they have reached the age of 14, of females before they have reached the age of 12); thus, by common judgement, Lessius, Tanner, Valentia and Saurez [refs]. The same is to be said about a guardian in respect of a ward. A mother indeed may not take the place of guardian, unless the guardian has died; because she has not, but the guardian has, paternal power. The reason is that before the age of puberty children do not seem capable of obliging themselves to God, unless dependently on the will of the father or guardian, to whom their wills are made subject. The vows made by those below the age of puberty may also be invalidated by the aforesaid people after the children have arrived at the age of puberty, as is well argued by those cited, because with the passage of time they do not lose the power which they had, and those vows had the tacit condition 'unless the parent or guardian should contradict it' etc., which proves the point. This argument is also understood to apply if they vow that they will do something when they come to puberty, as Lessius shows well. I reply secondly that the father, or the guardian (male or female) cannot invalidate the vows of those who have reached the age of puberty, unless they obstruct the discipline of the family or the power of the father. Thus, Lessius and Tanner, from the common judgement. This is clear because the vows of these children are only subject to the parents etc. by reason of parental control in material matters, and not because of the dominion of parents over the wills of their children. Hence, a vow of religion, chastity, holy orders, etc. cannot be invalidated, but vows of fasting, long pilgrimage etc. may be, because they have an impact on the management of the household. Vows regarding property may also be invalidated (unless the children have military or clerical income, over which they retain property rights)¹⁵⁵ by the aforesaid adults, until the children reach the age

---

¹⁵⁵ *Bona castrensia*, 'the goods of the camp', signified money or other property derived from military service; *quasi-castrensia* meant money or other property derived from ecclesiastical benefices, or the liberal professions (because 'the clergy are spiritual soldiers',

of 25, because before that age they do not have control over property. It is different however concerning vows about property which refer to a future time when they will have their own rights, because that does not hinder the management of parents, or of guardians, as Lessius shows well in the place cited, following the common judgement.

[139] Quae conditiones requiruntur ad ludum iustum, et an, qui ludo vetito aliquid est lucratus teneatur ad illud restituere et qui ludo vetito perdidit, an teneatur in conscientia solvere? Respondeo ad 1^m. requiri 3. conditiones ad ludum iustum, et licitum. 1^a. vt ludentes habeant liberam dispositionem rei, quam in ludum exponunt. 2^a. vt alter non pertrahat alterum ad ludendum per gravem iniuriam vt nimis fraude etc. vt si se simulet imperitum, cum sit peritus. etc. quia si sic pertractus, prodat, alter est causa eius damni, per gravem iniuriam, quia iure naturae. contractum irritat ex communi. Molina tamen et Garcias putant ex contrario fundamento probabili dictum coactorem victorem acquirere dominium lucri et non teneri ad restitutionem ante sententiam Iudicis. 3^a. vt ludentes vt[156] vtantur fraude contra leges ludi; quia id esset iniuste decipere. possunt tamen licite et iuste vti fraudibus, et astutiis communi consuetudine receptis. vide Less. l. 2. c. 25. d. 2. Tan. d. 4. q. 6. dub. 11. Respondeo ad 2^m. eum qui lucratum est aliquid ludo vetito, iure, vel a republica non teneri restituere ante sententiam Iudicis ita ex communi Tan. s. n. 306. Less. d. 3. et Sal. d. 5. de ludo. probatur quia iure naturali per talem lusum transfertur dominium: ius enim civile vel Ecclesias-ticum id non impedit, sed solum dat actionem ad repetendum in iudicio, quod perdidit. Adverte tamen non esse mortale ludos lege vetitos exer-cere, quia tales leges censentur solum leviter obligare [fo. 89] pro saecu-laribus, vt docent Doctores communiter: secus pro Clericis, si saepe ludant aleis, et ludis vetitis in iure canonico peccant enim mortaliter contra canones, et Trident. s. 22. c. 1°. de reform. Erit tamen solum veniale, vel omnino nullum, si semel, bis, terve tantum Clericus sic luserit, vt bene Less. S^a. et Sal. d. 24. recte explicant c. penult. de vita, et honest: clericorum et alias leges Ecclesiasticas de assiduitate, ludendi aleis, et taxillis, non autem pro vna, vel altera vice, etsi magna sit quantitas. Ex dictis sequitur non posse eum, qui perdidit vti secreta, et furtiva recompensatione ad recuperandum, quod ludo vetito perdidit ita Less. Tan. cit. Sal. d. 28. Respondetur ad 3^m. Medin: apud Less. d. 4. tenere solvendum in foro conscientiae quod ludo vetito perditum, quia iure naturali quisque tenetur implere promissa, repetere tamen potest

---

see L. Lessius, *De iustitia et iure* (Antwerp, 1612), l. 2, c. 4, dub. iii). Apparently, children had full rights over such property.
156   This looks like a miscopy for: *non*

in iudicio. Less. tamen cum Nav. negat in iure Caesareo communiter solvendum quia illic sancitum est, vt victus non cogatur solvere atqui parum est non cogi in foro externo, si cogatur in interno. ergo.

Case 139. *What conditions are required for a just game; and is a person who has won something in a forbidden game bound to restore it; and is a person bound in conscience to pay what he has lost in a forbidden game?*

I reply to the first question that three conditions are required for a game to be just and lawful. Firstly, that the players must have free disposition of the property they expose to risk in the game. Secondly, that one person does not entice another to play by using grave injustice or great fraud etc.; for example, by pretending to be unskilled, when he is skilled, etc. Thus, if having enticed the other in this way, he beats him in the game, he is the cause of the latter's loss, by practising grave injustice; and by the law of nature this invalidates a contract (for example, to play a game) according to the common judgement. Molina, however, and Garcias de Loaisa think from a different starting point that it is probable that the said winner of the money acquires ownership of it, and is not bound to restore it before the sentence of a judge. The third condition for a just game is that the players should not use fraud contrary to the laws of the game, because that is to deceive unjustly. They may however lawfully and justly use the frauds and craftiness which are accepted by common custom; see Lessius and Tanner [refs]. I reply to the second question that if someone has won something in a forbidden game, he is not bound by law or by the state to restore it before the sentence of a judge; thus, from the common judgement, Tanner, Lessius and Salas [refs]. This is proved, because, by the law of nature, ownership of property is transferred by such a game, and the civil and ecclesiastical law do not impede this transfer, but only give people leave to seek in the courts restitution of what they have lost. Notice however that it is not a mortal sin to play games forbidden by law, because such laws are judged not to impose a heavy obligation on laymen, as the doctors commonly teach. It is different with the clergy if they frequently play at dice and games forbidden by canon law, for they sin mortally against the canons and the Council of Trent [ref.]. It will however only be a venial sin or none at all, if a clergyman only plays in this way once, twice, or three times, as is well shown by Lessius and Salas [refs], who rightly explain that the canon [ref.] and other laws of the Church concerning the frequency of playing at dice and backgammon do not however apply for one, or two occasions, even if the number of games played on each occasion is great. From what has been said it follows that the loser may not use secret and furtive methods of compensation to recover what he has lost in a forbidden game; thus, Lessius, Tanner and Salas [ref.]. It is replied to the third question by Medina, cited by Lessius [ref.], that a man who has lost money in a forbidden game is bound in conscience to pay it, because by the law of nature everyone is bound to keep his promises; however, he may reclaim it afterwards in the courts. Lessius, however, with Navarre, deny that Roman law commonly requires payment, because there it is decreed that the loser is not bound to pay, suggesting that it is wrong to argue that there is a conscientious duty to pay, if the courts do not enforce this; which proves that judgement.

[140] An qui ludo, vel sponsione certum moraliter de victoria ob peritiam etc. potest iuste lucrum tenere? <u>Respondeo partem affirmantem</u> esse sat probabilem, si absit fraus, vel simulatio, quae ludo, vel sponsioni causam dedit, tunc enim pars negans est certa ex dictis casu praecedente ad 1^m. ita Tan. S^a. n. 313. citans Decium et Covar. et probabilem putat Sal. d. 22. quia in his quaeritur victoria vel fortunae, vel industriae, vel scientiae, vnde si tua scientia etc. sit maior, non teneris eam patefacere, sed satis est, si fraude, vel simulatione non tegas, qua Adversarius decipiatur. quisque enim, in ludo vel sponsione censetur suas partes agere, igitur alter suae imprudentiae, temeritate etc. [fo. 89^v] tribuat, quod ignotum prouocaverit, vel provocatus, periculo prodendi se exposuerit, non examinata Adversarii peritia. <u>contrariam tamen. Less. d.</u> 5 et Sal. S^a. tenet, estque communior. probat Sal. quia in ludo vel sponsione par debet esse conditio ludentium etc. alias non servatur aequalitas iustitia, [sed recte]^{157} quia error, vel dolus dat causam contractui, si enim hic alterius peritiam nosset, nollet cum eo suam committere. Sed recte <u>respondet Sal. hoc fundamentum esse minus</u> solidum, quia error sine dolo vel fraude, et qui non est circa substantiam contractus, iure naturali, nec irritat contractum nec reddit irritabilem, sed nostro casu nil horum intervenit. ergo.

Case 140. *May someone who is morally certain of victory in a game or wager, because of his skill etc., justly keep the winnings?*

I reply that it is probable enough that he may, if he used no fraud or pretence to initiate the game or wager; for if he did, it is certain that he may not, according to what has been said to the first question in the previous case; thus, Tanner [ref.], citing Decius and Covarrubias. Salas [ref.] thinks it is probable that he may keep his winnings, because the victory is gained in these games either by fortune, industry or knowledge. Hence if your knowledge etc. is greater, you are not bound to make it clear; but it is sufficient that you do not conceal it

---

157 Bracketed thus in MS, indicating a correction.

by fraud or pretence, so that your adversary is deceived. If he does not act in this way, anyone who takes part in a game or wager is judged to have played his part acceptably; and his opponent may attribute it to his own imprudence and rashness if through ignorance he challenged someone to a game, or accepted a challenge, and exposed himself to the danger of losing, without having looked into the skill of his adversary. The contrary, however, Lessius and Salas [refs] hold, and it is more common. Salas gives as proof of this judgement, that in a game or wager the abilities etc. of the players should be equal, otherwise equity and justice are not served, and the contract agreeing to play was made through error or deceit; for if he had known then of the skill of the other person, he would not have committed himself to play against him. But Salas rightly responds that the foundation of this judgement is less solid than that of the previous one, because error without fraud or trickery, and which does not concern the substance of a contract (none of which is present in this case), by natural law does not invalidate that contract, and does not render it susceptible to invalidity, which proves our judgement.

[141] Quotuplex rerum venalium pretium? Respondeo duplex. ita ex communi Salas. dis. 4. de empt. alterum esse legitimum, quod lege principis, vel reipublicae vel eorum autoritate taxatum est: alterum, vulgare seu naturale, seu forense quod sine humana lege ex rerum naturis conditionibus, et circumstantiis oritur, et a vulgo vel foro defenditur. pretium legitimum consistit in indivisibili, vnde non licet plus recipere, et omnis excessus est restituendus. pretium vulge, seu naturale non consistit in indivisibili, sed latitudinem habet, supremum v.g. 105. medium 100. infimum. 95. seu rigorosum moderatum vel pium, minimum, vnde licet rem eandem iuxta triplicem hanc aestimationem vendere, si tanti valeat. vtrumque est. S. Th. 2. 2ᵃᵉ. q. 77. a. 1. ad 1. Less. 2. c. 21. dis. 2. et communis.

Case 141. *How many types of price are there for the sale of goods?*
I reply, two types; thus, from the common judgement, Salas [ref.]. One type is the legitimate price which is fixed by the law of the prince or state, or by their authority. The other type is the vulgar, natural or market price, which without the intervention of human law, arises from the nature of the goods, their condition and the circumstances, and is maintained by the people or the market. The legitimate price remains invariably fixed; so it is not lawful to receive more, and everything in excess must be restored. The vulgar or natural price does not remain invariably fixed, but has latitude; for example, the highest or rigorous price, 105; the medium, moderate or just price, 100; the worst or lowest price, 95. Hence it is lawful to sell the same article according to this

three-fold estimation, if it is worth it. Both prices are dealt with by St Thomas Aquinas, Lessius [refs], and commonly.

[142] An liceat res pretiosas et raras, v. g. Falcones canes insignes, aves Indicas, statuas antiquas picturas etc. vendere quanti velit Dominus? Respondeo 1º. multos negare, quos citant, et sequuntur Less. l. 2. c. 21. d. 3. et Sal. d. 5. de venditione. probant 1º. [fo. 90] quia iustum pretium talium rerum est limitatum iuxta prudentem aestimationem peritorum mercatorum, ergo iniuste plus accipitur. 2º. quia talium rerum datur pretium certum et determinatum in ordine ad vsus humanos. 3º quia alioquin venditor, rem aestimans bona fide 10. posset eam 100. vel 1000. vendere, si videret principem aliquem ea delectari, quod absurdum. Respondetur melius affirmative. ita Sa. v. venditio. n. 14. vbi hanc regulam universalem tradit: cum non est pretium taxatum rebus ad vitam non necessariis, vt aureis, argenteis, margaritis etc. potest accipi quantum emens sciens et prudens. Sot. l. 6. de iust. q. 2. a. 3. fin. Tol. 8. sum. c. 48. n. 2. dicens non esse contra iustitiam accipere 4000 aureos pro statua antiqua, gemma etc. Val. d. 5. q. 20. de empt. p. 2. et 30. Ban. Ledes. Man. Medin. apud Sal. Sª. Probatur 1º. quia huiusmodi res, non habent pretium determinatum autoritate principis, nec communi vsu fori: ergo sola voluntate contrahentium 2º. quia cum hae res non sint necessariae vitae humanae eo ipso quod emptor velit dare tantum pretium, quantum exigitur vltra pretium naturale censetur excessum donare quia alioquin non emeret tanto pretio, cum non necessitetur ad emendum. Venditio ergo et emptio praedictorum habent admixtam donationem liberalem adeoque licet ratio venditionis praecise non potest plus accipere, quam valeat res naturaliter. potest tamen ratio donationis admixtae. confirmatur 1º. quia vt ex Nav. admittit Less. cit. n. 17. si venditor sit valde affectus erga rem suam, potest hunc suum affectum aestimare si bona fide id fiat, ergo a priore etc. 2º. quia praxis totius fere orbis a nobis stat.

Case 142. *Is it lawful for the owner of precious and rare things (for example, falcons, pedigree dogs, birds from the Indies, antique statues, pictures etc.) to sell them at the price he wishes?*
I reply firstly that many deny this: they are cited, and followed, by Lessius and Salas [refs]. They prove this firstly, because the just price of such things is fixed according to the prudent estimation of skilful merchants; therefore, it is unjust to accept more. Secondly, because such things are given a price which is certain and settled according to the uses to which people put them. Thirdly, because otherwise the seller valuing the thing in good faith at 10, could sell it at 100 or at 1000 if a prince should see it and be delighted with it; which is absurd. But the question is better answered in the affirmative; thus, Sa [ref.], where he

gives this universal rule: since there is no fixed price for things which are not necessary for life, like gold, silver, pearls, etc., as much may be accepted as a prudent and knowledgeable buyer is willing to give. Soto and Toletus [refs] say it is not against justice to accept 4000 gold pieces for an antique statue, a jewel etc; see Valentia [ref.], Bannes, Ledesma, Manuel, and Medina, cited by Salas. This is proved firstly, because things of this sort do not have a price laid down by the authority of the prince, nor by the common use of the market; therefore the price can only be decided by agreement between the contracting parties. Secondly, since these things are not necessary to human life, and since the buyer wishes to give such and such a price (as much as is demanded beyond the natural price), he is judged to donate the excess to the seller, because otherwise he would not buy at such a price, since he is not forced to buy it. The sale and the purchase therefore of the aforesaid things have mixed with them a free donation. Hence, although by reason precisely of the sale, the seller ought not to accept more than the thing is naturally worth, he may however do so by reason of this admixed donation. This is confirmed, firstly because, as Lessius admits, following Navarre [ref.], if the seller is very fond of his possession, he may give his affection a value, if he does so in good faith; this proves the point *a priori*. Secondly, because the practice of almost the whole world stands with us.

[143] An liceat transgredi legem taxantem triticum etc. dummodo servetur pretium, quod seclusa lege [fo. 90ᵛ] iustum esset. <u>Respondetur negative ita ex communi Sal. d. 6. de</u> emp. quia leges civiles, quae respiciunt bonum commune quales sunt taxantes pretia frumenti etc. venalis obligant graviter sub peccato mortale quia gravissima alioquin incommoda, et perturbationes orirentur nisi tales leges possint sic obligare. Et hinc infertur in magna sterilitate taxam non cessare, quia a magistratu iuste imponitur pro bono communi. ergo obligat. ita Sal.

Case 143. *Is it lawful to break the law fixing the price of wheat etc., as long as the price is observed, which, if there were no law, would be just?*
    The answer is no; thus, from the common judgement, Salas [ref.]. This is because civil laws which concern the common good, such as are those which limit the price at which corn etc. may be sold, oblige gravely under pain of mortal sin, because very grave problems and disturbances would arise, if such laws could not oblige in this way. And hence it is concluded that in times of serious harvest failure, the limit on prices should not cease, because it is justly imposed by the magistrate for the common good. Therefore it obliges; thus, Salas.

[144] An liceat vendere pretio currente, quando scitur pretium mox minuendum? Respondetur 1º. S. Th. 2. 2ᵃᵉ. q. 79. a. 3. ad 4. Caiet. ib. Sylv. v. empt. q. 15. quos citant et sequuntur Molin. d. 354. Less. c. 21. dub. 5. et Sal. dub. 32. citans Val. Rebel. Sotum, et alios affirmant cum Diogene licere, licet venditor sciat pretium mox minuendum, et maximam copiam mercium statim affuturam, idque ignoret emptor. Probatur 1º. quia res licite vendi potest iuxta communem aestimationem tunc vigentem; quia pretium iustum est, quod vel principis imperio, vel communi aestimatione imponitur: probatur 2º. quia privata scientia venditoris sensum et aestimationem non mutat, sicut nec privata scientia emptoris, quia alioquin emptor non posset emere pretio currente si sciret pretium postea valde augendum, quod tamen falsum est. vt ex c. 41. Gen. constat. vbi Ioseph omne frumentum Aegypti pretio currente comparavit, cum tamen Divina revelatione scirisset ante maximum fore annonae caritatem. Haec sententia est valde probabilis, et ex ea sequitur 1º. si scias obsidionem futuram, posse te celeriter merces vendere, non monitis emptoribus de periculo impendente. 2º. posse te elocare domum pretio solito, licet scias pretia locationum [fo. 91] minuenda, ob Aulae v. g. defectum. 3º. posse te vendere triticum pretio currente, licet scias magistratum edidisse decretum de eo minuendo, si tamen nondum sit publicatum 4º. idem dicendum de pecuniae commutatione, et alienatione etc. Respondeo 2º. Joan. de Med. q. 35. de rest. et Conradus¹⁵⁸ q. 62. et 3. de contract. teste Less. Sᵃ. et Rodrig. 2. p. Sᵃ. c. 81. n. 10. negativam tenent, cum Antipatro, et Cicerone, l. 3. off. probatur quia moraliter loquendo, et in ordine ad vsus homanum dictae merces, in casibus dictis vere sunt vitiosae sicut si essent furto ablatae, et obnoxiae restitutioni vel naturaliter ineptae vsibus, pro quibus venduntur et emuntur, ergo talis venditio iure naturali est invalida, vt est venditio mercium vitiosarum, et inutilium. secundum hanc sententiam etiam probabilem falsa sunt 1ᵃᵉ. 4. praecedentiae.

Case 144. *Is it lawful to sell at the current price when it is known that the price must soon go down?*

The reply is firstly that St Thomas Aquinas, Caietan, and Sylvester [refs] who are cited and followed by Molina, Lessius and Salas [refs], citing Valentia, Rebellus, Soto and others, affirm with Diogenes¹⁵⁹ that this is lawful. It is lawful even though the seller knows that the price soon must go down, because a large quantity of the merchandise is imme-

---

¹⁵⁸ The MS seems to read 'Iradius', but Conradus is referred to at this point by Lessius (*op. cit.* at n. 155), l. 2. c. 21. d. 5.
¹⁵⁹ Diogenes of Babylon, the Stoic philosopher, according to Cicero in *De Officiis*, believed that it was justifiable to pass on in payment forged money which you had received from somebody else.

diately about to be available, and the buyer is ignorant of that. This is proved firstly, because the merchandise may lawfully be sold according to the common valuation which then prevails; and also because the price which is imposed by command of the prince, or by the common valuation, is the just one. It is proved secondly, because the private knowledge of the seller does not change the understanding and valuation of the goods, just as the private knowledge of the buyer does not, because otherwise the buyer could not buy at the current price if he knew that the price would afterwards greatly increase, which however is false. This is clear from Chapter 41 of Genesis, where Joseph bought all the corn in Egypt at the current price, when however by divine revelation he knew that before long there would be a dearth of corn. This judgement is most probable, and from it follows, firstly, that if you know there will be a siege, you may quickly sell your merchandise, not warning the buyers of the impending danger. Secondly, you may let a house at the customary price although you know that the rent ought to be reduced because, for example, of a defect in the hall. Thirdly, you may sell wheat at the current price although you know the magistrate has issued an edict reducing the price, but the edict has not yet been published. Fourthly, the same is to be said about the exchange and sale etc. of money. I reply secondly, that Juan de Medina and Conradus [refs], according to Lessius, Sa and Rodriguez [ref.], hold the judgement which is in the negative, with Antipater[160] and Cicero in *The Offices* [ref.]. This judgement is proved because morally speaking and following the usage of men, the said merchandise in the said cases truly is defective, just as if it had been stolen by thieves and was liable to restitution, or was naturally incapable of the use for which it was being bought and sold; therefore such sale by natural law is invalid, as is the sale of goods which are defective and useless. Following this judgement, which is also probable, the four resolutions in the first reply are false.

[145] An liceat minoris emere ob anticipatam solutionem? Respondeo 1º. per se non licere, quia hoc esset re ipsa lucrari aliquod practicalem sortem ex vi implicitae mutuationis, quod tamen est vsurarium. ita Doctores communiter, quos sequuntur Less. Sª. d. 9. et Salas. d. 43. Respondeo 2º. licere tamen per accidens, vt si per illam anticipationem emptor patiatur damnum emergens vel lucrum cessens. item si esset periculum fraudis in venditore, quod vel merces non traderet, vel non stato tempore quia haec omnia pretio sunt aestimabilia. Demum quia

160 The Stoic, Antipater of Tarsus, argued (against his former master, Diogenes of Babylon), according to Cicero in *De Officiis,* that it was contrary to the 'office' or duty of a good man to make a profit by using unscrupulous business practices such as those discussed here.

hic modus vendendi inducit raritatem emptorum, et multiplicationem venditorum, adeoque facit rem decrescere.

Case 145. *Is it lawful to buy at a lower price by making an early payment before taking possession of the goods?*

I reply firstly that in itself it is not lawful, because it involves in practice making a profit on the transaction itself, by virtue of an implicit loan, which is usury. Thus, the doctors commonly teach, whom Lessius and Salas follow [refs]. I reply secondly it is, however, lawful by accident; if, for example, as a result of the early payment, the buyer should suffer unforeseen expenses, or a loss of income. Also, if there were danger of fraud on the part of the seller,[161] either because he might not deliver the goods, or not at the agreed time; this is because all these things are to be considered in estimating the price. Indeed, it is lawful because this method of selling induces a rarity of buyers, and an increase in sellers, and so it makes the goods decrease in price.

[146] An liceat illa Hispaniae aliarumque gentium praxis, qua antisipata solutione minoris emuntur lanae, quam valeant tempore emptionis. Respondeo 1º. Nav. in man. c. 23. n. 82. Medin. q. 38. de restit. in 6ª. caa. Val. q. 20. de empt. p. 2. c. 6. Rebel. l. 9. citans Mend. Pedraz. Garciam etc. [fo. 91ᵛ] condemnant praedictam consuetudinem vt vsurariam quia ratione anticipatae pecuniae atque adeo ratione mutui vsualis, quidquid dicant adversarii, vt arguit Rebel. pro reliquis lucrum intendi videtur. Respondeo 2º. Sot. l. 6. de iust. q. 4. a. 1º. ad 4. Mol. d. 360. Sa. v. empt. n. 4. Less. d. 9. et Salas d. 47. citans Tol. Angl. Caiet. Ban. Salon etc. praedictam consuetudinem probabilius excusant 1º. ratione Damni emergentis et lucri cessantis 2º. paucitatis emptorum; 3º. metus perfidiae et fraudis. 4º. quia talis venditio est ementi minus commoda. 5º. quia alia ratione non emeretur pluris quam nunc per anticipatam solutionem; quae rationes simul acceptatae talem emptionem et venditionem licitam reddunt nec est cur in re non adeo clara graves Theologi condemnentur.

Case 146. *Is the practice followed in Spain and other nations lawful, by which they buy wool, making an early payment, before taking possession of the wool, at a lower price than it would be worth at the time of delivery?*

---

[161] The terms used by casuists to justify receiving interest on a loan as a compensation were: *damnum emergens*, the emergence of a loss as a result of making a loan; *lucrum cessans*, the loss of an income to be derived from the money if it were not lent; and *periculum fraudis*, the risk of being defrauded of the loan by the borrower. See B. W. Dempsey, *Interest and Usury* (London, 1943).

I reply firstly that Navarre, Medina, Valentia, and Rebellus [refs], citing Mendoza, Pedraza, and Garcias de Loaisa etc., condemn the aforesaid custom as usurious. This is because, by reason of the early payment of the money, and by reason of the loan for use by the borrower, whatever adversaries say (as Rebellus argues, speaking for the rest), interest seems to be intended. I reply secondly that Soto, Molina, Sa, Lessius, Salas [refs], citing Toletus, Angelus, Caietan, Bannes, Salon etc., give a more probable judgement, and excuse the aforesaid custom. They do so, firstly, because of the danger to the buyer of the emergence of some expenses, and of the loss of income; secondly, because of the paucity of the buyers; thirdly, because of the fear of perfidy and fraud; fourthly, because such sale is less convenient for the buyer; fifthly, because for some other reason the merchandise might not be bought in the future for more than it is now by early payment. Which reasons, taken together, make such buying and selling lawful, and there is no reason in a matter which is not very clear, that serious theologians should condemn it.

[147] An Chyrographa, vel credita possint emi minoris, quam contineant. v. g. an ius ad 100 solvenda intra annum, possint modo emi 96. vel 7. et an chyrographa, seu librantiae possint interdum emi dimidio pretii, si difficilis, vel ambigua sit solutio? Respondetur ad 1ᵐ. negative, vt ex communi probat bene Mol. d. 361. Less. d. 8. de empt. Rebel. q. 13. et Salas d 39. probatur quia secluso omni damno emergenti et lucro cessanti periculo sortis dictae talis contractus est vsura, quia videtur implicite ratione solius temporis vel commutationis vindicans auctum supra sortem. contrarium tamen tenet Nav. Man. c. 15. n. 231. Caiet. Armil. Rosel. Bellar. olim Lovanii, et Parra Romae¹⁶² apud Salam; nec puto improbabilem, licet ab ipso debitore fiat emptio, vt docet Sa. v. deb. n. 21. quia talia debita minoris [fo. 92] putantur, quam pecunia praesens. ergo. Respondetur ad 2ᵐ. affirmative, vt bene Mol. Sᵃ. et Less. d. 9. et Sal. d. 40. probatur quia illa res in se, et venditori, non valeat nisi ½ pretium; tum quia iustum pretium pendet ex publica aestimatione, et non ex modo vnius, vel alterius ergo. hinc infertur militum chyrographa, vel librantias posse minoris emi quam valeant a mercatoribus, vel aliis aurialiabus, qui tamen obtinere solent summam integram imo et a ministris regiis, modo absit scandalum, et causa non sint, quod non fuerint solutae.

---

¹⁶² The MS reads: 'parva Roma', which is a copyist's error for 'Parra Romae'; see I. de Salas, *Commentarii in Secundam Secundae* (Louvain, 1618), p. 75. Southwell was following Salas quite closely at this point. Parra was the Jesuit teacher of Bellarmine at the Collegio Romano in the early 1560s (and it is interesting that Southwell associates the two men here), and a great Thomist; see J. Broderick, *Robert Bellarmine* (London, 1950), I 378ff.

Case 147. *May bonds or credit notes be sold for less than their face value, for example may the right to 100 to be paid within a year be sold now at 96 or 97? And may bonds or credit notes sometimes be sold at a lower price than their face value, if their final payment might be difficult or doubtful?*

It is to be replied negatively to the first, as from the common judgement Molina, Lessius, Rebellus, and Salas prove well [refs]. This is proved because, if there are no expenses likely to emerge, no loss of profit, and no danger to the said capital, such a contract is usurious, because it seems implicitly to be claiming interest on the capital, by reason of the passage of time alone or the exchange. The contrary however is held by Navarre [ref.], Caietan, Armilla, Rosella, and Bellarmine, when he was at Louvain, and Parra at Rome, as quoted in Salas. Nor do I think it improbable, even if the debtor himself makes the purchase, as Sa [ref.] teaches, because such a debt is thought to be worth less than present money. This proves the judgement. It is to be replied to the second affirmatively, as is well shown by Molina, Lessius, and Salas [refs]. This is proved because the credit note, both in itself and to the seller, may not be worth more than half its face value; in addition, because the just price depends on public estimation and not on the valuation of only one or two people. This proves the judgement. So it can be concluded that the bonds or credit notes of soldiers may be bought for less than they are worth by merchants or other money-changers, even if they usually obtain the whole sum from royal ministers, as long as there is no scandal caused and they are not the reason why the soldiers have not been paid.

[148] An si scias occulte debitorem tuum non esse solvendo, possis iis qui id nesciunt, vendere illud [pretium][163] debitum pretio ordinario? Respondetur esse iniustum, ita Less. d. 10. et Salas d. 44. quia debitum illud est intrinsece vitiosum moraliter, sicut est ius fructum in agro sterili, vel equus alienus restitutioni obnoxius. quae autem obiici possunt, sunt solum vitiosa extrinsece, et fortuiter. ergo.

Case 148. *If you know secretly that your debtor is not going to pay, may you sell the debt at its face value to people who do not know this?*

The reply is that it is unjust; thus, Lessius and Salas [refs]. This is because such a debt is morally speaking intrinsically damaged; like the right to the product of a sterile field; or a stray horse which is liable to restitution. These analogies may be objected to, however, on the grounds that such things are only extrinsically damaged, and by chance, which proves the objection.

---

163 Bracketed thus in MS, indicating a correction.

[149] An venditor teneatur emptori defectum rei venditae declarare, vti de praxi vendendi Equos vitiosos in Anglia? <u>Triplex est vitium in rebus:</u> 1^m. circa substantiam, vt si vendatur stannum pro argento. etc. 2^m. in quantitate libra v. g. pro ½ librae. etc. 3^m. in qualitate, vt si equus caecus etc. pro non caeco etc. <u>ad 1^m. vel 2^m.</u> reducitur venditio tritici mixti, et vini lymphati pro non mixtis. ita ex S. Th. 2. 2. q. 77. a. 2 Molin. D. 353. Less. d. 11. et Salas d. 345. quinque igitur regulis absolvitur quaestio. <u>1ª. vendens rem vitiosam</u> tanto. quanto si vitiosa non esset graviter peccat contra aequalitatem decipiendo, et obligatur ad restitutionem. ita omnes, vt certum. <u>2ª. non tenetur emptori</u> manifestare vitia manifesta, quae videre potest, ita Sal. [fo. 92ᵛ] d. 34. n. 3. additque bene si emptor ex negligentia ignorat, vel inadvertentia haec non videat sibi imputet, quia si negligens non esset manifesta videret. secus est si advertere nequit, vt si sit caecus, vel in ea re imperitus, tum enim venditor eum decipit, non ipse se ipsum. <u>3ª. si vitium sit occultum</u> non sat est si minuatur pretium iuxta exigentiam rei, sed tenetur (sub onere restituendi omnia damna) vitium in his tribus casibus declarare. <u>1º. si vitium sit</u> periculosum emptori. si v. g. Equus sit furiosus etc. <u>2º. si ad finem</u> emptoris res sit pars vtilis, vel invtilis, licet non sit noxia, vt invtilis medicina etc. <u>3º. si probabiliter scias</u> eum ad revendendum, si enim non aperias vitium, vendetur maiori pretio, quam res valet. in his enim fit gravis inaequalitas, si non aperiatur vitium. <u>4º. quod extra hos</u> 3 casus sufficit non dicto vitio pro eius exigentia in pretio distendere, ita Sal. Sª. n. 15. datur enim res bona, et vtilis, in quantitate debita, et aequalis pretii ergo non est iniustitia; et hoc licet emptor vitium sciens nollet rem emere: si tamen venditor non dolo nec mendacio vtens, solum negative se habet, alias enim innumerae venditiones essent iniustae, et deterrerentur emptores ab emendo, in contractu autem est aequalitas, animus vero emptoris contractui est plane extrinsecus, nec de essentia emptionis ergo. si tamen dicat emptor nolle se emere nisi vitio careat, venditio nulla, sive vitium occultum sit, sive non, sive grave, sive non, quia tunc non¹⁶⁴ ponitur conditio essentialis et expressa. ita Salas. vnde praxis Angliae. in equis vitiosis iniusta est, et ad restitutionem obligans.

5º. Emptor etiam tenetur occultas rei virtutes sibi soli notas venditori manifestare, vel saltem [fo. 93] pretium augere, si pretium rei augeat. ita Salas d. 36. n. 1. ex communi. patet ex dictis a paritate quia venditor non magis est obligandus, quam emptor vnde si venditor putet rem esse vitiosam, et emptor sciat esse sanam etc. obligatur. potest tamen non manifestando dare infimum, sicut in contrario venditor exigere supremum, vt ex Mol. Sal. Sª. <u>Licet tamen emere agrum</u> in quo latet thesaurus, vel fasciculum, in quo est herba pretiosa, quia talia commu-

---

¹⁶⁴ Thus in the MS, presumably a miscopy.

niter non aestimantur nisi ratione intrinsecae virtutis, ita communis sententia licet Angel. Armill. et Ban. probabiliter negent quia ratione vitii, mihi soli noti, teneor minuere pretium, ergo ratione virtutis mihi soli notae teneor augere.

Case 149. *Is a seller bound to declare to the buyer the defects of the thing which is for sale; for example, in the practice of selling good-for-nothing horses in England?*

Three types of defect are to be found in goods. First, concerning substance; if for example someone should sell tin as silver, etc. Second, in weight; for example a quarter sold as half a pound, etc. Thirdly, in quality; for example, if a blind horse, etc. is sold as a sighted one, etc. In either the first or second categories may be placed the sale of mixed wheat for unmixed, and watered wine for pure. Thus, from St Thomas Aquinas, Molina, Lessius, and Salas [refs]. The question is resolved by five rules. (1) Firstly, the person selling the defective goods at the same price as if they were not defective sins gravely against equity by deceiving, and is obliged to make restitution; thus, everyone, as certain. (2) Secondly, the seller is not bound to show defects to the buyer which are obvious and which the buyer can see for himself; thus, Salas [ref.]. He is right to add that if the buyer through negligence is ignorant of, or by inadvertence does not see these defects, this should be imputed to the buyer himself because if he were not negligent he would see things which were evident. It is different if the buyer could not see the defects, if for example he were blind or had no expertise in valuing these goods, for then the vendor deceives him, he does not deceive himself. (3) Thirdly, if the defect is hidden, it is not enough that the seller reduce the price according to what the defects require, but he is bound (under the penalty of restoring all the loss) to declare the defect in the three cases which follow. (a) First, if the defect is dangerous to the buyer; if for example a horse is wild etc. (b) Second, if for the purposes of the buyer the goods are only partly useful, or are useless, although they are not dangerous, as in the case of useless medicine etc. (c) Third, if you know probably that the article will be resold, for if you do not reveal the defect, the buyer will sell it at a greater price than it is worth, and in doing this, grave inequity will be done, if the defect has not been revealed. (4) Fourthly, outside these three cases (a–c above) it is sufficient to reduce the price according to what the defect requires, without mentioning it; thus, Salas [ref.]: for what is presented for sale is good merchandise, useful and in the quantity required, and at a fair price, therefore there is no injustice. And this is true even though, if the buyer knew the defect he would not want to buy the article, and even if the seller, without using trickery or lies, says nothing. For otherwise innumerable sales would be unjust, and buyers would be deterred from buying. However, there is equity in such a contract (as outlined in (4, above)), and indeed the intention of the buyer is clearly extrinsic to the contract and not of the essence of the purchase. This proves the judgement. If however the buyer says he does not wish to buy unless the article is without defects, the sale is null, whether the defect is secret or not, and whether it is serious or not, because then an essential and express condition is placed on the agreement. Thus, Salas. Hence the practice of England in the sale of good-for-nothing horses is unjust, and obliges to restitution.

(5) Fifthly, the buyer is also bound to show to the seller the hidden virtues of the merchandise known only to him, or at least to raise the price, if he may, of the merchandise. Thus, Salas [ref.], from the common judgement. This is clear from what has been said, as a matter of parity; because the seller is not to be placed under heavier obligations than the purchaser. Hence if the seller thinks the goods are defective and the buyer knows them to be good etc., he is obliged to say so. However, Salas [ref.] argues, from Molina [ref.], that without showing the defect, the purchaser may give the lowest price, just as on the other side the seller may demand the highest. So, it is lawful to buy a field in which treasure is hidden, or a bunch of flowers in which there is a valuable plant, because the value of such things is commonly not estimated except by reason of their intrinsic virtue. This is the common judgement, although Angelus, Armilla and Bannes deny it, with a probable judgement, arguing that by reason of defects known only to me, I am bound to reduce the price, and therefore by reason of a virtue known only to me I am bound to increase it.

[150] An venditiones et emptiones reciprocae eiusdem rei, Hispaniae Baratras et moratras. Italiae Itochalas, et varochalas, sint licitae? Petrus v. g. petit a Paulo mercatore 100. mutuo, renuit mutare, merces tamen vult ei vendere pretio supremo, vt possit eas cuilibet vendere numerata pecunia. reemit igitur vel potius redemit numerata pecunia, sed pretio infimo, vel medio Quaeritur an hae emptiones et venditiones licitae sint. Respondetur affirmative, 3. servatis conditionibus 1ª. vt non sit pactum implicitum vel explicitum de retrovendendo easdem Paulo. tunc enim esset vsura palliata: imponeretur enim onus vltra pretium, pretio astimabile 2ª. vt quando vendantur merces credito, non excedatur iustum pretium summum, vel infimum, quando reemuntur numerata pecunia. ita Less. l. 2. c. 21. d. 16. Salas 6. 37. et alii. 3ª. vt absit scandalum, vel magna paupertas seu necessitas mutuantis, quia in his casibus esset contra charitatem, licet non contra iustitiam. [fo. 93ᵛ] ratio est, quia prima venditio fieri potest cuicunque, ergo fieri potest Petro et secunda Paulo.

Case 150. *Is the reciprocal sale and purchase of the same thing lawful: in Spain, what is called 'Baratras and moratras'; in Italy, what is called 'Itochalas and varochalas'*[165]? *For example, Peter asks the merchant Paul for a loan of 100. Paul refuses to lend, but wishes to sell him some merchandise at the highest price, so that Peter can sell it to someone else for ready money. Peter then re-sells the goods to Paul, or rather Paul redeems them, for ready money, but at the lowest price, or the medium price. The question is, are these purchases and sales lawful?*

The answer is in the affirmative, with three reservations. First, that there is no implicit or explicit agreement to sell back the same goods to Paul, for then it would be usury in disguise, since the burden of a higher price would be imposed on Peter beyond the price at which the goods were re-sold. Second, that if merchants sell merchandise on credit, the just price (the highest or lowest) is not exceeded when it is sold back for ready money. Thus, Lessius and Salas [refs], and others. Third, that there is no scandal, and the person borrowing the money is not in great poverty or necessity, because in these cases it would be contrary to charity, even if it is not contrary to justice. The reason for the affirmative answer is that the first sale could be made to anyone, therefore it could be made to Peter; and the second sale could be made to Paul, for the same reason.

[151] An omnia monopolia sint iniusta. monopolium est vnius, vel solius in civitate venditio, vel vnica et singularis venditio. signatque apud Theologos machinationem seu industriam mercatorum, vt ipsi soli vel aliquid vendant, vel certo pretio vendant. Respondeo 1°. si fiat autoritate publica, vel aliquo pretio, vel alio modo impetrant a principe, vt sibi solis liceat aliquod genus mercium invehere, ac vendere, licitum esse vt docet Less. et Salas, si causa sit iusta, si autem merces sint necessariae reipublicae ad victum etc. tenetur princeps taxare pretium, ne monopolita vendant inique. si vero solum spectent ad luxum vel delicias, non tenetur. quod si concedatur sine iusta causa, erit etiam iniustum; fit enim iniuria emptoribus et venditoribus aliis, et sic vtrique fieri debet restitutio 1°. quidem loco ab impetrantibus privilegium quia sunt causae principales damni; 2°. a concedentibus, vt docent citati.

---

[165] The meaning of these terms is made clear in the text. Lessius (*op. cit.* at n. 155, l. 2. c. 21. dub. xvi) uses the singular forms *baratas* and *mohatras*, plural *baratae* and *mohatrae*. Salas (*In Secunda Secundae* (Louvain, 1618), p. 68) uses 'moharras', 'varatras', and 'stochalas', 'varochalas'. Cf. R. Naz, *Dictionnaire de droit canonique*, V (Paris, 1953), *s.v.* Intérêt et usure; B. Pascal, *Les Provinciales*, ed. L. Cognet (Paris, 1965), 139–41. Cognet says the word 'mohatra' derives from the Arabic for chance, risk.

Case 151. *Are all monopolies unjust? A monopoly is the sale in a city either of a unique, single commodity, or by only one person; and it means, according to the theologians, that these merchants alone may sell something they have manufactured or traded, or sell it at a fixed price.*

I reply first that if it is done by public authority; that is, if for some price or by some method, these merchants obtain from the prince the sole right to import some sort of merchandise and sell it, it is lawful, if the reason is just, as Lessius and Salas teach. However, if the goods are necessary to the commonwealth, for life etc., the prince is bound to limit the price, so that they do not sell the monopolised goods unjustly. If indeed the monopolies only involve luxuries or delicacies, the prince is not bound in this way. If the monopoly was conceded without just cause it will also be unjust, for harm is done to buyers and other sellers, and thus compensation should be made to both; in the first place, indeed, by those who obtained the privileges, because they are the principal cause of the damage; secondly by those who made the concession, as the authors cited teach.

Cases Concerning Marriage

Casus de Matrimonio R. P. Tho: Southw:[166]
(Cases concerning marriage
by the Reverend Father Thomas Southwell)

[M1] [fo. 13ᵛ] 1ᵘˢ. Quae sit materia et forma sacramenti Matrimonii? de qua re Sanch. de matr. l. 2. d. 5. Laym. de matr. p. 2. c. 2. etc. Suppono matrimonium esse proprie sacramentum nouae legis, vbi definitur in Flor. et Trid. s. 7. et 24. et cap. Abolendam de Haereticis, et sumitur ex 5. ad Ephes. Sacramentum[167] magnum. Loquitur autem ibi de matrimonio fidelium, et hoc ait significare speciali modo vnionem Christi cum Ecclesia vtque ex speciali Christi institutione atque adeo practice (id est) causando hanc vnionem et faciendo, vt sicut ciuiliter nubunt inter se coniuges, ita spiritualiter etiam nubant Christo.[168] Patres citat Bellar. l. 1. de matr. c. 3: Respondeo itaque illam esse materiam et formam huius sacramenti, quae est materia et forma matrimonii quatenus est contractus ciuilis: ita communiter[169] Theologi. ratio est quia Christus eleuauit ad sacramenti dignitatem illud ipsum matrimonium prius vsitatum;[170] quare tantum requiritur vt ponatur illa materia et forma, quae ad contractum ciuilem sufficiunt.

Hinc infero contra Canum[171] et Esthium[172] aliosque[173] Recentiores (quorum sententiam censurant alii Theologi[174]) formam[175] non esse verba sacerdotis, quia sic matrimonia clandestina olim non fuissent sacramenta, imo nec modo vbi non recipitur Trid:[176] imo nec matrimonia contracta coram Parocho et testibus sine verbis sacerdotis. Porro sine verbis istis erit materia et forma contractus validi. ergo.

Infero 2°. corpora contrahentium non esse materiam Sacramenti. ita Sanch. cit. Coninck de matr. d. 24. d. 3. Bonac. de matr. q. 2. p. 9.

---

166 S reads: *De Matrimonio*
167 S adds: *hoc*
168 S adds: *et hac de causa est signum vere magnum et efficax*
169 S adds: *fere*
170 S reads for the last two words: *quod antea non erat sacramentum*
171 S adds: *l. 8. de locis. c. 5. ad 3um*
172 S adds: *in 4°. dist. 26. §11*
173 S reads: *paucosque*
174 S reads: *Imo eorum sententia manifeste falsam, improbabilem, nota dignam, temerariam censent Vasq de matr: to: 4. in 3ᵃᵐ. partem dp. 3. Pontius, Tann, Sotus.*
175 S adds: *huius contractus*
176 S adds: *sess. 24. c. 1.*

Suar. tom. 3. p. d. 2. s. 1. et alii contra Vasq. Laym.[177] et Pontium. quia corpora sunt materia solum remota contractus, et circa quam,[178] non proxima ex qua;[179] siquidem contractus hic, sicut et caeteri est in genere actus transeuntis.

Infero 3°. contra Nauar.[180] materiam non esse merum consensum internum, [fo. 14] formam vero verba externa, quia sic tota materia sacramenti foret quid insensibile.

Dico itaque materiam et formam esse ipsos coniugum actus, qui in quantum sunt traditio suorum corporum sunt materia; in quantum acceptatio, forma ita Sanch.[181] Coninck[182], Bonac.[183] Suar. cit.[184] cum Bellar.[185] et Tan.[186] Ratio est quia contractus traditione et acceptatione essentialiter perficitur; traditio autem praecedit vt quid informe per modum materiae, acceptatio sequitur et determinat per modum formae.[187]

Case M1. *What is the matter and what the form of the sacrament of matrimony? On which subject, see Sanchez, Laymann etc. [refs].*

I lay down as a basis for our discussion that matrimony is properly speaking a sacrament of the new law, as defined at the Councils of Florence and Trent [refs], and by canon law [ref.], and derived from Ephesians 5, where St Paul calls it, 'this great sacrament'. Here he speaks, moreover, of the marriage of the faithful, and his words signify in a special way the union of Christ with the Church, by the special institution of Christ, who brings that union into practical existence; so that, as the faithful marry each other civilly, they also spiritually marry Christ. And so, for that reason, it is truly a great and powerful sign. Thus, the Fathers, whom Bellarmine cites [ref.].

I reply therefore that the matter and the form of this sacrament are

---

[177] S adds: *de matrim: p. 2. c. 2. n. 3.*
[178] S reads: *solum materia remota circa quam contractus*
[179] S adds: *intrinsece constitutur*
[180] S adds: *enchir: c. 22. n. 20*
[181] S adds: *de matrim: l. 2.dp. 5.*
[182] S adds: *de mat. dp. 24. db. 3.*
[183] S adds: *de mat. q. 21. pun : 41.*
[184] S reads: *tom: 3. in 3ͭᵃᵐ. partem dp. 9. l. 1*
[185] S adds: *de matr: l. 1. c. 6. et 7.*
[186] S adds: *hic q. 2. n. 37*
[187] S adds: *Confirmatur ex Florentino vbi nihil aliud ad matrimonium requiritur, quam consensus internus verbis aut alio signo expressus.*

Obiicies; Acceptatio potest praecedere traditionem, vt patet in postulante, nam si alter annuat, proficitur contractus, sine vlteriori actu postulantis. Argum: l. 1. § si quis de verb. obligatione, ergo non est maior ratio, cur haec sit forma quam traditio. Respondeo Acceptationem nunquam praecedere. Ad instantiam dico, postulantem dare postea acceptare saltem per taciturnitatem, et non reclamationem: Alioqui si statim reclamaret, nullus foret contractus.

the matter and form of matrimony in so far as it is a civil contract; thus, almost all theologians. The reason is that Christ elevated marriage, which had previously been used but had not been a sacrament, to the dignity of a sacrament. Hence, all that is required in order that matter and form are in place, is what is sufficient for a civil contract.

Hence I disagree with Cano, Estius and a few others of the more recent writers [refs], whose judgement other theologians censure, and which is indeed manifestly false, improbable and worthy of note for its temerity, according to Vasquez [ref.], Pontius, Tanner and Soto. I disagree with their view that the words of the priest are the form of the contract, because, if that were true, clandestine marriages as formerly contracted would not have been sacraments. Indeed, neither would marriages contracted before the parish priest and witnesses be sacraments now, where the Council of Trent is not received [ref.], without the words of a priest. But it is agreed that without these words, there will be the matter and form of a valid contract, which proves the point.

I infer secondly that the bodies of the contracting parties are not the matter of the sacrament; thus, Sanchez, Coninck, Bonacina, Suarez [refs], and others, against Vasquez, Laymann [ref.] and Pontius. This is because the bodies are only the matter from which the contract is indirectly and remotely formed, and do not closely or intrinsically constitute it, since this contract, like others, is in essence a transient act.

I infer thirdly, against Navarre [ref.], that the matter is not merely internal consent, and the form in truth the external words, because, if this were true, the matter of the sacrament would be something immaterial.

I say therefore that the matter and form are those acts of the people getting married, which in so far as they are the surrender of their bodies are the matter, and in so far as they are the acceptance of each other's bodies are the form; thus, Sanchez, Coninck, Bonacina and Suarez, with Bellarmine and Tanner [refs] The reason is that the contract is essentially perfected by surrender and acceptance. The surrender, however, comes first, in the manner of matter, as something without form; the acceptance follows and completes, in the manner of form. This is confirmed by the Council of Florence, where nothing more to marriage is required than internal consent expressed in words, or by some other sign.

You will object that acceptance may precede surrender, as is clear when someone makes a request, for if the other person nods assent, the contract is agreed, without any further act of the person making the request; as is clear from the civil law [ref.]. So there is no reason why acceptance rather than surrender should be the form. I reply that acceptance never precedes surrender. At the instance, I say, of the person making the request the surrender is made; afterwards it is accepted, at least by silence, and by not refusing. If, on the other hand, the person immediately refused, there would be no contract.

[M2] 2.[188] An omne omnino matrimonium inter fideles sit sacramentum, etiam celebratum inter absentes, aut acatholicos, aut eos, qui nollent intendere facere, quod facit Ecclesia, et quid si infideles ad fidem conuertantur? de qua re Laym. cit. Kon. db. 2. Sanch. d. 9. 10. et 11. Bonac. et alii.

Respondeo omne omnino matrimonium inter fideles contractum esse sacramentum. ita Sanch.[189] Laym.[190] Kon.[191] Tan.[192] quia Trid. s. 24. absolute pronuntiat matrimonium in noua lege esse sacramentum. atque omne baptizatorum matrimonium est uere matrimonium nouae legis, et sortitur speciales effectus proprios[193] huius status quoad indissolubilitatem, impedimenta, forum, ex quibus omnes recte colligunt matrimonium esse sacramentum. 2°. quia Christus eleuauit fidelium matrimonium ad esse sacramenti, nec plus requirit, quam vt sit verum matrimonium gratis enim plus configitur.[194]

Hinc sequitur matrimonium per Procuratores contractum esse sacramentum ita cit. cum Pontio[195] contra Canum, Victoriam et Caiet. sequitur 2°. contra Vasq. Pontium,[196] Bonac: et Rebellium non posse fideles separare a suo contractu rationem sacramenti, sed vel nihil facturos, si absolute plane nolint conficere sacramentum, vel si absolute velint contrahere futurum sacramentum, etiamsi id ipsi nollent, quia erit nolitio inefficax, qualis est illa Caluinistarum nolentium in baptismo conferre gratiam inhaerentem, etc. sequitur 3°. duos baptizatos, qui apud Turcas essent educati inscii omnis Christianitatis conficere sacramentum, si contrahant.[197] Intendunt enim[198] ritum sacrum, et quod facit Ecclesia saltem indirecte se volendo aliquid necessario cum eo connexum, alias certe si eiusdem intentio non sufficeret, Haeretici credentes matrimo-

---

188 Thus in A.
189 S adds: *l. 2. dp. 9. 10. et 11.*
190 S adds: *p. 21. c. 21. et n. 2. et c. 3. n. 6.*
191 S adds: *dp. 24. db. 21*
192 S adds: *q. 2. a nu: 46*
193 S reads: *primarios*
194 S reads: *confingitur*
195 S adds: *Bonac.*
196 S adds: *l. 1. c. 90*
197 S adds: *Dices, Requiritur intentio faciendi quod facit Ecclesia, s: ritum aliquem sacrum, non mere actionem ciuilem, quod hi non faciunt.*
198 S reads: *Respondeo Eos intendere*

nium esse solum ciuilem contractum non conficerent [fo. 14^{v199}] sacramentum contrahendo.

Ad vltimam partem questionis responsio probabilius esse matrimonium infidelium eo ipso, quod vterque vterque,[200] baptizetur postea, fieri sacramentum. ita San. d. 9. Tan.[201] Palud. Argens. contra Vasq. Kon.[202] Pontium, et Dianam[203], qui putant nunquam fieri sacramentum: item contra Bonac: Laym. et Henriq: qui saltem requirunt, vt de nouo consentiant. sed probatur quia[204] dubio pleraque ex matrimoniis fidelium de quibus Apostolus ad Ephes. 5. erant contracta ante baptismum et tamen de omnibus pronuntiat sacramentum hoc magnum, quo indicabat esse sacramenta iuxta Trid. s. 24 initio. 2°. quia eo ipso, et quidem sine nouo consensu matrimonium hoc fit ratum c. quarto.[205] de diuortiis, fit signum sensibile vnionis Christi cum Ecclesia, fit indissolubile, fit materia fori Ecclesiastici, aliaque grauamina matrimonii fidelium subit. ergo.[206]

Dices, coniuges infideles non poterant conficere sacramentum, tunc ergo opus est saltem nouo consensu. Respondeo potuisse conficere sacramentum imperfectum et in potentia, nec id mirum, cum et infidelis possit ministrare baptismum.

Case M2. *Is every marriage between the faithful always a sacrament; even if it is celebrated between people who are absent; or between non-Catholics; or between those who do not intend to do what the Church does? And what if infidels are later converted to the faith? On which, see Laymann, Coninck, Sanchez, Bonacina and others [refs].*

I reply that every marriage contracted between the faithful is always a sacrament; thus, Sanchez, Laymann, Coninck, and Tanner [refs]. This is because the Council of Trent [ref.] absolutely pronounces matrimony in the new law to be a sacrament; and every marriage of those who have been baptised is truly a marriage of the new law; and marriage acquires particular properties which are specific to this status, as concern indissolubility, impediments, and legal enforcement. From which, all rightly conclude that marriage is a sacrament. Secondly, because Christ elevated the marriage of the faithful to the status of a sacrament, and no more is

---

[199]   Along the top of A fos. 14^{v}–15 is the heading: *De Ministro Matrimonii et de // deliberatione requisita*, referring to Cases M3 and M4.

[200]   Thus in A.

[201]   S adds: *q. 21. n. 51*

[202]   S reads: *Conin.*

[203]   S adds: *de Sacram. resol. 253*

[204]   S adds: *sine*

[205]   S reads: *5°.*

[206]   S adds: *nulla est ratio cur non etiam sit Sacramentum, quia haec connexa sunt, et aeque facile intelligitur vnum atque aliud.*

required for it to be a sacrament than that it is a true marriage; and to claim more is pure invention.

Hence it follows that marriage contracted by proxies is a sacrament; thus, those who have been cited, with Pontius and Bonacina, against Canus, Victoria [ref.], and Caietan. It follows secondly, against Vasquez, Pontius [ref.], Bonacina and Rebellus, that the faithful cannot separate the idea of a sacrament from their marriage. But if they do not wish absolutely plainly to perform a sacrament they should either do nothing, and not marry; or, if they wish absolutely to contract a non-sacramental marriage, it will become a sacrament, even if they do not want it to do so, because their unwillingness will be ineffective, like the unwillingness of Calvinists to believe that baptism confers inherent grace, etc. It follows thirdly that two people who have been baptised but who have been educated in the territory of the Turks and have no knowledge of Christianity at all, perform a sacrament if they get married. You will say that for marriage to be a sacrament requires an intention on the part of those marrying to do what the Church does; that is, to perform a sacred rite of some sort, not merely a civil action; but in this case these people do not do this. I reply that they intend a sacred rite, and to do what the Church does, at least indirectly, by voluntarily engaging in something, which is necessarily connected to a sacred rite. Otherwise, certainly if this intention is not sufficient, then heretics who believe that marriage is only a civil contract do not perform a sacrament when they marry.

To the final part of the question the more probable reply is that the marriage of infidels, as soon as each of them is afterwards baptised, becomes a sacrament; thus, Sanchez, Tanner, Palude, Argent [refs], against Vasquez, Coninck, Pontius and Diana [refs], who think that it can never become a sacrament; also against Bonacina, Laymann and Henriquez, who at least require that they get married anew. But this is proved, because without a doubt many of the marriages of the faithful, of which the Apostle speaks, in Ephesians 5, were contracted before baptism, and nevertheless he pronounces them all to be 'this great sacrament', by which he indicated that it is a sacrament, as the Council of Trent [ref.] says. Secondly, because the marriage becomes lawful immediately, and indeed without a new statement of consent, according to the canon law [ref.], and becomes a real symbol of the union of Christ with the Church, becomes indissoluble, becomes a matter for the Church courts, and is placed under the other restrictions which the marriages of the faithful are. Therefore there is no reason why this marriage should not also be a sacrament, because these things are connected to it, and it is understood to be a sacrament just as easily as any other marriages is.

You will say, infidel spouses may not perform a sacrament, therefore there is at least need for a new statement of consent. I reply that they may perform an imperfect, but potential sacrament, and that is no surprise since even an infidel may administer baptism.

[M3] 3[us]. Quis sit minister huius sacramenti, et an peccet mortaliter, qui ministrat, aut assistit, aut benedicit extra statum gratiae? de qua re Sanch. l. 2. d. 6. Bonac. q. 2. p. 4. Laym. de matr. p. 2. c. 2.[207] Respondeo ipsos contrahentes esse ministros, ita cit. omnes cum Kon. Suar. et aliis passim, contra Canum et Esthium, putantes sacerdotem esse ministrum. Ratio nostra est quia coniuges ponunt totam materiam et formam: et Flor. ait causam efficientem matrimonii esse consensum de praesenti exterius expressum. ergo soli consentientes conficiunt sacramentum.[208]

Hinc infero sacerdotem assistentem in peccato mortali non peccare mortaliter, quia ad summum fecit solum quod sacramentale.[209] ita Sanch.[210] Kon.[211] Tan.[212] Infero 2°. eum qui scienter contrahunt[213] cum alio in peccato mortali [fo. 15] peccare mortaliter, nisi iustam habeant[214] excusationem, quia ministrant[215] sacramentum indigne. Caeterum contrahentes in peccato praecise qua conficientes sunt, non peccant mortaliter, quia non ministrant solemniter, nec ad hoc sunt peculiariter ordinati; peccant tamen qua recipientes sunt iuxta omnes, voluntarie admittendo obicem graciae.

Case M3. *Who is the minister of this sacrament, and does someone sin mortally by administering, or assisting, or blessing it, if he is not in a state of grace? On which matter, see Sanchez, Bonacina, Laymann, Coninck, and Suarez [refs].*

I reply that those who contract marriage are themselves the ministers; thus all those cited, with Coninck, Suarez and others, against Cano, and Estius, who think the priest is the minister. Our reason is that the people getting married compose both the form and the matter of the sacrament; and the Council of Florence says the efficient cause of matrimony is consent for the present expressed externally. Therefore only those giving their consent perform the sacrament. You ask whether one of them administers the sacrament only to himself or herself; whether

---

207 S adds: *n. 2. Konin: dp: 24. n. 24. Suar: 16. s. 4.*
208 S adds: *Petes, an quilibet sibi tantum ministret, an alter, an vterque? Respondeo Ministrare et sibi ipsi et sibi mutuo. Ita Tan: q. 3. n. 7. quia essentia matrimonii consistit in contractu, hic autem essentialiter et indiuisibiliter est ab vtroque.*
209 S adds: *benedictionem v.g. etc:*
210 S adds: *cit. n. 5.*
211 S adds: *n. 24.*
212 S adds: *n. 9. et alii.*
213 S reads: *contrahit*
214 S reads: *habeat*
215 S reads: *ministrat*

they do it to each other; or both. I reply that each administers it to him or herself, and they also do so mutually, one to the other; thus, Tanner [ref.]. This is because the essence of matrimony consists in the contract, which moreover is essentially and indivisibly made by each of them. Hence I infer that a priest in mortal sin who assists at a marriage does not sin mortally, because at the most all he does is sacramental, by for example giving a blessing; thus, Sanchez, Coninck, Tanner and others [refs]. I infer secondly that those who knowingly contract marriage with someone who is in mortal sin, sin mortally, unless they have a just excuse, because they minister the sacrament unworthily. Moreover, those in sin who contract marriage do not sin mortally precisely as ministers of the sacrament, because they do not minister solemnly, and they are not peculiarly ordained to do so; they sin however in that they are recipients, according to all, by voluntarily accepting an impediment to grace.

[M4] 4ᵘˢ. Quaenam deliberatio ad Matrimonium sit necessaria, num sufficiat ea, quae ad peccandum mortaliter sufficit.²¹⁶

Respondeo requiri tum ad Matrimonium tum ad sponsalia deliberationem plenamque aduertentiam eius quod agitur, ita vt possis conferre actum cum eius opposito. ita omnes, quia alioqui non esset actus humanus et voluntarius. Hinc furiosi, amentes, non possunt contrahere, nisi habeant lucida interualla, sic neque ebrii aut dormientes, etiamsi in vigilia²¹⁷ id intendissent,²¹⁸ at naturaliter distractus potest, quia manebit intentio virtualis.²¹⁹

Respondeo 2ᵒ. sufficere ad matrimonium eam deliberationem, quam ad peccandum mortaliter est sufficiens, ita Sanch. l. 1. d. 8. Kon. d. 21. n. 13. Vasq. Pontius,²²⁰ Tan.²²¹ Ratio est, quia sufficit plena libertas, nec plus requiritur ab vllo iure naturali vel positiuo.²²² Nec in re²²³ discrepat S. T. in supplem. q. 43. a. 2.²²⁴ et Bonac. q. 1. p. 4. cum aliis, qui requirunt plus viz: prouidentiam²²⁵ circa futura nam in puberibus

---

²¹⁶ S adds: *Sanch: l. 1. dp. 8. Kon: dp. 21. n. 13. Vasq. dp. 5. c. 1. Bonac: de matrim: q. 1. pun: 4. n. 4.*

²¹⁷ S adds: *aut sobrietate*

²¹⁸ S adds: *Sanch: dp: 8. n. 15.*

²¹⁹ S adds: *de quo in materia de Sacramentis*

²²⁰ S adds: *l. 4. c. 1.*

²²¹ S adds: *q. 1. n. 23.*

²²² S reads: *Ratio est, quia sufficit plena libertas, sine fundamento autem plus hic requireretur, cum nec iure naturali nec positiuo id probari queat.*

²²³ S adds: *vt opinor*

²²⁴ S adds: *corp: et ad 21ᵘᵐ.*

²²⁵ S reads: *prudentiam aliquam*

hoc non deest, quando adest vsus rationis. Vnde hi autores[226] excludant solum pueros ante septennium, qui forte possent peccare mortaliter, nec tamen haberent satis prouidentiae circa futura, vt statum eligant, quod concedo: nam certum est homines communiter prius maturos esse ad peccandum mortaliter, quam ad contrahendum, imo prius maturos ad peccandum mortaliter in vna materia, quam in alia; deliberatio itaque hic sumitur prout opponitur inaduertentiae in persona caeteroque matura.

Hinc infero 1º. cum Sanch. Vasq. et Pont. valere matrimonium aut sponsalia contracta in feruore iracundiae, amoris, etc. [fo. 15ᵛ[227]] modo ratio non fuerit absorpta.[228] 2º. valere etiamsi resiliat, quia non arguit defectum consensus statim mutare.[229] In dubio tamen hinc sumi potest aliqua controuersia.[230] 3º. surdos et mutos posse contrahere modo doceantur.[231]

Dices quod in calore iracundiae fit, ratum non est nisi postea eo cessante perseueretur. l. quicquid 48. ff. de reg. iuris. et c. diuortium de poen. dist 1. et c. si quis iuratus 2. q. 3. Respondeo hoc iuris positiui esse, nec obligare in hac materia de qua non loquitur,[232] sed de contractibus, qui rescindi possunt. ita Suar.[233] Vasq. Pontius.

Case M4. *What deliberation is necessary in preparation for matrimony? Is what is sufficient for a mortal sin enough? See Sanchez, Coninck, Vasquez, and Bonacina [refs].*

I reply that both for marriage and for betrothal, deliberation and full attention concerning what is being done is required, so that you can compare the action with its opposite; thus, everyone, because otherwise it would not be an action which is human and voluntary. Hence, the mad and fools cannot contract marriage, unless they have lucid intervals; in the same way, neither can those who are drunk or asleep, even if they had intended to marry when they were awake or sober; see Sanchez [ref.]. But those who are naturally distracted in some way may marry, because the virtual intention will remain; on which, see the discussion in *Concerning the Sacraments.*

I reply secondly that the deliberation which is sufficient to commit a mortal sin is sufficient for marriage; thus, Sanchez, Coninck, Vasquez,

---

226 S reads: *S: Tho: per hoc solum excludit*
227 In A, along the top of fos. 15ᵛ–16 (referring to Case M5) is the heading: *An qui ficte contrahit teneatur//ad implenda permissionem*
228 S adds: *quod raro in similibus praesumi potest. Sanch. Vasq: Pont. et alii.*
229 S adds: *animum*
230 S reads: *coniectura. Sanch. n. 8. Tan: n. 26.*
231 S adds: *Sanch: n. 12. Imo non repugnat absolute vt surdus mutus et caecus doceantur; vt bene Tan: q. 1. n. 30.*
232 S reads: *nec loquitur de matrimonio*
233 S adds: *l. 1. de voto. c. 9. n. 8.*

Pontius, and Tanner [refs]. The reason is that full liberty is enough, and no more is required by any law, either natural or positive. Nor, in my opinion, in this matter does St Thomas [ref.] disagree; neither do Bonacina [ref.] and others, although they require more, that is, prudence about the future, for in those who have reached puberty that is not absent, when they have the use of reason. Hence, these authors only exclude children before the age of seven, who, although they may perhaps commit a mortal sin, do not have enough prudence concerning the future for them to choose a status like marriage. This I concede, for it is certain that men are commonly mature enough to sin mortally before they are mature enough to marry; indeed, mature enough to sin mortally in one matter, before they are in another. Therefore, deliberation is assumed in this case in so far as it prevents inadvertence in a person otherwise mature.

Hence I infer firstly, with Sanchez, Vasquez, and Pontius, that marriage or betrothal contracted in the heat of passion or of love etc. is valid, as long as the use of reason is not overwhelmed, which, it is presumed, does happen rarely in similar cases. Secondly, it is valid even if one party should withdraw, because it does not argue a defect of consent to change one's mind immediately. In doubtful cases, however, some controversies can arise from this. Thirdly, the deaf and the mute may marry, as long as they are instructed; see Sanchez [ref.]. Indeed, it does not seem completely out of the question that the deaf, the mute and the blind may be instructed; as Tanner shows well [ref.].

You will say that what is done in the heat of passion is not valid unless afterwards when the passion has ended it is persevered with, according to both civil and canon law [refs]. I reply that these references are to positive law, and do not oblige in this matter of matrimony, about which they do not speak, but about contracts which can be rescinded; thus, Suarez [ref.], Vasquez, and Pontius.

[M5] 5us. An qui ficte contraxit i.e. sine animo contrahendi aut se obligandi teneatur stare contractui. de qua re Sanch. l. 1. d. 11. Lay. p. 2. c. 6.[234] Less. l. 2. de iust. c. 10. db. 3.[235] Respondeo eum qui ficte contrahit. i.e. absolute nolens contrahere aut se obligare, nihil facere etiamsi exterius consentiat. Est certa et communis omnium. et patet ex cap. Tuae. et c. Tua nos. de sponsal. et c. Tuas de sponsa duorum, et Flor. dicente causam efficientem[236] esse consensum. Hinc infero contra Vasq.[237] et

234 S adds: *et p. 1. c. 1. n. 11. Nauar: Enchir: c. 16. n. 18.*
235 S adds: *Bonac: q. 1. pun: 2. Vasq: dp. 6. c. 345. Kon: dp: 21. n. 7 et dp. 22. n. 37.*
236 S adds: *matrimonii*
237 S adds: *dp: 6. c. 2.*

Ponte,[238] nec promissionem, votum, emptionem, aliumue contractum valere, si absque consensu interno verba dentur ita Less. l. 2. c. 17. db. vlt. Sanch. d. 9. n. 3.[239]

Respondeo 2°. qui ficte contrahendo obtinuit a foemina copulam, tenetur stare contractui, et de nouo contrahere, si ipsa velit, nec sufficit alia via damnum sarcire. ita Less. cit. n. 20. aiens esse communem. Tan.[240] Nauar.[241] Molin.[242] Bonac: Sanch: ratio est, quia ipsa iam partem suam impleuit in contractu oneroso[243] intuitu promissionis ab ipso factae. ergo iustitia plane exigit, vt ipse impleat[244] suam. Excipe nisi potuerit facile fraudem animaduertere, tunc enim sibi imputet foemina. Idem dicunt Sotus, Sanch. Bonac. et Less. si sciuerit promittentem esse melioris longe conditionis; et est pobabile; probabilius tamen puto cum Laym. cit. n. 11. hoc praecise non excusare, si vere ipsa syncere crediderit, ipsum serio agere, vnde merito potest tanti suum pudorem [fo. 16] facere,[245] et nolle aliam compensationem siue virgo fuerit siue vidua honesta, aut alias bonae famae, modo tamen scandala et mali exitus non timeantur. vt bene Laym.[246]

Respondeo 3°. etiam copula non secuta, si tamen aliud damnum inde immineat, tenebitur stare contractui. v. g. quia altera pars tenebitur manere interrupta velit, nolit; et quia hoc regulariter sequitur, etiam regulariter ficte consentiens, tenebitur stare contractui: et hoc ad minimum docent Sanch. l. 1. d. 11. n. 5. Laym.[247] et Pont.[248] Sotus[249] et Tan: ratio est eadem, quae ante. Respondeo 4°. si nec copula nec aliud damnum sequatur, adhuc tenetur fictor stare contractui: probabile tamen est non esse obligationem ita strictam vt rationabili de causa non potuit excusari. Priorem partem docent Laym. Sotus et Pont. ratio est quia iustitia exigit vt faciat verba sua vera, alias euerteretur hominum societas. Alteram partem docent Sanch. cit.[250] et Diana;[251] quia nec ex

238 S adds: l. 2. c. 4.
239 S adds: et alii, quia est omnium quoad hoc eadem ratio: Matrimonium enim plus non requirit, quam quod ad essentiam cuiusuis contractus exigitur. Gratis enim plus fingeretur. Est ergo de essentia omnis contractus fieri cum vero consensu interno; et argumenta aduersariorum probantia sola verba externa sufficere, hic omnia solui debent.
240 S adds: hic q. 1. n. 13. et to. 3. dp: 4. q. 6. n. 136.
241 S adds: enchir: c. 16. n. 18.
242 S adds: tra: 2. dp. 105. n. 4.
243 S reads: interno
244 S adds: partem
245 S reads: aestimare
246 S adds: c. 6. cit. n. 21.
247 S adds: c. 6. cit.
248 S adds: l. 2. c. 4.
249 S adds: dist. 27. q. 1. a. 3. versic. Alia
250 S adds: n. 5.
251 S adds: de Sacram: resol: 247.

vi contractus tenetur, cum nullus fuerit, nec ratione damni. ergo saltem cum magno incommodo probabile est non teneri; dixi probabile, quia vere etiam probabile est quod teneatur ob rationem dictam; videtur enim fere aeque obligatoria, ac sit ipse contractus.

Case M5. *Is someone who contracts marriage deceitfully, that is without the intention of contracting or of obliging him or herself, bound to stand by the contract? On which matter, see Sanchez, Laymann, Navarre, Lessius, Bonacina, Vasquez and Coninck [refs].*

I reply that he who deceitfully contracts marriage, that is, who absolutely does not wish to contract or to oblige himself, does nothing, even if he consents externally. This is certain and common to all, and is clear from canon law [refs] and the Council of Florence, which says that the efficient cause of marriage is consent. Hence I infer, against Vasquez and Pontius [refs], that neither a promise, a vow, a sale nor any other contract is valid, if the words are given without internal consent. Thus, Lessius, Sanchez [refs] and others, because the reason is the same in this case as in all others; for marriage does not require more than is demanded as the essence of every contract, and it is fruitless to invent more. It is therefore of the essence of every contract that it should be done with internal consent, and the arguments of the opponents who try to prove that external words alone are sufficient, must all fail this point.

I reply secondly that a man who, having deceitfully contracted marriage, obtains copulation from a woman as a result, is bound to keep the contract, and to contract marriage anew, if she wishes, and no other way is sufficient to repair the harm he has done her; thus, Lessius, who says this is the common opinion, Tanner, Navarre, Molina, Bonacina and Sanchez [refs]. The reason is that she has already fulfilled her part of the onerous contract in consideration of the promise made by him; therefore, justice plainly demands that he should fulfil his part. The exception is if she could easily have noticed the fraud, for then the harm would be the woman's own fault. Soto, Sanchez, Bonacina and Lessius say it is the same if she knew that the man making the promise was of a far better condition than she; and that is probable. More probably, however, I think with Laymann [ref.] that this precisely does not excuse him, if in truth she did sincerely believe that he was acting seriously. Hence it is right that she values her honour at such a price, and does not wish for other compensation (apart from marriage), if she is a virgin, or an honest widow, or otherwise of good fame, as long however as scandals and an evil outcome are not feared; as Laymann shows well [ref.].

I reply thirdly that even if copulation has not followed, but if some other harm is threatened from his deceit, he will be bound to stand by the contract; for example, because otherwise the other party will be left

suspended, incapable of another marriage, whether she likes it or not.
And also because it regularly follows, that those deceitfully consenting
are regularly bound to stand by the contract; and this at least is taught
by Sanchez, Laymann, Pontius, Soto, and Tanner [refs]. The reason is
the same as before. I reply fourthly (1) that if neither copulation nor
any other harm should follow, still the deceiver is bound to stand by
the contract. It is probable, however (2) that this obligation is not so
strict that it cannot reasonably be excused. The first part (1) is taught
by Laymann, Soto and Pontius. The reason is that justice demands that
he should keep his true words, otherwise human society would be over-
thrown. The other part (2) is taught by Sanchez and Diana [refs], on the
grounds that he should not be bound by the force of a contract when it
is null, nor bound by reason of the harm that might result. Therefore at
least in cases of great inconvenience, it is probable that he is not bound
by the contract. I have said 'probable', because truly it is also probable
that he is bound for the reason (1) given; for it seems almost equally as
obligatory as the contract is itself.

[M6] 6ᵘˢ. An ad valorem Matrimonii sufficiat mere consensus internus
sine externa manifestatione? an praeter verba sufficerent alia signa? de
qua re Sanch. l. 2. d. 30 et 31.²⁵² Bonac. q. 2. p. 1.²⁵³ Respondeo certum
esse ad essentiam Matrimonii requiri signa externa. ita omnes ex Flor.
et c. licet²⁵⁴ de sponsa duorum. quia omnis humanus contractus praeter
internum consensum requirit essentialiter intimationem sensibilem.
Obiices c. Tuae de spons. dici verba esse necessaria quoad Ecclesiam.
ergo non ad Matrimonium in se. Respondeo sensum esse, quod verba (id
est) voces humanae ordinarie et regulariter requirantur, alias ordinarie
vix satis constaret Ecclesiae, cum alia signa sint valde obscura. In rigore
tamen consensus internus quouis signo vel nutu satis expressus, validum
facit [fo. 16ᵛ²⁵⁵] matrimonium quia surdi et muti valide contrahunt, et
olim sponsi per copulam contrahebant c. is qui de sponsal.

Nota tamen eos, qui loqui possunt teneri saltem sub veniali ordinarie
vti verbis, non aliis signis iuxta Ecclesiae consuetudinem. imo probabile
est esse obligationem sub mortali, vt docent multi apud Sanch. l. 2. d. 21.
Nota 2°. nullam certam verborum formam esse necessariam. standum
tamen regulariter pleno verborum sensui, si de mente contraria certum
non esset. Vnde si sint²⁵⁶ de futuro erunt tantum sponsalia, si de praesenti

---

²⁵² S adds: *Kon: dp. 28. n. 8.*
²⁵³ S adds: *n. 3. et 4.*
²⁵⁴ S reads: *Dicet*
²⁵⁵ In A, along the top of fos. 16ᵛ–17 (referring to Case M7) is the heading: *Quid sit
metus cadens in // virum constantem reuerentalis.*
²⁵⁶ S adds: *verba*

matrimonium: itaque si dicat; Accipio te in meam vel contraho tecum, vel, ex nunc habebo te in vxorem, erit matrimonium c. ex parte. 9. et c. penult. de sponsal: si dubium sit an sint de futuro, an de praesenti, censenda sunt sponsalia, quia in obscuris minimum est sequendum, praesertim si mali exitus timeantur. ita Kon.[257] et Tan.[258] Nota 3°. quoad alia signa pendere ex circumstantiis, et consuetudine quaenam sufficiant, vbi non constat de mente contrahentium. Sic traditio annuli, arrlae, iocaliae, manuum coniunctio, traductio in domum, non sunt vi sua traditio[259] sufficiens, esse tamen possunt tale, si accedat consuetudo etc. Sanch. l. 1. d. 22. Kon.[260] et Pont:[261] Taciturnitas etiam coram parente contrahente sufficit ad sponsalia. c. vn. de sponsal. impub: in 6. Idem est probabiliter, si sit quasi parens et curam gerat. Laym. 1. p. c. 1. n. 13. Sanch. l. 1. d. 23. n. 7. Tan[262] et Pont.[263] Imo sufficit ad matrimonium iuxta communem a paritate rationis, licet contrarium sit probabile cum quibusdam apud Pont. Nota vltimo, valide contrahi matrimonium per Procuratorem, vt patet ex praxi Ecclesiae, et c. final. de Procurat: in 6. Nec Trid: ius hoc correxit. Idem dicendum de litteris modo adsint sufficienter Parochus et testes. ita Sanch. l. 2. d. 11. et 12. et alii passim.

Case M6. *Is merely internal consent without any external manifestation sufficient for the validity of a marriage? Are other signs, apart from words, sufficient? On which matter, see Sanchez, Coninck and Bonacina [refs].*

I reply that it is certain that marriage essentially requires external signs; thus, all, following the Council of Florence and the canon law [ref.]. This is because all human contracts require essentially, beyond internal consent, an outward declaration. You will object that the canon law [ref.] says that words are necessary as far as the Church is concerned; therefore they are not required for matrimony in itself. I reply that the meaning is that words (that is, human voices) ordinarily and regularly are required, otherwise ordinarily it would scarcely meet with the approval of the Church, since other signs can be most unclear. In rigorous terms, however, internal consent, satisfactorily expressed by whatever sign or nod, makes a marriage valid, because the dumb and mute may validly marry, and formerly the betrothed used to contract marriage through copulation, according to the canon law [ref.].

---

[257] S adds: *cit. n. 27.*
[258] S adds: *q. 3. n. 97. Vide Sanchem l. 1. dp. 18.*
[259] S reads: *signum*
[260] S adds: *dp. 21. n. 22.*
[261] S adds: *l. 2.c. 21.*
[262] S adds: *q. 3. n. 95.*
[263] S adds: *c. 12. contra Sanchem l. 1. dp. 23. n. 7.*

Note, however, that those who can speak are bound at least under
venial sin ordinarily to use words, not other signs, according to the
custom of the Church. Indeed, it is probable that it is an obligation
under mortal sin, as many teach; see Sanchez [ref.]. Note secondly that
no particular form of words is necessary, but the rule is that it is necessary to stand by the plain meaning of the words, as long as it is not
certain that the intention is contrary. Hence, if they are words for the
future it will only be a betrothal; if words for the present, it will be a
marriage. Therefore, if he says, 'I accept you as mine', or 'I contract
with you', or 'from now on I will have you as wife', it will be marriage,
according to canon law [refs]. If there is doubt whether they are words
for the future or for the present, it is judged to be a betrothal, because in
obscure matters, the least is to be followed, especially if evil outcomes
are feared; thus, Coninck, Tanner and Sanchez [refs]. Note thirdly that
as far as other signs are concerned, it depends on circumstances, and
any signs accepted by custom are sufficient, when there is no agreement
about the intention of those contracting marriage. Thus, the gift of a ring,
a token, a jewel, the joining of hands, carrying the bride into the house,
are not a sufficient sign by their own force; but they may, however, be
sufficient if custom agrees; see Sanchez, Coninck and Pontius [refs]. In
addition, silence in the presence of a contracting parent is sufficient for
betrothal, according to canon law [ref.]. The same is probable if it is
performed by a parental substitute, in whose care the child is placed; see
Coninck and Pontius, against Sanchez [refs]. Indeed, this is sufficient
for marriage according to the common judgement, for similar reasons,
although the contrary is probable according to some; see Pontius. Note
finally that marriage is validly contracted by proxies, as is clear by the
practice of the Church and the canon law [ref.]. Nor has the Council of
Trent corrected this. The same is to be said about letters, as long as the
parish priest and witnesses are sufficiently in attendance; thus, Sanchez
[ref.] and others everywhere.

[M7] 7ᵘˢ. Quinam dicatur metus cadens in virum constantem: an metus
mortis, infamiae, amissionis bonorum? et quid de metu reuerentiali, et
precibus importunis? de qua re²⁶⁴ Less. de iust. l. 2. c. 17.²⁶⁵ Bonac.
q. 3. p. 8.²⁶⁶ Lay. p. 2. c. 5²⁶⁷. et l. 1. c. 6.²⁶⁸ tr. 2. et l. 4. tr. 4. c. 5.²⁶⁹

---

²⁶⁴ S adds: *Kon. dp. 28. db. 2.*
²⁶⁵ S adds: *db. 6. n. 35.*
²⁶⁶ S adds: *n. 6.*
²⁶⁷ S adds: *n. 2.*
²⁶⁸ S adds: *n. 4.*
²⁶⁹ S adds: *n. 6.*

Sanch. fuse l. 4.[270] Respondeo metus grauis hic dicitur ille, qui merito commouere possit virum fortem et constantem, eumque ad non leuia [fo. 17] incommoda subeunda impellere eius vitandi causa; esto hic et nunc non liceat, nec deceat eum vitare, vt Martyribus contigit; tamen ipsum malum ex se aptum est[271] vt valde moueat; et tunc erit metus grauis. ita Kon. hic d. 28. d. 2. Huiusmodi est mors, mutilatio, infamia, amissio bonorum omnium, stuprum et apud Less. cit. imo amissio rei probabilis,[272] inquit Bonac: cum Sanch.[273] amissio lucri notabilis puta ad quod aliunde titulum habes; secus si solum offeratur ad inuitandum ad matrimonium vel religionem. ita Sanch.[274] et Pont:[275] denique definire in particulari quis sit metus grauis pertinet ad iudicem. Sanch cit. d. 5.[276] Accipienda est autem grauitas haec respectiue ad aetatem, sexum, etc. leg. metus, ff. ex quibus causis. ita vt respectu pueri, foeminae, rustici, sufficit quod constantem puerum, foeminam aut rusticum solet commouere.[277] ita Kon.[278] Sanch.[279] Less. Denique sufficit si timeas vel tibimet, vel altero valde coniuncto, parentibus, vxori, liberis, magno amico, imo consanguineis vsque ad 4m. gradum, inquit Sanch.[280] cum Pont:[281] Hoc tamen prudentis iudicio[282] relinquendum.

Metus reuerentialis purus aliud non est, quam metus resistendi iis, quibus reuerentiam debemus, etiamsi aliud malum non timeatur, id est parentibus, curatoribus, Praelatis, etc. Is autem per se non est grauis, aut cadens in virum constantem iuxta communem. At si huic reuerentiae accedant minae, dura tractatio, asperitas vultus diurturna, erit grauis, et cadens in virum constantem.[283] Idem est si cum reuerentia iungantur preces importunae: Sanch:[284] Less:[285] Kon:[286] Lay: et Bon: imo Pontius[287] putat solas preces importunas sufficere, sed minus probabiliter. Porro ad metum grauem requiritur vlterius, vt malae haec timeantur non vane

270 S adds: *dp. 1. et sequentibus, praesertim 5.*
271 S reads: *esse potest*
272 S reads: *notabilis*
273 S adds: *dp. 5. n. 25.*
274 S adds: *cit. n. 28.*
275 S adds: *l. 4. c. 4. n. 10.*
276 S adds: *n. 1.*
277 S adds: *etiamsi respectu viri non sufficeret.*
278 S adds: *n. 29. et 30.*
279 S adds: *dp. 3.*
280 S adds: *l. 4. dp. 4. n. 12.*
281 S adds: *c. 3. n. 4.*
282 S adds: *arbitrio censeo.*
283 S adds: *quia difficile est admodum hominibus haec subire ab aliis quibus subsunt.*
284 S adds: *dp: 67.*
285 S adds: *c. 17. n. 35.*
286 S adds: *n. 35.*
287 S adds: *c. 5.*

sed probabiliter. l. 6. et 7. ff. quod metus causa vnde requiritur, vt qui minatur sit potens minas exequi. idque [fo. 17v288] soleat, quodque non sit alius euadendi modus. Sanch.289 Kon.290

Case M7. *What may be said to be the sort of fear which would affect a constant man: would it be fear of death, of dishonour, or of the loss of goods? And what about reverential fear, and importunate requests? On which see Coninck, Lessius, Bonacina, Laymann and Sanchez [refs].*

I reply that grave fear is said by these authors to be that fear which may justly move a strong and constant man, and such as would impel him to undergo considerable difficulties in order to avoid its causes, even if in some circumstances it was not lawful, and not proper, that he should avoid them, as is the case with martyrs; the evil causing this fear in itself is liable, moreover, to affect him greatly; and then it will be described as 'grave fear'. Thus, Coninck [ref.]. Examples of the evils which cause such fear are death, mutilation, dishonour, the loss of all goods, disgrace, and, according to Lessius in the place cited, even the probable loss of property; Bonacina says, with Sanchez [ref.], that a further example is the loss of a notable sum of money, to which otherwise you have a title. It is different if the money is only offered as an inducement to marry or to enter religion; thus, Sanchez and Pontius [refs] Finally, to define in particular what is grave fear is a matter for a judge; see Sanchez [ref.]. The gravity of this fear however is to be understood in relation to the age, sex etc. of the person concerned, according to the civil law [ref.]. So, in respect of a child, a woman, a rustic, it means what generally affects a constant child, woman or rustic, even if it would not be sufficient in respect of a man; thus, Coninck, Sanchez, and Lessius [refs]. Finally, Sanchez, with Pontius [refs], says it is sufficient if you fear on your own account, or for another closely connected to you: a parent, wife, one of your children, a great friend, or a blood relative to the fourth degree. This, however, I consider, should be left to the judgement of a prudent man.

Reverential fear, considered by itself, is no other than the fear of resisting those to whom we owe reverence, even if we fear no other evil; that is, parents, guardians, prelates etc. It is however not grave fear, nor such as to intimidate a constant man, according to the common judgement. But if this reverence is connected to threats, harsh treatment, unpleasant looks every day, it will constitute grave fear, and such as would intimidate a constant man, because it is very difficult for men to

---

288   In A, along the top of fos. 17v–18 (referring to Case M8) is the heading: *Qualis metus irritat matrimonium.*
289   S adds: *dp. 1. a. n. 15.*
290   S adds: *n. 23.*

undergo such treatment from those to whom they are inferior. The same is the case if reverence is combined with importunate requests. Sanchez, Lessius, Coninck, Laymann, Bonacina and even Pontius [refs] think that importunate requests alone are sufficient, but less probably. Indeed, for grave fear it is required further that fear of these evils is realistic and probable, according to the civil law [ref.]. Hence, it is required as a cause of this fear that the person who makes the threats has the power to carry them out, and is accustomed to do so, and that there is no other way of avoiding them; thus, Sanchez and Coninck [refs].

[M8] 8us. An metus irritans matrimonium esse debeat grauis, iniustus, et ad matrimonium extorquendum incussus.[291] et quid si a 3ª. persona, ipso contrahente inscio incutiatur. Sanch. l. 4. d. 12. et 13.[292] Laym. p. 2. c. 5. Bonac. q. 3. p. 8.[293] Less.[294] l. 2. c. 40. d. 3.[295] Respondeo probabilius esse, debere esse grauem argum. c. veniens 2. c. consultat de sponsal. et c. penult. de his quae vi. quia irrit non iure naturali, sed positiuo, hoc autem de solo[296] graui loquitur, vt patet ex iuribus cit: Probabile tamen est ob Doctorum autoritatem etiam leuem irritare matrimonium siue carnale siue spirituale. ita Nauar.[297] Rodr.[298] Diana.[299] et Tan. si autem comperte incutiatur;[300] et probabile censent Sanch. d. 17. Less. et Bonac. cit.

Debet esse incussus ab extrinseco non ab intrinseco. Hinc valet matrimonium si quis contrahat metu, ne alioqui sanitas periclitetur, aut ne peccet et damnetur. Sanch. d. 12. debet iniuste incuti, nam si iuste incutiatur, sibimet imputet. Hinc valet matrimonium si cogaris a iudice metu poenarum implere sponsalia, aut ducere quam corrupit spe nuptiarum. Sanch. d. 13. Debet incuti ad extorquendum matrimonium nam si quis te iniuste incarcerasset ob alias causas, et tu pro liberatione offerres te sponte[301] ad ducendam eius filiam, valent nuptiae, sponte enim eligis hunc medium euadendi. quod a fortiore est verum, si carcer sit iustus. ita Sanch.[302] Kon.[303] Lay. Bonac. Diana.[304]

---

291   S reads: *illatus*
292   S adds: *Kon: dp: 28. db. 1.*
293   S adds: *n. 8.*
294   S adds: *de iustitia*
295   S adds: *Nauar: c. 22. n. 51.*
296   S adds: *metu*
297   S adds: *enchir: cap: 22. n. 51.*
298   S adds: *in sum: par: 2. c. 8. n. 10.*
299   S adds: *de dub. regul: resol. 92.*
300   S puts the last four words in brackets, and adds: *hic q. 3. n. 42.*
301   S reads: *sponsum*
302   S adds: *dp. 12.*
303   S adds: *n. 21.*
304   S adds: *de Sacram: resol: 228.*

Addunt Sanch.[305] Kon.[306] Bonac.[307] et Tan:[308] etiamsi iniustus incarcerator offerat libertatem modo ducas[309] filiam: mihi tamen contrarium aeque videtur probabile cum Less. cit:[310] i.e. hoc moraliter eum cogere, cum aliunde teneatur ipsum liberare.[311] Alia est ratio si tertius aliquis suggerat incarcerato vt matrimonium offerat. Similiter si medicus nolit curare aegrotam, nisi ei nubat, non valet matrimonium nisi forte extraordinaria aliqua [fo. 18] cura esset suscipienda. ita Kon. et Sanch.[312] Irritat autem siue compars cogat, siue alius quicunque etiam illa inscia aut inuita. quia Iura voluerunt consulere libertati matrimonii c. cum locum. et c. veniens. 2. de sponsal. idque siue cogat ad hanc determinate siue ad aliam vage. ita Sanch.[313] Laym. Tan.[314]

Case M8. *Must the sort of fear which invalidates a marriage be grave, unjust, and inflicted in order to extort marriage; and what if it is inflicted by a third party, with the person contracting the marriage unaware?* See Sanchez, Coninck, Laymann, Bonacina, Lessius and Navarre [refs].

I reply that it is more probable that it should be grave fear, according to canon law [refs], because it invalidates marriage not by the law of nature, but by positive law, which only talks about grave fear, as is clear from the canons cited. It is probable, however, that on the authority of the doctors even light fear may invalidate matrimony, either carnal or spiritual;[315] Navarre, Rodriguez, Diana, Tanner (who says it must be known on good authority that such fear was inflicted), Sanchez [refs], Lessius and Bonacina, in the places cited, judge that this is probable.

It must be fear inflicted by an external agency and not internally generated. Hence, marriage is valid if someone marries out of fear that if he does not his health will decline, or he will sin and be damned; see Sanchez [ref.]. It must be fear which is unjustly inflicted, for if it is justly inflicted, then the person who becomes afraid is to blame himself. Hence a marriage is valid if you are forced by a judge under fear of punishment to marry in order to fulfil the terms of the betrothal; or if a man is forced to take the hand of a woman he corrupted by making

---

305 S adds: *n. 11.*
306 S adds: *n.10.*
307 S adds: *n. 20.*
308 S adds: *q. 3. n. 27. valere*
309 S adds: *eius*
310 S adds: *c. 40. cit. n. 16.*
311 S reads: *quia cum teneatur aliunde eum liberare, nolle id facere nisi ducat, est moraliter eum ad hoc cogere.*
312 S reads: *Ita Kon: n. ii. contra Sanch: dp: 12. n. 15.*
313 S adds: *disp. 12. n. 19. et 20.*
314 S adds: *et alii.*
315 That is, either entry into religion, or marriage.

her hope for marriage; see Sanchez [ref.] The fear should be inflicted in order to extort marriage, for if someone unjustly incarcerates you for some other reasons, and you voluntarily offer to marry his daughter in order to gain your freedom, the marriage is valid, for you chose voluntarily this method of escaping. This is true with even stronger reason if the imprisonment is just; thus, Sanchez, Coninck, Laymann, Bonacina, and Diana [refs].

Sanchez, Coninck, Bonacina and Tanner add that the marriage is valid, even if the unjust incarcerator offers you freedom on condition that you marry his daughter. However, to me the contrary seems equally probable, with Lessius [ref.]; because since he is bound for other reasons to free you, he should not do this on condition that you marry, and it is morally speaking a way of forcing you to do so. It is another matter if some third party suggests to the imprisoned person that he should offer marriage. Similarly, if a doctor refuses to cure a sick woman unless she marries him, the marriage is not valid, unless perhaps some extraordinary cure had been employed; thus, Coninck, against Sanchez [refs]. Moreover, a marriage is invalid whether it is a spouse that applies the force, or someone else, even if the spouse is unaware and does not wish this. This is because it is the intention of the laws to favour the liberty of marriage, as the canons show [refs]. This is true whether he forces you to marry this person specifically, or indiscriminately to marry anyone; thus, Sanchez, Laymann, Tanner and others [refs].

[M9] 9us. Sitne matrimonium metu contractum ita prorsus irritum, vt nec ipse, qui metum incussit teneatur ei stare altero postea volente? Sanch. l. 4. d. 15. Laym. p. 2. c. 5.[316] Bonac. p. 8. cit. n. 29.[317] Respondeo matrimonium metu contractum esse ipso iure prorsus irritum, non vero irritandum. (hoc enim in matrimonio est impossibile) nec solum in foro externo sed interno. ita S. T. in supplem. q. 47. a. 3. et theologi omnes. et patet ex c. cum locum, c. veniens. 2. despol. c. 2 de eo, qui duxit. docent 2as. nuptias valere, relictis primis ex metu contractis. sed neque per copulam carnalem confirmatur contractus, stante causa metus, etiamsi animo maritali habeatur (cuius tamen contrarium probabiliter docent Palud. Sotus. Ledesm. Angles, et alii apud Sanch. d. 18.)[318] cessante metu, et cognita priori inualiditate confirmatur per copulam, vbi Trid. non est receptum. Sanch. Bonac.[319] Kon.[320]

Coactorem teneri ratificare contractum, si pars coacta velit, negant

---

316 S adds: *n. 1.*
317 S adds: *Nauar: c. 22. n. 33. Kon: dp: 28. n. 9.*
318 S adds: *n. 13.*
319 S adds: *n. 24.*
320 S adds: *db. 4.*

Sanch.[321] Laym. Bonac. Tan.[322] affirmant Nauar.[323] Pont:[324] Kon.[325] et hoc verum censeo, si copula sit secuta vel aliud damnum, secus damno secluso, vt de fictore supra diximus. Merito tamen in foro externo, volente innocente, cogendus esset semper.

Case M9. *Is marriage contracted out of fear so completely invalid that the person who inflicted the fear is bound to accept this invalidity even if the other party afterwards is willing to keep to the contract? See, Sanchez, Laymann, Bonacina, Navarre and Coninck [refs].*

I reply that marriage contracted out of fear is for that reason completely invalid, but not in such a way as to invalidate marriage in the future (for that is impossible in marriage), not only in the law courts, but also in conscience. Thus, St Thomas [ref.] and all theologians; and it is clear from canon law [refs]. The canons teach that the second marriage is valid, when the first marriage contracted through fear is at an end. But the contract of marriage is not to be confirmed by carnal copulation, with the cause of the fear remaining, even if the copulation is done with marriage in mind, although the contrary is taught as probable by Palude, Soto, Ledesma, Angelus, and others, cited by Sanchez [ref.]. If the fear has ended and they are aware of the previous invalidity, it may be confirmed by copulation, where the Council of Trent is not received; see Sanchez, Bonacina, and Coninck [refs].

That the person who applied the force is bound to ratify the contract if the person in whom the fear was inspired wants this to be done is denied by Sanchez, Laymann, Bonacina, and Tanner [refs], and is affirmed by Navarre, Pontius, and Coninck [refs], and I judge this latter judgement to be true, if copulation has followed, or there is some other evil; but it is different if there is no evil, as concerning deceivers we have said above. Deservedly, however, in the law courts, if the innocent party wants it to be done, the guilty should always be forced to ratify the contract.

[M10] 10[us]. An error personae inualidet matrimonium v.g. Petrus ducit Catherinam, putans esse Ioannam, quaeritur an valeat? et quid si aeque libenter duxisset Catherinam si sciuisset. Sanch. l. 7. d. 18.[326] Bonac. q. 3. p. 2.[327] Laym: p. 4. c. 2.[328] Respondeo matrimonium contractum cum

---

[321] S adds: *dp: 15.*
[322] S adds: *q. 3. n. 23.*
[323] S adds: *c. 22. n. 33.*
[324] S adds: *c. 15.*
[325] S adds: *n. 9.*
[326] S adds: *n. 5.*
[327] S adds: *n. 2.*
[328] S adds: *n. 1. Konin: dp: 31. n. 9. Nauar: c. 22. n. 32.*

errore in substantia inualidum esse iure naturae. ita omnes. ratio est, quia
error [fo. 18ᵛ³²⁹] facit inuoluntarium, quare si erretur in substantia, iam
tota actus substantia est inuoluntaria iuxta illud iuris: nihil magis contrarium consensui, quam error: Leg. 15. ff. de iurisd. et errantis nulla est
voluntas. Leg. 8. l.³³⁰ de iuris et facti ignor. et colligitur ex c. Tua nos de
sponsal. Quid autem in vnoquoque contractu sit eius substantia, pendet
ex particulari eius natura, fine, caeterisque proprietatibus; et quod in vno
contractu est substantiale in alio erit accidentale, vt bene Vasq. 1. 2. d.
30.³³¹ n. 27. et Pont:³³² vniuersim autem illud dici potest substantiale,
quod tanti momenti esse solet in eo contractu, vt homines prudenter et
passim non solum non contraherent, si scirent illud deficere (hoc enim
non est satis.) sed etiam nolint actum suum seu contractum aliter valere,
nisi adsit ea conditio, siue ea nolitio sit expressa, siue confusa, quatenus
volunt more aliorum contrahere.

In matrimonio autem vbi datur corpus pro corpore ad substantiam
ex parte obiecti tantum videtur pertinere, quod non erretur in persona.
itaque si ducat Catherinam putans esse Ioannam est error in substantia,
et actus nullus, vt docent omnes. Quod verum est etiamsi aeque libenter
duxisset Catherinam si sciuisset. ita San: cit.³³³ Vasq.³³⁴ et Pont:³³⁵ quia
adhuc non est consensus in hanc, sed tantum fuisset, si sciuisset. Ignorantia autem³³⁶ concomitans, qualis est ista, facit vt actus non sit voluntarius. vt 1. 2. q. 6. docent theologi.³³⁷ Nota non solum inuincibilem
errorem sed etiam crassum et vincibilem vitiare matrimonium quia
adhuc deerit consensus. ita Sanch. et Kon. cit.

Case M10. *Does an error concerning the person invalidate a marriage?*
For example, Peter marries Catherine, thinking she is Joan, is this
marriage valid? And what if he would have married Catherine equally

---

³²⁹ In A, along the top of fos. 18ᵛ–19 (referring to Case M10) is the heading: *An error*
personae inualidet // matrimonium.
³³⁰ S omits the last number and adds *codice*
³³¹ S reads: *3.*
³³² S adds: *l. 4. c. 20. n. 4.*
³³³ S adds: *n. 6.*
³³⁴ S adds: *cit: n. 30.*
³³⁵ S adds: *n. 21.*
³³⁶ S reads: *enim*
³³⁷ S adds the following (replacing the last sentence in A): *Dices, esse multa alia*
contra substantiam matrimonii; vt ducere matrem, ducere aliquam ad tempus, et similia.
Respondeo Haec esse contra substantiam siue sciantur siue ignorentur, vnde et nullitas
actus non est ascribenda errori; at conditio illa substantialis, cuius error vitiat, est
tantum quod diximus. Petes, quisnam error vitiet? Respondeo Non solum inuincibilem,
sed crassum etiam et vincibilem, quia adhuc deerit consensus. Sanch: cit. n. 7. et Kon:
n. 9.

willingly, had he known? See, Sanchez, Bonacina, Laymann, Coninck and Navarre [refs].

I reply that a marriage contracted with a substantial error is invalid by the law of nature; thus, all. The reason is that the error makes the marriage contrary to the will of the spouses, and so if the error was one concerning the substance of the marriage, then the whole substance of the marriage is contrary to their will, according to these maxims of the civil law: 'nothing is more contrary to consent than error' [ref.]; 'a man who is in error has no will'[ref.]; and this is gathered also from to the canon law [ref.]. What, however, in each contract is its substance depends on its particular nature, its end, and its other properties; and what is substantial in one contract in another may be accidental; as Vasquez and Pontius [refs] show well. Universally, however, that can be said to be substantial in a contract which is thought customarily to be of such moment that prudent men not only would never agree to the contract if they knew it was lacking (for that is not enough), but also they would not wish their contract to be valid, unless it contained that condition, whether their unwillingness is explicit, or implicit, that they wish to marry in the same way as other people.

In marriage, however, where body is given for body, all that seems to be pertinent to the substance, as far as the subject treated (marriage) is concerned, is that there should not be an error concerning the person. Therefore if he marries Catherine, thinking her to be Joan, it is a substantial error, and the act is null, as all teach. This is true even if he would equally as willingly have married Catherine if he had known; thus, Sanchez, Vasquez and Pontius [refs], because at the time of the marriage he did not consent to marry Catherine, but he only would have done, if he had known it was her. Accompanying ignorance, however, such as this is, makes it such that the act is not voluntary, as the theologians teach [ref.]. You say, there are many other things against the substance of matrimony; such as, to marry your mother, to marry someone for a limited period of time, and similar. I reply that these are contrary to the substance whether they are known or not, whence the nullity of the act is not to be ascribed to the error; but the only subject of our discussion is that substantial condition, which error invalidates. You will ask, what sort of error invalidates? I reply, not only invincible error, but also crass error, and vincible error, because there will still be no agreement based on such error; see, Sanchez and Coninck [refs].

[M11] 11[us]. Vtrum error qualitatum accidentalium inualidet matrimonium v. g. Titus[338] ducit Bertam credens esse nobilem, opulentam,

---

[338] S reads: *Titius*

sanam, integram, cum sit plebeia, inops, leprosa, corrupta quod si sciret nullo modo contraheret, quaeritur an valeat. Sanch.[339] Laym.[340] Bonac. cit.[341] sup. Respondeo 1°. errorem [fo. 19] praedictarum qualitatum non vitiare matrimonium ita omnes cit.[342] ratio est quia non sunt de substantialia, sed accidentalia. Huius autem ratio vlterior est, quia censentur homines ita matrimonium contrahere, vt velint illud valere, etiamsi hae conditiones non subsistant. Cum enim sit contractus perpetuus, et maximi momenti, solet passim cum magna deliberatione suscipi per modum contractus[343] perpetui, et quem suscipiens intendit vt perpetuum, etiamsi in minoribus decipiatur, modo subsistant illa, quae apud omnes essentialia[344] censentur; hic enim est communalis agendi modus in huiusmodi; vnde haec censenda est ordinarie mens omnium.

Respondeo 2°. valet matrimonium etiamsi error iste det causam contractui, hoc est, etiamsi esses ita affectus, vt si scires nullo modo contraheres, ita Sanch. n. 18. et 22. et Bonac. n. 5. Laym.[345] Less.[346] quamuis non omnino improbabiliter contrarium teneat Pontius. l. 4. c. 21. aiens ita fuisse iudicatum in Hispania. sed probatur quod diximus; quia aliud est me etiam expresse noluisse contrahere, si defectum talem sciuissem; aliud posito, quod contraherem, noluisse contractum valere, nisi hac conditione subsisse.[347] Horum vnum[348] potest esse iustissimum alterum stultum, et iniustum. v. g. potest quis dicere, nollem ducere Mariam, si putarem Annam esse liberam a 1°. matrimonio at ducere Mariam cum hac conditione, vt nolim actum valere, si post constiterit Annam esse viduatam, esset impium. ergo ex eo quod quis ita sit affectus, vt nollet ducere hanc, si sciretur esse pauper etc. non sequitur eam duci sub ea conditione. similiter posset Monachus recte dicere nollem profiteri in hoc Monasterio, si putarem Abbatem esse seuerum, esse hunc vel illum defectum in eo; at velle profiteri, ita vt actus aliter non valeat, foret absurdum. Porro mentem contrahentium hoc pacto esse ordinarie interpretandam suadet et communis [fo. 19v349] sensus et sententia: et quia grauitas et perpetuitas contractus exigit, vt hoc animo suscipiatur, nimirum vt valere velis, quamdiu substantialia non desunt. Limitat 1°.

---

[339] S adds: *l. 7. dp. 18. n. 17.*
[340] S adds: *cit: n. 2. Kon: cit. n. 11.*
[341] S adds: *n. 5. Nau: n. 32 cit:*
[342] S adds: *et Vasq: cit. n. 27.*
[343] S reads: *status*
[344] S reads: *substantialia*
[345] S adds: *n. 2.*
[346] S adds: *c. 17. n. 29.*
[347] S reads: *re subsistente*
[348] S adds: *saepe*
[349] In A, along the top of fos. 19v–20 (referring to Case M13) is the heading: *De consensu conditionato praeterita vel futura.*

hoc Tan: q. 3. n. 45. et 49. nisi error qualitatis proueniat ex decep-
tione iniusta compartis, estque probabile, sed contrarium probabilius[350]
et commune. ita Bonac. Laym.[351] Limitant 2°. omnes,[352] nisi expresse
contrahas sub hac conditione, vt sit diues, nobilis, etc. i.e. mente saltem
intendens non aliter contrahere. ratio est quia tunc conditio illa fit essentialis respectu huius consensus hic et nunc.

Case M11. *Does an error in accidental qualities invalidate marriage?*
For example, Titius marries Berta, thinking she is noble, rich, healthy,
and a virgin, when she is plebeian, not wealthy, leprous and not a virgin,
which if he had known he would not in any way have married her; the
question is, is the marriage valid? See, Sanchez, Laymann, Bonacina,
Coninck and Navarre [refs].

I reply firstly that an error of the aforesaid qualities does not render
a marriage invalid; thus, all who have been cited, and also Vasquez
[ref.]. The reason is that they are not errors concerning substantial, but
accidental matters. The reason for this judgement is further that men
are judged to contract marriage in such a way that they want it to be
valid, even if those conditions described in the question are not met.
For since it is a perpetual contract and of the greatest importance, it
is accustomed to be undertaken everywhere with the greatest consideration. This is the way with all perpetual contracts, which a person
undertakes, intending them to be perpetual; even if in minor matters
he is deceived, he considers the contract satisfactory as long as those
things, which according to all are judged to be essential, are present. For
this commonly is the way of behaving in such matters, and hence this is
ordinarily judged to be the intention of everyone who does so.

I reply secondly that the marriage is valid even if that error itself was
the reason for making the contract, that is, even if your intention had
been such that if you had known you would in no way have contracted
marriage. Thus, Sanchez, Bonacina, Laymann, Lessius [refs], although
Pontius [ref.] holds that the contrary is not entirely improbable, saying
that it had been judged thus in Spain. But what we have said may be
proved: because it is one thing for me even expressly not to wish to
marry if such-and-such a defect should be known to me; and another
thing, assuming that I have married, that I do not want the contract to
be valid unless this condition has been met. The first of these positions

---

350 S adds: *est etiam in hoc casu valere Matrimonium.*
351 S adds: *dicentes esse communem: Quia stando in ipso contractus natura consensus*
fertur in solam actus substantiam; in caetera autem secundario, ergo semper erunt acci-
dentalia, dolus enim hoc non mutat, cum sit idem semper consensus obtentum. Et alioqui
nimis facile corruerent Matrimonia, cum saepe fraudis aliquid interueniat.
352 S adds: *et bene*

may often be most just; the second, stupid and unjust. For example, someone may say, 'I would not wish to marry Maria, if I thought Anna were free from her first marriage. But I am marrying Maria under this condition, that I do not want my act to be valid if afterwards it is clear that Anna is a widow'; which is impious. Therefore, because a man might have the desire not to marry this woman if he knew she was poor, it does not follow that he married her under that condition. Similarly, a monk might rightly say, 'I do not wish to join this monastery, if I think the abbot is severe, or that there is this or that defect in it'; but if he then said, 'However, I do wish to join, in such a way that my action is otherwise invalid', this would be absurd. Moreover, common sense and judgement persuade that the intention of those who make a contract is ordinarily to be interpreted in the following manner; that is, that you want it to be valid, as long as the substantial elements are not lacking, and the gravity and perpetuity of the contract demands that it should be undertaken in this spirit. Tanner [ref.] firstly limits this by saying that it is true unless an error of quality arises from the unjust deception of the spouse; and this is probable. But the contrary – that even in this case the marriage is valid – is more probable. Thus, Bonacina and Laymann, who say that this is the common judgement, because arguing from the nature of a contract, agreement is given primarily to the substance of the action, but secondarily to other things; which will always be accidental, for the fraud does not change this, since the object of the agreement is always the same. And otherwise too many marriages would be ruined, since there is often some fraud involved. Secondly, all writers rightly limit this judgement by saying that the marriage is valid unless you expressly contract with the condition, 'that she is rich, noble etc.'; that is, with the intention that you will not otherwise marry. The reason is that if this is done, then such a condition becomes essential in respect of this particular agreement, here and now.

[M12] 12ᵘˢ. An error qualitatis in personam aliquando redundet, e.g. Titius intendit contrahere cum filia vnica cuiusdam regis, sed eius loco adducitur ei alia quam coram ducit, quaeritur an valeat? Sanch. d. 18. n. 25. Laym.[353] Kon.[354] et Bonac.[355] Respondeo matrimonium illud Titii nullum esse, quia directe et primario intendit filiam talis Regis, secondario vero hanc praesentem quatenus putatur esse filia dicta, vnde errat in persona. At vero valeret, si intenderet contrahere cum illa praesente, absolute, putans falso eam esse Regis filiam, quia foret error quali-

---

[353] S adds: *cit. n. 2.*
[354] S adds: *n. 11. et 12.*
[355] S adds: *n. 7.*

tatis tantum. Itaque error qualitatis aliquando in personam redundat, aliquando non, aliquando vitiat, aliquando non. vt autem sciamus quando redundat, optima est regula quam dat Kon: d. 31. n. 15. et Bonac. q. 3. p. 2. n. 7. tunc errorem qualitatis redundare in personam, quando determinat mentem contrahentis ad certam aliquam personam distinctam ab ea, cum qua de facto contrahit, secus si non determinat ad aliam personam.[356]

Case M12. *Does an error of quality sometimes become an error concerning the person? For example, Titius intends to marry the only daughter of a certain king, but in her place another woman is brought to him, whom he marries publicly; is this marriage valid? See Sanchez, Laymann, Coninck, and Bonacina [refs].*

I reply that this marriage of Titius is null, because directly and primarily he intended to marry the daughter of this king, and secondarily, in truth, this present woman in so far as she was thought to be the said daughter; hence, he made an error concerning her person. But truly the marriage would be valid if he intended absolutely to marry the woman who was present, thinking falsely that she was the daughter of the king, because that would only be an error of quality. Therefore, an error of quality sometimes becomes an error concerning the person, sometimes not; sometimes it makes a marriage invalid, sometimes not. In order to know when an error of quality does become an error concerning the person, the best rule is that given by Coninck and Bonacina [refs]: an error of quality becomes an error concerning the person, when it decisively influences the intentions of the person who is getting married towards a particular person distinct from the one, whom he does in fact marry; it is different if it does not influence his intentions towards this other person, as is clear from the example which has been given.

[M13] 13. Quem effectum habeat matrimonium sub conditione honesta et possibili contractum?[357] v. g. contraho tecum si heri missam audieris; si sis meus conciuis; si cras nauis mea appulerit ex India: et quid si ante conditionis [fo. 20] euentum alter resiliat aut aliam ducat? Sanch. l. 5. d. 6. Laym. p. 2. c. 7.[358] Kon. d. 29. n. 8.[359] Bonac. q. 2. p. 10.[360] Respondeo consensum conditionatum esse illum, qui necdum plene existit, sed pendet suspensus a futuro euentu, vnde requirit 1°. vt conditio, sub qua fit, sit de futuro; nam si sit de praeterito vel praesente, vt si heri missam

---

[356] S adds: *Vt patet in exemplo posito.*
[357] S reads: *celebratum*
[358] S adds: *n. 1. et 2.*
[359] S adds: *9. 10.*
[360] S adds: *n. 20*

audieris, si sis conciuis, etc. non fit matrimonium proprie conditionatum id est suspensum, sed purum, nam si subsistat conditio, statim valet, si deficiat statim corruit; vnde non sunt vere conditiones istae. Conditio est enim adiectio suspensiua, vt recte Sanch.[361] et Pont:[362] requiritur[363] vt conditio sit possibilis; nam si impossibilis sit, non suspendit, sed vel statim vitiat si non reiiciatur, vel statim actus valet, si reiicienda sit conditio. Sanch. d. 3. et 4. Requiritur 3°. vt conditio sit contingens, quia si sit necessaria, et certo euentura reputatur pro iam posita: quare matrimonium erit purum.[364] Itaque conditio de futuro possibili contingenti adiecta suspendit matrimonium donec impleatur. ita Sanch. d. 6. addens conditionem debere esse honestam. sed hoc verum non est loquendo de conditione suspensiua, vt infra dicetur. Obligat autem contractus conditionatus, vt partes expectent conditionis euentum, sed si non eueniat sunt liberi: Quod si ante euentum alter resiliat, vel alteri nubat, licet peccet, tamen factum tenet. Sanch. d. 8. et Kon:[365] Quod si carnaliter misceantur ante euentum conditionis, in locis vbi Trid: non est receptum, fiet matrimonium quia per copulam censentur recessisse a conditione priori, vt expresse deciditur c. de illis de conditione oppos: et docent omnes. Ratio horum omnium est quia hoc est natura conditionis in aliis contractibus;[366] in matrimonio autem nihil contrarium statuit Ecclesia[367]. Aduerte modum adiectum non suspendere, quia non est conditio, sed tantum onus aliquod seu qualitas adiecta puro contractui, vt contraho tecum ea conditione vt des fratri meo 100 florenos.

Case M13. *What effect does a marriage[368] have which is contracted under a condition which is honest and possible? For example, 'I contract with you, if yesterday you heard Mass; if you are my fellow-citizen; if tomorrow my ship arrives from India'. And what if before the outcome of the condition, the other person should withdraw, or marry someone else? See Sanchez, Laymann, Coninck, and Bonacina [refs].*

I reply that conditional consent is consent which does not yet fully exist but which hangs suspended from a future event. Hence it requires firstly that the condition under which it is made should be one which concerns the future. For if it is concerning the past or the present, like

---

[361]　S adds: *cit: dp. 1ᵃ. n. 2.*

[362]　S adds: *l. 3. c. 1. n. 3.*

[363]　S adds: *2°.*

[364]　S adds: *Sanch: dp. 2.*

[365]　S adds: *n. 10.*

[366]　S adds: *vt patet consideranti.*

[367]　S adds: *quoad hoc, ergo sequitur naturam caeterorum contractuum.*

[368]　It should be borne in mind here, and in the cases on conditional marriage which follow, that 'marriage' can mean a contract for the present (which we call marriage), or a contract for the future (which is also called betrothal).

'if yesterday you heard Mass' or 'if you are a fellow-citizen' etc., it does not make it properly a conditional, that is, a suspended marriage, but a pure or unconditional marriage. For if the condition is fulfilled, the marriage immediately is valid; if it is deficient, it is immediately over-turned; hence those are not truly conditions. For a condition is a suspensive addition, as Sanchez and Pontius [refs] rightly say. It is secondly necessary that the condition is possible; for if the condition is impossible, it does not suspend consent, but either immediately invalidates it if the condition is not rejected, or the act is immediately made valid if the condition is rejected; see, Sanchez [ref.]. It is required thirdly that the condition should be contingent, because if it is necessary and certainly will happen it is considered already fulfilled; for which reason the marriage will be pure, and not conditional; see Sanchez [ref.]. Therefore a condition added which concerns the future and is both contingent and possible suspends a marriage until it is implemented. Thus Sanchez [ref.], adding that the condition must be honest; but this is not true when speaking of a suspensive condition, as will be said below. Moreover a conditional contract obliges the parties to wait for the outcome of the condition, but if it does not happen, they are free. If, therefore, before the outcome, one party withdraws, or marries another, although he or she sins, the fact nevertheless binds; see Sanchez and Coninck [refs]. If, therefore, they have carnal intercourse before the outcome of the condition, in places where the Council of Trent is not received it becomes marriage because by copulation they are judged to withdraw from the prior condition, as is expressly decided by canon law [ref.] and all writers teach. The reason for all this is that this is the nature of a condition in other contracts, as is clear by considering the matter; in marriage, moreover, the Church has decided nothing to the contrary as far as this is concerned; therefore the nature of other contracts should be followed. Notice the type of addition which does not suspend, because it is not a condition, but only a certain burden or quality added to the pure contract; such as, 'I contract with you, on condition that you give my brother 100 florins'.

[M14] [fo. 20ᵛ³⁶⁹] Casus 14ᵘˢ. Vtrum matrimonium sub conditione futura celebratum posita conditio fiat eo ipso purum, absque nouo consensu, aut etiam conditionis positae cognitione. Sanch. 8. d.³⁷⁰ Layn. n. 2. Kon. n. 6. et 11. Bonac: n. 20.³⁷¹ Respondeo matrimonium posita conditione

---

³⁶⁹ In A, along the top of fos. 20ᵛ–21 (referring to Cases M14 and M15) is the heading: *De conditionibus irritantibus seu // non irritantibus matrimonium.*
³⁷⁰ S adds: *n. 5.*
³⁷¹ S adds: *Nauar: tr: 22. n. 63. et 64.*

eo ipso purum effici sine nouo consensu, ita cit, omnes. contra Sotum[372] Pont:[373] et Tan:[374] probatur quia ita est in omnibus aliis contractibus,[375] imo et in actibus aliis longe nobilioribus, vt lege humana, definitione fidei etc. potest enim ad suum valorem exigere publicitatem in tali loco, qua posita statim valeat, et nihilominus conditio illa impleri potest, Concilio dissoluto, Pontifice dormiente, etc.[376] ergo. vnde infero contra Kon.[377] nec opus esse, vt partes sciant conditionem esse positam, vt patet ex aliis contractibus, ita in matrimonio etiam per Procuratores.[378]

Case M14. *Does a marriage celebrated under a future condition become pure or unconditional, immediately that condition is met, without new consent, or even without knowledge that the condition has been met? See Sanchez, Laymann, Coninck, Bonacina and Navarre [refs].*

I reply that after the condition has been met, the marriage becomes by that very fact pure or unconditional, without a new consent. Thus all those cited, against Soto, Pontius, Tanner and Bonacina [refs], and as far as Christians specifically are concerned, Tanner [ref.] agrees strongly. These writers cite St Thomas [ref.], where he calls conditional marriage a betrothal; but he is talking of the time before the condition is fulfilled. Our point is proved, because all other human contracts may be made dependent on a condition, so that as soon as that condition is fulfilled the contract is valid; indeed even in other, far nobler acts, for example in human law, in the definition of faith etc. For if a contract demands for its validity, publication in a certain place, when this has been done, it immediately becomes valid, and that condition can be fulfilled even if the Council is dissolved and the Pope sleeping etc; as Tanner himself rightly shows [ref.]. Therefore the same can be said about marriage. The

---

[372] S adds: *in 4°. dist. 29. q. 2. a. 1. can: 3.*

[373] S adds: *cap: 14.*

[374] S reads in place of the last two words: *Bonacinam, et quoad Christianos praecise acriter cum his stat Tann: q. 3. n. 83. et citant Sanctum Tho: supple: q. 47. a. 4. vbi vocat matrimonium conditionatum sponsalia; sed loquitur ante conditionem impletam.*

[375] S reads: *Probatur quia omnes alii contractus humani celebrari possunt dependenter a conditione, ita vt ea posita statim valeant:*

[376] S adds: *vt recte ipse Tan: de fide q. 4. n. 263. ergo idem dici debet de matrimonio. Patet consequentia, quia Christus eleuauit ad rationem Sacramenti illum ipsum naturalem contractum, qui ante fuit, nec nouas adiecit conditiones, sed neque Ecclesia aliquid quoad hoc innouauit.*

[377] S adds: *n. 6.*

[378] S adds: *contracto. Ita Praepos. q. 3. dub. 8. Obiicies: In nullo alio Sacramento sufficit consensus conditionatus, ergo neque hic. Nego consequentiam, quia matrimonium sequitur naturam contractus, in reliquis Christus determinauit res et verba quibus nihil addi potest. Obiicies 2°. cap: super eo, condit. appos. dicitur consensus iste non esse de praesenti. Respondeo Non esse ante impletam conditionem, bene tamen postea. Vide Con: et Sanch:*

consequence is clear, because Christ raised to the status of a sacrament that same natural contract, which had existed before, and he added no new conditions, and neither has the Church made any innovations as far as this is concerned. Hence I infer, against Coninck [ref.], that there is also no need for the parties to know that the condition has been met, as is clear from other contracts; this is also true in marriage contracted by proxies; thus, Praepos [ref.]. You will object: in no other sacrament is conditional consent sufficient, and therefore not in this. I deny the consequence, because matrimony follows the nature of a contract; in the other sacraments, Christ determined the truth and words, to which nothing can be added. You will object secondly that the canon law [ref.] says that such consent is not for the present. I reply that it is not before the condition has been fulfilled, but it certainly is afterwards; see Coninck and Sanchez.

[M15] 15us. Quam vim habeant hae conditiones? contraho tecum si Deo et Ecclesiae placuerit? si cras oriatur³⁷⁹ sol? Sanch. d. 1. et 2.³⁸⁰ Bonac. q. 2. p. 10.³⁸¹ Respondeo conditiones generales, vt si Deo placuerit, si non sis consanguinea etc. non suspendere matrimonium aut reddere conditionatum quia iure insunt. At vero si alio modo exprimantur, quam ex natura rei insint, tunc suspendent. vt si dicas: contraho tecum si non constiterit te esse consanguineam: sensus est enim, volo vt prius res examinetur, et tunc si constet non esse, erit matrimonium.³⁸² Hae et similes necessariae conditiones, v. g. contraho tecum, si cras oriatur sol, non suspendunt contractum, cum habeantur moraliter per ipsis positis³⁸³ nisi forte constet mentem contrahentium fuisse expectare crastinum. Sanch.³⁸⁴ et alii. Petes de hac conditione; contraham si Papa dispenset. Respondeo eam recte apponi posse. Nam quod aiunt Legistae conditionem a Principis voluntate pendentem censeri impossibilem leg. continuus 137. ff. de verb. oblig: intelligi debet, quando est res valde odiosa, et raro [fo. 21] concedi solita, vt v.g. si dicas; dabo tibi 100. pro coemiterio, si Papa patiatur fieri profanum. actus enim non valeret. Sanch. d. 5.

---

³⁷⁹ S reads: *luccat*
³⁸⁰ S adds: *Con: dp. 29. dub. 2. et n. 8.*
³⁸¹ S adds: *n. 5.*
³⁸² S adds: *Idem est si quis diceret, si comperero rem Deo et Ecclesiae ingratam non esse. Quare haec, contraho si Deo et Ecclesiae placuerit, vt sonat, non videtur efficere actum conditionatum.*
³⁸³ S reads, in place of the last six words: *quare statim valebit matrimonium vt supra diximus.*
³⁸⁴ S adds: *dp: 2. n. 6.*

Case M15. *What force do these conditions have: 'I contract with you if it please God and the Church'; 'If tomorrow the sun should rise'? See Sanchez, Coninck and Bonacina [refs].*

I reply that general conditions, like 'if it please God', 'if you are not related to me in blood' etc., do not suspend marriage or render it conditional, because they are present by law anyway. But if indeed they are expressed in another way, rather than according to the nature of the contract they are already found in, then they will suspend it. If for example you say: 'I contract with you if it does not emerge that you are related to me in blood'; for the meaning is, 'I will that the matter is first examined and then if it is agreed that it is not the case, this will be marriage.' It is the same if someone should say, 'If I discover that the matter is not disagreeable to God and the Church.' For which reason, this saying, 'I contract if it please God and the Church', on the face of it, does not seem to make a conditional act. These and similar necessary conditions (for example, 'I will contract with you if tomorrow the sun should rise') do not suspend the contract, since morally they are contained in the contract itself; unless perhaps it is agreed that the intention of the person contracting the marriage was to wait until tomorrow. See Sanchez [ref.], and others. You will ask about this condition: 'I may contract with you if the Pope grants a dispensation.' I reply that it can be rightly attached. For when the civil lawyers say [ref.] that a condition depending on the will of the Prince is to be judged impossible, it should be understood to mean when the matter is very odious and customarily only conceded rarely. As for example, if you say, 'I will give you 100 for the church-yard, if the Pope will allow it to be profaned', for the act would not be valid; see Sanchez [ref.].

[M16] 16us. An conditiones appositae contra substantiam matrimonii eam vitient. v. g. contraho tecum si generationem euites; donec aliam pulchriorem inueniam; si te adulterandam tradas. Sanch. l. 5. d. 9. Laym. l. 2. c. 7.[385] Less. l. 2. c. 18. d. 15.[386] Respondeo et dico 1°. conditiones adiectas praedictas per modum modi vitiare matrimonium ita expresse Gregor. 9. c. fin: de condit: appos.[387] et omnes Doctores. ratio est, quia matrimonium est essentialiter contractus obligans ad contrarium viz: ne procures abortum, adulteres etc. ergo velle obligare se obligare[388] ad

---

[385] S adds: *n. 8. Conin: dp: 29. dub. 3. Bonac: q. 2. pun: 10. n. 8.*
[386] S reads: *l. 2. de iustitia c. 18. dub. 15. n. 122.*
[387] S adds: *his verbis. Si conditiones contra substantiam coniugii inserantur, puta, si alter dicat alteri: contraho tecum si generationem prolis euites, vel, donec aliam digniorem inueniam, si pro quaestu adulterandam te tradas, matrimonialis contractus, quantumcunque sit fauorabilis, caret effectu*
[388] Repeated thus in A.

istam est velle se aliquid pugnans cum matrimonio. Hoc autem intellige de voluntate seria et absoluta;[389] nam si secundario tantum ista intende- rentur, sicut secundario intendit Haereticus significare suos errores per formas sacramentales valeret ex natura rei matrimonium. Forte tamen iure poisitiuo esset etiam tunc irritum, quia videtur Pontifex in odium sceleris irritare saltem in foro externo.[390] Dico 2°. si conditiones prae- dictae addantur per modum verae conditionis suspensiuae in futurum, ita vt sensus sit; contraho tecum, si prius prolem ex me susceptam, eneces, si cum tali concubueris, etc. matrimonium[391] iure naturae esse validum. ita San: cit. n. 40. Pontius et Praepos:[392] ratio est, quia iure naturae in caeteris valet is contrahendi modus, licet impius sit: iure etiam positiuo non videtur irritus, quia probabilius est Pontificem non agere de condi- tionibus de futuro, sed tantum de modis, vt bene Praepos: et alii.[393]

Case M16. *Do additional conditions, which are against the substance of marriage render it invalid? For example, 'I marry you if you avoid having children'; 'until I find another more beautiful woman'; 'if you commit adultery'. See Sanchez, Laymann, Coninck, Bonacina and Lessius [refs].*

I reply and say, firstly, that the aforesaid conditions, added to modify a contract of marriage invalidate it; thus expressly, Gregory IX [ref.], in these words, 'If conditions contrary to the substance of marriage are inserted, for example, if one says to the other: "I contract with you if you avoid having children", or "until I find someone else more worthy", "if you will commit adultery for money", the marriage contract, however much it may be favourable, will not have its effect.' All the doctors agree on this. The reason is that marriage is essentially a contract which obliges us to do the opposite; that is, not to procure an abortion, or not to commit adultery, etc. Therefore, to wish to oblige yourself to this is to wish something which is the enemy of marriage. However, you must understand this to refer to a serious, absolute and efficacious will, for if this is only meant secondarily, just as a heretic may intend his errors secondarily, through sacramental forms, the marriage would be valid by its very nature. Perhaps, however, the marriage would still also be invalid by the positive law, because it seems that the Pope, acting out of a hatred of evil, would invalidate it, at least in the legal forum. I say, secondly, if the aforesaid conditions are added in the manner of

---

389 S adds: *et efficaci*
390 S adds: *semper praesumetur irritum.*
391 S adds: *impleta conditione*
392 S reads instead of these references: *Ita Coninck .n. 40. Pontius. l. 3. c. 9. n. 11. Praepos: de matri. q. 3. dub. 7. n. 88.*
393 S adds: *mox citandi.*

a true, suspensive condition for the future, so that the meaning is: 'I contract marriage with you, if you will quickly kill the children you have by me', or 'if you will sleep with such a man', etc., the marriage by the law of nature would be valid; thus, Sanchez, Pontius, Praepos, and Coninck [refs] The reason is that by the law of nature this mode of contracting is valid in other matters, even though it is impious. By positive law also it does not seem to be invalid, because it is more probable that the Pope would not act concerning conditions about the future, but only concerning modifications to a contract, as Praepos shows well, and others who will soon be cited.

[M17] 17ᵘˢ. Vtrum conditiones aliae turpes vel impossibiles matrimonio adiectae, ipsum vitient. v. g. contraho tecum si omnes orientis gemmas mihi attuleris, si latrocinia mecum exercueris. Sanch:³⁹⁴ d. 3. et 15. Laym. cit. n. 11. Kon. d. 29. d. 3.³⁹⁵ Respondeo stando in ipsa rei natura videndum esse quid intendant: [fo. 21ᵛ³⁹⁶] nam si velint reuera non contrahere nisi ponatur talis conditio turpis aut impossibilis, reipsa nihil fiet nec potest Ecclesia facere vt valeat quia consensum supplere nequit, vt bene Rebellius pars. 2. de oblig. l. 2. q. 10. s. 4. Sanch. cit. d. 1. n. 4. Less. Kon. Difficultas est quia Greg: 9ᵘˢ. c. fin. cit. docet conditiones has haberi pro non adiectis, et matrimonium valere perinde ac si adiectae non essent. Omissis variis dicendi modis, dico Pontificem non loqui hic de conditionibus suspensiuis, sed modificantibus tantum, et per modum pacti; hae autem actum non vitiant vt in aliis etiam docet Molin: tr. 2. d. 208. Sanch. d. 19.³⁹⁷ Ratio est, quia cum adiiciantur per modum accessorii et appendicis supponere debent consensum absolutum in matrimonium ipsum. Et de huiusmodi conditionibus Pontificem loqui³⁹⁸ docent Rebell: Less.³⁹⁹ et Pont:⁴⁰⁰ cum Laym.⁴⁰¹ et Praepos:⁴⁰² Quare si esset conditio impossibilis suspensiua serio apposita, actus foret nullus.⁴⁰³

Dices etiam quando per modum⁴⁰⁴ adiicitur, potest serio, absolute et plane efficaciter adiici, ita vt nolis aliter valere matrimonium aeque ac

---

³⁹⁴ S adds: *l. 5.*
³⁹⁵ S adds: *Bonac: n. 16.*
³⁹⁶ In A, along the top of fos. 21ᵛ–22 (referring to Case M18) is the heading: *An valeat matrimonium sub conditione // continentiae.*
³⁹⁷ S adds: *n. 7.*
³⁹⁸ S reads: *Porro de huiusmodi conditionibus tantum, non vero de suspensiuis loqui Pontificem*
³⁹⁹ S adds: *cit. n. 122.*
⁴⁰⁰ S adds: *l. 3. c. 4. n. 9.*
⁴⁰¹ S adds: *n. 11.*
⁴⁰² S adds: *sub. 7. cit. n. 91.*
⁴⁰³ S adds: *vt bene illi.*
⁴⁰⁴ S adds: *pacti*

potest conditio contra substantiam matrimonii nam quoad hoc non est disparitas. ergo vitiabit. Respondeo posse ita adiici et tunc vitiaturam in foro conscientiae. Caeterum Pontifex propter fauorem Matrimonii vt ipse loquitur, statuit, vt semper praesumatur matrimonium absolute intentum, conditio vero tantum secundario. et statuendo hoc facit etiam, vt fideles censendi[405] ordinarie hoc modo contrahere, nisi expresse constet de opposito, quia intendunt ipsi ordinarie vt ipsorum verba et pacta intelligantur eo modo, quo similia accipi consueuerunt. Quare nisi constet clare de opposita mente ipsorum, etiam in foro conscientiae censendum erit matrimonium primario intentum, atque adeo validum.

Case M17. *Do other conditions, added to a marriage, which are dishonourable or impossible invalidate the marriage? For example, 'I contract with you of you will give me all the jewels of the Orient', or 'if you will commit robberies with me'. See Sanchez, Laymann, Coninck, and Bonacina [refs].*

I reply that, basing my decision on the very nature of marriage, what the prospective marriage partners mean must be examined; for if they truly wish not to marry unless such a dishonourable or impossible condition is added, truly nothing may be done about it, and the Church cannot make the marriage valid, because the couple cannot give consent to such a contract, as Rebellus, Sanchez, Lessius and Coninck [refs] make clear. The difficulty is that Gregory IX [ref.] teaches that we must hold that these conditions have not been added, and hence that the marriage is valid as if they had not been added. Setting aside other things that might be said here, I say the Pope does not speak here about suspensive conditions, but only about modifications, and those done through the medium of an agreement, which moreover do not invalidate the act, as Molina and Sanchez [refs] also teach in other matters. The reason is that they were added as an accessory and appendix, and so they should imply absolute consent to the marriage itself. And, according to Rebellus, Lessius, and Pontius, with Layman and Praepos [refs], it is concerning this sort of condition that the Pope speaks, not in fact about suspensive conditions. Hence, if it had been an impossible, suspensive condition seriously added, the act would be null, as the writers cited above say correctly.

You will say that even when it is added as a modification, it can be seriously, absolutely, and plainly efficaciously added, so that you only wish the marriage to be valid in the same way as a condition against the substance of marriage may, because there is no difference between such a condition and such a modification. Therefore, it will make it

---

[405] S adds: *sint*

invalid. I reply that if it is added in that way, then the marriage will be invalid in the forum of conscience. However, the Pope, out of good will for marriage, as he himself says, ordained that marriage should always be presumed absolutely to be intended, with any condition truly only secondarily intended. And by ordaining this, the result is that the faithful are ordinarily to be judged to contract in this way, unless it is expressly agreed to the contrary, because they themselves intend ordinarily that their words and agreements are to be understood in the way in which similar things are customarily accepted. Hence, unless it is agreed clearly that these people were of an opposite mind, even in the forum of conscience it will be judged that marriage was primarily intended, and so it is valid.

[M18] 18us. An valeat matrimonium sub hac conditione, vt continentiam seruemus? Sanch. d. 10. Laym. cit. n. 9.[406] Respondeo si efficaciter adiiciatur, ita vt sibi mutuo remittant ius reddendi carnale debitum probabilius est matrimonium non valere: ita S. T. Supplem. q. 47. a. 5. Sanch. Laym. cit. et Tan.[407] Henr. [fo. 22] et alii[408] contra Vasq. 3. p. d. 125. Kon. Pont.[409] et Bonac.[410] Probatur quia licet non sit de substantia matrimonii aut copula aut voluntas eam petendi, bene tamen voluntas efficax sese ad eam obligandi, vel potius vera obligatio ad copulam, saltem quantum ex vi iuris, et nisi aliquo extrinseco impedimento detineatur alter ne petat. Nihil enim aliud esse potest traditio corporum, nisi talis voluntas, qua viz: dicatur: volo vt liceat tibi a me petere debitum, et nequeo ex parte mea illud negare.[411] confirmatur, quia est contra substantiam matrimonii conditio haec, ac turpes supradictae, neque turpitudo facit, vt sint contra substantiam, sed quia obligant ad aliquid contrarium obligationi coniugali.

Obiicitur. B. Virgo verum contraxit matrimonium non tamen consensit in copulam; hoc enim fuisset contra Virginitatem perfectam. Respondeo eam consensisse remote in copulam modo iam dicto, vt docet S. Aug. c. B. Maria. 27. q. 2. et indicat S. T. cit. q. 48. a. 1.[412] fecit tamen id instinctu Dei, a quo certo sciuit S. Iosephum non petiturum: et forte etiam habuit ipse Castitatis votum, absque tamen iuris renunciatione.

Obiicitur 2°. haec obligatio superueniens matrimonio contracto non pugnat cum eo, ergo nec ab initio. Nego consequentiam sicut de virilium

---

[406] S adds: *Con: dp: 24. n. 43. Bonac: cit. n. 13.*
[407] S adds: *q. 3. n. 74. Sotus*
[408] S adds: *apud Sanchem*
[409] S adds: *l. 3. c. 11. n. 6.*
[410] S adds: *citatos cum aliis*
[411] S adds: *Hic inquam est consensus matrimonialis, habetque pro obiecto suo copulam.*
[412] S adds: *corp: et ad 1um.*

abscissione omnes debent dicere, quia semel contractum satis intelligi
potest manere in ordine ad alios effectus secundarios cohabitationis etc.
at initio debet constitui per ordinem ad suum effectum primarium.
Obiicitur 3°. Duo ligati voto simplici Castitatis, idque scientes,
valide matrimonium contrahunt. ergo obligatio ad copulam non est de
essentia matrimonii. Probatur consequentiam cum neuter possit licite
petere copulam, nec alter tenebitur ei reddere; cooperaretur enim eius
peccato, quod non possit, nedum tenetur, vt patet ex dictis de scandalo,
et dicetur infra casu 57. Respondeo saltem teneri[413] quantum est ex vi
iuris sui praecise, ita vt titulo iuris nequeat negare. vnde si alter petat a
Pontifice dispensationem voti sui, vel si aliunde cessaret obligatio eius,
eo ipso vellet nollet teneretur alter reddere: quod satis[414] intelligatur ius
remotum ad copulam, et vera corporum traditio. at si remittant sibi ius,
verbo tenus contrahunt, non reipsa.

Case M18. *Is a marriage valid under this condition, 'that we remain
chaste'?* See Sanchez, Laymann, Coninck and Bonacina [refs].

I reply that if it is added, so that it really has the effect that they
both mutually give up their right to render their carnal dues, it is probable that the marriage is not valid; thus, St Thomas, Sanchez, Laymann,
Tanner, Soto, Henriquez, and others cited by Sanchez [refs], against
Vasquez, Coninck, Pontius and Bonacina [refs], with others. This is
proved because, although neither copulation nor the desire to request it
are of the substance of marriage, the efficacious desire to oblige oneself
to perform copulation, or rather the true obligation to copulation, is at
least to oblige oneself as much as is required by the force of the law,
and unless one spouse is prevented from requesting their dues by some
external impediment. For the surrender of bodies can be nothing else
but such a desire, by which in fact we say: 'I wish that it were lawful
for you to request me to perform my marital dues, and I do not wish,
for my part, to deny them to you.' This, I say, is matrimonial consent,
and it has for its object copulation. This is confirmed because the condition proposed in this case is contrary to the substance of marriage in
the same way as the dishonourable conditions of the previous case are;
and it is not the dishonourableness that makes them contrary to the
substance of marriage, but because they oblige to something which is
contrary to the conjugal obligation.

An objection to this judgement is that the Blessed Virgin contracted a
true marriage, but did not however consent to copulation, for this would
have been contrary to her perfect virginity. I reply that she remotely

---

[413] S adds: *reddere*
[414] S adds: *est vt*

did consent to copulation in the way which has already been said, as St Augustine teaches [ref.], and St Thomas [ref.] declares. She however acted under the guidance of God, as a result of which guidance she knew for certain that St Joseph would not ask for his marital dues; and perhaps also he had himself taken a vow of chastity, without however renouncing his right.

A second objection is that this obligation (to chastity), when it dates from after the matrimonial contract, does not militate against it; therefore, it would not do so from the beginning. I deny the consequence, just as everyone should say concerning male castration. This is because once it has been contracted, marriage can satisfactorily be understood to continue, in order to achieve other secondary effects, like cohabitation etc. But at the beginning it should be constituted in order to achieve its primary effect.

A third objection is that two people bound by a simple vow of chastity, and both aware of this, may contract marriage validly; therefore, the obligation to copulation is not of the essence of matrimony. The consequence is proved since neither may lawfully request copulation, and the other is likewise not bound to render it; for that would be to co-operate in the other's sin, which should not be done, and which one is certainly not bound to do, as is clear from what has been said about scandal,[415] and what is said below, in Case 57. I reply that the spouse is at least bound to perform his or her marital duties precisely as a matter of legal duty, so he or she cannot deny them as if it were a right to do so. Hence, if one of them requests a dispensation from the vow of chastity from the Pope, or if in some other way this obligation should cease, then immediately whether he or she likes it or not, the other spouse is bound to render their marital dues, which may sufficiently be understood as demonstrating that there is a remote right to copulation, and the true surrender of bodies. But if they give up this right, they contract marriage, only verbally, not in reality.

[M19] [fo. 22ᵛ] 19ᵘˢ. An filius contrahens insciis seu inuitis parentibus peccet mortaliter. Sanch. l. 4. d. 22. et 23. Lay. p. 1. c. 1.[416] Bonac. q. 4. p. 17.[417] Respondeo esse per se loquendo peccatum mortale contrahere insciis parentibus: tenetur enim filius consulere parentes de suis nuptiis, ita omnes.[418] Con. Tan.[419] Pont.[420] Bellar. l. 1. c. 19. imo

---

415 Presumably a reference back to the English cases.
416 S adds: *n. 12. Coninck. dp. 28. dub. 5.*
417 S adds: *a. n. 15.*
418 S adds: *Sanch. Laym: Bonac.*
419 S adds: *q. 3. n. 103*
420 S adds: *t. 2. c. 1.*

tenentur expectare eorum consensum ordinarie loquendo, et quidem sub mortali, vt putant Bellar. et Tan. et fauent varii canones antiqui c. aliter. c. nostrates. 30. q. 5. c. honorantur. c. 32. q. 2. Verum alii forte probabilius docent esse solum peccatum veniale irreuerentiae sine consensu parentis nubere. nisi aliunde parens ob grauissimas causas[421] inuitus. ita Sanch. Lay. Kon. et Bonac. Caeterum si parens esset nimis durus, et filio appetenti coniugium non sine periculo incontinentiae[422] adhuc tergiuersaretur, aut similis causa subsit, non esset peccatum eo inscio contrahere. ita Tan.[423] Est enim hoc iuris naturalis, quod nequit parens filio eripere, vnde nec cogere possunt ad certas nuptias filios aut prohibere eas, quas rationabiliter expetunt. solum possunt consulere, et moderate etiam suadere.[424] Illud certum est, si filius contrahat insciis parentibus, matrimonium[425] esse validum, esto peccet, ita definit Trid. s. 24. c. 1. declarans in hoc ius antiquum[426] canonum, qui requirebant consensum parentum non tanquam aliquid de valore actus, sed solum de praecepto. ita Sanch : et Bellar.[427] Vtrum filia nubens indigno contra Parentis voluntatem possit exhaeredari, vide apud eosdem. Posset hoc lege introduci, licet[428] non videatur introductum,[429] cum non recenseatur inter causas exhaeredationis authent. vt cum de appelat. nouella 115. c. 3. ita Tan.

Case M19. *Does a son contracting marriage without the knowledge or permission of his parents sin mortally? See Sanchez, Laymann, Coninck, and Bonacina [refs].*

I reply that, in itself, it is a mortal sin to contract marriage without the knowledge of parents, for a son is bound to consult his parents about his marriage. Thus, all; Sanchez, Laymann, Bonacina, Coninck, Tanner, Pontius and Bellarmine [refs]. Indeed, they are bound to wait for their parents' consent ordinarily speaking, and indeed under mortal sin, as Bellarmine and Tanner think, and various ancient canons favour [refs].

---

421 S adds: *esset*
422 S reads: *inconuenientiae*
423 S adds: *n. 105.*
424 S adds: *Sanch. dp. 22. n. 7.*
425 S reads: *contractum*
426 S adds: *Idem colligitur ex cap. Tuae fraternitatis de sponsal: cap: cum causa de Rapt. cap: cum virum de reg:* S then reads in place of the next three words in A: *canones vero antiqui requirentes*
427 S adds: *et patet, quia et multa alia requiriunt, quae nullus dixerit esse substantiale. Pontius tamen l. 2. c. 1. putat olim in primis illis Ecclesiae saeculis Parentum consensum fuisse necessarium ad valorem; quod tamen ex iis canonibus non satis probatur.*
428 S adds: *de facto*
429 S reads in place of the final clause from here: *vnde nec potest ei negari legitima. Ita Tan: n. 107. Neque enim inter causas exhaeredationis quae recensentur authent. vt cum de appelat. Nouella 115. cap. 3. ponitur ista.*

But in truth, others, perhaps with more probability, teach that it is only to commit the venial sin of irreverence to marry without the consent of a parent, unless, however, the parent was unwilling for most serious reasons; thus, Sanchez, Laymann, Coninck and Bonacina. Moreover, if the parent is too harsh, and so far has often refused the son who is desirous of marriage and in danger of incontinence, it would not be a sin to contract marriage without the parent's knowledge; thus Tanner [ref.]. For by the law of nature a parent should not forcibly remove anything from his son; hence parents may not force their sons into certain marriages, or prohibit those which the sons on reasonable grounds choose. The parents may only give advice, and gently persuade their sons; see Sanchez [ref.]. It is certain that if the son contracts marriage without the knowledge of his parents, the marriage is valid, even if he sins in doing so. The Council of Trent [ref.] laid this down, declaring in this law that the ancient canons [refs] which required the consent of the parents did so, not in so far as it affected the validity of the act, but only as a precept. Thus, Sanchez and Bellarmine, and it is clear because many other things are also required by canon law, which no one would say are essential. Pontius [ref.], however, thinks that once, in the first centuries of the Church, the consent of parents was necessary to the validity of a marriage; but this cannot be satisfactorily proved from these canons. Whether a daughter who marries unworthily against the will of her parent can be deprived of her inheritance, is discussed in the same writers. This form of disinheritance might indeed be introduced by law, but in fact it does not seem to have been. Hence, a legitimate inheritance may not be denied to her; thus, Tanner [ref.]. Nor is it to be found among the causes of disinheritance listed in the Canon Law [ref.].

[M20] 20ᵘˢ. An matrimonium contractum sine Parocho et testibus sit invalidum in omni prorsus casu vbi receptum est Tridentinum v. g. in articulo mortis absente Parocho; inter haereticos in locis Catholicis, in locis catholicis vbi Parochi nulli sunt amplius,⁴³⁰ aut solum occulti. Sanch. l. 3. d. 17. Laym. p. 2. c. 4.⁴³¹ Bonac. q. 2. p. 8.⁴³² Respondeo. 1ᵒ. matrimonium sine Parocho et testibus vbi receptum est Tridentinum esse nullum. haec est certa et communis [fo. 23] habeturque in C. Trid. s. 24. c. 1. de reformatione matrimonii vbi tamen statuitur, ne obliget, nisi post dies 30. in singulis Parochiis respectare. Ratio est, quia Concilium ista statuit ad multa mala impedienda. Porro cum haec sit lex irritans formam praescribens contractui, et personas aliter contrahentes inhabili-

---

⁴³⁰ S reads in place of the preceding clause: *denique inter Catholicos in locis vbi Parochi et Episcopi nulli sunt amplius,*

⁴³¹ S adds: *n. 1. et 7. Con: dp: 27. dub. 1.*

⁴³² S adds: *a n. 1. 2. et 11.*

tans, obligat in omni casu, quia nec mortis articulus, vel vlla necessitas contrahendi in absentia Parochi potest facere, vt contractus subsistat sine sua forma substantiali, aut vt personae inhabiles agant valide, vnde non datur in istis epikeia.⁴³³ Respondeo 2º. in locis ubi semel promulgatum est Tridentinum postea vero haereticis ea occupantibus, iam vel nulli sunt Pastores, vel ita occulti, vt tuto adire nequeant, vt in ditione Hollandorum contingit, valet matrimonium sine Parocho, modo adsint duo testes. ita Kon. d. 27. d. 1. Praepos: de matr. q. 4. d. 8. Laym. cit. Estque Romae declaratum a Cardinalibus qui ita dicuntur respondisse Nuncio Bruxellensi, et Vicario Hollandiae an: 1600, et 1603. vt refert Praepos. et Kelisonus q. 45. a. 5. d. 2. et Konink ait ita declarasse Clement. 8ᵐ. Decretum enim C. intelligi debet, si adsint Parochi, vel alii Sacerdotes delegati. Caeterum cum iam sint in Hollandia multi Sacerdotes, putat Kelisonus Catholicos ibi inualide contracturos, si facile aliquem habere possint, et nisi metus grauis excuset. Caeterum in Anglia alia est ratio, cum ibi nunquam publicatum sit hoc Decretum. Quoad Haereticos⁴³⁴ vbi publicatum est Tridentinum aliqui censent eos valide contrahere sine Parocho Catholico etiam in locis, vbi adhuc publice degunt Parochi Catholici Pontifice viz: tacite indulgente: ita Laym. cit. et Tann.⁴³⁵ quod ea ratione videtur posse suaderi, quia plerumque⁴³⁶ intercedit aliqua pactio inter haereticos et Catholicos vt vtrique pacifice iuxta suam religionem viuant, quam vtpote etiam Catholicis commodam censetur approbare Pontifex, tanquam pars omnis Communitatis Catholicae. Nihilominus in rigore videtur verius illorum matrimonia esse [fo. 23ᵛ⁴³⁷] inualida et dissolui posse. ita Praepos. aiens ita responsum esse a Cardinalibus Vicario Hollandiae 1603. et similis declaratio extat in declarationibus ex Bibliotheca Bellar. impressis Lugduni s. 24. c. de matrimonio. Illud tamen circa has Cardinalium declarationes C. Trid: semel notasse sufficit. eas omnes quae sine sigillo et subscriptione Congregationis circumferuntur, siue impressae, siue manuscriptae, nullam fidem facere in iudicio vel extra ex Decreto S. D. N. Vrbani 8. 2. Aug. 1631. His adde peregrinos quoscunque in locis, vbi Concilium est receptum non posse sine Parocho contrahere. ita Sanch. d. 18. quia lex formam actibus praescribens, obligat etiam peregrinos.

Case M20. *In places where the Council of Trent is received, is marriage contracted without a parish priest and witnesses invalid in absolutely*

⁴³³ S adds: *vt diximus de leg. casu 50.*
⁴³⁴ S adds: *in locis*
⁴³⁵ S adds: *q. 3. n. 122:*
⁴³⁶ S reads: *communis*
⁴³⁷ In A, along the top of fos. 23ᵛ–24 (referring to Case M21) is the heading: *Quinam Parochus // requiratur*

all cases? For example, without a parish priest, at the point of death; between heretics in Catholic places; in Catholic places, where there are not enough parish priests and bishops, or they are only in hiding? See Sanchez, Laymann, Coninck and Bonacina [refs].

I reply firstly that in places where the Council of Trent is received, marriage without a parish priest and witnesses is null. This is the certain and common judgement and is to be found in the decrees of the Council of Trent [ref.], where however it is enacted that this law only obliges after it has been received for 30 days in individual parishes. The reason is that the Council decreed it thus to prevent many evils. Moreover since this is a law which invalidates, which lays down the form for a contract, and can also render people unsuitable to make a contract, it obliges in all cases; because not even the moment of death, nor any necessity requiring marriage in the absence of a parish priest, can make the contract exist without its substantial form, or allow unsuitable people to act with validity. Hence no leniency is shown in these matters, as we have said in *Concerning Laws*, Case 50. I reply secondly that in places where the decrees of the Council of Trent were once promulgated but which were actually afterwards occupied by heretics, and now either there are no pastors, or they are so much in hiding that they cannot safely attend, as is the case in the dominion of Holland, matrimony without a parish priest is valid, as long as there are two witnesses. Thus, Coninck, Praepos, and Laymann [refs]. And this was declared at Rome by the Cardinals who are said to have replied in this way to the Nuncio at Brussels and the Vicar of Holland in the years 1600 and 1603, as Praepos and Kellison relate [refs]; and Coninck says that Clement VIII declared it thus. For the decree of the Council should be understood to mean 'if there are parish priests, or other priests who have been delegated with such powers'. However, since there are now in Holland many priests, Kellison thinks Catholics would contract marriage there invalidly, if any priests could easily be had there,[438] and unless grave fear excuses them. However, in England the reason is different, since this decree of the Council of Trent was never published there. As far as heretics are concerned, in places where the Council of Trent's decrees have been published, some people judge that they validly contract without a Catholic parish priest, even in places where Catholic parish priests still live publicly (that is, with the tacit indulgence of the Pope); thus Laymann and Tanner [refs]. It seems possible that this judgement might be persuasive, for the reason that some agreement often develops between heretics and Catholics that they should each live peacefully according to their religion, which the Pope is also judged to approve

---

[438] That is to say, 'and they got married without a priest'.

in order to secure the well-being of Catholics, as part of the whole Catholic community. Nevertheless, taking a rigorous line, it seems to be more true that the marriages of these heretics are invalid and may be dissolved. Thus, Praepos, saying that this was the reply of the Cardinals to the Vicar of Holland in 1603. And the same declaration is extant in the Declarations from the Library of Bellarmine, printed at Lyon [ref.]. It is sufficient, however, for us to note here, concerning those declarations of the Cardinals about the Council of Trent,[439] that all those which circulate without the seal and subscription of the Congregation, either printed or manuscript, are not to be trusted, either in the law courts or outside, as a result of the decree of S. D. N. Urban VIII of 2 August 1631. Add to these points that any pilgrims in places where the Council is received may not contract marriage without a parish priest; thus, Sanchez [ref.], because a law which prescribes the form for such acts obliges even pilgrims.

[M21] Casus 21. Quisnam Parochus requiratur? num contrahentium proprius? num alterutrius sufficiat,[440] idque siue assistat in sua Parochia, siue extra? Sanch. l. 3. d.16.[441] Laym. p. 2. c. 4.[442] Bonac. q. 2. p. 8.[443] Respondeo certum esse, sufficere alterutrius Parochum siue Sponsi, siue Sponsae, si sit in propria Parochia. Ita omnes et expresse habetur in Rituali Pauli 5. Nomine autem Parochi a fortiori venit Episcopus, Papa, Nuntius Apostolicus, Vicarius Generalis, Abbas Episcopali gaudens iurisdictione et similes, de quibus Sanch. d. 27. Difficultas est an Parochus proprius possit assistere in Parochia aliena. Negat Pontius l. 5. c. 16. et Nauar.[444] fundatur in Cardinalium Declarationibus, sed hae fidem non faciunt, et si facerent, pro contrario afferri possent, ita enim habetur in Declarationibus ex[445] Bellar. s. 24.[446] c. 1. declar. 36 matrimonium contractum in [fo. 24] Parochia mulieris coram Parocho viri, et e conuerso, valet etiamsi Parochiae viri et mulieris sint in diuersis dioecesibus. Melius vrgeri possit Rituale Pauli 5. sed solum vult, vt assistat omnino

---

[439] This refers to the Congregation of the Council, the body of cardinals set up to see to the execution and observance of the decrees of the Council of Trent in 1564 by Pope Pius IV. Southwell refers occasionally to an edition of their 'Declarations' published in 1621 by Gallemart, of which he strongly disapproves, and which, as he says, was denounced by the Pope. Southwell approves, however, of an edition of the Declarations drawn from the library of Cardinal Bellarmine and published by Durand at Lyons in 1633. See the list of Southwell's Authorities above, and compare Case M26.
[440] S adds: *siue viri siue mulieris?*
[441] S reads: *19*
[442] S adds: *n. 3.*
[443] S adds: *n. 1. 10. 16. et 17.*
[444] S adds: *de clandes: de sponsal. consil. 3. n. 1.*
[445] S adds: *biblioth:*
[446] S reads: *25.*

licite, debere assistere in propria Parochia; est enim culpabile sine causa extra eam assistere, vt docent Tan. et Bonac. quamuis forte non mortaliter, vt volunt Kon. et Sanch.

Dico ergo Parochum proprium assistere valide extra suam Parochiam ita citati omnes cum Tan.[447] et Diana.[448] 1°. quia Tridentinum plus non requirit, quam vt sit Parochus proprius.[449] 2°. quia potest Parochus extra Parochiam audire Confessiones suorum, ministrare iis Sacramentum Eucharistiae et similia, quae contentiosa non sunt, vt vniuersim docet Sanch. l. 3. d. 19.[450] ergo et matrimonium est enim eadem ratio. 3°. quia ante Tridentinum poterat assistere extra Parochiam eo modo, quo tunc requirebatur assistentia scilicet ne esset clandestinum. ergo et iam idem potest, quia Tridentinum non correxit ius antiquum, quoad hoc, sed tantum annullat actum sine eius praesentia factum.

Case M21. *Which parish priest is required? Should it be the priest of the people getting married? Would it be sufficient to have the priest of either the man or the woman; and should he assist at the marriage in his own parish or outside it? See Sanchez, Laymann and Bonacina [refs].*

I reply that it is certain that it is sufficient to have the parish priest of either betrothed, man or woman, if he is in his own parish. Thus, all, and this is expressly said in the Ritual of Paul V. Under the name 'priest', however, are included with even stronger reason, bishop, pope, apostolic nuncio, vicar general, abbot enjoying episcopal jurisdiction, and similar; on which see Sanchez [ref.]. The difficulty is whether their own parish priest can properly assist in a different parish. Pontius and Navarre [refs] deny it, basing themselves on the Declarations of the Cardinals, but these are not trustworthy, and if they are, they can be alleged on the contrary side, for thus it is said in the Declarations from the library of Bellarmine [ref.]. Marriage contracted in the parish of the woman before the parish priest of the man, and the converse, is valid even if the parishes of the man and the woman are in different dioceses. The Ritual of Paul V might have a stronger argument, but it only wants the priest to assist in his own parish so that he assists completely lawfully; for he is culpable if he assists outside it without cause, as Tanner and Bonacina teach, although perhaps not gravely blameworthy, as Coninck and Sanchez would have it.

I say therefore that their own parish priest may assist outside his own parish; thus, all those cited, with Tanner, Diana and at length Pontius

---

[447] S adds: *q. 3. n. 116. et 120.*
[448] S adds: *de Sacram: resol. 232. et tandem Pontius c. 29. n. 9. sibi manifeste contradicens.*
[449] S adds: *vt patet legenti*
[450] S adds: *n. 8.*

[refs], who manifestly contradicts himself. My judgement is because, first, Trent does not require more than that it should be their own parish priest. Second, because the parish priest outside his parish may hear confessions of his parishioners, minister to them the sacrament of the Eucharist and similar things, which are not contentious, as Sanchez teaches in general terms; therefore this is also true of marriage, for the reason is the same. Third, because before Trent he could assist outside his parish, for the same reason as his assistance would now be required, that is, so that the marriage is not clandestine. Therefore he can also do the same now, because Trent has not corrected the ancient law, as far as that is concerned, but only annulled the action if it is done without his presence.

[M22] 22. Quis dicatur hic proprius Parochus, an Parochus originis, an potius habitationis? an quaeuis modica habitatio sufficiat etiam[451] animo permanendi? quid de iis, qui duo habent domicilia? quid de vagis, qui nullum habent? quid de militibus et scholaribus, vbi praeter Paro-chum habitationis, alium habent castrensem aut Academicum. Sanch. l. 3. d. 23. 24. 25. Bonac. q. 2. p. 8.[452] Kon. d. 27. n. 18.[453] Respondeo Parochum hic proprium esse eum, in cuius Parochia habitas, non vero in cuius [fo. 24ᵛ454] Parochia olim natus es, alias vagi haberent[455] proprium.[456] Habitationis autem Parochus ille est 1º. in cuius Parochia manes animo fixe permanendi, etiamsi tantum hodie eo peruenisti. 2º. etiam illa, vbi habitas animo permanendi maiori anni parte, licet alibi habeas domicilium fixum, vt scholaribus, militibus et Mercatoribus vsum erit, ita Sanch.[457] Kon. Pont. 3º. etiam ille, vbi habitas, animo manendi aliquot mensibus, etiamsi non maiori anni parte. ita Lay. c. 12. de leg. cum Nauar.[458] In 1º. casu dicitur acquisitum domicilium, in 2º. et 3º. quasi domicilium. Habens autem in vno loco domicilium, in alio quasi domicilium, potest coram alterutro pro libito contrahere, vt bene

451 S adds: *sine*
452 S adds: *a nu: 1º. vsque ad 10ᵘᵐ.*
453 S adds: *19. 20.*
454 In A, along the top of fos. 24ᵛ–25 (referring to Case M22) is the heading: *Quis est proprius Parochus // vagorum, habitantium in 2. locis, etc.*
455 S adds: *parochum*
456 S adds: *cuius contrarium supponit Concilium. Sanch. dp. 23. n. 7. Pont. l. 5. c. 13. n. 6.*
457 S adds: *cit. n. 13.*
458 S adds: *de iubilaeo notab. 32. n. 43. et colligitur ex l. Haeres absens Numquid. ff. de iudiciis;*

Pont.[459] contra San.[460] quod a fortiori est dicendum[461] quando quis habet duo domicilia fixa, aestiuum v.g. et hyemale, aut quando in eadem Parochia sunt duo Parochi in solidum. Et idem censent viri docti de militibus hic in Belgio praesidiariis aut in hibernis, qui praeter Parochum[462] loci habent[463] sacellanum castrensem.[464] Sed in hoc spectanda[465] consuetudo, et Praelatorum voluntas:[466] Tan. de Poen. q. 9. n. 57. post Suar. et Valent. ait alicubi non licere Academicis Parocho loci, sed Academico.

Quoad vagos, proprius illorum Parochus est non solum ille, in cuius Parochia versantur, sed quiuis alius, vnde a quouis possunt coniungi matrimonio et alia sacramenta accipere, cum nulli sint subiecti. ita Sanch.[467] Bonac.[468] Tan.[469] et Pont:[470] satis autem est si alter sit vagus. Porro vagus censetur, qui nullibi sedem habet, aut qui domicilio relicto, proficiscitur ad nouas sedes. [fo. 25] Peccat autem Parochus vagos coniungens sine venia ordinarii ob praeceptum Trid. c. 7. factum tamen tenet.

Superest difficultas de peregrinis, an possint contrahere coram Parocho, vbi pro tempore existunt, etsi breuissimo tantum tempore ibi mansuri sint? Affirmat Pont:[471] cum Sa[472] nixus Declarationibus Cardinalium de quarum fide iam diximus cas. 20.[473] Quare contrarium est communi Doctorum.[474] 1°. quia fuit ita decisum in Rota, teste Pontio. 2°. quia tam breuis mora non facit domicilium aut quasi domicilium, nec vt quis sit subditus, licet quoad aliqua sacramenta maioris necessitatis ex priuilegio sufficiat. 3°. quia Tridentinum punit Parochum coniungentem

---

[459]   S adds: *cit: n. 9.*
[460]   S adds: *vterque enim est proprius.*
[461]   S adds: *cum ipso Sanche dp: 24.*
[462]   S reads: *Pastorem*
[463]   S adds: *suum*
[464]   S reads instead of the last word: *per modum Parochi Castrensis; coram vtroque enim possunt contrahere, vt censent viri docti.*
[465]   S adds: *sit*
[466]   S replaces the final clause of this paragraph with: *Nam alicubi in Vniuersitatibus, vbi assignatur Discipulis Parochus Academicus, non licet iis vti Parocho loci; vt testatur Suar: 3. p. to: 4. dp. 2. sec: 2. n. 6. Valent. de poenitentia q. 10. pun: 2. Tan: de poenitentia. q. 9. n. 57. Tota enim haec licentia vtendi Parocho vbi fixe non habitas consuetudine et necessitate est introductum; quare et iuxta consuetudinem limitanda est.*
[467]   S adds: *dp. 25.*
[468]   S adds: *n. 9.*
[469]   S adds: *q. 3. n. 121.*
[470]   S adds: *c. 14*
[471]   S adds: *c. 13. n. 4.*
[472]   S adds: *verb. Parochus. n. 7. et verb. Matrim: n. 2.*
[473]   S reads for the last seven words: *sed iam diximus eas fidem amplius non facere:* Then adds: *Et praeterea forte solum volunt sufficere paruum tempus, modo adsit animus diutius permanendi; vt recte Tann: cit.*
[474]   S adds: *et Diana resol. 231. de Sacram:*

sponsos alterius Parochiae.[475] Non tamen[476] contraria est improbabilis, praesertim si peregrini non in fraudem eo, se contulerint, vt limitat Rebell.[477] et fauet Rituale Rom: in praeambulis.[478]

Case M22. *Who is properly called here one's parish priest? Is it the parish priest of origin, or rather of where one lives now? Does any small period of habitation suffice when one also has the intention of remaining there permanently? What about those who have two domiciles? What about travellers,*[479] *who have none? What about soldiers and scholars, who apart from the parish priest of their home, have another in their camp or academy? See Sanchez, Bonacina and Coninck [refs].*

I reply that your parish priest here is the priest in whose parish you live, not really in whose parish you once were born; otherwise travellers would have their own parish, which is contrary to what the Council of Trent supposes; see Sanchez and Pontius [refs]. The parish priest of your habitation is, firstly, he in whose parish you stay with the intention of remaining fixed, even if you only got there today. Secondly, also of the parish where you live with the intention of remaining for the major part of the year, although you have a fixed domicile elsewhere, as will be the case with scholars, soldiers and merchants; thus, Sanchez [ref.], Coninck, and Pontius. Thirdly, also of that place where you live with the intention of staying for some months, even if not for the major part of the year; thus, Laymann, with Navarre [refs]; and this is gathered from the civil law [refs]. In the first case, this is called the 'acquired domicile'; in the second and third cases, it is a 'quasi-domicile'. Someone who has, moreover, in one place a domicile, in another a quasi-domicile, may contract marriage in either, according to his preference, as Pontius [ref.] says well, against Sanchez; for either is his own parish. This must be said, with even stronger reason, when someone has two fixed domiciles, one a summer residence, the other a winter residence; or when in the same parish there are two parish priests working jointly. And the same judgement is made by learned men about garrison soldiers or those in winter quarters here in Belgium, who besides the parish priest of their locality, have a garrison chaplain, who is a sort of parish priest for the camp; for they can contract marriage before either. But in this

---

[475] S adds: *Supponit ergo Parochum non posse omnes ibi quomodocunque commorantes coniungere.*

[476] S adds: *ausim dicere*

[477] S adds: *par: 2. l. 2. q. 8.*

[478] S reads for the last two words: *dum in praeambulis indicat, tam peregrinos quam vagos posse licentia Episcopi obtenta coniungi.*

[479] Modern usage allows this translation. Southwell has in mind largely those of no fixed abode, rather than people going from A to B. 'Vagabonds' seems too harsh a term.

matter it is important to consider the custom, and the will of the prelates; for in those universities where an academic parish priest is assigned to the students, it is not lawful for them to use the parish priest of the place, as Suarez, Valentia and Tanner [refs] testify. Indeed, this licence to use the parish priest where you do not have a fixed home was introduced by custom and out of necessity; for which reason it is also limited according to custom.

As far as travellers are concerned, their own parish priest is not only he in whose parish they are staying, but any other; hence they may be joined in matrimony by, and accept other sacraments from, whoever they like, since they are subject to none; thus, Sanchez, Bonacina, Tanner and Pontius [refs]. Moreover, it is enough if only one of the two spouses is a traveller. Indeed, a traveller is judged to be someone who has a home nowhere, or who having left his domicile travels to a new home. However, the parish priest sins by marrying travellers without permission from his ordinary, on account of the commandment of the Council of Trent [ref.]. However, if it is done without such permission, the marriage holds.

There remains the difficulty of pilgrims. May they contract marriage before the parish priest where they are staying temporarily, even if they will remain there only for the briefest time? Pontius, with Sa [refs], says yes, relying upon the Declarations of the Cardinals, but we have already said in Case 20 that complete trust cannot be placed in this source. And besides, perhaps they are only willing and able to stay a little time, although there is present the desire to remain longer; as Tanner rightly says in the place cited. Therefore, the contrary is the common judgement of the doctors, and Diana [ref.]. First, because it was decided thus in the Rota, according to Pontius. Second, because such a brief delay does not make a domicile or a quasi-domicile; nor does it make someone a subject, although as far as other sacraments of greater necessity are concerned, by privilege it is sufficient to do so. Third, because Trent punishes parish priests who join in marriage betrothed couples from another parish. It presumes, therefore, that the parish priest cannot marry all those who are staying there in whatever way. The contrary, however, I dare to say, is not improbable, especially if the pilgrims do not come there fraudulently, as Rebellus [ref.] limits it, and as the Roman Ritual favours in its preambles, where it says that both pilgrims and travellers may marry, having obtained a licence from the bishop.

[M23] 23us. Vtrum praeter Parochum necessarii sint duo testes, et sufficiat quiuis, foeminae, infames, aut consanguinei, an si coacti intersint,[480]

---

[480] S reads, instead of the last four words: *An sufficiat quod intersint etiam coacti?*

et quid si illis tantum audientibus, et non vocatis aut adhibitis contrahatur. Sanch. d. 39. et 41. Bonac.[481] Kon. cit. d. 4.[482] Respondeo requiri ad minimum duo testes praeter Parochum vt valide contrahatur, sufficiunt autem foeminae, infames, aut consanguinei etc. ita passim Doctores quia Trid: non requirit testes omni exceptione maiores et quia Parochus supplebit quod iis deest. Debent autem Parochus et testes scire quid agatur; non enim fit te praesente nisi intelligas. leg. coram Titio 209. ff. de verb. sig. Sufficit autem si vi sint adducti. non tamen sufficeret Parocho transeunte contrahere, [fo. 25ᵛ483] sed debet esse aliqua ratione adhibitus cum testibus rogando vt adesse velint, vel vi adducendo ita Pont.[484] et Bonac.[485] sicque saepe dicuntur Cardinales respondisse, licet Sanch. aliter sentiat. Denique peccatum est Parocho inuito contrahere, vt bene Kon.[486] et Laym. p. 2. c. 4. n. 6. nisi necessitas vrgeret.

Case M23. *In addition to a parish priest, are two witnesses necessary, and is it good enough to have anyone as a witness; for example, women, infamous people, or blood relations? Is it good enough to have those who are forced to be present? And what if the marriage is contracted with the witnesses only listening, and not speaking or playing a part? See Sanchez, Bonacina, Coninck and Laymann [refs].*

I reply that at the minimum two witnesses are required in addition to the parish priest, in order that the marriage is validly contracted. Moreover, women, the infamous, or blood relations etc. are good enough. Thus, the doctors everywhere. This is because the Council of Trent does not require, with any exception, witnesses of a superior status, and because the parish priest will provide what is lacking in them. The parish priest and witnesses should, however, know what is being done; because, according to the civil law [ref.], you are not really present unless you understand. It is satisfactory, however, if they are brought there forcibly. It is not satisfactory, however, to marry with a parish priest who is inattentive, but he should behave resonably, and must ask the witnesses whether they wish to be present or whether they have been brought there by force; thus, Pontius and Bonacina. And it is often said that the Cardinals have responded in this way,[487] although Sanchez feels otherwise. Finally, it is a sin to marry if the parish priest is unwilling,

---

481 S adds: *cit. n. 44. et sequentibus.*
482 S reads: *dp: 27. dub. 4.* and adds: *Laym: par: 2ᵃ. c. 4. n. 6:*
483 In A, along the top of fos. 25ᵛ–26 (referring to Cases M24 and M25) is the heading: *An quiuis Clericus sufficiat pro // Parocho. An benedictio et denuntiatio etc.*
484 S adds: *c. 21.*
485 S adds: *n. 4.*
486 S adds: *n. 25.*
487 See n. 439 above.

unless there is a necessity to do so, as Coninck and Laymann [ref.] show
well.

[M24] 24ᵘˢ. An sufficiat ex licentia Parochi quiuis alius Sacerdos, aut
Clericus non Sacerdos, et an licentia generalis administrandi omnia
sacramenta ad hoc sufficiat. Laym. cit.⁴⁸⁸ Kon. d. 3. Bonac.⁴⁸⁹ Sanch. d.
35. Respondeo posse ex licentia Parochi vel Episcopi,⁴⁹⁰ alium assistere
loco eius: debet tamen esse sacerdos, vt patet ex verbis Trid:⁴⁹¹ Nec opus
est, vt haec licentia scripto detur;⁴⁹² imo sufficeret ratihabitio de praesente (non vero de futuro) item licentia generalis administrandi omnia
sacramenta, nisi ex circumstantiis aliud constet, quia nomine omnium
sacramentorum, venit etiam matrimonium vt bene Bonac. contra Kon:
denique sufficit siue ad assistendum siue ad substituendum, quod sit
Pastor, etsi non sit Sacerdos, quia etiam non Sacerdos est verus Pastor,
sic et Episcopus non consecratus: neque enim est actus Ordinis iste.⁴⁹³
sufficit enim ille, qui communiter existimatur Pastor, etsi reipsa non
sit, quia ius supplet ita omnes cum Sanch. d. 22. Imo bene Pont. contra
Sanch. et alios, ait,⁴⁹⁴ opus non esse vt habeat titulum coloratum, id est
collatum a legitimo superiore⁴⁹⁵ modo putetur vulgo verus, quia ratio
communis vtilitatis etiam in hoc casu militat, estque [fo. 26] textus
optimus Nouelli 44. de tabellion: c. 1. in fine. denique valide assistit
Parochus etiam suspensus, excommunicatus, aut interdictus, aut quem
prohibuisset Episcopus assistere, quia adhuc est Parochus, neque enim
est actus iurisdictionis, sed tantum testimonium personae qualificatae.
ita Kon.⁴⁹⁶ Bonac.⁴⁹⁷ Sanch.⁴⁹⁸ At vero Pastor excommunicatus non toleratus inualide daret licentiam assistendi alteri, vt docent Suar. Kon et
Lay. (sed aliter sentit Sanch.⁴⁹⁹) dare enim alteri licentiam videtur actus
iurisdictionis, qua talis priuatur.⁵⁰⁰

Case M24. *Is it sufficient, with the licence of the parish priest, to have
some other priest, or a cleric who is not a priest; and is a general*

488 S adds: *n. 4.*
489 S adds: *cit. n. 12. et 13.*
490 S adds: *a fortiori*
491 S adds: *nec sufficeret Clericus non sacredos.*
492 S adds: *cum id nullibi statutum sit, vt bene Bonac: cit contra Rebellum.*
493 S adds: *Sanch: dp. 20. citarique solent Cardd:*
494 S adds: *l. 5. c. 20.*
495 S adds: *sed sufficere intrusum*
496 S adds: *n. 28.*
497 S adds: *n. 21. et 22.*
498 S adds: *dp: 21.*
499 S adds: *cit. n. 6.*
500 S reads for the last three words: *qua priuat excommunicatio.*

licence to administer all the sacraments sufficient for this? See Laymann,
Coninck, Bonacina and Sanchez [ref.].

I reply that it is possible, with a licence from the parish priest, or,
with even stronger reason, from the bishop, for someone else to assist
in his place; but it should be a priest, as is clear from the words of the
Council of Trent. Nor is a cleric who is not a priest good enough. Nor
is it necessary that this licence should be given in writing, since this is
nowhere laid down, as Bonacina shows well, against Rebellus. Indeed,
approval for the present (not, however, for the future) is sufficient; also
a general licence to administer all the sacraments, unless according to
the circumstances something else is agreed, because in the description
'all the sacraments' marriage is also included, as Bonacina shows well,
against Coninck. Finally, it is good enough, that someone who assists
or substitutes is a pastor, even if he is not a priest (because even a
non-priest is a true pastor), and thus also a non-consecrated bishop;
for this is not an act dependent on Ordination. See, Sanchez [ref.]; and
the Cardinals[501] are generally cited here. Someone who is commonly
judged to be a pastor is good enough, even if he in fact is not, because
he fulfils the law; thus all, with Sanchez [ref.]. Indeed, Pontius says
well, against Sanchez [ref.] and others who have been cited, that it does
not matter if he has a fraudulent title, that is, one claiming that he has
been collated by a legitimate superior. It is good enough that, even if
he has been intruded, his title is commonly thought to be true, because
the reason of common utility also serves in this case; and the best text
here is in the Code of Justinian [ref.]. Finally, a parish priest assists
validly even if he has been suspended, excommunicated or interdicted,
or if the bishop has prohibited him from assisting, because he is still a
parish priest, and this is not an act of jurisdiction, but only the witness
of a qualified person; thus, Coninck, Bonacina and Sanchez [refs]. But,
in truth, a pastor who has been excommunicated and is not tolerated
would invalidly give a licence to assist to another, as Suarez, Coninck
and Laymann teach, although Sanchez [ref.] feels otherwise. For, to give
a licence to another seems to be an act of jurisdiction, of which such a
person has been deprived by excommunication.

[M25] 25. An sit peccatum mortale matrimonium contrahere omissa
trina denunciatione praeuia, aut consummare ante Ecclesiae ceremonias.[502] Sanch. d. 11. et 12. l. 3. Kon. d. 27. db. 5.[503] Laym. p. 2. c.
4.[504] Bonac. q. 2. p. 6. Respondeo esse mortale sine trina denunciatione

---

501   See n. 439 above.
502   S reads: *benedictiones*
503   S adds: *et 8.*
504   S adds: *a num: 9°. vsque ad 13ᵘᵐ.*

praeuia contrahere, cum ita praecipiat Ecclesia Trid: s. 24. c. 1. et Later. c. final. de clandest. despons: Excipe 1°. nisi[505] ex causa dispenset.[506] Nomine autem Ordinarii non intelligitur solum Episcopus,[507] imo in casu necessitatis posset Parochus declarare vim praecepti cessare vt si ante mortem ducenda esset concubina ita Laym.[508] Causae dispensandi sunt periculum impedimenti malitiosi, nobilitas, pudor ob senium aut disparitatem etc.[509] Excipe 2°. si solum omittatur vna ex tribus sine causa; videtur enim tantum veniale, vt bene Sanch.[510] quamuis mortale putent Laym. et Kon.[511] Respondeo 2°. non esse mortale consummare ante benedictionem Ecclesiae, nam Tridentinum solum hortatur coniuges ne id faciant; imo forte non [fo. 26ᵛ⁵¹²] est venali ita Sanch:[513] Kon.[514] Laym.[515] Iure communi tantum benedici deberent nuptiae, quando vterque primo nubit, at consuetudo obtinuit, vt id fiat,[516] etsi alteruter necdum benedictiones acceperit,[517] vide[518] citatos.[519]

Case M25. *Is it a mortal sin to contract marriage without the three banns having been read previously, or to consummate the marriage before the ceremonies of the Church have been performed? See Sanchez, Coninck, Laymann and Bonacina [refs].*

I reply that it is a mortal sin to marry without the three banns having been read previously, since the Church commanded this at the Council of Trent and the Lateran Council [refs]. The first exception is if the ordinary for some reason grants a dispensation, according to the Council of Trent. However, by ordinary is not just meant bishop, whatever Pontius [ref.] says. Indeed, in a case of necessity a parish priest may overrule this law; for example, if before death, a concubine is to

505 S adds: *Ordinarius*
506 S adds: *iuxta Tridentinum cit:*
507 S adds: *quicquid dicat Pontius c. 31.*
508 S adds: *n. 11.*
509 S adds: *de quibus Conin: dub. 6.*
510 S adds: *l. 3. dp. 5. n. 8.*
511 S adds: *et alii,* and continues: *Debent autem denunciationes istae fieri tribus diebus festis continuis, si non multum interpolatis; inter Missarum solennia vt mandat Tridentinum vel etiam tempore concionis. In vtriusque autem Parochia deberent in rigore fieri, de quo tamen consulenda consuetudo. Vide Laym: n. 10. Con: n. 50.*
512 In A, along the top of fos. 26ᵛ–27 (referring to Case M26) is the heading: *Vtrum qui in facie Ecclesiae contraxit invalide // debeat iterum coram Parocho contrahere.*
513 S adds: *dp: 22.*
514 S adds: *n. 71.*
515 S adds: *n. 12.*
516 S reads: *vt benedicantur* and adds: *si sponsa Virgo sit.*
517 S adds: *atque ita dicitur concessum a Ioanne 22.*
518 S adds: *Coninck. n. 72. Sanch: lib. 7. dp. 82. Laym: cit:*
519 S adds: *Vtrum vero in Anglia permittendae sint a Catholicis denunciationes istae, dixi in casibus Anglicanis cas: 24.*

be married. Thus, Laymann [ref.]. The causes of granting a dispensation are: the danger of a malicious impediment, nobility, shame about old age or a disparity in age etc.; on which, see Coninck [ref.]. The second exception is if only one of the readings of the banns is omitted without cause; for it only seems a venial sin, as Sanchez [ref.] shows well, although Laymann and Coninck and others think it is a mortal sin. These banns should, however, be read on three successive feast days, if not much time intervenes, at the time of the solemnisation of the Mass, as Trent commands, or even at the time of a sermon. They should, taking a rigorous line, be read in both parishes, on which the local custom should be consulted; see, Laymann and Coninck [refs]. I reply secondly that it is not a mortal sin to consummate marriage before the blessing of the Church, for Trent merely exhorts couples not to do it. Indeed perhaps it is not a venial sin; thus Sanchez, Coninck and Laymann [refs]. By common law, nuptials should only be blessed when both marry for the first time, but the custom has developed that it is done if the bride is a virgin; also if either one has not yet received blessings. And it is said that this was conceded by John XXII; see, Coninck, Sanchez and Layman [refs]. Whether indeed these banns are to be used in England by Catholics, I have said in the English Cases, Case 24.

[M26] 26. Vtrum illi, qui contraxerunt in facie Ecclesiae sed inualide ob impedimentum dirimens occultum, debeant iterum cognito et sublato impedimento contrahere coram Parocho et testibus. Sanch. l. 2. d. 37. Kon. d. 24. n. 83. Bonac. q. 2. p. 9.[520] Laym. c. 9.[521] n. 1. et p. 4. c. 14. n. 4.

Supponendum hic matrimonium valere non posse donec auferatur impedimentum, etiamsi sit solum iuris humani, vnde potius mori deberet coniux, quam debitum reddere ante dispensationem obtentam.[522] vide Sanch. l. 2. d. 39. Suppono 2°. si irritum fuerit vel ob defectum Parochi et testium, vel etiam ob impedimentum aliud, quod[523] probari possit, necessum est vt coram Parocho[524] iterum contrahant, hoc enim est forma essentialis matrimonii et necessaria quantum opus est ad impediendam clandestinitatem. Quaestio igitur est de impedimento omnino occulto,[525] vt si sponsus occulte cognouisset sororem sponsae.

---

[520] S adds: *n. 10.*
[521] S reads: *6.*
[522] S adds: *vt colligitur ex c: literas. 13. de restit. spol: cap: Inquisitioni. de sent. excom.*
[523] S adds: *notum sit, et*
[524] S adds: *et testibus*
[525] S adds: *nec probari possit in foro externo*

Pontius[526] affirmat contrahendum denuo coram Parocho et testibus,
1°. quia ita declararuit Clem. 8. consultus a P. Stephano Tuccio.[527] 2°.
quia declarunt Cardinales.[528] Dicendum tamen satis est quod clam renou-
etur, et ita declarauit Pius 5. teste Nauar. c. 22. n. 70. vbi ait esse praxim
Poenitentiariae,[529] et sequuntur Laym. Sanch.[530] Kon. Bonac. Rodrig.[531]
Binsfeld. Diana[532] etc.[533] Nam hoc non est ex casibus in Tridentino
comprehensis, cum non sit aptum [fo. 27] generare scandala, aut alia
incommoda, et in eo cessat totaliter finis legis. ergo. vnde haud dubio in
casu proposito Clem. 8°. impedimentum poterat probari, aut saltem esset
dubium an non posset, et poterat forte sine incommodo matrimonium
coram Parocho contrahi.[534] Quoad Cadinales dictum est supra cas. 20. et
Sanch. cit. n. 3. affert contrariam declarationem Cardinalium.[535]

Case M26. *Should those who have contracted marriage in church, but
invalidly, on account of a secret impediment which renders the marriage
null and void, once the impediment is known and removed, contract
marriage again in the presence of a parish priest and witnesses? See
Sanchez, Coninck, Bonacina and Laymann [refs].*
It must be understood that this marriage cannot be valid until the
impediment is removed, even if it is only a matter of human law. Hence
a spouse should die rather than render marital dues, before a dispensation has been obtained, as is clear from the canon law [refs]; see Sanchez
[ref.]. I maintain secondly that if the marriage was invalid either on
account of the lack of a parish priest or of witnesses, or because of
another impediment which is known and can be proved, it is necessary that they should marry again in the presence of a parish priest and
witnesses, for this is the essential form of marriage, which is necessary
as far as it can be done, in order to prevent clandestine marriages. The
question, therefore, concerns an impediment which is entirely secret,

---

[526] S adds: *l. 5. c. 6.*
[527] S adds: *vt refert Comitolus apud ipsum.*
[528] S adds: *apud Farinacium.*
[529] S adds: *et c. 16. n.* [illegible number] *ait esse praxim quotidianam:*
[530] S adds: *l. 2. dp. 37. Tann: q. 3. n. 58. et 102.*
[531] S adds: *to: 1. c. 219. n. 2.*
[532] S adds: *tract. 1. miscell. resol. 5.*
[533] S reads: *Praepos: et alii.*
[534] S reads, instead of the last sentence (from *vnde*): *Ad Clem: 8ᵘᵐ. Respondeo 1°. oppo-
nendo Pium 5ᵘᵐ. 2°. Dico eum locutum quando impedimentum poterat probari in foro
externo: vel solum respondisse Tuccio quid in eo casu vellet fieri, cum id tutius sit, potuis-
setque fieri sine incommodo.*
[535] S reads, instead of the last sentence: *Quoad Cardinales oppono alios apud Sanchem,
n. 3. et dico eas declarationes amplius fidem non facere, nisi constet esse authenticatas.*

and cannot be proved in a law court; for example, if a man had secretly known the sister of his betrothed.

Pontius [ref.] affirms that the marriage should be contracted anew in the presence of the parish priest and witnesses. First, because Clement VIII declared it thus after having been consulted by Father Stefano Tucci,[536] as Comitolus himself relates. Second, because the Cardinals declared this; see, Farinacius. However, it should be said that it is enough that the marriage is privately renewed, and Pius V laid this down, according to Navarre [ref.], who says it is the practice of the Penitentiary, and adds that it is daily practice. And this judgement is followed by Laymann, Sanchez, Tanner, Coninck, Bonacina, Rodriguez, Binsfield, Diana, Praepos [refs] and others. For this is not among the cases included in the decrees of the Council of Trent, since it is not apt to generate scandal, or other inconveniences; and hence the purpose of the law totally ceases, which proves the point. To Clement VIII, I reply first by opposing Pius V. Second, I say he spoke of a case when the impediment could be proved in a court of law, or there was doubt whether or not it could be; or he merely replied to Tucci with what in that case he wished should be done, since it was safer, and a marriage contracted in the presence of a parish priest might be done without inconvenience. As far as the Cardinals are concerned, I oppose contrary declarations of theirs cited by Sanchez [ref.] and I say, as I have said above in Case 20, that no further trust should be placed in their Declarations, unless it is agreed that they have been authenticated.[537]

[M27] 27. An ficte consentiens aut ex metu, si postea ex plena libertate matrimonium ratificet, altero minime monito, illud conualidet? et an sufficiat solus consensus internus, aut copula coniugalis? Sanch. l. 2. d. 32.[538] Kon. d. 24. n. 89. Laym. p. 2. c. 6.[539] Bonac. q. 2. p. 9.[540] Respondeo matrimonium conualescere, si fictor aut metum passus, aut qui errauit in persona, iterum clam consentiat, altero minime monito, aut nouum consensum praestante. ita cit. omnes[541] cum Nauar. Tan.[542] Diana[543] contra Pontium[544] fretum responso dicto[545] Clem. 8.[546] Probatur

---

536 Stefano Tucci, an Italian Jesuit who flourished c. 1585.
537 See n. 439 above.
538 S adds: *a numo. 8°.*
539 S adds: *n. 1.*
540 S adds: *n. 2. Nauar: c. 22. n. 51.*
541 S adds: *Sanch. Con: Bonac: Laym:*
542 S adds: *q. 3. n. 100.*
543 S adds: *de Sacram: resol: 292*
544 S adds: *l. 4. c. 24.*
545 S reads for the last two words: *autoritate illa*
546 S reads: *de qua supra.*

quia altera pars vere consentit ex parte sua, ergo sufficit quod pars ista ponat nunc suum consensum libere, quia plus non requiritur ad contractum humanum, maxime bonae fidae, qualis est iste, vbi solent partes quantum possunt sincere cupere, vt actus valeat omni meliori modo, quo potest, idque in perpetuum. Nec obstat quod dici posse ponatur iste consensus, quia cum alter non reuocauerit suum, vt patet ex eo, quod petat et reddat debitum, hoc censendum est sufficere. nam sine dubio potest habere hanc vim consensus noster, si velimus: sufficit autem consensus mere internus, vt probabiliter sentiunt Laym: Bonac. Sanch. quia externa signa [fo. 27ᵛ] iam olim sunt posita, vel recte si cum Kon. et Rebellio requiratur nouus consensus externus, quod satis est probabile, dico saltem sufficere copulam⁵⁴⁷ ex affectu maritali, vt iam⁵⁴⁸ patebit.⁵⁴⁹

Case M27. *If someone has consented to marriage deceitfully, or out of fear, and afterwards, in complete freedom, ratifies the marriage, and the other spouse is not warned about this, does this validate the marriage? Is internal consent alone enough, or conjugal copulation? See, Sanchez, Coninck, Laymann, Bonacina and Navarre [refs].*

I reply that the marriage becomes valid if (1) the deceiver, or the one who suffered fear, or who made a mistake as to the person of the spouse, privately consents again, without the other party (2) being warned, or offering new consent. Thus, all, with Sanchez, Coninck, Bonacina, Laymann, Navarre, Tanner, Diana [refs], against Pontius (ref), who relies on that reply of Clement VIII, on which see above. This is proved, because the other party (2) truly gave consent on his or her behalf; therefore it is sufficient that the first party (1) now gives his or her free consent, because no more is required to a human contract, especially one based on good faith such as this is, where the parties are accustomed, as much as they can, to desire sincerely that the contract should be valid in the best way it can, and in perpetuity. Nor is it an objection that it can be said that the first party (1) should give his or her consent,⁵⁵⁰ because since the other one (2) has not revoked his or hers, as is clear because he or she sought and rendered his or her marital dues, which is judged to be sufficient. For, without doubt, our consent can have this force, if we wish. Laymann, Bonacina and Sanchez feel it is probable that merely internal consent is sufficient, because the external signs have already been given. Alternatively, if, as Coninck and Rebellus think, external consent is required, which is probable enough,

⁵⁴⁷ S adds: *coniugalem*
⁵⁴⁸ S reads: *melius*
⁵⁴⁹ S adds: *ex casu 28º*.
⁵⁵⁰ Presumably the meaning is 'with a new public declaration'.

I say that conjugal copulation with marital affection is at least good enough, as now will be made more clear in Case 28.

[M28] 28. Vtrum ad conualidandum matrimonium irritum ob impedimentum dirimens occultum, opus sit vt pars vtraque nullitatem prius sciat, et de nouo deinde contrahat? Petrus ducit Catharinam occulte prius cognitam a fratre Petri, nec audet ei Catharina impedimentum detegere, quaeritur an obtenta occulte dispensatione, sufficiat mera copula maritalis ad conualidandum matrimonium? Sanch. l. 2. d. 36.[551] Bonac. q. 2. p. 9.[552] Laym. p. 4. c. 14.[553] et Kon. cit.[554] n. 95. Respondeo Copulam in eo casu conualidare;[555] modo tamen C Trid: ibi non sit receptum,[556] vel si sit receptum, contractus sit antea in facie Ecclesiae celebratus, et impedimentum occultum sit. id est quod probari nequit in foro externo, aut quod non sit periculum vt probetur;[557] item modo non fuerit impedimentum ex metu aut errore personae (modo tenens se ex parte nescientis dispensationem obtentam aut obtinendam.) hanc sententiam probabilem putat Sanch. et Bonac. et colligitur ex Angelo,[558] Caiet,[559] Soto,[560] Rodrig:[561] Probatur 1°. ex similibus casibus conuersis a iure, vt de eo, qui nescius duxit seruam et postea sciens eam carnaliter cognoscit.[562] c. proposuit et c. finali de coniugio seruor. et Vasq. 1. 2. d. 66. n. 28. et Tan. hic q. 3. n. 58.[563] idem de eo, qui secundam duxit viuente prima. de quo c. Veniens. 7. de eo qui duxit.[564] Probatur 2°. quia copula carnalis ex

---

[551] S adds: *Nauar: c. 22. n. 17.*
[552] S adds: *n. 7.*
[553] S adds: *n. 4.*
[554] S reads: *dp. 24.*
[555] S reads: *Respondeo Obtenta dispensatione conualidari matrimonium*
[556] S adds: *vt in Anglia,*
[557] S adds: *iuxta Henriq: l. 11. matrim: c. 2. n. 6.*
[558] S adds: *verb. matrim: 3. impedim: 13. n. 5.*
[559] S adds: *to: 1. opusc: 12. q. 2. et in summa verb: matr: tit: contractus matrim: etc.*
[560] S adds: *in 4. dist. 29. q. 2. a. 1. dub. vlt. et dist. 28. q. 1. a. 2. conclus. 3. et dist. 35. q. vnica. a. 2: versiculo, sed est praeterea.*
[561] S adds: *in Summa to: 1. c. 219. n. 2.*
[562] S reads, for the last sentence: *Probatur 1°. quia varia iura hoc videntur aperte dicere, viz. sufficere copulam maritali ex affectu, etiamsi compars nihil sciat de impedimento sublato. v. g. si quis per errorem ducat seruam, et postea resciscens eam esse talem, libere nihilominus eam postea cognoscat, eo ipso est matrimonium, vt manifeste dicitur.*
[563] S adds: *aiens esse communem: ergo etiamsi vxor nihil sciat, nec rogetur vt de nouo consentiat; mere per consensus viri, sublato ipsius erroris impedimento, matrimonium conualescit per copulam.*
[564] S reads, from the last footnote: *Item cap: Veniens. 7. de eo qui duxit: Ille qui viuente prima duxerat aliam insciam, permittitur post mortem primae manere cum secunda, nec iubetur eam de nullitate monere vt de nouo consentiat, sed tantum maritali affectu ei adhaerere. Supponit ergo quod mere per copulam ex parte illius foeminae, matrimonium prius irritum nunc conualidetur. Idem colligitur ex cap: Ad id 21. de Sponsal:*

affectu maritali[565] est verus consensus de praesente [fo. 28] non verbo sed facto;[566] est quippe realis corporum traditio mutua, idque non animo fornicario,[567] sed cum affectu coniunctionis perpetuae argum. c. is qui et c. ad id. 21. de sponsal. cap. sui de conditione appos: et cap veniens 7. de eo qui duxit. ergo si personae sint habiles per impedimenti sublationem nec opus sit Parocho et testibus, nihil ei deesse poterit ad constituendum matrimonium. vnde et iura cit. aperte supponunt, hoc vniuersaliter esse verum vt copula inter non impeditos semper sufficiat, modo fiat animo maritali. Vnde tota praesumptio et incertitudo in eo versatur iuxta iura, quando talis animus sit praesumendus. At eo supposito, vt certissimum supponunt, esse verum matrimonium. In nostro autem casu clarum est adesse affectum maritalem.

Dixi modo non fuerit impedimentum ex metu,[568] errore personae, quae non tam limitatio est quam declaratio assertionis. Non enim dicimus quod penitus cessante hoc impedimento non sufficiat copula, sed solum quod in his speciale videatur, quod impedimentum penitus non cesset, donec pars errans aut metum passa, non solum amplius metum non patiatur, aut erret; sed etiam vlterius sciat, se non teneri stare contractui facto.

Nam si cessante metu adhuc pergat consentire ideo quia putat se teneri, sane metus ille adhuc saltem virtualiter manet, et dat causam huic contractui,[569] sicut ante, non proxime in se, sed in suo effectu; vnde adhuc impedit: idemque [fo. 28ᵛ] dicendum de errore; quia iura intendunt in his impedimentis, vt pars restituatur suae libertati, quod non fit, nisi sciant nullitatem. At vbi consensus ante fuit liber, et impedimentum aliunde ortum sufficit, vt tollatur, et sequatur copula. Quamuis et improbabile non sit, quod etiam in istis non sit opus semper rescire nullitatem. sunt enim qui docent, matrimonium ingenui cum serua conualidari per copulam, si ipsa clanculum manumittatur, illo inscio; quod tenent multi apud Sanch. cit. n 3. et probabile putat Tan. q. 3. n. 57.

Dices 1º. semper esse consensum ex errore, quia alter accedit putans matrimonium prius valuisse. Respondeo hunc errorem non esse substantiae nec vllius qualitatis magni momenti: consentis enim nunc per copulam in eam, quam antea liberrime elegeras. Quod autem prior consensus alia ex causa fuerit irritus, quid refert in praesenti?

Dices 2º. solum intendit ratificare priorem consensum. Respondeo id falsum esse, tunc enim quantumcunque sciens accederet, non conuali-

---

565 A reads in the margin here: *Copula Carnalis ex affectu Maritali.*
566 S adds: *vt loquuntur iura,*
567 S adds: *seu ad libitum,*
568 S adds: *aut*
569 S reads: *consensui*

daret, intendit ergo ratificare, non vtcunque sed per veram repetitionem eiusdem consensus non verbo, sed facto.

Dices 3°. Qui soluit pecuniam ex errore putans esse debitam, errat in substantia. ergo et hic. Nego consequentiam quia hic solum est de [fo. 29] substantia cognoscere personam, in aliis aliae qualitates esse possunt esse[570] substantialis: quod enim in vno contractu est substantiale, in alio esse potest accidentale.[571] vt bene Vasq. 1. 2. d. 30. n. 27. Vide casum 28. de Anglicanis.

Caeterum si possit sine periculo moneri coniux, et[572] de nouo contrahi, id consulendum, quia tutius ob communem fere Recentiorum sententiam in contrarium et quia fauet stylus Curiae Romanae.

Case M28. *In order to validate a marriage which has been rendered invalid by a secret impediment capable of rendering a marriage null and void, is it necessary that both parties should first know of the nullity of the marriage, and then contract anew? Peter marries Catherine who had previously been known secretly by the brother of Peter, and Catherine does not dare reveal the impediment to Peter; the question is, having secretly obtained a dispensation, does mere marital copulation suffice to validate the marriage? See Sanchez, Navarre, Bonacina, Laymann and Coninck [refs].*

I reply that copulation in this case validates the marriage, but only where the Council of Trent is not received, as in England. In places where Trent is received, this is also true, if the contract was first celebrated in church, and if the impediment is secret (that is, one which cannot be proved in the law courts, or one of which there is no danger that it might be proved there, according to Henriquez [ref.]). This is also the case as long as the impediment had not resulted from fear, or an error in the person (as long as the matter is considered from the point of view of the party who does not know a dispensation has been obtained or ought to be obtained). Sanchez and Bonacina think this judgement is probable, and it is gathered from Angelus, Caietan, Soto, and Rodriguez [refs]. It is proved, first, because various laws seem openly to say this, that is, that marital copulation with marital affection is sufficient, even if the spouse knows nothing about the impediment which has been removed. For example, if someone out of error marries a slave girl, and afterwards discovering her to be such, nevertheless freely has carnal knowledge of her, by that action it is made a marriage, as is clearly said in the canon law [refs], by Vasquez and by Tanner

---

570 Repeated thus in A.
571 In A this word is written above *substantiale*, which is crossed out.
572 In the margin of A is written in bold, and slightly larger than the text, the letter *N*.

[refs], who says it is the common judgement. Therefore, even if the wife knows nothing, and is not asked to consent anew, merely by the consent of the man, with the impediment of this error removed, the marriage becomes valid by copulation. Also the canon law [ref.] says that if a man, while his first wife is alive, marries another who does not know about this, he is permitted after the death of the first, to remain with the second; nor is he ordered to warn the second wife about the nullity, in order that she may consent anew, but only to adhere to her with marital affection. The law supposes, therefore, that merely by copulation on the part of this woman, the marriage which was first made invalid is now made valid. The same is gathered from a different canon [ref.]. It is proved, secondly, because carnal copulation with marital affection is true consent for the present not in words, but by actions, as the laws say, because it is the real mutual surrender of bodies, and not with the intention of a fornicator or libertine, but with the affection of perpetual conjunction, as the canons say [refs]. Therefore, if the persons are suitable, as a result of the removal of the impediment, there is no need for a parish priest and witnesses, and there is nothing lacking to constitute a marriage. Hence, the laws cited openly grant that it is universally true, that copulation between those who are not under an impediment always suffices, as long as it is done with marital affection. Hence, all the prejudice and uncertainty in this matter is overcome, according to the laws, when marital affection can be presumed. And if that is accepted, as the doctors accept as most certain, it is true marriage. In our case, moreover, it is clear that marital affection is present.

I have said 'as long as the impediment had not resulted from fear or an error in the person', which is not so much a limitation on the judgement as a declaration of agreement with it. For we do not say that when this impediment is completely gone copulation does not suffice, but only that in these matters especially it seems that the impediment may not cease entirely, until the party in error or suffering from fear, not only does not suffer any longer from fear or error, but also knows in addition that he or she is not bound to keep to the contract that was made.

For, if the fear has ceased and he or she still continues to consent on that account because he or she thinks he or she is bound to do so, clearly that fear still, at least virtually, remains, and is the reason for his or her consent, just as it was before, not closely in itself, but in its effects; hence it still is an impediment. The same is to be said about error, because the laws intend with reference to these impediments, that one party should be restored to his or her liberty, which is not done unless he or she knows of the nullity of the marriage. But where the consent was freely given before, and the impediment arose from something else, it is enough that it should be removed, and copulation should follow. Although it is also not improbable that even in these cases (of fear and error) it is not always necessary to be informed of the nullity of the marriage. For, there are those who teach that the marriage of a free man with a slave girl is validated by copulation if she has been secretly freed, with him unawares; which many hold, cited by Sanchez [ref.], and which Tanner [ref.] thinks is probable.

You will say, firstly, that there is still consent through error, because the other party agrees thinking erroneously that the prior marriage is valid. I reply that this error is not of substance nor of any quality of great moment; for you consent now, by copulation, in what before you chose freely. Moreover, since the prior consent was invalid for a different reason, what does it matter at present?

You will say, secondly, he or she only intends to ratify the prior consent. I reply that this is false, for if it were true, however much he or she agreed while in a state of knowledge, it would not validate the marriage. But he or she does intend to ratify it, not in the way suggested, but by a true repetition of the same consent, not by words, but by actions.

You will say, thirdly, that someone who pays money in error, thinking it is owed, errs in substance; therefore this is also true in this case. I deny the consequence because here it is only a matter of substance to know the person; in other cases other qualities can be substantial. For what in one contract is substantial, in another may be accidental, as Vasquez shows well [ref.]. See Case 28 in the English cases.

However, if the spouse may without danger be warned, and the marriage be contracted anew, that is to be advised, because it is safer on account of the almost common judgement of the more recent writers (who argue against the opposite judgement), and because the custom and practice of the Roman Curia favour it.

[M29] 29us. Vtrum Pontifex, an Episcopus, an Princeps saecularis poterit statuere impedimenta matrimonium dirimentia? an Christiani Infidelibus subiecti teneantur impedimentis ibi receptis, aut econtra Christianis infideles Christianorum subditi? Sanch. l. 7. d. 1. et 3. Con. d. 30. dub. 1. Laym. p. 4. c. 1. Bon. q. 3. p. 1.

[573]Posse Ecclesiam seu Pontificem constituere impedimenta pro fidelium matrimoniis, vt docet Tridentinum s. 24. can. 3. et 4. idque siue pro omnibus, siue aliquibus tantum: debet tamen subesse causa, cum restringat libertatem naturalem. ita Sanch: d. 1. Praeter hos nulli hoc possunt; non Episcopi in sua dioecesi, quia hoc est ex reseruatis Pontifici: non Principes terreni in suis regnis pro fidelibus, Christiani saltem vt docent omnes contra Petrum Soto lect. 4. de matr. estque certum vt ait

[573] S inserts here: *Respondeo*

Tan: q. 3. n. 18. siue quia iure diuino ita est statutum, vt sentit Pontius
l. 6. c. 2. siue quia ita praescriptum est ab Ecclesia vt cum Bellar. [fo.
29ᵛ] l. 1. c. 32. caeteri.

Pro Infidelibus impedimenta constituit Princeps saecularis siue fidelis
sit, siue infidelis. Cum enim matrimonium sit contractus ciuilis, possunt
ei, sicut caeteris adiici conditiones, formae, et solemnitates, sine quibus
non valeat. Quod et de Iudaeis intelligendum, nec enim lege Leuitica,
qua tali tenentur amplius.

Petes an infidelis Princeps possit pro fidelibus suis subditis impedimenta constituere? Videtur enim[574] posse, cum Ecclesia nihil iuris
potuerit eripere, aut ab eo ad se aliquid reuocare. Ita sentiunt Sanch.
et Con: sed contrarium puto verius cum Tan: q. 4. n. 20. et Laym. n.
3. quia ipsa materia, vtpote spiritualis potuit ab Ecclesia eximi, et foro
sacro subiici. Vnde et Apostolus 1. Cor. 7. scribens ad fideles infidelibus
subiectos, satis ostendit, se plenam hac in re habere potestatem. Prae-
cipio non ego sed Dominus: et iterum: Ego dico, non Dominus etc. sine
vlla a Principe dependentia.

Case M29. *May the Pope, or a bishop, or a secular prince, lay down
what are the impediments which render a marriage null and void? Are
Christians who are subject to infidels bound by the impediments received
there? Or, on the other hand, are the infidel subjects of Christians bound
by Christian impediments? See Sanchez, Coninck, and Laymann and
Bonacina [refs].*

The Church or the Pope may lay down the impediments to the
marriages of the faithful, as the Council of Trent [ref.] teaches; either
for all or only for some. However, there should be a reason for doing
so, since it restricts natural liberty; thus Sanchez [ref.]. Apart from the
Church or the Pope, no one can do this; even bishops in their dioceses
may not do so, because this is among those things reserved to the Pope.
Temporal princes in their kingdoms, at least the Christian princes may
not do this with respect to the faithful, as all teach, against Petrus
Soto [ref.]. And this is certain, as Tanner says[ref.]; either because
it is ordained by divine right, as Pontius [ref.] feels, or because it is
commanded by the Church, as others, with Bellarmine [ref.] hold.

The secular prince may lay down impediments for infidels, whether
he is one of the faithful or an infidel himself. For, since matrimony
is a civil contract, princes may add conditions, forms and solemnities,
without which it is not valid, as they could add them to other contracts.
This is also to be understood concerning the Jews, but not the Levitical
law by which they are further bound.

---

[574] In A this word is written above a crossed out *non*

You will ask whether an infidel prince may lay down impediments for his Christian subjects; it seems possible, since the Church could take no rights away from him, nor revoke anything to itself from him. This is what Sanchez and Coninck feel, but the contrary I think is more true, with Tanner and Laymann [refs], because this matter itself is spiritual, and so the Church may take it away from him, and make it subject to the sacred forum. Hence also the Apostle, in 1 Corinthians 7, writing to the faithful who are subject to infidels, shows well enough that he has full power in this matter, without any dependence on a prince: 'Not I, but the Lord teaches this'; and again, 'I say this, not the Lord etc.'.

[M30] 30ᵘˢ. Quot sit impedimenta dirimentia? Sanch: l. 7. 6. Con. Laym. Bonacin: locis cit. Respondeo esse 14 ex quibus duo vltima sunt noui iuris a Tridentino constituta. Comprehenduntur autem his versibus:

Error, conditio, votum, cognatio, crimen,
Cultus disparitas, vis, ordo, ligamen, honestas,
Si sis affinis, si forte consentire nequibis.
Si Parochus testesque absint, si rapta tenetur.
Haec socianda vetant connubia, facta retractant.

Case M30. *How many impediments are there which render a marriage null and void?*[575] *See Sanchez [ref.], and Coninck, Laymann, and Bonacina, in the places cited.*

I reply that there are fourteen, of which the last two are of the new law, laid down by Trent. They are, moreover, listed in these verses:

Error, condition, vow, kinship, crime,
Difference of religion, force, order, bond, honesty;
If you are related by marriage; if perhaps you will refuse consent;
If parish priest and witnesses are absent; if she is abducted and held.
These forbid you to join in wedlock, and if you do they nullify it.

[M31] [fo. 30] 31ᵘˢ. An seruitus ignorata matrimonium dirimat? etiam cum alio seruo? et quid si contrahat cum libera putans eam esse seruam? Sanch. l. 7. d. 19. Laym. p. 4. c. 2. Bonac. q. 3. p. 3. Con: d. 30. d. 2. Respondeo si pars libera contrahat cum mancipio ignorans conditionem seruilem, matrimonium non valere, vt docent omnes: seruitus enim ignorata dirimit: non iure naturae, cum non sit error in substantia, sed ex iure positiuo. Cap. si quis ingenuus 29. q. 2. cum aliis ibidem. èt cap. 2. et 4. de coniugio seruorum.

Dixi <u>pars libera,</u> quia si seruus contrahens cum serua putans esse

---

575   Generally known as diriment impediments, and contrasted with prohibitory or impedient impediments, discussed in M53.

liberam, valet: nam ius positiuum solum procedit in iis, qui inde redduntur conditionis deterioris. Dixi <u>cum mancipio</u>, quia si ingenuus duceret liberam putans esse seruam valeret. non enim fit deterioris conditionis: ita S. T. Supplen: q. 52. a. 1. ad 5. Sanch. cit. n. 23. Debet autem esse verum mancipium ex iis, quae vendi possunt: nam cum seruis originariis et ascriptitiis, hoc est, addictis glebae seu agris colendis, valide contrahitur, quia non sunt vere serui. Sanch. d. 24. Dixi <u>ignorans</u>, quia seruitus secundum se non est impedimentum, sed vt ignorata vt bene Durandus. sufficit tamen ignorantia crassa, et vincibilis, ita Sanch. n. 20. At si affectasset ignorantiam, sibi imputet, vel si probabiliter dubitasset, vt bene Pont. c. 43. n. 3.

Nota, seruos valide contrahere inuitis Dominis, vt docet S. T. a. 2. et Sanch. d. 21. cum communi, argum. c. 1. de coniugio seruorum. Tenentur tamen ad consueta seruitia adhuc. si Dominus in nuptias consenserit, tacite sese [fo. 30ᵛ] obligat, ad eum non ita vendendum in partes remotas, vt coniugio vti non liceat, si <u>nesciuerit,</u> posset in rigore iustitiae eum, quo vellet vendendum mittere; ex aequitate tamen et charitatis lege tenetur non impedire vsum moderatum matrimonii, atque ad id a Iudice compelli potest. Con: n. 37. et 38. Laym. n. 4. et fortius Sanch: d. 22. et Pontius c. 42.

Si liber post cognitam seruitutem copuletur, quid iuris vide casu 28.

Case M31. *Does servitude which is unknown render a marriage null and void, even with another slave? And what if a slave marries a free woman thinking her to be a slave? See Sanchez, Laymann, Bonacina and Coninck [refs].*

I reply that if a free person contracts marriage with a slave while ignorant of this servile condition, the marriage is not valid, as all teach, for servitude which is unknown renders a marriage null and void, not by the law of nature, since there is no error in substance, but by positive law, according to the canons [refs].

I have said, 'a free person', because if a male slave marries a female slave thinking she is free, it is valid; for the positive law only applies to those who would be reduced to a worse condition by marriage. I have said, 'with a slave', because if a free man should marry a free woman, thinking she was a slave, it would be valid; for he is not given an inferior condition as a result. Thus, St Thomas and Sanchez [refs]. It should however be a true slave, one of those that can be sold. For with villeins, that is, those who are tied to the glebe or to the cultivation of fields, marriage may be validly contracted, because they are not true slaves; see Sanchez [ref.]. I have said 'while ignorant', because servitude in itself is not an impediment, but ignorance of it is, as Durandus shows well. Moreover, it is enough if it is crass and vincible ignorance and of the sort which can be overcome; thus Sanchez [ref.]. But if he had pretended to be ignorant, he is to blame, or if he had had doubts about the probability of servitude; as Pontius [ref.] shows well.

Note that slaves may contract marriage validly against the will of their masters, as St Thomas and Sanchez [refs] teach, with the common judgement based on canon law [ref.]. But they are still bound in this matter by the custom which governs their servitude. If the master consents to the marriage of a slave, he tacitly obliges himself not to sell the slave into distant regions, where he could not enjoy the marriage. If the master did not know about the marriage, he could in strict justice send him wherever he wanted to sell him, but in equity and by the law of charity the master is bound not to impede his slave's moderate use of the marriage, and he could be compelled not to do so by a judge. See Coninck, Laymann, Pontius and, more forcefully, Sanchez [refs].

On the question of what the law says if the free man, after discovering the servitude of his spouse, should copulate with her, see Case M28.

[M32] 32us. An votum solemne Religionis et Sacri Ordinis et Vota simplicia Societatis Iesu matrimonium contrahendum dirimant?[576] et quid de voto continentiae, quod in saeculo faciunt mulieres illae, quarum viri sacros ordines suscipiunt? Sanch. l. 7. d. 26. 28. et 40. Con. d. 20. n. 116. et d. 31. dub. 6. Lay. p. 4. c. 3. Bonac. q. 3. d. 9. Vasq. 3. p. tom. 3. d. 246. c. 3. Respondeo Votum solemne Ordinis vel Religionis dirimit matrimonium contrahendum. Est de fide ex Trid. sess: 24. can. 9. et cap. vnico de voto in 6. c. 1. 2. cap. Meminimus, cap. fin: Qui Clerici et vouentes: fuitque olim declaratum ab Innoc. 2. in C. Rom: vt refertur cap. vt lex 27. q. 1.

An autem semper in Ecclesia olim fuerint ista matrimonia irrita non est ita certum. Negat Pontius l. 7. c. 14. Tan. tom. 3. d. 5. q. 4. n. 69. Affirmat Bellar: l. 2. de Monachis c. 34. Less. c. 41. d. 8. Con. d. 20. n. 116. Sanch. Lay. et alii et huc magis propendet Suar. tom.[577] de relig. l. 9. c. 21. licet putet rem non plane certam. Suadetur haec pars [fo. 31] inde, quod multi canones antiquissimi praecipiant sic coniugatos separari; et hoc vniuersaliter non distinguentes an pars altera conscia fuerit, an non. Quod si matrimonium esset validum, foret onus intollerabile innocenti separari, sine spe alterius coniugis, vt est euidens. Ita Innoc. 1. ep. 2. c. 12. Siricius ep. 1. c. 6. Greg. 1. l. 11. ep. 59. Tol 1. can. 16. Calced. can. 16. Turon. 2. can. 16. Tol. 4. c. can. 51. Triburiens. can. 23. Tol. 8. can. 7. Carth. 4. can. vlt. Calixt. 2. cap. Presbyteris dist. 27. cum aliis dist. 28. et causa 27. q. 1. Verum est S. Aug. de bono viduit. c. 10. et 11. ex professo docere haec esse vera coniugia; sed agnoscit

---

[576] S reads: *irritent*
[577] S adds: *3.*

alios tunc aliter sensisse. Et hoc postea generaliter fuit receptum, licet tempore ipsius fortassis non esset constanter et vbique introducta haec vis irritans; pendet enim ex iure positiuo Ecclesiae, vt suppono.

2°. Certum est Vota Simplicia Societatis Iesu, siue Coadiutorum formatorum, siue Scholasticorum habere hanc vim irritantem, saltem post Decretum Gregor. 13. Extrauag. Ascendente Domino. An vero a principio id habuerit,[578] alibi diximus. sane Clementina Vnic. de consanguineis, excommunicantur Religiosi contrahentes, nulla facta restrictione Voti solemnis. Vnde et nostros ea censura comprehendi docet Sanch: l. 7. d. 48. n. 17. sed de [fo. 31ᵛ] hoc alibi.

Quoad eas, quae Castitatem vouent in saeculo, dum mariti ordinantur Sanch. d. 40. Laym. Bonac. cum Azorio docent esse impedimentum dirimens idque videtur innui cap. quia sunt, cap. si se. cap. si quae dist. 28. cap. seriatim: dist. 32. Contrarium tamen puto probabilius cum Soto l. 7. de iustitia q. 5. a. 3. ad. 2. et Pontio l. 7. c. 25. Nam cap. vnic. de voto in 6. aperte deciditur solum Votum Ordinis; et Religionis dirimere. Nec satisfacit, si dicas cum Sanche: eas esse inhabiles, non ex vi voti, sed ex statuto Ecclesiae, quia Ecclesia strictissime exigit ab his votum eo fine, ne nubant cap. 1. cap. Coniugatus, et aliis de conuers: coniugat: idque iure antiquo statutum est cap. Episcopus. cap. Agathota. et aliis 27. q. 2. ergo si ex vi voti non sint inhabiles, neque erunt ex vllo alio capite.

Case M32. *Does the solemn vow of religion and of holy orders, and do the simple vows of the Society of Jesus render the contracting of marriage null and void? And what about a vow of continence, which in the secular world those women make, whose men take up holy orders? See Sanchez, Coninck, Laymann, Bonacina, and Vasquez [refs].*

I reply that the solemn vow of holy orders, or of religion, renders the contracting of marriage null and void. This is a matter of faith, from the Council of Trent [ref.] and by canon law [refs]; and it was once declared by Innocent II in the Council of Rome [ref.].

Whether, however, in the Church these marriages were always invalid in the past is not so certain. Pontius and Tanner [refs] deny it; Bellarmine, Lessius, Coninck, Sanchez and Laymann [refs] and others affirm it; and on these Suarez [ref.] greatly depends, but he thinks the matter is not clearly certain. An argument in support of those who affirm this view is that many of the most ancient canons order that those who have married in this way should separate, and this universally, not distinguishing whether the other party was aware or not. The reason for this judgement is that, if the marriage had been valid, it would be an intoler-

---

[578] S reads: *habuerint*

able burden for the innocent party to separate, without hope of another spouse, as is clear. Thus, Innocent I, Siricius, Gregory I, the first Council of Toledo, the Council of Chalcedon, the second Council of Tours, the fourth Council of Toledo, the Council of Trebur, the eighth Council of Toledo, the fourth Council of Carthage, and Callixtus II [refs]. It is true that St Augustine [ref.] teaches openly that these are true marriages, but he acknowledges that others at that time felt differently. And this generally afterwards was accepted, although at that time perhaps the order invalidating these marriages was not constantly and everywhere introduced; for it depended as I suppose on the positive law of the Church.

Secondly, it is certain that the simple vows of the Society of Jesus, either of coadjutors or scholastics, have this power to render marriage null and void, at least after the decree of Gregory XIII [ref.]. Whether truly they had that before that decree, we have said elsewhere. Truly, by canon law [ref.] the religious who marry are excommunicated, with no restriction made to those who have taken solemn vows. Hence, our people[579] are also included in that censure, Sanchez [ref.] teaches; but of this, elsewhere.[580]

As far as those women are concerned who take a vow of chastity in the secular world, while their husbands are ordained, Sanchez [ref.], Laymann, Bonacina, with Azor, teach that this is an impediment rendering marriage null and void, and it seems that this is suggested by various canons [refs]. However, I think the contrary is more probable, with Soto and Pontius [refs]. For the canon [ref.] openly decided that only a vow of orders and of religion rendered marriage null and void. Nor is it sufficient if you say with Sanchez that these women are unfit, not on the strength of their vow, but by the statute of the Church, because the Church most strictly demands from them a vow in order to prevent them marrying [refs], and this was enacted by the ancient law of the Church [refs]; therefore, if on the strength of their vow they are not unfit, neither will they be under any other head.

[M33] 33[us]. Vtrum ordo Sacer ante annos discretionis, aut pubertatis etiam vi et metu susceptus, dirimat matrimonium? Sanch. l. 7. d. 29. et 30. Con: d. 20. d. 14. Bonac. q. 3. d. 9. Vasq. 3. p. tom. 3. d. 246. c. 3. De puero ordinato triplex est sententia. 1[a]. teneri ad Continentiam etiam ordinatum in Infantia. ita Pontius l. 7. c. 29. n. 15. et multi apud Sanch. 2[a]. est non teneri ordinatum ante annum 16. quia ante illum annum non valet Professio: parificate autem videntur quoad hoc Ordo Sacer et

579 Members of the Society of Jesus.
580 The reference here and in the last sentence seems to be to *De Voto*, but the discussion in Case 133 is also rather on the same lines.

Religio. ita Sanch. d. 30. [fo. 32] n. 8. Tan. hic q. 4. n. 38. 3ᵃ. et probabilior est infantem ante vsum rationis ordinatum non teneri, nisi postea
ratificet; at impuberes post vsum rationis sufficientem Ordinatos teneri,
ita Con: Bonac. cit. et Suar. tom. 3. Relig. l. 9. c. 17. Ratio prioris partis
est, quia nimis durum est, vt obligentur⁵⁸¹ ad Caelibatum, vnde quicquid
sit, an Ecclesia hoc possit praecipere, certe praesumendum non est de
facto, nisi luce clarius id constaret.

Ratio 2ᵃᵉ. est, quia iure naturae tunc votum valet, nec Ecclesia vllibi
illud irritat: estque alia ratio de Professione, quae ad plura obligat.

Metu graui ordinatum ad continendum obligari tenet Pontius, loc.
cit. Sed contrarium est dicendum est dicendum⁵⁸² cum caeteris cit: Suar.
Tan: et aliis, et colligitur ex cap. ad audientiam de his quae vi metuue
fiunt. Quae vi metuue fiunt carere debent robore. Quod si postea ratificet,
obligatur iuxta omnes. Vide⁵⁸³ plura de hoc vide supra casu 7. et 8. et in
materia de voto casu 10. et sequentibus, vbi diximus esse debere metum
ab intrinseco⁵⁸⁴ iniuste incussum: grauem vero censeri amissionem rei
notabilis, imo et magni lucri interdum, vt censet Pont: l. 4. c. 4. n. 10. ex
rota et Farinacio. Item metum reuerentialem, si coniunctae sint preces
importunae. Adde quod solum metum [fo. 32ᵛ] reuerentialem sufficere
doceat Diana de dubiis Regul: resol. 92. et 3. pars. tr. 5. miscel. resol.
20. et solas preces importunas sufficere ad metum grauem tenet Pontius
l. 4. c. 5. n. 17. Vterque minus probabiliter, quamuis non careat probabilitate, tum ob ipsorum autoritatem, tum aliorum dicentium et metum
leuem sufficere ad irritandum matrimonium siue carnale, siue spirituale;
vt Nauar. Rodrig. Veracruz, et alii cit. loc. dictis.

Case M33. *Do holy orders taken before the age of discretion, or puberty,
or taken as a result of force or fear, render marriage null and void? See
Sanchez, Coninck, Bonacina and Vasquez [refs].*

Concerning the ordination of a boy, the judgement is three-fold. First,
even those who were ordained in infancy are bound to continence; thus,
Pontius and many, cited by Sanchez [refs]. Second, no one is to be
ordained before the age of 16, because before that age the profession is
not valid, and it seems to be the same for those who enter religion, as
for holy orders; thus Sanchez and Tanner [refs]. And it is more probable
(1) that a child ordained before he has the use of reason is not to be held
to this, unless it is ratified afterwards. But (2) children after they have
acquired sufficient use of reason are to be held to their ordination; thus
Coninck, Bonacina, and Suarez [ref.]. The reason for the first part of this

---

⁵⁸¹ S adds: *inuiti*
⁵⁸² Repeated thus in A.
⁵⁸³ S reads: *Verum*
⁵⁸⁴ S reads: *extrinseco*

answer (1) is that it is too hard that they should unwillingly be bound to celibacy. Hence, whatever may be the case, whether the Church can command this or not, it certainly must be presumed that it does not in fact do so, unless further research reveals that the contrary should be agreed.

The reason for the second part of the answer (2) is that by the law of nature the vow is valid at this stage, and the Church does not invalidate it anywhere; it is a different matter in the case of Profession, which obliges to more things.

Someone who was ordained out of grave fear is obliged to continence, Pontius holds, in the place cited. But the contrary should be said, according to Suarez, Tanner and others who have been cited, and is gathered from the canon law [ref.]. Those things which are done through fear or force must lack validity. But if he ratifies the oath afterwards, he is obliged by it, according to all. See more about this above, in Cases 7 and 8, and in the work *Concerning the Vow*, Case 10 and following, where we have said that to qualify as grave fear (that is, the sort of fear which invalidates an oath), it should be fear inflicted unjustly by an external agent. Grave fear is also judged to include the fear of the loss of any notable property, and indeed sometimes of great wealth, as Pontius [ref.] judges, from the practice of the Rota, and from Farinacius. Reverential fear, if it is combined with importunate requests, also falls into this category. In addition, reverential fear alone is enough, Diana [ref.] teaches; and Pontius [ref.] holds that importunate requests alone suffice to create grave fear. Both judgements are less probable, although they do not lack probability, both because of the authority of these writers, and also because others say that light fear is enough to invalidate marriage, either carnal or spiritual; as Navarre, Rodriguez, Veracruz and others, who have been cited, say in the places cited.

[M34] 34ᵘˢ. Quid sit cognatio consanguinitatis, quae eius lineae? et quo pacto gradus numerandi? v. g. in quo sint gradu Iacob et Esau fratres, in quo eorum filii, in quo nepotes, pronepotes? Sanch. l. 7. d. 50. Conin: d. 32. d. 1. n. 1. et 2. Lay. par. 2. c. 4. Bonac. q. 3. pun. 5. Respondeo Cognationem carnalem definiri a S. T. hic q. 54. a. 1. et aliis; Vinculum personarum ab eodem propinquo stipite descendentium, carnali propogatione contractum. Quae tamen de lineatione⁵⁸⁵ maxime conuenit lineae transuersali. Nam Pater et filius sunt consanguinei v. g. Adam et Sethus sine ordine ad alium stipitem: sed hoc facile subintelligitur, et ideo retinenda recepta definitio. Continetur autem haec consanguinitas

---

585   S reads for the last two words: *linea*

quibusdam lineis et gradibus, quo[586] explicare[587] oportet vt ipsa cogno-
scatur.

Lineae sunt duae, recta, inter ascendentes et descendentes: late-
ralis seu transuersalis inter eos, qui ex eodem stipite propagantur, vt
sunt fratres et eorum liberi. Singulae vero ex his lineis [fo. 33] plures
complectitur gradus, i.e. habitudines distantiae a stipite, ratione quarum
plus vel minus se contingunt. Tota autem series linearum et graduum
vocatur arbor consanguinitatis, de qua Gratianus 35. q. 5. et eam prae
caeteris bene proponit Laym. p. 4. c. 4. Pro cognoscendis porro his
gradibus tres afferuntur regulae[588] a Doctoribus passim, quas tamen ad
duas reducit Kon: cit.

Prima regula. In linea recta tot sunt gradus, quot personae, vna
dempta. e.g. Abraham, Isaac, et Iacob faciunt duos gradus. Isaac distat
ab Abrahamo in 1°. gradu, Iacob ab eodem in 2°. et sic de reliquis. 2ª.
Regula in linea transuersa aequali tot gradibus distant inter se, quot a
communi stipite. e. g. duo fratres sunt in 1°. gradu, duo consobrini in 2°.
horum filii in 3°. et nepotes in 4. ita Alex. 2. cap. ad sedem, et Zacharias
cap. Parentelae 35. q. 5. Alia est[589] numerandi in iure ciuili vbi tot sunt
gradus quot sunt personae. leg. 1. ff. de grad. lib. 38. tit. 10.

3ª. Regula, In linea transuersa inaequali tot gradibus distant inter se,
quot distat ille a stipite, qui est remotior, e. g. Iacob distat ab Isaac[590]
stipite in 1°. gradu, filius Esauui distat ab Isaac in 2°. ergo Iacob et filius
Esauui distant inter se in 2°. gradu. filius Iacobi et nepos Esauui in 3°.
Nepos Iacobi, aut ipsemet Iacob et pronepos Esauui in 4°. ita expresse
Greg: 9. cap. finali de consang: et omnes Doctores.

Vnde sequitur 1°. eos, quorum vnus est in 4°. gradu, alius in 5°. a
stipite esse in 5. gradu, atque adeo non egere [fo. 33ᵛ] dispensatione ad
contrahendum cap. fin. de consang.

Sequitur 2°. si tales petant dispensationem; sufficere quod dicant se
in 3. vel 4. gradu versari, absque eo, quod explicent mixtionem 2ⁱ. aut
3ⁱ. gradus propinquioris: vere enim mixtus ex 2°. et 3°. est 3ᵘˢ. et mixtus
ex 3°. et 4. est 4ᵘˢ. vnde sufficit dicere esse 4ᵐ. atque ita declarauit Pius
5us. vt refert Sanch. l. 8. d. 24. n. 25. Excipe, nisi alter esset in 1°. gradu
a stipite, vt si patruus vellet ducere fratris sui filiam, non enim sufficit
dicere esse in 2°. gradu, quia Pontifex non intendit in hoc casu dispensare. ita Sanch. cit. n. 32.

Nota consanguinitatem aliquando duplicari in eodem subiecto v.
g. duo fratres ducunt duas sorores: filii istorum fratrum sunt consan-

---

586 S reads: *quos*
587 In A this word is a correction of *explicatur*
588 S adds: *35. q. 5. et*
589 S adds: *regula*
590 In A this word is written above *Esau*, which is crossed out.

guinei[591] in 2°. gradu bis, et ex parte patrum, et ex parte matrum. si duo fratres ducerent duas consobrinas, filii haberent duplicem consanguini-tatem, vnam in 2°. gradu, aliam in 3°. quod notandum est pro dispensa-tionibus, de quo Sanch. l. 8. d. 24. n. 4.

Case M34. *What is the kinship of consanguinity, and what are its lines? And in what way are its degrees to be counted? For example, in what degree are the brothers Esau and Jacob, and in what degree their sons, and their grandsons, and their great-grandsons? See Sanchez, Coninck, Laymann and Bonacina [refs].*

I reply that carnal kinship is defined by St Thomas [ref.] and others, as the bond which is contracted by sexual reproduction, between persons who are related by descent from the same related stock. This definition, however, when it comes to the lines of consanguinity agrees best with what are called the 'transverse' lines. But father and son are also consan-guineous, for example Adam and Seth, without reference to another stock; but this is easily understood, and so the received definition should be retained. This consanguinity is continued, moreover, in certain lines and degrees, which must be explained in order that consanguinity can be understood.

There are two lines; the direct line between direct ascendants and their descendants; and the lateral or transverse line, between those who were propagated from the same stock, as are brothers and their chil-dren. Each of these lines, in truth, encompasses many degrees; that is, the conditions of distance from the stock, by reason of which they are related, to a greater or lesser extent to each other. The whole series, moreover, of lines and degrees is called the tree of consanguinity, on which see Gratian [ref.]; and Laymann [ref.] explains it better than others. To understand these degrees further, three rules [ref.] are adduced everywhere by the doctors, which, however, Coninck in the place cited reduces to two.

The first rule: in a direct line there are as many degrees as persons, minus one. For example, Abraham, Isaac and Jacob make two grades. Isaac is distant from Abraham in the first degree, Jacob from the same in the second degree, and thus concerning the rest. The second rule: in a transverse line people from the same generation are distant among themselves by as many degrees as they are from the common stock. For example, two brothers are in the first degree, the two children of two sisters in the second, the children of these are in the third degree, and the grand-children in the fourth. Thus, Alexander II [ref.] and Zacharias

---

[591] In A, written above, is: *cognati*, which is what S reads.

[ref.]. Another rule for counting is used in the civil law, where there are as many degrees as there are persons [ref.].

The third rule: in the transverse line, people from different generations are distant one from another in as many degrees as the more remote of the two is distant from the stock. For example, Jacob is distant from Isaac, the stock, in the first degree; the son of Esau is distant from Isaac in the second; therefore Jacob and the son of Esau are distant one from the other in the second degree; the son of Jacob and the grandson of Esau in the third; the grandson of Jacob, or Jacob himself and the great-grandson of Esau in the fourth. Thus, explicitly, Gregory IX [ref.] and all doctors.

Hence it follows, first, that those, of whom one is in the fourth degree, the other in the fifth, are in the fifth degree from the stock, and so they do not need a dispensation in order to marry, according to canon law [ref.].

It follows, second, that if such people seek a dispensation, it is enough that they say they are in the third or the fourth degree, without explaining the mixture of the second or third degree of kinship; for, truly, a mixture of second and third is the third; and a mixture of the third and fourth is the fourth, and hence it is enough to say it is the fourth. And thus Pius V declared, as Sanchez [ref.] relates. The exception is if one is in the first degree from the stock, for example if a paternal uncle wanted to marry the daughter of his brother, for it would not be enough to say he was in the second degree, because the Pontiff did not intend to dispense in this case; thus Sanchez [ref.].

Note that consanguinity is sometimes duplicated in the same subject, for example if two brothers marry two sisters, the children of these brothers are consanguineous in the second degree twice, both on the side of the mother and on the side of the father. If two brothers marry the two children of sisters, the children have double consanguinity, one in the second degree, the other in the third, which is to be noted for dispensations; on which, see Sanchez [ref.].

[M35] 35us. Ad quot gradus dirimat matrimonium consanguinitas? et quo iure? num iure diuino inualidum sit inter Patrem et sororem, Matrem et filium caeterosque gradus Leuit. 18. prohibitos? et quinam illi sint? Sanch. l. 7. d. 51 et 52. Kon. d. 32. d. 1. Laym. p. 4. c. 6. Bonac. q. 3. pun: 5°. a num. 7. Bellar. l. 1. de matr. Respondeo olim dirimisse vsque ad 7. cap. ad sedem. 35. q. 5. et aliis iuribus ibid. q. 2. non tamen plane constanter, vt patet ex cap. propinquis, ibid. Tandem C. Later. sub Innoc. 3°. reuocauit ad 4m. consanguinitatis et affinitatis inclusiue; et [fo. 34] huic iuri nunc stamus. Iam vero indubitatum est gradum 2^m. aequalem, et inferiores deinceps non dirimere nisi iure Ecclesiastico. Difficultas est de reliquis, praesertim iis, qui habentur Leuit. 18. id est Patris cum filia aut nepote; matris cum filio aut nepote; fratris cum sorore, nepotis cum amita (non tamen auunculi cum nepote) vitrici cum priuigna, vel eius filia; soceri cum nuru; nouercae cum priuigno, fratris cum fratria; nepotis cum relicta patrui; sororii cum sorore vxoris seu glore, vxore tamen viuente.

Dico 1°. matrimonium in his gradibus esse per se loquendo iure naturae illicitum, nisi adsit causa excusans. ita Sanch. d. 52. n. 7. Tan. q. 4. n. 50. Bellar. l. 1. matr. c. 27. et antiqui, S. T. Bonau. Durand. Caiet. Petr. Soto, Dominicus Soto, Angelus et alii apud Sanch. 1°. quia Scriptura Leuit. 18. et 20. vocat has nuptias turpes, Ne polluamini; et damnantur ob haec ipsi Gentiles c. 18. v. 24. et c. 20. v. 23. 2°. quia cap. litteras, de rest. spol. vocantur iure diuino prohibiti. 3°. idem colligitur ex Conciliis Agathensi c. 61. Epaunensi can. 30. Auralian. 3°. can. 10.

Dico 2°. Probabilius videri etiam iure naturae, matrimonium in istis gradibus[592] esse inualidum per se loquendo. ita aperte S. T. Bonau. Durand., et fauet Trid. sess. 24. can. 3. si attente legatur, fauet et Innoc. 3us. cap. fin. de diuortio, aperte supponens matrimonium pagani cum relicta fratris esse nullum. Ratione probatur quia cum hae nuptiae sint iure naturae[593] illicitae, non quod ipse [fo. 34v] contractus in se sit prohibitus, sed ob copulae indecentiam, sequi videtur contractum, qui est essentialiter obligatio ad hanc copulam, esse ex natura rei nullum, vt in simili Laym. c. 6. n. 1.

Dico 3°. Posse tamen ob graues causas licite in[594] multis ex his gradibus contrahi, Pontifice dispensante in iure positiuo, et declarante cessare ius diuinum. Est de fide definitum in Trid: cit. contra haereticos modernos in fauorem matrimonii Henrici 8ui. cum Catharina. Probatur euidenter quia Deutr. 25. conceditur vt frater ducat relictam fratris ad suscitandum semen defuncto. Quod et Gen. 38 fecerunt filii Iudae. Iacob duxit duas sorores gen. 29. Amram duxit suam amitam. Exo. 6. Abraham duxit sororem suam. gen. 20. vt omittam filios Adami. Vnde et fratres et sorores non inualide contrahere existimo[595] in iure naturae, si adsit sufficiens necessitas, vt expresse tenet Pontius l. 7. c. 32. cum Caiet. 2. 2. q. 154. a. 9. Scot. in 4. dis. 40. Con: d. 32. n. 19. quod probat exemplo filiorum Adami: et probabilius est Abrahamum idem fecisse gen. 20. vero soror mea est, filia Patris mei.

Imo[596] inter patrem et filiam posset esse matrimonium ipso iure, si fingeretur id necessarium ad conseruationem generis humani, vt si

---

592 Written above this word in A is *casibus*, which S reads.
593 S reads: *ex natura rei*
594 In A *his* is crossed out at this point.
595 S adds: *stando*
596 In A this word replaces *Quomodo*, which is crossed out.

Adamus ex Eua solas filias suscepisset. ita Sanch. d. 51. n. 10. cum Soto et aliis contra Caiet. et Estium.

Quoad affinitatem in 1°. gradu etiam rectae lineae, dico probabilius esse, in eo posse Pontificem dispensare v.g. vt contrahas cum nuru, priuigna, socru, nouerca, etc. Ita Sanch. d. 66. Pont. c. 34. Bonac. p. 12. et probari potest ex Agathensi. [fo. 35] Epaun: Aurelian cit. Ratio est, quia iure naturae praecise non videtur tanta in hoc indecentia, namque per copulam fornicariam aeque contrahitur haec affinitas, et tamen in eo casu valde parum reuerentiae conciliatur erga consanguineos Amasiae. Contrarium tamen quoad rectam lineam probabiliter tenent Tan: q. 4. n. 123. Laym. c. 6. Coninck. cit. n. 53.

Case M35. *To how many degrees does consanguinity render marriage null and void; and by what law? Is it invalid by divine law between father and sister, mother and son, and other degrees prohibited by Leviticus 18, and what are they? See Sanchez, Coninck, Laymann, Bonacina, and Bellarmine [refs].*

I reply that canon law [refs] once used to prevent marriage up to the seventh degree, although not entirely consistently, as is clear from another canon [ref.]. At length, the Lateran Council under Innocent III revoked it to the fourth degree of consanguinity and affinity inclusive, and we now keep to this law. Now it is truly indubitable that the second degree of the same generation, and the lesser degrees afterwards, do not render marriage null and void, except by ecclesiastical law. The difficulty is with the rest, especially those which are found in Leviticus 18: that is, a father with his daughter or granddaughter; a mother with her son or grandson; a brother with his sister; a grandson with his paternal aunt (but not a maternal uncle with his grandchild); a step-father with his step-daughter, or with her daughter; a father-in-law with his daughter-in-law; a step-mother with her step-son; a brother with his sister-in-law; a grand-son with the widow of his paternal uncle; and a sister's husband with the sister of his wife, but while the wife is still alive.

I say firstly that marriage in these degrees is in itself by the law of nature unlawful, unless there is a reason which excuses it; thus, Sanchez, Tanner, Bellarmine [refs]; and the ancients, St Thomas, St Bonaventure, Durandus, Caietan, Petrus Soto, Dominic Soto, Angelus, and others, cited in Sanchez. This is because, first, Scripture (Leviticus 18 and 20) calls these marriages dishonourable, saying, 'Defile not yourself', and the Gentiles themselves were condemned because of this [refs]. Secondly because in the canon law [ref.] such marriages are described as being prohibited by divine law. Thirdly, the same is gathered from the Councils of Agatha, Pamiers, and the third Council at Aurillac [refs].

I say secondly that, in itself, it seems more probable that even by the law of nature, marriage in these degrees is invalid. Thus, openly,

St Thomas, St Bonaventure, Durandus; and the Council of Trent [ref.] agrees, if it is carefully read. Innocent III [ref.] also agrees, openly maintaining that the marriage of a pagan with the widow of his brother is null. This is proved by reasoning that, since these marriages are unlawful by the law of nature, not because the contract in itself is prohibited, but because of the indecency of the copulation, it seems to follow that the contract which is essentially an obligation to that copulation is by the nature of the matter null; as, in a similar discussion, Laymann [ref.] argues.

I say thirdly that it is possible for grave reasons, however, to marry lawfully in many of these degrees, if the Pope grants a dispensation from the positive law, and declares that the divine law ceases. It was defined as a matter of faith at the Council of Trent, in the place cited, against the modern heretics, in favour of the marriage of Henry VIII with Catherine. It is proved clearly because Deuteronomy 25 conceded that a brother should marry the widow of his brother, in order to raise up seed for the dead man, which is also what the sons of Judah did in Genesis 38. Jacob married two sisters; see Genesis 29. Amram married his father's sister; see Exodus 6. Abraham married his sister; see Genesis 20. Not to mention the sons of Adam. Hence, I believe that even brothers and sisters may marry lawfully, by the law of nature, if there is sufficient necessity, as is expressly held by Pontius, with Caietan, Scotus, and Coninck [refs], which he proves with the example of the sons of Adam. And it is more probable that Abraham did the same; see Genesis 20, 'she is truly my sister, the daughter of my father'.

Indeed, between father and daughter there may be marriage, by that law, if it were claimed that it was necessary for the conservation of the human race; for example, if Adam and Eve only had daughters. Thus, Sanchez [ref.], with Soto and others, against Caietan and Estius.

As far as affinity in the first degree is concerned, even in the direct line, I say that it is more probable that the Pope may grant a dispensation; for example, so that you can marry your daughter-in-law, stepdaughter, mother-in-law, or step-mother, etc. Thus, Sanchez, Pontius, and Bonacina [refs], and it may be proved from the Councils of Agatha, Pamiers and Aurillac, which have been cited. The reason is that precisely by the law of nature there does not seem to be such indecency in this, and by fornication this affinity would equally well be contracted, and moreover in that case much less reverence and friendship would be shown towards the blood relatives of the mistress. The contrary, however, as far as the direct line is concerned, is held as probable by Tanner, Laymann, and Coninck [refs].

[M36] 36us. Vtrum inter omnes ascendentes et descendentes in recta linea sit iure naturali, aut positiuo irritum matrimonium? Sanch. d. 51.

a. n. 12. Con. d. 32. n. 16. Laym. c. 6. n. 2. Bonac. q. 3. p. 5.[597] n. 8. Respondeo probabilius, hos gradus iure naturae non dirimere in infinitum, sed ad 2. vel 3 iure naturae, ad 4. iure positiuo; atque adeo extra eum valiturum omni iure matrimonium. ita Sanch. cit.[598] Tan. cit. n. 54. Bonac. contra Con. Petrum Soto, et Iustinian: instit. de nuptiis. Ratio est, quia consanguinitas non potest esse infinita, cum paulatim minuatur vis sanguinis communicati, vt etiam indicat C. Later. cap. penult. de consanguin: 2o. quia durum nimis videtur, vt Adamus et Noe, si fuisset mature viduati, tam diu viuerent sine nuptiis.

Case M36. *Is marriage between all ascendants and descendants in the direct line invalid by natural or by positive law? See Sanchez, Coninck, Laymann and Bonacina [refs].*

I reply that it is more probable that these degrees do not render marriage null and void by the law of nature into infinity, but to the second or third degree by the law of nature, to the fourth degree by the positive law; and so outside these degrees marriage will be valid by every law; thus Sanchez, Tanner (refs,) and Bonacina, against Coninck, Petrus de Soto and Justinian [ref.]. The reason is that consanguinity cannot be infinite, since little by little the concentration of the inherited blood diminishes, as the Lateran Council [ref.] also shows. Secondly, because it seems too harsh that Adam and Noah, if they had been widowed as mature men, should have lived so long without marriage.

[M37] 37[us]. Quid sit cognatio spiritualis? et inter quas personas versetur? An uxor et filii Patrini eam contrahat[599] cum prole baptizata eiusque Parentibus? et quid in hoc statuerit Trid: s. 24. c. 2. de matr. Sanch. l. 7. d. 54. Conin: d. 32. n. 24. Laym. par. 4. c. 8: Bonac. q. 3. p. 5. n. 2. Respondeo cognationem spiritualem esse propinquitatem personarum ortam ex statuto Ecclesiae propter collationem Baptismi aut Confirmationis. Sanch. cit. de ea fit mentio. 30. q. 1. 3. 4. et titulo de cognatione spirituali. [fo. 35ᵛ] tam extra, quam in 6°. Porro in 6°. c. 1. et 3. habetur eandem esse rationem quoad[600] baptismi et Confirmationis. De huius ceremoniae antiquitate ex Dionysio et Tertulliano, Augustino agit Suar. 3. p. q. 67. a. 7.

Triplex in iure est eius species; 1ᵃ. paternitas; hanc contrahunt tam baptizator, quam susceptores cum baptizato, censentur enim quasi Patres, vt explicit S. Tho: q. 56. a. 3. Hanc immutauit Tridentinum cit: tollendo paternitatem indirectam, vt mox dicetur; item praefiniendo numerum

---

597   S adds: *2.*
598   S reads: *dp. 51.*
599   S reads: *contrahant*
600   S adds: *hoc*

susceptorum. 2ª. species est compaternitas; haec directe contrahitur a baptizante et susceptoribus cum Patre et matre carnali baptizati. Olim vero indirecte transfundebatur ad vxorem mariti suscipientis, et ad virum susceptricis: modo post consummatum matrimonium susciperent. v.g. Petro suscipiente filium Pauli, vxor Petri ante ab eo cognita, fiebat matrina pueri, et commater Pauli. c. 1. et c. Martinus de cognatione spirituali in 6º. Verum indirectam hanc cognationem sustulit Tridentinum loc. cit. 3ª. species est fraternitas, quam olim contrahebant omnes tam baptizantis, quam susceptorum filii siue ante, siue post geniti cum baptizato, non tamen cum eius fratribus c. 1. de cognatione spirituali in 6º. verum hanc penitus sustulit Tridentinum cit. vnde hodie vbi recipitur Tridentinum haec cognatio solum versari potest inter baptizantem et suscipientes[601] ex vna parte, et inter baptizatum et Parentes eius ex alia. Et in his conueniunt Doctores omnes. Recte autem Bonac. cit. n. 4. monet, nunquam inter ipsos susceptores mutuo contrahi hanc cognitionem solitam. quare maritus et vxor, si eundem suscipiant, non perdunt [fo. 36] inde ius petendi debitum. Suar. cit. a. 8. imo id licitum ait Sanch. et consuetum d. 51. n. 5. licet olim cap. quod autem. 3º. q. 4. id tanquam minus decens censeatur. Hanc doctrinam carmine hoc complexus est, S. Tho. cit. a. 4.

Vnus semper erit compatrum spiritualis
Alter carnalis, non fallit regula talis.

Porro quod iuris pro Anglia quoad cognationes per Tridentinum sublatos vide in casibus Anglicanis 23.

Case M37. *What is spiritual kinship? And between which persons does it exist? Do the wife and children of the godfather contract it with the child that has been baptised, and with its parents? And what did the Council of Trent [ref.] enact on this matter? See Sanchez, Coninck, Laymann and Bonacina [refs].*

I reply that spiritual kinship is the relationship of persons which arises from the law of the Church, on account of the connection they form at baptism or confirmation; see Sanchez in the place cited. The canon law makes mention of it in various places, both in the Sext and elsewhere [refs]. Indeed, in the Sext [ref.] it is said that the same argument applies to both baptism and confirmation. Suarez [ref.] discusses the antiquity of the latter ceremony, following Dionysius, Tertullian and Augustine.

There are three forms of spiritual relationship according to the law. The first form is paternity. The person who baptises and the godparents

---

[601] In A this word is written above *baptizatos*, which has been crossed out.

contract this with the baptised, for they are judged to be like fathers, as St Thomas [ref.] explains. The Council of Trent, as cited, changed this, removing indirect paternity, as will be discussed shortly, and also by laying down the number of godparents. The second form is co-paternity; this is contracted directly by the person baptising and the godparents, on the one hand, with the natural father and mother of the baptised person, on the other hand. Indeed, this kinship used to be transferred indirectly to the wife of a godfather, and to the husband of a godmother, as long as they had become godparents after the marriage had been consummated. For example, if Peter acted as godfather to the son of Paul, but Peter's wife had previously been known by Paul, she would become both godmother of the boy, and co-mother with Paul; see the canon law [ref.]. However, the Council of Trent, in the place cited, abolished this indirect relationship. The third form is fraternity, which formerly every child, both of the person who baptised, as well as of the godparents, contracted with the baptised person, whether they were born before or after the baptism; but they did not contract it with the baptised person's brothers; see the canon law [ref.]. Truly, the Council of Trent, as cited, entirely abolished this relationship. Hence, today, where Trent is accepted, this spiritual kinship can only exist between the person who baptises and the godparents, on the one hand, and the baptised person and his parents, on the other. And in these matters all the Doctors agree. Rightly, however, Bonacina [ref.] warns, that kinship never used to be mutually contracted between the godparents themselves. Therefore, a husband and wife, if they are godparents to the same child, do not as a result lose the right to seek their marital dues; see Suarez [ref.]. Indeed, Sanchez [ref.] says this is lawful and customary, although once the canon law [ref.] judged that it was less decent. This doctrine is summed up in this poem, from St Thomas [ref.]:

One will always be spiritual co-father;
The other carnal: such a rule does not deceive.

However, for what the law is in England, as far as this kinship which has been abolished by Trent, see in the English cases, Case 23.

[M38] 38us. An ad contrahendam hanc cognationem spiritualem requiratur, vt Patrini realiter teneant Infantem ad fontem; vt Baptismus sit verus, et solemnis: vt adsit animus suscipiendi: et an suscipiens per procuratorem eam vere contrahat? Sanch. l. 7. d. 56. 58. 59. et 62. Conink. d. 32. dub. 2. Laym. p. 4. c. 8. a. n. 4. et de Baptis. c. 9. n. 5. Bonac. q. 3. p. 5. §. 2. a n. 8. Respondeo quoad baptizantem, vt contrahat hanc cognationem solum requiri vt baptizet, siue solemniter siue aliter, siue ex necessitate, siue sponte. Sanch. dp. 62. Bonac. n. 11. Quoad susceptores requiruntur variae conditiones.

1ᵃ. vt vere teneant physice contingendo saltem mediis vestibus, et hoc vel dum actu baptizatur, vel saltem immediate eum suscipiendo ex manibus baptizantis. Quare declaratum est a Cardinalibus quod Abulae, vbi Patrinus, solebat infantem tenere, et statim post matrinae eum tradere, haec cognationem non contraheret. Ratio est, quia iura exigunt contactum et ex alia parte haec cognatio restringi debet, quantum potest, vt suo exemplo indicat Tridentinum. Ita Sanch. [fo. 36ᵛ] Conink Bonac Pontius. Sufficit tamen tenere etiamsi non respondeat, quamuis et hoc faciendum sit. Sanch. dp. 56.

2ᵃ. requiritur vt teneat animo suscipiendi, non vero materialiter assistendi causa sine tali intentione. Sanch. dp. 58. Vnde infero valde esse probabile non valere, si erret in persona, suscipiens Petrum cum sit Paulus. Sanch. n. 7. Alia est ratio de baptizante; hic enim tenetur ferre intentionem in praesentem, siue sit Petrus siue Paulus.

3ᵃ. requiritur vt sit verum et validum sacramentum; itaque si fuerit ex vllo capite irritum, aut si solum supplebantur exorcismi et ceremoniae, non contrahitur cognatio. Sanch. dp. 62. n. 5. et omnes.

4ᵃ. debet esse baptismus solemnis, id est, a sacerdote cum ceremoniis consuetis celebratus. Nam quando ex necessitate celebratur a Laico aut sine ceremoniis, non est adhibendus Patrinus. Sanch. dp. 62. n. 14. Vnde et probabiliter idem tenet non contrahi cognationem, etiamsi intendas contrahere. Quamuis quoad hoc alii contradicant. Suar: Con: Tan. Laym.

5ᵃ. debet habere vsum rationis, et hoc sufficit. Sanch. dp. 61.

6ᵃ. debet esse baptizatus, alias legibus Ecclesiae non est subiectus.

7ᵃ. post Tridentinum debet esse designatus: et quidem probabilius existimo cum Sanch. dp. 57. n. 12. Suar: 3. par. q. 67. n. 8. contra Bonac. Tan. Laym. hanc conditionem requiri a Concilio vt essentialem; ita vt si nullus designetur, nullus sit susceptor, etiamsi tangant et teneant; quia amplianda est haec cognationis restrictio, [fo. 37] cum sit fauorabilis. Illud certum, si vltra designatos alii tangant, eos nihil facere, vt statuit Concilium.

Debet autem designari vnicus, vt etiam iure antiquo habetur, cap. Non plures. 101. de consecr. dist. 4. et cap. fin. de cogn. sprial. in 6°. vel ad summum, vnus et vna. Tridentinum. c. 2. cit. Nec potest Episcopus concedere vt sint duo viri vt duae foeminae, vbi Tridentinum est receptum. Sanch. dp. 57. n. 7. Quod si de facto plures designentur, et a Parocho admittantur, probabile est, omnes cognationem contrahere, quia Concilium factum non irritat: Ita Sanch. cit. n. 14. quamuis contrarium probabile etiam teneat Suar. cit.

Vltimo dicendum, posse aliquem per Procuratorem suscipere, et cognationem contrahere. ita contra Sanch. dp. 59. docent alii.⁶⁰² Bonac.

---

⁶⁰² S adds: *n. 40.*

n. 34. Laym. c. 8. n. 5. Tan. q. 4. n. 70. Pont. n. 10. Et probatur 1°. ex consuetudine Principum, non enim est verosimile, quod in iis casibus nullus vere suscipiat. 2°. quia potest quis per Procuratorem quicquid potest per seipsum, nisi expresse prohibeatur. leg. 1ª. ff. de Procuratoribus. §.Vsus. l. 3. tit. 3. et cap: Potest. de reg: iuris in 6°.: hic autem nulla est prohibitio nec actus est talis naturae, vt ei repugnet per alium fieri.

Case M38. *In order to contract this spiritual kinship, is it required that the godparents should really hold the infant at the font; that the baptism should be true and solemn; that the godparents should possess an intention to act as such; and does the godparent really contract this relationship through proxies? See Sanchez, Coninck, Laymann, and Bonacina [refs].*

I reply that as far as the person baptising is concerned, in order to contract this kinship, it is only required that he or she should baptise, either solemnly or otherwise, either out of necessity or of his own free will; see Sanchez and Bonacina [refs]. As far as the godparents are concerned, various conditions are required.

The first condition is that they should physically hold the child, by at least touching it through its clothing, either during the act of baptism, or at least immediately taking the child from the hands of the person who baptised it. For which reason, it was declared by the Cardinals that in Avila, where the godfather was accustomed to hold the infant and immediately give it to the godmother, he did not contract that kinship. The reason is that the laws demand contact, and from another point of view this kinship ought to be restricted, as much as it can be, as the Council of Trent shows by its example. Thus, Sanchez, Coninck, Bonacina and Pontius. However, it is enough to hold the child, even if he does not make the responses, although that also ought to be done; see Sanchez [ref.].

The second condition requires that they should hold the infant with the mind of a godparent, not just for the sake of assisting physically, without such a mind; see Sanchez [ref.]. Hence I infer that it is most probable that it is not valid if they make a mistake as to the person, taking Paul, thinking that it is Peter; see Sanchez [ref.]. It is a different matter with the person who is baptising; for he or she is bound to carry out his or her intentions with respect to the child which is present, whether it is Peter or Paul.

The third condition requires that it should be a true and valid sacrament. Therefore, if it was in any respect invalid, or if only the exorcism and ceremonies were performed, the relationship is not contracted; see Sanchez [ref.] and all the authorities.

The fourth condition requires that it should be a solemn baptism, that is, one which is celebrated by a priest with the customary ceremonies. For when it is celebrated out of necessity by a lay-person or without ceremonies, a godparent does not have to be provided; see Sanchez [ref.]. Hence, Sanchez holds, with probability, that you do not contract kinship then, even if you intended to do so. However, as far as this is concerned, other writers contradict this; see Suarez, Coninck, Tanner and Laymann.

The fifth condition is that the godparent should have the use of reason, and this is enough; see Sanchez [ref.].

The sixth condition is that the godparent should have been baptised himself; otherwise, he or she is not subject to the laws of the Church.

The seventh condition is that, after Trent, he or she should be formally designated as godparent, and indeed I consider this more probable, with Sanchez and Suarez [refs], against Bonacina, Tanner, and Laymann. This condition is required by the Council as essential, so that if no one is designated, no one may be a godparent, even if he or she touches and holds the child, because this is a restriction on how far this sort of kinship should extend, which is pleasing. It is certain that if people beyond those designated as godparents touch the child, it has no effect on them, as the Council enacts.

Moreover, a single godparent should be designated, as also is laid down by the ancient law [refs]; or at most a godfather and a godmother; see the decree of the Council of Trent [ref.]. Nor, where Trent is received, may a bishop concede that there should be two men and two women; see Sanchez [ref.]. If in fact more are designated and admitted by the parish priest, it is probable that they all contract a relationship, because the Council does not invalidate what has been done. Thus, Sanchez [ref.], although Suarez, in the place cited, also holds the contrary to be probable.

Finally it must be said that anyone may act as a godparent by proxy, and contract kinship, as is taught by Bonacina, Laymann, Tanner and Pontius [refs], against Sanchez [ref.]. And it is proved, firstly from the custom of princes; for it is not likely that in such cases no one truly 'takes the child from the font'.[603] Secondly, because anyone may do by proxy whatever he can do for himself, unless it is expressly prohibited, as the civil and canon law [refs] say. Moreover, there is no prohibition here, and the action is not of such a sort that it should be repugnant to him for it to be done by someone else.

[M39] 39[us]. Quot susceptores esse possint in Baptismo aut Confirmatione? An infans ante vsum rationis possit esse susceptor? An maritus et

---

[603]   There is a play on words here; the phrase can be taken literally (which is the point of the discussion in this case), or simply to mean 'no one becomes a godparent'.

vxor possint eundem suscipere. Sanch. l. 7. dp. 57. et 61. Con. dp. 32. n. 28. et 37. Bonac.cit. n. 17. et 24. Laym. de baptismo l. 5. trac. 2. c. 9. Patet ex dictis, esse debere vnum et vnam ad summum, debere habere vsum rationis, et posse vxorem et maritum eundem suscipere. Porro quae de Baptismo diximus, locum habent in Sacramento Confirmationis.

Case M39. *How many sponsors may there be in baptism or confirmation? May an infant before it has the use of reason be a sponsor? May a husband and wife be sponsors to the same person? See Sanchez, Coninck, Bonacina and Laymann [refs].*

It is clear from what has been said that there should be at most one male and one female, they should have the use of reason, and a wife and husband may be sponsors to the same child. Moreover, what we have said about baptism applies also to the sacrament of confirmation.

[M40] 40us. Quid sit cognatio legalis? quaenam eius species? et [fo. 37^v] ad quas personas pertineat? Sanch. l. 7. dp. 69. Con. d. 32. d. 3. Laym. p. 4. c. 7. Bonac. q. 3. p. 5. §. 3. Respondeo Cognatio legalis est propinquitas consurgens ex adoptione. Eam dirimere matrimonium. patet ex 30. q. 3. c. 1. 5. et 6. et cap. vn. de cognat. leg: approbante Ecclesia in hoc ius ciuile. Probabilius est non consurgere ex adoptione imperfecta, sed tantum ex perfecta illa, quae vocatur arrogatio, quia stricte facienda est interpretatio; et quia sola arrogatio cohabitationem infert. Ita contra Pont. et alios Sanch. Conin: Bonac. Tan. q. 4. n. 74.

Triplex est eius species. 1^a. linea recta inter adoptantem ex vna parte, et adoptatum eiusque decendentes[604] ex alia. Includuntur autem solum ii, qui in patria potestate tunc existunt, non vero qui prius emancipati, aut post geniti, aut spurii. ita Sanch. n. 63. 34. Tan. n. 72.

2^a. species est fraternitatis inter adoptatum et filios carnales legitimos adoptantis. cap. vn. de cog. leg. Dixi carnales, quia inter adoptiuos nullum reperitur statutum impedimentum. Sanch. n. 28. Laym. contra Angelum. Dixi legitimos, quia spurii non sunt in patria potestate, vnde nec contrahunt. Sanch. Con. Laym. Durat hoc impedimentum solum quamdiu vterque est sub patria potestate, et cessat ea cessante; cum tamen prior species maneat soluta adoptione, vt habetur instit. de nupt.

3^a. est cuiusdam affinitatis inter vxorem adoptantis, et adoptatum, eiusque descendentes supradictos, quae etiam durat soluta adoptione, instit. de nupt.

[fo. 38] At vero inter adoptantem et parentes adoptati nulla est

---

604 S adds: *in adoptione inclusos*

cognatio, sicut neque inter filios filiae adoptiuae, quia foemina non habet patriam potestatem in liberos. Bonac. n. 8.

Case M40. *What is legal kinship? What are its forms? And to what persons does it pertain? See Sanchez, Coninck, Laymann, and Bonacina [refs].*

I reply that legal kinship is a relationship which arises from adoption. It renders marriage null and void, as is clear from civil law [ref.], with the Church approving this in the canon law [ref.]. It is more probable that it does not arise from imperfect adoption, but only from perfect adoption, which is called 'arrogation', because it must be interpreted strictly, and because only 'arrogation' brings cohabitation with it. Thus, against Pontius and others, Sanchez, Coninck, Bonacina and Tanner [ref.].

It has three forms. The first (1) is the direct line between the adopter on the one hand, and the adopted and his descendants on the other. Only those are included, however, who are, at that time, in the father's power, not indeed those who have been previously emancipated, or those born afterwards, or who are illegitimate; thus, Sanchez and Tanner [refs].

The second form is fraternity between the adopted and the legitimate children of the body of the adopter, according to canon law [ref.]. I have said 'of the body' because between adopted children no impediment has been found to have been enacted; see Sanchez [ref.] and Laymann, against Angelus. I have said 'legitimate', because bastards are not in the power of the father and therefore they do not contract this kinship; see Sanchez, Coninck and Laymann. This impediment only lasts as long as each is under the power of the father, and ceases when that ceases. However, the first form of kinship discussed above (1) remains when the adoption is at an end, as the Institutes of Justinian [ref.] say.

The third form is a sort of affinity between the wife of the adopter and the adopted child, and his descendents aforesaid, which also lasts after the adoption is over, according to the Institutes of Justinian [ref.].

But truly between the adopter and the parents of the adopted there is no kinship, just as there is none with the sons of an adopted daughter, because a woman does not have paternal power over children; see Bonacina [ref.].

[M41] 41[us]. Quaenam crimina matrimonium dirimant? An coniugicidium sine adulterio? an adulterium solum? an adulterium cum machinatione coniugicidii, aut cum matrimonio, aut matrimonii promissione? Sanch. l. 7. d. 78. et 79. Con. d. 31. d. 5. Laym. p. 4. c. 10. Bonac. q. 3. p. 6. Respondeo Crimina dirimentia esse coniugis occisionem, et adulterium, modo adsint conditiones requisitae. cap. relatum. cap. si quis 30. q. 1. et aliis citandis. 1°. sufficere potest solum vxoricidium (eadem est ratio de mariticidio[605] c. si quis, et cap. laudable de conuers. infidel. vt docent omnes cit: contra Victoriam et Ledesm. id immerito negantes.) sine adulterio,[606] patet cap. c. 1. de conuers. infidel. debet autem habere[607] 4. conditiones. 1°. quod vterque communi consilio machinentur mortem coniugis. vnde si Petrus inscia Catharina occidit, vel vxorem suam, vel eius maritum, nullum ex hoc praecise inter eos sequetur impedimentum. 2°. debent realiter occidere, vel per se, vel per alium, nec sufficit conatus sine effectu, aut ratihabitio post factum. Sanch. d. 78. n. 13. 3°. quod machinentur eo fine, vt postea contrahant. Nauar. c. 22. n. 46. Sanch. n. 13. Pont. l. 7. c. 45. n. 4. Con. n. 51. Bonac. n. 5. Laym. n. 2. ob quorum autoritatem probabilis est haec 3ª. conditio, cum sit fauorabilis; licet mihi non videatur satis ex iure colligi; et contrarium videatur potius indicari cap. laudable. quod etiam docent Caiet. et Armilla. 4°. quod saltem [fo. 38ᵛ] alter sit fidelis, et hoc sufficit, vt et infidelis post baptismum maneat impeditus; secus si tunc ambo essent infideles.

2°. dirimit vxoricidium cum adulterio coniunctum, etiamsi vnus tantum ex contrahentibus adulteris coniugem siue suam, siue complicis e medio tollat, altero ignorante cap. si quis viuente cit. et cap. super hoc de eo qui duxit. Debet autem occidere eo fine, vt contrahat, Immo haec intentio contrahendi debet esse nota complici, vt docet Pont. l. 7. c. 45. n. 5. cum S. Tho. q. 60. a. 2. Nec sufficit intentio liberius fornicandi. 2°. debet adulterium praecedere occisionem alias non dirimit cap. super hoc. et cap. veniens de eo qui duxit. 3°. debet esse adulterium verum cum seminatione intra vas; item cum iniuria matrimonii veri, non existimati tantum.

3°. Dirimit adulterium, si accedat contractus matrimonialis inter ipsos. cap. litterarum. cap. veniens. cap. fin: de eo, qui duxit. Requiruntur autem hae conditiones. 1°. quod sit verum adulterium intra vas naturale 2°. quod vterque sciat esse adulterium; vnde si foemina contrahat cum altero coniugato putans esse solutum, non impedit. cap. 1. et c. veniens de eo, qui duxit. 3°. debet tam contractus, quam adulterium fieri viuente altero coniuge, tempore vnius et eiusdem matrimonii cap. fin. de eo, qui duxit. Sa.

4°. Dirimit adulterium si accedat promissio matrimonii de futuro post mortem coniugis: vtique ne detur causa captandae mortis alienae: cap. finali. de[608] eo qui duxit. Requiritur autem 1°., vt sit verum [fo. 39] adulterium, vt sciatur ab vtroque vt tam fides data, quam adulterium

---

605 S reads: *matricidio*
606 S adds: *vt*, which is crossed out in A.
607 S adds: *tunc*
608 In A the last three words are written above the following four, words which are crossed out (and miscopied from the next line): *vt sciatur ab vtroque.*

fiant viuente vno, et eodem coniuge, vt in precedente casu dictum est.
2°. specialiter hic requiritur vt sit promissio non ficta, sed seria. Laym.
n. 4. Bonac. n. 8. Diana de Sacr: resol. 198. contra Sanch. et Con:
quia ficta promissio non est promissio, nec aeque dat ansam captandae
mortis ex parte promittentis. 3°. requiritur quod promissio acceptetur;
non tamen requiritur mutua promissio, vt contra Henriquem, cui fauet
Laym. docent Sanch. Pontius, et alii, quia sufficit fides data, cap. sigficasti: de eo qui duxit. ad hoc autem sufficit sola promissio acceptata sine
repromissione. Imo sufficit sola acceptatio per solam taciturnitatem ad
hoc enim est fides data Con. n. 58. Pont. n. 2. contra Sanch. n. 25. et
Bonac.n. 9.

Ex dictis infertur solum adulterium nunquam dirimere sine machinatione, aut fide data, vt habetur cap. sigficasti cit. quare iura antiqua
31. q. 1. intelligenda sunt de adulterio cum conditionibus praedictis, a
iure posteriori declaratis. Similiter solum coniugicidium ab vno solo
factum non dirimit. Denique certum est haec crimina non impedire
contrahendum cum aliis, sed tantum cum complicibus supradictis cap.
litter. de eo, qui duxit.

Case M41. *What crimes render marriage null and void? Does killing
a spouse without adultery? Does adultery alone? Does adultery with
a plot to kill a spouse, or adultery with marriage, or adultery with the
promise of marriage? See Sanchez, Coninck, Laymann and Bonacina
[refs].*

I reply that the crimes which render marriage null and void are the
killing of a spouse, and adultery, as long as the requisite conditions are
present; see the canon law [refs]. (1.) First, the killing of a wife alone
can be enough, without adultery, as is clear from the canon law [refs].
The same is the case with the killing of a husband, according to canon
law [refs], as all those cited teach, against Victoria and Ledesma, who
deny this unreasonably. However, there should then be four conditions.
(1a.) First, both by common agreement must plot the death of the spouse.
Hence, if Peter, without Catherine being aware, kills either his wife or
her husband, no impediment between them follows precisely from that.
(1b.) Second, they should really kill the wife, either themselves, or by
employing another; and an unsuccessful attempt, or approval after the
deed, is not enough; see Sanchez [ref.]. (1c.) Third, they should plot
the murder in order to marry afterwards; see Navarre, Sanchez, Pontius,
Coninck, Bonacina and Laymann [refs], on account of whose authority
this third condition seems probable, since it is fair. However, it does not
seem to me to be satisfactorily drawn from the law, and the contrary
seems rather to be indicated by the canon [ref.], which Caietan and
Armilla also teach. (1d.) Fourth, that at least one is a Christian, and this

is sufficient for the infidel after baptism to remain under the impediment; it is different if both were infidels then.

(2.) Second, the killing of a wife, accompanied by adultery, renders marriage null and void, even if only one of the adulterers contracting marriage killed either his spouse or the spouse of his accomplice, with the other one in ignorance; see the canon law [refs]. (2a.) First, he should kill in order to marry; and indeed that intention of marrying should be known to the accomplice, as Pontius teaches with St Thomas [refs]. Nor, if the intention was to commit fornication more freely, is that sufficient. (2b.) Second, adultery should precede the killing, otherwise it would not render marriage null and void, according to the canon law [refs]. (2c.) Third, it should be true adultery with semination inside the vessel; also with detriment to the true marriage, not just a presumption of detriment.

(3.) Third, adultery renders marriage null and void if it encourages a contract of marriage between the adulterers; see the canon law [refs]. There are required however these conditions. (3a.) First, it should be true adultery within the natural vessel. (3b.) Second, both should know that it is adultery. Hence, if a woman contracts marriage with another person who is married, thinking him to be free, it is not an impediment, according to the canon [ref.]. (3c.) Third, both the contract and the adultery must be done while the other spouse is alive, at the time of one and the same marriage; see the canon [ref.] and Sa.

(4.) Fourth, adultery renders marriage null and void if it encourages a promise of marriage in the future, after the death of the present spouse; this requirement is to prevent such a promise giving cause to seek the death of another; see the canon [ref.]. It is required, however (4a.) first, it should be true adultery, known to be such by both, and they must make a promise to commit adultery and carry it out, while one and the same spouse is living, as is said in the preceding case. (4b.) Second, it is specially required here that they should make a sincere and not a false promise; thus, Laymann, Bonacina, and Diana [refs], against Sanchez and Coninck. This is because a false promise is not a promise; nor, equally, does it give occasion to seek the death of the spouse on the part of the person promising. (4c.) Third, it is required that the promise of one is accepted by the other. However, a mutual promise is not required (as Sanchez and Pontius and others teach, against Henriques, who is favoured by Laymann), because it is sufficient that trust is given, as the canon [ref.] says. Moreover, for this all that is needed is a promise accepted without a re-promise. Indeed, tacit acceptance alone is sufficient for this, for it is trust given; see Coninck and Pontius [refs], against Sanchez and Bonacina [refs].

From what has been said, it is inferred that adultery alone never renders marriage null and void, without plotting, or a promise of marriage, as is said in the canon [ref.]. Hence the ancient laws on the subject of adultery [ref.] are to be understood with the aforesaid conditions, which are declared by the later law. Similarly, wife-killing done by one person alone does not render marriage null and void. Finally, it is certain that these crimes do not prevent marriage with others, but only with the aforesaid accomplices; see the canon [ref.].

[**M42**] 42us. An matrimonium fidelis cum infideli seu non baptizato, aut haeretico, sit aut irritum, aut illicitum, et quo iure? Sanch l. 7. d. 71. et 72. Con. d. 31. d. 3. Lay. p. 4. c. 14. Bonac: q. 3. pun. 7. Respondeo et Dico 1°. Matrimonium fidelis cum infideli seu non baptizato esse nullum. ita S. Tho. q. 59. Suppl. a. 1. et omnes [fo. 39^v] Theologi apud Sanch: d. 71. non quidem iure diuino, aut naturali, sed Ecclesiastico; quamuis de claro textu vix constet. Fauet canon 67. Hiscaeni,^609 ex Arabico; iubentur enim separari. Caeterum illicita esse haec connubia dictat ratio, ob periculum peruersionis, et malae educationis educationis^610 prolium; vnde a Deo olim prohibita. Exodi 34. Deut. 7. 3. Reg. 11. idem colligitur ex 1°. Cor. 7. tantum in Domino. et 2. Cor 6. Nolite iugum ducere cum infidelibus, vt late Cornel. et Pont. c. 46. quare fidelis^611 inualide duceret catechumenam. vt recte S. Tho:

Dico 2°. matrimonium Catholici cum haeretica esse validum, vt est certum apud omnes. Sanch. d. 72. Est tamen illicitum, et ab Ecclesia prohibitum. de quo, in casibus Anglicanis. casu 22.

Case M42. *Is the marriage of a Christian with an infidel, or an unbaptised person, or with a heretic, invalid or unlawful; and by what law? See Sanchez, Coninck, Laymann and Bonacina [refs].*

I reply and I say, firstly that the marriage of a Christian with an infidel or an unbaptised person is null; thus, St Thomas [ref.] and all theologians, according to Sanchez [ref.]. Not indeed by divine law, or natural law, but by ecclesiastical law. However, according to which law precisely there is hardly any agreement. One of the Arabic canons of the Council of Nicaea [ref.] favours this judgement; for they are commanded by it to separate. However, reason dictates that this marriage is unlawful, on account of the danger of perversion and of the bad education of the children; hence these marriages were once prohibited by God: Exodus, 34; Deuteronomy, 7; 3 Kings 11. The same is gathered from 1 Corinthians 7, 'only in the Lord', and 2 Corinthians 6, 'bear not the yoke with unbelievers'; as Cornelius and Pontius [ref.] show at length. Hence,

---

609 Thus in S and A: a misreading for *Nicaeni*
610 Repeated thus in A.
611 In A at this point, *infidelis* is crossed out.

the marriage of a Catholic with a catechumen would be invalid, as St Thomas rightly says.

I say secondly that the marriage of a Catholic with a heretic is valid, as is certain according to everyone; see Sanchez [ref.]. It is however unlawful and prohibited by the Church; concerning which, see Case 22, in the English cases.

[M43] 43us. Vtrum 2^m. matrimonium valeat priore coniuge adhuc viuo? quid si 2^m. sit consummatum, et prius ratum tantum? quae denique certitudo sufficit de morte primi coniugis, vt liceat 2as. nuptias capescere? Sanch. l. 7. d. 80. et l. 2. d. 46. Bonac. q. 3. p. 10. Con: d. 25. d. 3. Laym. p. 3. c. 3. Respondeo 2m. non valere, quia 1m. est iure diuino indissolubile, et Πολογαμία omnis eodem iure irrita. vt definit Tridentinum sess. 24. can. 2. et Innoc. 3us. cap: gaudemus de diuort. Amplia si^{612} 1um. sit solummodo ratum, posterius vero consummatum, adhuc enim praeualet 1^m. vt expresse decisum est c. 3. et cap. fin: de sponsa duorum.

[fo. 40] Haec autem vnitas et perpetuitas matrimonii, nec mero iure naturali, vt existimo, subsistit; nec solo iure humano; sed iure diuino positiuo, quod indicauit Adamus, quando dixit, Erunt duo in carne vna, vt interpretatur Christus Mat: 19. Et licet Patriarchis olim concessa sit dispensatio ad plures vxores, et diuortia seu repudia, adueniente tamen Christo reuocata illa est, non solum pro Christianis, sed pro toto mundo. Nisi quod in fauorem fidei infidelis conuersus posset deserere suam compartem, si cohabitare nolit sine iniuria Creatoris, de quo alibi.

Iam vero vt licite contrahat 2°. requiritur moralis certitudo de morte prioris coniugis, hanc enim exigit rei grauitas, et ius 3^{ae}. personae: Nec sufficiunt coniecturae, aut etiam mera probabilitas qualiscunque quando enim agitur de graui damno alteri inferendo, non sufficit mera probabilitas, sicut sufficit quando agitur solum de peccato vitando. Sanch. l. 2. d. 46. n. 6. Bonac. Con. Tan. q. 4. n. 106. et colligitur ex cap. In praesentia. 19. de sponsal. vbi exigitur certus nuntius, multo^{613} minus poterit iudex permittere publice, vt in tali casu ineatur 2^m. matrimonium vt bene Laym.

Nihilominus probabile est in foro conscientiae sufficere notabilem aliquam probabilitatem siue praesumptionem, vt tenent Armilla, Antoninus, Lopez, Syluest. et alii apud Sanch. et Laym. qui et dicunt hoc probabile; et sequitur Diana de Sacr. resol. 214. quam sententiam puto etiam veram in casu magnae [fo. 40^v] necessitatis; haec enim facit, vt minor certitudo sufficiat, vt suppono ex materia de conscientia cum Sanch. l. 1. in Decal. c. 9. n. 33. et colligitur ex cap. cum per bellicam.

---

612 S reads: *etiamsi*
613 S reads: *multoque*

34. q. 2. vbi ponderatur quod foeminae illae sollicitudine cogente, nupserint: et infra Inculpabile iudicandum, quod necessitas intulit. Porro quousque sufficiunt fama aut testis vnus, est iudicis arbitrari: posse enim haec sufficere, si talia[614] adsint adminicula existimo cum Sanch. d. 46. n. 12. Tan. n. 107. Con: n. 21. Bonac. n. 13. Illud certum, comparente priore marito deserendum esse posteriorem, cap. cum per bellicam cit. et cap. Dominus de 2^{is}. nuptiis.

Case M43. *Is a second marriage valid while the first spouse is still alive? What if the second marriage is consummated and the first was not yet consummated? Finally, what certainty is sufficient concerning the death of the first spouse, in order for a second marriage to be lawfully undertaken? See Sanchez, Bonacina, Coninck and Laymann [refs].*

I reply that the second is not valid, because the first is by divine law indissoluble, and all polygamy is invalid by the same law; as the Council of Trent laid down [ref.] and Innocent III [ref.]. Further, even if the first marriage had not been consummated, and the next one had been truly consummated, the first would still prevail, as was expressly decided in the canons [ref.].

However, this unity and perpetuity of marriage, is not, as I judge, merely a matter of the law of nature; nor merely by human law; but by the positive, divine law, which Adam showed when he said 'and they two shall be in one flesh', as Christ interpreted it in Matthew 19. And although a dispensation was once conceded to the patriarchs that they could have a number of wives, and could practice divorce or repudiation; however, with the advent of Christ, however, this was revoked, not only for Christians but for the whole world. The exception is a case where, to benefit the faith, a converted infidel might desert his wife, if he did not wish to cohabit with her to the detriment of the Creator; which is discussed elsewhere.

Moreover, so that he or she might lawfully contract for a second time, moral certainty is required concerning the death of the previous spouse, for the gravity of the matter requires this, and so do the rights of the third party. Nor do conjectures suffice, or even mere probability of whatever kind. For when it is a matter of inflicting grave harm on another person, mere probability is not sufficient, despite the fact that it is sufficient when the matter only concerns the avoidance of sin; see Sanchez, Bonacina, Coninck, and Tanner [refs]. This is gathered from the canon law [ref.], where correct information is required. Much less may a judge permit that in such a case he or she may enter publicly upon a second marriage, as Laymann shows well.

---

[614] S reads: *alia*

Nevertheless it is probable that in the forum of conscience some notable probability or presumption is enough, as is held by Armilla, Antoninus, Lopez, Sylvester and others, cited by Sanchez and Laymann, who also say that this is probable. Diana [ref.] also follows this, and I think this judgement is also true in a case of great necessity; for this means that lesser certainty is enough, as I suppose is the case in matters of conscience, with Sanchez [ref.]. This is also gathered from the canon law [ref.], where the case is considered of those women who are driven by hardship to marry, and the judgement is: 'what necessity forces must be judged free from blame'. Indeed, how far rumour, or one witness, is sufficient is for judges to decide; for this may be sufficient, if other evidence is present. That is my judgement, with Sanchez, Tanner, Coninck and Bonacina [refs]. It is certain, that if the first husband is found, the second one must be deserted, according to canon law [refs].

[M44] 44us. Vtrum impedimentum publicae honestatis ex sponsalibus de futuro oriatur: si ea vllo modo sint inualida, etiam ob defectum pure occultum, aut si ex mutuo consensu dissoluantur? ad quot gradus dirimat, et respectu quarum personarum? num affinium aeque ac consanguineorum sponsae? Sanch. l. 7. d. 68. et 69. Kon. d. 32. d. 5. Laym. par. 4. c. 9. Bonac. q. 3. p. 11. a. n. 1. vsque ad 9. Certum est, ex sponsalibus de futuro oriri impedimentum dirimens inter sponsum, et consanguineas sponsae, et e conuerso, vt expresse habetur cap. vnic. de sponsal. in 6°. et patet ex cap. inuenit. cap. ad audientiam. cap. sponsam de sponsal. cap. litteras, cap. accessit de sponsal. impub. Non est affinitas cum non fundetur in copula carnali, sed est quasi affinitas, et definiri potest ex S. Tho: q. 55. a. 8. Supppl: Propinquitas orta ex sponsalibus propter honestatem aut decentiam.

[fo. 41] Olim ex sponsalibus etiam inualidis oriebatur, modo ex defectu; modo ex defectu[615] consensus non procederet inualiditas. cap. vn. de sponsal. in 6°. At iure nouo Tridentino ex quocunque capite sint inualida (loquimur in hoc casu tantum de sponsalibus de futuro) siue ex defectu consensus, siue quod essent consanguinei, alioue impedimento obstricti, nullum nascitur impedimentum, vt docent omnes: idemque dicendum de sponsalibus incertis aut conditionatis cum Sanch. d. 69. Amplia etiamsi sit defectus pure occultus, ob fictionem internam. contra Sanch. d. 68. n. 14. vt recte Kon. n. 69. Bonac. n. 3. et 14. Laym. n. 4. quia Tridentinum loquitur absolute: Ecclesia tamen quae de[616] iudicat, praesumit ea valida.

Quod si ex mutuo consensu dissoluantur, quae prius erant valida

[615] Repeated thus in A.

[616] S adds: *occultis non*

omnino verum existimo remanere hoc impedimentum cum Sanch. d. 68.
n. 21. Bonac. n. 7. Laym. n. 5. qui id bene confirmat ex cap. accessit de
sponsal. impub. Ratio est, quia semel fuerunt valida et impedimentum
exortum. ergo nulla est ratio cur cesset magis, quam per mortem alterius ex sponsis, per quam non extingui impedimentum hoc in comparte
est indubitatum. Denique verba Concilii habent, vt vbi valida fuerint,
oriatur, etc. Nihilominus contrarium tuentur Sa hic n. 12. Tan. q. 4. n.
109. Pont: l. 7. c. 36. n. 9. Rebel: 2: p. l. 1. q. 14. n. 2. et acriter Diana
de Sacr. resol. 222. fundantque se in quadam declaratione Cardd: apud
Gallemart. [fo. 41^v] sed non est iis adhibenda fides, vt saepe diximus et
in declaratione ex bibliotheca Bellarmini habetur contrarium.

Dirimebat olim honestas haec ad 4 gradum iuxta omnes, et patet ex
cap. sponsam: supra. At iure nouo Tridentino. sess. 24. cap. 3. statuitur,
vt 1^m. gradum non excedat. Dirimit porro cum sponsae consanguineis
tantum, non vero cum affinibus. Itaque sponsus mortua sponsa de futuro
ducere nequit eius matrem aut sororem, quia sunt eius consanguineae in
1°. gradu. At posset ducere eius nouercam, priuignam aut nurum, quia
sunt affines tantum in 1°. item consobrinam, quia non est consanguinea
in 1°.

Case M44. *Does the impediment of public honesty arise from betrothal,
if for any reason the betrothal was invalid even on account of a purely
secret defect, or if the betrothal was dissolved by mutual consent? To
how many degrees does it render marriage null and void, and in respect
of which persons? Does it affect relations by marriage as much as
blood relations of the betrothed? See Sanchez, Coninck, Laymann and
Bonacina [refs].*

It is certain that there arises an impediment from betrothal rendering
marriage null and void between the male betrothed and the blood relations of the betrothed woman, and vice versa, as is expressly stated in
the canon law [ref.] and is clear from other canons [refs]. There is no
affinity, since it is not founded on carnal copulation, but it is a virtual
affinity, and can be defined from St Thomas [ref.], as a kinship arisen
from betrothal on account of honesty or decency.

Formerly, the impediment used to arise from betrothal, even invalid
betrothal, as long as invalidity did not proceed from a defect of consent;
see the canon [ref.]. But by the new law of Trent, for whatever reason
a betrothal (we are speaking here only about betrothal) is invalid,
whether from a defect of consent, or because they were consanguineous, or restricted by some other impediment; from this, no impediment arises, as all teach. The same is to be said about an uncertain
or conditional betrothal, as Sanchez teaches [ref.]. Furthermore, this is
true, even if it is a purely secret defect, on account of internal deceit, as
Coninck, Bonacina and Laymann [refs] say rightly, but which Sanchez

[ref.] opposes; because Trent speaks absolutely on this subject, and the Church, moreover, does not judge concerning secret matters, and presumes that it is valid.

But if the betrothal, which was previously valid, was dissolved by mutual consent, I judge that it is entirely true that this impediment remains, with Sanchez, Bonacina, and also with Laymann [refs], who confirms the judgement well from canon law [ref.]. The reason is that at one time the betrothal was valid, and the impediment arose as a result; therefore, there is no reason why it should cease now any more than it would by the death of one of the betrothed; and it is not to be doubted that by such a death, this impediment is not extinguished in the partner. Finally, the words of the Council are that 'where the betrothal was valid, the impediment arises, etc'. Nevertheless, the contrary is held by Sa, Tanner, Pontius, Rebellus, and strongly by Diana [refs], and they base themselves on a certain Declaration of the Cardinals, edited by Gallemart; but no trust is to be placed in them, as we have often said; and the contrary is said in a Declaration from the Library of Bellarmine.

This impediment of honesty formerly rendered marriages null and void to the fourth degree, according to all, and as is clear from the canon [ref.]. But the new law of Trent [ref.] laid down that it should not go beyond the first degree. It renders marriages null and void, however, only with respect to the blood relatives of the betrothed, not in truth with respect to the relations by marriage. Therefore, the male betrothed, on the death of his betrothed, cannot marry her mother or sister, because they are his blood relatives in the first degree. But he can marry her stepmother, stepdaughter or daughter-in-law, because they are only relations by marriage in the first degree; also a cousin, because she is not consanguineous in the first degree.

[M45] 45ᵘˢ. Vtrum ex matrimonio rato, non consummato et inualido oriatur impedimentum honestatis publicae? et quot ad gradus dirimat? Sanch. d. 70. Kon. d. 32. n. 70. Laym. c. 9. n. 5. Bonac. q. 3. p. 11. n. 9. Respondeo.⁶¹⁷ Certum esse ex matrimonio rato, non consummato oriri impedimentum dirimens, vt docent omnes. Et quamuis Sanch. putet nullum de hoc extare textum, verius tamen est contrarium. Nam saltem cap. si quis vxorem, et cap. si quis desponsauerit 27. q. 2. de hoc casu loquuntur. Est autem honestas publica, non affinitas, vnde nec cum hoc impedimento contrahentes incurrent⁶¹⁸ Excommunicationem Clement.

---

⁶¹⁷ In the margin of A at this point is written: *matrimonium ratum non dirimit sponsalia iuxta communem.*
⁶¹⁸ S reads: *incurrerent*

latam contra contrahentes cum affinitate [fo. 42] Sanch. d. 64. n. 23.
Dirimit respectu consanguineorum, non vero affinium, vt praecedens.

In hoc impedimento nihil mutauit Tridentinum vt declarauit Pius
5us. itaque oritur ex matrimonio inualido alia ratione quam ex defectu
consensus. v. g. si quis contrahat infans, amens, ebrius, coactus non
consurgit; secus si cognatus, monachus etc. imo si sine Parocho et
testibus; quamuis hoc non improbabiliter neget Sanch. cit. n. 13. Imo
Nauar. c. 22. n. 58. Couar. et Lopez putant apud Sanch. non oriri, si
vllo ex capite sint inualida: quod non improbabile censet Tan: n. 113.
sed post Pii 5ⁱ. Declarationem non video multum in hoc probabilitatis.
Denique ob eandem causam dirimit vsque ad 4^m. gradum, sicut[619] olim,
vt declarat etiam Pius 5. et docent Sanch. Con: Laym. Bonac. Tan: quare
Toletus et Lopez negantes, non videntur legisse hanc Pii 5ⁱ. declarationem.

Case M45. *Does the impediment of public honesty arise from a marriage
which has been legally celebrated, but has not been consummated and
is invalid? And to how many degrees does it render marriage null and
void? See Sanchez, Coninck, Laymann and Bonacina [refs].*

I reply that it is certain that from a marriage legally celebrated but
not consummated, an impediment able to render marriage null and void
arises; thus all teach. And although Sanchez believes that none of this is
apparent textually, the contrary however is truer, for at least two canons
[refs] speak of this matter. It is, however, public honesty, not affinity;
hence those marrying with this impediment do not incur the excommunication of Clement imposed on those who marry with affinity; see
Sanchez [ref.]. It renders marriage null and void in respect of those who
are relations by blood, but not those related by marriage, as is said in
the preceding case.

In this impediment Trent changed nothing, as Pius V declared. Therefore it arises from a marriage which is invalid for another reason apart
from defect of consent. For example, if someone marries as a child,
when mad or drunk, or when forced to do so, it does not arise; but it is
different if he is a relation, or a monk etc. Indeed, it arises if he marries
without a parish priest or witnesses, although Sanchez [ref.] denies this,
not improbably. Indeed, Navarre, Covarruvius and Lopez [refs] think,
according to Sanchez, that it does not arise, if the marriage is invalid
under any heading; which Tanner [ref.] judges is not improbable. But
after the declaration of Pius V, I do not see much probability in this.
Finally, for the same reason, it renders a marriage null and void as far
as the fourth degree, just as in the past, as Pius V also declared, and as

---

[619] In A this word is written above *licet*, which is crossed out.

Sanchez, Coninck, Laymann, Bonacina and Tanner teach. Wherefore, Toletus and Lopez, who deny this, do not seem to have read this declaration of Pius V.

[M46] 46us. Quid sit affinitas? ad quot gradus dirimat ex copula siue coniugale, siue fornicaria? Vtrum affinis vxoris sit etiam affinis mariti? et e contra? An coniugum consanguinei sint inter se affines? Sanch. l. 7. d. 64. et 67. Con: d. 32. d. 4. n. 45. 46. et 56. Laym. p. 4. c. 5. Bonac. q. 3. p. 12. Respondeo Affinitas recte definitur a Nauar. c. 22. n. 42. Propinquitas duarum personarum quarum vna cum consanguinea alterius habuit copulam.

[fo. 42^v] Ex hac definitione colligitur haec regula generalis ad affinitatem dignoscendam: semper eam esse inter 2as. personas, quarum vna sit carnaliter cognita, altera cognoscentis consanguinea. Itaque duae Virgines nunquam sunt vere affines, quia neutra est carnaliter cognita. Item si non sis consanguineus proprie personae cognitae, sed affinis tantum, non contrahis affinitatem.

Necessaria est autem vera copula cum seminatione intra vas ad fundandam affinitatem, nec sufficit quiuis alius congressus; praeposterus etc. sufficit porro copula etiam fornicaria, vel etiam per vim, aut in somno extorta; cap. discretionem. de eo qui cognouit, et docent omnes. Addit San: sufficere, si semen virile siue attractione, siue alia via quacunque in vterum peruentat. sed contrarium credo probabilius cum Pont. c. 33. n. 2. quia canones requirunt copulam, et quia non fiunt vna caro, nisi communicando semen cum mutua adhaesione naturali. iuxta illud 1. Cor. 6. Qui adhaeret meretrici, vnum corpus efficitur, de quo recte Vasq. 3. p. tom. 3. d. 204. c. 4.

Dirimit affinitas ex copula coniugali vsque ad 4^m. gradum inclusiue. cap. non debet. de consangu. si vero sit ex copula fornicaria iure nouo Tridentino s. 24. c. 4. dirimit non amplius vsque ad 4^m. vt olim, sed in 1°. et 2. gradum tantum [fo. 43] itaque si quis duceret sororem vel consobrinam eius, quam deflorauit, inualide ageret: secus si in gradu inferiori esset cognita.

Olim affinitas gignebat affinitatem variis modis. de quibus Sanch. d. 67. n. 1. At Concilium Lateran. cap. non debet de consang. sustulit omnes[620] modos[621], excepto iam supra explicato, inter personam cognitam et consanguineos cognoscentis. Possunt ergo duo fratres vnius familiae ducere duas sorores alterius familiae, quia duobus contrahentibus reliqui duo non sunt inter se affines. Possunt duo vidui contrahere, simulque eorum filius et filia ex priori thoro. Potest vir vxore mortua

[620] S adds: illos
[621] S reads: modo

ducere fratrissam suae vxoris, i.e. viduam relictam a fratre vxoris: similiter et relictam vitrici, aut priuigni. Et ratio horum omnium est, quia
affinis vxoris non est vere affinis mariti. Nec coniugum[622] consanguinei
fiunt affines inter se cap. non debet. cit. et docent omnes.

Case M46. *What is affinity? To how many degrees does it render a
marriage null and void, as a result of either conjugal copulation or
fornication? Is a marital relation of the wife also a marital relation of the
husband, and vice versa? Are the blood relations of the spouses related
by marriage between themselves? See Sanchez, Coninck, Laymann and
Bonacina [refs].*

I reply that affinity is correctly defined by Navarre [ref.] as the kinship
of two persons, one of whom has copulated with the blood relation of
another.

From this definition is derived this general rule in order to distinguish affinity: it must always be between two persons, one of whom has
been carnally known by someone who is a blood relation of the other.
Therefore, two virgins are never truly affined, because neither has been
carnally known. Also if you are not properly a blood relation of the
person who has had carnal knowledge, but only a relation by marriage,
you do not contract affinity.

It is necessary, however, that it is true copulation with semination
within the vessel in order to constitute affinity, and any other, perverted
sort of congress is not sufficient. However, fornication is also sufficient,
even if it has been forced, or extorted in sleep, according to the canon
[ref.], and as all teach. Sanchez adds that it is sufficient if the virile semen
arrives at the uterus either by being inserted, or in some other way. But
I believe the contrary is more probable, with Pontius [ref.], because the
canons require copulation, and because the two people concerned do
not become one flesh, except by communicating the semen with natural,
mutual attachment, according to 1 Corinthians 6, 'who is joined to a
harlot is made one flesh'; on which Vasquez [ref.] comments correctly.

Affinity through copulation renders marriage null and void to the
fourth degree inclusive, according to the canon [ref.]. If, in truth, the
affinity is a result of fornication, by the new law of Trent [ref.] it renders
marriage null and void not, as formerly, so far as the fourth degree,
but only to the first and second degrees. Therefore, if a man marries
the sister or niece of a woman whom he has deflowered, he would act
invalidly; it is different if the woman is in an inferior degree.

In the past, affinity produced affinity in various ways, on which see
Sanchez [ref.]. But the Lateran Council [ref.] removed all ways except

---

[622] At this point in A the word *affines* is crossed out.

that which has already been explained above, between the person who has been carnally known and the blood relations of the perpetrator. Therefore, two brothers from one family may marry two sisters from another family, because with the first two married, the other two are not between themselves affined. Two people who have been widowed may marry, and their son and daughter from the previous marriages may marry. A man whose wife has died may marry the sister-in-law of his wife, that is, the widow of the brother of his wife; similarly, also the widow of his step-father, or of his step-son. And the reason in all these examples is that a relation by marriage of the wife is not really a relation by marriage of the husband. Nor do the blood relations of the spouses become relations by marriage among themselves, as the canon says [ref.] and all teach.

[M47] 47ᵘˢ.⁶²³ An matrimonium in primo gradu lineae rectae aut transuersae affinitatis sit iure naturae irritum? v. g. cum socru, nuru, nouerca, priuigna, fratrissa, glore, etc. Sanch. d. 66. Con. d. 32. n. 51. et 53. Laym. p. 4. c. 6. a n. 5. Bonac. p. 12. cit. n. 7. Respondeo videndum casum 35. supra. vbi diximus, hos omnes esse dispensabiles a Pontifice magna aliqua de causa. quod de linea transuersa est certum absque iusta causa videri ipso iure naturae non solum illicitum, sed etiam inualidum in iis [fo. 43ᵛ] contrahere. videantur ibi dicta.

Petes⁶²⁴ in affinitate cognoscendum sit 1ᵘˢ. gradus? quis 2ᵘˢ. quis in linea recta, vel transuersa? Respondeo eosdem esse hic gradus, qui in consanguinitate. Personae enim copulatae carnaliter sunt quasi stipes; deinde in quo gradu vnus est consanguineus alicui, in eodem gradu alter erit illi affinis: vnde dici solet; persona iuncta personae mutat genus, non gradum: hoc est, mutat consanguinitatem in affinitatem retento gradu. Sanch. d. 64. n. 3. et 4.

Petes an detur duplex affinitas in eadem persona sicut et dari potest duplex consanguinitas. Respondeo affirmatiue. Qui enim cognosceret duas sorores Bertae v. g. foret dupliciter affinis; vnde et in petenda dispensatione hoc deberet exprimi. Sanch. l. 8. d 24. n. 4. Pont. l. 8. c. 17. n. 26. Filuci: tom. 1. tr. 10. p. 2. c. 10. n. 329. At duplex affinitas non est eandem consanguineam bis cognoscere, sicut neque quod cognoscat eam, quae sibi est consanguinea bis, quia proxima radix affinitatis adhuc est vnica viz: copula cum persona consanguinea. vnde nec stylus Curiae exigit, vt hoc exprimatur, vt patet ex Filucio et aliis.

---

⁶²³ In the margin of A is written a little unclearly: *affinitas in 1o. gradu iure naturae aut diuino. ita Bonac. San. Henr. Con. Gutierez ne quidem ex matrimonio secondaria probabilis*
⁶²⁴ S adds: *quomodo*

Case M47. *Is a marriage in the first degree of affinity, either in the direct line, or in the transverse line, invalid, according to the law of nature? For example, with a mother-in-law, daughter-in-law, step-mother, step-daughter, sister-in-law, step-sister, etc. See Sanchez, Coninck, Laymann and Bonacina [refs].*

I reply that Case 35 above should be consulted, where we said that all these marriages are dispensable by the Pope for an important reason. As far as the transverse line is concerned, it is certain that without a just cause it seems, by the law of nature itself, not only unlawful but also invalid for them to marry: see what is said in that case.

You will ask what is to be understood as the first degree of affinity; who is in the second degree; who in the direct line; or the transverse line.

I reply that these grades are the same as in consanguinity. For the persons who have copulated carnally are in a sense the 'stocks'. In addition, in the degree that one person is related in blood to another; in the same degree another person will be related to him in marriage. Hence, it is customarily said that a person joined by marriage to someone changes the type of relationship, not the degree; for this changes consanguinity into affinity, with the degree retained. See Sanchez [ref.].

You will ask, may double affinity be judged to exist in the same person, just as double consanguinity may. I reply affirmatively. For if a man were to have knowledge of the two sisters of, for example, Berta, he would be doubly related to her by affinity. Hence in requesting a dispensation this should be explained; see Sanchez, Pontius, and Filliuci [refs]. But it is not double affinity to know the same blood relation twice, just as it is not double affinity when a man has known a woman who is in a double consanguineous relation to him. This is because the real reason for the affinity in these cases is single; that is, copulation with a blood relation. Hence, the practice and custom of the Curia does not demand that such facts should be explained, as is clear from Filliuci and others.

[M48] 48ᵘˢ. Quid sit affinitas matrimonio superueniens? ad quot gradus extendatur? an priuet iure petendi [fo. 44] debitum sub peccato mortali etiam occulta, et ante sententiam iudicis. Sanch. l. 9. de matr. disp. 27. et 30. Laym. p. 4. c. 5. n. 3. Bonac. q. 3. p. 12. n. 20. et q. 4. p. 2. Respondeo Affinitatem tunc superuenire matrimonio quando coniux cum consanguinea vel consanguinea coniugis copulam adulterinam exercet. v. g. vir cum sorore vxoris; fit enim inde frater affinis vxoris suae. Extendebatur olim ad 4. gradum, nunc vero ad 2ᵐ. tantum post Tridentinum quia cum Concilium c. 4. cit: affinitatem ex copula illicita restrinxerit vsque ad 2. gradum, consequenter effecit, vt non sit amplius incestus habere rem cum consanguinea coniugis in 3. et 4°. gradu.

Effectus huius affinitatis ex incestu, est priuare incestuosum iure petendi debitum, ita statuente Ecclesia variis in canonibus, vt colligitur ex cap. 1. cap. discretione. cap. tuae fratern. de eo qui cognouit, etc. cap. si quis dormierit. 27. q. 2. Cuius rei praebuit exemplum Dauid abstinens se a concubinis, quas polluerat Absolon, cum iam factae essent ei quasi nures. 2. Reg. 20. Priuat autem hoc iure ipso facto ante sententiam Iudicis, et sub mortali. Nauar. c. 16. n. 35. Soto in 4. dist. 37. q. vn. ad 2. conclus. 2. Sa, Pont. Sanch. Bonac. Lay. etiam[625] Angelus et Syluest. apud Sanch. requirant incestum publicum, et Veracruz ibid. n. 9. putat [fo. 44ᵛ] esse tantum veniale. sed contrarium est iuri conforme, quia etiam per occultam copulam aeque incurritur affinitas, et materia videtur plane grauis.

Debet autem nocens debitum reddere, si petatur, quia innocens non est priuandus iure suo cap. discretionem et cap. vlt. et penult. de eo qui cognouit. et docent omnes. Vnde et vir petere subinde potest in gratiam vxoris, quia hoc est ipsi[626] reddere, vt bene Sotus, et Sa. sed non aliter. Denique ad petendum dispensare possunt Episcopi et Regulares Priuilegiati.

si vterque incestum committat, vterque priuatur iure petendi, vnde nec debent reddere Sanch.cit. d. 28. Excipe nisi malitiose id facerent, animo sese mutuo priuandi. arg. cap. si vir de cognate. spil. ita Pont. l. 9. c. 7. n. 3. et alii.

Vt contrahatur haec affinitas debet esse copula intra vas naturale perfecta; item voluntaria, non per vim extorta, quia poena supponit culpam: Imo probabile est copulam culpabilem per metum grauem extortam non inducere hanc poenam, vt cum Nau: et Rebello docet Bonac. p. illo 2. n. 5. licet Sanch. et Pont. dicant quamuis culpabilem sufficere. Denique scire debet nocens, se et incestum committere, et hoc specialiter ab Ecclesia esse prohibitum. Bonac. n. 6.[627] ratio incestus ignoratur. At sufficit matrimonium esse ratum, nec consummatum, quia adhuc aeque contrahitur affinitas.

Case M48. *What is the affinity which arises after marriage? To how many degrees does it extend? Does it deprive a spouse of the right of asking for his or her marital dues, even if it is secret, and before the sentence of a judge has been given? See Sanchez, Laymann and Bonacina [refs].*

---

[625] S reads: *etiamsi*
[626] S reads: *quasi*
[627] S adds: *alias*

I reply that affinity arises after marriage when the husband practices adulterous copulation with a blood relation, or with a blood relation of his wife. For example, if a man copulates with the sister of his wife, for he becomes by doing so the brother by affinity of his wife. It extended once to the fourth degree, but now after Trent in truth only to the second degree, since the Council [ref.] restricted affinity by illicit copulation up to the second degree. Consequently this means that it is no longer incestuous to have to do with a blood relation in the third and fourth degree of one's wife.

The effect of this affinity through incest is to deprive the incestuous husband of the right of asking for his marital dues; the Church has laid this down in various canons [refs]. The example of David proved this, when he abstained from the concubines whom Absalom had polluted, since they had then been made his virtual daughters-in-law; see 2 Kings 20. Moreover, this removal of conjugal rights takes effect by law immediately, before the sentence of a judge, and under mortal sin. See Navarre, Soto [refs], Sa, Pontius, Sanchez, Bonacina, and Laymann; even if Angelus and Sylvester, cited in Sanchez, require the incest to be publicly known, and Veracruz [ref.] thinks it is only a venial sin. But the contrary is consistent with the law, because affinity is incurred as much by secret copulation as by copulation that is publicly known, and because the matter clearly seems grave.

However, the culprit must perform his marital duties, if asked, because the innocent party is not to be deprived of her rights, as the canon law says [refs] and all teach. Hence a man may also ask for his rights immediately afterwards, in order to please his wife, because that is to perform his obligations to her, as Sotus and Sa say well; but not otherwise. Finally, bishops and privileged regulars may grant a dispensation for him to seek marital rights.

If both commit incest, both are deprived of the right of seeking their marital dues, and hence they should not perform them; see Sanchez [ref.]. The exception is if they do it maliciously with the intention of mutually depriving each other; see the canon [ref.], Pontius [ref.], and others.

In order that this affinity is contracted, it should be copulation perfected within the natural vessel, and also voluntary, not extorted by force, because a punishment supposes a crime. Indeed, it is probable that criminal copulation extorted by grave fear does not incur this punishment, as Bonacina [ref.] teaches, with Navarre and Rebello; but Sanchez and Pontius say that although it is criminal, it still suffices. Finally, the guilty party should also know that he or she has committed incest, and that this is specially prohibited by the Church; see Bonacina [ref.], for otherwise he is ignorant of the fact that the reason for the impediment

238 CAROLINE CASUISTRY

is incest. However, it is enough if the marriage has been celebrated but
not consummated, because affinity is also contracted at this point.

[M49] 49ᵘˢ. Vtrum impotentia dirimat?⁶²⁸ v. g. si sint [fo.
45] malefi-
ciati: si vir sit frigidus, Eunuchus, aetate decrepita: si mulier arcta, et ad
pariendum inepta: Et quid si scientes ita contrahant? Sanch. l. 7. d. 92.
et 97. Con. d. 31. dub. 7. conclus. 1 et 2. Laym. p. 4. c. 11. Bonac. q. 3.
p. 13. Respondeo impotentiam perpetuam dirimere matrimonium quia
inanis est traditio corporum ad actum impossibilem, et hoc iure naturae,
vt recte Sanch. d. 98. et sumitur ex cap. 2. et sequentibus de frigidis et
maleficiatis. Consistit autem in eo, quod coniuges nequeant consum-
mando matrimonium effici vna caro: ad hoc autem requiritur penetratio
vasis foeminei cum seminatione iuxta illud arg. c. 5. de digamis, et
docet Sanch. d. 92. qui recte d. 99. n. 37. cum Tan: q. 4. n. 131. docet
non sufficere, vt artificio aliquo infundatur semen, sed necessariam esse
vasis penetrationem; dirimit autem siue nascatur ex intrinseco defectu,
siue ex maleficio daemonis, siue ex improportione respectiua, vt docent
omnes, et patet ex iuribus citatibus.

Itaque impotentia est, si vir sit frigidus. i.e. destitutus calore, spiri-
tibus aut vero semine ad congressum, vel e contra si adeo calidus, vt
semper seminet antequam ad vas perueniat. 2°. impotens est Eunuchus
vero semine destitutus: Sanch. d. 92. n. 17. quod multo est certius post
motum proprium Sixti V. ad Nuncium Hispaniae, in quo declarat Eunu-
chos vtroque testiculo carentes esse inhabiles. Probabilius autem est
ipsum non condere nouum [fo. 45ᵛ] ius, sed ius naturale declarare, vt
docet Sanch. cit. n. 18. Tan. n. 137. Laym. n. 13. Praepos. q. 7. d. 20.
3°. Senectus per se non impedit; adhuc enim spermatisonum exercere
possunt, licet sterilem, et patet ex praxi. si tamen esset valde exhaustus
vel simpliciter, vel respectiue, quia viz: ducta virgine nequit ob debilitatem ingredi claustra pudoris, esset inualidum. Sanch. d. 92. n. 23.
Laym. n. 6. Tan. n. 137. contra Tabienam, Nauar. Rodr. Vegam apud
Sanch. censentes hoc esse per accidens, nec dirimere. 4°. impotentia
est, si foemina ita sit arcta, ex claustri constrictione, vt viri ingressum
non admittat: vel saltem⁶²⁹ viri istius ob eius improportionem, vel debilitatem. Quod si ferro, aut medicinis aptari queat sine graui periculo,
matrimonium valet ab initio, vt habetur cap. frater: de frigid. Sanch.
d. 93. n. 15. 5°. impotentia non est quod sint steriles, aut foemina ad
pariendum inepta, quia adhuc effici possunt, vna caro, nam et steriles
semen emittunt, sed non prolificum. Ita Sanch. d. 93:⁶³⁰ n. 25. et 140.

⁶²⁸ S adds: *matrimonium*
⁶²⁹ S adds: *non*
⁶³⁰ S reads: *92.*

Idem dicendum de morti proximis cum Laym. n. 6. et Bonac. n. 17.
Caeterum Filucius hic n. 65. cum aliis probabile tenet, foeminam, quae
parere nequit, censendam impotentem. Sed probabilius est sufficere
quod fieri vna caro possint.

Porro ita dirimit impotentia, vt nequeant huiusmodi personae valide
contrahere, etiamsi cedere velint iure suo ad copulam, quia ius ad
copulam atque adeo potentia ad illam est de essentia matrimonii [fo.
46] vt bene Sanch. d. 97. Con. n. 79. Bonac. n. 12. etiamsi contrarium
contendat Pontius 1. 7. c. 56. cui fauet S. T. Addit: q. 58. a. 1. ad 4m.
Verum S. T. non intelligit posse hos contrahere verum matrimonium
iure diuino indissolubile, sed tantum contractum vitae socialis ad mutua
obsequia. In quo sensu cap. consultaoi de frigidis dicitur, tales debere
cohabitare, vt fratres et sorores. In quo etiam sensu intelligo Tan. n.
139. Interim si pars potens cum alio contraheret, vere teneret hic 2us.
contractus, quod signum est, priorem non fuisse verum matrimonium vt
colligitur ex cap. requisisti. 33. q. 1.

Dices impotentiam superuenientem non dirimere matrimonium
contractum. ergo nec contrahendum, quia stare potest, cum matrimonii
essentialibus. Respondeo vt matrimonium semel initum conseruetur,
minus requiri, quam ad 1m. constitutionem, vt dixi ad casum 18. praesertim quia vt supra dixi, omnimoda haec insolubilitas ex iure positiuo
Dei oritur, qui voluit, vt in hoc casu sufficeret, quod deseruire possit ad
secundaria matrimonii officia. Excipe nisi foemina sexum mutaret, quod
Compluti suo tempore accidisse narrat Pontius 1. 7. c. 58. n. 2. tunc enim
solueretur matrimonium cum turpe sit duos viros manere coniunctos
etiam in ordine ad officia secondaria qualia sunt oscula, tactus, etc.

Case M49. *Does impotence render a marriage null and void: for
example, if they are bewitched; if the man is frigid, a eunuch, of a
decrepit age; if the woman is too narrow, and incapable of child-birth?
And what if they married knowing this? See Sanchez, Coninck, Laymann
and Bonacina [refs].*

I reply that perpetual impotence renders marriage null and void
because the surrender of bodies to an impossible act is stupid; and this
is according to the law of nature, as Sanchez [ref.] says rightly, and as
is drawn from the canon law [refs]. The essence of impotence, moreover, is that the spouses cannot by consummating marriage be made one
flesh. Moreover, for consummation is required penetration of the female
vessel with semination, according to canon law [ref.], and as Sanchez
[ref.] teaches. Sanchez, with Tanner [ref.], rightly teach that it is not
enough that the semen is poured in by some artifice, but penetration of
the vessel is necessary. Moreover, impotence renders marriage null and
void, whether it results from an intrinsic defect, or from the witchcraft

of a demon, or from differences in the respective proportions, as all teach, and as is clear from the laws that have been cited.

Therefore, it is impotence if the man is frigid, that is lacking the heat, spirits, or indeed semen, needed for congress; or on the contrary if he is so heated that he always ejaculates before he reaches the vessel. Secondly, a eunuch who is truly destitute of semen is impotent; see Sanchez [ref.]. This is much more certain after the *Motu Proprio* of Sixtus V to the Nuncio to Spain, in which he declared that eunuchs lacking both testicles were unfit for marriage. It is more probable, however, that this did not establish a new law, but declared what was the natural law, as is taught by Sanchez, Tanner, Laymann and Praepos [refs]. Thirdly, old age in itself is not an impediment to marriage, for old men can still produce sperm, albeit sterile; and this is clear from practice. If however an old man was very exhausted, either simply or in respect of this task, because, that is, he could not, due to debility, enter the virginal duct which was closed through shame, the marriage would be invalid. See Sanchez, Laymann and Tanner [refs]; against Tabiena, Navarre, Rodriguez and Vega, cited by Sanchez, who judge that this is an accidental factor and does not render a marriage null and void. Fourthly, it is impotence if the woman is so narrow, from closed constriction, that she will not admit the ingress of a man, or at least of this man, because of his disproportion or debility. But if she can be opened by force or by medicine, without grave danger, the marriage is valid from the beginning, as the canon [ref.] says, and Sanchez [ref.]. Fifthly, it is not impotence if they are sterile, or the woman is not suitable for child-birth, because they can still be made one flesh, for even the sterile emit semen, although it is not fertile; thus, Sanchez [ref.]. The same must be said about those who are close to death, with Laymann and Bonacina [refs]. However, Filliucci [ref.], with others, holds that it is probable that a woman who cannot bear children, should be judged to be impotent. But more probably it is sufficient that they can be made one flesh.

Moreover, impotence makes marriage null and void to such an extent that such people cannot validly contract marriage, even if they wish to give up their own right to copulation, because the right to copulation, and thus the power to do it, is of the essence of marriage; as is shown well by Sanchez, Coninck and Bonacina, even if the contrary is maintained by Pontius [ref.]. This judgement is favoured by St Thomas [ref.], who, in truth, does not see that these people can contract a true, indissoluble marriage by divine law, but only a contract for a social life of mutual respect. In which sense, the canon [ref.] says that such people should cohabit as brother and sister. In which sense also I understand Tanner [ref.]. Meanwhile, if the potent party should contract marriage with another person, truly this second contract would hold, which is a sign that the prior contract was not a true marriage, as is gathered from the canon [ref.].

You will say that impotence which arises after marriage does not annul the marriage contract; therefore, it does not prevent a contract being made, because it can stand with the essentials of marriage. I reply that marriage once started should be preserved, but less is then required than was needed to constitute it at first, as I have said in Case 18, especially because as I have said above, this indissolubility arises entirely by the positive law of God, who wished that in this case it should be enough that the impotent party could serve the secondary duties of marriage. The exception is if a woman changes sex, which Pontius [ref.] says happened in Alcala de Hanares in his time; for then the marriage should be dissolved since it is shameful if two men remain conjoined, even in respect of secondary duties, such as kisses and touching etc.

[M50] 50us. Quaenam impotentia sit perpetua? num temporalis matrimonium dirimat? an impuberes[631] matrimonium contrahant? et quo iure? Sanch. l. 7. d. 93. a. n. 7. et d. 104. Con. d. 31. a. n. 82. Laym. c. 11. cit. Bonac. loc. cit. n. 12. et q. 1. p. 4. n. 10.

[fo. 46^v] Respondeo impotentiam esse perpetuam, quae tolli nequit sine miraculo, aut peccato, aut graui corporis laesione: temporalem, quae sine vllo ex his tolli potest. ita Sanch. d. 93. n. 7. et alii. Itaque si mulier tam arcta sit, vt aptari non possit, nisi fornicando cum alio magis proportionato, aut non sine graui laesione, matrimonium non valeret, ne quidem postquam tali modo indebito aptata esset, nisi de nouo contraherent. Sanch. Con. Lay. cit. argumentum cap. fraternitatis. Caeterum valet, si maleficium solui possit per Ecclesiae Exorcismos, quia remedium est, licet supernaturale, non tamen miraculosum. Bonac. cit. et Con: n. 85. si temporale sit impedimentum valet matrimonium etiam eo nondum sublato. cap. fraternitatis quia sufficit potentia ad copulam remota, et suo tempore exercendam. Itaque si constet si constet[632] arctitudinem posse facile tolli, valebit matrimonium etiamsi foemina ex morositate nollet pati aliquid remedium. Tenetur autem foemina pati dolores, incisionem, et remedia necessaria, modo moderata sint, ne vir cogatur viuere sine remedio fornicationis. Con. n. 83. Quod si tam acerba sint, vt pati ea non teneatur, meo sane iudicio censendum foret matrimonium nullum et separandum. vt a fortiori docet Pont. l. 7. c. 62.

[fo. 47] Petes quid si foemina nullo laborans vitio, mere ob Virginei sigilli clausuram sit viro debili imperuia; an censeri debeat impedimentum temporale, et ipsa obligata ad remedia moderata? Negat acriter

---

631 S adds: *inualide*
632 S repeats these two words thus, and then crosses out *de*

Pontius cap. illo 62. aiens esse separandos, quod foemina habeat ius ad naturalem apertionis modum: et probabile censet Diana de Sacr. resol. 199. sed multo est probabilius matrimonium valere, ipsamque pati debere incisionem moderatam. ita expresse S. T. addit: q. 58. a. 1. ad 5. Sanch. d. 93. n. 26. Tan. n. 141. iuncto n. 134 et probatur ex cap. fraternitatis vbi generaliter decisum est, impedimentum non esse perpetuum, quod praeter diuinum miraculum per opus humanum absque corporali periculo potuit remoueri.

Ex dictis infero impuberes doli capaces stando praecise in iure naturae valide contrahere, quia habituri sunt potentiam generandi; at iure positiuo inualide id faciunt, antequam vir habeat annos 14. et foemina 12. ita Sanch. d. 104. Excipe nisi malitia suppleat aetatem, nomine autem malitiae intellige et discretionem, et etiam generandi potentiam cum Sanch. n. 21.

Case M50. *What is perpetual impotence? Does temporary impotence render marriage null and void? Do those below the age of puberty contract marriage invalidly, and by what law? See Sanchez, Coninck, Laymann and Bonacina [refs].*

I reply that impotence is perpetual, when it cannot be taken away except by a miracle, or by a sin, or by grave harm to the body; temporary impotence is impotence that can be removed without any of these. Thus, Sanchez [ref.] and others. Therefore, if a woman is so narrow that she cannot be made suitable for marriage, except by fornication with someone better proportioned, or not without grave injury, the marriage is not valid; and indeed if afterwards she was made fit by some unworthy method, not unless they contracted marriage anew. Thus, Sanchez, Coninck, and Laymann as cited, referring to the canon law [ref.]. However, it is valid if the witchcraft causing impotence can be dissolved by the exorcisms of the Church, because the remedy is, although supernatural, not miraculous; see Bonacina, as cited, and Coninck [ref.]. If the impediment is temporary, the marriage is valid, even if the impotence has not yet been removed, according to the canon law [ref.], because it is sufficient if there is potency for postponed copulation, exercised in its own time. Therefore, if it is agreed that the narrowness of the woman can easily be removed, the marriage will be valid, even if the woman does not wish to undergo any remedy out of squeamishness. The woman is, however, bound to suffer pains, incision, and the necessary remedies, as long as they are moderate, lest the man is forced to live without the remedy of fornication; see Coninck [ref.]. But, if the remedies would be so harsh that she is not bound to suffer them, truly in my judgement, the marriage should be judged null and they should separate; as Pontius [ref.] forcibly teaches.

You will ask, what if the woman is suffering from no physical problem, but it is merely that, due to the closure of the hymen, she is impervious to a feeble man. Should this impediment be judged to be temporary and should she be obliged to undergo a moderate remedy. Pontius [ref.] denies it strongly, saying they must separate, because the woman has a right to the natural method of opening, and Diana [ref.] thinks it is probable. But it is much more probable that the marriage is valid, and that she should undergo a moderate incision; thus, expressly, St Thomas, Sanchez and Tanner [refs], and it is proved from the canon law [ref.], when it is generally decided that the impediment is not perpetual, because without a divine miracle, it could be removed by human effort without physical danger.

From what has been said, I infer that those below the age of puberty who are 'capable of mischief', standing precisely on the law of nature, contract marriage validly, because they will in the future have the potency to reproduce. But by positive law they marry invalidly before the male has reached 14 years and the female 12. Thus, Sanchez [ref.]. The exception is if according to the legal maxim 'malice supplies age' although by 'malice' you should also understand discretion, and even the potency to reproduce.[633] See Sanchez [ref.].

[M51] 51ᵘˢ. Vtrum in dubio an impotentia sit perpetua, possint coniuges tentare copulam per triennium, etiam cum periculo pollutionis extra vas? an aliquando vltra triennium? et quid faciendum si non succedat? Sanch. l. 7. d. 107. et 108. et l. 9. d. 17. n. 18. et 24. Conin: d. 31. n. 83. Lay. p. 4. c. 11. n. 4. 5. et in fine capitis.

[fo. 47ᵛ] Respondeo si impotentia sit euidens, vt quia vir caret instrumentis, etc. non esse concedendam experientiam triennalem cum actus illi sint clare illiciti: Conceditur ergo haec experientia vbi est dubium, quo tempore vacare debent rei maritali, et remediis vti, maxime precibus et exorcismis in casu maleficii. Quod si elapso triennio maneat impotentia, vel possunt simul manere tanquam simul manere tanquam[634] fratres et sorores, si velint; vel separare, si malint. Hoc tamen fieri debet autoritate Iudicis, non priuata autoritate, et accepto prius iuramento tam coniugum asserentium se non consummasse, quam septimae manus propinquorum, id est septemorum testium ex parte vtriusque, qui deponant se credere non consummasse. Parti autem potenti concedendae sunt aliae nuptiae, imo vtrique si impotentia credatur respectiua. Quod si contractis aliis nuptiis deprehendatur clare Ecclesiam in priori iudicio

633 The legal maxim, 'malitia supplet aetatem', meant that the age of criminal responsibility could be reduced below 14 if the culprit's actions showed malice equivalent to that of someone older.
634 Repeated thus in A.

deceptam fuisse, et impotentiam fuisse solummodo temporalem, restaurandum est prius coniugium, quod tamen facile non est praesumendum, etiamsi vterque alias nuptias consumment, quia posset esse impotentia respectiua. Quae omnia patent ex cap. laudabile de frigidis et communi Doctorum. Sanch. et aliis.

Nota etiam vltra triennium posse quandoque proferri hanc experientiam etiam cum periculo pollutionis extra vas 1º. si videatur esse ex defectu minoris aetatis. Sanch. 100. et Pont. infra cit:[635] 2º. si triennium fuerit notabiliter interruptum; debet enim suppleri Sanch. d. 111. [fo. 48] Pont: cit. c. 66. n. 1. 3º. Si post triennium petant a Iudice dissolutionem, potest ipse vel triennium, vel aliud tempus arbitrarium assignare adhuc. Pon. n. 12. 4º. si trienniis tempore constet remedia non adhibita, a quibus omnino credatur tollenda. 5º. si coniuges elapso triennio non essent adhuc dubii, sed habeant spem aliquam bene fundatam consummandi, credo eos posse adhuc pergere, vt aperte docet Caiet. 2. 2. q. 154. a. 1. in solu: 4ⁱ. par: ad 2ᵐ. vero. aiens quendam qui genuerat ex priore vxore tentasse cum 2ª. ex piorum consilio 6. annos, et tandem genuisse. 6º. si impotentia superueniat matrimonio semel valido, possunt tentare quamdiu est spes. Sanch. l. 9. d. 17. Tan. 155.[636] Laym.

Case M51. *In cases of doubt about whether impotence is perpetual, may spouses test their ability to copulate for three years, even with danger of pollution outside the vessel? Is it sometimes possible beyond three years? And what is to be done if it does not succeed? See Sanchez, Coninck and Laymann [refs].*

I reply that if the impotence is manifest, for example because the man lacks an instrument etc., the triennial experiment is not to be conceded, since these acts are then clearly unlawful. Therefore, this experiment is conceded where there is doubt, and during this time the couple should devote themselves to their marital relations, and use remedies, especially prayers, and exorcisms in the case of witchcraft. But if after three years the impotence remains, either they may remain together as brother and sister, if they wish; or separate, if they prefer. This, however, should be done not by private authority, but by the authority of a judge, and having first accepted the oath, both of the spouses swearing that they have not consummated the marriage, and also with the help of seven neighbours, that is of seven witnesses on behalf of each, who depose that they believe they have not consummated the marriage. Moreover, another marriage should be allowed to the potent party; indeed, to both if the impotence is believed to be specific to this marriage. But if after

635 S reads: *c. 66. n. 1.*
636 S reads: *153.*

they have married other spouses the Church clearly discovers that it had been deceived in the previous judgement, and the impotence had only been temporary, the previous marriage is to be restored; this, however, is not an easy inference to draw, for, even if each one had consummated their new marriage, it could have been a case of specific impotence. All of which is clear from the canon [ref.] and the common judgement of the doctors; see Sanchez and others.

Note also that beyond the three years they may continue this experiment for a further period, even with the danger of pollution outside the vessel, under the following conditions. First, if it seems the impotence arose from the defect of their youth; see Sanchez and Pontius [refs]. Second, if the three years were notably interrupted, the lost time should be made up; see Sanchez, and Pontius [refs]. Thirdly, if after the three years they seek from a judge a dissolution of the marriage, he may himself assign a further three years or other period according to his judgement; see Pontius [ref.]. Fourthly, if after three years it was agreed that a remedy had not been found which it was believed would totally remove the problem. Fifthly, if the spouses after the three years had elapsed, were not still doubtful, but had some well-founded hope of consummating the marriage, I believe that they might still persevere; as Caietan [ref.] openly teaches, saying that in truth someone who had had children with his previous wife, tried with his second wife following the advice of pious men for six years and at length did have children. Sixthly, if the impotence developed in a marriage which previously had been valid, they might try as long as there was hope; see Sanchez, Tanner [refs] and Laymann.

[M52] 52[us]. Vtrum raptus dirimat matrimonium? an dirimat perpetuo? et quas conditiones requirat? num vt abducatur foemina de loco in locum? num sufficiat quod ipsa assentiente soli Parentes sint inuiti? Sanch. l. 7. d. 12. et 13. Molin: de iustitia. tr. 3. d. 105. Lay. p. 4. c. 13. Bonac. q. 4. p. 18. Con. d. 3.[637] dub. 4. Respondeo Raptus est abductio foeminae siue solutae, siue coniugatae de loco in locum, vel contrahendi matrimonii vel explendae libidinis causa, inuita[638] ipsa, vel saltem eius parentibus, aut Tutoribus, Mol. Sanch. Lay. Bona. Tan. q. 4. n. 78. Dicitur abductio, etc. quia licet vi foeminam opprimere contineat specialem raptus malitiam in Confessione,[639] at in praesenti iura loquuntur solum de raptu et abductione. ita omnes citati. Dicitur siue solutae, etc. quia iure canonico consideratur, vis illata siue sit virgo, siue vidua, siue meretrix. etc.

---

637 S reads: 31
638 S adds: vel
639 S adds: explicandam

cap. eos. 36. q. 2. <u>Dicitur vel ipsa, etc. quia duae</u> sunt [fo. 48ᵛ] raptus species; altera, si foeminae vis inferatur: altera, si ipsa in abductionem consentiente Parentes resistant. Probabilius autem est fore raptum, si Parentes inuiti sint, etiamsi nec vis inferatur, nec ipsi id sciant: sicut Dominus saepe absens, et ignorans est inuitus, vt bona furto rapiantur. Ita Mol. n. 2. contra Sanch. n. 13. Tan. et satis colligitur ex cap. raptoribus. 36. q. 1. cap. Nullus ibid. q. 2. et c. raptor. 27. q. 2. Excipe, nisi foemina et consentiat in discessum, et etiam in matrimonium legitime contrahendum: tunc enim raptus non erit ob parentum renitentiam. cap. lex. 36. q. 1. et cap. cum causa de raptor: secus si solum consentiat in fornicationem.

His positis, Dico, nouo iure Tridentino ses. 24. c. 6. statutum esse, vt nullum sit matrimonium inter raptorem et raptam, quamdiu ipsa in eius manet potestate, idque etiamsi ipsa iam mutata volunte id cuperet. Itaque dirimit non perpetuo, sed donec loco tuto sit restituta. <u>Iure antiquo non dirimebat, modo</u> abesset metus. cap. fin: de rap. Quod in Anglia hodie seruandum.⁶⁴⁰ Sufficit autem ad hoc impedimentum, quod soli Parentes sint inuiti, quia est verus raptor in sensu Concilii, cum tam iure canonico, quam ciuili censeatur talis, quae est communior sententia. ita Henr. l. 12. c. 14. n. 4. Sa. hic n. 9. Bonac. n. 5. Tan. n. 80. Praepos q. 7. n. 142. Laym. n. 4. Rebell. Nauar. Rodrig. et alii apud ipsos, contra Sanch. Con. Dianam resol. 260.

[fo. 49] Idem existimo cum Bonac. n. 5.⁶⁴¹ si abducta sit per dolum, qui aequiparetur violentiae et a fortiori⁶⁴² magicis incantationibus, et philtris dementata fuerit, quia est verus raptus. l. vn. cod. de rapta. par. prunas. verb. nisi odiosis artibus circumuenerit. et fatentur omnes, quo posito nulla est ratio cur talis raptus⁶⁴³ non dirimat, quia Tridentinum loquitur generaliter.

At si foemina rapiat virum, non videtur hoc impedimentum procedere, licet aliqui aliter censeant. ita Praepos. contra Henr. similiter si rapta sit non matrimonii, sed libidinis causa, non esse impedimentum putat Diana de sacr. resol. 261. Similiter nec si rapta sit ab alio inscio sponso. quia Concilium dicit inter raptorem et raptam Praepos. similiter nec si abducta sit, vt in seruitutem redigatur, quia non est raptus, vt ex definitione constat et docent omnes.

Case M52. *Does the forcible seizure of a woman render marriage null and void; does it do so perpetually; and what conditions are required*

---

⁶⁴⁰ In A at this point in bold, and slightly larger than the text is written in the margin: *NB.*
⁶⁴¹ In A a long indecipherable word is crossed out here.
⁶⁴² S adds: *si*
⁶⁴³ S adds: *etiam*

for it to do so? Does the woman have to be abducted from place to place? Is it sufficient if the woman herself assents, and only her parents are unwilling? See Sanchez, Molina, Laymann, Bonacina and Coninck [refs].

I reply that forcible seizure involves the abduction of a woman, either free or married, from one place to another, for the sake either of contracting marriage or of satisfying lust, with either the woman herself unwilling, or at least her parents or guardians unwilling; see Molina, Sanchez, Laymann, Bonacina and Tanner [ref.]. We say, 'abduction etc.', because although to oppress a woman by force shares the particular wickedness of abduction, and must be explained in confession; nevertheless, at present the laws speak only about forcible seizure and abduction; thus, all those cited. We say, 'either free etc.', because by canon law [ref.], what is considered is the force inflicted, whether it is on a virgin, a widow or a prostitute etc. We say, 'either the woman herself unwilling etc.', because there are two sorts of forcible seizure: one, if force is inflicted on the woman; the other, if she herself agrees to the abduction and the parents oppose it. More probably, moreover, it will qualify as forcible seizure if her parents are unwilling, even if no force is inflicted, and her parents do not know about it, like a master who is often absent, and hence is ignorant when his goods are taken, against his will, by a thief. Thus, Molina, against Sanchez [refs], and Tanner; and the judgement is drawn satisfactorily from the canon law [refs]. The exception is if the woman both consents in running away and also in legitimately contracting marriage; for then it will not be 'forcible seizure' simply on account of the opposition of the parents; see the canons [refs]. It is different if she only consents to fornication.

Having laid this down, I say that by the new law of Trent [ref.], it was decided that there was to be no marriage between the abductor and the abducted, as long as she remained in his power, and even if she herself, having now changed her mind, should desire it. Therefore, it renders marriage null and void, not perpetually, but until she should be restored to a place of safety. The ancient law did not render a marriage null and void as long as there were no fear, according to the canon [ref.], which must today be observed in England. It is enough, however, for this impediment to arise, that the parents alone are unwilling, because that is a true, forcible seizure in the sense of the Council of Trent, and according to both canon and civil law this is judged to be the case. This is the more common judgement; thus, Henriques, Sa, Bonacina, Tanner, Praepos, Laymann, Rebellus, Navarre, Rodriguez and others cited by them; Sanchez, Coninck, Diana [refs] disagree.

I consider it is the same, with Bonacina [ref.], if she had been abducted by cunning, which is equivalent to force, and especially if she was made mad by magic incantations and philtres, because that is true abduction. As the civil law says [ref.], 'unless he attacked using odious arts'; and all say this. Having laid this down, there is no reason why such an abduction does not also render marriage null and void, because Trent speaks generally.

But if a woman abducts a man, it does not seem that this impediment applies, although others judge otherwise; thus, Praepos, against Henriquez. Similarly, if she was abducted for the sake, not of marriage, but of lust, it is not an impediment, thinks Diana [ref.]. Similarly, not[644] if she was abducted and her betrothed was ignorant of it, because the Council of Trent says, 'between abductor and abducted'; see Praepos. Similarly, not if she was abducted in order to be reduced to servitude, because that is not 'forcible seizure', as is clear from the definition, and all teach.

[M53] 53us. Quaenam sint impedimenta tantum impedientia, et an obligent nunc omnia sub peccato mortali. Sanch. l. 7. d. 6. et 17. Con. d. 30. dub. 3. Laym. p. 4. c. vlt. Bonac. q. 3. p. 14. Impedimenta impedientia vocantur illa quae impediunt matrimonium contrahendum; sed non dirimunt contractum. numero sunt 12. 1°. Interdictum Eccelsiae, viz. quando Praelatus vel Pastor prohibent[645] aliquos ne contrahant, siue vt inquiratur de impedimentis, siue ob temporis reuerentiam, etc. 2°. Tempus prohibitum. 3°. Sponsalia cum alia persona. 4°. Votum simplex Castitatis extra Religionem. 5°. Cognatio spiritualis ex Catechismo. 6°. Incestus. 7°. Raptus alienae sponsae. 8°. Vxoricidium. 9°. [fo. 49^v] leuare propriam prolem ex fonte malitiose. 10°. occisio Presbiteri. 11°. publica Poenitentia. 12°. Matrimonium cum Moniali. Ex his 7. vltima impediunt in poenam, cum sint crimina. Caeterum vsu exoleuisse obligationem docent Nauar. c. 22. n. 75. et 85. Sanch. d.17. n. 4. Con: n. 25. Lay. cit. Tan: q. 4. n. 29. Pont. c. 14. n. 4. Diana resol. 258. contra Bonac: Nihilominus laudabile est vt Confessarius his suadeat continentiam perpetuam; cum et in dispensatione pro incestu soleat ex stylo Curiae addi, vt mortua vxore maneat sine spe coniugii.

5um. id est, cognatio ex catechismo contrahitur ab eo, qui respondet in baptismo nomine infantis, vtique quando respondet alius, quam patrinus. de quo cap. 2. de cognat. spr. in 6°. Probabilius est non obligare sub mortali, quia vt ait Bonifacius 8us. cap. cit. ex cap. contracto: extra: de cognat spir: vix affert impedimentum. saltem non esse in vsu docet Sotus in 4. dist. 42. q. 1. a. 2. versiculo vrgentius. Denique post Tridentinum videtur penitus sublatum, nam Ses. 24. c. 2. tollitur omne

---

644 That is, no impediment to her marrying her betrothed arises from her being abducted without him knowing about it.
645 S reads: *prohibet*

impedimentum cognationis spiritualis, praeter ibi proposita. Ita Sanch.
d. 10. Bonac. n. 6. Con. n. 24. Pont. l. 6. c. 11. Lay. n. 2. contra Nauar.
3ᵐ. et 4ᵐ. impediunt ex natura rei, vt est manifestum. Porro⁶⁴⁶ Castitatis esse seruandum: atque adeo impedire, etiamsi grauissimae postea
oriantur carnis tentationes diximus in materia de voto. [fo. 50] casu 23.
Neutrum dirimit, nam matrimonium cum vna contra sponsalia priora
cum alia, habetur ab omnibus validum. similiter et post votum simplex.
cap. Rursus, qui Clerici et vouentes. Igitur 2°. sunt tantum impedimenta
quae iure positiuo impediunt, nunc in vsu, et sub mortali obligantia,
interdictum viz. Ecclesiae et tempus prohibitum, quorum duorum solum
meminit S. Tho. q. 50. a. 1. et hoc carmine proponit.

Ecclesiae vetitum, necnon tempus feriatum,
Impediunt fieri, permittunt iuncta teneri.

De Interdicto agitur toto titulo de hac re, vbi cap. 2. deciditur factum
tenere. obligat sub mortali regulariter vid. Sanch. d. 17. De posteriori
cas. seq:

Case M53. *Which impediments are merely 'impedient',*⁶⁴⁷ *and do
they all now oblige under pain of mortal sin? See Sanchez, Coninck,
Laymann and Bonacina [refs].*

'Impedient' impediment is the name given to those which prevent a
marriage being contracted, but do not make the contract null and void
once it has been made. There are twelve. (1.) The interdict of the Church,
that is, when a prelate or pastor prohibits people from contracting
marriage, either so that an inquiry might be made about impediments, or
on account of reverence for the time of year proposed for the marriage,
etc. (2.) A prohibited time. (3.) Betrothal to another person. (4.) A simple
vow of chastity by someone who is not in religion. (5.) Spiritual kinship,
from the Catechism.⁶⁴⁸ (6.) Incest. (7.) The abduction of someone else's
betrothed. (8.) Killing a wife. (9.) To take one's own child maliciously
from the font. (10.) The killing of a priest. (11.) Public penitence. (12.)
Marriage to a Religious. Of these, the last seven impede as a punishment, since they are crimes. The obligation to observe the others has
grown up through use; as is taught by Navarre, Sanchez, Coninck,
Laymann, Tanner, Pontius and Diana, against Bonacina. Nevertheless,

---

⁶⁴⁶ S adds: *Votum*
⁶⁴⁷ Generally known as prohibitory or impedient impediments, and contrasted with the
diriment impediments discussed in Case M30.
⁶⁴⁸ The Roman Catechism, published first in 1566 on the instructions of the Council of
Trent and Pope Pius V, says in Part II, chap. ii, q. xxvi that 'the spiritual affinity contracted
in baptism impedes and annuls matrimony'; see J. Donovan, *Catechism of the Council of
Trent* (Dublin, 1908), 155.

it is laudable that the confessor should, in these cases, advise perpetual continence; since, as in the case of a dispensation for incest, it was generally added, following the practice and custom of the Curia, that, when the wife died, the man should remain without hope of marriage.

The fifth is kinship contracted, according to the Catechism, by someone who responds during a baptism in the name of a child, and who responds otherwise than as a godfather; on which see the canon law [ref.]. It is more probable that this impediment does not oblige under mortal sin, because as Boniface VIII says [ref.], it hardly even brings an impediment with it. At least, it is not in use, as Soto teaches [ref.]. Finally, after the Council of Trent, it seems surely to be withdrawn, for Trent [ref.] took away all impediments of spiritual kinship, apart from that proposed here. Thus, Sanchez, Bonacina, Coninck, Pontius and Laymann, against Navarre [refs].

The third and fourth impede from the nature of marriage itself, as is manifest. Indeed, a vow of chastity must be kept, and so it is an impediment, even if the most grave temptations of the flesh should arise afterwards; as we have said in the work *Concerning Vows*, Case 23. Neither impediment renders a marriage null and void, for marriage with one woman, when judged against a prior betrothal to another, is held by all to be valid. It is the same, also, after a simple vow, according to canon law [ref.]. Therefore, there are only two impediments which impede by positive law, which are now in use, and oblige under mortal sin; that is, the interdict of the Church, and a prohibited time. St Thomas [ref.] only mentions these two, and does so in this poem:

The prohibition of the Church, and forbidden times
Are impediments to contracting marriage,
But permit it to continue, after they have been joined.

Concerning the interdict there is a whole title in the Council's decree [ref.] on this matter, where it is decided that if there had been a marriage despite the interdict, it should continue. This impediment obliges as a rule under mortal sin, see Sanchez [ref.]. On the impediment of time, see the next case.

[M54] 54us. Vtrum sit peccatum mortale contrahere et consummare matrimonium in Aduentu et quadragesima? et quid si id cum benedictione fiat? Sponsae solemni traductione? aliisque publicae laetitiae signis? Sanch. l. 7. d. 7. Con: d. 30. n. 36. Lay. cit. n. 1. Bonac. cit. n. 4. Tempora pro nuptiis prohibita sunt ab Aduentu vsque ad Epiphaniam inclusiue, iure tam antiquo, quam nouo. Deinde iure antiquo a Septuagesima vsque 8am. Paschae et a Dominica Rogatium vsque ad Sabbatum Pentecostes. Sanch. d. 7. At iure nouo Trid: ses. 24. c. 10. tantum a 1. die quadragesimae vsque ad 8am. Paschae inclusiue.

His positis Respondeo prohiberi his temporibus non ipsas nuptias in se, sed nuptiales tantum solemnitates, quae in tribus consistunt, in benedictione sacra, in ceremoniis et tripudiis, etc. denique in solemni traductione sponsae in domum sponsi. Colligitur [fo. 50ᵛ] ex Tridentino cit. vetante nuptias solemnes et cap. Capellanus de feriis, et ex vsu. Sanch. Con: Bonac Lay. Pont. Nisi forte alicubi strictior sit consuetudo. Hoc modo celebrare nuptias esset mortali, nisi Episcopus dispensaret ex causa: secus priuatim contrahere, et consummare matrimonium cum moderata etiam aliqua festiuitate.

Case M54. *Is it a mortal sin to contract and consummate marriage in Advent or Lent; and what if it is done with a blessing, with the solemn delivery of the bride,*[649] *and with other signs of public joy? See Sanchez, Coninck, Laymann and Bonacina [refs].*

The times prohibited for marriage are from Advent to Epiphany inclusive, by both the ancient and new law. Then by ancient law from Septuagesima until the Sunday after Easter, and from Rogation Sunday until Pentecost Saturday; see Sanchez [ref.]. But by the new law of Trent [ref.], only from the first day of Lent to the Sunday after Easter inclusive.

Having laid this down, I reply that marriage in itself is not prohibited at these times, but only solemn weddings, which consist of three things: a holy blessing; ceremonies and dances etc.; finally, the solemn delivery of the bride into the house of the bridegroom. This is gathered from Trent, as cited, which forbids solemn nuptials, from the canon law [ref.], and from use; see Sanchez, Coninck, Bonacina, Laymann and Pontius. However, in some places the custom may perhaps be stricter. This solemn way of celebrating nuptials is forbidden as a mortal sin, unless a bishop has a reason to grant a dispensation. It is different if the marriage is contracted and consummated privately with some moderate festivities.

[M55] 55ᵘˢ. Quis possit dispensare in impedimentis dirimentibus? an id possit Episcopus, saltem in graui necessitatis casu? idque non solum post contractum matrimonum sed etiam ante. Sanch. l. 2. d. 40. Bonac. q. 3. p. 15. Con. d. 33. d. 3. Lay. l. 1. de leg. c. 22. n. 4. Respondeo in dirimentibus solus dispensat Pontifex per se loquendo. ita omnes passim. Patet ex praxi, et recursu quotidiano ad Romanam Curiam. Item quia inferior non potest dispensare in lege superioris, nisi forte id sit ei concessum. argum. Clemena. Ne Romana de elect. dispensat[650] in iis

---

649 The bridegroom carrying the bride over the threshold of their home.
650 S adds: *porro*

solis, quae iura humano sunt statuta. vel etiam declarando cessare ius diuinum in quibusdam aliis, vt casu 35. est dictum.

Excipe 1°. nisi matrimonium sit bona fide contractum in facie Ecclesiae cum impedimento, iamque timeatur scandalum ex separatione incontinentiaeue periculum, nec sit recursus ad Pontificem; tunc enim dispensare potest Episcopus, vt recte Vasq. de leg. d. 178. n. 6. Laym. cit. Tan. hic q. 4. n. 142. Sanch. Bonac. [fo. 51] et caeteri statim citandi; censetur enim ob necessitatem id Pontifex concedere, et colligitur ex cap. quia circa de consang: quicquid dicant aliqui. Caeterum si vel scienter contrahant in gradibus prohibitis, vel ignoranter quidem, sed omissis culpabiliter denunciationibus, tunc nequit dispensare Episcopus, cum nec dispensare soleat Pontifex, vt decernit Trid: ses. 24. c. 5.

Excipiunt 2°. aliqui, si necessitas valde vrgeat, etiam ante contractum. ita omnium 1us. docuit Sanch.cit. n. 7. quem sequuntur Bonac, cit. n. 6. Pont. 1. 8. c. 13. n. 6. Salas de leg. d. 20. l. 3. n. 27. Reginald: n. 31. n. 205. Polao tr. 3. d. 6. p. 5. n. 7. Diana tr. 2. miscell. resol. 19. citans Molfesium, Homobonum et alios, ob quorum autoritatem est probabile; debet tamen necessitas esse valde vrgens, et extraordinaria.

Excipe 3°. Nisi alicubi consuetudine sit introductum, vt in quibusdam dispenset ordinarius, vt hic Leodii praetenditur pro 3°. et 4°. gradu in quibusdam circumstantiis.

Excipiunt 4°. aliqui, quando dispensatio Papalis fuit surreptitia, volunt enim posse conualidari ab Episcopo, quod probabile putat Pontius l. 8. c. 13. n. 7. argum. quia circa de consang: qui tamen textus loquitur post contractum vid Sanch. d. 38.

Denique in impedimentis matrimonio contracto superuenientibus dispensat Episcopus ad petendam debitum, sicut et cum habente votum simplex castitatis, vt petat; Idemque possunt Regulares priuilegiati, vt docet Sanch. d. 12. n. 4. Huiusmodi impedimentum est incestus cum consanguinea vxoris iuxta dicta casu 48. an idem faciat cognatio spiritualis [fo. 51v] superueniens, v. g. si coniux prolem coniugis baptizet, vel suscipiat, vid. Con. d. 34. d. 8. id neruose confutantem.

Case M55. *Who can dispense with impediments which render a marriage null and void? May a bishop do so, at least in a case of grave necessity; and may he do so not only after the marriage has been contracted, but also before? See Sanchez, Bonacina, Coninck and Laymann [refs].*

I reply that, *per se*, only the Pope may dispense with impediments that render a marriage null and void; thus, all writers everywhere. This is clear from practice and the daily recourse to the Roman Curia. In addition, because an inferior cannot dispense with the law of a superior, unless perhaps the power to do so has been granted to him; see the canon law [ref.]. However, the Pope dispenses in only those matters which are laid down by human law. In addition, the Pope may declare that divine law ceases in some other areas, as has been said in Case 35.

The first exception is if the marriage was contracted in good faith, in church, despite the impediment, and now scandal is feared from a separation, or from the danger of incontinence, and there is no recourse to the Pope. For then the bishop may grant a dispensation; thus, correctly, Vasquez, Laymann, Tanner, Sanchez, Bonacina [refs], and others who will be cited below. For it is judged that the Pope would concede this, because of the necessity; and it is gathered from the canon law [ref.], whatever others may say. However, if they contract marriage in the prohibited degrees, either knowingly, or indeed ignorantly, but culpably omitting the banns, then the bishop may not dispense, since the Pope is also not accustomed to dispense in such a case, as Trent [ref.] pronounces.

Secondly, exception is made in some cases, if necessity strongly urges it, even before the contract. Sanchez taught this first of all, and he is followed by Bonacina, Pontius, Salas, Reginald, Castro-Palao and Diana [refs], citing Molfesius, Homobonus and others; on account of their authority, this is probable, but the necessity must be very urgent and extraordinary.

The third exception is if it was introduced in some places by custom that in some things, the ordinary might dispense; as, here in Liège, it is claimed that in certain circumstances this can be done for the third and fourth degrees.

Fourthly, some commentators argue there is an exception that, when a papal dispensation has been acquired surreptitiously, the bishop should be able to validate it; which Pontius [ref.] thinks is probable, following canon law [ref.], although this text speaks about action after the marriage has been contracted, see Sanchez [ref.].

Finally, there is an exception in the case of impediments which arise after the marriage has been contracted, and here the bishop may dispense concerning the right to ask for marital dues, as is also the case with someone who has taken a simple vow of chastity. And the same power to grant such dispensations is also held by regulars who have this privilege, as Sanchez [ref.] teaches. An impediment of this sort is that incurred if a man commits incest with a blood relative of his wife, according to what has been said in Case 48. On whether the same may be done in cases of spiritual kinship which arise after the marriage – for example if one spouse baptises a child of the other, or acts as a godparent – see Coninck [ref.], who vigorously refutes this.

[M56] 56[us]. Quaenam causae excusent a reddendo debito coniugali? an vxor quae parere nequit sine maximo vitae discrimine, aut non nisi foetum mortuum teneatur, aut possit debitum reddere? Con. d. 34. dub.

2. et 3. Lay. p. 3. c. 1. n. 5. Sanch. 1. 9. d. 24. et l. 7. d. 102. n. 11. Bonac. q. 4. p. 1. Respondeo coniux, qui negat debitum coniugi serio petenti peccat mortaliter et a fortiori, si nunquam velit reddere, nisi raro et cum difficultate, committit enim iniustiam in re graui. ita omnes. Vnde et mortaliter peccat, qui voluntariis pollutionibus, aut immoderatis ieiuniis facit se impotentem ad reddendum debitum. ita Sanch. d. 3. Quod si non petat ita serio, si tergiuersanti facile acquiescat, si raro admodum saepe petenti negetur, non erit nisi veniale ob materiae paruitatem.

Excusatur a reddendo coniux, si id nequeat sine graui detrimento sanitatis; vt si laborat febri aut vulnere: si ex copula morbum contraheret grauem: si coniux leprosus sit, adsitque horror, aut infectionis periculum; si moreretur in partu; si vxore grauida foret abortus periculum; quod tamen raro subesse teste experientia docet Sanch. d. 22. n. 7. et Con: n. 77. si sit amens, aut ebrius; nisi vt maius vitetur malum. Bonac. n. 10. At non excusatur vxor a reddendo eo quod foetum viuum nequeat parere quia melius est foetui sic esse, quam omnino non esse: neque [fo. 52] quod siccanda essent vbera ex conceptu, quia prolem[651] aliis alimentis vtcunque nutrire potest; neque ideo ne supra facultates multiplicentur proles, si vir acres patiatur stimulos. Con. n. 24. et Tan: q. 6. n. 41 quia ius habet absolute coniux ad copulam, vt ex Apostolo docet Alex: 3. c. 2. de coniugibus lepr. Reddere potest vxor tempore menstrui, si facile nequeat detrectare. Vir vero tunc scienter petens peccat, sed non nisi venialiter. nam grauior illa prohibitio. Leuit. 20. et Ezech: 18. ad legem pertinet ceremonialem. ita Sanch: d. 21. et Pont. l. 10. c. 14. Potest etiam foemina reddere etiam cum certo vitae periculo in pariendo quia non tenetur abstinere cum incontinentiae periculo, licet non teneatur reddere. ita Sanch. 1. 7. d. 102. n. 11. Tan. q. 6. n. 39.

Case M56. *What reasons excuse a spouse from rendering conjugal dues? Is a wife who cannot bear children without great danger to her life, or only if the foetus is dead, bound to render her conjugal dues; is she allowed to do so? See Coninck, Laymann, Sanchez and Bonacina [refs].*

I reply that a spouse who denies the marital dues to his or her spouse when he or she seriously requests them, sins mortally, and with even more reason if he or she never wants to render them, except rarely and with difficulty. For the spouse commits injustice in a grave matter; thus all. Hence he or she sins mortally by becoming unable to render conjugal dues through voluntary pollutions, or immoderate fasting; thus, Sanchez [ref.]. But if he or she does not request the conjugal rights so seriously, if turning his or her back he or she easily acquiesces, if he

---

651 S adds: *lactentem*

or she is rarely refused when he or she often requests, it will only be a venial sin, because of the smallness of the matter.

A spouse is excused from rendering what is due if she cannot do so without grave detriment to her health; if, for example, she suffers from a fever or wound; if she would contract a grave illness as a result of copulation; if her husband is leprous, and there is horror or danger of infection; if she would die in childbirth; if, for a pregnant wife, there is a danger of abortion, which, however, experience teaches rarely happens, as Sanchez and Coninck [refs] teach; if he is insane, or drunk; if she refuses in order to avoid a greater evil; see Bonacina [ref.]. But the wife is not excused from rendering what she owes because she cannot bear a living foetus, because it is better for the foetus to have existed thus than for it never to have been. Nor because her breasts will become dry after conception, because the child drinking the milk may be fed with other nourishment in some way. Nor, if the man is sexually very active, so that her children do not multiply beyond her strength; see Coninck and Tanner [refs]. This is because the spouse has an absolute right to copulation, as Pope Alexander III [ref.] teaches, following the Apostle. A wife may render what she owes in the time of menstruation, if she cannot easily refuse. In truth, a man who knowingly asks at that time sins, but only venially, for that prohibition in Leviticus 20 and Ezekiel 18, which belongs to the sacred law, is more grave; thus, Sanchez and Pontius [refs]. A woman may also render what she owes even with certain danger to life in childbirth, because she is not bound to abstain if there is danger of incontinence, although she is not in this case bound to render what she owes; thus Sanchez and Tanner [refs].

[M57] 57ᵘˢ. An si coniux illicite petat, possit alter nihilominus reddere? v. g. Titius post votum Castitatis simplex ducit vxorem, et petit debitum, an teneatur, aut an possit ipsa reddere? Sanch. l. 9. d. 6. Con. d. 34. d. 4. Lay. p. 3. c. 1. n. 7.⁶⁵² Bonac. q. 4. p. 3. Respondeo et dico 1°. si illicite petat tantum ex malo fine, aut aliquo errore, aut simili circumstantia, quam posset ipse petens deponere, tunc licite alter reddit; quia actus absolute bene fieri potest hic et nunc. ergo. si male fiat, petenti soli imputandum, nec curandum ab altero iuxta dicta de scandalo in Anglicanis. cas 11. Dico 2°. si petenti ob circumstantiam personae eius (puta ob Castitatis votum alteri cognitum.) [fo. 52ᵛ] sit absolute illicitum hic et nunc exercere copulam, etiam erit illicitum alteri reddere per se loquendo. est contra Sanch. Con. Bonac. Lay. citatos et Dianam resol. 296. de sacra: sed asseritur a Pontio l. 10. c. 3. et probatur, quia cooperari proxime ad peccatum alterius, admittendo, amplexando, etc. est

---

⁶⁵² S reads: *17*

malum et illicitum, quandoquidem actus petentis malus est non ex mera
eius voluntate, sed ex se hic et nunc, ita vt non possit non esse malus.

Dixi per se, quia non est hoc ita intrinsice malum, quin metus mortis,
aut similis mali excusaret, nam redditio, vt suppono, illicita foret, non
ex obiecto (vt esset, si subesset impedimentum dirimens occultum, aut
abortus certo esset secuturus.) sed mere quatenus est cooperatio[653] ad
actionem illicitam alterius: cooperari autem etiam proxime ad peccatum
alienum ob grauissimam necessitatem excusari potest, vt si quis Excom-
municato ob metum mortis daret Eucharistiam iuxta dicta de leg. cas.
20. et 21. Imo probabile existimo cum Sanch. d. 6. citata contra Con:
quod etiamsi foemina sciuisset hoc votum viri sui ante matrimonium
aut si ipsa etiam votum haberet communi consensu emissum, non tamen
teneretur cum vitae periculo viro illicite petenti negare debitum, quia
non obligat votum cum tanto periculo; quod a fortiori dicendum, si
actus esset tantum iure humano prohibitus, puta ob circumstantiam loci,
etc. aut si venialiter tantum malus, in hoc enim casu semper excusari
reddentem a [fo. 53] veniali malitia docet Sanch. n. 6. Con: n. 27. non
improbabiliter.

Case M57. *If a spouse unlawfully asks for his marital rights, may the
other nevertheless render them? For example, Titius after a simple vow
of chastity marries and asks his wife for what he is owed, is she bound
to, or may she, render what she owes? See Sanchez, Coninck, Laymann
and Bonacina [refs].*

I reply and say firstly that if his request is unlawful only because it
is made with evil intent, or from some error, or from a similar circum-
stance, which he himself could explain while making his request, then
his spouse lawfully renders what she owes, because her action may
absolutely be well done here and now; which proves the point. If the
one who asks acts badly, he alone is to blame, and the other party must
not be concerned, according to what has been said about scandal in the
English Cases, Case 11. I say secondly if copulation is absolutely, here
and now, unlawful for the spouse requesting his conjugal rights, on
account of the circumstances of his person (for example, on account of
a vow of chastity known to the other spouse), it will also be unlawful
in itself for the other to render these rights. This judgement is against
Sanchez, Coninck, Bonacina, and Laymann, who have been cited, and
Diana [ref.], but it is asserted by Pontius [ref.], and proved, because
to co-operate closely in the sin of another, by complying with him,
embracing him etc. is evil and unlawful, when the act of the spouse

653 In A this word is written above a crossing out of *mer*

asking for his rights is indeed evil, not merely from his unlawful intention, but in itself here and now, so that it cannot be other than evil.

I have said 'in itself', because this is not so intrinsically evil that fear
of death or similar evil does not excuse it. For the rendering of marital
dues, as I suppose, would be unlawful, not as an action which the spouse
performs (as it would be, if there had been a secret impediment which
makes the marriage null and void, or if abortion would certainly follow),
but merely in so far as it is co-operation in the illicit action of another.
However, to co-operate, even closely, in the sin of another on account of
most grave necessity may be excused; for example, if someone should
give the Eucharist to an excommunicate out of fear of death, according
to what is said in *Concerning Laws*, Cases 20 and 21. Indeed, I consider
this probable, with Sanchez [ref.], against Coninck, because even if the
woman had known about this vow of her husband's before the marriage,
or if she herself also had made such vow by common consent with
him, she would still not be bound, with danger to her life, to deny
her marital obligations to her husband, who was unlawfully requesting
them, because a vow does not oblige with such danger. This, with even
more reason, must be said if the act were prohibited only by human
law, for example on account of circumstances of place etc., or if it were
only a venial sin, for in this case rendering marital obligations is always
excused from venial wrong, as is taught by Sanchez and Coninck [refs],
not improbably.

[M58] 58ᵘˢ. An dubitans de valore sui matrimonii possit dubio stante
debitum reddere, aut etiam petere?⁶⁵⁴ Sanch. l. 2. d. 41. a. n. 42. Con.
d. 34. n. 100. et seqt. Laym. l. 1. tr. de conscien: c. 5. n. 24. Bonac.
q. 4. p. 4. Respondeo si vterque mala fide contraxerit, neutrum posse,
dubio stante, vel petere vel reddere. ita passim omnes. Ratio est quia
nulla possessio suffragatur, vbi est mala fides. Et quidem cum mala fide
contrahunt ordinarie loquendo, qui cum dubio de matrimonio⁶⁵⁵ contrahunt, quia tenentur coniuges scire quod sint habiles. si tamen erant iam
in possessione iuris sui ad contrahendum, et superueniat dubium. v. g.
an dispensatio obtenta sit valida, tunc facta diligentia, si vinci nequeat
dubium, possunt bona fide contrahere et consummare: ita Con: d. 34.
n. 104. praesumitur enim valida, et sic de caeteris. si vero bona fide
vterque contraxerit, et dubium postea superueniat, tenetur dubitans
inquirere veritatem; et interea temporis reddere debet, sed non petere.
Reddere quidem, quia alter non est priuandus iure suo, ob tuum dubium:

---

⁶⁵⁴ In A this word is written above a crossing out of *reddere*
⁶⁵⁵ S reads: *impedimento*

non vere petere, quia non potest se exponere fornicationis periculo, donec inquisierit: foret enim id temerarium, ita passim Doctores. Difficultas praecipue est, an si post factam diligentiam adhuc perserueret dubium, teneaturne abstinere semper a petendo? affirmat Vasq. l. 2. d. 66. c. 4. et Tan: q. 6. n. 361. et alii quia cap. Domini de 2^{is}. nupt. et cap. Inquisitioni de sent: excom: ita videtur decisum. Probabilius tamen est post factam diligentiam posse in dubio etiam petere, quia possessor bonae fidei nunquam est priuandus suo iure in dubio est enim hoc nimis durum ex ipsa rei natura, et in [fo. 53^v] quacunque materia. ita Sanch. l. 2. d. 41. n. 47. Con. 105. Lay. Bonac. cit. Ad cap. Domini respondeo sermonem esse de iis, qui mala fide contraxerunt. Ad cap. Inquis: respondeo solum dici ad quid dubium obliget vi sua praecise, id est antequam facta sit inquisitio veritatis. Ex his infertur, si vnus contrahat bona fide, et alter mala, debere hunc reddere, sed non petere; nisi forte non dubius, sed certus esset matrimonium esse nullum, tunc enim potius deberet sustinere excommunicationem humiliter quam reddere, vt habetur cap. inquis. citato et docent omnes.

Case M58. *If someone is doubtful about the validity of his marriage, may he, while the doubt still stands, seek or even render his marital dues? See Sanchez, Coninck, Laymann and Bonacina [refs].*

I reply that if each spouse married in bad faith, neither may, with the doubt still standing, either ask or render; thus, all, everywhere. The reason is because no possession helps a case, when there is bad faith. And, indeed, those who marry with doubts about the marriage, do so in bad faith, ordinarily speaking, because spouses ought to know that they are suitable for marriage. If, however, they were in possession of the right to marry, and a doubt arose (for example, over whether the dispensation which had been obtained was valid), then having used due diligence, if the doubt could not be overcome, they might with good faith contract and consummate the marriage; thus Coninck [ref.]. For, the marriage is presumed to be valid, as is true in other matters of a similar sort. If in truth each had contracted marriage in good faith, and the doubt afterwards arose, the doubting spouse is bound to inquire about the truth, and in the meantime should render his dues, but not ask for his rights. Indeed, he should render his dues, because the other spouse is not to be deprived of her right, on account of your doubt; but he should not ask, because he may not expose himself to the danger of fornication, while the inquiries are being made, for that would be rash; this is the judgement of the doctors, everywhere.

The difficulty principally is, whether, after due diligence, and the doubt still continuing, he is bound to abstain for ever from asking for his conjugal rights. Vasquez and Tanner [refs] and others affirm it, because two canons [ref.] seem to have decided it in this way. However, it is more probable that having done diligence, he may, while still in doubt, also ask for his conjugal rights, because the possessor of good faith is never to be deprived of his right when in a state of doubt; for this is too hard by the very nature of the question, and this is true in all similar matters. Thus, Sanchez, Coninck [refs], Layman and Bonacina, as cited. To one of the canons [ref.] cited by those who take the opposite view, I reply that the discussion there is about those who have married in bad faith. To the other canon [ref.], I reply that it only speaks about what doubt obliges us to do precisely by its own force; that is, before an inquisition has been made into the truth. From what has been said, it is inferred that if one party contracted in good faith, and the other in bad, the latter should render conjugal dues, but not ask for them; unless perhaps it is not doubtful, but certain, that the marriage is null, for then he should rather undergo excommunication humbly, than render them, as is said in the canon [ref.], and as all teach.

[M59] 59us. Sitne peccatum mortale exercere copulam coniugalem modo indebito, non seruando viz. vas legitimum, situmque naturalem? Et quid si inchoatam copulam adrumpant, aut generationem impediant. Sanch. l. 9. d. 16. 17. et 19. Con: d. 34. n. 80. Lay. l. 3. s. 4. n. 14. et 19. Bonac. q. 4. p. 11. n. 12. et p. 13. et 6. n. 16. Respondeo exercere copulam non seruato vase legitimo esse peccatum mortale grauissimum: similiter et seminare extra vas naturale, vt patet ex facto Onae gen. 38. vnde potius mori debet vxor, quam copiam sui ad ista facere.

Dico 2°. seruato vase naturali, modus concumbendi innaturalis tunc solum erit mortalis, quando generationem impedit, vt quia semen totum effluxerit, etc. ita Sanch. d. 16. Pont. c. 11. Bonac. Con: Lay. sunt quidem peccata veniala valde crassa, et acriter a Confessario reprehendenda, solius voluptatis causa hos situs quaerere ineptos, sed non mortifera, imo si necessitas postulet, culpa vacant. Vnde si vir ita petat, potest vxor se illi conformare, imo melius est id facere, et forte tenebitur [fo. 54] ad vitandas rixas, sed solum ex charitate. vt docet Lay. Sanch. Pont. At probabilius existimo eam ex iustitia ad has turpitudines non obligari cum Bonac. p. 3. n. 9. et 10. Less. l. 4. c. 3. d. 13. n. 89. contra Dianam et Sanch. Denique conceptum semen nefas est eiicere. de quo videri potest Sanch. d. 16. n. 5. et d. 20.

Dico 3°. Copula semel inchoata nequit alter interrumpere[656] altero inuito, cum vterque ius habeat ad copulam completam et prolificam. Si ambo consentiant, et iusta subsit causa, puta ob valetudinem, vel ne excrescat prolium numerus, nullum erit peccatum si vir se retrahat, modo nec vxor seminauerit, nec sit periculum pollutionis in alterutro;

---

[656] S reads: *abrumpere*

si iusta causa non adsit, erit veniale. Ratio cur non sit mortale cessantibus his periculis est quia non impeditur generatio contrarie, sed tantum priuatiue. Sanch. d. 19. Lay. Bonac. Diana resol. 204. et 224.[657] At impedire generationem contrarie vt eiiciendo semen, et similia, est peccatum grauissimum.

Case M59. *Is it a mortal sin to perform conjugal copulation using an unwarranted method; that is, not using the legitimate vessel, and the natural position? And what if they break off from copulation after it has begun, or impede generation? See Sanchez, Coninck, Laymann and Bonacina [refs].*

I reply that to perform copulation not using the legitimate vessel is a most grave mortal sin. Similarly, also to seminate outside the natural vessel, as is clear from the case of Onan; see, Genesis 38. Hence a wife should rather die than give her permission for that to be done.

I say secondly that if the natural vessel is used, an unnatural method of copulation will only be a mortal sin when it impedes generation, or because all the semen overflows etc.; thus, Sanchez, Pontius, Bonacina, Coninck and Laymann [refs]. To seek these improper positions for the sake of pleasure alone, is indeed a most gross venial sin, and strongly to be condemned by the confessor, but it is not a mortal sin; indeed if necessity requires, it is not to be blamed. Hence if a man asks, his wife may conform herself to him, indeed it is better to do so, and perhaps she will be bound to do so to avoid quarrels, but only out of charity, as Laymann, Sanchez and Pontius teach. But I consider it more probable that she is not bound to do these disgraceful acts, with Bonacina and Lessius [refs], against Diana and Sanchez. Finally, it is wrong to remove the semen after it has been received by the woman; on which, see Sanchez [ref.].

I say thirdly that once copulation has started neither spouse may interrupt it against the will of the other, since each one has a right to completed and productive copulation. If both consent, and there is a just cause, for example on account of health, or so that the number of children does not increase, there will be no sin if the man withdraws, as long as the wife has not seminated, and there is no danger of pollution for both of them; if there is no just cause it will be a venial sin. The reason why in this case it is not mortal when these dangers do not apply is because generation has not been impeded by an injurious action, but only by inaction; see Sanchez, Laymann, Bonacina and Diana [refs]. But to impede generation by an injurious action, for example by the woman removing semen, and similar things, is a most grave sin.

---

[657] S reads: *227.*

[M60] 60us. Vtrum oscula, aspectus, et tactus turpes sint in coniugibus peccata mortalia extra copulam, et quid si coniux in absentia coniugis morose delectetur, aut seipsum impudice tangat. Sanch. l. 9. d. 44. et 45. n.[658] 2. Con. d. 34. d. 11. Lay. l. 3. s. 4. n. 12. et l. 1. tr. 3. c. 6. n. 14. Bonac. p. 8. n. 12. et p. 9. n. 6. Respondeo omnia haec licita esse quando actu ordinantur ad copulam, vt docent omnes. quod si non ordinentur, sed solius voluptatis causa fiant, adhuc non erunt mortalia. ita Sanch. Bonac. Vasq. l. 2. d. 113. n. 3. aiens neminem contradicere. quod ampliandum censeo ad oscula obscoena, cum Diana de sacra. resol. 225. Filucio tr. 30. n. 195. Lay. cit. Sanch. [fo. 54^v] et aliis contra Rodr. et Syluest. damnantes oscula pudenda inter coniuges peccati mortalis, quia reuera et ista sunt media ad copulam. ergo non sunt mortifera. Limitata, nisi esset periculum pollutionis extra vas, cum Sanch. d. 45. n. 33. et aliis, tunc enim sunt per se loquendo mortalia. id est nisi sit causa excusans. v. g. vt honeste et moderate amorem coniugalem testentur. vt alter alteri haec petenti morem gerat ad vitandum offensionem, etc. Verum tactus et oscula plane pudenda hoc nomine vix possunt esse necessaria; quare si fiant cum pollutionis periculo erunt communiter mortalia.

Dico 2°. in absentia coniugis potest sine peccato mortali morose delectari de coniuge absente, etiamsi sequatur membrorum commotio, modo absit pollutio. ita contra Nauar. c. 16. n. 10. et Sa verb. Lux: n. 14. caeteri fere omnes, Vasq. Sanch. Lay. Con. Dian. Bonac. quia ad fouendum amorem coniugalem hoc videtur concedendum. At seipsum tangere impudicem non potest in coniugis absentia, quia hoc nec est medium ad copulam hic et nunc, nec ad amorem coniugalem fouendum. ita sentio cum Vasq. d. illa 113. n. 4. Diana. resol. 215. Lay. n. 12. Bonac. n. 12. licet hos tactus a mortali excuset non improbabiliter Sanch. d. 44. n. 16. modo absit pollutio. Et ex his patet, quid de aspectibus et verbis impudicis inter coniuges sentiendum. de quo San. loc. cit.

Case M60. *Are shameful kisses, looks and touching mortal sins in spouses apart from during copulation, and what if one spouse in the absence of the other, indulges in morose delectation,*[659] *or touches*

---

[658] S reads: *q*.

[659] At the very beginning of the Ampleforth manuscript (before what is numbered fo. 1) is a brief note which helps explain this phrase: *Delectatio morosa, non dicitur a mora temporis cum 1 momento perfici possit, sicut alia peccata: sed per morosam delectationem intelligimus plenam ac deliberatam acceptationem delectationis de opere malo, seu liberum consensum ad illam habendam etiamsi voluntas sit opus ipsum non patrandi. Deducitur ex D. Tho. l. 2. q. 74. a. 6. ad 3. ex P. Comit. tom. priore. p. 473.* This can be translated as follows: Morose delectation is not given this name on account of a delay in time, since it may be completed in one moment, as other sins may be. But by morose delectation we understand a full and deliberate acceptance of delight concerning an evil

himself immodestly? See Sanchez, Coninck, Laymann and Bonacina [refs].

I reply that all these things are lawful when their performance is directed towards copulation, as all teach. But if they are not directed in this way, but only done for the sake of pleasure, still they will not be mortal sins; thus, Sanchez, Bonacina, and Vasquez [ref.], who says that no one contradicts this. This I consider should be extended to obscene kisses, with Diana, Filliucci [refs], Laymann as cited, Sanchez and others, against Rodriguez and Sylvester, who condemn shameful kissing between spouses as a mortal sin. But truly these are also a means towards copulation, therefore they are not mortal sins. This is limited if there is danger of pollution outside the vessel, as Sanchez [ref.] and others say, for these things are then in themselves mortal sins; that is, unless there is a cause which excuses; for example, so that honestly and moderately they prove their conjugal love, and so that one spouse behaves in such a way as to avoid giving offence to the spouse who is asking for this, etc. Truly, touching and kisses, which are clearly shameful by this definition can hardly be necessary; therefore, if they are done with danger of pollution, they are commonly seen as mortal sins.

I say secondly that in the absence of a spouse, the other may without mortal sin practise morose delectation about the absent spouse, even if commotion of the members should follow, as long as there is no pollution. Thus (against Navarre and Sa [refs]), almost all others; Vasquez, Sanchez, Laymann, Coninck, Bonacina. This is because in order to foster conjugal love it seems that this should be conceded. But a man may not touch himself immodestly in the absence of the spouse, for this is neither a means to copulation here and now, nor to fostering conjugal love; this is my opinion, with Vasquez, Diana, Laymann and Bonacina [refs], although Sanchez [ref.] not improbably excuses such touching from mortal sin, as long as there is no pollution. And from what has been said, it is clear what should be thought concerning immodest looks and words between spouses; on which, see Sanchez in the place cited.

[M61] 61[us]. Vtrum ob adulterium coniugis liceat facere diuortium etiam ante iudicis sententiam? quid si adulterium culpabile non fuerit? aut ipse illud condonarit? [fo. 55] aut certe idem crimen commiserit, licet occultissime? Lay. tr. 10. p. 3. c. 7. n. 7. Con: d. 35. d. 1. et 2. Bonac. hic q. 4. p. 5. Sanch. l. 10. d. 3. 4. 5. 6. 12. 14. Respondeo certum esse, licere facere diuortium, quoad thorum et habitationem, propter adulterium. Patet ex Mat. 19. Nisi ob fornicationem, etc. et docent omnes.

---

act, or free consent to having it, even if the will is not to do this act. This is deduced from St Thomas, as cited by P. Comitolus [ref.].

Dico quoad thorum, etc. quia vinculum propterea dissolui non potest, vt docent omnes cum C. Trid. sess. 24. can. 7. Nomine adulterii comprehenditur quaeuis alia copula consummata, cum alio supposito siue sit sodomia actiua, vel passiua, siue bestialitas, per quas coniux diuidit suam carnem. Secus pollutio secreta, tactus impudici, etc. ita omnes. sed nec sufficit copula sodomitica cum propria vxore ad diuortium perpetuum, vt ex probabiliori docet Sanch. d. 4. Bonac. n. 4. Lay. n. 7.

Quando crimen est notorium non est opus alteri expectare sententiam Iudicis, vt diuertat, sed potest statim discedere, aut adulteram e domo pellere. ita San: d. 12. n. 5. et 31. Lay. n. 8. Con. n. 2. Bonac. n. 10. Pont. l. 9. c. 18. Praepos. q. 5. n. 102. sin occultum existat, plerumque ob scandalum opus erit Iudicis sententia eo secluso potest innocens etiam ob crimen occultum negare thorum, atque etiam cohabitationem, discedendo in longinqua, quia Christus Mat. 19. concedit veniam absolute dimittendi adulteram. ita omnes cit: praeter [fo. 55ᵛ] Pontium, qui putat requiri sententiam, vt negetur cohabitatio.

Diuertere autem non potest 1º. si adulterium fuerit inculpabile, vt quia vi oppressa; aut quia putabat esse virum proprium, qui latenter accessit, aut quia putans ipsum mortuum 2º. nupsit. At probabilius est non excusare, quod metu mortis consenserit in scelus, quia tenebatur potius mori. 2º. si iam illud condonarit⁶⁶⁰ siue expresse, siue etiam tacite: quod fit, quando sciens et volens admittit partem nocentem ad thorum, ad oscula, ad conuictum, vt fuse Sanch. d. 14. Huc pertinet, si aut ipse⁶⁶¹ vxorem prostituerit, aut veniam dederit, etc. 3º. nec potest diuertere si⁶⁶² adulterium committat, cap. significasti de diuortiis, et docent omnes. Ratio est quia fit compensatio, et⁶⁶³ abolitur iniuria, et inaequalitas, quae est fundamentum diuortii. Vnde et sequitur idem dicendum, etiamsi alter et prius, et saepius, et atrocius peccauerit, alter vero postea, et⁶⁶⁴ occultissime, quia est eadem ratio iniuriae quoad substantiam. ita Sanch. d. 6. et reliqui cit. et Praep. n. 100. qui tamen ait, non esse improbabile quod occultus adulter possit diuertere ab eo, cuius crimen est notum. Denique nota, quoad ius diuortii pares esse virum et foeminam ex ipsa natura huius contractus, nec potest vnquam praescribi in contrarium (licet quoad alios effectus et poenas peior [fo. 56] sit causa foeminae) vt docent omnes contra Caietanum.

Case M61. *Is it lawful to divorce on account of the adultery of a spouse, even before the sentence of a judge? What if it was not culpable adul-*

---

660 In A these two words follow the same two crossed out.
661 S adds: *directe*
662 S adds: *ipse*
663 S adds: *sic*
664 S adds: *solum*

tery, or if the other spouse condoned it, or if the other spouse certainly committed the same crime, although most secretly? See Laymann, Coninck, Bonacina and Sanchez [refs].

I reply that it is certain that it is lawful to divorce, as far as bed and board are concerned, on account of adultery; this is clear from Matthew 19, 'except it be for fornication' etc., and all teach this. I say 'as far as bed etc.', because the marriage bond cannot be dissolved for this reason, as all teach, with the Council of Trent [ref.]. In the term 'adultery' is included whatever other forms of copulation have been consummated with the other person, whether it be active sodomy, or passive, or bestiality, by which the spouse 'divided his or her flesh'. Secret pollution is different, and shameful touching etc.; thus, all. But sodomy with one's own wife is not sufficient for perpetual divorce, as Sanchez, Bonacina and Laymann [refs] teach as more probable.

When the crime is notorious it is not necessary for the other party to wait for the sentence of a judge in order to divorce, but he may immediately leave, or expel the adulterous woman from the house; thus, Sanchez, Laymann, Coninck, Bonacina, Pontius and Praepos [refs]. If the crime is secret, it will be necessary, in order to avoid many scandals, to obtain the sentence of a judge, but without that, the innocent party may also, on account of a secret crime, deny bed, and even cohabitation, moving far away, because Christ in Matthew 19 conceded absolutely permission to send away an adulterous woman; thus everyone cited, except for Pontius, who thinks that a judicial sentence is required in order to deny cohabitation.

However, divorce is not possible, firstly, if the adultery was committed without blame: for example, because she was raped; or because she thought he was her own husband who came to her in secret; or because she thought he was dead, and she had married a second person. But it is more probable that she is not excused, if she consented to the crime out of fear of death, because she is bound rather to die. Secondly, if the husband had already condoned it, either expressly, or even tacitly, which was done by knowingly and willingly admitting the guilty party to the bed, to kisses, to living together; as Sanchez [ref.] says more fully. It is the same if he directly prostituted the wife, or gave her permission to commit adultery, etc. Thirdly, he cannot divorce if he himself committed adultery, according to the canon [ref.], and as all teach. The reason is that by doing so he is compensated, and the injury and inequality is abolished, which is the foundation of divorce. Hence it also follows that the same must be said, even if one spouse sinned first, and often, and atrociously, while the other in truth did so afterwards, and only most secretly, because as far as the substance of the matter is concerned, the reason is the same; that is, both have suffered injury. Thus, Sanchez [ref.], and the others who have been cited, and Praepos [ref.], who, however, says that it is not improbable that a secret adulterer can divorce one whose crime is known. Finally, note that, as far as the law of divorce is concerned, men and women are equal by the very nature of the contract, and it cannot ever be judged to be different (although as far as the other effects and penalties are concerned, the case of a woman is worse), as all teach, against Caietan.

[M62] 62ᵘˢ. An teneatur coniugem adulterum iam emendatum recipere? an possit eo inuito Religionem ingredi? an si innocens post latam diuortii sententiam cadat in adulterium, teneatur alterum redire volentem recipere? Lay. cit. n. 14. et 16. Con. cit. n. 13. et 25. Bonac. n. 19. et 23. Sanch. l. 10. d. 9. et 11. Respondeo non teneri innocentem vnquam admittere sontem quantumcunque emendatum per se loquendo: est quidem opus laudabile, et magnae charitatis id facere. Fieri etiam potest, vt innocens ad vitandum propriae incontinentiae periculum ad id videri possit obligatus, at nunquam ex iustitia, quamdiu ipse manet innocens. Vnde et potest eligere statum vitae immutabilem siue Religionis siue ordinis sacri altero inuito, vt docent omnes.

Quod si ante diuortium ipse adulteretur, amittit ius diuertendi iuxta communem, vt supra diximus. At si id contingit post diuortium iam publice et perfecte celebratum multi censent non acquiri inde alteri ius reuertendi, quod res facta sit iam irreuocabilis, et nocens omni iure suo spoliatus. ita Sanch. d. 9. n. 30. Lay. n. 14. Bonac. n. 19. Tan. et alii. Mihi tamen contrarium videtur probabilius, atque adeo posse reuocari, nisi forte iam ad ordines, aut Professionem ascendisset. quia ius diuortii nascitur ex ipsa natura contractus, sententia autem Ecclesiae solum declarat ius istud: atqui [fo. 56ᵛ] stando in natura contractus, ille qui postea labitur, amittit eo ipso ius diuertendi. ergo et⁶⁶⁵ post sententiam haec enim accidentaliter se habet ad iuris istius substantiam. 2º. quia sententia non tribuit ius fornicandi. ergo tenetur aeque seruare fidem, ac ante, coniugi adultero, at ante ita tenebatur, vt faceret illi veram iniuriam, qua compensaretur adulterium,⁶⁶⁶ ergo et iam. ita Con: n. 13. et 14. cit. et Pont. l. 9. c. 20. n. 6. aiens esse communiorem, Mol. et alii apud Lay. et quoad⁶⁶⁷ praxim alii non admodum discrepant; concedunt enim posse saltem Ecclesiam cogere talem ad rescindendum diuortium.

Case M62. *Is a spouse (1) bound to take an adulterous spouse back once he or she has reformed? May the first spouse (1) enter religion against the other's will? If the innocent party, after the sentence of*

---

⁶⁶⁵ S adds: *amittit*
⁶⁶⁶ In A this word is written above *iniuriam*, which has been crossed out.
⁶⁶⁷ Crossed out at this point in A: *ab*

divorce, falls into adultery, is he or she bound to return to his or her spouse if the latter is willing to receive him or her back? See Laymann, Coninck, Bonacina and Sanchez [refs].

I reply that *per se* the innocent party is not bound ever to take the guilty party back, however much he or she has reformed. It is, of course, a laudable work, and of great charity to do so. It may also be said that the innocent party, in order to avoid the danger of his or her own incontinence, might seem to be obliged to do so, but never out of justice, as long as he or she should remain innocent. Hence he or she may also choose an immutable state of life either in religion or by taking holy orders, as all teach.

But if the innocent party himself or herself should commit adultery before the divorce, he or she loses the right to divorce the other, according to the common view, as we have said above. But if it should happen after the divorce has been publicly and completely executed, many consider that he or she does not in this way acquire the right to return to the other, because what has been done is now irrevocable, and the guilty party has been deprived of all his or her rights; thus, Sanchez, Laymann, Bonacina, Tanner [refs] and others. To me, however, the contrary seems more probable, and so he or she may be recalled, unless perhaps already he or she has ascended to holy orders or a religious profession. This is, first, because the right to divorce derives from the very nature of the marriage contract, and moreover, the sentence of the Church only declares that right. By basing his or her case on the nature of the marriage contract, a spouse (1) who committed adultery after the other spouse had done so, lost, as a result, the right to divorce, after the sentence of the Church; for the action of this first spouse (1) is accidentally the substance of the right. Secondly, because the sentence of the Church does not give the right to fornicate; therefore a spouse is still bound to keep faith with the adulterous spouse as much as before. Before, the marriage bond allowed the innocent party (1) to injure the adulterous spouse in order to be compensated for adultery (by divorcing), and hence he or she must still be bound to him or her now. Thus, Coninck, and Pontius [refs], who says this judgement is more common, Molina and others, cited by Laymann; and as far as practice is concerned others do not very much disagree, for they concede that it is at least possible that the Church may force such a person to rescind the divorce.

[M63] 63us. An dentur aliae causae diuortii, praesertim perpetui, vt haeresis, saeuitia, et similia? Con. cit. dub. 4. Lay. cit. a. n. 16. Bonac. cit. a. n. 25. Sanch. cit. d. 15. 17. et 18. Respondeo fide certum esse, posse etiam ob alias causas fieri diuortium ad certum, incertumue tempus. vt contra Haereticos definit Tridentinum s. 24. can. 8. licet sola sit fornicatio, ob quam praeciso omni alio iuris positiui adminiculo, possit[668] iure suo dimittere coniugem in perpetuum. Causae hae sunt haeresis, saeuitia, sollicitatio ad peccatum, graui corporis periculum, mutuus consensus ad vouendam continentiam in Religione, vel extra. Quod si criminosus in praedictis tempestiue corrigatur, [fo. 57] semper est recipiendus. At in haeresi post Ecclesiae sententiam eum haereticum declarantem, non tenetur Catholicus[669] eum recipere etiam emendatum Sanch. Con. Lay. Pont. c. 22. et sumitur ex cap. de illa de Diuortiis: quod certius est adhuc si Religionem velit ingredi, argum. cap. fin: de conuers. coniug: potest enim Ecclesia priuare haereticum hoc iure, sicut et multis aliis.

Nomine saeuitiae veniunt insidiae, verberatio grauis, frequentes et valde molestae rixae, et similia, Sanch. d. 18. et si nulla sit emendationis spes, potest Iudex eos perpetuo separare et innocens Religionem ingredi. Sanch. ibid. n. 49.

Per alia coproralia pericula intelligimus morbum contagiosum, furorem atrocem, quod vxor sit venefica, de quo recte Con: db. 4. n. 21. non enim tenetur coniux cum tam graui suo incommodo debito coniugali satisfacere; in particulari tamen cauendum scandalum.

Damna spiritualia ad diuortium sufficientia sunt, si maritus sollicitet vxorem ad sodomiam, ad meretricium, aliaue peccata, potest enim recedere donec corrigatur iuxta illud Christi, si oculus tuus scandalizat te etc.

Case M63. *Are there other grounds for divorce, especially perpetual divorce; for example heresy, cruelty and similar things? See Coninck, Laymann, Bonacina and Sanchez [refs].*

I reply that it is truly certain that divorce, for either a fixed or indeterminate period, is possible for other reasons; for example, the Council of Trent [ref.] lays this down as an action to be taken against heretics. However, it is only for fornication that one spouse may exercise the right to separate in perpetuity from the other with the precise support of positive law, and excluding everything to the contrary. The other grounds for divorce are: heresy; cruelty; soliciting a spouse to engage in sin; grave bodily danger; and mutual consent to take a vow of chastity, in religion or outside it. If someone who is accused of the aforesaid crimes is corrected in good time, he should always be taken back. But in the case of heresy, after the sentence of the Church has declared someone to be a heretic, a Catholic is not bound to take the heretic back, even when he has been reformed; see Sanchez, Coninck, Laymann and

---

[668] S adds: *coniux*
[669] In A this word is written above *haereticus*, which is crossed out.

Pontius [refs], and this judgement is drawn from the canon law [ref.]. This is more certain if he wishes to enter religion, according to the canon [ref.]; for the Church can deprive a heretic of this right, just as of many others.

Under the term 'cruelty' are included: crafty devices, grave beating, frequent and most troublesome quarrels, and similar things; see Sanchez [ref.]. And if there is no hope of improvement, the judge may separate them perpetually, and the innocent party may enter religion; see Sanchez [ref.].

By other physical dangers we understand: contagious disease; atrocious fury; that the wife is a sorceress;[670] on which, Coninck [ref.] writes correctly. For the spouse is not bound to fulfil his marital duties with such grave personal trouble; however, scandal in particular must be avoided.

Spiritual harms are sufficient grounds for divorce, if the husband solicits his wife to sodomy, prostitution, or other sins. For he can go away until he is corrected, according to the saying of Christ, 'if thy eye scandalises thee' etc.

De Sponsalibus
(Concerning betrothals)

[M64] 64us. Quid sint sponsalia? quidnam[671] aetas ad ea contrahenda requiratur? An obligent sub mortali? an sponsi cogi possint ad ea implimenda a Iudice, aut [fo. 57v] etiam per adiectionem poenae conuentionalis? Lay. de Matr. p. 1. c. 1. a. n. 1. ad 8.[672] Con. d. 2. d. 1. et 5. et d. 22. d. 2. et 5. Bonac. de Matr. q. 1. p.[673] vlt. Sanch. l. 1. d. 1. n. 7. d. 16. 27. 29. et 30. Respondeo Sponsalia sunt futurarum nuptiarum promissio. ita Nicolaus 1us. cap. Nostrates. 30. q. 5. S. Tho. in Supplem: q. 43. a. 1. et reliqui. Quare non sunt simplex promissio sed mutuus contractus, vt docet Sanch. d. 5. cum communi. Potest tamen vnus alteri promittere nuptias, et hic acceptare sine repromissione quo in casu non erunt Sponsalia, sed simplex promissio matrimonii ex vna tantum parte. vt bene Sanch. d. 5. n. 12. et Lay. n. 2. contra Vasq. Sponsalia requirunt deliberationem sufficientem, de qua satis dictum supra, sicut etiam de fictione, de verbis externis, de metu et errore, casu 4. et seqbus. Hic solum superest dicendum, quod iure canonico debeant 7um. annum expleuisse

---

670 The Latin *venefica* can also mean 'poisoner'.
671 S reads: *quaenam*
672 S reads: *n. 1. 2. 3. 4. 7. 8. 16.*
673 S adds: *num. 1 et 2. et punc. 2. n. 1. et 2. et punc. 4. n. 1. 2. 3. et punc.*

ad sponsalia contrahenda. argum. cap. litteras. et cap. accessit de spons. impub. ita S. T. supplem: q. 43. a. 2. et alii. Ante quod tempus expletum non valebant nisi constet malitiam supplere aetatem. Ita Sanch. d. 16. a. n. 4. Lay. n. 16.

Obligant haud dubio sub mortali. ita Lay. n. 3. Bonac. p. 2. et alii, quia est contractus iustitiae in re graui. vnde et sequitur posse eum qui iniuste resilit, [fo. 58] cogi a Iudice per Censuras ad ea implenda. sicut ad tribuendum in caeteris ius suum argum. cap. ex litteris 10. de sponsal. Caeterum ob periculum mali exitus non sunt nimium vrgendi, quia matrimonia debent esse libera. Sanch. d. 29. Con. d. 22. d. 2. Lay. n. 4. argum. cap. requisiuit de sponsal. idque siue iurata siue non.

Poena sponsalibus adiici potest, ita vt obliget etiam eum, qui iuste resiliret, vt docent omnes ex cap. gemma de sponsal. Immo multi valde probabiliter affirmant in omni casu poenae adiectionem esse irritam, nec vnquam⁶⁷⁴ obligare. ita Sanch. d. 30. Bonac. p. vlt. alios citans. Mihi tamen videtur probabilius posse adiici, ne iniuste resilias, quia hoc non est contra Matrimonii libertatem, sed per se licitum et ex alia parte iura intelligi possunt, ne apponatur pro resiliente iuste ita Con. d. 22. d. 5. et Pont l. 12. c. 19. n. 8. Caeterum si soluatur etiam a iuste resiliente potest retineri; quia iura non irritant translationem dominii, vt docent omnes cit. Alia est ratio de arrhis, quas licite apponi in pignus fidei docent omnes cit. De quo videri potest Sanch. d. 35. et Bonac. loco citato.

Case M64. *What is betrothal? What age is required to contract it? Does it oblige under mortal sin? May the betrothed be forced to carry out the terms of the betrothal by a judge, or even by the addition of an agreed penalty? See Laymann, Coninck, Bonacina and Sanchez [refs].*

I reply that betrothal is the promise of future marriage; thus Nicholas I [ref.], St Thomas [ref.] and the rest. It is not, therefore, a simple promise, but a mutual contract, as Sanchez [ref.] teaches, with the common view. Moreover, one person could promise to marry another, and the other could accept without making a promise in return, in which case it is not a betrothal, but only a simple promise to marry by only one party; as Sanchez and Laymann show well, against Vasquez. Betrothal requires sufficient deliberation, about which enough has been said above, just as also about deception, about external words, about fear and error, in Case 4 and those which follow. This alone remains to be said, that to contract betrothal, by canon law [refs] they should be over seven years of age; thus, St Thomas [ref.] and others. Before this age, betrothal is

---

⁶⁷⁴ At this point in A *valere* is crossed out.

not valid, unless it is agreed that 'malice supplies age';[675] thus, Sanchez and Laymann [refs].

Betrothal obliges, without doubt, under mortal sin; thus, Laymann, Bonacina [refs] and others, because it is a contract of justice in a grave matter. Hence it also follows that he who unjustly withdraws may be forced by a judge by censures to keep to it, in the same way as he must in other matters perform his duty; see the canon law [ref.]. However, because there is a danger of an evil outcome, the betrothed must not be subjected to too much pressure, because marriage should be free; see Sanchez, Coninck and Lymann [refs], using the canon law (ref). And this is true whether they have taken oaths or not.

Penalties may be added to betrothal, so that they even oblige a person who withdraws justly; as all teach, from the canon law [ref.]. However, many affirm, very probably, that in every case the addition of penalties is invalid and never obliges; thus Sanchez, and Bonacina [refs], who cites others. It seems more probable to me that they may be added to prevent you from unjustly withdrawing, because this is not against the liberty of marriage, but is in itself lawful, and also because the laws may be interpreted to prevent such a penalty being used against the person who justly withdraws; thus, Coninck and Pontius [ref.]. Besides, if it (i. e. the penalty) is paid even by one who justly withdraws, it may be kept; for the laws do not invalidate the transference of property, as all those cited teach. The presents which all those cited teach are lawfully given as pledges of faith are a different matter. About which, Sanchez [ref.] and Bonacina, in the place cited, may be consulted.

[M65] 65[us]. Vtrum in locis, vbi receptum est Tridentinum matrimonium ob defectum Parochi et testium inualidum vim habeat [fo. 58ᵛ] Sponsalium de futuro? Lay. supra n. 18. Con. d. 21. dub. 1. Bonac. q. 2. p. 8. n. 51. Sanch. l. 1. d. 20. Respondeo probabilius mihi videri, quod tale matrimonium vim habeat sponsalium. ita Con. d. 21. d. 4. Licet contrarium etiam probabiliter teneat Sanch. et Bonac. cit. Ratio est, quia in contractu bonae fidei partes censentur sese obligare meliori modo quo possunt, iuxta illud Iurisperitorum: si actus non habeat[676] vt ago, valeat eo modo, quo valere potest. Ex quo fundamento decisum est. cap. vn. de desponsal. impub: in 6º. matrimonia impuberum valere vt sponsalia, eadem autem prorsus videtur[677] ratio hic. quia ad sponsalia non requiritur Parochus et testes. ergo sunt habiles ad illa et intendunt quantum possunt se obligare. ergo.

675 See n. 633 above.
676 S reads: *valeat*
677 S adds: *esse*

Dices Tridentinum annullare actum, eique resistere. Respondeo mere ei resistere, qua matrimonium est. de sponsalibus nihil prorsus statuit, nec vlla ratione aduersatur scopo Concilii, vt valeat actus in ratione sponsalium. ergo non est cur dicamus non esse relictum suae naturae. confirmatur, quia lex correctoria, non est extendenda talis autem est illa Tridenti. ergo extendi non debet ad sponsalia.

Case M65. *In places where the Council of Trent is received, when a marriage is invalid on account of a defect in the need to have parish priest and witnesses, does the marriage have force as a betrothal for the future? See Layman, Coninck, Bonacina and Sanchez [refs].*

I reply that it seems more probable to me that such a marriage has the force of a betrothal; thus, Coninck [ref.]. However, Sanchez and Bonacina in the places cited hold, also probably, the contrary. The reason is that in a contract made in good faith, the parties to it are judged to oblige themselves in the best way they can, according to that saying of the jurists: 'if the action is not valid in the way I act, it is valid in whatever way it can be valid'. On which basis it is decided in canon law [ref.] that the marriages of children before they have reached puberty are valid as betrothals; moreover, the same seems to be exactly the reason here, because for a betrothal, a parish priest and witnesses are not required. Therefore, the parties involved are suitable for betrothal, and they intend to oblige themselves to as much as they can, which proves the point.

You will say Trent annuls this action, and opposes it. I reply that it merely opposes it as a marriage; but as a betrothal, it enacts precisely nothing. There is no reason why to consider that this action is valid as a betrothal, goes against the intention of the Council; therefore, there is no reason why we should say this action should not be taken for what it naturally is, a betrothal. This is confirmed, because an amendment to the law should not be extended; but what is laid down by Trent is such an amendment, and hence it should not be extended to betrothals.

[M66] 66ᵘˢ. Petrus contrahit Sponsalia cum Catharina, deinde contrahit alia etiam de futuro cum Susanna cum eadem perficiens copulam; quaeritur vtrinam contractui stare debeat? Lay. cit. n. 5. Con. d. 23. d. 4. Bonac. q. 1. p. 5. a. n. 7. ad 11.⁶⁷⁸ Sanch. l. 1. d. 49. et 50. Respondeo In locis, vbi Tridentinum non est receptum sponsalia 2ª. [fo. 59] per copulam transire in matrimonium ex praesumptione Ecclesiae: matrimonium autem cum secunda dirimit sponsalia cum priori, vt supra est dictum. quare 2ⁱˢ. est standum ibi: At vbi Tridentinum est receptum 1°.

---

⁶⁷⁸ S reads: *n. 7. 8. 9. 10.*

certum est posse Catherinam in eo casu resilire ob iniuriam, quam ei
Petrus facit. 2°. etiam certum videtur, quod in pari causa, i.e. si nulla
sequatur copula cum secunda Petrum manere obligatum ad priora si
ipsa velit, quia cum secunda sunt iniusta nullam pariunt obligationem,
ne quidem extinctis primis, quia nulla erant. ita Sanch. cit. Pont. l. vlt.
c. 14. et alii passim. 3°. dico, si copula habita sit cum secunda ignara
prioris contractus, probabile valde est, et practice tutum, quod possit, et
debeat stare secundis, quia ratione damni ius secundae videtur fortius.
ita Con. cit. et Pont. c. 14. n. 4. Probabilius tamen mihi videtur, quod in
rigore iustitiae valeant adhuc prima. ita Lay. et Sanch. cit: quia secunda
sunt contra iustitiam et irrita, idque etiamsi iurata essent, non enim[679]
prior per iniquitatem partis[680] priuari iure suo. Fateor tamen, quod si
prima parum sit iactuarae passura,[681] posterior vero valde multum, obligabit charitas, vt potius contrahatur cum secunda et poterit iudex ad id
obligare.

Obiicies, Qui post votum simplex Religionis, data fide matrimonii
extorqueret copulam, teneretur ad nuptias omissa Religione. ergo et in
casu nostro. Respondeo antecedentem ab aliquibus negari apud Sanch.
l. 1. d. 45. sed eo concesso, dico, disparitatem esse, quia votum non
obligat ex iustitia, et quia mitius in istis agitur cum Deo, quam cum
hominibus, Deus quippe non suam spectat [fo. 59ᵛ] in iis vtilitatem sed
nostram.

Case M66. *Peter contracts a betrothal with Catherine, then he contracts
another one, also for the future, with Susanna and with her he performs
copulation; the question is, which contract should he abide by? See
Laymann, Coninck, Bonacina and Sanchez [refs].*

I reply that in places where Trent is not received, according to the
presumption of the Church, the second betrothal becomes a marriage
through copulation. The marriage, moreover, with the second person
renders the betrothal to the first null and void, as has been said above.
Therefore the second contract is to be upheld here. But where Trent is
received, it is certain, first, that Catherine may in this case withdraw, on
account of the injury that Peter has done to her. Second, it also seems
certain that in case where the two betrothals were the same, that is, if
no copulation had followed with the second, Peter would have remained
obliged to the first if she wished, because since the betrothal to the
second was unjust, it carried no obligation. This is true even if the first
betrothal had become extinct, because the second betrothal was null.

679 S adds: *potest*
680 S reads: *compartis*
681 S reads: *perpessura*

Thus, Sanchez in the place cited, Pontius [ref.], and others everywhere. I say, thirdly, if copulation was performed with the second person and she was ignorant of the first contract, it is most probable and in practice safe, that he might and should stand by the second woman, because by reason of the damage she suffered the right of the second seems stronger; thus, Coninck in the place cited, and Pontius [ref.]. However, it seems more probable to me that in strict justice the first still is valid; thus, Layman and Sanchez in the places cited. This is because the second betrothal is against justice and invalid, even if they swore oaths to it; for the first woman should not be deprived of her right through the iniquity of her partner. I confess, however, that if the first woman has suffered little loss, and the second has really suffered very much, charity will oblige him to contract marriage with the second, and a judge could oblige him to do that.

You will object that if someone takes a simple vow of religion, and then having promised to marry, extorts copulation, he is bound to marry, and leave religion; therefore the same should apply in our case. I reply that the antecedent is denied by some; see Sanchez [ref.]. But having conceded it, I say that there is a disparity because the vow does not, out of justice, oblige, and because these things go more kindly with God than with men, and God certainly does not consider His own utility in these matters, but ours.

[M67] 67us. <u>An patiens defectum occultum teneatur eum manifestare</u> comparti, aut a Sponsalibus abstinere? Con. d. 23. d. 12. Bonac. q. 4. p. 5. n. 22. Sanch. l. 6. d. 27. a. n. 7. <u>Respondeo aliquos esse defectus, qui solum reddunt</u> nuptias minus expetibiles, non tamen perniciosas, vt quod foemina sit corrupta, cum putetur Virgo, quod sit infirma, etc. et hos defectus non tenetur manifestare; nullo enim iure ad id tenetur, cum sit in se valde durum et damnosum hos defectus aperire, nec moribus ita receptum, sitque alterius sibi cauere, modo absit dolus. Imo potest dissimulare se esse corruptam, si interrogaretur, quia non est hoc discendum ab ipsa: et a fortiori contractis nuptiis artificio aliquo vti, ne in congressu deprehendatur vitium, quia iam peracto[682] contractu hoc ipsi viro melius est. ita Sanch. cit. Con. cit. et Pont: l. 12. c. 18. Diana de Sacr. resol. 287. Quod si defectus redderet nuptias valde perniciosas, videtur sane obligandus eum aperire etiam ex iustitia, praesertim, si alter inquirat, multoque magis videretur contra charitatem id non facere, vt docet Con. cit. iuxta doctrinam Lessii de iure[683] l. 21. c. 2. d. 11. et probabile censet Pontius, indicans tamen certum non esse, quod teneatur vnquam

---

[682] S reads: *pacto*
[683] S adds: *et iustitia*

occultos illos defectus aperire. c. 18. n. 6. Talia sunt lepra, morbus Gallicus, grauis infamia personalis, etc. si tamen constaret alterum, si sciret, nihilominus contracturum, non erit opus ea detegere.

Case M67. *Is someone who is suffering from a secret defect bound to reveal it to the partner, or to abstain from the betrothal? See Coninck, Bonacina and Sanchez [refs].*

I reply that there are some defects which only make marriage less desirable, but not, however, pernicious. For example, if the woman is not a virgin when she was thought to be one, if she is unwell etc., she is not bound to reveal these defects. For she is not bound to do so by any law, since it is most hard and damaging to make these defects known, and it is not the custom to do so. And it is up to the other party to beware, as long as there is no trickery. Indeed, she may dissimulate the fact that she is not a virgin, if she is interrogated, because this matter does not have to be learned from her; and with even more reason, when the marriage has been contracted, she may use some artifice, so that the defect is not discovered during congress, because once the contract has been made, this is better for the man himself; thus, Sanchez, Coninck, Pontius and Diana. But if the defect would render the marriage very pernicious, it seems clear that the spouse is bound to reveal it, even out of justice, especially if the other party asks, and it seems much more to be against charity not to do so, as Coninck in the place cited teaches, according to the doctrine of Lessius [ref.]. Pontius [ref.] also considers it probable, indicating, however, that it is not certain, because a person is always bound to reveal these hidden defects. Such defects are leprosy, the French disease,[684] grave personal infamy etc. If, however, one party is certain that if the other party knew, he or she would nevertheless contract marriage, there is no need to reveal these defects.

[M68] [fo. 60] 68us. An dissoluantur sponsalia per rerum mutationem superuenientem. v.g. si alteruter fornicetur, si incidat in egestatem, morbum incurabilem, deformitatem grauem?[685] aut si voueat Castitatem in saeculo non solemniter? Lay. p. 1. c. 2. n. 6. 10, et 18. Con. d. 23. n. 25. et 54. et dub. 8. Bonac. q. 1. p. 8. et 5. n. 13. Sanch. l. 1. d. 55. et 57. et seqq. et d. 46. Respondeo dissolui sponsalia per quamcunque mutationem notabilem superuenientem, quae merito retraheret a contrahendo, aptaue sit infelices creare exitus. Promissio enim intelligitur si res permaneat in eodem statu absque mutatione notabili. Argum. cap. quemadmodum de iureiurando, et cap. fin: de coniug. lepros. ita autores

---

684 Syphilis.
685 S adds: *etc.*

citati, et cum iis Pontius l. 12. c. 17. Itaque si alter incidat in lepram, morbum gallicum, infamiam, egestatem, si amittat oculum, nares, aures, etc. potest alter resilire: item si deprehenderetur esse malignis moribus; quia paria quoad hoc censentur, non esse, ac[686] non apparere, quando contrahis. ita omnes cit. 2º. si alter fornicetur, potest alter resilire, vt patet a fortiori ex dictis de diuortio. si fornicetur vterque neutrum posse resilire docet Bonac. p. 8. cit. n. 6. at probabilius est, virum saltem posse, cum sponsae fornicatio sit longe turpior. ita Sanch. d. 55. n. 9. Diana resol. 284. Lay. n. 12. Imo vtrumque resilire posse satis probabiliter docet Tan: q. 1. n. 62. quia cum mulier fornicante viro ius sit adepta dissoluendi, non potest per suam fornicationem de nouo ligari. Denique si foemina vi esset cognita, aut solum [fo. 60ᵛ]turpibus actibus dedisset operam, possit reiici, quia est notabiliter vilior, quae tamen in viro non videntur procedere. ita Sanch. Lay. Con: Bonac. cit.

3º. Dissoluuntur Sponsalia per votum Castitatis in Religione iuxta omnes, cum et matrimonium ratum inde dissoluatur. Imo per solum ingressum in[687] Nouitiatum dissoluuntur ex parte deserti iuxta omnes; at deserens videtur solum liber, si profiteatur, adeoque si egrediatur, cogendus erit[688] contrahere: quia fauor Religionis, et natura rerum aliud non petunt. ita Lay. n. 3. Con: n. 23. Pont. c. 10. Tan. q. 1. n. 147. licet et hunc liberum esse statim a Sponsalibus teneat Sanch. d. 42 et Bonac. p. 5. n. 3. estque probabile. Quoad votum simplex Castitatis factum post Sponsalia[689] multi negant per illud dirimi sponsalia priora, quia videtur esse votum illicitum et Deo ingratum, vtpote contra fidem datam. ita Sanch. d. 46. Lay. Con. et alii. estque probabile, et practice tutum, vt bene Tan: citandus. Mihi tamen contrarium videtur probabilius cum Tan: q. 1. n. 5. Bonac. n. 13. Pont. c. 12. et multis aliis apud Tan: quia cum coelibatus sit beatior status, vt definit [fo. 61] Tridentinum censetur haec conditio inesse Sponsalibus, Nisi ad statum perfectiorem velim ascendere. et fauet Apostolus 1. Cor. 7. Dico non nuptis, bonum est, si sic permaneant. et confirmat Pontius ex cap. Veniens. Qui Clerici et vou: Vnde a fortiori idem dicendum de susceptione ordinis sacri.

Case M68. *Is a betrothal dissolved by a change of circumstances which arises; for example if one of the couple fornicates, if he or she falls into extreme poverty, or contracts an incurable disease or grave deformity, or if he or she vows perpetual chastity, but not solemnly? See Laymann, Coninck, Bonacina and Sanchez [refs].*

I reply that a betrothal is dissolved by any notable change which

---

686 In A this word is written above *et*, which has been crossed out.
687 In A at this point the word *Religionem* is crossed out.
688 In A at this point the letters *eg* are crossed out.
689 In A at this point the word *priora* is crossed out.

arises, which reasonably would have dissuaded them from making the contract, or is apt to create unhappy outcomes. For the promise made at betrothal is understood to mean, 'if things remain in the same state without notable change'; see the canon law [refs], the authors cited, and with them, Pontius [ref.]. Therefore, if one of the betrothed falls into leprosy, the French disease, infamy, great poverty, if he or she loses an eye, nose, ears etc., the other one may withdraw; also if he or she is discovered to have bad habits. This is because these problems were not judged to exist or did not appear when you made the contract; thus, all those who have been cited. Secondly, if one party fornicates, the other may withdraw from the contract of betrothal, as is clear with even more reason from what has been said about divorce. If each one fornicates, neither may withdraw, Bonacina [ref.] teaches, but it is more probable that at least the man may, since the fornication of the female betrothed is far more shameful; thus, Sanchez, Diana and Laymann [refs]. However, Tanner [ref.] teaches with enough probability that each one may withdraw, because when the man fornicates the woman acquires the right to dissolve the betrothal, and she cannot by her own fornication be bound again to it. Finally, if the woman has been raped, or even if she gave occasion to shameful acts, she may be rejected, because she is notably more worthless as a result; but this does not seem to happen in the case of a man. Thus, Sanchez, Laymann, Coninck and Bonacina as cited.

Thirdly, betrothal is dissolved by taking a vow of chastity in religion, according to all, since an unconsummated marriage is also dissolved in that way. Indeed, betrothal is dissolved on behalf of the deserted person, simply by entry into the novitiate, according to all. But the person who is deserting seems only to be free from the betrothal, if he or she continues in religion. Hence, if he or she leaves religion, he or she should be forced to contract marriage, because the benefit of religion and the nature of the matter ask for nothing else; thus, Laymann, Coninck, Pontius and Tanner [refs]. However, Sanchez and Bonacina [refs] think he or she is immediately free from the betrothal, and it is probable. As far as a simple vow of chastity made after the betrothal is concerned, many deny that this renders the prior betrothal null and void, because it seems to be an unlawful vow and one which is not pleasing to God, since it is against the promise that has been made. Thus, Sanchez [ref.], Laymann, Coninck and others; and it is probable, and in practice safe, as Tanner, who must be cited, shows well. The contrary, however, seems more probable to me, with Tanner, Bonacina, Pontius [refs] and many others, cited by Tanner. This is because celibacy is a more blessed state, as the Council of Trent explains. This condition is judged to be contained in the betrothal; 'unless I wish to ascend to a more perfect state'. And the Apostle favours this, in 1 Corinthians 7, 'I say to the unmarried, it is good for them if they so continue'; and Pontius confirms it from the canon law [ref.]. Hence with even stronger reason, the same must be said about taking holy orders.

[M69] 69us. An dissoluantur sponsalia ex mutuo consensu? aut per elapsum diei praefixae, etiamsi alter inculpabiliter fuerit impeditus? Lay. cit. n. 1. et 16. Con. d. 23. dub. 1. et 6. Bonac. q. 1. p. 10. n. 1. et p. 6. n. 6. Sanch. l. 1. d. 52. 53. Respondeo mutuo consensu dissolui sponsalia iuxta omnes, argm. cap. 2. de sponsal. Quod si impuberes contraxissent, posset alter pubes factus resilire etiam altero inuito; sed neuter ante pubertatem, vt docet Sanch. d. 51. n. 6. et 9. debet autem resilire pubes statim, alioquin ea confirmare censetur: statim autem fieri dicitur, quod intra triduum fit iuxta Sanch. n. 14. consentit Pont. c. 9. addens contra Sanch. posse resilire, etiamsi ea iuramento confirmasset. Denique dissoluuntur sponsalia per lapsum termini praefixi ex parte eius per quem non stetit, altero manente obligato. arg. cap. sicut 22. de sponsal. Quod intellige, quando dies praefixus est ad faciendam690 obligationem, non ad eam sollicitandam, Vtro autem ex [fo. 61v] his modis sit praefixus, colligi debet ex verbis, intentione, et circumstantiis, vt bene Pont. c. 16. praesertim an ab initio sit adiectus, an non.

Sed quid si is per quem stetit, sine sua culpa fuerit impeditus? Negat tunc dissolui Sanch. n. 7. Bonac. p. 6. cit. Affirmant Lay. et Conin: Mihi videtur 1o. mens eorum inspicienda, an solum culpabilem moram caueri voluerint, vel saltem aliam voluntariam. Quod si non constet; videtur sane sententia Sanchii aequior et probabilior 1o. quia ex reg. 66. iuris in 6o. videntur haec accipi de mora voluntaria. et cap. Sicut, indicat Pontifex; iubet enim moroso iniungi Poenitentiam, si per ipsum steterit, vtique sua culpa (supponitur enim quod non distulisset ob Religionis ingressum.) alias sensus foret absurdus. Denique non videtur aequum, vt inuoluntarie impeditus damnum patiatur; multo minus vt ipso manente obligato, vt vult Con: n. 46. cum aliis alter exsolutus maneat; hoc enim poenale est, nec sine culpa tam691 iniungendum.

Denique nota, si causa dissolutionis sit manifesta, non esse opus adire iudicem, quia contractus est ita celebratus, vt liceat ex iusta causa [fo. 62] recedere. At si Sponsalia essent manifesta, et causa dissolutionis non liquida, tunc adeundus est Iudex. Quamuis secluso graui scandalo non videtur mortale aliter facere. ita Tan: q. 1. n. 72. Con: d. 32.692 n. 70. Lay. c. 2. n. 28. Sanch. d. 69. modo recedas ex causa vere probabili; et693 ex mere dubia. Finis.

---

690 S reads: *finiendum*
691 S adds: *facile*
692 S reads: *23.*
693 S adds: *non*

Case M69. *Is betrothal dissolved by mutual consent; or by the passing of the date arranged for the marriage, even if one party was prevented without blame from keeping it?* See Laymann, Coninck, Bonacina and Sanchez [refs].

I reply that betrothal is dissolved by mutual consent, according to all, following the canon law [ref.]. If they had contracted as youths below the age of puberty, either may withdraw once they have reached puberty, even if the other is unwilling; but neither may do so before puberty, as Sanchez [ref.] teaches. The one who has reached puberty should withdraw immediately, otherwise he is judged to confirm the betrothal: it is said to be done 'immediately', however, when it is done within three days, according to Sanchez [ref.]. Pontius [ref.] agrees, adding against Sanchez that he may withdraw, even if he had confirmed the betrothal with an oath. Finally, betrothal is dissolved by the expiry of the term prefixed, on the part of one person, whose fault it is, with the other party keeping to the obligation; according to the canon law [ref.]. This should be understood to mean, the date arranged for the fulfilment of the obligation, rather than for the beginning of the process. For which of these two events, however, the date was arranged should be gathered from the words, the intention and the circumstances of the contract, as Pontius [ref.] shows well; especial attention should be paid to whether these conditions were added to the contract from the beginning or not.

But what if the person who allowed the time to lapse, was prevented without being to blame? Sanchez and Bonacina [refs] deny that it is then dissolved. Layman and Coninck affirm that it is. It seems to me that, firstly, the intentions of the contracting parties should be examined, whether they only wanted to prevent culpable delay, or at least other voluntary delay.[694] If this is not agreed, the judgement of Sanchez given above seems clearly more equitable and probable. First, because according to the canon law [ref.], this seems to be the accepted way of treating voluntary delay, and another canon [ref.] agrees, for it orders penitence for the betrothed person who delays, if he was the cause, that is, it is his fault (for it is supposed that he had not put off the marriage because he had entered religion); and any other meaning would be absurd. Finally, it does not seem fair that the person who was impeded involuntarily should suffer harm; much less that the innocent person who remained obliged should also suffer harm, as Coninck [ref.], with others, wants, and that the other person should also remain bound; for that is penal, and not so easily to be imposed on someone who is without blame.

---

[694] Presumably this means, whether or not the intention was to take a delay (deliberate or not) as breach of contract.

Finally, note that if the cause of the dissolution of the betrothal is manifest, there is no need to go to a judge, because the contract is made in such a way that it is lawful to reject it for a just cause. But if the betrothal was manifest and the cause of the dissolution not clear, then it is necessary to go to a judge. However, if there is no grave scandal, it does not seem to be a mortal sin to do otherwise; thus Tanner, Coninck, Laymann and Sanchez [refs], as long as you withdraw for a reason which is truly probable, and not merely because of doubt.

The End

Appendix

[MS Sancroft 37, fo. 105ᵛ]
[MA] <u>De Osculis</u>

Certum est oscula quae fiunt tantum honestae beneuolentiae causa iuxta patriae consuetudinem non esse peccata. Certum item est esse mortalia, quando quis per ea intendit allicere ad concubitum, vel in iis repraesentat sibi delectationem copulae extra matrimonium, imo communior et tutior opinio non esse mortalia, licet solum intendat illam voluptatem carnalem quae ex osculo oritur: Quamuis in hoc vltimo puncto contraria opinio sit etiam probabilis, cuius rationes fuse persequitur Lessius. quia est difficile condemnare peccati mortalis toties quoties iuuenes et puellas, procos et procas, inter quos oscula et delectatio inde orta moraliter loquendo non possunt euitari. Vnde Caietanus et Armilla, quando condemnant oscula peccati mortalis sic loquuntur. Qui osculis vacant libidinose. Vbi videntur solum loqui de osculis replicatis, et cum mora et ardore libidinis ob periculum enim consensus vlterioris vel pollutionis haec sunt mortalia. At amplexus, oscula, et tactus qui non sunt impudici, si solum habeantur ex ioco, vanitate leuitate, absque delectatione venerea intenta, vel si ea insurgat reprimatur, non excedunt culpam venialem quia materia est exigua. Turpiloquium, eius auditio, cantus leues, et visus inhonestus non sunt mortalia, nisi fiant cum mora, mala intentione, vel periculo consensus vel pollutionis. Aspicere bruta cöeuntia non est mortale, nisi fiat cum mora et periculo delectationis libidinosae, sed famuli qui ea quadam libidine contrectant genitalia pecorum, peccant mortaliter. Aspectus viri concumbentis cum muliere est omnio vitandus sub graui peccato ob periculum, quia mouet efficaciter, vnde grauiter peccare possunt coniuges qui in suo cubiculo habent pueros, ancillas.

[fo. 106] Filucius Poenitentiarius de choreis. Rustici diebus festis non sunt prohibendi a choreis, modo fiant post Missam, tum quia otio aliter vacarent, quod peius esset, tum quia fiunt pro more regionis et coram aliis publice, ideoque magna ex parte aufertur libidinis occasio, tum quia videntur conciliatrices omnis benevolentiae inter adolescentes et puellas, vnde saepius contrahuntur matrimonia inter illos. Tollendi tamen sunt abusus. tract. 33. in 6°. praecepto.

Puella quae per vim attingitur inhoneste vel etiam constupratur, non peccat coram Deo mortaliter, si obnitatur et non det consensum, licet aliquam percipiat delectationem. quoad forum autem exterius illa praesumeretur consensisse quae non clamauit, cum satis esset propinqui qui iuuarent. Sed id non est necessarium in foro interiori, vt expresse docet ex Soto Nauarrus. Imo Sotus dicit non teneri etiam in propriis membris resistere, eo quod satis sit non se componere ad actum obscoenum, quod verum erit si ex timore non audet resistere. Aptare autem ad id membra, tibias aperire, vestem eleuare, aut quid simile agere, censet Nauarrus esse quodammodo cooperari, et non solum pati, licet non adesset consensus interior pro fornicatione vel delectatione.

Non tenetur quis abstinere a re licita, licet inde soleat sequi pollutio, modo absit periculum consensus. vt patet in Confessario, studioso, medico, nec euigilans reprimere coeptam in somno, sed sufficit non placere. Sa.

Appendix

MA *Concerning kisses*

It is certain that kisses which are performed only out of honest benevolence according to the custom of our country are not sinful. It is also certain that they are mortal sins when a person intends by using them to draw someone gently into fornication, or creates for himself through kissing the pleasure of extra-marital copulation. On the other hand, the more common and safer opinion is that it is not a mortal sin even if his only intention is to derive the carnal pleasure which arises from kissing (although on that last point the contrary opinion is also probable, the reasons for which are shown more fully by Lessius). This is because it is difficult to condemn as guilty of committing a mortal sin so many young men and girls, courting couples, among whom kisses and the pleasure arising from them cannot morally speaking be avoided. Hence, when Caietan and Armilla condemn kissing as a mortal sin they speak about those who linger lustfully over kisses; they seem only to speak of repeated kisses, performed slowly with libidinous ardour, for because of the danger of ulterior consent and pollution such kisses are mortal sins. But an embrace, a kiss, and a touch, if they are chaste and happen in play, from vanity, levity, without sexual intent (or if it breaks through, it is repressed); these do not exceed venial culpability, because the matter is slight. Immodest speech, and listening to it, worthless songs, and dishonest looks are not mortal sins, unless they are done for a long time or with bad intent, or with the danger of consent or pollution. To watch animals copulating is not a mortal sin, unless it is done for a long time, and with the danger of lustful pleasure. But servants who handle the genitals of their animals with some lust, sin mortally. To watch a man copulating with his wife is entirely to be avoided under pain of grave sin because of the danger that it has a powerful effect on those who watch. Hence, married couples may sin gravely if they have boys and servant girls in their bedrooms.

Filliuci in the *Poenitentiary*, concerning dances says rustics on feast days are not prohibited from performing in dances, as long as they do so after Mass. First, because otherwise they will use their leisure in some other way which may be worse. Second, because they do it according to the custom of their region and publicly in front of others, and so in great part the occasion of lust is removed. Third, because the dances seem to be very useful matchmakers between adolescent boys and girls, and as a result marriage is often contracted between them. Abuses should however be removed [ref.].

A girl who is dishonestly taken by force or even ravished does not sin mortally before God, if she struggles and does not give assent, although she experiences some pleasure. As far as the external forum is concerned, she is judged to have consented if she does not call out, when there are enough people in the vicinty who would help. But that is not necessary in the internal forum as Navarre expressly teaches from Soto. Indeed, Soto says she is not even bound to resist with her own limbs, so it is enough that she does not agree to an obscene act, which will be true if through fear she does not dare to resist. But to get her limbs ready for it, to open her legs, to raise her clothing, or to do something similar, is judged by Navarre to be in a way to co-operate and not simply to endure, even though there was no internal consent for fornication or pleasure.

No-one is bound to abstain from a lawful action, even though pollution usually results from it, as long as there is no danger present of consent (as is clear for the confessor, student, doctor), nor if he represses it when he wakes up, if it begins in sleep; but it is enough that it does not give pleasure. See Sa.

Cases Concerning Ecclesiastical Fasts

[MS Sancroft 37, fo. 17]

Casus aliqui de Ieiunio Ecclesiastico
(Some cases concerning ecclesiastical fasts)

[F1] <u>Casus 1us</u>. Quinam teneantur praecepto ieiunii Ecclesiastici? Num Adolescentes ante annum aetatis 21um. in Anglia? Num senes post annum sexagesimum? S. Tho: 2. 2. q. 147. a: 4. Nauar: enchir: cap. 21. n. 16. Laym: l. 4. tra: 8. cap: 3. n. 1. et 2. Less. de iust. l. 4. c. 2. db. 6. Fil: tra: 27. p. 2. c. 6. q. 4. Azorius 2ª. p. mor: l. 7. c. 17. q. 2. 3. et 4.

Respondeo Adolescentes non obligari ante annum 21um. nec mares nec foeminas, etiamsi fortes sint, nec Religiosos, nisi quatenus obligentur in regula. Ita cum S. Thoma Omnes. Quia cum sint in statu incrementi vsque ad 3um. septennium, expediebat non obligari. Amplia, quod ad nulla omnino teneantur cum Fagund. Sanch: et Bonac: contra Palud: et Angelum volentes eos teneri ad aliqua. Itaque si ieiunio egeant ad vitia carnis reprimenda, praescribendum id erit a Confessariis. Limitanda, quoad legem vnicae refectionis, nam a carnibus et cibis prohibitis tenentur abstinere, statim ac vsum rationis habent, sicut ad caetera praecepta iuxta omnes. Denique nec tenentur in Anglia ante annum 21um.

Quoad senes, communis est sententia excusari eos, qui vere senes sunt, hoc est in notabili virium detrimento: Est enim senectus morbus incurabilis. Quoad annum, Dico probabilius nullum esse certum. Vnde si constet sexagenarium satis esse robustum, tenebitur ieiunare. Ita Caiet: Azor: Fagund: Bonac: Less. de iustitia l. 4. c. 2. db. 6. et Laym: l. 4. tract. 8. c. 3. [fo. 17ᵛ] Facile tamen praesumitur sexagenarius esse vere senex et excusatus, imo id praesumendum est, nisi euidenter constet oppositum; vt aiunt Caiet. Less. Fil. Sanch: Addo non carere probabilitate, quod omnes sexagenarii sint eo ipso excusati, siue constet de robore siue non. Ita Sanch: Sa. Diana atque alii apud ipsos. Non est tamen probabile foemina quinquagenarias passim excusari.

Case F1. *Which people are bound by the commandment to keep the fasts of the Church? Are adolescents under the age of twenty-one in England bound in this way? Are the elderly after the age of sixty? See St Thomas, Navarre, Laymann, Lessius, Filliuci, and Azor [refs].*

I reply that adolescents under the age of twenty-one are not obliged to fast; neither male nor female, even if they are strong; nor the religious, except in so far as they are bound to do so by their Rule. Such is the view of all writers, with St Thomas. This is because until they have reached their third septennial, they are growing and so it is necessary that they should not be obliged to fast. Furthermore, Fagundez, Sanchez and Bonacina argue that adolescents are entirely exempt, which is against the judgement of de Palude and Angelus, who wish them to be obliged to something. Therefore, if they need to fast in order to repress the vices of the flesh, this should be prescribed to them by their confessors. This judgement (exempting adolescents from fasting) applies only to the law which lays down that only one meal a day should be eaten, for they are bound to abstain from meat and prohibited foods as soon as they have the use of reason, in the same way as they are bound to other commandments, according to all writers. In conclusion, people in England are not bound to fast until they are twenty-one.

As far the elderly are concerned, the judgement that those who are truly old should be excused is the common one, for fasting is most detrimental to their strength, and old age is an incurable illness. As far as the precise age is concerned I say that it is more probable that nothing is certain. Hence if it is clear that a sexagenarian is strong enough, he will be bound to fast. Thus, Caietan, Azor, Fagundez, Bonacina, Lessius and Laymann [refs]. It may, however, easily be presumed that a sexagenarian is truly an old man and that he is excused. Indeed it must be presumed that this is true, unless the opposite is obvious; as Caietan, Lessius, Filliuci, and Sanchez say. I add that it does not lack probability that all sexagenarians are simply by virtue of their age excused, whether or not there is clear evidence of their strength. Thus, Sanchez, Sa, Diana, and others cited by them. It is not however probable that female quinquagenarians are always to be excused.

[F2] Dico 2º. Excusari omnes infirmos, debiles, conualescentes, foeminas praegnantes, nutrices, pauperes. Ita Laym: et Less. locis cit: S. Th. 2.2. q. 147. a 4. Fil: Azorius. Nauar: etc. Quoad infirmos quibus prodesset ieiunium docet Sanchez eos etiam non teneri, quia Ecclesia, inquit, semper infirmos excipit, ne afflictio addatur afflicto. Vnde peccabunt contra temperantiam solummodo, si nocentia comedant. Nota tamen pauperes eo die, quo habent iustum prandium, per se loquendo videri obligatos, pro eo die, vt docet Sanch: consil: 15. Caeterum quia fere contingit esse debiles, ex inedia praeterita, vel in periculo magnae inediae futurae, plerumque excusari poterunt.

Case F2. I say secondly that all the following are to be excused: the sick, the weak, convalescents, pregnant women, those who are nursing babies, and the poor. Thus, Laymann, Lessius, St Thomas, Filliuci, Azor and Navarre etc. [refs]. As far as the infirm, who might be harmed by fasting, are concerned, Sanchez teaches that they also are not bound to fast, because he says the Church often excepts the infirm, lest affliction be added to the afflicted. Hence such people sin only against temperance if they eat forbidden foods. Note, however, that the poor who on a particular day have a meal of the sort which is lawful on that day are obliged,[695] speaking of the matter in itself, as Sanchez teaches [ref.]. However, because they possibly may be weak through lack of food in the past, or are in great danger in the future of a great lack of food, most of them may be excused.

[F3] <u>Dico 3º</u>. Omnes artifices non excusari, sed tantum laboriosos, quicquid resistat Fagundez c. 8. n. 4. l. 1. in 4º. praec:, quia Eugenius 4us., cuius priuilegio ille nititur, expresse meminit artium laboriosarum: et ita docent caeteri omnes. Tales sunt mechanicae fere omnes inquit Lessius, etiam Sutoria, cum Lessio, Tannero, Bonac: et modernis plerisque contra Toletum. Sartores et Barbitonsores verisimilius est non excusari; ita Less. Laym: Azor: Bonac: Tannero, Reginaldo, Sanchez. Eos tamen [fo. 18] excusat Fagundez, sed falso vt dixi nixus fundamento. Diana resol: 8. citans Ledesmium.

Denique Concionatores, Confessarii, Ludimagistri et similes eatenus excusantur, quatenus eorum labor ieiunium non compatitur. Nec refert vtrum ex obligatione an ex charitate gratis an ob stipendia haec faciant. Addit Sanchez n. 7. Magistros Scholarum Grammaticae in Societate nunquam teneri ad ieiunandum tota quadragesima, etiamsi fortes sint, quia constat vires postea valde debilitari. Ad summum, inquit, tenebuntur ad 3. dies in Septimana.

Case F3. I say thirdly that all workers are not excused, but only labourers; and all other writers teach this (although Fagundez disagrees [ref.]), because Eugenius IV, on whose privilege Fagundez himself relies, expressly mentions the laborious crafts. Such are almost all mechanics, says Lessius, even the shoemakers; and Lessius, Tanner, Bonacina and many of the modern authors agree, against the opinion of Toletus. Tailors and barbers are more probably not to be excused; thus, Lessius, Laymann, Azor, Bonacina, Tanner, Reginaldus, and Sanchez. Fagundez however excuses them, but, as I have said, relying on a false foundation; see Diana [ref.] citing Ledesma.

Finally, preachers, confessors, schoolmasters and similar people are excused in so far as their work is not compatible with fasting. Neither does it matter whether they do this work on account of an obligation, or freely out of charity, or for a stipend. Sanchez [ref.] adds that the masters of grammar schools in the Society are never bound to fast for the whole of Lent, even if they are strong, because it is agreed that their

---

695   Presumably, to abide by the rules of fasting and abstinence which apply on that day.

strength would be afterwards greatly reduced if they did. At most, he says, they are bound to fast for three days in a week.

[F4] Dico 4º. Pedibus iter agentes excusari possint iuxta omnes. Intellige, si multum itineris conficiant, vt si magnam diei partem proficiscantur, inquit Sanch. consil. 10. Aut 12. aut 15 milliaria Italica inquit Filuc: trac: 27. p. 2. n. 122. Equitantes communiter non excusari docent omnes. Laym: Filuc: Sanch. Bonac: Excipe primo, nisi iter sit multorum dierum. 8. v.g. vel 10. nec absque concussione notabili, tunc enim non teneris. Ita Laym: Fil. Sanch: Excipe 2º., si sit periculum magnae lassitudinis aut debilitatis. Ita Sanch: et Bonac: 3º. si non inuenias sufficientem refectionem in via pro vna vice, Sanch: 4º. Nisi curratur equis dispositis, vulgo a posta, est enim magnus labor. Sanch: cit: Vnde patet muliores et agasones plerunque excusari, habent enim multum laboris.

Case F4. I say fourthly that, according to all, those undertaking a journey on foot may be excused. You should understand this to mean that they are on a long journey, and are travelling for a large part of the day, says Sanchez [ref.]; travelling either twelve or fifteen Italian miles, according to Filliuci [ref.]. All teach, however, that travellers on horseback are not excused: thus, Laymann, Filliuci, Sanchez and Bonacina. There are four exceptions: first, if their journey lasts many days, for example eight or ten, and involves notable jolting, for then you are not bound to fast; thus, Laymann, Filliuci and Sanchez. Second, if there is danger of great tiredness or debility; thus, Sanchez and Bonacina. Third, if on one stage of the journey you do not find sufficient refreshment; thus, Sanchez. Fourth, if you are riding on horses hired at stages of the journey, vulgarly called 'post horses', for that is very laborious; thus, Sanchez in the place cited. Hence, it is clear that muleteers and grooms are mostly excused, for they have to work hard.

[F5] Dico 5º. Eum, qui de industria se defatigat, nulla alia de causa quam vt ieiunium subterfugiat, peccare mortaliter [fo. 18ᵛ] dando occasionem, sed iam defatigatus poterit coenare; Vnde ludentes pila, venatores, latrones grassantes, licite ieiunium soluunt; ita Azor: Laym: Filuc: cit: Sanch: consil. 7º. n. 15. et consil. 11. n. 5. Qui habet causam iustam nihil peccat; iusta autem est causa, si sit ob maius aliquod lucrum vel commodum, etiamsi necessaria non sit. Vt si Paterfamilias pedes lustret suos operarios, etiamsi habeat oeconomum qui id praestet. Sanch: Similiter lusus pilae et venatio interdum licite suscipiuntur in quadragesima cum solutione ieiunii, quia nimis durum foret continuo abstinere, Sanch: consil. 7º. n. 18. Caeterum, si causa turpis sit, aut superflua, vt frequenter ludere ac venari, peccas eam ponendo, praeuidens inde ieiunium violandum; quia praeceptum Ecclesiae sicut obligat ad ieiunium, ita etiam ne absque vlla necessitate ponas impedimenta impletionis eius, sicut vsu uenit in caeteris omnibus praeceptis, vt dici solet in materia de legibus. Ita Sanch: cit. et reliqui. Diana tamen absolute pronunciat resol: 40. non peccari dando causa coenationi siue per recreationem, siue per opus illicitum, vt visitando amasiam, etc. citatque Medinam et ex parte Ledesmium; sed tenendum quod diximus.

Dices, licitum esse consulto se transferre in locum in quo non ieiunatur, vt vitetur ieiunium, ergo et se defatigare. Respondeo concesso antecedente cum Diana resol: 19 et negando consequentiam, quia in priori casu acquiro exemptionem a ieiunio adeundo locum liberum, ad quod ius habeo, nec fraudem facit qui vtitur iure suo: sicut nec ille qui priuilegium aut [fo. 19] dispensationem quaerit; At in posteriori pono impedimentum legis obseruationi, meque reddo inhabilem, stante de caetero hic et nunc legis vigore, hoc autem non licet, quia lex finem praecipiens, media etiam censetur praecipere, quale est hoc non se reddere impotentem. Scio licet vitare obligationem Missae, eundo in oppidum vbi non est festum; non vero eundo in syluas, vnde redire nequeam tempestiue ad sacrum audiendum. Sic etiam Sacerdoti non licet breuiarium in mare proiicere, licet sit illius Dominus, ergo neque in casu nostro. Nec est credibile mentem fuisse Ecclesiae obligare homines sub mortali ad ieiunium, et simul permittere vt stultis et illicitis cursitationibus se inde expedire possent, lucrum ex scelere reportantes: Hoc enim foret occulte homines timore ieiunii instigare ad peius terendum tempus, quam si non ieiunaretur.

Case F5. I say fifthly that someone who tires himself out by working for no other reason than to avoid the fast sins mortally by being the cause of this fast-breaking, but if he is already tired may dine. Hence, those who play ball, huntsmen, and hunt servants,[696] may lawfully break the fast; thus, Azor, Laymann, Filliuci and Sanchez [refs]. Someone who has a just reason to do something does not sin. Moreover, a just reason may be doing something to gain some great monetary reward or benefit, even if it is not a necessary action. For example, if the father of the house goes round on foot to supervise his labourers, even if he has an overseer to perform this function; see Sanchez. Similarly, it may be sometimes lawful to play a game of ball, or go hunting in Lent, and hence break the fast, because continual abstinence from such pursuits would be too harsh; see Sanchez [ref.]. Otherwise, if the reason for breaking the fast is dishonourable, or unnecessary, for example if you play ball or hunt frequently, you sin by doing so, when you foresee that as a result you will violate the fast, because the commandment of the Church obliges

---

696 *Latrones grassantes* may mean 'highway robbers'.

you to fast and also not to place any impediments in the way of doing so without any necessity, as is the case with all other commandments. This is generally said in discussions of the law; thus, Sanchez in the place cited, with the rest. Diana [ref.], however, declares that it is absolutely not a sin for a man to give himself a reason to eat a meal, as the result either of recreation, or of an unlawful act, like visiting a lover etc., and he cites to support this Medina and, in part, de Ledesma. But we consider that it is necessary to keep to what we have said.

You will say that it is lawful to move deliberately into a place in which the fast is not practised, in order to avoid the fast, and hence it would also be lawful deliberately to make oneself tired. I reply that although the antecedent point may be conceded with Diana [ref.], the consequence should be denied, because in the prior case I acquire exemption from the fast by going into a place which people may visit freely, which I have a right to do; and no one commits fraud if he uses his right, in the same way that a man may ask for a privilege or dispensation. But in the second case I place an impediment on the observance of the law, and I put myself outside the reach of a law which otherwise should apply in this place and at this time. This however is not lawful because when a law lays down an end it is also judged to lay down the means, of which this is one, so that the law does not render itself powerless. I know that it is lawful to avoid the obligation to hear Mass, by going to a town where it is not a feast day; but not in truth by going into the woods, from whence I cannot return in time to hear Mass. In the same way it is not lawful for a priest to throw his breviary into the sea, even though it is his own property; therefore, neither are similar things lawful in our case. Nor is it credible that the intention of the Church was to oblige men to fast under mortal sin, and at the same time to permit them to be able to escape by stupid and unlawful courses, like a man carrying off the prize by cheating. For this would be secretly to encourage men out of fear of fasting, to spend their time doing something worse than if they had simply not fasted.

[F6] Dico 6º. Magnam difficultatem in ieiunando esse iustam dispensandi causam; Ita Sa. Tann: Bonac. Imo Bonacina contra Filucium asserit, hanc esse causam per se excusantem; quod si ita sit, poterit Confessarius talem declarare excusatum: Tutius tamen foret dispensationem petere. Qui soluit ieiunium bona fide putans se habere iustam causam, cum vere non habeat, non peccat mortaliter, quia Eccelsiae praecepta hoc praesertim non ita seuere obligant. Ita Caiet: Sanch. Nauar: Filuc: et Laym: cit. n. 6. Et vniuersim ignorantia vincibilis, modo crassa non sit aut affectata, excusat in lege humana; vt docent Sanch: Valentia, Bon: Reginal: et Azorius.

Case F6. I say sixthly if someone would experience great difficulty by fasting, it is a just reason for dispensing with the obligation to fast; thus, Sa, Tanner, and Bonacina. Indeed, Bonacina, against Filliuci, asserts that 'great difficulty' is a reason which in itself[697] excuses, and if this is the case, a confessor may declare such a person to be excused. But it would be safer to seek a dispensation. If someone breaks the fast in good faith, thinking he has a just reason, when in truth he does not have one, he does not sin mortally, because the commandments of the Church, especially in this matter, do not oblige so severely. Thus, Caietan, Sanchez, Navarre, Filliuci and Laymann [ref.]; and it is universally held that vincible ignorance, as long as it is not crass or feigned, excuses where human laws are concerned, as Sanchez, Valentia, Bonacina, Reginaldus and Azor teach.

[F7] Dico 7ᵒ. In Quadragesima, oua, lacticinia, lardum, seu sagimen communi iure esse vetita. Probatur argumento cap: Denique dist. 4. et decreto Sextae Synodi generalis. Ita etiam [fo. 19ᵛ] interpretante consuetudine et communi Doctorum Sententia vt S. Th: 2.2. q. 147. a. 8. Laym: l. 4. tract. 8. c. 1. Less. Filuc: Azor: Sanch. Bonac: et alii, quibus immerito se opponit Fagundez contendens non esse obligationem sub mortali, sed veniali tantum. Dixi iure communi, quia speciali consuetudine videmus contrarium in Belgio quoad lacticinia introductum. At vero extra Quadragesimam licita sunt oua et lacticinia, nisi consuetudo loci ea excludat: ita Omnes. Caeterum lardum in condiendis cibis per se loquendo licitum non esse probabilius est istis diebus. Ita San: Filuc: Laym: nisi vbi mos obtinuit. Non tamen est improbabile, iis, qui vesci possunt ouis et laticiniis etiam in Quadragesima, licitum esse vsum lardi seu sagiminis; ita Glossa, Hostiensis, Abbas, Syluester apud Laym: item Azor: et Diana citans Graffium et Fagundez. Item Layman tenet esse prohibitum istis solum sub veniali.

Dispensatus ad carnes mere quia pisces non suppetunt, aut quia non congruunt temperamento tuo, teneris adhuc ad vnicam tantum refectionem, sicut tenentur ii, qui dispensantur ad oua; quia qui potest partem praecepti implere, tenetur ad eam, cum nequeat totum. Secus esset, si ob debilitatem dispensaretur tecum. Ita Less. Filuc: Laym: Bonac: contrarium tamen docent Fagun: Azor: Tolet. Suar: estque probabile.

Case F7. I say seventhly that in Lent, eggs, dairy products, lard, or seam,[698] by common law are forbidden. This is proved by the canon

---

697 That is, without a dispensation.
698 Pork lard.

law [ref.], by the decree of the sixth general synod, and also by the interpretation of custom, and the common judgement of the doctors like St Thomas, Laymann, Lessius, Filliuci, Azor, Sanchez, Bonacina and others, to whom Fagundez wrongly opposes himself, maintaining that this is not an obligation under pain of mortal but only of venial sin. I have said 'by common law', because by special custom we see that the contrary, as far as dairy products are concerned, has been introduced in Belgium. But truly outside Lent, eggs and dairy products are lawful, unless the custom of the place excludes them; thus, all our authors. However, lard, when used in preparing food, speaking of the matter in itself, is more probably not lawful on those days (thus, Sanchez, Filliuci, and Laymann), except where the custom of doing so prevails. It is not however improbable that those who may eat eggs and dairy products even in Lent, may also lawfully use lard or seam. Thus, the Gloss; Hostiensis; Abbas; Sylvester, cited by Laymann; also Azor; and Diana, citing Graffeus and Fagundez. In addition, Laymann holds that it is prohibited to them only under pain of venial sin.

If you have a dispensation to eat meat merely because fish is not available, or because it is not suitable to your constitution, you are still bound to take only one meal, in the same way that those who have a dispensation to eat eggs are; because a person is bound to fulfil part of the commandment if he can, when he cannot keep the whole of it. It is different if you have a dispensation on account of debility. Thus, Lessius, Filliuci, Laymann and Bonacina; the contrary, however, is taught by Fagundez, Azor, Toletus and Suarez, and is probable.

[F8] <u>Dico 8º</u>. Potum lactis, iusculi, et similium, quae sumi solent principaliter ad nutriendum, vsurpari non posse extra horam refectionis sine violatione; vere enim habent rationem cibi, etiamsi bibantur; ita Laym. Filucius et alii passim. Caetera omnia enumerata non frangunt ieiunium, vt vinum, ceruisia, electuaria per modum medicinae, modo non [fo. 20] excedatur quantitas in electuariis caeterisque comestibilibus.

Vnde nec erit peccatum veniale modicum sumere, ne potus noceat, aut vrbanitatis causa cum amico, aut ratione officii, si pincerna sit aut coquus. Potus vero vini in quauis quantitate non frangit ieiunium iuxta S. Thomam et Recentiores communiter, contra Halensem, Rosellam, et alios Antiquiores, qui putarunt vino mane sumpto vel ad sedandam famem, violari ieiunium. Imo etiamsi consulto eo fine bibatur, vt fames sedetur, corpus nutriatur, minusque sentiatur ieiunii difficultas, non est peccatum mortale, vt contra Regin: docent Sanch: Diana et alii, quia Ecclesia noluit potum prohibere: Quamuis facile ea ratione perdatur ieiunii meritum, vt docet S. Tho: cit. a. 8. De sumendo modico Vrbanitatis causa dubitat Azor; sed potius negat; at id fieri posse probabilius docent Bonac: Fagund. Diana.

Petes quid sit faciendum ei, qui mane per incogitantiam ientat? Respondeo. Debere adhuc seruare ieiunium, dilata scilicet in vesperam coena, vel simili aliquo modo, ita vt ientaculum seruiat loco refectiunculae vespertinae. Quod si hoc circumstantiae non ferant, poterit iuxta Nauar: et alios gerere se perinde, ac si nihil comedisset. Vide Lessium l. 4. c. 2. db. 3. n. 18. Fagund: c. 4. n. 6. Nauar: et Bonacinam.

Case F8. I say eighthly that drinking milk, broth and similar things which are taken principally for nutrition, may not be done except at meal times without violation, for truly they have the effect of food even if they are drunk; thus Laymann, Filliuci and others everywhere. All other drinks listed[699] do not break the fast, such as wine, beer, cordial used as a medicine, provided the quantity of cordial and other things consumed is not excessive.

Hence neither will it be a venial sin to take a little food, lest the drink is harmful,[700] or out of civility if you are with a friend, or by reason of your office, if you are a wine-server or a cook. In truth, to drink wine in any quantity you like does not break the fast, according to St Thomas and the more recent authors commonly, against Alexander of Hales, Rosella and the other more ancient writers, who thought that to drink wine in the morning or to remove hunger violated the fast. However, even if it is drunk deliberately in order to remove hunger and so that the body is fed, and so that the difficulty of the fast is felt less, it is not a mortal sin, as Sanchez, Diana and others teach (against Reginaldus) because the Church does not wish to prohibit drinking. However, by that reasoning the merit of the fast might easily be lost, as St Thomas teaches [ref.]. Concerning taking a little for the sake of civility, Azor is doubtful, and he is inclined to oppose it; but that it may probably be done is taught by Bonacina, Fagundez and Diana.

You will ask what should be done with someone who in the morning absentmindedly breakfasts. I reply that he should afterwards keep the fast, that is by delaying his dinner until the evening, or in some other similar way, so that the breakfast takes the place of the evening supper. But if circumstances do not allow this, he should, according to Navarre and others, behave as if he had eaten nothing; see Lessius, Fagundez, Navarre and Bonacina [refs].

---

699 *enumerata*, 'listed': this suggests that there was a list of drinks in the question at the head of the case, which our copyist chooses to leave out (after the first case) in this collection of cases.

700 This seems to mean, 'lest the drink taken without food is harmful'.

[F9] <u>Dico 9º</u>. Eum qui necdum satis sumpserat in prandio, aut qui inten-
derat redire, si forte auocetur, posse adhuc reuerti et prandium absoluere, quia ex intentione censetur vnica comestio; sicut est eorum, qui
in Monasteriis lecturi aut ministraturi sunt, partem prandii ante caeteros
[20ᵛ] accipiunt. Ita Caiet. Laym: Less. Azor. Filucius: et quoad moram
intermediam Bonac. pun: 3. n. 10 ait posse esse longum tempus. Sanch:
consil. 24. Horam mediam vel integram, Ioan: Sanchius apud Dianam.
resol. 32. duas horas, Azorius iudicio prudentis relinquit. Quod si quis,
sat cibi sumpto per totum tempus meridianum cogatur interrumpere
comestionem, reuerti non potest, nisi ad Collationem vespertinam, quia
tam vastum interstitium non permittit, vt censeatur vnica refectio, quantumcunque id ipse intendisset: Quod si sat cibi nutrimentalis non sump-
sisset, potest 2º. refici, sed soluet meo iudicio ieiunium in eo casu, at
licite, quia excusatur. Ita colligo ex Bonac: pun: 3. n. 8: et Sanch: consil.
28. n. 8. Porro si quis surgat e mensa animo finiendi, non potest iterum
reuerti; ita Laym: Probabile tamen est, si duret adhuc prandium, aut si
statim animum mutet, illudque instauret, non esse peccatum mortale.
Ita Less. et Filucius.

Case F9. I say ninthly that a person who had not yet eaten enough at
the midday meal, and who was perhaps called away, but intended to
return to the meal, might when he returned complete the meal, because
his intentions show that this should be judged to be a single meal; just
as it is in the case of those who in monasteries act as the readers or
as servants, and receive part of the midday meal before the others.
Thus, Caietan, Laymann, Lessius, Azor, Filliuci; and as far as a break
in the middle of the meal is concerned, Bonacina [ref.] says it may be
a long time. Thomas Sanchez [ref.] says half an hour, or an hour. John
Sanchez, cited in Diana [ref.], says two hours. Azor leaves it to the
judgement of a prudent man. Hence, someone, who has eaten enough
food, and is then forced to interrupt his meal for the whole midday
period, may not return to the table until the evening collation, because
it is not permissible to consider that if he returns after a long absence
he has eaten a single meal, whatever he himself had intended; but if
he had not eaten enough nutritious food, he might have a second meal,
but in my judgement he would break the fast in this case, but lawfully,
because he would be excused. I gather this from Bonacina and Sanchez
[refs]. But if someone should leave the table believing he had finished,
he may not come back; thus, Laymann. It is however probable that if
the midday meal was still in progress, or if he immediately changed his
mind and started the midday meal again, it would not be a mortal sin;
thus, Lessius and Filliuci.

[F10] <u>Dico 10º</u>. Azorium l. 7. c. 11. q. 4. Sanch: consil. 28. Nauarrum et Fagundem docere mortale esse peccatum horam prandii praeuenire notabiliter, comedendo v. g. hora 9ª. vel 10ª. estque probabile. Probabilius tamen est tantum esse veniale, ita Less. l. 4. c. 2. db. 2. Laym. l. 4. tract. 8. c. 1. Filucius, Bonac: Diana Tolet: et alii, quia adhuc seruatur substantia, nec videtur nunc dierum tanti fieri horae circumstantia. Causa autem iusta praeueniendi erit iter, hospitalitas, et similia.

Case F10. I say tenthly that Azor, Sanchez, Navarre and Fagundez [refs] teach that it is a mortal sin to move the time at which the midday meal is eaten forward by any notable amount, by eating for example at nine or ten, and this is probable. It is more probable, however, that it is only a venial sin to do so; thus, Lessius, Laymann, Filliuci, Bonacina, Diana, Toletus and others [refs]. This is because the substance is still observed if the meal is eaten at this time, and it does not seem that nowadays so much should be made of the circumstances of the time. Moreover, a just reason for moving the time forward would be a journey, hospitality and similar things.

[F11] <u>Dico 11º</u>. Non licere in vespertina refectiuncula quouis genere cibi quadragesimalis vti in exigua quantitate. Ita Laym: Less. citat. Nauar: Azor: Filucius, et alii plurimi, quos fuse refert et sequitur Diana; [fo. 21] contra vnum Bonacinam asserentem posse sumi ex quouis cibi genere, modo seruetur quantitas. Solum ergo licet vti, praeter modicum panis, pomis, bellariis et similibus, quae in ientaculis extra refectionem solidam sumi solent. Pisciculum fumo duratum concedit cum Azorio Laym; modicum casei vel butyri Laym. Iusculum ex pane et aqua Azorius et Bonacina: quod tamen negant Filuc: et Laym: eo quod actione ignis fiat substantia nimis nutrimentalis. Ego puto cum Laym: non fore graue peccatum vti tali iusculo in moderata quantitate, imo nullum, si adsit causa specialis. Denique in his omnibus consuetudo timoratorum est spectanda. Quantitas debet esse exigua, quaeque censeri nequeat esse coena. Ita omnes, estque per se clarum. In particulari quantum, iudicio prudentis relinquitur, consideratis locis, personis, indigentia etc. In Brittania solitas sumi maiores Collationes quam in Gallia ex Maiore refert Azorius cit. c. 8. q. 8. Aliqui 6 vncias definiunt, vt Filucius. Alii 8. vt Fagun: aiens ita saepe respondisse Suarium, et sequitur Diana resol. 1. Denique Filu: Reginal. Laym. concedunt 4ᵗᵃᵐ. partem iustae coenae, quod est satis aequum, licet Diana putet laxum; talis enim nec coenatus, nec semicoenatus dici potest.

Case F11. I say eleventhly that it is not lawful in a small evening meal to eat Lenten foods of whatever sort you like in small quantities; thus, Laymann, and Lessius in the place cited, Navarre, Azor, Filliuci, and many others, whom Diana refers to at greater length and follows. There is one writer who disagrees, Bonacina, who asserts that it is possible to eat whatever sort of food you like, as long as the rules concerning quantity are observed. Therefore, it is only lawful, besides a modicum of bread, to have fruit, or sweetmeats and similar things which, apart from solid food, it is the custom to eat at breakfast. Laymann concedes with Azor, that a small, dried, smoked fish may be eaten; and a modicum of cheese or butter, according to Laymann. Broth made from bread and water is permitted, according to Azor and Bonacina; which however Filliuci and Laymann deny, because these ingredients are made too nutritious when cooked. I think with Laymann that it would not be a grave sin to use such broth in moderate quantities, and no sin if there were a special reason. Finally, in all these things the custom of the God-fearing is to be observed. The quantity should be small, so that the meal cannot be judged to be a dinner, according to all writers, and as is clear in itself. The particular quantities are to be left to the judgement of a prudent man, who has considered the places, persons and their needs etc. In Britain they are accustomed to eat larger collations than in France, as Azor reports, using Major[701] [ref.]. Some, like Filliuci lay down a permissible quantity as being six ounces; others eight, as Fagundez does, saying that Sayer often replied in this way, and Diana [ref.] follows this. Finally, Filliuci, Reginaldus, and Laymann allow the fourth part of a full dinner to be eaten, which seems fair (although Diana thinks it lax), for such a person cannot be said to have dined, nor half dined.

[F12] Dico 12º. Non licere sine causa vespertinam refectiunculam mane sumere, dilata in vesperam coena. Ita contra Anglem et Lopem caeteri, viz: Nauar: Laym: Less. Azor: Filuc: Sanch. Bonac: Fagund: Diana, quia seruanda est consuetudo, cum tota huius Collationis ratio nitatur consuetudine: Item curanda vniformitas; et alioquin subest periculum laxitatis et corruptelarum. Existimo tamen esse tantum [fo. 21ᵛ] Veniale hanc mutationem facere, quia videtur res exigua, Ita Less. Laym: Filuc: Bonac: Diana, contra Nauar: Sanch. et Azorium. Rationabiles porro causae ad mutandum sunt, iter, somnus, conciliandus, negotia interdiu, concio, lectio, complexionis debilitas, studendi commoditas; hae inquam sufficiunt sine dispensatione; ita Autores Citati.

Case F12. I say twelfthly that it is not lawful without reason to take the small evening meal in the morning, if you delay dinner until the

---

[701] John Major, or 'Scotus', was of course a native of Scotland; hence Southwell says 'Britain' here and not 'England'.

evening. This is the view of many (although Angelus and Lopez disagree): Navarre, Laymann, Lessius, Azor, Filliuci, Sanchez, Bonacina, Fagundez, and Diana. They say this because custom is to be observed, since the whole reason for this meal rests upon custom. Also uniformity is to be observed, otherwise there is a danger of laxity and corruption. I consider however that it is only a venial sin to make this change, because it seems a small matter; thus, Lessius, Laymann, Filliuci, Bonacina, Diana (who disagrees with Navarre), Sanchez and Azor. Reasonable causes for such a change are: a journey, sleep, discussions, daily business, preaching, lecturing, weakness of constitution, and the requirements of study. These I say are sufficient without a dispensation; thus, the authors who have been cited.

Appendix

Festa Angliae Obligationis

[Ampleforth, fo. 94ᵛ]

			Dominicae.
	Ian:	VI.	Circumcisio.
		VI.	Epiphania.
Vigil.	Feb:	II.	Purificatio.
Vig:		XXIV.	S: Matthias.
	Mar:	XIX.	S: Iosephus.
Vig:		XXV.	Annunciatio.
	Apr:	XXIII.	S: Georgius.
	Maii.	I.	SS: Philip: & Iacobus.
		III.	Inventio S: Crucis.
Vig:	Iun.	XXIV.	S: Ioan: Bapt:
Vig:		XXIX.	SS: Petri & Pauli.
Vig:	Iul:	XXV.	S: Iacobi.
		XXVI.	S: Annae.
Vig:	Aug:	X.	S: Laurentii.
Vig:		XV.	Assump: B: V.
Vig:		XXIV.	S: Barthol:
Vig:	Sept.	VIII.	Nativ: B. V.
Vig:		XXI.	S: Mathaeus.
		XXIX.	S: Michael.
Vig:	Oct:	XXVIII.	SS: Simon. & Iudae.
Vig:	Nov:	I.	SS: Omnium.
Vig:		XXX.	S: Andr:

Vig:	Dec:	XXI.	S: Thom: Ap.
Vig:		XXV.	Nativ: Dni.
		XXVI.	S: Stephanus:
		XXVII.	S. Ioannes.
		XXVIII.	SS: Innocent:
		XXIX.	S: Thom: Cantuar:
		XXXI.	S: Silvest:
			Pascha cum duobus diebus sequentibus.
			Dies Ascentionis.
Vig:			Pentecostes, cum duobus diebus sequentibus.
			Corpus Christi.

[fo. 95]   Ieiunia.

Quatuor Tempora. Vigilia Annunciationis (nisi cadat infra hebdomadam paschatis). Omnibus feriis Sextis (excipe infra 12 dies Nativitatis Domini, et a Paschate vsque ad Ascensionem.)

Abstinentiae.

Omnibus Dominicis in Quadragesima. Omnibus diebus Sabbatinis. Feria secunda et tertia et quarta ante Ascensionem Domini. Die S. Marci abstinetur a carnibus, nisi cadat infra hebdomadam paschatis.

Feasts of Obligation in England

			Sundays
	January	6	Circumcision
		6	Epiphany
Vigil	February	2	Purification
Vigil		24	St Matthias
	March	19	St Joseph
Vigil		25	Annunciation
	April	23	St George
	May	1	Sts Philip & James
		3	Invention of the Holy Cross
Vigil	June	24	St John the Baptist
Vigil		29	Sts Peter & Paul
Vigil	July	25	St James [the Greater]
		26	St Anne
Vigil	August	10	St Lawrence
Vigil		15	Assumption of the Blessed Virgin

Vigil		24	St Bartholomew
Vigil	September	8	Nativity of the Blessed Virgin
Vigil		21	St Matthew
		29	St Michael
Vigil	October	28	Sts Simon & Jude
Vigil	November	1	All Saints
Vigil		30	St Andrew
Vigil	December	21	St Thomas the Apostle
Vigil		25	Nativity of our Lord
		26	St Stephen
		27	St John
		28	Holy Innocents
		29	St Thomas of Canterbury
		31	St Sylvester
			Easter with the two following days
			Ascension Day
Vigil			Whitsun with the two following days
			Corpus Christi.

Fasts

The four Ember Days. The Vigil of the Annunciation (unless it falls within Easter week). All Fridays (except within the 12 days of the Nativity of our Lord, and from Easter to Ascension Day).

Days of Abstinence

All Sundays in Lent. All Saturdays. Monday, Tuesday, Wednesday and Thursday before Ascension Sunday. St Mark's Day is a day of abstinence from meat, unless it falls within Easter week.

Appendix: Faculties

[Ampleforth fo. 93ᵛ]
**Facultates pro NN. pro omnibus dominiis
Regis Angliae, excepta Hibernia.**

1º. Absolvendi ab haeresi, et Apostasia a fide, et schismate, quoscunque etiam Ecclesiasticos, tam Saeculares, quam Regulares: non tamen qui ex locis fuerint, vbi Sanctum Officium exercetur, nisi in locis missionum, in quibus impune grassantur haereses, delinqueunt, nec illos qui iudicialiter abiuraverint, nisi isti nati sint vbi impune grassantur haereses, et post iudicialem abiurationem illuc reversi in haeresim fuerint relapsi, et hos in foro conscientiae tantum.

2. Absolvendi ab omnibus casibus, etiam in Bulla coenae.

3. Dispensandi in 3. et 4. simplici et mixto consanguinitatis, et affinitatis gradibus in contractis matrimoniis [fo. 94] cum personis Catholicis aut haeresim relinquentibus; et prolem susceptam legitimam declarandi.

4. Restituendi ius petendi debitum amissum.

5. Administrandi omnia Sacramenta etiam parochialia, Ordine et Confirmatione exceptis.

6. Celebrandi missam quocunque loco decenti, etiam sub dio; sub terra; vna hora ante Auroram et alia post meridiem; bis in die si necessitas exigat: si tamen in prima non sumpsit ablutionem; et super altare portabile etiam fracto aut laeso, aut sine SS. reliquiis et praesentibus haereticis, aliisque Excommunicatis si aliter celebrari non possit et non sit periculum sacrilegii; dummodo inserviens missae non sit haereticus vel Excommunicatus.

7. Deferendi SS. Sacramentum occulte ad Infirmos sine lumine, vbi est periculum.

8. Recitandi Rosarium vel alias preces si Breviarium secum deferri non possit, vel Divinum Officium ob aliud impedimentum legitimum recitare non possit.

9. Tenendi et legendi quoscunque libros prohibitos praeter contentos in Bulla coenae; et praeter opera Caroli Molinaei et Nicolai Macchiavelli; et libros de Astrologia Iudiciaria principaliter vel incidenter, vel alio quovis modo de ea tractantes. Dandi etiam licentiam Laicis ex iusta causa vt libros Catholicorum contra haereticos Anglico idiomate scriptos et Sacras Scripturas in idem idioma fideliter versas legant.

10. Dispensandi et commutandi vota simplicia ex rationabili causa exceptis votis Castitatis et Religionis.

11. Benedicendi paramenta et alia vtensilia ad Sacrificium Missae necessaria vbi non intervenit vnctio.

12. Dispensandi quando expedire videtur super esu carnium Ovorum et Lacticiniarum etiam tempore quadragesimae.

13. Concedendi Indulgentiam plenariam primo conversis ab haeresi et fidelibus quibuscunque in articulo mortis, saltem contritis, si confiteri non possint.

14. Concedendi singulis Dominicis et aliis diebus festis decem annorum Indulgentiam iis, qui eorum concionibus intervenerint, et plenariam iis, qui praevia sacramentali peccatorum suorum confesssione Sacram Eucharistiam sument in festis natalis Domini, Paschatis [fo. 94ᵛ] et Assumptionis Beatissimae Virginis.

15. Lucrandi sibi easdem Indulgentias.

16. Secundis feriis non impeditis officiis 9. lectionum vel si impeditis, die immediate sequente, celebrandi missam de requiem, in quocunque altari etiam portabili, liberandi animarum secundum eorum intentionem, e purgatorio per modum suffragii.

Quas facultates concedimus ad septennium duntaxat ita tamen vt antea etiam revocari possint ad placitum nostrum sine vllius causae expressione, easque manu nostra propria firmari.

Cardinalis Protector.

Faculties for NN for all the dominions of the King of England, except Ireland

1. Of absolving from heresy, and apostacy from the faith, and schism, all persons whatever, even ecclesiastics, both seculars and regulars. Not, however, those who might be from the places where the Holy Office operates, unless they have committed crimes in missionary places where heresies rage with impunity; and not those who have judicially abjured, unless they are those who were born where heresies rage with impunity, and, after judicial abjuration, they have relapsed again into heresy; and these people only in the internal forum.

2. Of absolving from all cases, even those in the Bull *In Coena Domini*.

3. Of dispensing in the third and fourth degrees of simple and mixed consanguinity and affinity in marriage contracts, with Catholic persons, or those giving up heresy; and of declaring children begotten by them legitimate.

4. Of restoring the right to ask for conjugal dues after it has been lost.

5. Of administering all the sacraments, even the parochial ones, apart from Orders and Confirmation.

6. Of celebrating Mass in any decent place, even in the open air; or underground; one hour before dawn, and one hour after mid-day; twice in one day if necessity demands it, as long as he has not taken the

ablutions in the first one; and on a portable altar, even one broken or damaged, and without the relics of saints; and with heretics and other excommunicated people present, if it cannot be celebrated otherwise, and if there is no danger of sacrilege, as long as he who serves the Mass is not a heretic or excommunicate.

7. Of carrying the Holy Sacrament secretly to the sick without a light, where there is danger.

8. Of reciting the Rosary or other prayers if he cannot carry a Breviary with him, or he cannot recite the Divine Office on account of another legitimate impediment.

9. Of possessing and reading any prohibited books, apart from those contained in the Bull *In Coena Domini*, and apart from the works of Charles du Moulin and Niccolo Machiavelli,[702] and books principally or incidentally of judicial astrology, or in any other way dealing with it. Of giving also licence to the laity for a just cause that they may read the books of Catholics written against heretics in the English language, and Holy Scriptures faithfully translated into the same language.

10. Of dispensing and commuting a simple vow for a reasonable cause, except for vows of chastity and religion.

11. Of blessing vestments and other utensils necessary for the Sacrifice of the Mass where anointing is not involved.

12. Of dispensing when it seems necessary concerning eating meats, eggs and dairy foods, even during Lent.

13. Of granting a plenary indulgence to people when they are first coverted from heresy, and to all the faithful at the point of death, at least those who are contrite, if they cannot be confessed.

14. Of granting an indulgence of ten years, for every Sunday and for other feast days, to those who attend their sermons; and a plenary indulgence to those, who having previously confessed their sins sacramentally, take the Holy Eucharist on the feast of the Lord's Nativity, Easter and the Assumption of the Blessed Virgin.

15. Of gaining for themselves the same indulgences.

16. On Mondays, if it is not impeded by the reading of the office of nine readings, or if impeded, on the day immediately following, of celebrating a requiem mass, on any altar, even a portable altar, for freeing souls, according to their intention, from purgatory by means of suffrages.

Which faculties we concede for seven years at least, provided however that they may be revoked before that, at our pleasure, without any reason to be given, and confirmed with our own hand.

The Cardinal Protector of England.

---

[702] See above, Introduction, xxiii, and p. 96, n. 137.

Index

The index covers only the English text. Authorities cited, including the Bible, papal decrees and councils, are listed on pages xxxvii–xlvi and are not indexed here, except for the Council of Trent. References are to page numbers, not cases.

travellers, parish priests of   185–6

unity, of marriage   227
usury   131, 132, 133, 137
    see also trading and business

validity
    and affinity   233–4, 235
    of baptism   218–19
    betrothal   229–30, 269–70
    of chaste marriage   175–6
    and consanguinity   212–13, 214
    and crime   23–5
    dubious, and marital rights
        258–9
    and force   246–8
    impotence and   239–40, 242–3,
        244–5
    of marriage   xxix, 95, 148,
        173–4, 180, 194–5
    of mixed marriages   225–6
    ordination   63–4
    of second marriage   227–8
    and substantial error   160–1
    of vows   204–5, 206–7
    of wills   87–8
    see also marriage
vestments   xxiv–xxv
    blessing, 299
    ceremonies without   37–8
    Mass without   28
viaticum
    multiple celebrations of Mass   58
    time of   29

without fasting   57
without vessels and ornaments
    28
virginity   274
vocations, of seminarists   xxxi
vows
    anti-gambling   121
    and betrothal   273, 276
    of chastity   205
    invalidation
        by guardians   122–3
        by parents   122–3
        by spouse   120
    and validity of marriage   204–5,
        206–7

water
    blessing of   37–8
    consecration   56
weddings, heretic, taking part in
    9–10
wills
    interpretation of   88, 89
    validity of   87–8
wine, consecration   56
witchcraft   xix, 108–9, 239–40, 242,
    244
    see also magicians; superstitions
women
    forcible seizure   247–8
    purification of   37–8
    serving Mass   29